AF361384

The James Scarth Gale Library of Korean Literature

General Editors: Ross King and Bruce Fulton

Redemption and Regret

MODERNIZING KOREA IN THE WRITINGS OF JAMES SCARTH GALE

James Scarth Gale

Edited by Daniel Pieper

UNIVERSITY OF TORONTO PRESS
Toronto Buffalo London

ISBN 978-1-4875-0434-2 (cloth)   ISBN 978-1-4875-2997-0 (EPUB)
                                        ISBN 978-1-4875-2996-3 (PDF)

The James Scarth Gale Library of Korean Literature

Library and Archives Canada Cataloguing in Publication

Title: Redemption and regret : modernizing Korea in the writings of James
    Scarth Gale / James Scarth Gale ; edited by Daniel Pieper.
Names: Gale, James Scarth, 1863–1937, author. | Pieper, Daniel, 1980– editor.
Description: Series statement: James Scarth Gale Library of Korean Literature
    series | Includes bibliographical references and index.
Identifiers: Canadiana (print) 20210123664 | Canadiana (ebook) 20210123699 |
    ISBN 9781487504342 (cloth) | ISBN 9781487529970 (EPUB) |
    ISBN 9781487529963 (PDF)
Subjects: LCSH: Korea – History. | LCSH: Korea – Civilization. | LCSH:
    Korea – Social life and customs. | LCSH: Korea – Foreign relations –
    1864–1910. | LCSH: Korean language.
Classification: LCC DS902 .G156 2021 | DDC 951.9/02–dc23

This work was supported by the Academy of Korean Studies Grant funded
by the Korean Government (MEST) (AKS-2011-AAA-2103), as well as by the
Centre for Korean Research at the University of British Columbia.

University of Toronto Press acknowledges the financial assistance to its
publishing program of the Canada Council for the Arts and the Ontario Arts
Council, an agency of the Government of Ontario.

*This book is dedicated to James Scarth Gale: Translator,
Koreanist, and Literatus*

Contents

PART TWO: OLD COREA

Series Preface

The James Scarth Gale Library of Korean Literature brings together in one series the many literary translations and scholarly essays of James Scarth Gale (1863–1937), Canadian missionary to Korea, that are preserved in the Gale Papers at the Fisher Rare Book Library at the University of Toronto. During his forty years in the mission field, from 1888 to 1927, and with the assistance of several Korean Christian "pundits," Gale translated numerous Korean literary works into English, the vast majority of which were written in Literary Sinitic (Classical Chinese, or *hanmun,* as it is called today in Korean) rather than in vernacular Korean. Most of these translations were never published and remain in manuscript or typescript form. Thus, this series presents Gale's translations from a century and more ago of Korean literary texts dating as far back as the eleventh century, in a format congenial to the present-day reader: romanizations have been updated; Gale's prose style has been polished wherever possible without sacrificing his distinctive voice; each volume is provided with a scholarly introduction and an annotated apparatus to facilitate contextualization and understanding; and the original texts in Literary Sinitic or vernacular Korean are included so as to allow advanced students of traditional Korea's two main literary languages to make easy comparisons with Gale's translations.

In addition to edited reproductions of Gale's literary translations and essays, the series will include an index to the Gale Papers and occasional research monographs on James Scarth Gale's multifaceted activities as a pioneering Western scholar, translator, and interpreter of Korea's literary heritage. The following is a preliminary list of volumes forthcoming in the series:

Hyangsoon Yi, ed. *"P'alsangnok": The Eight Marks of the Buddha*, translated by James Scarth Gale

Ross King. *"I Thank Korea for Her Books:" James Scarth Gale, Korean Literature in* Hanmun, *and Allo-Metropolitan Missionary Orientalism*

Caleb Park, ed. 500 nyŏn kidam: *Strange Tales from Korea's Five-Hundred-Year Chosŏn Dynasty*, translated by James Scarth Gale and Caleb Park

Vincenza D'Urso, ed. *Footprints of the Wild Goose: A Trip to the Diamond Mountains and the East Coast by Miss Kim Kŭmwŏn (1830)*, translated by James Scarth Gale

Ross King and William S. Wells, eds. *Index to the James Scarth Gale Papers, University of Toronto*

Gregory Evon, ed. *Selected Works of Yi Kyubo (1169–1241 AD)*, translated by James Scarth Gale

Ross King, ed. *Korean Poets and Poetry of the Koryŏ Dynasty, 918–1392 AD: Translations by James Scarth Gale*

Joohee Baik, ed. *Translation of a Korean Gentleman's Trip from Seoul to Peking, 1712–1713 AD*, translated by James Scarth Gale

James Lewis, ed. *A Trip to Japan, 1718 AD, by Sin Yuhan (Member of Korean Embassy)*, translated by James Scarth Gale

Illustrations and Tables

Illustrations

Tables

Acknowledgments

Over the course of preparing this book I have incurred many debts. My involvement with the writings of James Scarth Gale dates back to 2012 when I, along with several other UBC Work Study students, began to process the vast *Nachlass* of Gale housed at the Thomas Fisher Rare Book Library at the University of Toronto. That work was supported by an Academy of Korean Studies, Korean Studies Laboratory grant titled "Cosmopolitan and Vernacular in the Sinographic Cosmopolis: Comparative Aspects of the History of Language, Writing and Literary Culture in Japan and Korea" (2011–16, led by Ross King). The generous support of this grant facilitated my ongoing graduate studies while deepening my knowledge of Korean literature and history through the intangible guidance and mentorship of a pioneer scholar in Korean studies. I am grateful for the opportunity to have gained such insight into the mind of a visionary scholar and the burgeoning of the field of modern Korean studies.

Years of sifting through thousands of nearly indecipherable pages of handwritten manuscripts eventually yielded a number of works of nearly publishable quality, primarily because, unlike the vast majority of pages in the James Scarth Gale Papers, they were thankfully rendered in typescript format. Two of these typescripts – *Pen Pictures of Old Korea* (ca 1912) and *Old Corea* (ca 1923) – are presented in this volume. My gratitude goes to Ross King of the University of British Columbia for bringing these to my attention and supporting my publication of them as part of the James Scarth Gale Library of Korean Literature. I would like to also express my gratitude to Dr King for his ongoing support with myriad aspects of this project and for tracking down various primary sources that Gale frustratingly neglected to cite in detail. My thanks also goes to Bruce Fulton of the University of British Columbia for his thorough editing and thoughtful feedback. This manuscript was immensely improved thanks to the input of these scholars.

I am also indebted to the Korea Foundation and the support it afforded through the Fellowship for Postdoctoral Research in North America (2017–18), during which the bulk of the manuscript was prepared. Without the generous support of the Korea Foundation, this project never would have come to fruition. My gratitude is also due to Washington University in St Louis, whose members of the East Asian Languages and Cultures Department graciously opened their doors to me during my postdoctoral fellowship there and offered their invaluable support during a critical period of the manuscript's preparation. I also want to express thanks to the University of British Columbia for providing the academic and moral support necessary to complete this book in a timely fashion.

Finally, I want to express my everlasting gratitude to my family for their unending love, support, and kindness.

REDEMPTION AND REGRET

Introduction

These sketches pertain to Old Korea and not to Korea of the immediate present. The same old Korea has receded from us, and these records are souvenir-pictures of her part of the great Orient which has so recently disappeared beneath the tidal-wave of modern life. Some of the conditions and customs of the past we bid a hearty farewell to; some again we see pass with feelings of regret.

J.S. Gale, Pen Pictures of Old Korea, Seoul, June 1912

James Scarth Gale (1863–1937) was a Canadian missionary, scholar, and translator who served in Korea for nearly forty years. Hailing from rural Ontario, Gale received a bachelor's degree in language and literature from the University of Toronto before being dispatched to Korea on 15 December 1888, under the sponsorship of the University College Young Men's Christian Association. He was the first Canadian and first non-ordained missionary to set foot on Korean soil, where he would more or less remain until 1927.[1] During this time Gale developed into the foremost Western scholar of Korean history, language, and literature, completing the first translation of Korean literature into a Western language, the first translation of English literature into Korean, the first comprehensive Korean-English dictionary, and a pioneering

---

1 During this time, Gale spent roughly one year on furlough in North America and another year in Japan. For autobiographical details of Gale's life, see Rutt, *James Scarth Gale and His "History."*

Korean grammar.[2] He also left behind mountains of unpublished English translations of Korean literature in Literary Sinitic (*hanmun*, or Classical Chinese), which remain his most significant legacy to the field of Korean studies and Korean literature.[3]

Gale's tenure in Korea coincided with a tumultuous and transformative period that witnessed the country's transition from a "hermit" suzerain kingdom to an independent empire and finally to a colonial possession of Japan. These colossal changes are reflected in the shifting nature and content of Gale's writings. The present volume introduces two of Gale's unpublished typescripts that represent distillations of the pre-annexation and post-annexation eras, respectively, of his career. These typescripts are among the James Scarth Gale Papers, housed at the Fisher Rare Book Library at the University of Toronto and virtually untouched by academic research and largely unknown to the general public.[4] The present volume is the second in a series that attempts to shed light on Gale's vast *Nachlass* – his legacy of scholarship on Korea spanning nearly half a century.[5] As Ross King of the University of

---

2 The first English translation of Korean literature was *The Cloud Dream of the Nine* (*Kuunmong* 九雲夢, 1922), first written by Kim Manjung (金萬重, 1637–92) in the seventeenth century and set in Tang China (618–907). The first translation of English literature into Korean was *T'yŏllo ryŏktyŏng* (天路歷程 *The Pilgrim's Progress*), a Christian allegory written by John Bunyan (1628–88) that was one of the most significant works of religious literature in English. Gale's *A Korean-English Dictionary* (*Han-Yŏng chajŏn* 韓英字典, 1897) was a ground-breaking work of some 35,000 entries that had a profound effect both on subsequent bilingual dictionaries and monolingual Korean dictionaries. Gale's grammar was entitled *Korean Grammatical Forms* (*Sagwa chinam* 辭課指南, 1894, rev. 1903) and represented the first substantial grammar of the Korean spoken language in English.

3 These may be found mostly in manuscript form in the James Scarth Gale Papers, housed at the Fisher Rare Book Library at the University of Toronto.

4 For descriptions of this collection's content and import, see King, "James Scarth Gale, Korean Literature in *Hanmun*, and Korean Books"; Kwŏn, Han, and Yi, "Keil munsŏ (Gale, James Scarth Papers)." The only research of which I am aware that deals directly with either *Pen Pictures* or *Old Corea* is an article by Yi Sanghyŏn and Yi Chinsuk (2014), focusing only on Gale's translations of Korean *sijo* verses appearing in *Pen Pictures*. See Yi and Yi, "*Chosŏn p'ilgyŏng* (Pen-pictures of Old Corea [1912])."

5 The first volume is Gale, King, and Park, *Score One for the Dancing Girl, and Other Stories from the "Kimun ch'onghwa."*

British Columbia has demonstrated through his examination of the Gale Papers since 2004, the vast majority of these four-thousand-plus manuscript pages contained in nineteen ledgers, though misleadingly labelled "Diaries," are in fact unpublished English translations of Korean literature in *hanmun*.[6] Despite Gale's diverse activities in translation, education, lexicography, fiction writing, historiography, and of course evangelization, his unpublished work demands that we re-evaluate his legacy with the understanding that it is characterized most profoundly by *hanmun*-to-English literary translation.[7]

The first typescript in the present volume, *Pen Pictures of Old Korea* (朝鮮筆景, 1912; hereafter *Pen Pictures*),[8] consists of forty-three short essays written between 1894 and 1912.[9] The second typescript, *Old Corea* (ca 1923), follows a similar format, containing forty essays on various topics along with forty-nine short translations of Korean literature, mostly in Literary Sinitic.[10] The heavier focus on literary translation in the latter typescript mirrors the shift in Gale's scholarly career, starting in the 1910s, toward greater engagement with cosmopolitan literature in *hanmun*, and also reflects his increasing proficiency in this literary medium. More importantly, however, the literary turn evident in *Old Corea* demonstrates an increasingly active and, in Gale's mind, urgent curatorial intercession into the cosmopolitan literary tradition to preserve a fading written tradition for global posterity, a point I will return to later in this introduction. Although the diversity of the essays in these two typescripts confounds a clear-cut categorization, the following broad topics recur: language issues; Korean history, diplomacy, and international relations; Korea's noted women; religion; social issues; technology; archaeology; and superstitions and animism.

---

6 King, "James Scarth Gale, Korean Literature in *Hanmun*, and Korean Books."

7 King, "James Scarth Gale, Korean Literature in *Hanmun*, and Allo-Metropolitan Missionary Orientalism."

8 The sinographs 朝鮮筆景 (*Chosŏn p'ilgyŏng*) associated with the English title are not a reference to an existing work but were in fact chosen by Gale as the original Korean title of his book, demonstrating his increasing familiarity and facility with Literary Sinitic.

9 Judging by the essays explicitly dated by Gale, the bulk of them were penned between 1894 and 1906.

10 The *OC* version presented here has been considerably condensed because duplicate essays also appearing in *Pen Pictures* have been omitted. Differences between the versions have been footnoted throughout *Pen Pictures*.

This introduction highlights some of these major themes and discusses their wider significance in the context of Korea's ongoing modernization. In contrast to the vast majority of the Gale Papers, in the typescripts featured here Gale often injects his own opinions and interpretations in a style akin to that of his *Korean Sketches* (1898) and *Korea in Transition* (1909).[11] The composite of opinions, observations, and ruminations expressed in these works paints the conflicted portrait of a knowledgeable, sympathetic, and dedicated Koreaphile, animated nonetheless by unshakeable notions of Christian superiority and Western triumphalism. Through a close reading of *Pen Pictures* and *Old Corea* and other of his contemporary writings, I demonstrate how the sentiments expressed therein reflect a pronounced ambivalence toward the passing of the traditional order, an ambivalence rooted in the conflict between Gale's personal and literary proclivities and his Western missionary identity.

A second theme I explore is Gale's all-pervasive evangelical strategy, which sought to establish a "coevalness" among the Judeo-Christian religious tradition, the Confucian cosmological order, and at times nativist beliefs.[12] In the process I join King[13] in questioning the classic Orientalist paradigm that positioned the West as the unquestioned source of cultural and religious authority, in opposition to an unenlightened Orient, highlighting instead Gale's conferral of equal status or even superiority upon an ancient and enlightened, if by some measure "heathen," Sinological tradition.

A third point addressed in this introduction is Gale's complex and evolving relationship with Japan. By examining various chapters in *Pen Pictures* as well as other unpublished writing by Gale, I demonstrate his deeply ambivalent views toward the Japanese presence in Korea: he saw Japan simultaneously as a positive force for material growth and progress as well as an irreconcilably impotent cultural and spiritual model for Korean modernity, a view that paralleled his broader fraught

---

11 Indeed, many short excerpts and several larger passages from *Pen Pictures* and *Old Corea* found their way into these published books. The overall content and style of *Pen Pictures* coincides more closely with *Korean Sketches* and *Korea in Transition* and agrees chronologically, whereas the content of *Old Corea* tends toward the more apolitical, literary bent of Gale's later career.

12 Fabian, *Time and the Other*.

13 King, "I Thank Korea for Her Books": *James Scarth Gale, Korean Literature in* hanmun, *and Allo-Metropolitan Missionary Orientalism*.

relationship with Korean modernization. A further argument pertains to Gale's seemingly anti-national and retrogressive project of cosmopolitan literary translation. Korean literature in Literary Sinitic, rather than merely a nostalgic reversion to antiquarian tradition, was for Gale proof of Korea's literary and cultural greatness. Gale's personal writings and translations in *Pen Pictures* and *Old Corea*, therefore, should be understood as a broader project to establish Korea's literary heritage and participation within the broader Sinographic cosmopolis.[14] Standing as they do in opposition to the "legitimate" historical trajectory of nationalistic Korean language and literature championing "democratic" vernacularization over "feudal" *hanmun*,[15] Gale's language ideologies and broader scholarly project may be dismissed as anachronistic, Sinocentric, and anti-nationalistic, but this characterization rather misses the mark.[16] I argue that Gale, in affirming Korea's thoroughgoing, vibrant, and at times superior participation in a tradition of transnational textual exchange, is affirming a sort of pro-Korean, nationalistic ideology, albeit within a premodern context.

An overarching theme connecting *Pen Pictures*, *Old Corea*, and indeed much of Gale's writing is a pervasive sentiment of ambivalence and loss in the face of Korean modernization. A knowledgeable and astute "Student of the Orient,"[17] Gale heaped praise upon the Literary Sinitic tradition while recognizing that modern literature in the vernacular was the inevitable wave of the future, causing him

---

14 For a definition of the Sinographic cosmopolis, see Koh, *Infected Korean Language*. For various perspectives on aspects of the Sinographic cosmopolis, see King, ed., *Cosmopolitan and Vernacular in the World of Wen* (forthcoming).

15 See Yu Cho, "Diglossia in Korean Language and Literature"; Peter Lee, "Early Twentieth-Century Poetry," 337. Whether a piece was composed in the Korean alphabet has been construed as a sort of ontological litmus test for genuinely "Korean" literature. See Kichung Kim, "What Is Korean Literature?," in *Introduction to Classical Korean Literature*, 1–10; Koh, *Infected Korean Language*.

16 Heinz Insu Fenkl, for example, dismisses Gale's translation of *Kuunmong* (*Cloud Dream of the Nine*) and indirectly his entire scholarly project by deeming it the work of an antiquated "Catholic priest." See Fenkl, "*Kuunmong*, A Translator's Note." A much more common approach to Gale and his perceived antiquarian, religion-inspired scholarly project is either neglect or a perfunctory, superficial treatment.

17 This was the nom de plume Gale frequently used in his writing for *Korea Magazine*.

to deplore the lack of a modern vernacular literary idiom that could properly replace the cosmopolitan tradition he saw dissolving before him. His attempts to establish consanguinity between Western and Eastern religions at times produced contradictions that challenged his missionary identity, resulting in alternately empathetic portrayals and moralistic condemnations.[18] Perhaps Gale's greatest source of ambivalence was the spectre of Japan, a simultaneously irresistible yet menacing model of material progress and inevitable failure. Gale's scholarly legacy itself is conflicted within both Western and Korean academia, complicated by his supposed pro-Japanese leanings, his scholar-missionary identity, and the "anachronistic," "anti-nationalistic" nature of his wider cosmopolitan literary project. It is the goal of this book to disentangle the complex work and legacy of the foremost scholar-missionary on Korea through an examination of two of his unpublished works, thereby illuminating at a personal level the process of Gale's intercultural interface and Korean modernization.

Dedicated Koreaphile or Western Triumphalist?

Gale first arrived on Korean soil on 15 December 1888, and quickly distinguished himself from most of his missionary colleagues by "going native," attempting to conform to Korean life, staying in Korean homes, and eating Korean food, an approach that gained him, according to one of his missionary colleagues, the trust of the Korean people.[19] Gale assessed the lay of the land immediately after his arrival in 1888, describing the foreign community as insular and expressing his desire to live among Koreans. In one of his many letters to his sister Jen, he writes, "This [meeting foreign dignitaries] is necessary, I understand, but I don't like it at all, at all. On Monday eve next Christmas I am invited to a gathering and among others invited is Col. Charlie Long, General Gordon's friend. I don't like this at all and am going to withdraw from it and become a Corean. There are so few foreigners in this great city that they naturally cling [zzz] together and meet more than

---

18 Gale's supposed liberalism also brought on clashes with more dogmatic, sectarian colleagues. See Rutt, *James Scarth Gale and His "History."*

19 The colleague was Samuel Moffett (1864–1939), pioneering Presbyterian missionary to Korea and one of Gale's close friends. For an account of Gale's early years in Korea, see Yu Yŏngsik, *Ch'akhăn mokchya*, 807–15.

they otherwise would."[20] Gale's activities and lifestyle for the next decade would embody this ethos. After a failed attempt to acquire a residence in the Hwanghae Province capital of Haeju, where no Westerner had yet ventured, Gale spent the spring and early summer of 1889 in the remote west-coast village of Sorae, the site of the first Christian church in Korea, where he began his language and cultural studies in earnest.[21] Gale next travelled to Pusan, then a sleepy backwater port being developed by the Japanese, where no Western missionaries were yet stationed.[22] In the spring of 1891, after a short stint in Seoul, Gale travelled with his friend, the American Presbyterian missionary Samuel Moffett, to Mukden, Manchuria, to visit the Scottish Presbyterian missionaries, especially John Ross, who had made the first translation of the New Testament into Korean.[23] After getting married in 1892 to Harriet Elizabeth Gibson, the late Dr Heron's widow,[24] Gale settled down with his new family in the east coast port of Wŏnsan, a new mission station with a minuscule foreign population. He would remain there until 1897.

It was during this period of "in-culture proselytization," marked by far-flung excursions, limited contact with the foreign community, and immersion in Korean lifestyle and culture, that Gale began to develop pro-Korean sentiments and the deep knowledge of Korean language and culture that would ultimately blossom into a lifelong affinity for

---

20 Jim S. Gale, "Letter to Jen," Seoul, December 1888, reproduced in Yu Yŏngsik, *Ch'akhǎn mokchya*, 517. In another letter to his sister the following year, Gale elaborates on his approach to life in Korea and how it related to evangelization: "A few who are already on the ground I think are making the mistake in trying to make Koreans like ourselves. We can't do that. The changes if anything must be the other way. We must become like Koreans, for they can still be Koreans and Christians at the same time." Gale, "Letter to Jen," Seoul, 1 August 1889, reproduced in Yu, *Ch'akhǎn mokchya*, 533.

21 Gale describes his travails in Haeju in vivid detail in his *Korean Sketches*. For a further discussion of this church and its significance, see the introduction to the section titled "Miscellaneous" in *Old Corea*, this vol. In this section, Gale includes a travelogue of an ill-fated journey to Sorae in "A Trip to Sorae Beach," *Old Corea*. Sorae is also where Gale would meet his future "pundit" and lifelong friend, Yi Ch'angjik. Rutt, *James Scarth Gale and His "History,"* 13–15.

22 Rutt, *James Scarth Gale and His "History,"* 15.

23 Ibid., 18–19.

24 Dr John William Heron (1858–90) arrived in Korea in June 1885 as a medical missionary from the American Presbyterian Church. He died five years later of dysentery and was the first to be buried at what would become Yanghwajin Foreign Missionary Cemetery.

Korean studies. Gale's rapid acculturation in the mission field bore fruit almost immediately when in June 1890 he joined the American missionaries H.G. Underwood (1859–1916) and Homer Hulbert (1863–1949) and others in founding the Korea Tract Society (Han'guk sŏngsŏ sahoe), later to become the Christian Literature Society of Korea.[25] In February of the following year he was appointed to the Permanent Executive Bible Committee of Korea, in which capacity he began a decades-long affair with Bible translation that culminated in his ignominious exit from that organization in 1923.[26] Gale assisted Hulbert in the preparation of Underwood's *Concise Dictionary of the Korean Language in Two Parts* (1891)[27] and followed in 1897 with his own landmark contribution to Korean lexicography, *A Korean-English Dictionary*. In between these two projects, in 1894, he published *Korean Grammatical Forms*, a pioneering work steeped in cultural context and reflecting his keen ear for reportage of the spoken Korean language that he had experienced living across the peninsula.[28] The Wŏnsan years also witnessed the publication of the groundbreaking translation *T'yŏllo ryŏktyŏng* (*The Pilgrim's Progress*, 1895). Gale began to write with authority on matters of Korean language, literature, and culture in various missionary magazines and scholarly journals,[29] and published his first book, *Korean*

---

25 Rutt, *James Scarth Gale and His "History,"* 18.

26 Ibid. The name Permanent Executive Bible Committee was changed to Board of Official Translators in 1893. Gale would eventually have vehement disagreements with his missionary colleagues over Bible translation. Gale believed in producing a more readable, "beautiful" form of Korean that "spoke to the soul of the Korean," and consequently his translations were criticized for being insufficiently literal. For a discussion of this debate, see ibid., 72–5.

27 Although Gale's expertise in Korean was likely minimal at this time, one of the reasons he was approached for the job was because of his knowledge of French. Many definitions for Korean words were carried over from Felix Clair Ridel's *Dictionnaire coréen-français* (韓佛字典, 1880), published by French missionaries a generation earlier. However, the experience was undoubtedly informative and prepared him for his own monumental undertaking, *A Korean-English Dictionary* (*Han-Yŏng chajŏn*), first published in 1897. See Rutt, *James Scarth Gale and His "History,"* 18.

28 Rutt, *James Scarth Gale and His "History,"* 21.

29 These include but are not limited to the *Transactions of the Royal Asiatic Society – Korea Branch* (1901–30), *Korean Repository* (1892, 1895–8), *Korea Magazine* (1917–19), *Korea Review* (1901–6), *Open Court* (1887–1936), *Men and Missions*, and *North China Daily News*.

Sketches, in 1898. By the time Gale returned to Seoul in 1898 and began writing many of the essays that would form *Pen Pictures*, he was already one of the foremost Western linguists, lexicographers, translators, and ethnographers on Korea.

Gale's mission, though, was ultimately evangelical, and his writings display a continual interplay between his developing Koreaphilia and ongoing Western/modernist triumphalism. Gale's attempts to preserve the last vestiges of "Old Corea" through detached ethnographic observation and translation stemmed from his profound knowledge of and respect for Korean culture, particularly its literary legacy, yet his Western missionary identity also coloured his world view, producing a complex prism through which he came to perceive traditional Korea. On the one hand, Gale was deeply knowledgeable of Korean customs and culture, held profound respect for the scholar of old and the tradition that elevated him, and eventually gained a vast knowledge of Korean literature in Literary Sinitic. As suggested by the aforementioned letter to his sister, his writings echo a conscious and all-encompassing drive to exist in communion with "the natives," to empathize as much as possible with their cultural, literary, and linguistic Weltanschauung. On the other hand, Gale's writings could be extremely triumphalist in tone, viewing the spread of Christianity as an unquestionably positive force in dispelling outdated and wasteful customs, folk religions, and superstitions. This ambivalent view of "Old Corea" thus stemmed in part from a conflict between Gale's "nativist" conservative language ideology – exalting the Literary Sinitic tradition while maligning the as-yet-feeble Korean attempts at modern vernacular literature – and his triumphalist missionary posture.

Like much discourse of his day, Gale's writing was at times informed by Anglo-Saxonism and the Social Darwinist paradigm of competition among the races, with Christian conversion proffered as the promise of progress and victory. In the following account in *Pen Pictures*, Gale confidently predicts the triumph of Christian logic over Oriental geomantic beliefs:

The great building [Myŏngdong Cathedral] sits on the back of a terrestrial dragon that lies sprawled out under the city, on the good treatment of which depends the prosperity of the reigning house of Yi. Last summer a missionary built his home on a spur of the hill, which, in the old maps of geomancy, is marked "The Dragon's Head." At once the brute resented it and there was no rain; consequently this year of famine. The weight of

> the Cathedral is helping to squeeze the life out of the Dragon, and on his
> putrid carcass we hope one of these days to see a solid, up to date, Chris-
> tian city.[30]

Despite the clear tone of triumphalism, here as in much of his writing Gale assumes the voice of the "native" in describing the perceived effect of this geomantic calamity, presenting a parallel outlook that, while unapologetically Christian in orientation, is in no way uninformed or unsympathetic. This world view resulted therefore from a combination of deep cultural knowledge and normalized expressions of Western teleological superiority. Over the course of Gale's career the combination of (or conflict between) these outlooks resulted not in triumphant resolution but in even more profound ambivalence. In the *Pen Pictures* essay "Korea's Receding Pantheon," a description of Korea's fading religious traditions, his ambivalence is more pronounced:

> These twelve forms of worship that have beckoned the Korean of the past
> to pay his vows, his prayers, his tithes, his tears, are receding into the vis-
> tas of the by-gone and forgotten. Soon we shall see them only in folk-lore
> records, and among customs defunct and dead. We watch them recede
> with something akin to sorrow, unless a better be on hand to take their
> place, and make good the defects that were inherent in them.[31]

Despite Gale's Christian missionary identity, the disappearance of traditional Korea's decidedly non-Christian religions was to be met not with unbridled joy but with "something akin to sorrow." The emphasis is placed not on "logic" or the polytheistic underpinnings of Korean beliefs, but on the behaviour that they evoked, the "vows, prayers, tithes, and tears." Moreover, these beliefs need not be rejected wholesale but could be "supplemented" by "making good their defects," an allusion to his evangelical strategy informed by fulfilment theory.[32]

Another theme that surfaces in Gale's typescripts is the repeated infantilizing of the Korean monarch Kojong (高宗, 1852–1919; r. 1863–1907). This was often achieved metaphorically, with Gale describing a country

---

30 Gale, "Korea's Electric Shocks," *Pen Pictures*, this vol.

31 Gale, "Korea's Receding Pantheon," *Pen Pictures*, this vol.

32 Fulfilment theory, the progressivist missionary view that Christianity should
    be presented as the fulfilment rather than the annulment of other religions,
    will be discussed in more detail below.

of hapless children entering an adult's diplomatic universe it scarcely understood. Many of Gale's most blistering critiques of Kojong appeared in *Pen Pictures*, essays penned following his move to Yŏnmotkol, Seoul, in 1899; his remaining years in Korea would be spent there. Essays dating from this period until roughly 1910 represent the most political writings of his career,[33] and his commentary and predictions as to Korea's future were often insightful and remarkably prescient. Gale arrived in Seoul in the midst of epochal changes in Korea's cultural and geopolitical landscape. The Kabo Reforms (1894–6) had ushered in a host of changes, including the abolishing of the civil service examination (*kwagŏ*) and the elevation of the vernacular script (*ŏnmun*) to the level of "national script" (*kungmun*), two changes that would have a profound effect on Korea's literary and linguistic landscape and Gale's perception of it. Meanwhile, Japan's victory in the Sino-Japanese War (1894–5) removed direct Chinese influence from the peninsula and began a period of Russian and Japanese rivalry for influence in Korean affairs. Against this backdrop, Gale depicts a deeply superstitious and dangerously ignorant monarch at the helm of a doomed vessel:

> [King Kojong] has never advanced in the way of true reform, and yet he takes a deep interest in the drawing room touches of Western life. He knows the exact differences between the uniforms of the representatives that appear before him, and just how many gold strings there are in each country's epaulettes. He has studied clocks, watches, and barometers, not as articles for use, but as ornaments. He likes machine-guns, not to fire off but to make-believe with. He is indeed a spoiled child that regards his little country as something created for his special delectation, and all the people as flocks and herds intended for his slaughter. He is as incapable of grasping the meaning of the age he lives in as a ten-year old boy would be of taking Port Arthur.[34]

Kojong's ignorance of international affairs and geopolitical realities was for Gale not just a matter of regret or pity but a potential disaster for the entire Korean nation. In a chapter aptly titled "Unconscious Korea," Gale expresses exasperated frustration with Kojong's incompetence,

---

33 The March First Independence Movement stimulated another brief flurry of political writings, in which Gale decried the brutal Japanese response.

34 Gale, "All Good Things Are Three," *Pen Pictures*, August 1904, this vol. Port Arthur was a major battlefront in the Russo-Japanese War, which was raging when Gale penned this essay.

the result of which he views as the decline of a hapless and credulous
populace into oblivion:

> He is an absolute monarch, though all unaware of the actual world he
> lives in. His unconscious subjects, too, dare have no thoughts whatever
> about their country. They are to take quietly what he and fate decree. Piti-
> ful beyond expression is the position of the Korean people. A kinder more
> loveable race never lived. We who have known them for years, and have
> never met with insult, who have had access to every home and to many
> a heart, know how to appreciate and sympathize with them in this their
> time of helplessness. As for their future – a race of slaves we fear.[35]

These and other of Gale's political writings during this period depict
a backward monarchy in paternalistic, slightly patronizing tones. Yet
sentiments expressed by Gale elsewhere suggest that such writings
were the expression of a concerned though increasingly pessimistic
ally rather than that of a critic bemoaning an outmoded monarchical institution in an era of republicanism and Western triumphalism.
Following the March First Independence Movement in 1919, in a letter
to Lord James Bryce, a former British ambassador to the United States
(1907–13), for example, Gale describes a long and proud Korean history
of monarchical rule in pleading Korea's present case for independence:

> Only twice during this long period [AD 668–1910] did her reigning house
> fall and a new family come to the throne … During these 1200 years she
> has lived happily under many good kings. Sometimes under kings of less
> worth she has gone back. For all that time there were no civil wars like our
> Wars of the Roses, not one.[36]

In characteristic fashion, Gale compares Korea favourably to the
supposedly more advanced West, attributing greater stability and
longevity to a country under a monarchical form of government.
Moreover, Japan's complicity in the murder of Queen Min[37] and its

---

35 Gale, "Unconscious Korea," *Pen Pictures*, March 1901, this vol.

36 Gale, "Letter to the Right Hon. Viscount Bryce," 10 March 1919, 1–5. This and
    many of Gale's private letters have been photographically reproduced in Yu
    Yŏngsik, *Ch'akhăn mokchya*. The letter to Lord Bryce appears on pp. 639–41.

37 Queen Min, or Empress Myŏngsŏng (明成皇后, 1851–95), was assassinated
    in the early morning of 8 October 1895 on the palace grounds, by Japanese

subsequent machinations in Korea provoked more sympathetic portrayals of his former target, suggesting that his criticisms were propelled not by malicious intent toward Kojong or the teleological belief in a hopelessly backward Orient but rather by concerns about the future of Korea.

> On the following morning [after the queen's murder], while still fearing for his life, the King was forced to sign documents that gave over all power into the hands of men who were under Japanese influence. This made him a prisoner in his own palace, until he was able to escape and find asylum in the Russian legation. From there he called together his friends, reorganized his government, and lost little time in punishing his enemies who had been in power over him. This act of the King embittered the Japanese against Russia, opened the door for Russian intrigue, and hastened if it did not actually cause the Russo-Japanese War.[38]

Far from a helpless child ignorant of circumstances, Kojong here is accorded more agency in foreign affairs. Though in Gale's view Kojong's actions resulted in the Russo-Japanese War, the king is more sympathetically portrayed in confrontation with malicious international forces that threatened Korea's independence. Gale's sentiments about the state of Korea in the international arena and the actions of Kojong in the years preceding annexation are marked by the same ambivalence and conflict. Ranging from paternalistic and condescending to laudatory and defiant in the face of foreign aggression, Gale's political writings in *Pen Pictures* and other contemporary venues expose the sentiments of an emotionally and scholarly invested Koreaphile confounded by the international state of affairs and exasperated by inaction and lack of reform. These writings served to disentangle the salvageable remnants of a proud cosmopolitan tradition and to rectify such vestiges with his own totalizing Western missionary world view.

---

agents hired by the consul to Korea, Miura Gorō (三浦梧楼). The empress was viewed as an impediment to the reform efforts in Korea promoted by Japan. Miura and fifty-six other parties were put on a farcical trial but acquitted for lack of evidence.

38 Gale, "Why Japan Has Failed in Korea," unpublished article, 5, reproduced in Yu Yŏngsik, *Ch'akhăn mokchya*, 646–51; 647.

Gale's Evangelical Strategy: A Holistic Approach to Scholarship

This ongoing rectification engendered continual conflict in Gale's writing and created a sort of iconoclastic approach to the mission field in Korea distinct from the posture of most of his colleagues. Perhaps the most enduring and systematic of Gale's approaches to Korean studies was the missionary-scholarly ideological matrix through which he viewed his subject matter. The representative example of this ideology was his equation of the Judeo-Christian God with the Confucian "God" (天 *ch'ŏn*), an evangelization-strategy-cum-scholarly-framework that was extended to a greater or lesser degree to other aspects of Korean culture during the course of his career and that served as a sort of litmus test for what was salvageable of "Old Corea." I argue that this ideological matrix formed the apparatus through which Gale approached his work, creating an inseparable fusion of the religious and the scholarly that forces us to consider holistically Gale's academic and missionary identities, with all the contradictions and conflict inherent in such a synthesis.

Comparatively little scholarly research has been conducted on James Scarth Gale; even less research deals with his scholarly and translation activities, especially after 1910.[39] Most Korean-language treatments of Gale and other Western missionaries are to be found in church and mission histories, which have witnessed a boom since the 1970s. As Ross King has noted, "research by *Korean* scholars on Gale tends to have been concentrated in the hands of historians of Protestant Christianity in Korea, who focus either on his work as a Bible translator … or on his activities in converting upper-class highly educated Koreans to Christianity in the first years of the 20th century."[40] In other words, there has been a tendency in Korean academia, especially its non-secular branch, to attempt a separation of the religious and secular pursuits of scholar-missionaries such as Gale, subsuming the former activities under the purview of church history and mostly disregarding the latter. For example, in his lengthy and purportedly comprehensive *Han'guk Kidokkyohoesa* (The History of the Christian Church in Korea, 2000), Min Kyŏngbae dedicates considerable attention to the religious activities of Gale and other missionaries but gives little to no consideration to their scholarly achievements. Although Min acknowledges the contributions of Gale to the field of Korean studies

---

39 Two recent exceptions are the massive two-volume *Ch'akhăn mokchya* by Yu
    Yŏngsik, and Yi Sanghyŏn's *Han'guk kojŏn pŏnyŏkka ŭi ch'osang* (2012).
40 King, "James Scarth Gale, Korean Literature in *Hanmun*, and Korean Books," 241.

when he writes that "Gale's position in modern Korean literary[41] and cultural history is so great as to be incomparable,"[42] he dedicates a mere five pages of this six-hundred-page tome to the combined scholarly output of all Western missionaries in Korea.[43] Rather than separating Gale's missionary and scholarly legacies, I argue, a holistic consideration of Gale's missionary-scholar identity is necessary to shed light on his own contemporary perspective and to explain his larger religio-academic project, notably his conflation of Eastern and Western theism.

An additional trend in Korean church histories is to privilege the indigenous impetus in church formation while dichotomizing Korean and "foreign" contributions to church history. The corollary to this is the conflation of the ethno-national independence struggle with church history, presenting Korean Christianity as a form of liberation theology.[44] While indigenous Korean converts did play a more significant role in Korean church history than in most other societies worldwide where missionaries were active, dividing church history along ethnic lines and placing overwhelming emphasis on indigenous actors not only has the potential to essentialize the motivations and actions of religious actors according to racialized constructs, but also downplays potentially unifying theological or intellectual concerns in favour of totalizing ethno-national identities. In contrast, Yi Sanghyŏn, who has written more extensively on Gale than perhaps any other scholar, offers fresh perspectives on the life, identity, and scholarship of Gale.[45] In his *Han'guk*

---

41 "Modern" is misleading in that subsequent research has demonstrated that Gale's most profound contribution was to premodern Korean literature in English translation.

42 Min, *Han'guk Kidokkyohoesa*, 285.

43 Ibid., 282–6.

44 For representative examples, see Min, *Han'guk Kidokkyohoesa*; Yŏksa p'yŏnch'an wiwonhoe, *Han'guk Kidokkyo 100 nyŏnsa*; Yi Chaejŏng, *Taehan Sŏnggonghoe paengnyŏnsa*; Yi Manyŏl, *Han'guk Kidokkyo wa minjok undong*; Yi Manyŏl, *Han'guk Kidokkyo wa minjok ŭisik*; Chu, "Han'guk Kidokkyo paengnyŏnsa"; Yi Tŏkchu, *Nara ŭi tongnip, kyohoe ŭi tongnip*; Sŏ, *Kyohoe wa minjok ŭl saranghan saramdŭl*.

45 Yi has written mainly on Gale's literary and translation activities, lexicography, and evangelization strategy. For a representative sampling, see the following: Yi Sanghyŏn, "Han'guk sinhwa wa Sŏnggyŏng"; "*Yumong ch'ŏnja* sojae Yŏng-Mi munhak chakp'um kwa Keil (J.S. Gale) ŭi kukhanmunch'e pŏnyŏk silch'ŏn"; "Ijungŏ sajŏn kwa kaenyŏmsa kŭrigo Han'gugŏ munhak"; "Keil ŭi Han'guk kososŏl pŏnyŏk kwa kŭ t'onggukkajŏk maengnak."

kojŏn pŏnyŏkka ŭi ch'osang (Portrait of a Translator of the Korean Classics, 2012), for example, he states that his purpose is to portray Gale not as an "Orientalist depicting Korea from a Western perspective ... or as a foreigner who loved Korea" but rather as a "translator of Korean classical literature," an approach at direct odds with the dominant church history paradigm and more consistent with recent offerings by Si Nae Park and Ross King.[46] Yi's initial statement belies the radicalness of his proposition, one that subverts the dominant ethno-nationalist paradigm in Korean history. By focusing on Gale as a *translator* of classical Korean literature into English and not as a *foreigner* per se, Yi prioritizes the linguistic over the ethno-national, in the process aligning Gale's textual positionality with that of Korean readers of his time, the only difference being that Gale approached the *hanmun* text linguistically once removed from the original, that is, through translation.[47]

Yi's approach thus transcends the ethno-national dichotomy inherent in most previous research, accepting Gale as an effectively Korean (though Anglophone) translator of the Korean classics while simultaneously challenging the previous neglect of his extensive translation activities. While Yi's work offers illuminating possibilities for future research and constitutes a welcome counterbalance to religiously oriented church histories, in the present volume I seek to theorize Gale's identity and scholarly work in a holistic manner. In other words, I present Gale as both foreign missionary *and* indigenized Koreaphile, Canadian preacher *and* a-national translator, proposing in this way to highlight and discuss the zones of articulation that arose from this hybrid identity, as well as the themes of conflict and resolution inherent therein.

Gale's ontology of the Korean religious universe represents one such zone of articulation, his mode of contextualizing Korean Confucian praxis with Judeo-Christian theology. Gale's strategy of equating Confucian "heaven" (*ch'ŏn*) with the Christian God emerged sporadically during his earliest years in Korea and had crystallized into an ideological matrix by the time he composed *Pen Pictures*. In the writings and translations in *Old Corea* and in translations from his later years, Gale routinely substituted "God" for any mention of a higher

---

46 Yi Sanghyŏn, *Han'guk kojŏn pŏnyŏkka ŭi ch'osang*, 3; King, "James Scarth Gale and the Christian Literature Society"; King, "James Scarth Gale, Korean Literature in *Hanmun*, and Korean Books"; Gale, King, and Park, *Score One for the Dancing Girl*.

47 Yi Sanghyŏn, *Han'guk kojŏn pŏnyŏkka ŭi ch'osang*, 18.

power – mostly in a Confucian context but not exclusively. This evangelization strategy should therefore be understood as a universal ideology that informed Gale's entire Korean studies project. Gale was not alone in his adaptation of Christianity to native religious traditions, although he was ahead of the curve. Indeed, his thinking was linked to so-called fulfilment theory (*sŏngch'wiron*), which was officially adopted at the World Missionary Conference in Edinburgh in 1910 and applied by mainline Protestant missionaries to their work in China and Korea. Yi Sanghyŏn describes the underpinnings of this theory as follows: the "truth, ethics, and revelations of non-Christian religious traditions were a form of preparation for the Gospel, as well as a point of contact from which to enter into a dialogue with Christianity. Christianity had the ability to complete the commandments and prophecies of Confucianism, fulfilling the fundamental spiritual desires of other religions."[48]

Gale wrote explicitly on religious themes in several chapters of *Pen Pictures* and *Old Corea*, and throughout his career the tone of his writing was informed by Christian fulfilment theory. In "Korea's Preparation for the Bible," Gale indicates five characteristics of traditional Korea that would facilitate the acceptance of Christianity: "Thus has Korea prepared a way for the glad reception of the Gospel, by her special name for God,[49] by the attributes ascribed to Him, by the associations of every day life, by the place accorded to literature, and by her easy and comprehensive writing."[50] In "Korea's Receding Pantheon," appearing in the typescripts of both *Pen Pictures* and *Old Corea*, Gale provides an inventory of Korea's traditional religious beliefs, writing with confidence of their gradual demise but suggesting finally that they not be effaced through Christianity but instead be considered a step toward fulfilment: "We watch [these beliefs] recede with something akin to sorrow, unless a better be on hand to take their place, and make good the defects that were inherent in them."[51] In *Old Corea*'s "The Corean's

---

48 Ibid., "Han'guk sinhwa wa Sŏnggyŏng," 43.

49 Gale is referring to the supposedly native term *Hananim* which he promoted as the equivalent of the Christian "God." Although there was a heated debate among Western missionaries over which term to adopt, with some missionaries preferring the Catholic term *Ch'ŏnju* (天主 Lord of Heaven), *Hananim* eventually won out. For a discussion of the etymology of these terms, see Baker, "Hananim, Hanŭnim, Hanŭllim, and Hanŏllim."

50 Gale, "Korea's Preparation for the Bible," *Pen Pictures*, this vol.

51 Ibid., "Korea's Receding Pantheon," *Pen Pictures*, this vol.

View of God,"[52] Gale presents perhaps his clearest distillation of his view of Korean theism and contextualizes his own approach with the consensus among foreigners:

> Corea has been said by more than one foreigner to be a land without religion, and the statement might at first seem to be correct. It is due to the fact that she has but few fixed dogmas to rule her world. Dogma, however, does not always represent the highest and purest kind of faith. While without a definitely clear-cut religion, Corea has never been without a deep-rooted conviction that God lives and that He is near at hand.[53]

The religion-themed essays in *Old Corea* demonstrate a further development of Gale's Korean theological thought. Over the roughly two decades that separate the bulk of the two typescripts, Gale's writing shows evidence of a more systematic and universalistic approach to Korean religious thought and its relationship to Christianity. In "The Corean's View of God," Gale draws on the authority of the Korean historical record – quotations that supposedly would "speak for themselves" – to prove the presence of God throughout Korea's history. In evoking this textual tradition, Gale was attempting to connect evangelically with the soul of the literati class by connecting with the mind of the scholar through the Literary Sinitic tradition. These quotations were, according to Gale, "selected from over a hundred examples spanning a period of nearly two thousand years."[54] Extending his parallel discourse development beyond a mere Ch'ŏn-God equivalence, Gale subsumes the entire spectrum of religious deities under the Judeo-Christian banner through recourse to the ancient Hebrew pantheon:

> As the Hebrew wrote El, Elohim, Eloah, El-Shaddai, Jehovah, etc., expressive of the deity's different attributes but all the one God, so the Corean has used many names that point to the same Spirit, infinite, eternal and unchangeable, Who, though he dwells unseen to the mortal eye, controls all the doings of the earth. Some of these names are Hananim and Ch'ŏn

---

52 Although the *Old Corea* typescript version is undated, a comparable version appeared in the *Korea Mission Field* 11 (1916): 66–9.

53 Gale, "The Corean's View of God," *Old Corea*, this vol.

54 This longer list of quotations may be found in Gale's unpublished ledgers. These and other unpublished writings show clear evidence of a sustained and focused evangelical strategy inspired by fulfilment theory.

(天), the One Great One, Sangje (上帝), the Supreme Ruler; Sinmyŏng (神明), the All-seeing One; Taejujae (大主宰), the Master; Ch'ŏn'gun (天君), the Divine King; Ch'ŏn'gong (天功), the Celestial Artificer; Okhwang (玉皇), the Prince of Perfection; Chohwaong (造化翁), the Creator; Sin (神), the Spirit, and many others.[55]

Also, during the 1910s, Gale seems to have been delving more deeply into the Tan'gun narrative and its religious import. In "The Corean's View of God," penned around 1916, Gale writes, "If we put aside the tradition of the god-man, Tan'gun, not yet fully investigated, we find that Corea received her first revelation of God about the time of the Hebrew prophet Samuel. The announcement came from China, of a great Creator. He sits high above the heavens untouched by earth's frailties, sin, change, or decay. He was the God of the Chu Dynasty."[56] In contrast, in the September 1917 issue of *Korea Magazine*, Gale includes a lengthy explication of the religious import of the Tan'gun myth, describing Hwanin (桓因 "God"), Hwanung (桓雄 "the Spirit"), and Hwan'gŏm (桓儉 "God-man") as a "Triune Spirit" equivalent to the Holy Trinity of Christianity.[57] By broadening the Tan'gun myth pantheistically to include all major religious traditions in Korea, and in turn accepting the pre-Confucian animism and totemism of the Tan'gun myth as an earlier yet unfulfilled iteration of Christianity, Gale in effect accorded universal legitimacy – or at least redeemability – to the pantheon of Korean religious thought:

In our country there is a deep and mysterious religion which indeed includes the three great cults, Confucianism, Buddhism, and Taoism and forms the basis of our national life. If we speak of filial piety, or loyalty to the king, we think of the great Teacher of the No Kingdom (Confucius).[58] If, on the other hand, we pretend to the impossible and things beyond

---

55 Gale, "The Corean's View of God," *Old Corea*, this vol.

56 *Chu* here is the Sino-Korean pronunciation of 周 (Ch. Zhou). Gale seems to be referring to the Duke of Zhou (周公), who is credited with consolidating the Zhou dynasty in the eleventh century BC and who is renowned as a cultural hero and paragon of sage rule. That Gale should equate the Duke of Zhou's sagacity with divine inspiration, however, is striking.

57 "Tangun," *Korea Magazine* (September 1917): 404.

58 "No" here is the Sino-Korean rendering of 魯 (Ch. Lu), the home state of Confucius.

human kind, we say it is the religion of Noja.[59] Again, if it is a question of doing no evil but good only, it is ascribed to the great teacher of India (Buddha), but Tangun taught them all.[60]

This inclusion of Buddhism within the realm of legitimate religions was in line with Gale's gradually softening stance toward that faith. Gale initially viewed Buddhism with suspicion as a corrupt "sect," echoing the dominant Confucian discourse of the time. In *Korea in Transition* (1909) he writes,

[Buddhism's] long course of history has been marked by various degrees of corruption and by dark deeds. In delightfully secluded corners and in the shade and quiet of the hills are its temples. So separated are they from the wicked world and so shut away into the silent lands of meditation and repose, that you would think them the habitation of the holy, but it proves not to be so ... The fall of the Koryŏ dynasty in 1391 [*sic*] AD was supposed to be due to the corrupt influence of Buddhism, and since then the state has looked down upon it as an outcast religion.[61]

However, in the same section on Buddhism, Gale paints a more ambivalent portrait of the religion and its legacy.

What shall we say in commendation of Korea's form of Buddhism? Perhaps it is that Sakyamuni has taught a lesson in tenderness and compassion. There is a gentleness in some of the old priests and a dreamy mystic something that inspires one to go softly and to put all iron and hardness out of the soul. But Buddhism, with its gilded idols and its awful representations of the Ten Hells that await mortals and its unintelligible litany and its immoral priesthood, constitutes but a poor portal for the soul of the man.[62]

By the 1920s, however, when many of the essays constituting *Old Corea* were penned, Gale was expressing syncretic views on theology in an attempt to harmonize Confucian, Buddhist, and Christian beliefs

---

59 I.e., 老子 (Ch. Laozi).

60 "Tangun," *Korea Magazine* (September 1917): 406.

61 Gale, *Korea in Transition*, 79–80.

62 Ibid., 81.

more fully. Upon his retirement in 1927, Gale addressed the many friends and colleagues he had amassed over four decades; on the subject of religion he had this to say:

> In religion, too, the East has given us Confucianism, Buddhism, and Taoism. What do I think of this? The more I study them the more I honour the sincerity, the self-denial, the humility, the wisdom, the devotion that was back of the first founders, great priests of the soul. Their one desire was to overcome evil and step upward and upward, nearer to God. In this we are all alike – Confucian, Buddhist, Christian – all brothers. Kind and sympathetic we should be to one another. Christ came to fulfill the ideals of each and every one of us. In Him, whatever our religion may be, we shall find the ideal of the soul.[63]

Thus, by the late 1910s Gale seems to have developed a universalistic conception of Korean religious thought based on a systematic construction of theistic parallels with Judeo-Christian theology – a conception he would maintain for the rest of his life. Although Gale was not alone in adopting fulfilment theory as an evangelical strategy, there is evidence that from his earliest days in Korea he had adopted a relatively more accepting view of religious thought, and that for the rest of his career he worked to integrate the Judeo-Christian and Sinitic thought worlds more systematically. The primary medium by which Gale attempted to approach the Eastern religious tradition was Literary Sinitic; unlike his other missionary colleagues, Gale focused on classical Korean literature in *hanmun*, extensively citing Korean histories in *hanmun* to bolster and legitimize his religious arguments in the eyes of a classically educated Korean audience. Universalizing Korean religious thought under the Judeo-Christian banner was for Gale not a straightforward matter of epistemic synthesis, nor was it a

---

63 Gale, untitled, 1927, reproduced in Yu Yŏngsik, *Ch'akhăn mokchya*, 801. Gale expresses a similar sentiment in the introduction to his English translation of *Kuunmong* (*Dream of the Cloud Nine*): "*The Cloud Dream of the Nine* is a revelation of what the Oriental thinks and feels not only about things of the earth but about the hidden things of the Universe. It helps us toward a comprehensible knowledge of the Far East"; "Confucian, Buddhist and Taoist ideas are mingled throughout the story, but everyone speaks with confidence of Heaven as a place." See Kim, *The Cloud Dream of the Nine*, trans. Gale, 7; 37.

process of Sinitic effacement at the hands of totalizing Christian discourse. Rather, it was a continual and conflicted project of reassessing and re-evaluating the Sinographic order against his own missionary mode of thought.

Japan and the Vacuity of Material Modernity

As I have mentioned, most of the Korean-language scholarship on Gale has been conducted by church historians, who have tended to focus more on indigenous figures. But there seems to be another reason for the minimal attention paid to Gale's contributions: the perception that he harboured pro-Japanese sentiments. The exact origin of this impression is unclear, but Gale himself was aware of it. In a 1906 letter to the American missionary and statesman Dr Arthur J. Brown, who wrote extensively on Christian missions in Asia and shared Gale's ambivalent views toward Japan's role in Korea,[64] Gale refers to this "misperception" while affirming his true loyalties:

> These are days of intense interest in Korea. Politically the country is fast under lock and key and has entered on a period of great distress and humiliation. I have always been reckoned as pro-Japanese by some of my fellow labourers but I am by no means so. I am out and out pro-Korean but it seems wise to me and others too I am not alone in keeping on good or favorable terms with the Japanese. Herein lies hope for Korea. I realize however how hard it is for the average Korean to willingly submit to the ordeal. It has brought down the proudest to a place of humility and God is richly blessing them.[65]

64　Arthur Judson Brown (1856–1963) served as Secretary of the Presbyterian Board of Missions, among other positions, and travelled extensively throughout Asia, writing in detail about his journeys. His account of Korea may be found in Brown, "A Reading Journey in Korea." Brown's prolific bibliography includes *The Mastery of the Far East* (1921), in which he provides a well-researched and relatively even-handed account of Japan's administration of Korea. This work cites the "Reverend Dr. James S. Gale" several times and in general seems to share Gale's perspective on Japan, acknowledging certain material advances brought by Japan but faulting the heavy-handed Japanese administration.

65　Gale, "Letter to Dr. Brown," 10 March 1906, reproduced in Yu Yŏngsik, *Ch'akhăn mokchya*, 589.

The following passage from the *Diary of Yun Ch'iho* is often invoked as conclusive evidence of Gale's pro-Japanese orientation:

2nd. Wednesday. [June 1927]. Bright. Hot. Seoul home. To the station to see Dr. Gale and his family leaving Korea for good. His departure is a distinct loss to Korea. He has done more than any other single missionary to introduce the Korean literature to the world. No one to succeed him in sight. It's somewhat sad that his too pronounced pro-Japanism has to a great measure estranged the young men of Korea from him. So sorry to see him leave, perhaps forever.[66]

Although Yun's rather cryptic entry does not explain exactly why Gale is considered pro-Japanese, the matter-of-fact manner of the statement does suggest that this was a widely held belief, at least among "young men of Korea." However, Yun's observations also reveal the central conundrum of Gale and his legacy: his position as an allo-metropolitan Christian missionary as well as the foremost medium of Korean literature conveyance to the Western world.[67] Though a Koreaphile at heart and a lifelong advocate of Korean literary culture, Gale's outlying position as a missionary neither Korean nor Japanese endowed him with a relatively less partisan viewpoint not invested in ethno-national or dominant-subaltern debates. I argue that Gale's tendency toward emotional detachment on the question of Japanese governance of Korea has been differently construed by nationalist scholars of Korean church

---

66 Yun and Kim, *Yun Ch'iho ilgi*, vol. 9 (1927), 118. This quotation also appears in the following sources: Hwang and Yi, *Kaenyŏm kwa yŏksa, kŭndae Han'guk ŭi ijungŏ sajŏn*, 340; Yu Yŏngsik, *Ch'akhan mokchya*, 849. Although the overall tone of these sources does not depict Gale as overly pro-Japanese, the repetition of this quotation does tend to perpetuate the misperception.

67 I take the term "allo-metropolitan positionality" from Ross King to describe Gale's identity as a foreign missionary whose nationality did not coincide with that of the metropolitan power. Unlike British Orientalists in colonial India or Japanese scholar-officials who benefited from the full political, financial, and ideological support of their respective metropoles, Gale's allo-metropolitan status undercut the viability of his scholarly project and challenges the classic understanding of an empowered Orientalist agent representing a powerful hegemon. King also argues that Gale's allo-metropolitan posture serves to explain his being "consigned to oblivion." See King, "James Scarth Gale, Korean Literature in *Hanmun*, and Allo-Metropolitan Missionary Orientalism."

history more informed by the Korean ethno-nation (*minjok*) versus foreign dichotomy and politically invested in the legacy of colonial subjugation and collaboration. Moreover, considered within the broader category of foreign missionaries in Korea, Gale's characterization as more pro- than anti-Japanese is puzzling.[68] Given the continual pressure by the Government General of Korea (GGK) on missionaries to acquiesce to colonial rule, at least tacitly, any critique of Japanese administration more vociferous than that of Gale would likely have resulted in a missionary's expulsion from Korea. Missionaries such as Gale, if they wished to continue their work, were obliged to actively support the Japanese, self-censor, and remain tacit supporters, or else offer constructive critiques while quietly questioning the entire enterprise. Gale chose the last of these courses.

Capping a series of political essays in *Pen Pictures* in which Gale reported with exasperation the grim outlook of the country in the run-up to the Russo-Japanese War, "Japan's Task in Korea" expresses cautious optimism as to Japan's prospects in Korea: "Japan has before her the difficult and delicate task of placating Korea, and winning the hearts of this conservative people. It will cost nothing to take possession of Korea and Korea's government, but it will tax her skill to win Korea's heart and confidence … She [Japan] is wise, however, in her day and generation, and doubtless will win in this fight too."[69] Emboldened by the stunning outcome of the Russo-Japanese War, an unprecedented victory by an Eastern over a Western power, Japanese policymakers were confident of success in Korea. Gale's essay cautions against such hubris, noting the deeply ingrained hatred of Japan within the "bone and fiber" of the Korean people and the diametrically opposed character of the two nations. Crucially, despite their shared East Asian identities and common membership in the Sinographic cosmopolis, Gale points out the chasm between Japan and Korea in terms of literature, again appropriating the perspective of the Korean literatus:

> Still another reason for this dislike is the fact that their ideals are different. Japan is a land of *jiujutsu* [*sic*] and the two-handed sword. Mere babies of the Sunrise Empire wear soldier cape, carry make-believe guns and

---

68 Yu Yŏngsik suggests that the background of Gale's second wife, Ada Sale, contributed to the perception of Gale as pro-Japanese, writing that "Ada was able to 'mingle freely with the [Japanese] government people and [be] influential in harmonizing the official classes and the missionaries.'" Yu, *Ch'akhǎn mokchya*, 852.

69 Gale, "Japan's Task in Korea," *Pen Pictures*, 1905, this vol.

shout "*banzai.*" Their world is the battle-field and their ambition is to rout Kuropatkin.[70] The Korean has no such thought. The goal of his desire is scholarship where he can pose as Confucius or the Yellow Emperor, and lecture his fellow-citizens in the language of the ancients. One is the land of the sword and one is the land of the pen. With what contempt the Korean regards the Japanese cross-strokes, and down-strokes, and short-stops and dots of the written character. Not one of them will do, all is lacking in strength, finish and form. The rascal may rout 400,000 Russians, but he is not civilized, behold how badly he writes that character.[71]

Even Gale's initial open-mindedness toward the Japanese administration of Korea was tempered by what he viewed, from an optimistic perspective, as miscalculations caused by Japan's ignorance of Korea. At his most pessimistic, however, he believed that the entire Japanese enterprise in Korea was futile. His views on Japan, like those of many observers, evolved over time.[72] A sea change seems to have occurred, however, following the Japanese response to the March First Independence Movement. Gale wrote in stark and personal terms on the effect of this response in a June 1919 edition of the *Japan Advertiser*:

The writer used to imagine that Japan would prove an expert at reading the Korean mind, seeing that she was an Oriental herself, and was therefore within the charmed circle of the East, but he has changed his mind. Japan knows little or nothing of what Korea means or matters. The methods she adopts, the words she speaks, the announcements she makes prove her ignorance. It is not unfair to say that she is wholly unaware of the kind of being she has to deal with, and so today has resorted to the bayonet and gun-butt to solve her problems.[73]

---

70 Aleksei Nikolaevich Kuropatkin (Алексе́й Никола́евич Куропа́ткин, 1848–1925) was the Russian Imperial Minister of War from 1898 until his relief from command following Russia's initial defeats under his command in the Russo-Japanese War.

71 Gale, "Japan's Task in Korea," *Pen Pictures*, this vol.

72 Yu Yŏngsik argues that three "incidents" prompted Gale to change his mind toward Japan: the murder of Queen Min in October 1895, the censoring of his textbook *Yumong Ch'ŏnja* in 1908 by the Japanese Residency General, and the Japanese response to the March First Movement. While I agree that all three events influenced Gale's perception of Japan, I focus only on the final and most decisive incident. See Yu, *Ch'akhŭn mokchya*, 853–8.

73 In the handwritten manuscript version of this essay in the Gale Papers, Gale has written in the upper margin, "Written for the *Japan Advertiser* and

Gale was beginning to question the role of shared race – the definitive criterion in the waning Social Darwinist paradigm – in predicting
the course of modernization for Korea. In contrast, he began to claim
that his position as an allo-metropolitan foreign missionary superseded
shared ethnic identity in "winning the hearts" of Koreans, because his
were relationships not based in fear. In a letter to Lord Bryce written
shortly after the eruption of the March First Movement, Gale reported
on the 9 March meeting he attended with a Japanese administrator and
eight other foreign missionaries, at which he conveyed many of the
same sentiments:

Last Sunday evening (March 9th) the Director of Home Affairs, Mr. Usami,
asked for an interview with some of the oldest missionaries, and nine of
us gathered to meet him. He was very courteous and kind and I could see
that he deeply appreciated the gravity of the situation … He then asked
us to tell him plainly wherein we felt Japan had failed, and I mentioned
two points that seemed to stand out against her regime and being largely
responsible for the present situation. First, while Japan has done much for
Corea, made roads, given a secure government, instituted laws, opened
up ways of commerce, and safeguarded health, mentally she had placed
the Corean under a reign of terror. He does not dare utter the promptings
of his heart lest the spy and the gendarme or the soldier have him away to
prison with its medieval horrors. I said to Mr. Usami "You will pardon me
but I am sure I am right in saying that you can never get at a Corean's real
heart; I may, but not you. Why? Because while I am sure that he does not
fear you, he fears that machine that stands back of you and fills his soul
with terror. Ten years ago many Koreans were with Japan; today they are
all gone, miles away in heart.[74]

---

published therein July 15th, 1919. Three of its phrases were slightly softened
down to please censor." See Spectator, "Japan's Problem," *Japan Advertiser*,
11 July 1919. In *The Renaissance of Korea*, a sympathetic depiction of Korea's
plight, Joseph Waddington Graves introduces large excerpts from this article,
retaining Gale's anonymity with the following introduction: "In the *Japan
Advertiser*, July 11th, 1919, appears an illuminating article on the whole question of Japan's tragically mistaken policy in Korea. The writer is 'Spectator,'
a *nom de plume* which is understood to belong to a singularly well-informed
authority on matters Oriental." See Graves, *The Renaissance of Korea*, 40.

74 Gale, "Letter to Viscount Bryce," 10 March 1919, reproduced in Yu Yŏngsik,
    Ch'akhăn mokchya, 640.

A common current, which begins as a quietly voiced reservation in *Pen Pictures* and develops into a defiant denunciation in Gale's post–March First discourse on the Japanese role in Korea, is the distinction between material and spiritual modernization. Highlighting this distinction was for Gale the ultimate goal of his Korean studies project and the proper objective of any effective missionary in the country, an objective that was, however, impossible to realize within a ruling system maintained by fear and coercion, regardless of common language or ethnicity.

Gale's most blistering critique of Japan's role in Korea was his unpublished and bluntly titled "Why Japan Has Failed in Korea," a systematic criticism of Japan's history of violent coercion in Korean foreign affairs and its oppressive education, publication, and legal policies. Gale's detailed critique of Japan's actions in Korea from its earliest forays until the violent crackdown of March 1919 reflects not a sudden about-face by a pro-Japanese individual but rather the recognition of a devoted Korean sympathizer that he could no longer find any basis to even nominally support Japanese efforts. The vacuity of material modernity in winning Korean "hearts and minds," a recurring theme in much of Gale's writing on Japan, resurfaces here:

> The Korean is by nature a quiet, long-suffering, peaceful, and rather timid fellow, but at the same time can be resentful and determined when given sufficient provocation.
>
> It is, therefore, quite an interesting question to find out just what the Japanese have done to change these people, who, ordinarily, are so easily controlled and contented, into a resentful, protesting multitude, ready to sacrifice life, property, and, indeed, everything, just to be rid of the Japanese who in many respects have been their material benefactors.[75]

Gale elaborates on the failure of material progress to alter the deep-seated contempt of Japan held by Koreans:

> From the time when the mind of man runneth not to the contrary the Koreans have looked upon the Japanese as a race of inferior culture and barbaric tendencies worthy only to be feared. The recent strides that Japan has made in material progress have not greatly altered this ancient habit

---

75 Gale, "Why Japan Has Failed in Korea," reproduced in Yu Yŏngsik, *Ch'akhăn mokchya*, 646–51.

of thought. The average Korean thinks, that, given the same opportunities, his people would have accomplished all that Japan has done.[76]

Thus did Gale conclude in the aftermath of the March First Movement that Japan had ultimately failed in the difficult task outlined in the closing pages of *Pen Pictures*, a task he had viewed with a sceptical but nevertheless cautiously optimistic eye. The Japanese were now further from the "heart" of the Korean than they had been at annexation, a heart that he, the Koreaphile foreign missionary, was now paradoxically in a better position to understand. The depoliticized and more heavily literary content of *Old Corea* is evidence that the period around 1920 marked the end of Gale's political writing, even as he continued to develop his Judeo-Christian-Korean theological strategy and deepened his immersion in Korean literature in Literary Sinitic. The Japan question, therefore, like many aspects of Korea's modernization, evinced in Gale a mixture of ambivalence, frustration, and conflict, wrought by his complex identity as allo-metropolitan missionary, triumphalist modernizer, and Koreaphile literatus.

Koreaphilic Cosmopolitanism: Gale's Project to Establish Korea's Classical Literary Legacy

Gale had by the time of *Pen Pictures* developed a distinct ideology concerning the Korean linguistic and literary landscapes and Korean culture more generally. One of the primary foundations of his intellectual approach to East Asia was the relationship between "Chinese" and Korean culture, particularly in terms of language and literature. In the 1900 inaugural issue of *Transactions of the Royal Asiatic Society – Korea Branch* (RASKB), in an essay titled "The Influence of China upon Korea," Gale details China's long history of cultural hegemony on the Korean peninsula and depicts a contemporary Korean culture inundated with Sinitic influence.[77]

---

76 Ibid.

77 As Ross King pointed out in a 2017 presentation on Gale, this "debate" between Homer Hulbert and James Gale over the influence of China in Korean culture and history was staged by the RASKB so as to present caricatures of the two positions, in the style of a high-school debate, with Gale positing overwhelming influence from China and Hulbert averring the predominance of Korean indigenous influence. Yet these "caricatures" were far from fabricated and instead reflect to a large extent the respective ideologies of Gale and Hulbert,

The following excerpt demonstrates Gale's ideology regarding the linguistic element of this influence:

> Such being the nature of these centuries of Chinese influence Korea has to-day no life, literature or thought that is not of Chinese origin. She has not even had a permanent Manchu occupation to break the hypnotic spell of Confucianism. Even her language, while possessing a basis of form entirely different from that of China, has had the latter language so grafted into it, and the thought of the same so fully made a part of its very essence, that we need the Chinese character to convey it. This will account for the native contempt of the native script. *Ŏnmun* (諺文) has become the slave of *Hanmun* (漢文), and does all the coolie work of the sentence, namely, the ending, connecting and inflecting parts, while the *Hanmun*, in its lordly way, provides the nouns and verbs.[78]

Gale goes on to detail the influence of Chinese at the lexical level, his observations bolstered by his extensive expertise in dictionary compilation:

> Out of a list of 32,789 words, there proved to be 21,417 Chinese and 11,372 Korean, that is, twice as many Chinese as native words. At the present time, too, the language is being flooded by many new terms to represent incoming Western thought, and these are all Chinese.
>
> In the *Hanmun* dictionary, or *Okp'y ŏn* (玉篇), there are 10,850 characters. In reading these, the native endeavours as far as possible to mark each character by some native word, which will approximately give the meaning, so he says *Soe-kŭm* or "metal"-*kŭm*. In this search for native words that will approximately designate the character he finds himself lacking in the case of more than 3,000 characters. For 7,700 of them native words are found, but for the remainder nothing even approaching the meaning exists in the native speech.[79]

Gale's observations are snapshots of the premodern linguistic hierarchy in Korea, which positioned Literary Sinitic as the ultimate medium

---

evidenced by their subsequent scholarship. See King, "James Scarth Gale, Korean Literature in *Hanmun*, and Allo-Metropolitan Missionary Orientalism."

78 Gale, "The Influence of China upon Korea," *Transactions of the Royal Asiatic Society – Korea Branch* 1 (1900): 14.

79 Ibid.

of literature and the vernacular script (*ŏnmun*) as a tool for accessing *hanmun*. Gale wrote with all sincerity that to "sit down and write a story in the native language, or Anglo-Saxon, so to speak, is, we may say, impossible."[80] Gale is thus describing the mixed-script (*kukhanmun* 國漢文) form of writing, an inscriptional practice that may narrowly refer to the *t'o*-style translation-cum-reading tradition (*ŏnhae*) that characterized the premodern study of *hanmun* texts, but may more broadly define an emergent *compositional* technique that combined *hancha* (sinographs) and *han'gŭl* (vernacular) orthography in varying degrees of vernacularization – a technique just emerging among the intellectual class at the time of Gale's writing. What he was definitely *not* describing, however, was the *composition* of literature in pure *han'gŭl*, a feat the impossibility of which he was convinced.

In the same inaugural issue of *Transactions*, Homer Hulbert presents a prearranged rebuttal to Gale's paper, pointing out examples of indigenous Korean cultural heritage. Despite his nativist tone, Hulbert himself seems to acknowledge the immaturity of vernacular literature in the following lines:

As a medium of writing the Koreans adopted the Chinese character and they still continue to use it. There has never risen a man in Korea to do for his country what Chaucer, Dante and Cervantes did for theirs, namely, write a classic in the native tongue and begin the good work of weaning the people away from a foreign system which restricts the benefits of erudition to the meagrest minority of the people. And yet Korea has not been wanting in men who recognised the need of a change. The first of these was Sŭl-ch'ong [*sic*] (薛聽), to whom reference was made in the paper read last month as being one of Korea's great men. It is true; but the foundation of his greatness lies, it seems to me, in his attempt to make popular education possible in his native land. He it was who invented the *Ni-t'u* [*sic*] (吏套), which was a half-measure and therefore doomed to failure. But such as it was it was entirely anti-Chinese, at least in this respect that, by weaning the Koreans away from the Chinese grammatical system, the first step would be taken towards weaning them away from the whole system.[81]

---

80 Ibid., 14–15.

81 Homer B. Hulbert, "Korean Survivals and Discussions," *Transactions of the Royal Asiatic Society – Korea Branch* 1 (1900): 25–50; 30–1. There are two meanings of *idu* (*Ni-t'u*), one referring to a particular method among several others

Hulbert was in effect concurring with Gale's assessment of the lack of an established, venerated vernacular literature, but proposed a drastically different remedy: wean the readership from Literary Sinitic by offering a viable alternative.[82] The tone of Gale's "Influence of China upon Korea," on the other hand, is completely diametric. In contrast with Hulbert and the vast majority of Western missionaries and scholars of Korea, Gale embraces the influence of China, revels in its absoluteness, and further asserts Korea's cultural superiority by its participation in the cosmopolitan order it represented.

Although these diametrically opposed positions may be partially explained by the pre-arranged structure of the debate, the two men's perspectives on Korean history and culture were far from arbitrary assignments within a debate forum: Gale's entire scholarly project embodied a Sinocentric, cosmopolitan world view, while Hulbert's broader scholarship for its part evidenced a strong nativist streak. Moreover, in terms of the emergent field of Korean studies, the

---

for modifying a Literary Sinitic text to be read in "Korean," and the other to encompass all of these methods of modification. Here Hulbert is referring to its latter, generalized meaning. Although this "invention" is traditionally attributed to the Silla (668–935) scholar Sŏl Ch'ong (薛聰, 650–730), based on the account of his life in the *Samguk sagi*, evidence suggests that the system had already been developed in earlier Silla, whereas Sŏl Ch'ong was responsible for synthesizing the practice. Lee and Ramsey describe the *idu* method of writing in the following way: "In translating a Chinese-language text into Korean using *idu*, the scribe first changed the words of the text around into Korean syntactic order. Then he added Korean particles and verb endings and other function words using Chinese characters either phonetically or semantically to represent those function words." Although the earliest attempts at manipulating Literary Sinitic texts to "Koreanize" them are attested from the Three Kingdoms period, "it was in Silla that *idu* seems to have been developed into a functional transcription method." Unlike other vernacularization methods, *idu* continued to be utilized for centuries after the invention of the Korean alphabet, up until the late nineteenth century. See Lee and Ramsey, *A History of the Korean Language*, 53–62.

82 Hulbert would repeat such language ideologies in various other venues. His textbook *Samin p'ilchi* (士民必知 Necessary Knowledge for Scholars and Commoners, 1890), the first textbook to be written in pure *han'gŭl*, may be viewed as a contribution to this bolstering of native literature. For a discussion of Hulbert, his textbook, and language ideologies, see Pieper, "Korean as a Transitional Literacy," chap. 4.

Gale-Hulbert debate held much more significance than a staged deliberation over Korean history or a mere friendly rivalry between two scholar-missionaries. Metonymically, Gale and Hulbert represented cosmopolitan and nationalistic versions of Korean history writ small on the scholar-missionary stage. Even so, their positions extended to broader discussions of Korean culture and heritage among subsequent generations of Korea scholars and arguably constitute the dominant axis of philosophical inquiry in contemporary Korean studies in the East Asian context. To take just the example of language: Hulbert's concluding remarks in the aforementioned article portend the nationalistic argumentation in the field of Korean linguistics that legitimized vernacularization as the natural rectification of a legacy of Chinese domination over indigenous Korean culture. In his 2015 discussion of diglossia in premodern Korea, Ross King writes of this discourse that "perhaps more dangerous for the modern Korean context, though, is the way in which the inherent 'twoness' in diglossia [has] played into modern Korean script nationalism, leading most Korean researchers to cast *hanmun* and *han'gŭl* as villain and hero, respectively, in teleological grand narratives of the long struggle of *han'gŭl* to overcome adversity and discrimination in benighted pre-modern 'ideographic' times in order to finally win the day in an enlightened modern and phonographic Korea."[83] Appearing at the cusp of a revolution in Korean inscriptional practice and modern literature, the Gale-Hulbert debate provides a blueprint for subsequent developments in Korean studies. Partly because Hulbert presented a more nativist, even nationalistic portrayal of Korean culture in which the Korean vernacular is suppressed by Sinographic culture, subsequent treatments of Hulbert by Korean language sources, many of which echo his perspectives, have been much more generous and thorough.[84] Gale's project, by contrast – championing membership in a Sinographic cosmopolis that seemed increasingly antiquated and anti-nationalistic – has been viewed as antithetic to the modern, nation-based historical paradigm. Gale's tone and

---

83 For a number of examples of this language ideology, see King, "Ditching 'Diglossia,'" 8.

84 See for example Kim Tongjin, *P'aran nun ŭi Han'gukhon*. Although the Korean title may be translated as "The Blue-eyed Soul of Korea: Hulbert," the official English title is *Crusader for Korea: Homer B. Hulbert*. Also see Kim Kwonjŏng, *Han'guginboda Han'guk ŭl tŏ saranghan Migugin Hŏlbŏt'ŭ* [Hulbert: The American Who Loved Korea More Than Koreans].

philosophical perspective may have struck his readers as antiquated and anachronistic, an impression that has only deepened with time. And yet, I argue, it was precisely through this revelling in the antiquarian that Gale sought to affirm Korea's cultural greatness by dint of its participation in a transnational and diachronic sinographical tradition.

Although Gale from early on in his nearly four decades in Korea observed the monumental influence of Korea's neighbour to the West, he bore witness during that time to countless transformations, and his observations are reflected in the tone and content of his writing. One area of discourse that demonstrated a shift in his thinking was language ideologies in relation to Korean literature. In "Korean Literature," appearing in *Pen Pictures*, Gale prefaces his translation of Hong Yangho's "Setting Free the Wild Goose" (放鴈辭 Pang an sa), a work of Korean literature in *hanmun*, with the following observations of the state of "modern literature" in Korea:

Korea is a land without novels or newspapers.[85] Let anyone who suffers from nervous prostration, brought on by a vain effort to keep pace with the literature of the day, come here and rest. No regular story-writer is known to have lived in these parts for a thousand years. There are no publishing houses and no laws of copyright. Scholars have written short essays at rare intervals, but literature has never been reduced to the common levels of ordinary life. Books done in the colloquial and sold at ordinary street stalls, would be an abnormal thing in the eyes of the old-fashioned scholar.[86]

The observations in this 1902 essay reflect a still-compartmentalized linguistic landscape in which Literary Sinitic was the unassailable and unavoidable embodiment of "true" literature, and the vernacular was an instrument of access or else the medium of an "abnormal" literary curiosity. Significantly for Gale, the term *literature* was polysemous: it referred to both "true" literature in *hanmun* as well as literature in the Western sense, the literature at "the common levels of ordinary life,"

---

85 The typescript for this essay in *Pen Pictures* dates from 1905, but it had appeared already in the 21 June 1902 edition of the *Japan Weekly Mail*. Although Korea's first modern novel in the Western sense had yet to be written, there were a number of vernacular newspapers in circulation at this time, and so Gale's claim that newspapers did not exist is puzzling.

86 Gale, "Korean Literature," *Pen Pictures*, this vol.

which for Gale had yet to come to fruition. Gale reiterates this "compartmentalized" state of Korean language and literature in his essay "A Freak of Language" in *Pen Pictures*:

> Korea, which sleeps and dreams of Yo (堯) and Sun (舜), two Chinese Emperors who lived before the Flood,[87] has no less than three languages in which to express her dreamings: an eye-language, an ear-language and a hand-language.[88]
>
> The eye-language comes from China in the form of ideographs or pictures. Its soul lies not in the sound but in the shape, for the sound changes according to the place in which it exists, while the shape remains ever the same … Korean literature is nearly all written in the eye-language. It cannot be heard by any mortal ear. The eyes must see it, and the mind translate it, and the voice sing it out in colloquial before the ear can hear and understand. For that reason Orientals are great readers by the eye … This eye-language is a sign and wonder in the land of Sinim,[89] a marvel and a mystery among the sons of men. It is the oldest form of writing on the earth. It is the most widely distributed, being placarded on door-posts all the way from Tokyo to Tibet and from Harbin to Mandalay. It is the most sacred for its forms are worshipped by millions of the race, yet I suppose

---

87 Gale often provided parallel Western chronologies when discussing events in Asian history for the benefit of his Anglophone readers. In this case Gale claims that Yo (Ch. Yao) and Sun (Ch. Shun) predated the great biblical flood, but the flood's traditional dating to roughly 2300 BC suggests overlap with the life of Yo.

88 For a detailed description of the origins of European ideography and its application to Egyptian hieroglyphics and Literary Sinitic, see O'Neill, *Ideography and Chinese Language Theory*. Gale does not make any further mention of "hand-language," apparently some form of sign language, in his essay.

89 The land of Sinim is a reference to the following passage of the Old Testament: "Behold, these shall come from far: and, lo, these from the north and from the west; and these from the land of Sinim" (Isaiah 49:12, KJV). Many Bible scholars believe Sinim (Hebrew: מִינִים) to be a reference to China, in this case the Qin state founded in 778 BC, or less specifically, distant lands far to the east of the Holy Land. The latinization of Qin, Sinae, and the common occurrence of its root in various words such as sinology, sinograph, etc. suggest a Chinese connection. Gale seems to be using the term here as a stand-in for "the Orient."

it is the most hidebound and indefinite of all written languages. It has been the lurking place of subterfuge, evasion, white-lie, guile and duplicity. Through it men hint at what they are after, while covering up the real thought and motive that lies underneath, by it you can write one thing and mean another. It possesses no definite article and no indefinite, so that when it comes to an exact translation satisfactory results are impossible.[90]

For Gale, the sinograph is at once exotic and duplicitous, mysterious and yet notorious, a source of wonder and marvel with widespread currency throughout the Eastern world but equally "the lurking place of subterfuge, evasion," and "guile." What is clear from this passage is that for Gale this "eye language" (Literary Sinitic) commanded a vast amount of authority and legitimacy throughout East Asia on account of its wide distribution and antiquity. By Western standards, however, "the character" is inexact and nebulous and on that basis a dubious medium for modern literature and translation, which demands directness and precision, and crucially, intertranslatability with Western languages.[91] A language ideology such as this thus evokes a somewhat exoticized Orientalist perspective of a still-dichotomous literary landscape, where a "competent" modern vernacular idiom had yet to emerge to bridge the gap between "duplicitous" Literary Sinitic and nascent "common" literature in the Western sense.

The intervening decade separating *Pen Pictures* and *Old Corea*, however, was momentous in the evolution of Korean language and literature. As Im Sangsŏk has demonstrated, a rather dramatic shift in orthographic practice occurred during roughly the five years preceding annexation in 1910, resulting in a shift from *t'o*-style writing characteristic of earlier iterations of *kukhanmun* to more vernacularized writing that limited *hancha* increasingly to the semantic level.[92] The year 1917 would mark the publication of Yi Kwangsu's *Mujŏng* (Heartlessness), considered the first modern Korean novel. Following the inauguration of Japan's so-called Cultural Rule (*bunka seiji*) in the 1920s in the wake of the March First Movement, a renaissance of literary culture soon blossomed, offering myriad new directions in inscriptional practice

---

90 Gale, "A Freak of Language," *Pen Pictures*, 1901, this vol.
91 Pieper, "Korean as a Transitional Literacy," 172–3.
92 See Im, *20-segi Kuk-Hanmunch'e ŭi hyŏngsŏng kwajŏng*. For a discussion of this shift in the process of Korea's broader linguistic modernization, see Pieper, "Korean as a Transitional Literacy," 269–71.

and challenging Gale's earlier linguistic dichotomy. Gale's writings in *Old Corea* and other contemporary venues reflect changes in Korean literary culture as well as Gale's shifting perceptions. In *Korea Magazine*, for example, Gale writes on how to approach Korean literature:

> If anyone desires to make a study of Korean literature he must work through the medium of the Chinese character. The fact that there is little or no literature written in the *Ŏnmun* makes it necessary in the first place; and in the second, *ŏnmun* books that exist, are all heavily charged with Chinese words and combinations, so that they are if anything more difficult than the Chinese itself.[93]

Such a statement represented a more sophisticated articulation of Gale's literary and language ideologies in response to the developments he had observed in the Korean literature. No longer completely compartmentalized, the Korean literary landscape now came to be characterized by hybridization at the interface between the cosmopolitan and the vernacular. While Gale conceded the existence of "*ŏnmun* books," the student of Korean literature would nevertheless require knowledge of the character to parse the meaning of vernacular literature "heavily charged with Chinese words and combinations." Gale is in effect acknowledging the increasing transgression of the vernacular-cosmopolitan boundary by an emergent mixed-script vernacular idiom highly inflected by Sino-Korean (and Sino-Japanese) neologisms, but from a position still grounded in the cosmopolitan *hanmun* tradition. In the same essay, Gale clarifies his position by offering a reactive perspective on Korean literature that accords with the view of the traditional scholar but is incompatible with modern Korean literature:

> It need not therefore discourage any student of the East to think that he is not a Chinese scholar, for if he has a knowledge of the colloquial, and bends his energies to the attainment of whatever is possible in the way of Chinese, he can, with the aid of a good pundit, get at the thought that underlies Korean literature. As pertains to so many other aspects of

---

93 *Korea Magazine* 1 (July 1917): 297–8. The *Korea Magazine* contained many essays and literary translations that would constitute Gale's *Old Corea* typescript, and so these two works should be viewed as complementary components of a larger literary project, the coalescing of his life's work.

Oriental life, he must see through the teacher's eyes, and read by the aid and assistance of the teacher's brain.

To attempt, therefore, anything like an examination of Korean literature, the student requires at his elbow a scholar of the old school. A modern literary graduate knows little or nothing about the classic books which his fathers have written. *As little are they a part of his life as they are of the foreigner's* (emphasis mine).[94]

Despite Gale's conceding the emergence of "*ŏnmun* books," literature par excellence remained the purview of Literary Sinitic, a literary world that was closed to the foreigner and the Korean "modern literary graduate" alike. This was the perspective of the quintessential *yangban* literatus, based on the indispensable master-student relationship of canonical knowledge transference. The last line of this excerpt solidifies the extent of this rupture in the linguistic landscape and the degree of textual alienation wrought by it, to the extent that "the ignorant foreigner" and the "modern boy" now stood at a position of equal estrangement from the Sinographic cosmopolis. In an essay entitled "Father and Son" appearing in *Old Corea*,[95] Gale reiterates the effects of this rupture as he ruminates on the abrogation of the civil service exam:

In the old days an incentive was given to the study of Chinese by the honours of the *kwagŏ* or official examination.[96] The distinction and social standing that it gave meant a starry crown for all time. To win this place of honour, the children of the literati would study from dawn till dark, day in and out, and never know a weary hour. This has ceased … The writer foresees not many years hence when the literature of this land will be a closed and sealed book except to a few persons of exceptional and rare attainment. As the old man who now sits lonely in the shadow, says his farewells and withdraws into the eternal quiet, he will carry away with him one of the most interesting varieties of literary achievement that the world has ever seen.[97]

---

94 Ibid., 298.

95 This essay was also published in the *Korea Magazine* and the missionary periodical *Men and Missions*.

96 The civil service examination (*kwagŏ sihŏm*) was a mechanism by which talented men were selected for government service based on their erudition and knowledge of the Confucian corpus, mainly the *Four Books* and *Five Classics*, and literary composition.

97 Gale, "Father and Son," *Old Corea*, this vol.

Thus, during the late 1910s and 1920s, confronted with the breakdown of cosmopolitan-vernacular compartmentalization, the emergence of a viable yet "inferior" modern literary idiom, and the increasing estrangement of modern educated Koreans from "true" Korean literature, Gale responded with a curatorial intercession to preserve the vestiges of Korea's proud literary heritage for global posterity through translation of *hanmun* literature into English. Gale's literary and translation activities, particularly as distilled in *Old Corea*, constituted a broader missionary-scholarly project to confirm the cultural and literary greatness of Korea by establishing its active and robust participation in the transnational Sinographic cosmopolis. Rejecting the ascendant nationalistic framework rooted in notions of cultural autonomy and anti-toadyism, Gale embraced this transnational literary network from a premodern though staunchly Koreaphilic perspective. The voluminous English translations he left behind in the *Old Corea* typescript and especially in the James Scarth Gale Papers testify to this scholarly project. At the same time, their neglect by the scholarly community reflects the dominance of the nation-centred historical narrative in twentieth-century Korean historiography. This book attempts to re-examine and reinvigorate cosmopolitan aspects of Korea's premodern history and incorporate these into modern and contemporary Korean historical inquiry.

Gale's Project in Context: Parallels with China and Japan

Gale's career in Korea parallels similar efforts by Western personages in other areas of the Sinographic cosmopolis in the late nineteenth and early twentieth centuries. In Japan, slightly prior to Gale's career, William George Aston (1841–1911) of the British consular service was appointed as interpreter at the British legation in Edo in 1864, just five years after Britain established diplomatic relations with Japan in 1859 and four years before the Meiji Restoration in 1868. Aston would go on to become a foremost Japanologist, like Gale in Korea publishing groundbreaking grammars of the Japanese language, including *A Short Grammar of Japanese* (1869; revised edition 1888), the latter edition which represented, according to Peter Kornicki, the "first description of the Japanese language by a Westerner to eschew the grammatical categories of European languages, and the first attempt to capture the internal logic of Japanese."[98] Aston went on to publish *Grammar of the Japanese*

---

98 Kornicki, "Aston, William George."

Language (1872; revised editions 1877 and 1904), based on extensive research of Japanese grammarians, which was scholarly in tone and highly regarded in linguistics.[99] Aston was also like Gale a pioneering translator of Japanese and scholar of Japanese literature: his 1896 translation of *Nihon shoki* (*Chronicles of Japan*, 720) remained the definitive translation for many decades, while *A History of Japanese Literature* (1899) "was for eighty years the most thorough work of its kind in English," considering Japanese literature from the earliest times while also breaking "new ground in dealing with contemporary literature," something that Gale would largely eschew.[100] Aston also would make pioneering though limited forays into Korean studies, becoming the first British diplomat to reside in Seoul (1884) as consul general, where he become one of the first Western students of the language and prepared a set of notes on Korean grammar for his diplomatic colleague Ernest Satow (1843–1929), an exceptional linguist, diplomat, and Japanologist in his own right whose more glamorous though less scholarly rigorous career overshadowed that of Aston. In 1883 Aston and Satow, along with the Japanese linguist Basil Hall Chamberlain (1850–1935), published *A Manual of Korean Geographical and Other Place Names Romanized*, a modest yet pioneering work for its time that contributed to laying the groundwork for subsequent lexicography in Korea, in which Gale came to be deeply involved.

Chamberlain represents perhaps Gale's closest parallel in Japan. Arriving in East Asia slightly earlier than Gale, Chamberlain was first hired by the Meiji government as part of a retinue of *O-yatoi gaikoku-jin* (御雇い外国人), or foreigners hired for their expertise or specialized knowledge to assist with Japanese modernization, and appointed as an instructor at the Imperial Japanese Naval Academy (1874–82) and then as a professor of Japanese at Tokyo Imperial University (1886–90), demonstrating his command and knowledge of the language. Like Gale, Chamberlain was a pioneering translator, lexicographer, and cultural critic, publishing the first translation of the early eighth-century *Kojiki* (Record of Ancient Matters) in 1882, *A Handbook of Colloquial Japanese* (1888), his influential *Things Japanese* (1890), and *A Practical Guide to the Study of Japanese Writing* (1905). Chamberlain's *Bashō and the Japanese Poetical Epigram* (1902), moreover, represents the first treatment of haiku in a Western language, complete with a lengthy introductory

---

99 Ibid.
100 Ibid.

essay, echoing Gale's groundbreaking translations of the similar *sijo* poetic form presented in the first chapter of this volume.

Despite these numerous parallels with early Japanologists, Gale's project in Korea seems to draw more inspiration, both philosophically and textually, from experiences in China dating back to the late Ming dynasty. In particular, Gale's position as a mediator between the East and the West has been compared to that of Matteo Ricci (1552–1610), one of the founding members of the first Jesuit Mission in China.[101] The parallels, however, extend beyond their respective positions as cultural bridgeheads: Gale, like Ricci before him, focused his evangelization efforts on the literati class, believing that such an intellectual connection would not only be a more effective strategy for conversion but would serve to facilitate the philosophical acceptance of the religion based on the prevailing cosmological framework. Relating to this approach, both Ricci and Gale practised what has been called "inculturation" in their missionary work, adapting church teachings to their respective environments. In the most superficial sense this meant adapting – or at least accommodating – their own diet, lifestyle, and outlook to that of their adoptive countries, but in a deeper sense this involved a fundamental reconceptualization of Christian theology vis-à-vis East Asian cosmology. Ricci appropriated the indigenous though slightly obscure *Tianzhu*, "Lord of Heaven," as an equivalent term to the monotheistic God of the Christian religion, attempting to establish in the process a systematic connection with *Shangdi* (the Lord on High) and *Tian* (Heaven) described in the Confucian Classics; in a parallel fashion, Gale seized on the indigenous though conceptually limited Korean term *Hanŭnim* as both the semantic equivalent of "God" and textual proof of the potential theological harmony of Confucianism and Christianity. Ricci's own description of his evangelical strategy further evinces parallels with the text-based approach of Gale: "[I] endeavored to enlist Confucius, the leader of the sect of literati, on our side by interpreting in our favor some things left uncertain in his writings."[102] Thus, both scholar-missionaries resisted the summary dismissal of Confucian thought and practice, which brought them into conflict with their missionary colleagues and sometimes with church authority,[103] while

---

101 Gale and Kwŏn, *Han'guk ŭi Mat'eo Rich'i Cheimsŭ Keil*.

102 Quoted in Fontana, *Matteo Ricci*, 188.

103 In what became known as the Chinese Rites Controversy, Ricci and the Jesuits argued that certain Confucian rites such as venerating ancestors (*chesa* 祭祀)

simultaneously subsuming Confucian cosmology under a supreme Christian theological umbrella inspired by a form of fulfilment theory.

Another figure who perhaps represents an even more intimate point of comparison was the Sinologist and scholar-missionary James Legge (1815–97).[104] Sharing Gale's Scottish ancestry, like Gale in Korea Legge also resided in his adoptive home of Hong Kong for multiple decades, adopting an accomodationist outlook toward Chinese culture and thought. The parallels extend to their specific approaches to evangelization: Legge, best known for his pioneering translations of the Chinese classics, was like Gale and Ricci motivated by what Lauren Pfister has called a "missiological strategy" to connect with the traditional elitist culture of China.[105] Moreover, Legge had likewise adopted an accommodationist view of Confucianism, most distinctly expressed in his pamphlet *Confucianism in Relation to Christianity* (1877), a work prepared originally for the Shanghai General Conference of Missionaries but later deleted from the conference proceedings because of its controversial nature.[106] Such views on Confucianism became so closely associated with Legge that detractors later used the term "Leggism" to describe any accommodating attitude toward Chinese traditions.[107]

Similarities between the two scholar-missionaries are also notable in their respective approaches to translation. According to Pfister, writing on Legge's translation style and objectives,

> almost all Chinese leadership in civil society under the Manchurian despot, whether formal or informal, was placed into the hands of scholars who studied ... Chinese classical texts and had to pass a series of civil examinations devoted to their exposition. All speeches and writings among literate people were peppered with references to them. Therefore, if any Christian materials were to gain their attention and appreciation, they had to use an informed classical Chinese style. Legge's work was dedicated in

---

constituted secular traditions, whereas the Franciscans and Dominicans viewed such practices as forms of religious worship incompatible with Christianity, setting off a series of bans and reversals finally settled only in 1939 with a final authorization of such practices by Pope Pius XII.

104 For in-depth works on James Legge, see Girardot, *The Victorian Translation of China*; Pfister, *Striving for the Whole Duty of Man*.

105 Pfister, "The Legacy of James Legge," 79.

106 Ibid.

107 Ibid.

part to serve missionaries by giving them access in English to translations and interpretations to these treasured works of the Chinese gentry.[108]

Legge's translation philosophy also extended to the Chinese translation of the Bible: he wholeheartedly joined the call for a retranslation that bore fruit with the Chinese New Testament in 1847, a version that aimed to convey the Word in a relatively "stylish way" that would appeal to literati sensibilities.[109]

Here as well Gale was in agreement, championing a version of the vernacular Korean Bible that "spoke to the soul" of the Korean and eschewed the literalness and awkward woodenness of the previous translation, a position that fomented near-monolithic opposition from his colleagues on the Board of Official Translators. In his translations of the Chinese classics, however, Gale's particular style diverged considerably from that of Legge, and his ruminations on Legge's translations in fact reveal once again a nativized Korean outlook within the cosmopolitan Confucian tradition. The Gale Papers contain many of his draft translations of the classics, some accompanied by illuminating introductions that reveal his approach to the translation, like the following from 1921:

> *The Great Learning* [大學] has been done into English three times already: once in 1808 by a Baptist missionary, Marshman, of Serampore, India; once in 1828 by the Rev. David Collie of the London Missionary Society, Malacca, and finally by Dr. Legge, a Scotch missionary in Hongkong, in 1861. Two of these translations I have by me as I have worked out my own from the Korean point of view. The purpose of this version is to make known to my Korean and Foreign associates the thoughts of this famous book. The Korean renderings in this version have been greatly simplified while the translation, too, has been put into natural easy running English quite different from the ponderous periods of Dr. Legge. Four good Korean scholars, in council together, have had to do with the Korean renderings. It therefore represents a fair consensus of Korean opinion as well as can be arrived at.[110]

108　Ibid.

109　Ibid.

110　Gale, "*Taehak* 大學 The Great Learning, 1923," in Gale Papers, Box 6, Folder 43. Gale published his translation of the *Taehak* in 1924 through the Christian Literature Society.

Here Gale and his translation team stand at the nexus of both inter- and intratranslation, mediating the reception of the classics into what is judged a more "natural" and "easy-running" style of English, but also overseeing the vernacular Korean version based on a "fair consensus" of scholars of the old school.[111] Thus, by the 1920s Gale's full-scale Literary Sinitic translation project came to represent the culmination of his scholarly endeavours after four decades in the country and his curatorial vision for Korea's cosmopolitan literary heritage. Viewing previous translations by Legge and others as inadequate, Gale set out to publish his own "from the Korean point of view," based on the vernacular explications of his trusted "pundits," who in turn produced vernacular Korean renderings for a new age and readership increasingly estranged from the cosmopolitan medium. Gale therefore mediated intertranslation between the Latin and Sinographic cosmopoli, inspired by the philosophical tradition of Ricci and Legge but grounded in the Korean literati universe, while his co-translators stewarded the transition from intratranslation within the Sinographic cosmopolis to intertranslation between Literary Sinitic and vernacular Korean, a dual translational strategy which did justice, in their minds, to the rich literary heritage of a cosmopolitan Korea.

Concluding Remarks

In *Score One for the Dancing Girl*, Si Nae Park draws a connection between Gale's "nostalgic pangs" for traditional Korea and his literary technique in translating *yadam* (野談 unofficial talk). Park writes, "I wish to show how the nostalgic pangs that Gale developed for Korea's Sinitic literary tradition led him to treat his English translations as a space to emulate the habits and conventions of late-Chosŏn transmission of *yadam* ... To this end, I contextualize his *Kimun ch'onghwa* translations within the disappearance of Literary Sinitic ... at the turn of the twentieth century, the revival of interest in the 1910s and 1920s in old Korean books from the Chosŏn period, and the personal bond that Gale formed with his Korean co-translators."[112]

111　This passage reflects the method by which Gale and his team approached Literary Sinitic texts, whereby his Korean "pundits" would first "translate" a passage into *t'o*-style vernacular Korean, from which Gale would then render his English translation.

112　Park, "Translating to Inherit," xvii.

Building on this notion of "nostalgic pangs," I seek in this book to demonstrate the pronounced and continual ambivalence Gale felt toward Korean modernization, embodied most clearly in his unpublished typescripts *Pen Pictures* and *Old Corea*. More than a matter of influence on tone or translation technique, as Park has noted, this "nostalgia" defined the literary-evangelical philosophical matrix by which Gale approached his work in Korea, both scholarly and evangelical. His activities in Korea represented an ongoing effort to disentangle what he considered to be negative premodern characteristics from positive traits worthy of maintaining.

From a cultural-anthropological perspective, however, traditional Korea as a whole was worthy of at least cataloguing for posterity, and so Gale's typescripts also contain faithful and relatively neutral accounts of spirit worship and superstitions deemed beyond the pale by the typical Christian observer, though these descriptions are discretely interspersed with spasms of moral condemnation and Western triumphalism. Moreover, Gale's scholarly projects embodied an ongoing effort to disentangle the author's missionary, literary, and anthropological identities. The many hats that Gale wore at different times are manifest in his writing, providing a complex, diverse, and compelling reading experience.

The sentiments expressed in Gale's *Pen Pictures* and especially *Old Corea*, along with the English translations of *hanmun* literature in the latter, represent the crystallization of Gale's view of the Sinographic cosmopolis and Korea's position squarely within its orbit, a perspective he had been developing since his arrival in the 1880s. Writing at a time in which he believed "the old [had] disappeared but the new [had] yet to arrive,"[113] the inevitable eclipsing of the Literary Sinitic tradition was an ominous affair given the absence of a truly modern literature and the perceived unpreparedness of the vernacular for such a task. However, the continued modernization of the Korean language and the rise of an idiom of modern vernacular Korean literature in the late 1910s and especially the 1920s engendered in Gale a reactive and adverse response – Gale dug in his heels and redoubled his efforts at shoring up a "legitimate" Korean literary legacy through writing and especially translation projects, informed by a conservative and intractable

---

113 Gale, "Korean Literature," *The Christian Movement in Japan, Korea, and Formosa* (1923), quoted in Park, "Translating to Inherit," xv.

language ideology. *Old Corea* and *Pen Pictures* thus provide not only an intriguing glimpse into an informed outsider's perspective on a rapidly shifting linguistic and literary landscape, but also a fascinating backdrop to an entire generation of Korean literati stranded at the crossroads between nullified tradition and an uncertain future. The rise of modern Korean literature in a way magnified the ambivalence Gale already felt for the modernization process, sealing the fate of a tradition he held so dear.

Gale's Literary and Translation Style

In the first work in this series on James Scarth Gale, *Score One for the Dancing Girl*, the editors noted a number of stylistic quirks in Gale's literary and translation style. These are stylistic conventions that characterize Gale's entire literary career, and so were inevitably encountered in the texts presented in this present volume as well. The first is Gale's tendency to "domesticate" Korean terms and concepts for a largely uninitiated, Western audience, the most dramatic of which was his subsuming of various Sino-Korean terms for heaven, the heavens, the sky, and spirits under the umbrella of the Christian "God."[114] In this volume I have retained this particular stylistic strategy, as it reflects more faithfully the period during which he wrote and illuminates his identity as a scholar-missionary. However, for the sake of transparency I have footnoted wherever possible the original Sino-Korean terminology.

A second stylistic quirk is Gale's habit of referring to Literary Sinitic as "the character." As King points out, "the character" "was not simply a question of knowing Chinese characters; rather, the character for Gale was a metonym for Literary Sinitic (*hanmun*) writ large: sinographs, the long and arduous training process in Classical Chinese texts, and the entire canon of Literary Sinitic literature itself."[115] This idiosyncrasy is on display throughout the chapters in this volume.

A third convention that characterizes Gale's *yadam* translations, the texts in this volume, and indeed his entire translation philosophy is his strong belief in "thought" or "free translation," coupled with a strong denouncement of literal translation. The translations appearing in *Old*

---

114 King, "Further Contextualizing the Translations of James Scarth Gale," xliii–xlv.

115 Ibid., xlvii.

Corea, like his excerpts from *Kimun ch'onghwa*, display this same dedication to the production of a readable translation that "sings out" in the target language, which partially explains his tendency to "domesticate" his translations noted above: whereas his philosophy on Bible translation into Korean dictated a smooth, readable rendition that spoke to the "soul" of the Korean reader, his translations into English on the other hand necessitated the adoption of a Westernized idiom and language that could successfully domesticate unfamiliar concepts for a lay audience.[116]

Finally, in a departure from Richard Rutt's treatment and that of the editors of the previous volume in this series, in this volume I have largely retained Gale's frequent though somewhat irritating inversion of predicates. His own unique romanization style has furthermore been replaced by the McCune-Reischauer system, and mistakes in grammar and usage have been corrected. However, I have retained Gale's idiosyncratic vocabulary usage, which I believe gives his writing a quaint and slightly antiquarian tone.[117]

In sum, I seek in this volume to present Gale at his most raw and unvarnished, reflecting the pioneering nature of his work as well as his antiquarian proclivities. While his typescripts in the main text have been reproduced in his characteristic manner, devoid of precise references to primary sources – a style, incidentally, in harmony with the Literary Sinitic tradition of oblique allusions to classical texts – the footnotes serve to contextualize the scholarship and style of a century ago for the contemporary reader.

Editorial Conventions

• Gale rarely provided exact citations for his translations, making it often difficult to determine the authorship and title of the original.

---

116 Ibid., l–li. A final quirk noted by the editors is Gale's particular "system of equivalences for the many terms for government institutions and offices and governments posts and ranks," a system much more prominently displayed in his *yadam* translations. Ibid., li–lii.

117 Rutt writes, "I have altered his vocabulary where it was misleading or irritatingly mannered. (He constantly wrote *glass* for *cup* … and *pen* for *writing brush, writing* for both *literary composition* and *calligraphy*; he overworked *master* for *expert* or *great man, soul* for *mind, round* for *routine* or *course, thought* for *meaning, ever* for *always, but* for *only*, and *back of* for *behind*." See Rutt, *James Scarth Gale and His "History,"* ix.

However, in cases where the source has been confirmed, the original *hanmun* has been provided in hopes that the texts may be of use to readers of Literary Sinitic, and as pedagogical materials for advanced students of Korean literature.[118]

- *Hanmun* originals are provided only for Gale's lengthier translations; for shorter excerpts or quotations, only the citation is given.
- The □ symbol is used to indicate that a sinograph that is indecipherable, while [zzz] indicates an illegible section of the English text, with each group of three equalling what appears to be one English word in the original text.
- Editorial notes in `Courier` typeface are Gale's annotations. Bracketed material within *Pen Pictures* and *Old Corea* indicate a clarification by myself of a Korean term or historical event for non-specialist readers.
- Not all of Gale's individual chapters are dated. Those that are dated in the typescript conclude with the year in Courier typeface, indicating the date Gale pencilled in.
- Despite his Canadian provenance, Gale does not consistently employ British English but occasionally follows American spelling. He does, however, generally demonstrate internal consistency in spelling over time (i.e., "flavour" is always spelled as such, and his spellings show no tendency toward Americanisms in his long writing career). This particular quirk of Gale has been preserved.
- Many of the chapters in the *Pen Pictures* typescript also appear in the *Old Corea* typescript, usually with substantial edits. In this volume, such chapters have been omitted from *Old Corea*, but differences between the two versions are footnoted in *Pen Pictures*.
- Below the title of each chapter, I cite all known occurrences of the piece in other venues.
- Most photographs appearing in this volume have been placed according to Gale's exact positioning in the typescripts, though at times this renders their placement somewhat arbitrary, with little apparent relation to the surrounding text.

---

118 Many of these conventions follow those mapped out in the previous volume in this series, *Score One for the Dancing Girl*. See King, "Further Contextualizing the Translations of James Scarth Gale," liii–liv.

Bibliography

Periodicals

Japan Advertiser
Japan Weekly Mail
Korea Magazine
Korea Mission Field
Korean Repository
Korea Review
Men and Missions
North China Daily News
Open Court
Transactions of the Royal Asiatic Society – Korea Branch

Other Sources

Baker, Donald. "Hananim, Hanŭnim, Hanŭllim, and Hanŏllim: The Construction of Terminology for Korean Monotheism." *Review of Korean Studies* 5, no. 1 (2002): 105–31.
Brown, Arthur J. *The Mastery of the Far East: The Story of Korea's Transformation and Japan's Rise to Supremacy in the Orient*. New York: Charles Scribner and Sons, 1921.
– "A Reading Journey in Korea." *Chautauquan* (August 1905): 481–578.
Chu Chaegwang. "Han'guk Kidokkyo paengnyŏnsa: Minjung sagwan ŭi ipchang esŏ ŭi punsŏk kwa pip'an" [A Century of Christianity in Korea: A Minjung-Oriented Analysis and Critique]. *Sinhak yŏn'gu* 21 (1979): 199–216.
Fabian, Johannes. *Time and the Other: How Anthropology Makes Its Object*. New York: Columbia University Press, 2002.

Fenkl, Heinz Insu. "*Kuunmong*, A Translator's Note." *Azalea: Journal of Korean Literature and Culture* 7 (2014): 247–62.

Fontana, Michela. *Matteo Ricci: A Jesuit in the Ming Court*. Lanham, MD: Rowan and Littlefield, 2015.

Gale, James Scarth. *Korea in Transition*. New York: Eaton and Mains, 1909.

– *A Korean-English Dictionary (Han-Yŏng chajŏn* 韓英字典). 1897.

– *Korean Grammatical Forms (Sagwa chinam* 辭課指南). 1894. Rev. ed. 1903.

– "Korean Literature." *The Christian Movement in Japan, Korea, and Formosa* (1923): 465–71.

– *Korean Sketches*. New York: Fleming H. Revell, 1898.

– trans. *Score One for the Dancing Girl, and Other Stories from the "Kimun ch'onghwa": A Story Collection from Nineteenth-Century Korea*. Edited by Ross King and Si Nae Park. Annotations by Donguk Kim. Toronto: University of Toronto Press, 2016.

– trans. *T'yŏllo ryŏktyŏng* (天路歷程). Translation of *The Pilgrim's Progress*, by John Bunyan. Seoul: Trilingual Press, 1895.

Gale, James Scarth, and Kwŏn Hyŏgil. *Han'guk ŭi Mat'eo Rich'i Cheimsŭ Keil* [James Gale, the Matteo Ricci of Korea]. Seoul: Han'guk kodŭng sinhak yŏn'guwŏn, 2012.

Girardot, Norman. *The Victorian Translation of China: James Legge's Oriental Pilgrimage*. Berkeley: University of California Press, 2002.

Graves, Joseph Waddington. *The Renaissance of Korea*. Philadelphia: Philip Jaisohn, 1910.

Hwang Hodŏk and Yi Sanghyŏn. *Kaenyŏm kwa yŏksa, kŭndae Han'guk ŭi ijungŏ sajŏn: Oegugindŭl ŭi sajŏn p'yŏnch'an saŏp ŭro pon Han'gugŏ ŭi kŭndae* [Concept and History, Modern Korean Bilingual Dictionaries: Viewing Korean Linguistic Modernity through Foreigners' Dictionary Compilation Projects]. Sŏul: Pangmunsa, 2012.

Im Sangsŏk. *20-segi Kuk-Hanmunch'e ŭi hyŏngsŏng kwajŏng* [The Formation of Sino-Korean Mixed Script Style]. P'aju: Chisik sanŏp-sa, 2008.

Kim, Kichung. *An Introduction to Classical Korean Literature: From Hyangga to P'ansori*. London: Routledge, 1996.

Kim Kwŏnjŏng. *Hanguginboda Hanguk ŭl tŏ saranghan Migugin Hŏlbŏt'ŭ* [Hulbert: The American Who Loved Korea More Than Koreans]. Sŏul: Yŏksa konggan, 2015.

Kim, Manjung. *The Cloud Dream of the Nine: A Korean Novel of the Tangs of China, about 840 AD*. Translated by James Scarth Gale. London: Daniel O'Connor, 1922.

Kim Tongjin. *P'aran nun ŭi Han'gukhon. Crusader for Korea: Homer B. Hulbert*. Sŏul: Ch'am choŭn ch'in'gu, 2010.

Kim Tongni. "Munyŏdo" [The Shaman Painting]. *Chungang* 5 (1936).

King, Ross. "Ditching 'Diglossia': Describing Ecologies of the Spoken and Inscribed in Pre-Modern Korea." *Sungkyun Journal of East Asian Studies* 15, no. 1 (2015): 1–19.
– "Further Contextualizing the Translations of James Scarth Gale." In *Score One for the Dancing Girl, and Other Stories from the "Kimun ch'onghwa": A Story Collection from Nineteenth-Century Korea*, translated by James Scarth Gale, edited by Ross King and Si Nae Park, annotations by Kim Donguk, xxxvii–liv. Toronto: University of Toronto Press, 2016.
– "I Thank Korea for Her Books": *James Scarth Gale, Korean Literature in* Hanmun, *and Allo-Metropolitan Missionary Orientalism*. Toronto: University of Toronto Press, forthcoming.
– "James Scarth Gale and the Christian Literature Society: Salvific Translation and Korean Literary Modernity." In *Corea, una Aproximación Humanista a los Estudios Coreanos*, edited by Wonjung Min. Santiago: Pontificia Universidad Católica de Chile, 2014. E-book.
– "James Scarth Gale, Korean Literature in *Hanmun*, and Allo-Metropolitan Missionary Orientalism." Lecture delivered at the Royal Asiatic Society – Korea Branch, Seoul, South Korea, 11 November 2017. www.raskb.com/blog /2017/11/04/lecture-video-james-scarth-gale-korean-literature-hanmun -and-allo-metropolitan.
– "James Scarth Gale, Korean Literature in *Hanmun*, and Korean Books." In *Haeoe Han'gukpon komunhŏn charyo ŭi t'amsaek kwa k'ŏmt'o* [Examinations and Investigations of Overseas Historical Documents on Korea], edited by Sŏul taehakkyo Kyujanggak Han'gukhak yŏn'guwŏn, 237–64. Sŏul: Samgyŏng munhwasa, 2012.
– *Cosmopolitan and Vernacular in the World of Wen: Reading Sheldon Pollock from the Sinographic Cosmopolis*. Language, Writing and Literary Culture in the Sinographic Cosmopolis Series. Brill (forthcoming).
Koh, Jongsok. *Infected Korean Language, Purity vs. Hybridity, from the Sinographic Cosmopolis to Japanese Colonialism to Global English*. Edited and translated by Ross King. Amherst, NY: Cambria Press, 2014.
Kornicki, Peter. "Aston, William George." *Oxford Dictionary of National Biography*, 2019. https://doi.org/10.1093/ref:odnb/30488.
Kwŏn Sun'gŭng, Han Chaep'yo, and Yi Sanghyŏn. "Keil munsŏ (Gale, James Scarth Papers) sojae *Simch'ŏng chŏn, T'osaeng chŏn* Yŏngyŏkpon ŭi palgul kwa ŭiŭi" [The Discovery and Significance of Gale's English Translations of *Simch'ŏng chŏn* and *T'osaeng chŏn* Appearing in *The James Scarth Gale Papers*]. *Kososŏl yŏn'gu* 30 (2010): 419–94.
Lee, Ki-Mun, and S. Robert Ramsey. *A History of the Korean Language*. Cambridge: Cambridge University Press, 2012.

Lee, Peter H. "Early Twentieth-Century Poetry." In *History of Korean Literature*, edited by Peter H. Lee et al., 336–89. Cambridge: Cambridge University Press, 2003.

Min Kyŏngbae. *Han'guk Kidokkyohoesa: Han'guk minjok kyohoe hyŏngsŏng kwajŏng* [The History of the Christian Church in Korea: The Formation of a Korean National Church]. Sŏul: Yŏnse taehakkyo ch'ulp'anbu, 2000.

O'Neill, Timothy Michael. *Ideography and Chinese Language Theory: A History*. Berlin: Walter de Gruyter, 2016.

Park, Si Nae. "Translating to Inherit: An Introduction to James Scarth Gale's Translations from the *Kimun ch'ŏnghwa*." In *Score One for the Dancing Girl, and Other Stories from the "Kimun ch'onghwa": A Story Collection from Nineteenth-Century Korea*, translated by Jamed Scarth Gale, edited by Ross King and Si Nae Park, annotations by Donguk Kim, xv–xxxvi. Toronto: University of Toronto Press, 2016.

Pfister, Lauren. "The Legacy of James Legge." *International Bulletin of Missionary Research* 22, no. 2 (1998): 77–82.

– *Striving for the Whole Duty of Man: James Legge and the Scottish Protestant Encounter with China: Assessing Confluences in Scottish Nonconformism, Chinese Missionary Scholarship, Victorian Sinology, and Chinese Protestantism*. New York: Peter Lang, 2004.

Pieper, Daniel. "Korean as a Transitional Literacy: Language Education, Curricularization, and the Vernacular-Cosmopolitan Interface in Early Modern Korea, 1895–1925." PhD diss., University of British Columbia, 2017. http://hdl.handle.net/2429/61132.

Ridel, Felix Clair. *Dictionnaire coréen-français* [韓佛字典 Korean-French Dictionary]. Yokohama: C. Lévy, imprimeur-libraire, 1880.

Rutt, Richard. *James Scarth Gale and His "History of the Korean People": A New Edition of the History Together with a Biography and Annotated Bibliographies*. Sŏul: RASKB, Taewon Publishing, 1972.

Sŏ Chŏngmin. *Kyohoe wa minjok ŭl saranghan saramdŭl* [Those Who Loved Their Church and Nation]. Sŏul: Kidokkyomunsa, 1990.

Yi Chaejŏng. *Taehan Sŏnggonghoe paengnyŏnsa: 1890–1990* [A 100-Year History of the Anglican Church in Korea]. Sŏul: Paengnyŏnsa p'yŏnch'an wiwŏnhoe, 1990.

Yi Manyŏl. *Han'guk Kidokkyo wa minjok ŭisik: Han'guk Kidokkyosa yŏn'gu non'go* [National Consciousness and the Korean Church: The History of the Christian Church in Korea]. Sŏul: Chisik sanŏpsa, 1991.

– *Han'guk Kidokkyo wa minjok undong* [The Korean Christian Church and Nationalist Movements]. Sŏul: Posŏng, 1986.

Yi Sanghyŏn. *Han'guk kojŏn pŏnyŏkka ŭi ch'osang: Keil ŭi kojŏnhak tamnon kwa kososŏl pŏnyŏk ŭi chip'yŏng* [Portrait of a Translator of the Korean Classics:

James Scarth Gale's Discourse on Classical Studies and His Translations of Classical Fiction]. Seoul: Somyŏng ch'ulp'an, 2012.

– "Han'guk sinhwa wa Sŏnggyŏng, sŏn'gyosadŭl ŭi Han'guk sinhwa haesŏk: Keil ŭi sŏngch'wiron kwa Tan'gun sinhwa insik ŭi chŏnhwan" [The Bible, Korean Myths, and Their Interpretation by Missionaries: The Fulfillment Theory of James Scarth Gale and Changes in His Understanding of the Tan'gun Myth]. *Pigyo munhak* 58, no. 10 (2012): 41–83.

– "Ijungŏ sajŏn kwa kaenyŏmsa kŭrigo Han'gugŏ munhak: Keil kojŏnhak ŭl ilgŭl kŭndae haksulsajŏk munmaek, 'munhwajae wŏnhyŏng' kaenyŏm ŭi hyŏngsŏng kwajŏng kwa Han'gŭgŏ ŭi munhwa saengt'ae" [Bilingual Dictionaries, Conceptual History, and Korean Literature: The Modern Korean Academic Context Surrounding Gale's Classical Studies, the Emergence of the "Cultural Asset Preservation Prototype," and the Cultural Ecology of the Korean Language]. *Pan'gyo ŏmun yŏn'gu* 42 (2016): 47–97.

– "Keil ŭi Han'guk kososŏl pŏnyŏk kwa kŭ t'onggukkajŏk maengnak: *Keil Yugo* (Gale, James Scarth Papers) sojae kososŏl kwallyŏn charyo ŭi chonjae yangsang kwa kŭ ŭimi e kwanhayŏ" [The Transnational Context of Gale's Translations of Classic Korean Fiction: The Content and Significance of Documents on Classical Fiction in the James Scarth Gale Papers]. *Comparative Korean Studies* 22 (2014): 11–53.

– "*Yumong ch'ŏnja* sojae Yŏng-Mi munhak chakp'um kwa Keil (J.S. Gale) ŭi kukhanmunch'e pŏnyŏk silch'ŏn: Kaesin'gyo sŏn'gyosa ŭi kŭndae munch'e rŭl hyanghan kihoek kwa kŭ nojŏng 1" [American and British Literature Appearing in James Scarth Gale's *Yumong ch'ŏnja* and His Utilization of Mixed Script: A Protestant Missionary's Project and Journey toward Modern Korean Style]. *Sŏgang inmun nonch'ong* 42, no. 4 (2015): 99–154.

Yi Sanghyŏn and Yi Chinsuk. "*Chosŏn p'ilgyŏng* (Pen-pictures of Old Corea [1912]) sojae Keil [J.S. Gale] yŏngyŏk sijo ŭi ch'angjak yŏnwŏn kwa 'naejiin ŭi kwanjŏm'" [The Source and Composition of James Scarth Gale's English Translations of *Sijo* Appearing in His *Pen Pictures of Old Korea* (1912) and the "Naejiin" (Japanese) Perspective]. *Uri munhak yŏn'gu* 44, no. 10 (2014): 221–58.

Yi Tŏkchu. *Nara ŭi tongnip, kyohoe ŭi tongnip* [National Independence, Church Independence]. Sŏul: Kidokkyomunsa, 1988.

Yŏksa p'yŏnch'an wiwonhoe. *Han'guk Kidokkyo 100 nyŏnsa* [100 Years of Christian Church History in Korea]. Sŏul: Han'guk Kiddokkyo changnohoe ch'ulp'ansa, 1992.

Yu Yŏngsik. *Ch'akhăn mokchya: Keil ŭi salm kwa sŏn'gyo* [The Kind Preacher: The Life and Mission of Gale]. Sŏul: Chinhŭng, 2013.

Yu Cho, Young-mee. "Diglossia in Korean Language and Literature: A Historical Perspective." *East Asia* 20, no. 1 (2002): 3–23.

Yun Ch'iho and Kim Sangt'ae. *Yun Ch'iho ilgi (1916–1943): Han chisikin ŭi naemyŏng segye rŭl t'onghae pon singminji sigi* [The Diary of Yun Ch'iho (1916–1943): The Colonial Period Viewed through the Inner World of a Korean Intellectual]. Sŏul: Yŏksa pip'yŏngsa, 2001.

PART ONE

Pen Pictures of Old Korea

Korean Songs and Verses

Along with his pioneering efforts in lexicography, Bible translation, and prose translation, Gale was the first to publish translations of the *sijo* Korean poetic form into English, versions that first appeared in the *Korean Repository* (1895–8), a monthly periodical that published on various Korea-related themes, primarily for the foreign missionary audience in Seoul. As Kevin O'Rourke writes, for most of the twentieth century *sijo* was treated as primarily a literary text, but the roots of the poetic form, like so much Korean literature, lie in the oral and musical tradition. The term *sijo* itself is a modern concoction to refer to what was originally a subdivision of *kasa*, literally "music words," a blanket term used to describe all vernacular songs.[1] What are today called *sijo* were originally performed in five lines, or *chang*, accompanied by the *kagok-ch'ang*, which involved an accomplished singer and a large company of players. Over the course of the late nineteenth century the *sijo-ch'ang*, a simplified three-line *sijo* form, gradually replaced the earlier form and seems to be "the basis of the modern three-*chang* division of shijo adopted by Ch'oe Namsŏn and subsequent commentators."[2] Since then, the essential criteria of *sijo* have been firmly established: three *chang* (sections); fourteen to sixteen syllables in each section,

---

1 O'Rourke, *The Book of Korean Poetry*, 11–13; O'Rourke, *The Book of Korean Sijo*.

2 O'Rourke, *The Book of Korean Poetry*, 12–13. Scholars attribute the development of this simplified *sijo-ch'ang* form to Yi Sech'un, a renowned singer during the reign of King Yŏngjo (r. 1724–76). Shin, "A Reception Aesthetic Study on *Sijo* in English Translation," 178.

distributed between four distinct *ŭmbo* (breath groups); and not exceeding forty-five syllables in total.[3]

O'Rourke identifies the three major *sijo* compilations as *Ch'ŏnggu yŏng'ŏn* (青丘永言, 1728), compiled by Kim Ch'ŏnt'aek; *Haedong kayo* (海東歌謠, 1763), compiled by Kim Sujang; and *Kagok wŏllyu* (歌曲源流, 1876), compiled by Pak Hyogwan and An Minyŏng.[4] The selections appearing in *Pen Pictures*, however, were translated from *Namhun t'aep'yŏngga* (南薰太平歌 Southern Fragrant Song of Peace), an anonymously composed wood-block anthology of *sijo*, folk songs (*chapka*), and *kasa* originally published in 1863. Introducing a number of the translations in the *Korea Bookman* in 1922, Gale wrote the following on his acquisition of *Namhun t'aep'yŏngga*:

> Thirty years and more ago the father of the once famous Yang Kŭit'ak[5] had a Korean song book struck off from the plates owned by a friend of his which he presented to me with his best compliments … These songs carry in their wings the spirit of long ago, and breathe an Oriental message that has accompanied the Far East since the days of Tan'gun."[6]

In her study on Gale's *sijo* translation, Shin Eun-kyung describes Gale's chance encounter with *Namhun t'aep'yŏngga* as "an important literary event in translation history," noting that through the process of translation Gale rendered *sijo* into "an entirely different poetic form," resulting in the "destruction of pre-established norms of *sijo* and provid[ing] succeeding translations with a new model."[7] The significance of Gale's translation, however, extends beyond the realm of literary hermeneutics and should be understood within his broader scholar-missionary project to understand the Korean people through a comprehensive examination of their literature. Yi Sanghyŏn and Yun Sŏlhŭi argue that while

---

3 Subsequent commentators, though, have remarked on the large number of exceptions to these rules and have questioned these strict parameters. O'Rourke, *The Book of Korean Poetry*, 12.

4 Ibid., 12–13.

5 Yang Kit'ak (梁起鐸, 1871–1938) was a Korean independence activist and the head of the Korean Provisional Government in Shanghai from 1933 to 1935. Along with the British journalist Ernest Bethell, he established the vernacular newspaper *Taehan maeil sinbo* in 1904, which took a critical stance toward Japanese administration in Korea before the newspaper's closure in 1910.

6 Gale, "Korean Songs," *Korea Bookman* 3, no. 2 (June 1922): 27; quoted in Shin, "A Reception Aesthetic Study on *Sijo*," 178.

7 Shin, "A Reception Aesthetic Study on *Sijo*," 179.

Gale's project on the surface resembles the classic European Orientalist paradigm, Gale's continuous endeavours to forge a "nativist perspective" (*Naejiin ŭi kwanjŏm*) through his missionary and literary activities represented a fundamentally divergent paradigm.[8] On a practical level, moreover, Yi and Yun contend that Gale's exploration of vernacular *sijo* should be understood not in opposition to his interest in and translation of *hanmun* literature but as part of an increasingly integrated linguistic landscape: the growing interest that Gale displayed in *hanmun* literature from the 1890s suggests a desire to more effectively engage with the language and expressions of more vernacular literature. Gale's comprehensive literary project, moreover, reflected his dogged determination to master all forms of the Korean language, not only to further his scholarly explorations but to facilitate his evangelical duties.[9]

In his reissue of Gale's *History of the Korean People*, Richard Rutt writes that "there is justification for altering his verse translations because in his later letters he wrote of them as drafts with which he was not satisfied," and thus Rutt takes liberties with the translations appearing in that work, rearranging some verses and omitting certain words.[10] The verses and songs presented here remain untouched, except where noted, to serve as a point of comparison with *Old Corea* and to demonstrate the evolution of Gale's style and scholarship. Although his translations of Literary Sinitic poetry often resulted in his abandoning rhyme schemes for blank verse iambic pentameter, in the translations of vernacular verses featured below he has rendered highly readable English versions. Though his translations could at times strike the reader, even of his day, as quaint and outmoded, here Gale's token style blends seamlessly with the Korean vernacular idiom.

The original *Pen Pictures* typescript contains just three illustrations, all of them drawn by the Korean artist Kim Chun'gŭn (金俊根) and interspersed within this opening chapter on Korean songs and verses. Although very little is known about the artist himself, more than fourteen hundred of his pieces survive, housed in Korean, American, and European museums. Gale reported in January 1895 that he was working closely with Kim on his Korean translation of *The Pilgrim's Progress* (1678).[11] A Christian allegory written by John Bunyan (1628–88), *Pilgrim's Progress* was one of the most significant works of religious

---

8 Yi and Yun, *Oegugin ŭi Han'guk siga tamnon yŏn'gu*, 239.

9 Ibid., 238.

10 Rutt, *James Scarth Gale and His "History,"* x.

11 Pak Chŏngse, "Keil (J. Gale) ŭi *T'yŏllo ryŏktyŏng*."

Illustration 1. Kim Chun'gŭn, "Include my Name"

literature in English and among the earliest novels penned in the English language. The Korean version, titled *T'y'ŏllo ryŏktyŏng* (modern Korean *Ch'ŏllo yŏkchŏng* 天路歷程, 1895), was the first translation of English literature into Korean, and for this fact alone Gale's legacy in Korean literary history should be assured. Kim ended up providing forty-two illustrations for Gale's *Ch'ŏllo yŏkchŏng*, which were clearly modelled on the illustrations appearing in the 1874 reissue of *Pilgrim's Progress*.[12] Kim's artwork lends a distinct Korean folk feel, providing a glimpse into the culture of the late Chosŏn era.

---

12   For a side-by-side comparison of these illustrations, see ibid.

Table 1. Translations and Relevant Information on *Sijo* Appearing in *Pen Pictures*

Order in Pen Pictures	Gale's Numbering	English Title	Opening Line	Original Source	Other English Versions
1	I	Gale doesn't provide a title for this section, but in the *Korean Repository* they are described as "Korean Love Songs"	"Green clad mountains"	"Chyŏngsăna," *Namhun t'aep'yongga*, # 25	*Korea Bookman* 6, 1922 (reissue)
2			"Frosty morn"	"Saebyŏk sŏri," *Namhun t'aep'yŏngga*, #12	*Korean Repository* 2, 1895 (1st ed.); *Korean Sketches* (reissue)
3			"Silvery moon"	"Saebyŏk tal," *Namhun t'aep'yŏngga*, #39	*Korean Repository* 3, 1896 (1st ed.)
4			"The gates"	"Tyŏkmuinŏm chyunmun hŏnde," *Namhun t'aep'yŏngga*, #2	*Korea Bookman* 6, 1922 (retranslation)
5			"A mountain village"	"Sanch'on e," *Namhun t'aep'yŏngga*, #8	Unpublished
6			"In the first watch"	"Ch'ogyŏng e," *Namhun t'aep'yŏngga*, #21	Unpublished

(Continued)

Order in Pen Pictures	Gale's Numbering	English Title	Opening Line	Original Source	Other English Versions
7			"Farewell's a fire"	"Nibyŏri puri," *Namhun t'aep'yŏngga*, #61	*Korean Repository* 2, 1895 (1st ed.); *Korea Bookman* 6, 1922 (reissue)
8			"Fill the ink-stone"	"Ahoeya yŏnsyu," *Namhun t'aep'yŏngga*, #30	*Korean Repository* 2, 1895 (1st ed.); *Korea Bookman* 6, 1922 (reissue)
9			"That rock"	"Chyŏ kŏnnŏ kŏmŏ utstokhŏn pawi," *Namhun t'aep'yŏngga*, #48	*Korean Repository* 3, 1896 (1st ed.); *Korean Sketches* (reissue); *Korea Mission Field* 5, 1925 (reissue)
10	III	In the *Korean Repository* appears the title "Korean Songs (Free-will)." The section in *Pen Pictures* begins with the sentence, "The Korean, too, is human enough to have in his nature the voice that says, 'Eat, drink, and be merry for to-morrow we die.'"	"Third moon"	"Samwŏl samil," *Namhun t'aep'yŏngga*, #20	Unpublished
11			"The boys"	"Ahŭinŭn," *Namhun t'aep'yŏngga*, #3	*Korean Repository* 5, 1898 (1st ed.); *Korea Bookman* 6, 1922 (reissue)
12			"Man he dies"	"Saram i chyugŏ kasyŏ," *Namhun t'aep'yŏngga*, #171	Unpublished
13			"Heaven and earth"	"Ch'ŏnji nŭn," *Namhun t'aep'yŏngga*, #168	Unpublished

14	IV	"On Filial Piety"	"That ponderous"	"Man'gŭn soe rŭl," *Namhun t'aep'yŏngga*, #49	*Korean Repository* 2, 1895 (1st ed.); *Korean Sketches* (reissue); *Korea Mission Field* 5, 1925 (reissue)
15	V	"On Rank"; in *The Korean Repository* this work is titled "The People" under the section title "Korean Songs."	"Very small"	"Kamjangsăi chyakta hăgo," *Namhun t'aep'yŏngga*, #140	*Korean Repository* 5, 1898 (1st ed.)
16	VI	"The Pedlar"; in *The Korean Repository* this work is titled "Ode on the Pedlar" under the section title "Korean Songs."	"Here's a pedlar"	"Tŏkdŭl e Tongnanjŏt sapso," *Namhun t'aep'yŏngga*, #87	*Korean Repository* 3, 1896 (1st ed.)
17	VII	"A Piece of Extravagance"	"There is a bird"	"Pungmyŏng yu ŏ, ki myŏng wi kon" (北冥有魚, 其名為鯤), Soyoyu (逍遙遊), *Changja, Naep'yŏn* (莊子 內篇)	*Korea Review* 1, 1901 (1st ed.)
18	VIII	"Nevermind"	"Hollo!"		*Korea Mission Field* 6, 1926 (reissue)

Korean Songs and Verses
(Translations)
Korean Repository (1895–8);
Korea Review (1902)

I

Ambition for Fame
Green clad mountain bend thy head,
And tell me of the past that's dead;
Of the great, the wise, the rare,
When they lived, and who they were.
(In days to come if asked the same,
Kindly just include my name).

II

The greatest number of songs deal with the sorrows of the deserted wife. The long hours at night seem doubly lengthened. The birds calling as they pass suggest to her various existences of more felicity than her own. Each sound is a voice that heightens her sorrow. The return of fete days marks the years of his absence. The babblings of the brook tell that he still remembers her. Flowers and birds each have their message; even the ancient sages and history itself are filled with the burden of her grief. The sea, with its myriad flocks, the rocks and trees, are all in waiting on her, each speaking its message. To the Korean, this outlawed passion, Love, is nothing if it does not include all the universe.

Frosty morn and cold wind blowing,
Clanging by are wild-geese going,
Is it to the Sosang River,[13]
Or the Tongch'ŏn, tell me whither?

---

13 Gale's translation errs; this refers to the Xiao and Xiang Rivers (瀟湘江) in Hunan Province to the south of the Yangtze River, rivers depicted in the painting "Xiaoxiangtu" (瀟湘图) by the famous Southern Tang painter Dong Yuan (董源, ?–962). In its broader meaning, Xiaoxiang serves less as a precise geographic location than as a literary and poetic symbol for untamed, mysterious regions with picturesque landscapes.

Through the mid-night hours this crying,
Is so trying.
Silvery moon and frosty air,
Eve and dawn are meeting,
Widowed wild-goose flying there,
Hear my words of greeting:
On your journey should you see,
Him I love so broken hearted,
Kindly say this word for me,
That it's death when we are parted.
Flapping off the wild-goose clambers,
Says she will if she remembers.
The gates are closed, the silent hours,
Look with the moon upon the flowers,
While I behind the silken screen,
Deserted and heart-broken lean.
The distant hamlet cock now crows,
My loneliness who knows? Who knows?

Illustration 2. Kim Chun'gŭn, "Widowed Wild Goose Flying There"

A mountain village, night grows late,
Dogs in the distance bay,
I peek out through the bamboo gate,
The sky is cold, the moon is gray.
These dogs! What can such barking mean,
When nothing but the moon is seen?
In the first watch, the kingfisher,
In the second, the goatsucker,
In the third, and fourth, and fifth,
These wild geese in clangor lift
Their voices night by night,
And sleep has ta'en its flight.
Farewell's a fire that burns one's heart,
And tears are rains that quench in part,
But then the winds blow in one's sighs,
And cause the flames again to rise.
Fill the ink-stone, bring the water,
To my love I'll write a letter;
Ink and paper soon will see,
The one that's all the world to me;
While the pen and I together,
Left behind, condole each other.
That rock heaved up on yonder shore,
I'll chisel out and cut and score,
And mark the hair, and make the horns,
And put on feet and all the turns,
Required for a cow;
And then my love if you go 'way
I'll saddle up my bovine gray,
And follow you somehow.

III

The Korean, too, is human enough to have in his nature the voice that says, "Eat, drink, and be merry for to-morrow we die."

Third moon, third day,
Plum flower, peach spray,
Ninth day, ninth moon,
Maple and chrysanthemum.

Golden goblet full of wine,
Tongch'ŏn River, evening time,
Jovial comrade, wise and rare,
Drinking to the moon up there.

Illustration 3. Kim Chun'gŭn, "Moonlight and Snow"

The boys have gone to dig ginseng
While here beneath the shelter,
The scattered chess and checker-men,
Are lying helter-skelter.
Full up with wine, I now recline,
Intoxication, superfine!

Man he dies and goes away,
Will he not come back some day?
All have seen him go, but then,

None have seen him come again.
This is why men love to hear,
Jokeful songs and gleesome cheer.
Heaven and earth, creation's inn;
Time the lodger found within;
Life launched on eternity,
A grain of millet in the sea;
Like a dream is one's short day,
Why not spend it merrily?

IV
On Filial Piety

That pond'rous weighted iron bar,
I'll spin out thin, in threads so far,
To reach the sun, and fasten on,
And tie him in before he's gone;
That parents, who are growing gray,
May not get old another day.

V
On Rank

"Very small, my little man,"
Said the ostrich to the wren;
"But" the wren went on to say,
"I'll outfly you any day,"
"Size is nothing but a name,
Big or little, all the same."

VI
The Pedlar

Here's a pedlar passing me,
Calling Tongnan pickle.[14]

14　"Tongnan pickle" refers to *panggejŏt*, or salted shore crab (*helice tridens*) pre-
　　served in a soy sauce mixture. This is a translation of a *sijo* found in *Namhun
　　t'aepy'ŏngga* titled "Taekdŭlŭi tongnanjŏt sapso"; here Gale has romanized the

What can this word Tongnan be?
Some fresh dish, undoubtedly,
One's appetite to tickle.
Then the pedlar stops to state;
"Large feet two, and small feet, eight,
Looking upward, heaven-eyed,
Armour-plated, flesh inside,
Stomach-ink of black and blue,
Body round and cornered, too,
Creeping fore and aft mis-tickle (mystical)
Very best of Tong-nan pickle!"
(Looks into the Pedlar's basket).
"Pedlar, cease this rigmarole,
"Pickled crabs, well bless my soul!"[15]

VII
A Piece of Extravagance

There is a bird in the great North Sea,
Whose name is *kon*,[16]
His size is a bit unknown to me,
Though he stretches a good ten thousand *li**
Till his wings are grown,
And then he's a bird of enormous sail,

Korean dialect form "Tongnan" employed in the poem and domesticated the food item as "pickle."

15 This seems to refer to *kejang* or *kejŏt*, a fermented seafood dish prepared by marinating fresh, raw crabs in a soy sauce mixture. Although originally freshwater crabs were used, because of their scarcity, increasingly *kkotke* (horse crabs) are used. *Kejang* is a traditional cuisine of Chŏlla Province.

16 As Yi Sanghyŏn and Yun Sŏlhŭi demonstrate, there is a slight variation between the two versions of Gale's translation of this *sijo*, the first published in *Korea Review* as "The Opening Lines of Chang-ha [莊子] (4ᵗʰ Cent. B.C.)," in February 1902, and the second appearing in *Pen Pictures*: whereas the former version names the original animal a fish, the latter describes the initial animal as a bird. The original text describes the transformation of a fish (*kon* 鯤) into a bird (*pong* 鵬) as a metaphor extolling the possibilities of achieving higher consciousness. See Yi and Yun, *Oegugin ŭi Han'guk siga tamnon yŏn'gu*, 295.

With an endless back and a ten-mile tail,
And he covers the heavens with one great veil,
When he flies off home.[17]

*One *li* equals one third of a mile.

VIII
Nevermind

Hollo!
Who dyed thus black the crow?
Explain,
Or bleached so white the crane?
Who pieced the legs of the heron tall,
Or left the duck no legs at all?
I wonder.
Still, black or white, low-set, long-reached,
Pieced out or clipped, black-dyed or bleached,
Who cares? What matters it?

17 Gale's translation is a paraphrase of the following passage from the Inner
   Chapter (內篇) of the *Zhuangzi* (莊子), one of the two foundational texts of Taoism, attributed to the Warring States period (475–221 BC) philosopher Master
   Zhuang (莊子). The passage appears in "Enjoyment in Untroubled Ease" (逍
   遙遊), which Gale seems to have translated as "A Bit of Extravagance: "北冥有
   魚，其名「鯤。鯤之大，不知其幾千里也。化而「鳥，其名「鵬。鵬之背，不知其
   幾千里也；怒而飛，其翼若垂天之雲。是鳥也，海運則將徙於南冥。南冥者，天
   池也。"

Eternal Life

In "Eternal Life," Gale again attempts to draw parallels between Christian and Korean philosophical views on the afterlife. Central to the concept of *yŏngsaeng* (永生 eternal life) for the Korean is marriage and primogeniture, a subject that Gale broached in various writings.[1] Gale concludes this chapter with a discussion of the issue of child marriage in Korea, a topic that he did not often mention but one that concerned early Korean reformers and the missionary community alike. While the marriageable age in Chosŏn Korea was officially fifteen for girls and fourteen for boys, reports such as Gale's suggest that many families, especially of the lower class, defied this law, often for economic reasons. Following the first round of Kabo Reforms in 1894 that abolished the practice of child marriage,[2] the American missionary Homer Hulbert reflected on the significance of the law in an issue of the *Korean Repository*, stating, "We have here a resolution that is beneficent in every way and which can be opposed on no reasonable grounds." He goes on to say that child marriage is "a relic of barbarism and is the cause of untold suffering. It often happens that the girl is taken to the house of her betrothed many years before the wedding takes place and her position there is practically that of a slave to her future mother-in-law."[3]

---

1 See "Marriage in Korea," "The Family Line," and "A New Style of Courtship" in *Pen Pictures*, this vol.

2 The official reform reads: "男女早婚, 亟宜嚴禁, 男子二十歲, 女子十六歲以後, 始許嫁娶事." "Early marriages are strictly forbidden. A man must be twenty years old and a woman sixteen before they marry." English translation taken from Hulbert, "Korean Reforms," *Korean Repository* 2 (January 1895): 5.

3 Ibid.

In addition to worrying about the social ills caused by the practice of early marriage, Christian missionaries were concerned about the salvific import of marriage in Korea. A Rev. R.H. Sidebotham deployed in Pusan reported in a 1905 issue of the *Korea Mission Field* on the discussions in his congregation, claiming that "we discussed marriage, that topic of so much importance to our church, and after conference together, formulated several rules in addition to those already adopted by the Korean church as a whole … 'Do not betroth children before they are of a suitable age for marriage' 'Although parents must generally arrange for marriages, they must not force their children to marry' … 'Baptized girls must not be engaged to unbaptized boys.'"[4] As a missionary well steeped in the gospel of Christianity's reformative power, Gale was undoubtedly concerned with the social ramifications of early marriage, but in characteristic fashion his thoughts wander to broader philosophical questions: what is the Korean view of a higher power, and how do "peculiar" cultural practices such as child marriage explain such a view?

Eternal Life
Pen Pictures, 7–8; Old Corea, 36–7

Changsaeng[5] or *yŏngsaeng*[6] (Eternal Life)[7] are expressions well known to the Korean. The missionary will discourse upon them and the hearer will nod his head and respond, "Yes, eternal life is first and foremost; get it at all costs." The preacher is encouraged and feels that he

---

4 R.H. Sidebotham, "Enthusiastic Conference," *Korea Mission Field* 1 (1905): 66.

5 This seems to refer not to the characters *changsang*, as Gale originally wrote (elsewhere he renders *saeng* as *saing*), but *changsaeng* (長生 long life). In the *Old Corea* (hereafter OC) version, Gale writes "chang-sang pool-sa" (*changsaeng pulsa* 長生不死), meaning literally "long life without death," or immortality.

6 永生.

7 Gale's capitalization of "Eternal Life" likely contains religious import, that the idea conveyed through the phrase is a stand-in for "God," also demanding capitalization. This (attempted) equating with the Korean concept of eternal life is in line with Gale's ongoing strategy of establishing intertranslatability between the Confucian and Christian concepts of a higher power. For a focused and systematic presentation of this evangelical strategy, see "The Corean's View of God" in *Old Corea*, this vol.

is winning ground, and likely to have substantial results. But it is like Paul Laurence Dunbar, the negro, says of talking Greek to a [zzz zzz].[8]

"I'm for a republic" says the Chinaman; "So am I," says Uncle Sam.

"Then your mind and mine are just the same," says the Chinaman, but they are not. Uncle Sam's idea of a republic and the Chinaman's differ as widely as the missionary's idea of eternal life and that of the Korean.

The Korean has ten ideographs representing Eternal Life that he posts up in his front room in order that they may cast a beneficent spell over him. First and foremost are the everlasting hills. No man can understand their mystic meaning better than he, and he says their message is "forever;" second, the water, be it stream or sea, that lives and moves; then the plants that rise triumphant after winter, fresh and perfumed, sweet as [zzz];[9] the sun in its wanderings across the sky; the deer that come down from the hills with timid step, and whose dead are never seen; the clouds; the sacred crane; the bamboo; the turtle; the pine – all are emblems of Eternal Life.

Eternity is everything to him and time is nothing. If he can only make sure of the former he lets the latter go as it pleases. "Time is trash," says he in every act of life. I was once upon a time telling the literati of the famous poets of the West, and among other things attempted to translate this couplet from Goethe, thinking it might be good for his health[10] as well as for his literary delectation:

Mein Vermächtniss, wie herrlich weit und breit;
Die Zeit ist mein Vermächtniss, mein Acker ist die Zeit.[11]

---

8 Here the original typescript has been crossed out and a barely legible substitute is scribbled in the margin. The typescript reads "it is like Uncle Sam talking to Krüger about the word republic." However, throughout the rest of the analogy, Gale crosses out Krüger and replaces it with "Chinaman," which is the point of comparison he again employs in *Old Corea*. Paul Laurence Dunbar (1872–1906) was an African American poet and playwright who wrote the lyrics for *In Dahomey*, the first musical produced on Broadway entirely written and performed by African Americans. He is perhaps best known for his usage of antebellum African American southern vernacular English in his writing.

9 In the *OC* version, Gale has crossed out "fresh and sweet as ever."

10 *OC*: "good for his soul."

11 "My inheritance, how lordly wide and fair, Time is my estate; to time I'm heir." This translation appears in Carlyle and Shelston, *Thomas Carlyle: Selected Writings*, 11. Gale's German rendering of Johann Wolfgang Goethe's *Wilhelm Meister's Travels* contains a number of variant or simply incorrect spellings: "Mein Vermachtnisz, wie herrlich weit und breit, / Dei Zeit ist mein Vermachtnisz, mein Acker ist dei Zeit." The standard German is provided in the main text.

He did not see the point.

On an average the Korean does not live long and dies easily. He simply says "I am ill, I shall die," and lo, he is dead. Time slips through his fingers and is gone, which may account for his valuing it so lightly; but his eternity is priceless, and this he explains as "I, and my son, and my grandson, and my great grandson," etc. If this line is only left unbroken,[12] he will lie down and die with a smile, but if there is no son, unto him it is woe, woe, woe.[13]

As I write, before my window on one of the long dikes of the city, there is a New Year's stone-fight in process.[14] Thousands of spectators, packed close together, are moving forward one moment and rushing for their lives the next. This time-honoured custom has blossomed out afresh,[15] and the whole city is moved to go out and see. They use clubs, and stones, and slings, the object being to kill as many as possible in one afternoon.[16] I have never been able to fathom the meaning of the annual stone fight.[17] My friend Kwak says it is to prepare the nation to resist an enemy in time of war. I asked how he would do in the case of a four-point-seven gun. Kwak said, "*Kŭlsse*," which has a reflective force and means, "Really now, I wonder. I hadn't thought of that." One thing the stone fight does prove, namely, the worthlessness of time. The Korean sees no charm in tennis or cricket; his one and only terrestrial game is the fun of snuffing out somebody else's life. It illustrates the radiant bubble on which the Land of Morning Calm sails along.[18]

But he has his real anxieties, too, that the missionary perhaps sees more frequently than any other. "I am a great sinner" says he.

"And how so?"

"I have no son, I have lost eternal life; give me a son."

---

12 *OC:* "If this line is maintained unbroken."

13 *OC:* "but if there is no son he feels that his inheritance is woe, woe, woe."

14 *OC:* "When I wrote this some years ago, I saw before my window on one of the long dikes of the city a New Year stone fight was in progress."

15 *OC:* "This time-honoured custom had revived." This seems to suggest that the custom had died out sometime between the time of his writing in 1902 and the editing of the *OC* version in the 1920s.

16 *OC:* "in one fight."

17 This sentence has been omitted from the *OC* version.

18 This entire paragraph is rendered in the past tense in the *OC* version. This suggests an acknowledgment by Gale by the 1920s that Koreans' perception of time and eternal life had evolved.

This son may be the laziest child of all the earth, with a jungle of unkempt locks for head-gear, and a body fit only for a public bath-house,[19] but never mind, he is the unit necessary along which to pass the mystic current called life. To have a son is the *summum bonum*[20] of existence, and an overwhelming desire to attain this blessing has led Korea[21] into child marriage, concubinage, retirement of men from family cares in middle life, the degradation of women, and the ruin of the races generally.

No sooner is anxiety to have a son over with, than the father and mother begin to torment themselves with the thought of how he is to marry, and so accomplish another step in the life that must not end.

A month or so ago my gardener came to me and said he had a matter of importance to speak of. "My son, the Yellow Dragon,"[22] said he, "is eight years old, and I have made no provision as yet for his marrying, but there is a man in Righteous Town where the King lives, who is hard up and offers me his daughter, if I'll only take her and keep her. It is such an excellent chance, and the boy may live and die childless otherwise."

Such is a sample of the cares that have marked the gardener's face and weighed on the Korean's soul generally.[23]

"The Yellow Dragon!" said I, "who has eaten only nine years,[24] and can't feed himself or fly a kite? Nonsense!" But in matters of this kind the Korean is the most persistent man alive. "Heaven is good," said the gardener.

A day or two later I passed the gardener's house, when a sunny-faced little dot stood by the way to meet me. "And who are you?" I asked.

"My name is Poktong-i"[25] (Lucky-Girl) was the reply.

---

19 *OC*: "and a body fit only for the pest-house."

20 A Latin expression meaning "the highest good" or the ultimate goal.

21 The *OC* version is rendered "led Corea ages ago," again demonstrating the acknowledgment of progress by Gale.

22 This seems to refer to the Korean name Hwangyong (黃龍).

23 *OC*: "Such are the cares that have scored the gardener's face and weigh on the Corean national soul."

24 *OC*: "who has 'eaten' but nine summers." In Korean, one's age may be described as the number of years one has "eaten" (e.g., *nai mani mŏgŏssŏyo*, I have eaten many years [I am quite old]). The implication of this phrase is to emphasize the maturity, preparedness, or fitness of the subject for some action or behaviour.

25 This title is a combination of the name Poktong (福童), indeed meaning "lucky or fortunate child," and the diminutive affix ~*i*, (~이), which functions much the same as ~*ito*/*ita* do in Spanish (e.g., *perrito*, little [male] dog).

"Where do you live?"

"Right here," said she. I then realized that I was in the presence of the future wife of the gardener's heir, the Yellow Dragon.

By hook or by crook children must be obtained at the earliest possible stage, and so, finances permitting or not permitting, sons and daughters are married off from nine years old and upwards. Little or no account is taken of the personal appearance of the one to be married. The texture of her soul may be of sackcloth or silk, her face sunshine or thunder, the groom thinks nothing of it. Our ideas of choice, and consent, and love, and adoration, and infatuation are all the vagaries of foreign-devildom and belong not to Korea.[26]

When the wife has no children the concubine appears, the wife, Sarah-like,[27] often joining as earnestly in the search as does the husband. She regards it as no wrong to her. The missionary lady weeps over her Korean sister, but the sister is all unconscious of what the agony means. Her husband must have a son, does this peculiar foreign woman not know?

The Korean's spirit temple is the only thing in the country that accords with the eternal fitness of things of which he talks so much; for it is not a house built with hands, but a mound on a mountain spur, encircled by hills and covered over with the sky. Here he sacrifices, here he meets the spirits of the past, here he makes provision for the future, for as the grave is well chosen so is his eternal life rendered secure; a failure, and the family is lost; a successful choice, and there is wealth and honor, and sons forever.

(1902)

---

26 In the *OC* version this paragraph is also rendered in the present tense, suggesting that child marriage may have still been prevalent in the 1920s and contrasting with Gale's earlier implication.

27 This refers to the Old Testament Bible story in which Sarah, after being unable to bear a son for ten years with her husband Abraham, suggests that he take her handmaiden Hagar as a concubine. Hagar then gives birth to Abraham's first son, Ishmael.

Tobacco in Korea

The general consensus on the origin of tobacco in Korea is that it entered Chosŏn Korea in the early seventeenth century via Japan, which in turn had received it in the late sixteenth century through its trade with Portugal. Evidence also exists, however, that tobacco entered Korea via China, based on *The Diaries of the Royal Secretariat* (Sŭngjŏngwŏn ilgi 承政院日記), a daily record of the inner workings of the Chosŏn government from 1623 to 1894. According to this document, tobacco was widely circulating in the midst of trade-ransom negotiations for prisoners of war following the Second Manchu Invasion (Pyŏngja horan, 1636). Although Gale's claim of a Chinese route for the entrance of tobacco to Korea is possible, the date he provides of 1645 is problematic in that Prince Chang Yu (張維, 1587–1638) died well before his supposedly introducing the crop. Furthermore, according to Chang's *Kyegok manp'il* (谿谷漫筆 The Causeries of Kyegok, 1635), "The method for smoking tobacco [*namnyŏngch'o* 南靈草] first came from Japan. There they call it *tanpaku katamari* [淡泊塊 a bundle of tobacco], and they say the plant came from various lands in the southern ocean. It first arrived in our country some 20 years ago."[1] Whatever the exact origins of the crop, its popularity quickly spread in Chosŏn Korea, and records by foreign observers in the late nineteenth century uniformly note the nearly universal enjoyment of tobacco among men and women, young and old.[2]

1　See Sin and Sŏ, "Chosŏn hugi hŭbyŏn," 27, 30.

2　See, for example, Carles, *Life in Corea*. Carles noted that it was acceptable for men and women to smoke after marriage, which at that time would have meant children as young as ten.

Tobacco's popularity has continued into contemporary South Korea, although there is a marked gendered division that stands in stark contrast with premodern Korea: while the smoking rate among men as of 2017 was among the highest in OECD (Organisation for Economic Co-operation and Development) countries, at 36.2 per cent, smoking among women was by far the lowest, at 4.3 per cent.[3]

Gale begins the chapter with reference to William Woodville Rockhill (1854–1914), the United States diplomat, scholar of the Far East, and personal friend of Gale, perhaps best known for his authorship of the United States' Open Door Policy for China in the wake of the Boxer Rebellion of 1899–1901. In addition to serving as the minister to Russia (1910–11) and Turkey (1911–13) under President Taft, Rockhill also served as minister to Greece (1897–9), Serbia (1898–9), and China (1905–9) under President Roosevelt. Rockhill was a distinguished Orientalist scholar with significant contributions in sinology and Tibetology, among other fields, including extensive travelogues from China, Mongolia, and Tibet, and French translations of the Prātimokṣa Sutra. Concerning Korea, he published "Notes on Some of the Laws, Customs, and Superstitions of Korea" in *American Anthropologist* (1891). Gale's nephew, the sinologist Esson M. Gale, in his *Salt for the Dragon: A Personal History of China*, wrote:

> My own Chief of Mission, first among his compeers, was the Envoy Extraordinary and Minister Plenipotentiary of the United States, William Woodville Rockhill … Known generally for his aloofness and acid remarks, the Minister condescended to treat me with unexpected kindness. Away back, possibly sometime in the 1890's, I surmise, he and my Uncle James Gale had become friends during a trans-Pacific voyage to Korea. Their conversation had revolved about the curious similarity in Royal objections to the introduction of tobacco into England and Korea. Gale had written a sprightly monograph on the arrival of the weed in the latter land.[4]

Here Esson Gale could be referring either to Gale's "Tobacco in Korea" published in *Korea Magazine* (June 1917, 248–54), or maybe even to this piece. The Gale Papers contain quite a few references to tobacco.[5]

---

3 "Health Risks – Daily Smokers – OECD Data."

4 Esson Gale, *Salt for the Dragon*, 15.

5 Ross King, personal communication, 19 October 2018.

Tobacco in Korea
Pen Pictures, 9–10[6]

I once heard Mr. W.W. Rockhill, now U.S. Minister in St. Petersburg, say that the Koreans were the greatest smokers in the world. If measured by the time the pipe is in the mouth they certainly are; but if it be a question of tobacco consumed, the Korean may very easily fall behind the [zzz] foreigner. He is a deliberate, comfortable, unconscious smoker, so apathetic in his enjoyment of his long pipe, that you hardly know whether he holds the smoke or the smoke holds him. Cares and anxieties are whiffed away, and the fumes curl over his soul softly, benignly, sleepily. The foreigner, on the other hand, pulls actively, bites viciously the end of his cigar, swallows the fumes and then expels them by all the means of exit, nose, ears and eyes, the result being that in half an hour he consumed more tobacco than the Korean would in a day. To even matters up, however, Korean smoking means a united pull, "man, woman and boy," all at it, from first cock-crow of the morning till the curfew sings "lights out!" at night. It is as difficult to find a man who does not smoke, as it is to find a ten-year old son of a gentleman who is not married.

Tobacco was introduced into Korea about 1645 by Prince Chang Yu who went as ambassador to the first Manchu Emperor.[7] Prince Chang's daughter afterwards became queen of Korea, but his chief fame rests on the fact that he introduced the "weed" to his waiting nation. We are told that on his first introducing it, there was great opposition, so much so that the matter was taken to the courts, and the question discussed was as to whether a man had a right to sit and "eat" smoke or not. Prince Chang's father-in-law, whose name was Kim, was greatly scandalized, and told his son to keep out of his sight; said he,

"The odour that accompanies you is unspeakably nauseating, and the sight of you making a stovepipe of yourself is disgusting to look upon."

---

6   An abridged version of this essay appears in Gale, *Korea in Transition*, 9–10. Gale additionally broaches the subject in an *OC* chapter titled "Tobacco in Corea," but the content differs markedly. The *OC* chapter matches the article "Tobacco in Korea" appearing in *Korea Magazine* 1 (1917): 248–54.

7   More recent research on the origins of tobacco use in Korea places its introduction at a much earlier date, although all seem to agree on the seventeenth century as an entry date. See Sin and So, "Chosŏn hugi hŭbyŏn."

The account goes on to say, "For this reason, whenever he saw his father-in-law coming, Chang would whip the pipe out of his mouth and hide it. This explains why young people to-day may not smoke before those who are older."[8]

If Prince Chang's father-in-law, in this year of grace 1902, could only see his posterity sitting in long rows, pipe in hand, whiffing the hours away, and [zzz] the [zzz] essence of nicotine, what would he say? Tobacco made friends with small and great and possessed itself of the whole land even to the remotest corner.

In 1792, Mr. Yu Tŭkkong,[9] a famous scholar, was given the subject "Tobacco" and the rhyme character *Song* (meaning Luzon or Manila)[10] and asked to write a verse. His first line ran, "The Spiritual root [zzz] from Luzon." Already we see that it had worked its way up into the realm of the spiritual to be so designated; while Manila meant and still means to the Korean a land of outer darkness, so that Mr. Yu's line interpreted would read, "Tobacco took its rise in Hades but now sits among the Gods."

This gives one a hint as to its history during the hundred and fifty years that had passed. To-day it still holds its own in spite of all shocks, being reinforced by the cheap cigarette that is pushing hard at the long pipe. The evolution of the pipe I have not been able to follow, but it is

---

8 The more widely accepted theory as to the origins of the stigma placed on smoking in the presence of superiors is Confucian in nature, and while indirectly linked to Chang's "respectfully" concealing his habit from his father-in-law reflects much more ingrained social practices. C. Paul Dredge writes, "At least two things about smoking likely made it seem inappropriate in the presence of superiors from its very beginnings in Korea. They are that 1) smoking is a form of physical pleasure and that 2) smoking changes the nature of social space independently of the wishes of anyone but the smoker himself. To enjoy oneself or even to be comfortable physically is behavior that has traditionally been inappropriate in Korean social situations where superiors are present. The superior has some authority over the inferior, and expresses this symbolically in his control of the physical comfort of his inferior." See Dredge, "Smoking in Korea," *Korea Journal* 4 (1980): 28.

9 Yu Tŭkkong (柳得恭, 1748–1807) was a Chosŏn-era scholar, government minister, and poet during the reign of King Chŏngjo.

10 This character may refer to the second syllable of the transliteration of Luzon, the northernmost island of the Philippines and location of Manila, when using sinographs: Ch. Rusong (呂宋, Luzon).

so long in stem that the smoker cannot light it himself. When he has no servant by to help, he strikes the match, fits it into a chink or corner, and gets back far enough to reach it with the bowl. The coolie uses a shorter pipe that he carries up his sleeve, or down the back of his neck. The Korean pipe-bowl is about as large as that of China, but the mouthpiece is seldom made of jade or stone, and is not nearly as huge. It is a thin metal spear that, in any jostling, hustling country, would be likely to find its way through the back of the neck, but in Korea where the national spirit is passive and not active, a man might smoke a stiletto on Bell Street[11] (Broadway) and be in no danger whatever.

Tobacco plays a part in the sacred ceremony of sacrifice. When tables of food are brought in and placed before the tablet, the pipe is offered to the ancestral spirit, who accepts it with about as much visible animation, as the coolie does his day's work. It is not vulgar for a Korean woman to smoke, but it is vulgar indeed for her to know how to write Chinese or to read the native script, which however, is another story. Widows are said to be great smokers, as the pipe must serve as company in place of the absent husband. For the widow it is called *"mangsich'o"*[12] (the weed that scatters care).

Korean tobacco costs 1100 cash a catty, or about five pence English money per pound. The best quality grows up north, 240 miles distant from Seoul, in a place called Songch'on, that was the capital of ancient Korea (Koguryǒ) 37 BC.[13] In the cold far north it flourishes. They sow the seed early even before the frost is out of the ground, and wait for seedlings; then it is transplanted, and fertilized, and weeded, and topped and encouraged, so that the leaves grow rich and large. When the moisture or sap comes well up out of the ground, and when the plant is full and lazy, and ready to topple over at the sign of rain, clipping number one takes place; two others follow, altogether three in the year. It is then

---

11 This is a translation of one of the main east-west thoroughfares in Seoul, Chongno (鐘路), meaning literally "Bell Street."

12 Probably 忘時草, "weed for forgetting time."

13 Koguryǒ (高句麗, 37 BC–AD 668) was an ancient kingdom that encompassed the northern and central regions of the Korean peninsula and extended into southern and central inner and outer Manchuria. A formidable military power in ancient northeast Asia, it was eventually defeated by a Silla-Tang alliance in 668. Today's North Korea, sharing the kingdom's later capital of P'yǒngyang, draws on the military might and independence of ancient Koguryǒ as a source of nationalistic and historical legitimacy vis-à-vis the South.

woven in by the stems to straw ropes and hung up, and taken down, piled together, separated, shaken out, put back, crushed, and sat upon, until by slow degrees it is cured. Then the stems are removed, and the best, usually the first cutting, is put by to await the purchaser.

Korea is a land of pipes, and the pipe is an emblem of peace. While a fight is in progress the pipe is laid aside, words are multiplied, insults added, angels appealed to, streams of invective poured forth, with eyes aglare, veins distended, and the whole being ready to burst, both participants keyed up to the same tune, and throwing off about a million vibrations to the second, till the proper climax is passed, when everything collapses, and we hear the "tack" of the pipes being cleared for a smoke and now peace reigns once more.

(1902)

Concerning the Occult

In the opening lines of "Concerning the Occult," Gale writes, "It is undoubtedly true that the Korean has a bent in the direction of the occult and the unseen." This may also be said of Gale's own literary predilections. The Korean name that Gale adopted early on, Ki Il (奇一), means "strange," "fantastic," or "peculiar one," suggesting such a bent from early on in his career. Much of the Korean and English literature that he chose to translate was concerned with the supernatural, preternatural, and the occult, demonstrating a certain fondness for this subject matter. "Concerning the Occult" is dated from 1912, making it one of the last selections to be included in *Pen Pictures,* and this was roughly the time when Gale started to become aware of and gain an appreciation for the vibrant tradition of Korean occult literature. In 1913 Gale published his *Korean Folk Tales: Imps, Ghosts and Fairies,* featuring translations of various fantastic tales and weird anecdotes, some of which appeared in the *Taedong Yasŭng* (大東野乘 Tales of the Eastern Country) and others which were drawn from Im Pang's (任埅, 1640–1724) *Ch'ŏnyerok* (天倪錄 Records of the Invisible Workings of Heaven), *yadam* or "unofficial" fictional narratives compiled sometime between 1717 and 1724.[1] Gale continued this trajectory with his translation in 1921 of *Kŭmnyŏng chŏn* (金鈴傳 The Tale of Golden Bell), the anonymously authored late-Chosŏn vernacular tale of a golden bell with miraculous and supernatural abilities.[2] His taste for the supernatural extended to his selection

---

1 Rutt, *James Scarth Gale and His "History,"* 50.

2 Gale Papers, Ledger 18, pp. 167–86. The "Tale of Golden Bell" seems not to have been published and remains only in manuscript form in Gale's personal

of English literature for translation into Korean when in 1924 he published *Yŏng-Mi sinirok* (Strange and Marvelous Tales from England and America), a collection of English and American literature that conformed thematically to Gale's "inordinate interest in the preternatural."[3]

Gale's interest in the supernatural is, at first glance, not easily reconcilable with his missionary identity. Indeed, only one of the accounts included in this chapter contains any overtly religious themes, with the remaining accounts grounded in secular curiosity. Gale's potentially "unwholesome" preoccupation with such themes seems to have attracted attention, as the topic is explicitly broached in the preface to *Strange Stories*, penned by Gale's Korean "pundit" Yi Wŏnmo. When Yi is asked the reason for making such a book, whether the tales contained within were not "at some remove from the truth of the Holy Bible," Yi writes of the connections between the visible and the invisible in language accessible to the Korean reader: "We can see that the Heavenly Father in his omnipotence made not only our bodies but also our spirits, and that he governs not only the material world but also the spiritual."[4] Thus, it is clear that Gale had given careful consideration to the theological underpinnings of occult literature and had by the 1920s developed a rather sophisticated philosophical "cover" for his secular literary dalliances.

Concerning the Occult
Pen Pictures, 11–12; *Old Corea*, 82–3;
Korea Magazine (1917): 22–4

It is undoubtedly true that the Korean has a bent in the direction of the occult and the unseen more than he has toward the matter-of-fact concerns of life. He likes to hide himself away into regions of quiet, where he can meditate off into the realm of the spiritual to meet clairvoyant folks and telepathic doubles. Mind specters and familiar spirits

---

ledgers. But see Olsen, "Gendered Filiality and Heroism in the Tale of Golden Bell" for a discussion of this text.

3 Gale and Yi Wŏnmo, *Yŏng-Mi sinirok*; King, "James Scarth Gale and the Christian Literature Society," 19–21.

4 Gale and Yi Wŏnmo, *Yŏng-Mi sinirok*; quoted in King, "James Scarth Gale and the Christian Literature Society," 22.

he is familiar with. The old fortune-teller will sing out his formula and then end with a spasmodic rap of his wand-stick saying, "Come down, come down, ugh! come down." Possessions, exorcisms, floatings about in mid-air, necromancing through the night are all matters of common converse.[5] The automatic hand, too, he has discovered, and second powers of vision.

Speaking of the catastrophe of the *Titanic*[6] to a Korean friend, I mentioned how the world had lost an old familiar face and interesting personality in W.T. Stead.[7] The writer spoke of his efforts on behalf of the general weal of England, of his friendship for Russia, of his gifts as a writer, all of which interested the Korean only slightly; but when I told of his letters from "Julia," and the strange doings of that automatic hand of his, the friend awakened as from a deep sleep. Here was a familiar theme that was in accord with his own, and he at once told me of two happenings in his experience that were enough like the doings of Julia to merit repetition.

One was this: A friend, let's call him Kim, was taking a siesta one afternoon while an acquaintance was sitting at the foot of his mat reading a book. Sometime later a third party called, and then the two proceeded to comb over the Chinese together. They came to a passage difficult to construe, with a word in it that neither of them understood.

Kim, who was dozing, heard them discuss the passage in loud and emphatic tones. He grew tired of it and finally got up and said, "Don't you two ignoramuses know that the word *sukch'ŏng* means *honey*,"[8] but they paid no heed. "Look here," said he, "I tell you it means *honey*." They paid no attention but still they went on arguing. The afternoon sun shone square on the book while the two sat one on each side with the disputed characters between them. Kim, incensed at the thought

---

5 *OC*: "are all matters of every day talk."

6 *OC*: "Some years ago speaking of the catastrophe of the *Titanic*." At the time of the *Pen Pictures* version of this essay, the sinking would have been very fresh in the collective memory, but the *OC* version, though not dated, was clearly written years later, probably in the mid-1920s.

7 William Thomas Stead (1849–1912) was an English newspaper editor known as one of the pioneers of investigative journalism. Later in his life he turned increasingly to spiritualism, claiming that he was in contact with the spirit world through telepathy, and that he was capable of producing automatic writing inspired by a spirit medium.

8 熟淸.

of their taking no notice of him, said, "You fools, it means *honey*!" and went back and lay down. He fell asleep and when he awoke it was evening and the third party was gone.

"I say," said the friend, "but you did sleep."

"What's the use of staying awake," said Kim, "when folks pay no attention to what one says?"[9]

"What do you mean?" asked the friend.

"Why, I mean about *sukch'ŏng*, when you were arguing about it."

"Yes, we were, we just didn't know what it meant."

"But I told you that it was 'honey' and you paid no attention."

"*Honey*? You never said *honey* to us that we heard."

"Go away," said Kim, wearied out by it, "didn't Yi So-and-So call?"

"Yes."

"And didn't you and he read the book together?"

"Yes."

"And didn't you get into a dispute and argue in a loud and [zzz] way over *sukch'ŏng*?"

"Yes, we talked over that word, but only quietly; we did not wish to disturb you."

"But I got up and told you what it meant."

"Oh no, you didn't; you never got up at all, had no part in it and were sound asleep all the time."

Kim went on to explain certain features of the afternoon, the sunshine on the book, etc. showing that we was most definitely awake and aware of the conversation, while his friend vouched for it that he had been sound asleep all the time.

Still this might have been a dream or a piece of imagination on his part.

Here is another story, trustworthy witnesses still being on hand to vouch for it:

Chang fell ill and died. He had been an average, uninfluential Christian for a year or so. Great was the consternation[10] in the home, for Chang was the support of the household and was still a young man. Friends called to condole with the stricken family. All the accompaniments that bespeak Korean grief were present[11] – tears and desolation.

9　*OC*: "when folks pay as little attention to one as you did?"

10　*OC*: "distress."

11　*OC*: "All the accompaniments that bespeak a greatest loss that can overtake a Corean were present."

A startling thing happened in that home: five hours after the so-called death Chang suddenly rose up, shook himself back into consciousness, and spoke to the congregated mourners.

"Friends," said he, "I have seen wonders, have been all the way to heaven and back again to earth."

With startled faces they looked at him. Was it a dream, or was he alive, for of a surety, according to Korean custom, he had been dead? Inquiry was made as to where he had gone and what he had seen.

"When I died," said he "I was taken by a company of angels[12] into the high heaven where I met Yi Yodam, the Christian preacher of the town of Tamyo. He had just died."[13]

The assembled company knew of Yi Yodam, and the announcement of his death was a startling piece of news to them.

"We were carried up to heaven, where were indescribable delights, such as the heart never dreamed of.[14] We were both graciously welcomed, Yi especially. Passing by an archway that seemed to lead to the Eternal City, he was asked to enter while I was directed to another.[15] I separated from him with regret, but was shown a portico of such splendor as these eyes never before looked upon. Into it I entered but was stopped by an angel who said to me:

'Your companion, when on earth, was a faithful servant, and told others of God's goodness, and so has passed to great reward, but you are to go back to earth once more for a new and fresh opportunity to be faithful.'

"My regrets for having to return from such a region of bliss were very great. I begged that I might stay forever, but it was not to be, and so I am here and would tell of the mercy of God, and how we should all give our hearts to Him."[16]

"But how about Yi Yodam?" asked the company.

"Yi Yodam is in heaven" said Chang, "for I have just been with him and we have walked together on the celestial way."

So emphatic was he in the statement, that one of the hearers started at once on foot to Tamyo to see how it fared with Yi Yodam. Arriving at

---

12 *OC*: "I was taken by an angel."
13 *OC*: "who had just died also."
14 *OC*: "as I had never dreamed of."
15 *OC*: "while I was ordered forward."
16 *OC*: "and would tell of the mercy of God and how good He is."

the village, he inquired as to the leader of the church, where did he live and how about him?

"He is dead" said the man addressed.

"Dead?"

Sure enough, the signs of mourning were evident; on going to the house he found that the master and faithful leader of the church had passed away that day according to the message brought by Chang on his return from heaven.

These facts are correctly stated, though the proper names are changed. They are vouched for by one whose name stands high in Korea for Christian integrity, higher than Mr. Stead's does in England, while the story itself is hardly less wonderful than any messages from "Julia," and without the doubtful necromancy that goes with them.[17]

(1912)

---

17 "and without the doubtful necromancy that goes with them" does not appear in the *OC* version.

A Note of Warning

Korean Confucian literati first became acquainted with Christian thought through Jesuit missions in seventeenth- and eighteenth-century China. Though many Chosŏn officials who encountered Jesuits in the Qing capital were impressed by the technological innovations of the West, most found Western religious thought unconvincing at best. One of the primary arguments levelled against Christian theology was the foundation of selfishness upon which hopes for salvation were constructed, and traces of this line of reasoning may be detected in "A Note of Warning." Confucian thinkers such as Sin Hudam (慎後聃, 1702–61) contrasted the Confucian idea of moral perfectability with Christian morals when he wrote, "How could we even think it possible that it was because they wanted to win a reward that the sages and virtuous men of old took their ethical responsibilities seriously and worked ... at cultivating moral character?"[1] In "A Conversation on Catholicism," An Chŏngbok (安鼎福, 1712–91), like Sin a disciple of the renowned scholar Yi Ik,[2] writes of the selfish motivations of Christians: "[Jesus] tantalized

---

1 Sin Hudam, "Sŏhak pyŏn 西學辯," in Yi Manch'ae 李晩采, ed., *Pyŏgwi p'yon* 闢衛編, 1:40b–45b; quoted in Ch'oe, Lee, and de Bary, *Sources of Korean Tradition*, 2:128.

2 Yi Ik (李瀷, 1681–1763) was a late-Chosŏn government minister who has often been characterized as a Sirhak (Practical Learning) scholar, a modern neologism to describe a school of thought that emerged in seventeenth- and eighteenth-century Chosŏn that was concerned with social and political injustice. Yi Ik wrote on a number of social issues, including more equitable land distribution. Seth, *A Concise History of Korea*, 222–4.

people with promises of heaven if they did good and threatened people with hell if they did evil. In promoting moral behavior, the sages, however, focus on this world. They illuminate virtue and revitalize the people in order to educate and transform them. Jesus encouraged selfishness and the sages foster selflessness."[3]

The Korean preacher quoted by Gale applies this same religious philosophy, this time in defence of Christianity. The result is a hybrid, Koreanized Christian parable emphasizing the essential righteousness and perfectability of humankind that could nevertheless inspire selfless contribution to the service of the church. The original farmer in the story contributes his turnip (service) to the king (the church) out of genuinely moral motivations, not for personal gain, whereas the second farmer contributes his fatted calf based on a lust for personal gain, which may be interpreted as a greedy desire for eternal life. Gale did not often summarize or show general interest in the sermons of Korean preachers, and the reasons for his selection of this particular homily are uncertain, but the sentiments contained seem to have represented for Gale a poignant fusion of Confucian and Christian theology, a theme very much compatible with his general evangelical and literary strategy.

A Note of Warning
Pen Pictures, 13

A Korean preacher was heard to remark the other day, that contributions for Christian work, given in the hope of getting something bigger in return, were a miserable kind of service. To illustrate: Said he, "There was a man once who had a field of turnips in which grew one of enormous size, broad across, and tall up and down; such a turnip as no man had ever seen before, chief of all turnips. The farmer made up his mind that such a specimen was too good for a country village, and that he would carry it to Seoul and offer it to the king. Making his way thither he succeeded at last in getting word into the Palace, 'Just a humble country bumpkin who has a magnificent turnip from his field that he wishes to present to Your Majesty.'

---

3 An Chŏngbok, *Sunam chip* 順菴集, 17: 8a–26a; quoted in Choe, Lee, and de Bary, *Sources of Korean Tradition*, 2:131–2.

The turnip was brought in and king and courtiers were greatly interested and astonished. In return the countryman was given a rich present of gold and sent back to his home.

A neighbour on hearing this, made up his mind that he too would make an offering and exact something better still from the royal munificence. He fatted a calf and fed and stuffed him till he was round and sleek and [zzz], and then led him up to the capital. He made application at the Palace, 'Just a humble country bumpkin who has a magnificent calf from his stall that he wishes to present to Your Majesty.'

Word came back, 'His Majesty has plenty of cattle, well-fed and well-groomed, keep your calf for your family; they will enjoy it.' But this countryman's loyalty was deep and broad and long, 'Would His Majesty please accept the gift and so satisfy the heart of his humblest subject?' Thus pressed the king accepted it and in return sent word saying, 'Your present given in such a loyal spirit is greatly appreciated, in return I send the most wonderful thing I have on hand, which is a huge turnip given to me by a man in the country. Accept the turnip as a gift from your king.'

Disgusted and outraged, this countryman, in place of carrying a pocket full of gold, went home with the wretched turnip, convinced that the offering of gifts to kings was an unprofitable business."

"Let people beware" said the preacher "how they make contributions in God's service."

On and Off the Street Car

In 1897 the American businessman Henry Collbran and his junior partner, Harry Bostwick, secured the rights to construct an electric streetcar through the heart of Seoul, and when it began operations on 17 May 1899, it became the first such technology not only in Korea but throughout Asia. Henry Collbran was a savvy entrepreneur, a British-born naturalized U.S. citizen who had left the railroad business in Colorado to pursue opportunity in the emerging market of Korea. After forgoing an initial venture into Korean gold-mining, because of what he viewed as potentially excessive training and transportation costs, Collbran along with his partner Bostwick secured the rights to build Korea's first railroad, running from Chemulp'o (present-day Inch'ŏn) to Seoul.[1] The rights to this project had been secured thanks to the vigorous lobbying efforts of Dr Horace Allen, the Presbyterian missionary-physician who was among the first wave of Westerners to arrive in 1884 and who eventually served as head of the U.S. legation.[2] The railway was successfully completed and Collbran's reputation in the Korean business community grew. Shortly after, word spread that Emperor Kojong[3] sought to further modernize the capital through electrification, telephone service, and the installation of an electric trolley

---

1 Southerton, *Colorado's Henry Collbran*.

2 Ibid.

3 When Korea was officially elevated to the Korean Empire in October 1897, King Kojong became Emperor Kojong and Queen Min became Empress Min. However, the titles King/Emperor and Queen/Empress were often used interchangeably.

service, the latter at the urging of a Korean government official who had seen such a system first-hand on a trip to Washington, DC.[4] Collbran and Bostwick exerted pressure on Dr Allen to broker a deal secretly to forestall the efforts of competing interests, notably the Japanese. In February 1899, a contract was signed for the joint rights to operate all three technologies under the auspices of the newly established Seoul Electric Company (Hansŏng chŏn'gi hoesa).[5] The company continued to operate profitably until 1909, when Collbran was forced to sell his company to Japanese competitors, who had by then developed a near monopoly over the Korean economy.

The streetcar network expanded under the Japanese, increasing from thirty-seven cars in 1910 to a fleet of 154 in 1937; average daily passengers, meanwhile, increased from 9,810 in 1910 to 150,000 in 1935.[6] The Seoul streetcar had few competitors through the 1950s and remained the most popular mode of transportation, owing to the prohibitive cost or rarity of alternatives. By the mid-1960s, however, Seoul's by-then dilapidated streetcar system fell out of fashion, and on 30 November 1968, the last streetcar travelled the streets of Seoul.

Seoul's streetcar operated at the speed of about 10 miles per hour, measured some 8.7 metres, and could accommodate up to forty passengers.[7] The inaugural route extended from Sŏdaemun through Chongno, past Tongdaemun to Ch'ŏngnyang-ni, but additional routes were soon added. The carriages were open air, protected only by a roof, but there was a central compartment that was walled off and reserved for first-class passengers. Many have reported that Emperor Kojong maintained his own royal carriage, which he used to visit the grave of his murdered wife, Empress Min, but Donald Southerton claims that according to Collbran family records, the monarch, "although in possession of his own private car, never rode the system. Upon opening of the trolley line, Kojong agreed to sit in his car but would not let it move."[8] As with many of his writings appearing in this volume, Gale's primary concern here lies not with documenting the details of such a technological innovation but rather with the encounter between tradition and modernity that it engendered, an at-times physical collision comically

---

4 Ibid.

5 Ibid.

6 Lankov, *The Dawn of Modern Korea*, 79.

7 Ibid., 78–9.

8 Southerton, *Colorado's Henry Collbran*.

related in Gale's amusing anecdote of a *kisaeng*'s[9] first experience with this Western contraption.

On and Off the Street Car
Pen Pictures, 14–15;
"On and Off the Tram-Car," *Old Corea*, 124–5

A convenient car service now connects the two extreme ends of the city of Seoul. The laying of it has cost no end of high-skilled operation[10] – tearing up the former tracks, ripping out of old bridges, levelling off, straightening, ballasting, overhauling, and resetting; till now, two lines with heavy rails, level with the street, run direct as a rifle shot right across the city.[11] Cement bridges, lowered and widened, take the place of the hump-backed arches that used to span the streamlets and gutters.[12]

One day the writer saw a hard-[zzz], sun-tanned Japanese in charge of a gang of coolies, putting the finishing touches to the line. He had the divided foot-gear of the islands and the general make-up of a Japanese coolie gang-master. Occasion came to tap him on the shoulder, and ask a question, which he answered at once in good Korean.

"You, a Japanese, how comes it that you speak Korean?"

"Speak my own language," was the answer, "I'm a Korean, no Japanese about me."

---

9 *Kisaeng* (妓生), which may be translated as "students of the arts performed by females" were female entertainers who, according to Kathleen McCarthy, "participated in the full panopoly of social events that comprised the social lives of Korea's govering elite." Rosters of *kisaeng* were maintained at government offices throughout the provinces, and in the capital they were employed by the Court Entertainment Bureau and "presented elaborately choreographed music and dance pieces on festival days and occasions of state." Although one of the expectations of *kisaeng* was to provide sexual compansionship for government officials, this was not their sole or even primary role. McCarthy, "Kisaeng and Poetry in the Koryŏ Period," 6. Gale provides historical background on the origins of the *kisaeng* in "The Dancing Girl," *Old Corea*, this vol.

10 *OC*: "surgical operation."

11 *OC*: "run direct across the city."

12 *OC*: "that used to span the gutters."

"Then where did you learn to lay steel roadways so well?" I asked.

"Oh, I learned it years ago, and not a cent of money have I saved out of it either.[13] It ain't any use to learn when you can't save."

"You are wrong," I replied, "How many Japanese were employed in the laying of these cement bridges?"

"None at all," was the answer, "Koreans, every man of them."[14]

Thus it comes that in the wake of the Japanese who knows how, Koreans are learning, and a great company of useful men are under process of development in Seoul.

On these double tracks the unimpeded cars spin by, carrying an increasing number of passengers.

The fuss and hum of an electric wire were such in the early days, that the devout grandmother made her prayers to the god of sparks and fire that possessed it,[15] and bowed low to the wires and the pole; but to-day old customs are receding, and the same grandma who used to pray, prays no more, but rides the car complacently and makes a heap of inward grumbling when "no power" appears.[16]

The law of hard fact[17] and mathematical calculation comes in to appropriate the preserves, that were given up to the telegraph god and other quaint oddities that flourished for a day.

---

13 *OC*: "Oh, I just picked it up years ago, but there is no money in it, not a cent."

14 Although Korean labour was employed in the construction of the streetcar, all of the drivers were Japanese. On 26 May 1899, just ten days after the streetcar's inauguration, a five-year-old child was struck by a streetcar driven by a Japanese driver and killed. Horace Allen, the head of the U.S. legation in Korea, wrote in the *New York Times* shortly after the incident: "A child was run over and killed and the natives, who had never seen a trolley car in operation, regarded it as a too dangerous vehicle to be tolerated. They wrecked the car and started for the power house to demolish that, but before doing any further damage the rioters were quelled." Witnesses to the accident, suspicious of all things Japanese, considered the incident an intentional act of murder and rioted, destroying the carriage, while the Japanese driver and Korean conductor narrowly escaped with their lives. See Allen, "American Work in Korea: The United States Minister to the Hermit Nation Talks – Bad Start of a Trolley Road," *New York Times*, 18 July 1899; Lankov, *The Dawn of Modern Korea*, 78.

15 In the *OC* version, the words "that possessed it" have been deleted.

16 In the *OC* version Gale writes "no powa" [*sic*], which seems to be a representation of the Korean pronunciation (*p'awŏ*) of the English word "power."

17 *OC*: "hard reason."

The question now is, not how to propitiate the creature that controls the wire and the pole, but how to get safely on and off the car.[18] Altogether the nature of the thing is a mystery. A law governs the steel car and track that is quite outside the realm of old Korea's understanding. For example, all the bells may ring, conductor and motorman may pump volumes of discord from the hidden sources underneath, and the hum and noise may be at the highest pitch, but the countryman walking leisurely between the rails just ahead is oblivious. Only when the bump of the catcher impacts against his pantaloons, and the war-whoop of the driver breaks in on his meditations does he give the leap of his life, and wake up to the fact that a new era is upon him.[19] Just this morning did the writer behold a close shave that brought chills over him.[20]

Still the question of all questions that concerns the street-car is the getting on and off. By what possible law does *terra firma* suddenly play crack-the-whip with you[21] and send you and your goods and chattels to the four winds?

It was a mild day with a layer of soft mud over the landscape, including road and by-way. The car, however, rode clear of it and swung along at its accustomed pace. A loud-voiced female, young and rather good-looking, wearing a spotless suit of woman's gear, edged with ermine and no end of fluff and finery, got aboard. She was a modern dancing-girl going somewhere, when suddenly she changed her mind, spoke one or two high words with the serving-woman who accompanied her, and strode to the rear of the car in a business-like fashion. The conductor, who was busy, apparently making up his runs, gave her a side glance and a warning: "Look out," said he. She in return felt that her dignified personality was not within the comprehension of this clod-hopper of a conductor, and so suddenly pulled her skirts together and gave a bound into the blue azure. The car, going at the rate of fifteen miles an hour, left her spinning and ricocheting all over the place, till at last with a rebound of astonishing velocity, she flattened out on the miry surface. But she was on to her feet again like the mountain roe, though hopelessly bemired as to appearance. Meanwhile the car had stopped and the conductor shouted, "Mademoiselle, I told you to look out."

---

18 OC: "on and off the creature when in motion."

19 *OC*: "the 20th century is upon him."

20 OC: "Only this morning did the writer behold a close shave that brought hot sweats down his back."

21 *OC*: "with the careless rider."

"What do you mean by 'Look out' you son of an unwashed idiot?!"[22] Her words faded into the distance, for the two bells rang and away went the car, the conductor mumbling to himself words of offended indignation. That suit of spotless ermine was the cost of her special lesson in street-car riding. She doubtless rides to-day but no longer leaps off the platform in any such way.[23]

It is an everyday occurrence this jump from the whirling car.[24] The conductor boys are always kind and take all manner of care, "Grandpa, keep in your head or you'll crack that post and have to pay damages." "Wait now, mother, wait till it stops." "Don't be anxious. Sit still, I'll get you off."

Koreans when once trained are a very alert people,[25] and quick of foot. Those who learn to get on and off, like post-office men and telegraph boys, are experts who never fail. The law that governs getting on and off the street car is being learned. It appropriates large spaces in the understanding[26] that were formerly given up to Confucian dignity and the law of the *yang* and the *yin*.

More lines are to be laid and soon Seoul will be able to hurry you off to all points of the compass by a rapid, well-cushioned, well-lighted, commodious car.

---

22 Here "idiot" has been crossed out, replaced in the margin by something unreadable.
23 *OC:* "no longer leaps off when the stage is in motion."
24 *OC:* "It used to be an everyday occurrence."
25 *OC:* "agile people."
26 *OC:* "It occupies space in the same understanding."

A Sample of Korean Labour Song

Along with "Korean Songs and Verses," "A Sample of Korean Labour Song" is one of the few oral-vernacular selections in *Pen Pictures* and *Old Corea*, Gale preferring to engage with Literary Sinitic, what he considered the quintessential literary medium in Korea. Gale rarely provided detailed citations, and the oral nature of this particular selection makes the discovery of its origins virtually impossible. In the closing lines of this chapter Gale mentions that this was a rendition of a work song that he had heard "in the year 1889 when I first lived in a distant part of [this] country." Following his arrival in December 1888 in the midst of a cholera epidemic, in the spring of 1889 Gale lived in Haeju, the capital of Hwanghae Province, before moving to Sorae, a town on the Yellow Sea coast in the township of Changyŏn. It was then, in his lonesome early days as a missionary pioneer in far-flung locales of this newly opening country, that Gale would have encountered this song, and to recall this plaintive tune undoubtedly summoned a feeling of bittersweet nostalgia. The song itself bears some of the common hallmarks of work songs in many societies: the lampooning of local authority figures, and rhythmic repetition, which Gale has rendered "Yo-ho, yo-ho, o-yo, hurrah, there!"

A Sample of Korean Labour Song
Pen Pictures, 16–17

The Korean's soul is strung to a minor key. He is not a child to be called "laughter" as was Isaac.[1] Healthful hilarity has played but a poor part

---

1 The name Isaac is spelled יצחק or ישחק in Hebrew and comes from the verbs צחק (*sahaq*) and שחק (*sahaq*), meaning to laugh. The name alludes to the mother

in Chosen during the last twenty years. Yet the Korean keenly appreciated a good joke, but a really good one is almost as rare with him as it is in the funny pages of the *Ladies' Home Journal*. His ideal world lies far back in the impossible vistas of the past, and the widest rim of his horizon shows no evidence of any paradise peeking over. He is cast in a saddish mould as regards the present world, and a still sadder one as regards the "Yellow Springs" or "Underworld" to come.[2] He has music and songs – all races sing in some key or other – and out of his songs shimmer forth reflections of his inner soul.

Here is a sample that tells a story from one of his commonest pages. It is a labour-song, where the leading chorister, knee-deep in the mud, pipes out his statement, and then all his fellow-labourers come swinging in on the chorus, planting their seedlings meanwhile:

> Like a little round mat, a field of three rice measures,
> Off in the hills, 'tis quite a field of paddy,
> (chorus) Yo-ho, yo-ho, o-yo, aha aha there!
> Straight out we line, like the figure "one," (一)
> Round we swing, four-square like "mouth," (口)
> Yo-ho, yo-ho, o-yo, hurrah, there!
> With the fiery sun straight on the back,
> And the feet deep in muddy mire
> Thus do we farm, and when it's done,
> Who will eat of it I wonder?
> Yo-ho, o-ho, o-yo, hurrah, there!
> Let's feed the old folks, eh!
> And let the young wife have her fill,
> And see too the kiddies fed,
> And when we're old, we'll get our helping.
> Yo-ho, yo-ho, o-yo, hurrah, there!
> God made man, and Mother Earth supplies his need,
> Caring for us just like parents,
> We learned from Sillong[3] to grow paddy, and to sow the fields,
> Sin taught us fire and how to cook,
> And thus we flourished, became [zzz] a people.
> Yo-ho, yo-ho, o-yo, hurrah, there!

Sarah's reaction upon hearing that she, a woman of eighty-nine, would give birth to a son with her husband Abraham, a man of ninety-nine.

2 黄泉.

3 Sillong (神農 Ch. Shennong), meaning "Divine Farmer," is a figure in ancient Chinese mythology said to have lived some 4,500 years ago and is credited with teaching methods of agriculture and the cultivation and use of medicinal herbs.

In the basin of the rice-field,
With water a hand-span deep,
Pulling the comb-toothed harrow,
We break the clods, big [zzz] as wooden pillows.
Comb them out fine as lintel flour.
Yo-ho, yo-ho, o-yo, aha there!
Toward each clod goes out the hand,
And an effort made for every bunch of seedling,
We wonder to whom will fall the [zzz] of grain,
And to whom [zzz] shall pass the spoon?
Yo-ho, yo-ho, o-yo, hurrah, there!
Fill in, fill in, plant every inch of space,
The soil is poor and the owner short of cash;
Supplies for spring are gone, and hungry [zzz] he toils,
No grass from Takwan height, [zzz] of fertilizer.
Yo-ho, yo-ho, o-yo, hurrah, there!
Squire Pak of our village has fine fields this year,
Fields of one bag measure, and fields of four days ploughing,
A hundred loads of rich manure! – and that [zzz] too little,
So he piled it o'er with droppings from the oxen
Yo-ho, yo-ho, o-yo, hurrah, there!
But there's trouble in the wind, trouble for Squire Pak
Thick and warm his thatch, and high piled his store of savings
Still, before and behind rumors are rife, and spies are on his track.
If he's taken 'twill be no question [zzz] of wrong,
Shaken dry of every cash he'll be.
Yo-ho, yo-ho, o-yo, hurrah, there!
Citizen Ch'oe of our town, you know him? A bit close you know,
But a man [zzz] fault
Is the sin of a thousand bags and more
He was arrested by the prefect, and now wears the cangue,
He lives inside the prison and has not seen the daylight
For a half year and more.
Yo-ho, yo-ho, o-yo, hurrah, there!
The only son of three generations, lost his parents when a child,
Is now condemned for lack of filial piety.
I don't wonder he's a bit resentful in his soul.
His Excellency, the prefect, wears the honoured name of Chŏng,
Has long ears for the sound of money,
But no ears at all for righteous indignation.

Yo-ho, yo-ho, o-yo, hurrah, there!
Look here fellows, listen to me,
After all your toil at farming,
When you have enough to eat and wear and something over,
Don't think of laying by, never!
Drink your fill, and play your game,
And have a good time while you may.
This world is full of robbers,
If you're rich you'll suffer torture!
Yo-ho, yo-ho, o-yo, hurrah, there!

The flavour of this song is a faithful, though perhaps too outspoken an expression of the mind of my host in the year 1889 when I first lived in a distant part of his country, and listened to criticisms of the long-eared prefect who held office just over the way. In the host's mind, the magistrate, and all magistrates, were sons of Ishmael, worthy of being rendered immortal by just such a heartsome ode as this.

Marriage in Korea

Gale returned often to the topic of marriage in *Pen Pictures* and *Old Corea*, and he seemed particularly intrigued by the centrality of primogeniture. He claims that the true reason for marriage was not for love or "for selfish pleasure," but to obtain a son and nothing more. While many Korean husbands and wives undoubtedly came to love each other after marriage, Gale is accurate in describing traditional Korean marriages as based not on love but on arrangements by families through consultation of the *saju* (四柱), or "four pillars," determined by the year, month, day, and hour of birth.[1] Gale mentions toward the end of this chapter the Chosŏn government's recent stipulation that "boys be eighteen and girls sixteen before they marry," referring to the Kabo Reform legislation. However, by most accounts this law was not strictly enforced, at least not immediately, and children much younger than this continued to be arranged for marriage.[2] Even after child marriage had gradually disappeared, arranged marriages remained the norm for many decades.

In the final lines Gale makes a number of predictions as to the future of marriage in Korea, and much like his other predictions, these have all more or less come to pass, though he might have been surprised by how

---

1 Gale wrote about this topic in detail in Gale, "Selection and Divorce," *Transactions of the Royal Asiatic Society – Korea Branch* 4 (1913): 17–22.

2 Theodore Jun Yoo cites one study claiming that of 128,258 women who married in 1932, a total of 85,878, or 67 per cent, were under nineteen years of age, and 12,575, or 9.9 per cent, were under seventeen years of age. *Sin yŏsŏng* 9 (1933), unpaginated; quoted in Yoo, "The 'New Woman' and the Politics of Love, Marriage and Divorce," 306.

long certain customs persisted. Love marriages, or at least non-arranged marriages, have become the norm in present-day Korea, but this is a relatively recent development, perhaps from the 1980s. Many families still consult the prospective couple's "four pillars," though a non-propitious outcome rarely counts as grounds for cancelling pending nuptials. Perhaps the most persistent custom that Gale notes is the preference for sons. Only recently, since the late 1990s, has the centuries-long priority given to having a son finally started to break down.

Marriage in Korea
Pen Pictures, 18–19

If there is any matter in which the Korean's mental capacity comes to a perfect state of white heat, it is in regard to marriage. He is a born match-maker, a born marrier. He will have who married to whom, finished and done, before the sun goes down.

What money is to a son of the West, so marriage is to this child of East Asia; every man is after it. I have tried long and hard to see the full bearing of the question upon the race, but I feel that I am as yet a mere beginner in its mystery. The Korean's ideas are not ours. He never, never associates marriage with such a line as "Kiss me softly and speak to me low." Theoretically he says, "Let me be married in the spring, when the plum-blossoms show, and when the peach-flowers and apricots tint the hillside," and yet he never thinks of his bride as his peach or plum-blossom. Spring is the mating season, and he would mate. He wants to be married, not for selfish pleasure, nor because [zzz] hungry heart and soul. He wants a son, a son of his very own to be born; he wants a son, wildly – anything for a son. Wife, and love, and colourful idiom, and domestic joy, are unseen in his scramble for it, this gift of the gods, a son.

Recently rumours swept over the land to say that in a little while no marriages would be permitted between Koreans, that every marriageable Korean would have to be mated to a Japanese, and such a scurry in all the go-between circles was never seen. The bride's marriage boxes[3]

---

3 This refers to *ham* (函), wooden boxes that traditionally were sent by the family of the prospective groom to the home of the bride, bearing a marriage letter (*honsŏji*) containing the names of the groom and his parents, information about the family, and a gift, usually of silk.

ran up in price and at last were scarcely purchasable for any money. Everybody was seemingly out on the hot hunt to get one. Now, however, they know it was a "scare-head" rumor only, and trade has fallen off in the marriage interest.

In the choice of a bride, still as in China the old elements are consulted: metal, wood, water, fire and earth (kŭm-mok-su-hwa-t'o).[4] Everybody has his fixed element, according to the day, month, hour and year in which he was born. A girl marked "metal" is crossed off when a "wood" boy is in question. A "fire" girl and a "water" boy mated would mean fuss and steam and sizzle, while a "wood" girl and a "water" boy would fall within the sphere of good luck. Also an "earth" girl and a "metal" man might walk hand in hand and be partakers of harmony and never-ending posterity. A foreigner would go crazy under the weight and drag of it, but the Korean has kept faithfully to it for 3000 years.

When the lots were cast and the elements juggled sufficiently with, and the girl chosen and the day settled, with its heaps of sewing and stitching done and finished, the wedding takes place. The bride rides in a tiger-skin-bedecked chair, and the bridegroom on the back of a prancing palfrey.[5] They meet, not easily, but in the stiff manner of the East, drink, bow, and are married. She swims in all the colours of the summer sunset, but never smiles. Her face is daubed and pipe-clayed, and her eyes are fastened shut. The groom wears the garb of a courtier of the king, but looks scared and unmagnificent. They are married and live happily ever after. This is the only real marriage. Second, and third, and fourth marriages are mere makeshifts, and but a shadow of the real thing.

As for second marriages, Kim's home was desolate. Typhus had his wife in its grip and the chances were all against her. In the struggle she went under, and Kim leant over his bookcase, and cried an honest broken cry. The funeral was held and words of comfort were spoken for Kim. Two days later a hurried invitation comes, "Kim will marry at once, make haste to the wedding."

Kim was married and lives happily ever after.

For a land that takes a long time to move under ordinary conditions, Korea is quicker than Napoleon Bonaparte when it comes to marrying.

To-day my old friend of seventy-seven lost his wife. Says he, "I got her when she was a girl of seventeen, and we have lived sixty years

---

4 金木水火土.

5 Palfrey is a generic term for a type of riding horse highly valued by nobility during the Middle Ages.

together" and tears brimmed over from his old filmy eyes. Did they love? Why, yes, they seemed to, and yet I am not sure. The whole sex relationship is a great mystery.

The Government has recently enacted that boys be eighteen and girls sixteen before they marry. This is, in the mind of old Korea, red-handed.

I suppose ere long modern boys will wed when they please [zzz] and girls will consent in coy and bashful manner, the old days of juggling with wood, fire and water will depart into the shadows, and the intense desire for a son will give place to modern 20th-century feelings of indifference, or perhaps dislike of the burden of a son who might in his baby days interfere with one's own freedom.

Pak's Experiences

"Pak's Experiences" is a representative example of Gale's ambivalence toward the eclipsing of traditional Korean culture, a sentiment emanating from the conflict between his missionary identity and growing sympathy with his adopted environment. The piece also demonstrates his evangelical strategy of connecting aspects of Korean belief systems – in this case animism – with those of Abrahamic religions, which may be considered an attempt by Gale at reconciling this conflict. Pak, a "good Christian" for six years, nonetheless becomes convinced that he is being terrorized by malicious fire spirits, a decidedly non-Christian notion that Gale domesticates through the appellation "fire-devil." Gale's rational Western persona, upon hearing Pak's tale of woe, remarks coolly that arson is to blame, but the knowledge and detail, sincerity and sympathy infused into Pak's account betray the sentiments of a narrator not completely convinced by his own comforting, Western logic. Judgment of Pak is ultimately withheld; the "enlightened" Westerner, rather than condemning the Korean subject as a recalcitrant heathen relapsing into superstition, highlights the earnestness of his beliefs, hybrid though they be. The "experience" ends not with an "enlightened" Korean renouncing superstition in the name of Western logic and religion, but rather a repentant Korean Christian doubly convinced of the existence of malicious demons. For Gale, then, the method by which Koreans achieved salvation was secondary to the ultimate salvific quest, which speaks to his wider strategy of universalizing the discourses of Abrahamic faiths.

At one point in the account a *kut* (굿) is performed, which is a ritual conducted by a Korean shaman requesting the involvement of spirits in human affairs, usually for purposes of welfare and good fortune, or to dispel troublesome spirits. The *kut* involves elaborate spirit-induced dancing and singing/chanting, and unfolds in ceremonial phases called *kori*. A *kut* represents the intersection of three elements: spirits of gods, believers, and the shaman (*mu* 巫). An interesting parallel to this episode of competing religious rituals (Christianity and animism) related by Pak can be found in Kim Tongni, "Munyŏdo" (The Shaman Painting).

Pak's Experiences
Pen Pictures, 20–1; *Old Corea*, 80–1; Spectator, *Korea Magazine* (1917): 362–4

Pak is an old friend, headman of his town, a big town, too, with no end of timber interest and wood craft on the river.[1] Pak is rotund, and bald, and shiny. His beard is rather stringy and shot through with gray; his eyes filmy and blurred somewhat by the dust and cobwebs of fifty-five years. But they smile still and the round face beams with hospitality. Small beads of perspiration usually stand out along Pak's brow, and fringe the back wrinkles of his neck. These are not from heat or over exertion,[2] but simply from the tight rotundity and high pressure of his body.

I was invited[3] to dine with him in his home, so we dropped off our shoes and bowed our way into the inner room of his thatched dwelling. I sat cross-legged on the host's mat, friend Yi sat under the paper window,[4] while Pak himself was near the door. We three occupied nearly all of the space, for the room was only six feet by eight. There were several pieces of furniture in it, cases of books and other things piled up, that showed [zzz] the host a man of affairs. A Korean room lends itself easily to a close and intimate conversation. For him who can smoke, the room fills rapidly at a few well-distended puffs,[5] and the spirit of the raconteur develops. Pak does not smoke, and this is not a story but an experience.

---

1 The *OC* version reads "a big town too, that sends much timber down its river."

2 *OC*: "This is not because of the heat of overexertion."

3 *OC*: "I was invited with a friend."

4 *OC*: "I sat on the best mat; my friend Yi sat cross-legged under the paper window."

5 *OC*: "For the smoker, the room can be filled rapidly by a few well-directed puffs."

"We have not seen the like of this for years," said he. "The thing has got on to my nerves till I can feel it up and down my back.[6] It began in this way: There was an old pear tree that stood just behind the home, between the line fence of me and my neighbour, which the town had worshipped for a hundred years. I concluded, being headman and a Christian, to do away with the nuisance, and so cut down the tree. It was in no sense in accord with twentieth-century rules.[7] You may be sure there was a row.[8] The people of the town came out like bees, old and young, big and little, and made a formidable demonstration. But I explained that it was my pear-tree and that I had a perfect right to cut it down – all the devils in the world [zzz] to the contrary notwithstanding.[9] I felt at the time a crawling sensation up my back, and browsings round [zzz] my ears.[10]

Did the honoured stranger ever hear of fire-devils?[11] In Chosŏn, in old days we had no end of them,[12] goblins that placed fire on the outer rim of the thatch or along the paling, or in the middle of a tree, devil-fires enough. But of recent years they seem to have almost ceased. I had not seen a devil-fire, now, for a long time. Well, on the 10th day of last Moon, directly after I cut down the pear-tree, I was awakened at the first cockcrow by the cry of fire. Out we tumbled to find the whole place lighted up, the neighbour's back fence and outhouse going off in flames. I saw at once that it was a devil-fire, and after putting it out came back to sit down and meditate. Never before had I felt such strange sensations crawling up and down me, or whisking about under one ear and then under the other.[13] Here was a problem,[14] sure enough.

---

6 OC: "It has made the nerves of my back tingle."

7 In the OC version, this sentence has been deleted.

8 OC: "This caused a row."

9 OC: "cut it down, devils or no."

10 OC: "I confess I felt at the time a crawling sensation up and down my back and round my ears."

11 Gale's usage of the term "devil" may be seen as another attempt to universalize Abrahamic religious discourse in discussions of Korean animism, when less religiously charged terms such as "goblin" or "spirit" would have sufficed.

12 OC: "In Old Corea we had no end of them."

13 In the OC version Gale adds "heŭsal heŭsal like," which is the Korean mimetic expression ŭssŭl (-kŏrida) meaning to experience a shiver of fear, or more physically to feel one's skin crawl. Gale's variant spelling is likely due to his transcribing a non-standard dialect.

14 OC: "Here was a predicament."

Not only had I roused a whole village but here were a raft of fire fiends on my track.

Next day the village met in solemn conclave. Fire-devils were abroad and Pak the 'Papist' had done it[15] by cutting down the pear-tree. They then called together a religious séance, or sorcerers' *kut* of [zzz], witchmen, fortune-tellers, with drums, gongs, and squealing pipes. They made the whole place a pandemonium in their efforts to get at these evil spirits. I called in our religious people. We sang psalms and prayed in order to neutralize the confusion. They demanded that we stop, cease praying, and asked also a money contribution to help them;[16] but I said 'No, no! That's your way and this is ours; yours is yours, and ours is ours, I give you no money.' When they had done all the *kut*, they planted a new pear-tree, and bowed, and blessed, and prayed, and sacrificed,[17] and had a feast and then went home.

It was a time of anxiety such as I had never known before. I've been a Christian, you know, for these six years, but I never heard much of the Gospels except at meetings. Now, however, I felt constrained to read, and I did so, while up and down my back[18] went these devils," and Pak's brow was beaded with perspiration which bespoke the sincerity of his words. "Six times I went through those Gospels, and all my bad deeds and unfair words came back to me, all the lies I had told. My heart melted at the thought of the many wrongs I had done.[19] I made resolves to be a better man. Next night again fires blazed up, and it was my corner paling this time."

Western-like, I said, "Somebody set fire to your fence, Friend Pak."

"Ah, ha," said he "the Stranger has drunk much Eastern water, and yet he knows not the East. You Westerners may play with dynamite, but no Easterner ever 'fools' with this kind of thing, no, no. Besides, all our gates are closed, there is no entrance for a stranger, and certainly the neighbour across the way would not endanger his own thatch, by fooling with fire at second watch in the morning.[20] The Stranger never felt

---

15   *OC:* "had brought them."

16   *OC:* "The others demanded us to stop praying. They levied a money contribution on us."

17   *OC:* "blessed, prayed, had a sacrifice for it, and went home."

18   *OC:* "while *ŭssŭl ŭssŭl* up and down my back."

19   *OC:* "at the many sins I had committed."

20   In traditional Korea, time during the nightwas marked by a clepsydra, or water clock, the most well-known model of which was the self-striking water clock

them go up and down his back, did he? The Good Book, too, is in line with my experience. We have had nine devil-fires within the last month."

"Yes," said Yi, "I saw one with my own eyes, at four a.m. on the 8th."[21]

I went with Yi to examine the back paling. There was [zzz] about half gone and blackened. The neighbor's outhouse was roofless.

(Two months later, the fire-demons at last got their grip on the village, and in fiendish delight swept away Pak's home and the neighbors', thirty-two houses in all. We walked over the blackened ruins that marked the desolation. Pak, financially, is a ruined man, but he walks humbly, and remarks that for him and his house they still intend to serve the Lord).[22]

(1912)

(*chagyŏngnu* 自擊漏) designed by the Chosŏn Chief Court Engineer Chang Yŏngsil in 1434, during the reign of King Sejong. Consisting of large bronze vessels, smaller vessels, and long water tanks, the flow of water between these vessels precisely measured night hours according to a system of five *kyŏng* (更), which were in turn divided into twenty-one *chŏm* (點); the system was collectively called the *kyŏngjŏmpŏp* (更點法). Gale's references to watch numbers (first watch, second watch) throughout his writings suggest this traditional method of telling time; in this case, the second *kyŏng* is sometime shortly after midnight. The *OC* version records "second cock-crow of the morning," which suggests an impulse by Gale to domesticate an unfamiliar time-telling tradition for the foreign reader.

21 *OC*: "I saw one at four o'clock in the morning on the 8th." Pak uses the traditional time ("second watch"), whereas another Korean acquaintance, Yi, employs standard Western timekeeping, suggesting the overlapping usage of both systems for a time.

22 In place of this final paragraph, the *OC* version includes the following: "The village now concludes that its special pear tree is valueless and that the only way for it to find escape from terror is to become a Christian like Pak the Papist."

The Mystery of It

"The Mystery of It" employs Gale's common trope of cross-cultural comparison between the East and the West, this time expressing incredulity as to the economic solvency of the traditional Korean household. Although containing, like much of his writing, a measure of essentialization, differences undoubtedly existed between the cultures in financial matters, differences that were indeed exacerbated by the deepening of modernity. Certainly more assistive economic exchanges were occurring under the table than Gale seems to recognize – though he implies as much when claiming that "everybody is in debt to everybody" – and a family of seven would not necessarily have to survive only on the pittance earned from fashioning straw sandals but instead may have availed itself of community and familial support. One aspect of Gale's anthropological account of suicide in Korea that would have to be amended today is his truism that the Korean "never suicides because he is out of work, or in debt, or afraid that starvation awaits him, or from any feeling of disgrace at being a business failure." Studies have shown a strong correlation between the effects of the 1997 Asian financial crisis and the suicide rate in South Korea, a rate currently tenth in the world and the highest among OECD member nations.[1] Another change in suicide patterns resulting from the "fierce collision with the new regime" has been the skyrocketing instances of suicide among the elderly, possibly attributable to the breakdown of the extended family,

---

1 Kwon, Cho, and Cho, "A Closer Look at the Increase in Suicide Rates"; Singh, "The 'Scourge of South Korea.'"

the increasing isolation of the elderly population, and the inadequacy of the social safety net.[2]

Gale's point on the "glorious," redemptive potential of at least certain suicide acts is nonetheless well taken; the country has a long tradition of high-profile suicides of political protest, acts that were and are still viewed as legitimate and heroic forms of patriotism by many. Many Chosŏn government ministers, for example, committed suicide in protest against the signing of the Protectorate Treaty (1905) and Treaty of Annexation (1910), a tradition that continues in Korea's dissident culture, recently in January of 2017 when the Buddhist monk Chŏngwŏn died of self-immolation in protest against the Park administration's agreement with Japan on the issue of wartime sexual slavery.

The Mystery of It
Pen Pictures, 22

How lightly care sits on the soul of the Korean, is known to every one of his old-time acquaintances. In no part of the world is the text, "Your Heavenly Father feedeth them," accepted by believer and non-believer alike as a self-evident truth, as unquestioned as any mathematical axiom. He knows nothing of deep grinding care that goes down into the quick, with saline mixtures added. He is free altogether from these. Suicide exists, but never as due to financial embarrassment, or anxiety about to-morrow's supply. If he has a quarrel and loses "face," he may suicide on his enemy's doorstep to pay off old scores, which is the shortest and surest way of squandering accounts, though but what law of profit and loss it works out I do not know. Again if it is required that he make a special display of heroic virtue, he may do it through suicide. Suicide in itself is not a blood-besmeared cowardly act that leaves friends and relatives in disgrace; not at all. It more often is an act of a brave heart, that finds no other form of expression, but he never suicides because he is out of work, or in debt, or afraid that starvation awaits him, or from any feeling of disgrace at being a business failure.

Everybody is in debt to everybody. Clearing days come once a year or so, when there is the tug of all the seasons in settling up, and then

2 Kwon, Cho, and Cho, "A Closer Look at Suicide Rates."

again matters lapse back into the place where they were, and where food and clothing come of themselves and all are happy.

Some years ago a symposium was undertaken by which it was to be shown how Korea lived; what was back of the mystery of payment and receipt, profit and loss, prosperity and debt, but it died in the proposition, and to this day, after fifteen years of added time, the proposers are as much in the dark as ever as to how the ordinary Korean lives.

Over the way is a man with a family of seven: himself, wife, four children and mother-in-law. The children are very small. "How goes the world with you?" we ask.

"Very bad, indeed," he answers, "I hardly know where to-morrow's dinner is to come from."

"What do you work at?" we inquire.

"Straw sandals," says he.

"How many pairs do you make a day?"

"Three pairs, about."

"How much do you sell them at?"

"Five *sen*."[3]

Here is a clear fifteen *sen* a day for seven people to feed and dress on, and yet they live. If a foreigner undertook to keep that home he would have to pay fifteen yen a month at least, or they would starve on his hands. How they live no man knows and yet they are never anxious. Some law of survival that defies the scrutiny of the West to get at, exists till to-day, no care for the morrow. This law will surely come into fierce collision with the new regime, be shattered, and leave its crew shipwrecked.

The Korean is anxious politically, not financially, anxious as to how his country goes, not anxious as to the relation of his own efforts to national prosperity. Groups of idle people sit about discussing the why and wherefore of the present times, not realizing that to be up and doing is the only solution.

Doubtless in the changes that come, hard law conditions of cause and effect will follow, where we shall lose the mystery and charm that has governed Korean life for the last quarter of a century, in which no one seemed obliged to work, and all were well fed and clothed and had not a care in the world.

---

3 The *sen* is the smallest unit of Japanese currency, with 100 *sen* equalling one yen.

The Family Line

Gale wrote extensively on the topic of family lineage, and in particular what this revealed about Korea's general preoccupation with the past and neglect of the present. Surfacing time and again in his writings, Korea's supposed antiquarian orientation represented the primary contrast between Korea and the West and one of the potential stumbling blocks to modernization. Simultaneously, his own predilections for the antiquarian and his fascination with Korean history meant that he resisted a wholesale dismissal of this "obsolete" philosophy, evoking sentiments fraught with ambiguity and tension. Even in this chapter, a comparatively more critical assessment of Korea's attachment to a hackneyed past, an element of pathos as to the eclipsing of this tradition is betrayed.

Gale writes specifically of the Yŏnan Yi clan (Yŏnan Yi ssi 延安 李氏), one of the most illustrious and well-established of Korean clans tracing its origins to General So Chŏngbang (蘇定方 Ch. Su Dingfang) of Tang China, who aided Silla in the defeat of Paekche and the establishment of a unified peninsula in AD 660. The general's descendants established their ancestral seat (*pon'gwan*) – which combined with the family name determines the various clans in Korea – at Yŏnan in Hwanghae Province in present-day North Korea, and today include over 160,000 members. Although the importance of lineage has waned in contemporary South Korea, knowledge of one's clan is still virtually universal among Koreans, and in fact required information on most official government documents. The traditional prohibition on marriage between individuals with the same agnatic lineage was codified in 1957 with Article 809 of the Korean Civil Code and remained in force until it was finally deemed unconstitutional in March 2005. At the time of Gale's writing, however, regardless of the potential distance of relation, marriage between members of the same clan and ancestral seat was considered an unspeakable taboo, and Gale was probably not exaggerating the extent of ostracization endured by the couple. Just who the hapless foreign matchmaker was, however, remains a mystery.

The Family Line
Pen Pictures, 23

Koreans think the world and all of their ancestral seat, family line, genealogical table, etc. Pride of birth rides majestically over poverty and ignorance of every sort, as well as over every other man's success. Their greatness may be moth eaten and old beyond the days of Genghis Khan, may be but the threadbare remains of no end of reverse and grinding poverty, but the family seat is talked of and introduced into conversation with all the proud haughtiness of the first lord of the land.

The writer met a little five-year-old boy the other day. He had on a very soiled jacket and a wide and dusty pair of padded pantaloons. He was standing quite alone and seemed lost. I asked "Who are you?"

"I am a Yŏnan Yi" said the boy. Now the Yŏnan Yi's date their origin from General So of the Tangs, China,[1] who in 641 AD conquered Paekche, one of the early kingdoms of Korea.[2] Since then, these Yi's have been the most exclusive aristocrats, and have gone proudly by in a palanquin while the rest of the world walked. This little chubby-faced boy looked up at me and said, "I'm a Yŏnan Yi."

"Have you had breakfast?" I asked.

He nodded his head but uttered no word.

"Are you lost?" I inquired, but he wagged his little head to say no.

"Then who is your father?"

"He is a Yŏnan Yi," and that was all his little vocabulary would grant me. He had drawn with his first breath and consciousness of life, the fact that he was one of the earls of Yŏnan, and that his trousers might

---

1 General So Chŏngbang (蘇定方 Ch. Su Dingfang).

2 Paekche (百濟, 18 BC–AD 660) was one of three major kingdoms on the Korean peninsula during the so-called Three Kingdoms period, which lasted until Silla's unification of the peninsula in AD 668. Paekche occupied the southwestern portion of the peninsula, Silla the southeast, and Koguryŏ the northern portion extending far into the Asian continent into the region later known as Manchuria. The demise of Paekche is traditionally dated to 660, not 661 as Gale has written.

be soiled; a dark brush of breakfast might be on each cheek; the world itself might annex and go to destruction but he was a Yŏnan Yi! The pride of family is very great and any questionable cross blood that is brought in makes posterity hang its head for a thousand years.

A leading missionary in Korea once knew a young man who seemed suited to wed a girl of her acquaintance, and so she set about it in true Western fashion to make a match. All was settled till it was found that the bungling Westerner had fixed up two to wed who were of the same family line. They had been first cousins somewhere in the days of Augustus Caesar, and it was contrary to all the laws of heaven and earth for two such to wed. The girl's mother, with a long knife, a wild eye, and a mouth full of words, threatened to cut off the foreigner and all her posterity for planning such a marriage. There was fire and smoke and no end of shriek and fainting fit, but the marriage came off, for the Westerner, too, was set in her way. The family line was ruined and the old woman took herself off to Mexico with a lot of emigrants to escape the shame of it.[3]

---

3 Gale is referring to the emigration of 1,033 Koreans to the Yucatan Peninsula on 4 April 1905, the first Korean nationals to ever travel to Mexico. Their emigration was arranged by the British henequen plantation operator and labour recruiter John G. Mayers and the Colonial Continental Emmigration Association's Vice President Hinata Terumake (白向糧武), as part of an effort to alleviate the labour shortage in the Mexican agricultural sector. Advertisements in Seoul promised ample harvests and tantalizing economic opportunities for immigrants, but in actuality the 702 men, 135 women, and 196 children who arrived in Mexico suffered low wages, beatings and jailings for failing to meet quota, and the hardships of the Mexican Revolution (1910–20). In 1921, some 288 Koreans set off for Cuba, and roughly 800 of their descendants still live there. See Sŏ, "K'uba Hanin inminsa."

Korea's Electric Shocks

Written in December 1901, "Korea's Electric Shocks" began a series of writings on political intrigue and diplomatic machinations, probably inspired by the Gales' move to Seoul from Wŏnsan on the east coast in September 1899. Other than the various "political sketches" contained in *Pen Pictures*, Gale also wrote as a correspondent for the *North China Daily News* from October 1899 to August 1905 on topics ranging from the waning role of the eunuch in the royal court, to the coming Russo-Japanese War and the proper approach to an ascendant Japan.[1] Gale's move to Seoul to serve as pastor of the Yŏnmotkol Church (present-day Yŏndong Church) coincided with a period of intense reform and heightened tension in northeast Asia. Twelve converted members of the Independence Club (Tongnip hyŏphoe) became members of Gale's church during this time, including Yi Sangjae (李商在, 1850–1927), who played a leading role in modernizing Korean education, and Rhee Syngman (李承晩, 1875–1965), the future first president of the Republic of Korea. Gale's contact with such influential progressive leaders imbues his accounts during this time with credibility and urgency.

The Kabo Reforms of 1894–6 had begun an irreversible process of social and political transformation, while the Sino-Japanese War had removed Chinese influence on the peninsula, reordered the international hierarchy in northeast Asia, and triggered a competition between Russia and Japan for supremacy in Korea. As Gale notes, unlike the military machinations of Russia and Japan designed to

---

1 Rutt, *James Scarth Gale and His "History,"* 35.

demonstrate hegemony, the contribution of distant America to Korea's modernization was of a cultural and technological nature, but no less profound. Pioneering American entrepreneurs such as Henry Collbran began to make the first inroads into the Korean national psyche through their introduction of dramatic new technologies before eventually being forced out by Japan. Though initially limited in application, technologies such as the tramcar and electrification served as powerful symbols of a brave new world for those who beheld it.

Korea's Electric Shocks
Pen Pictures, 24–8;
"Electric Shock to Korea," *Outlook*
70 (1902): 377–80

In reading the *Memories of a Hundred Years* by Edward Everett Hale, I was specially drawn, by way of contrast, by a letter written by a Chinese envoy to Korea in 1487, which lies beside it on the table. In the *Memories of a Hundred Years*, a great continent is seen shaking itself from the sleep of ages and coming forth for action, to accomplish in one century the work of a millennium.[2] On the other hand, the envoy's letter pictures a Korea, in habit and custom so identical with that of the present, that you would think it was written but yesterday. Four hundred and fourteen years on this side of the salt Pacific have made no changes whatever, while one hundred on the other side has transformed a world.

In 1487 America was unborn; even the place of her future habitation was unknown; behold her now with hand upon the Orient trying to teach her grandmother, and scaring the life out of her by a variety of magic and spirit craft. It seems as though the whole Western world had combined to impress upon Korea the fact that there are other laws [zzz]

---

2 Edward Everett Hale (1822–1909) was an American literatus and Unitarian minister. The author of over 150 books and pamphlets, he championed progressive causes such as anti-slavery, the education of former slaves, and world peace. He founded the magazines *Old and New* (1870–5) and *Lend a Hand* (1886–97), which advanced a number of these causes.

beside those known to her, and that an eternal fitness of things exists that she never dreamed of.[3]

(Shock First)

In the shocks that have been felt during the last few years Germany has had a part. Perhaps the most stunning blow ever given to the imperial house of Yi[4] was at their hands. In 1899 word passed that the German Emperor's brother, Prince Henry, was coming.[5] Great were the preparations in view of this. Korea put on her best coat and spectacles, and lined up in Chemulp'o to receive him in a way befitting kings. He landed from his launch, jumped ashore, tipped his hat, stepped up to the horse waiting for him, tied the saddle, and, finding the girth slack, lifted the flap, tightened it, mounted, and rode off like any other officer of the German army. The high lord executioners of Korea, who had expected someone in robes like the Pope or the Archbishop of Canterbury, seeing him in ordinary dress were simply stunned. They gathered up their traps: spittoons, fans, umbrellas, and whatnot, and made a frantic effort to follow. The rate at which Prince Henry rode, and the lack of ceremony that attended all his movements, gave the Minister of the Household such a shaking up that to this day he says, "Under heaven and among men I never saw the like of it."

---

3 This is a prime example of Gale's reversal of the classic Orientalist trope. Whereas most missionaries insisted that the West was a far more advanced civilization than its eastern counterpart, Gale continuously reiterated the antiquity of Sinitic culture while faulting the West for being hopelessly "behind." This perspective, however, is counterbalanced by a strong dose of "stagnation theory," an influential discourse on Chosŏn Korea which averred the gradual decline of a once-resplendent Korean culture to a current state of stagnation and decay. Such a theory was most notably used by Japan as justification for intervening in Korea's domestic affairs, and Gale seems to have taken stock in such rhetoric (until the March First Movement of 1919, at any rate). This discourse has remained remarkably hegemonic in twentieth-century scholarship on late Chosŏn Korea.

4 The Yi dynasty, Chosŏn Korea.

5 In early August 1899, Prince Henry of Prussia arrived in Wŏnsan Harbor, and on 8 August the Gales hosted a party in his honour in the garden of their residence. Rutt, *James Scarth Gale and His "History,"* 32.

His Majesty the Emperor met this tall, sun-tanned, blue-eyed Westerner with speechless amazement. This was Prince Henry, brother of the German Emperor, with a calloused hand, and hardened muscle.

"See how tanned and brown he is," whispered the Emperor to the Crown Prince, and they fastened their eyes upon him, amazed to think of one so democratic sitting so high among princes.

During the many days that his ship hung at anchor he was frequently seen, followed by his little dachshund, stick in hand climbing the hills, or coming back mud-bespattered before the astonished gaze of king and coolie.

"They are watching you, sir," was a remark made to him, "and they are trying to reconcile your freedom with the greatness of the German Empire."

"What this country needs," said Prince Henry, "is to be shaken bodily out of itself and started afresh on new lines."

Once, too, he was dining with the Emperor and the Crown Prince, and "I did have a time of it," said Prince Henry "to make that dinner go. Once during the meal on account of some hitch in the supply department, our interpreter withdrew to straighten matters out. When he had gone there was an end to our conversation, what could I do? I looked at the Emperor and smiled, and he smiled at me, and we all smiled; but you cannot keep up a smile forever. What could I possibly do to help out the situation, and bridge over the time while the interpreter was away straightening out matters with the cook? Then a happy thought struck me," continued His Highness. "When I was a boy I had learned to blow rings with smoke, and as I had a cigarette at the time, I said to myself 'I'll blow a ring.' I blew one, a fine one, and upward it sailed. I blew another. The Emperor looked with animated wonder and gave the Prince a nudge to emphasize his interest. With my success in blowing smoke bubbles I saved the day."

One of the guests at the table remarked to the [zzz], "Behold how royalty entertain each other," at which Prince Henry laughed heartily.

From the world of kingship no shock could have been more powerful than that given to Korea by Prince Henry of Prussia.

(Shock Second)

France has had her part, too, in this electric method of shaking up the Far East. Her priests were here as early [zzz] in 1835, fifty years before the opening of the ports. They were beheaded, one relay after another, but still others stepped in bravely to fill the place.[6] France, whose creed is agnosticism at home and Roman Catholicism abroad, has forced her way through numberless difficulties, till at the present time she stands represented by the Cathedral,[7] the most prominent building in the city of Seoul, overshadowing all palaces and legations, and putting to shame Confucius, Buddha, the God of War, demons, goblins, and ancestral spirits. Were a less powerful hand than France back of it, the unsophisticated heathen would upset the Cathedral and make its site a rendezvous for music-men and dancing-girls, but France brooks no nonsense of that kind in her dealings with the Far East.

Below the hill on which the Cathedral stands there is a gate-house and an ancient decrepit gate-keeper in charge. He was strong once, for it was his hand that swung the sword under which the heads of the French priests fell in 1866.[8] He is forgiven now and guards the entrance to the sacred enclosure. This, too, is a mystery to the Eastern world. Korea's method would have been to take him and his son and his grandson and hang their heads up in a row in front of the Cathedral.

The great building sits on the back of a terrestrial dragon that lies sprawled out under the city, on the good treatment of which depends the

---

6 Although French Catholic priests from the Société des Missions Étrangères de Paris were the first foreign missionaries to set foot on Korean soil in 1835, Catholicism actually began many years earlier in 1784 with the baptism of Yi Sŭnghun in China, who had accompanied his father on a diplomatic mission to Beijing. Thus, from 1784 to 1835, Catholicism in Korea was an indigenous movement without direct foreign support. Throughout the nineteenth century, major persecutions of Catholics occurred in 1801, 1839, 1846, and 1866, resulting in nearly 10,000 martyrs. One of the greatest threats posed by this religion, according to the Chosŏn government, was the refusal of its believers to adhere to proper traditions of ancestral worship, which represented an affront to the ruling authority of the Chosŏn dynasty.

7 This is the Cathedral Church of the Virgin Mary of the Immaculate Conception, or the Myŏngdong Cathedral, on which construction began on 5 August 1892. It was dedicated on 29 May 1898 and still stands in the Myŏngdong neighbourhood, Chung-gu District, Seoul.

8 When the Regent Taewŏn'gun, father of the minor King Kojong, assumed power in 1864, there were twelve Jesuit priests living and preaching surreptitiously to a Catholic population of approximately 23,000. The Taewŏn'gun renewed a campaign against Catholic believers in Korea, including martyring twelve French missionaries. In response, France launched a punitive expedition in October and November 1886, finally securing the release of two surviving French missionaries.

prosperity of the reigning house of Yi. Last summer a missionary built his home on a spur of the hill, which, in the old maps of geomancy, is marked "The Dragon's Head." At once the brute resented it and there was no rain; consequently this year of famine. The weight of the Cathedral is helping to squeeze the life out of the Dragon, and on his putrid carcass we hope one of these days to see a solid, up to date, Christian city.[9]

(Shock Third)

Great Britain is here, of course as everywhere else. She does not go in for show specially, or for appearances that do not count for anything, but she has applied her string of the battery to Korea on more than one occasion. For many years the proceeds of the Customs have been in the hands of a chief commissioner, who is a subject of Great Britain, and who, though a successful financier, has the gift of offending those who would like to have a good time on Customs money. Even His Majesty has to say "Please" when he wants some of it to spend. Only last spring a difference arose between the Emperor and this king of the Customs service. Matters grew hot, and Great Britain stepped in to see that contracts were kept, Russia [zzz].[10] The Emperor said, "This is my country. I shall do as I please, and I have ten thousand soldiers ready to carry out my orders."

Six British men-of-war moved silently into Chemulp'o harbour, carrying several thousand men and some four-point-seven naval guns ready for action. There was a shock and a spasm, but contracts were kept and no one was hurt.

(Shock Fourth)

But what has America done? She has no princes to drop in and upset His Majesty, no cathedrals to show off with, and no desire to run five

---

9 Gale's account here of Christian logic overcoming Eastern superstition is somewhat uncharacteristically triumphalist in tone. Gale often passed judgment on Korea's "groundless" animistic beliefs, but typically through obliquely worded assessments, preferring that the reader draw his or her own conclusions. Even in this blatantly triumphalist sentiment, we nevertheless find a more or less informed, if not sympathetic description, of Seoul's geomantic landscape.

10 The original typescript reads "Russia stood hands off," but this has been crossed out and replaced with illegible scribbling in the margin.

inch guns up to the city; and yet she has startled Korea more than any other country. Near the centre of the city there is a beautiful marble pagoda that was brought from Peking about 1300, by one of the Mongol queens that came as bride to Korea. Her people at that time were shaking the whole known world, and under leaders like Genghis, Kublai and Tamerlane, were upsetting all the thrones of Asia, so that Korea still speaks of them with bated breath, and children know them by name. The marble pagoda still stands, a silent witness before the world of the great Mongol conquerors; but past its stony ear whizzes an American electric car every ten minutes, at ten miles an hour, regardless of all the Mongol shades. Along this main street of Seoul, one of the oldest streets in the world, stretch Western wires charged with a something that defies all the curiosity of the East to pronounce upon. A few days ago a broken strand hung temptingly from one of the poles, and the Far East determined to get hold of it to investigate, with result – one live wire, one dead man. A government notice was posted up: "If anyone is caught fooling with these thunder and lightning strings let him be paddled."

When the day of opening the electric road arrived, the ancient East Gate, built in 1395, creaked from weight and pressure of multitudes crushed into it, eager to see this United States spirit-wagon that would run with no push or no pull. Away it went, throwing off flashes of lightning when night came on, until the poor old woman took out tables of food and offered sacrifice to the god that lived in the wire and the rails.

"Oh, prince of sparks and fire," said she, "bless my old man, and keep away all the spooks and banshees, and don't misuse fire round our house, but warm us and feed us and be good, amen."[11]

But a shock like this could not pass without some eruption manifesting itself on the face of the city. Little by little, the heavens grew dry and the earth rolled up its clouds of dust, day followed day with no signs of rain, and the caking rice-fields grinned and gaped. What could be the cause of it? The geomancers and ground-doctors were consulted on all sides, and their one answer was: "The devil that runs the thunder and lightning wagon has caused the drought." Eyes no longer looked with curiosity, but glared at it, and men swore under their breath and cursed the "vile beast" as it went humming by, till, worked up beyond

---

11 Gale's use of the word "amen" in this animistic prayer to gods and spirits is another subtle attempt to equate indigenous religions in some way to Christianity, although this strategy is much more pronounced in his dealings with Confucianism.

endurance, there was a clash and an explosion, one car was rolled over and another was set on fire, and a mob of thousands of men took possession of the streets, foaming and stampeding like wild beasts. Soldiers and police and yamen runners and road guards were all away at breakfast, so the city had its own time of it, till a group of Americans, some of them measuring six feet six, came along in an extra car to clear off the debris. When the mob rolled up threateningly, an American from the State of Cork looked sideways at it and said "Be aff wid yees now, you and your ancestors, or ye'll git yourselves hurted."[12]

At the magic word the crowds melted away, and the line was once more set in motion, leaving the twentieth century uninterrupted to hum its tune to the gates and towers of ages so long gone by.

But His Majesty, seated on his cushions in the palace, did not see the riot or have a chance to enter into the spirit of the thing. He learned, however, that the lightening had won the day, and that now his best plan was to make friends with it and get it inside of the palace as soon as possible.

"Tell the American," said he, "that the brightest thing he has is what I want for the Audience Hall."[13]

---

12 A similar incident occurred in January 1904, when a rickshaw driver who refused to yield to a streetcar was killed when its icy brakes failed to stop in time. A crowd gathered at the accident site and overturned the streetcar before a platoon of U.S. marines was brought in to disperse the riot. See Southerton, *Colorado's Henry Collbran*. According to Keith Pratt, opposition to the streetcar also came "from accident victims who had been sleeping on the lines, using the rails for pillows … from nationalists who objected to the employment of Japanese drivers; and from disgruntled chair [palanquin]-carriers who saw their livelihood threatened." Despite this opposition, the streetcar continued unabated, becoming the backbone of Seoul's transportation infrastructure. Pratt, *Old Seoul*, 37–8.

13 Electricity was first introduced to Korea in the royal palaces in early 1885, just a few years after the technology itself had been invented. Following the signing of the United States–Korea Treaty of 1882 (Cho-Mi suho t'ongsang choyak), a Korean Diplomatic Special Mission was dispatched to the United States, Korea's first such mission to a Western nation. Among other activities, the mission met with representatives of Thomas Edison while staying in New York, and upon return to Korea mission members urged King Kojong to adopt this technological wonder. The Edison Light Company was commissioned to handle the palace electrical matters, and Korea thus became the first country in the region to enjoy an electrified palace, acquiring this technology several years before Tokyo or Beijing. Electricity for wider consumption, however,

"All right," says the United States, "an arc-light, two thousand candle power: you shall have it."

A day or two of poles and wires and bottle-ends and all was made ready; the glass globe hung harmlessly from the ceiling of the audience chamber; night came on and His Majesty and ministers repaired thither to see. In the mean time a couple of candles were placed in the corners to relieve the gloom at last. The word was given, "Ready," and suddenly the place blazed with an indescribable light perfectly appalling, while the spirit of the thing went fiz-z-z-z-whit-whit, enough to terrify the immortal gods.

"Tell What-you-may-call-him," says His Majesty, "to take it away, and take it away quick." Now, a cluster of incandescent luminaries shine in the place of the arc light that spat and swore and had no manners.

His Majesty has got over the shock and enjoys this artificial sunlight that has come to him from America, in the glow of which no hidden assassin can lurk, or night thief make his way. He remembers the dark night and the awful room in the Summer Palace where Queen Min was murdered, and he thanks his stars for the electric sunshine which these wizards have brought him.

In the toil and labor and sorrow of creating a new palace, doubtless his heart goes back to the Lotus Pavilion and Audience Hall that were his glory in days gone by; but Queen Min was murdered there and it rendered his Windsor unpropitious, so he moved away, and betook himself to the task of buying out all the odds and ends that occupied the quarter of the city where the electric lights now beam upon him.

The gate to the south has over it a signboard marked, "The Way of Love and Harmony." On its right stood a European variety shop built of boards and plaster that constituted one of the odds and ends, necessary for His Majesty to buy to round out his palace. A message came one morning, presenting the Emperor's compliments and asking the European how much he wanted for his boards, plaster, and tin roof.

---

did not arrive until a concession was granted to the Seoul Electric Company, established as a joint partnership between the royal family and the American businessmen Henry Collbran and Harry Bostwick, who were also in charge of constructing Korea's first railway (from Chemulp'o to Seoul) and the electric streetcar. Soon afterward, "electric lighting began sprouting up to illuminate the rail lines, stores, and homes of high-ranking officials," but remained a relatively scarce commodity until more widespread urban illumination was adopted in the late 1920s. Southerton, *Colorado's Henry Collbran*; Lankov, *The Dawn of Modern Korea*, 51–2.

"One thousand dollars," was the reply.

As no Korean ever buys short-off without conference, the messenger returned to say that His Majesty would take it over and pay the money in a week. The week went by and the variety shop was forgotten in the multitudinous cares of state. Long enough after, an indifferent kind of individual brought the thousand dollars round, with coolies on hand to pull down the variety shop.

"Hold up," says the European, "the price is five thousand to-day," which caused a financial shock in Korea's Wall Street equal to the blow given by the two-thousand-candle arc-light. No word from the palace for many days, till unexpectedly a messenger appeared to ask, "What is the price of your concern to-day?"

"Ten thousand dollars," was the reply.

There was a dire tussle, in which Oriental propriety had to take the ring with Western rough-and-tumble. Seven thousand five hundred was paid over, and the Emperor gradually recovered, which perhaps has tinged his view of the whole Western world.

On still nights, or when the wind blows softly from the south, the peculiar note of many metal plates and bars singing in unison is wafted to the city over the wall. Korea has talked for three thousand years about the primal element "metal," and how with its fellow constituents, wood, earth, water, fire, it enters every created thing; but she had to wait till the year 1900 to hear the song of a great steel bridge, tuned to its note in the far-off West.

"What's that noise?" asks the stranger.

"It's the spirit-bridge on the road of the fiery-wheel," is the reply. Already the sound has grown familiar, but the mystery that underlies it is as deep and unfathomable as ever. Two old Koreans stand and look in wonder, "Say, Bill," says one "did you ever see the like of that?"

"Umph!" says Bill, "it's the end of the world, that's why." "I say," says the other, as the train goes by, "Look at that. Any man that would create that kind of thing is doomed."

"Doomed! I should say," says Bill.

"Let's get away. What's good enough for my grandfather is good enough for me."

(Seoul Dec. 1901)

Broken Earthenware

"*Broken Earthenware*" belongs to the conversion narrative category of Gale's writings, other examples including "Happy Yi" and "The Korean Woman." These short accounts of his own parishioners or those of his colleagues typically depict the positive benefits of conversion to Christianity through Gale's characteristic blending of the literary and the religious. "*Broken Earthenware*" features Chŏng, a particularly rowdy drunk who turns his life around, thanks to the intervention of his converted daughter. What stands out about the piece, however, is not its moralistic argument for temperance but rather its vivid, evocative description of the intoxicated antics of the main character. Gale had a knack for bringing to life scenes of everyday life with a Victorian idiom that could be charmingly antiquated, and here this characteristic style shows through. As in other of his writings, despite the rather clear moralistic pronunciation on the dangers of drinking and the redemptive potential of conversion, "*Broken Earthenware*" somehow avoids a tone of sanctimonious condemnation, instead relaying a poignant, accessible, and perhaps relatable narrative. It is unclear whether the picture below, which accompanied the original typescript, depicted Chŏng, typical boozers, or simply members of the commoner class.

Broken Earthenware
Pen Pictures, 29–30; Old Corea, 120–1

Recently the writer[1] read a book by one Harold Begbie[2] called *Broken Earthenware*. It is an interesting and startling account of how the most

---

1 *OC:* "Some time ago the writer."
2 Edward Harold Begbie (1871–1929) was a British author and journalist who wrote nearly fifty books, many infused with a strong Christian moralist

Illustration 4. "Bits of 'Broken Earthenware'" (members of the laboring class),
in *Pen Pictures*

unsavoury odds and ends of what used to be men, can be gathered
together and made to live and be glad; of how dive "punchers" and
"copper bashers" may be constructed over into something as wonderful as a Saul of Tarsus.[3] By what law was it brought about? If the

element. *Broken Earthenware*, published in 1908, was his best-selling work and
dealt with the theme of alcoholism.

3 In the *OC* version, "of how dive 'punchers' and 'copper bashers' may be" has
been deleted. Saul of Tarsus came to be called Paul the Apostle, according to
Acts of the Apostles, following his conversion to Christianity. Formerly dedicated to the persecution of early Christians, while travelling from Jerusalem to

miner's method of extracting gold from tailings and heaps of rubbish be worth study, and if superfine stationery, born of rags and garbage heaps, can delight and surprise us, what shall we say of a science that takes fag-ends from the gutter and makes out of them good men and good women?

In *Broken Earthenware* it is not done by any law of physics, nor by logic or mathematical calculation, but by a very simple and unlikely agent indeed. A little Salvation Army lassie, not gifted at all but humble, gentle, and brave as the spirit of the prophets, by some method of more than mesmeric influence, gets into touch with, and lands her desire out onto solid ground, to be free forever. When decorations are given for life saving from the deep and awful sea, pin on her breast the best the world can show.[4]

This is by way of introduction. At the corner of the street just under the hill lives Chŏng.[5] He is a thatch vendor, which occupation has rendered him two benefits; one, money to buy drink with; and the other, rest and refreshment when he is over heavily laden.

Chŏng was no common drinker with only a red nose and bleared eye to show for it; not he. He was known to the world in general and to Seoul in particular as a man who could terrify invisible spirits by the awful manner of his spree. A hard raucous voice he had, and a pair of fog-horn lungs, a willowy kind of body, too, loosely put together, that would wave to and fro, double up and recover, go all ways at once and yet never lose its footing. But exercises were preliminary to a regular out-with-it-all in the middle of the street.[6] Chŏng took a few days to work up to his best pitch. He accosted every man that went by. If no reply was forthcoming he would swing off after the passer with curses and threatening.[7] Each retreating footstep added to the general weight of aggravation.[8] Something had gone wrong with the entire universe in

---

Damascus one day Saul is knocked from his horse and blinded by the appearance of the resurrected Jesus Christ. Upon regaining his sight three days later he dedicates his life to the preaching of the Word.

4 *OC*: "deep and awful sea, should she not be entitled also to a measure of recognition?"

5 *OC*: "lived Chŏng." Chŏng is referred to in the past tense throughout the remainder of the *OC* version, suggesting that he was deceased by the time of Gale's revisions.

6 In the *OC* version, Gale begins a new paragraph here.

7 *OC*: "curses and intuperatives."

8 *OC*: "general weight of woe."

the mind of Chŏng.[9] He talked to himself, kicked high at the stone wall just opposite, flung odds and ends about, cast dust in the air, swore oath on oath, called on the gods to smite him, "do it if they dare," roared, and burst, and blew. With all the rubber in his soul active,[10] he would jump, and whirl, and kick, till his widely voluminous garments would fairly burst with intensity of action.

In the knowledge of the writer this lasted for ten years and more. Certainly English "punchers" and "copper bashers"[11] may be deeper in black kinds of crime, but for a demon of uproar, none ever surpassed Chŏng. The police, like the Levite, went by on the other side, and the street periodically yielded up its ghost[12] and lay prone, while Chŏng had his innings.

Suddenly a day came when it ceased. Chŏng was gone. Someone looking a bit like him was seen going repeatedly with quiet step and softened manner to a neighbouring meeting-house. He carried a New Testament and was often seen with his face to the floor praying. The date arrived for the returning rampage but it did not materialize. Month followed month and the old demon of confusion was evidently dead. Chŏng is a quiet oldish man now, who frequently says that God has been good to him.[13]

How came the change about?[14] A little daughter of his was sent to the mission school. She learned her lessons, drank deep of the teaching, began to pray and read, and to tell others what she had found of interest. How she approached that wild father of hers, what she said, how her little girl faith grappled with his untamed soul; with what soft influences she wooed him in, I know not.[15]

---

9   "in the mind of Chŏng" has been deleted from the *OC* version.

10 *OC*: "With all the vibrating material in his soul active."

11 *OC*: Here "copper bashers" has again been deleted; perhaps Gale had concluded that the term was obscure or outdated.

12 *OC*: "the service yielding up the ghost."

13 The following has been added to the *OC* version: "Later he departed this life in company with the angels who had come to show the way."

14 *OC*: "How came it all about?"

15 *OC* "with what soft influences she wooed him away from his wild world and landed him safe in a region of calm I know not." The *OC* version adds this final passage: "She was but a plain low class little girl, a young woman now, with poor ancestry and homely face, but like Daniel of old the spirit of the 'eternal gods' was in her, a great and wondrous mystery that deals in 'broken earthenware.'"

Unconscious Korea

Coming a full three years before the outbreak of hostilities in February 1904, Gale's predictions as to the course of events in "Unconscious Korea" are remarkably prescient, though like most observations they vastly overestimate the strength of Russia, and suggest the degree of tension between Japan and Russia that had already been reached. This selection, perhaps more than any other, encapsulates Gale's exasperation and genuine concern about the "unconscious" state of the country as it staggered unwittingly into the modern diplomatic universe. At the helm was the frighteningly incompetent Emperor Kojong. On several occasions in *Pen Pictures*, Gale levelled unflinching criticisms against Kojong, describing the monarch as hopelessly out of touch with the modern world. In this chapter, coupled with Gale's ominous accounts of gathering clouds on the political horizon, the stakes of Kojong's ignorance are heightened from the level of hapless victim to dangerously naive leader. In the words of Gale, he was an "absolute monarch, though all unaware of the actual world he lives in."

Gale references midway through the chapter the so-called Triple Intervention. In its victory over Qing China in the Sino-Japanese War (1894–5), Japan won, among other concessions, the Liaodong Peninsula in southern Manchuria. However, due to the Triple Intervention of Russia supported by France and Germany, Japan was forced to relinquish control of the peninsula to Russia, which then proceeded to lease a naval base from the Chinese at Lushan (Port Arthur) and build other infrastructure to support its newly acquired warm-water port, developments that alarmed Japan. When the Japanese offer to recognize Russian autonomy in Manchuria in exchange for free rein in Korea was rebuffed, Japan staged a surprise attack at Port Arthur, leading to war. The Triple Intervention was viewed by Japan as an affront to its national dignity and emblematic of racist duplicity among Western actors on the international stage. Gale's prediction that this simmering animosity caused by the national humiliation of the Triple Intervention would erupt in war was an incredibly prescient observation, precisely what came to pass three years later.

Unconscious Korea
Pen Pictures, 31–4;
Outlook 68 (June 1901), 694–7[1]

The old-fashioned Korean[2] is the last man in the world to know his own whereabouts. Times and seasons with their accompaniments have no place in the region of his comprehension. It may be to-day, or it may be yesterday, or it may be a thousand years before the Flood, it is all the same to him. His grandfather lived, and his son lives – why should he care?

"What have I to do with[3] the eternal laws of heaven and earth?" is one of his oft-repeated questions.

He never dreams of material cause and effect, linked together, and ruling among men.[4] Every change and chance for him has its rise in some mysterious omen, or sign, or spirit rapping, or offended ancestral god. With him spirit is always greater than matter.[5] It moves and matter responds, and as you cannot hope to oppose spirit, leave matter alone also.[6]

---

1 A condensed version of this article appears under the title "Korean Characteristics" in *Missionary Review of the World*, vol. 12, September 1901, 691–3. An even more thoroughly condensed version appears in *Public Opinion*, vol. 31, 4 July 1901, 11.

2 *Outlook*: "The poor Korean."

3 *Outlook*: "What have I got to do fooling with."

4 *Outlook*: "and ruling among mortals."

5 *Outlook*: "greater far than matter."

6 Here Gale is referencing Confucian cosmology, referring to *ki* (氣) as "spirit" and *li* (理), often termed "principle," as "matter." The primary aspect that distinguished Neo-Confucianism from Confucianism was the belief in the primacy of principle over "spirit," which Gale seems to suggest is inimical to Koreans' true disposition.

Not long ago one of my friends managed by skill and patience to capture a tiger. He had painted a little pig with [zzz] acid[7] and made it fast to a tree. The tiger came by and ate the pig, but he repented forthwith, and proceeded to unburden his soul of all the undigested matter. While thus engaged, friend Kang shot him with his ancient flint-lock gun. Later another tiger was secured, but the wife tigress came to sit as sentry, and the flintlock was too uncertain; so Kang called on me for a rifle. A Martini-Henry I had,[8] a strong gun, sufficient to withstand much shock and jar. I gave it, saying,

"Be careful now; with the gun on one side and the tiger on the other, I am anxious, but I disclaim all responsibility."

"Oh yes, yes, I know all about it," said Kang, "Let tigers beware," and he marched off in triumph.

He shot off a cartridge to let his friends hear the noise, and then another for friends who had not heard the first; then he proceeded to wipe out the barrel with a wad of rag and the steel rod. In less time than I take to tell it he had rag and rod fast half way down. Out it would not nor would it in. He perforated his front garments, and nearly gave himself appendicitis by his efforts to push. Said he,

"The law that governs this affair contradicts everything I have seen in heaven and earth; I'll put a cartridge in and shoot it out."

There was a flash, a burst of artillery, with sparks of fire, and Kang for one instant wakened up to see if he was alive. He brought back the gun and reprimanded me:

"Don't you ever lend that kind of weapon again. Anything that bursts like that and flies all over is most dangerous."

I asked, "Are you alive?"

"Yes," said he, "but it was near death I was."

I replied, "After my warning, too, I have no words; I am speechless; go in peace."

Kang holds me responsible to-day for certain powder marks that disfigure his person. I have done him an injury, and the professor of logic in Oxford[9] itself could not put any other idea into his head. There is no such thing as a relation between cause and effect in Korea. The case of Kang represents the vast majority of the peninsula.[10] Think of it!

---

7 *Outlook*: "strong poison."
8 *Outlook*: "An American Martini I had."
9 *Outlook*: "Harvard."
10 *Outlook*: "the whole peninsula."

With recent wars and rumors of wars, came ten thousand rifles,[11] landed at Chemulp'o. This week they were distributed to the Korean soldiers, the old ones being cast aside. I stopped yesterday before a group gathered at a sentry box:

"These are the new rifles, are they?" I asked.

"Yes-s-s," in rather a monotonous tone.

"Are they not satisfactory?"

"The rifles are all right but the cartridges won't do."

"How is that? Don't they fit?"

"Oh, yes, they fit, but the odor – no powder about it at all, just a nasty fishy smell (`pirin nae naptaeda`);[12] we can never use them."

Of course the smell of the cartridge was more to him than the distance the ball will carry, or the extent of its power to perforate. Smell and spirit are about the same. I venture to say that if these soldiers had their way, they would dump every box of these cartridges into the river and let the fates take the country.

The Korean might well be placarded "The Unconscious Human." Just now round about him are gathering shadows and mutterings, the full import of which he seems to hear not; at any rate which he certainly understands not. He says the graves of his ancestors must be moved to some more propitious place. To this extent only is the national mind awake to the situation.

On the north is Russia bearing down slowly and steadily. She is like the glacier – not a good train to go by when you are in a hurry, but a through train nevertheless if you give her time. She is just far enough civilized to come within the limits of Oriental comprehension. For that reason she is the choice of the East before all other Western nations. Her flag flies over Manchuria, but of course she disclaims all intention[13] to annex the same, and the governments at home, busied over the despatch, forget all about the flag that flies; but the flag will fly, and places once called Maershan and Tŭnghwasŏng will be known hereafter as Muravieff and Kornoloff. All around these coasts go the ships of various nations. There are no light-houses, there is a tide of thirty-six feet off Chemulp'o; untold dangers to navigation abound throughout the Yellow Sea but the ships go on forever, and among

---

11 *Outlook*: "French rifles."

12 To emit a fishy smell: *pirinnae nanda* (비린내 난다).

13 *Outlook*: "thought."

them the Russian, in and out, taking Masanp'o[14] to-day when all eyes are on Manchuria, and withdrawing to-morrow, saying, "I have just given up Masanp'o, what more do you want? I shall also give up Manchuria when the time comes."[15]

How suspicious all are of Russia! Some years ago one bright June morning, three war-ships were sighted off the east coast of Korea. I watched them make the entrance into the outer harbour, all apparently with full steam ahead. Suddenly one stopped and let the others pass. In a set position she hung, steaming madly all day long, with no noticeable change. She did not even turn with the tide; there she stood planted as though not in water but on land. The other vessels wheeled about, lowered their boats, and there was great commotion. We learned at night that the "Vitchius" had a rock four feet through the bottom. The crew was landed on an island nearby, and the Far East said,

"Ah ha! A trick of Russia to secure a footing in Korea."

The Englishman came by and said, "By Jove! These rascals are up to something."

Japanese hove-to to "look-see."

All summer long the Russian fleet struggled with the ill-fated ship, and just when hope of success began to dawn, a wild autumn storm struck her, and the ship "herself went down by the island crags to be lost ever more in the main."

The Russians moved away, and the Far East still sometimes asks,

"What do you suppose they were after?"

Some of us would like to see Tolstoi write a novel on the Designs of Russia before he dies. The skilful way in which Russia manipulated her forces so as to gain Port Arthur and push the railway down from Nerchinsk,[16] before the world was aware what she was about, illustrates

---

14 In March 1900 Russia secured exclusive concessions for a settlement at Masanp'o and declared its intention to build a winter harbour for warships, which threatened Japan's growing influence on the Korean peninsula, specifically encroaching on Japan's passage from the East Sea to the Yellow Sea. Concessions were in the end awarded jointly to Russia and Japan. This was the first of a number of Russian attempts to gain a foothold in Korea, which escalated tensions between Russia and Japan, eventually erupting in the Russo-Japanese War of 1904–5.

15 *Outlook*: "I shall give up Manchuria in the same way."

16 Nerchinsk (尼布楚 Ch. Nibuchu) is a town and administrative center of Nerchinskii District in Zabaikalskii Krai, Russia. Following the Treaty of

her methods. She now has Port Arthur and Manchuria;[17] she has a solid footing at Masanp'o, a place of great influence in the question of Korea; and she is gathering her forces, fleet and army, for another glacial step forward. France in the meantime acts as her aide-de-camp. Russia is apparently after Korea, and unless more than ordinary diplomatic intelligence is displayed, she will outwit the other Powers and get possession, without the Korean soldiers having occasion to smell a single fishy cartridge.

This would undoubtedly prove true if Russia had to deal with European Powers only, which she has so long and so successfully hoodwinked; but here there is another factor to reckon with. An Oriental nation, awake, and armed, and ready, is watching every move. Japan was deceived once, and by it lost Port Arthur. She will never be deceived again. Russia gained by the acquisition of this point an open harbour and key to the Yellow Sea, but she won as well the eternal enmity of Japan, and a day of reckoning is surely coming. The little Japanese soldier, broad as long, game as any terrier, once stormed the heights and took this fortress from the Chinaman; he would enjoy the sport much more keenly to storm and take it from the Russian. No one knows what Japan will do; she is ready; she will fight to a finish, for it will mean to her life or death. It must come unless Russia yields Korea, or comes to some reasonable understanding in the matter of boundary line compensation. Will Russia do so? She may; she will if she is wise.

While the surrounding atmosphere is electric with coming possibilities, His Korean Majesty is busy with his dead ancestors, oblivious of the living. He is building a mausoleum[18] behind the United States Legation, where the pictures and tablets of his deceased ancestors are to repose. These pictures were copied from originals kept in Yŏnghŭng[19]

Nerchinsk in 1689, the first treaty between China and Russia, which established borders between the two countries in the Amur River basin, Nerchinsk became the primary centre of trade between Russia and China.

17 Port Arthur (Lushan) and Manchuria would later be sites of skirmishes in the Russo-Japanese War.

18 *Outlook*: "a beautiful mausoleum."

19 Yŏnghŭng is located in the current North Korean province of South Hamgyŏng. The "mausoleum" that Gale indicates is the Sŏnwŏnjŏn (璿源殿 The Hall of the House of Yi), a shrine on the grounds of Seoul's Kyŏngun Palace built for housing the royal portraits (*ŏjin* 御眞) of King Kojong's ancestors, the House of Yi. Just two months after its construction the shrine burned under mysterious circumstances and all the portraits contained within were

two hundred miles away. A wide and beautiful road was made across the peninsula, along which to escort them. A body-guard of several hundred officials, including the Prime Minister, accompanied them on their way. It was a great reality to His Majesty, this arrival of the pictures, while gunboats crowding into Chemulp'o and dangers threatening, north, south, east, and west are viewed simply as foreign phantasmagoria. As the smell of the smoking powder is more to the soldier than the force or direction of the bullet, so the pictures of his ancestors are more to the Emperor than all the eager crowding faces of the living.

So the weeks pass by, and his unconscious Majesty prattles them away with trifles. It was but a day or two ago that he was invested by the British representative with the most eminent order of the Indian Empire, the accompanying note then signed, "Victoria," and dated less than a month before she died. But what did he know of Victoria or the Indian Empire? The chain of solid gold, weighted down with hangings of elephants, tigers, and flowers, caught his eye for the moment, so that he smiled pleasedly and made a pretty little speech in reply.

Said he: "My joy is great, but yet is mingled with sorrow to think that she who gave it has gone back home."

It was the act of a play-house king, the speech and donning of the order. His eyes would glance aside to ask of his Ministers, "Have I said what I ought to? Have I said it right?"

He is an absolute monarch, though all unaware of the actual world he lives in. His unconscious subjects, too, dare have no thoughts whatever about their country. They are to take quietly what he and fate decree. Pitiful beyond expression is the position of the Korean people. A kinder more loveable race never lived. We who have known them for years, and have never met with insult, who have had access to every home and to many a heart, know how to appreciate and sympathize with them in this their time of helplessness. As for their future – a race of slaves we fear.

To-day the one call heard throughout Japan is "Attention! Forward, march!" and armies are answering, magnificently drilled. Battleships

---

almost completely destroyed. For an account of this event and its aftermath, see "The Burning of the Temple" and "A Royal Funeral," in *Pen Pictures*, this vol. The sole remaining portrait of King T'aejo, the founder of the Chosŏn dynasty, along with Kings Sejong, Yŏngjo, Chŏngjo, Ch'ŏlchong, Kojong, and Sunjong are preserved at the Royal Portrait Museum (Ŏjin Pangmulgwan) in Chŏnju, South Korea.

plow the sea, every jot and tittle up to date,[20] from admiral to quarter-master; each man ready and understanding how to do his duty. A whole Eastern question is pending, in which Korea is the storm centre, and from all decision in which she is hopelessly shut out. From her retreat in some Buddhist monastery or ancestral hill she will watch, one of these days, in a half-conscious way, a passage-at-arms that will rival Gettysburg, or a tournament on sea that will eclipse Trafalgar.

The other day an acquaintance, Mr. Yang, came breathlessly in, just arrived from P'yŏngyang, one hundred and ninety miles north, where his home is. He was in a state of great excitement, and his almond eye looked most appealingly upon me,

"I hear there is to be war between Ilbon and Arasa[21] (Japan and Russia). Is it so? What will we do about it?" said he. "Will they fight on land or on sea?"

"On both, I suppose."

"There now, I thought so. Then it's out of P'yŏngyang I get. The mischief that's in that place beats all. If it's on this red earth that mortal nations are to slaughter each other, of course they'll come miles and miles to do it inside the walls of P'yŏngyang. The luck veins in the miserable hills round about it have got the worst kind of blight on them.[22] My nephew speaks some Russian; do you suppose it would be wise for me to keep him at my house to help smooth matters over in case war comes? What do you think I had better do about it? My house and fields are all in P'yŏngyang, but never mind that; just say the word and I'll let the whole concern go, and get off into Hwanghae or some other corner.

---

20 In Matthew 5:17, Jesus assures his audience that he has not come to abolish the laws of the prophets but rather fulfil them when he states, "For verily I say unto you, till heaven and earth pass, one jot or one tittle shall in no wise pass from the law, till all be fulfilled" (KJV). A jot is the tenth letter of the Hebrew alphabet and the smallest, while a tittle is a pen-stroke letter extension that can differentiate one Hebrew letter from another. Together these emphasize that something has been done to completion, with not even one small amount or iota being overlooked.

21 "Arasa" (俄羅斯) is the transliteration of Russia using sinographs. Although this was common practice throughout East Asia in the nineteenth and twentieth centuries, it sounds decidedly old-fashioned in the contemporary Korean context.

22 *Outlook*: "the worst kind of devil." "Luck veins" refers to currents of energy thought to exist in geomantic theory.

We live in the vilest age. I saw Japanese and Chinamen fight in Kabo (1894) in front of my house, and the way they treated each other was most shameful. I assure you I was in the greatest kind of danger, though I had nothing to do with their wretched quarrel, didn't even know what they were fighting about. I shall not be caught again. Whew! That I ever lived to see such an age! I shall call," concludes Yang, "shortly, and we can talk over what I had better do about it."

Yang is some sixty years of age, an old-fashioned Korean, belonging to the official writer class, a man of influence, of some means, a man whose soul is full of ancient thought and civilization, and who represents a million of his countrymen in his views of the possible war.

(Seoul March 1901)

Korean Literature

In premodern Korea, very little attention was paid to the vernacular script, language, or literature in the vernacular more generally; Literary Sinitic was the *raison d'être* for the literate classes, and the vernacular existed principally as a mediating tool for access to "truth" in the cosmopolitan language. For this reason, one of the most common themes in Western missionary discourses on the Korean language in the late nineteenth century is disbelief at the lowly status of the vernacular. The extreme "otherness" of the language hierarchy encountered in Korea – the vaunting of the cosmopolitan and the disparaging of the vernacular – engendered among missionaries an almost perfunctory discourse on the unassailable position of the cosmopolitan (cast as an undifferentiated "Chinese"), the lamentable status of the vernacular (usually characterized as *ŏnmun*, the word for the vernacular script), and the impediment it represented to modern education and proselytization. Although the sentiments expressed by Gale in "Korean Literature" reinforce this Western discourse on the supposed backwardness of the Korean linguistic landscape, his own literary activities diverged sharply from his missionary colleagues. While most missionaries eagerly anticipated and hoped to abet the disappearance of the Literary Sinitic tradition, Gale's characteristically ambivalent attitude toward literary modernity caused him to chart an alternative path, preserving traditional Korean literature through his translation project while promoting a mixed-script style for expository writing, much like his Korean intellectual counterparts. This essay exposes the polysemy of the concept of "literature" for Gale: he denies the existence of "novels," "regular story-writers," or "publishing houses," but carefully translates an "elegant" work by Hong Yangho (洪良浩, 1724–1802), a piece composed in the legitimate literary idiom. This translation is characteristic of Gale's style: a quaint, Victorian-era idiom and poetic sensibility, clever rhyme scheme, and free translation more concerned with the sense than literal accuracy.

The photograph below is of Chibokchae (集玉齋), built in 1891 by King Kojong as his private study and library and located at the back of Kyŏngbok Palace by the gate that today opens toward the Blue House (Ch'ŏngwadae), the residence of the South Korean president. Chibokchae was closed to the public until the late 1990s but was opened in 2016 as a public library and book cafe. In Gale's day it also functioned as a venue for the king to receive foreign diplomats. Kojong is reported to have to have kept some forty thousand fascicles of rare titles here. According to Yi T'aejin, all the books originally housed here, excepting a few that eventually went to the Changsŏgak (藏書閣) Archives established by Yi Wangjik in 1918, are now housed in the Kyujanggak Royal Library.[1]

Illustration 5. "The Palace of Literature, Seoul" (Chibokchae 集玉齋), in *Pen Pictures*

---

1 Ross King, personal communication, 30 October 2018. See Yi T'aejin, "Chungguk pon tosŏ wa Chipokche tosŏ."

Korean Literature
Pen Pictures 35–7; *Old Corea* 135–3;
Esson Third, *Japan Weekly Mail*, 21 June 1902;
North China Herald, 1902[2]

Korea is a land without novels or newspapers.[3] Let anyone who suffers from nervous prostration, brought on by a vain effort to keep pace with the literature of the day, come here and rest. No regular story-writer is known to have lived in these parts for a thousand years. There are no publishing houses and no laws of copyright. Scholars have written short essays at rare intervals, but literature has never been reduced to the common levels of ordinary life. Books done in the colloquial and sold at ordinary street stalls, would be an abnormal thing in the eyes of the old-fashioned scholar.

Says he, "How could common words such as people use everyday in talk be printed in books?"[4]

2　Although Hong Yangho's prose/poetry work "Setting Free the Wild Goose" (Pang an sa 放鴈辭) appears in *Pen Pictures of Old Korea* and *Old Corea*, the respective essays within which it is placed differ markedly: this version is prefaced with Gale's thoughts on the current state of the literary landscape, while the *OC* version includes various mentions of the goose in Korean literature and the significance of the animal in East Asian culture and iconography. Furthermore, Gale's translations of Hong's piece exhibit considerable divergences, and it is unclear which version was penned first. An essay similarly titled "Corean Literature and History" opens the *OC* typescript, and while the subject matter touches on similar themes, the content is decidedly different, reading more as a history of thought and literature on the Korean peninsula. The typescript for this essay in *Pen Pictures* dates from 1905, but it had appeared already in a 21 June 1902 edition of the *Japan Weekly Mail* (hereafter *JWM*).

3　Although Korea's first modern "novel" in the Western sense had yet to be written, there were a number of vernacular newspapers in circulation at this time, and so Gale's claim that newspapers did not exist is puzzling.

4　This sentence seems to sum up Gale's definition of vernacular literature, that is, the representation of popular speech in written form. In this sense, Korea in 1905 was indeed lacking in "modern literature." In the version of "Korean Literature" published in *JWM*, the following sentence appears here: "In his attitude he reminds me somewhat of a callow secretary who had been loaned Mark Twain's

Literature in Korea is never vulgar. Education consists in a knowledge of the immortal Chinese Classics. Characters are sacred and no printed book can be tossed about, or trod upon without offending the soul. In the world of the literati, children begin with the *Thousand Character Classic* (Ch'ŏnjamun), and gradually see step by step,[5] till they come to the famous history, that explains the nature of the *yang* and the *yin* and other beliefs[6] of ancient China.[7] Then they read the *T'onggam* [通鑑],[8] a history of the Middle Kingdom from the fourth century BC to 959 AD, written by a famous historian, Sama Kwang;[9] then the *Great Learning* [Taehak 大學],[10] *Mencius*, the *Analects*, *Doctrine of the Mean*, the *Books of Poetry* and *History*, and finally the *Yŏkkyŏng*.[11] No work dealing with native subjects appears on the curriculum. It has been a law with Korea that a small state should serve a large one, and so in its education she has excluded everything that is not of pure Chinese origin, lest she should appear to exalt self above her [zzz].

   'More Tramps Abroad.' He brought it back, and the friend inquired as to how he liked it. 'Oh, I enjoyed it, but don't you think he's rawther vulgar?'" This portion, incidentally, was crossed out of the typescript version in *Pen Pictures*.

5 In the *JWM* version, "and gradually see step by step" is rendered simply as "and pass on to a history."

6 In the *JWM* version, "beliefs" are referred to as "fables."

7 This seems to refer to the *Book of Documents* (Sŏgyŏng 書經 Ch. Shujing) also called *Documents of the Elders* (Sangsŏ 尚書 Ch. Shangshu), one of the five Confucian Classics along with the *Classic of Poetry* (Si kyŏng 詩經), the *Book of Rites* (Yegi 禮記), the *Book of Changes* (Yŏkkyŏng/Chuyŏk 易經/周易), and the *Spring and Autumn Annals* (Ch'unch'u 春秋). The *Book of Documents* is a collection of speeches made by rulers and important government ministers from mythical times to the Western Zhou period (11ᵗʰ c. to 770 BC).

8 *Chach'i t'onggam* (資治通鑑 Ch. *Zizhi Tongjian*, Comprehensive Mirror in Aid of Governance) was written in AD 1084.

9 Sima Guang (司馬光, 1019–86) was a historian and scholar of China's Song dynasty.

10 *Taehak* (大學 Ch. Da Xue) was, along with *Doctrine of the Mean* (Chungyong 中庸), the *Analects of Confucius* (Nonŏ 論語), and *Mencius* (Maengja 孟子), one of the "Four Books" in Neo-Confucianism. They were selected by Zhu Xi during China's Song dynasty as the most important works of Neo-Confucian thought and became the core of the official curriculum for the civil service examination in Ming and Ching China. This curriculum was subsequently adopted by the Neo-Confucian-oriented Chosŏn dynasty (1392–1910).

11 The *Book of Changes* (易經).

The form of Chinese writing used by the Koreans is what is called *wenli*,[12] to distinguish it from the *kwanhwa* or Mandarin.[13] Very famous Korean writers have lived, a whole group of them in the fifteenth century, who wrote many books on history, ceremony, etc. Some of these scholars were highly honoured at the court in Nanking, but their books were laid aside and forgotten, or lost, or destroyed,[14] until it is almost impossible to get hold of such native literature, and even scholars know little or nothing of the literary history of their poor peninsula.

Of late books are coming out of unexpected holes and corners and offering themselves for sale. The other day an encyclopaedia, called the *Munhŏn pigo* (National Encyclopedia),[15] written about 1770, was sold to a foreigner for 194 yen. At about the same time I met a man with an armful of books on his way to the Japanese settlement. I inquired as to what they were and found them marked Igye [耳溪], someone's nom de plume, though no one seemed to know the possessor of the name. After search I found it was a Mr. Hong Yangho,[16] who was sent as the

---

12 *Wenli* (文理), literally "principles of writing or literature," was a term coined in the nineteenth century by Christian missionaries in China to refer to Classical Chinese or Literary Sinitic (文言文 *wenyanwen*), although it never gained the currency of the latter term outside of missionary circles.

13 *Kwanhwa* (官話 Ch. *Guanhua*) refers to the northern Chinese spoken vernacular, ancestor of what today would be called *Putonghua*, or Mandarin. In Korea an analogous term *Hanŏ* (漢語) was also used, but this word referred more generally to the spoken language of China as opposed to the written (*hanmun*) and did not denote Mandarin alone. The linguist Neville Whymant (1895–?), writing in 1922, placed *Guanhua* ("Kuan Hua") in the following categorization with other written and spoken forms of Chinese: "1. Wen-li – used by scholars. 2. Kuan Hua Proper – spoken by the general well-educated public and by officials. 3. Kuan Hua Patois – Spoken by the lower class generally; is No. 2 interspersed with localisms and replete with slang and slurred pronunciations. 4. The Classical Written Style – As extant in the days of Confucius, and still the *sine qua non* for University aspirants. 5. The Epistolary Style – Used solely in writing letters, etc." Missionary literature both before and after this piece by Gale (1905) seems to concur with this basic outline of the language and would have influenced Gale's perspective on the language. See Edkins, *A Grammar of the Chinese Colloquial Language*; Whymant, *Colloquial Chinese (Northern)*, 12–13. In the *JWM* version, this sentence reads quite plainly, "The Chinese of Korea is *Wenli*."

14 The *JWM* version adds here "or buried."

15 Hong Ponghan, *Tongguk munhŏn pigo* (東國文獻備考, Encyclopedia of Documents and Institutions of the Eastern Kingdom).

16 Hong Yangho (洪良浩, 1724–1802).

king's representative to the Court at Peking in 1795. He was also governor of the north of Korea, and is mentioned in the *Book of Famous Men*[17] as one of the distinguished literary men of the day.

The book begins with an essay on the wild goose. Its purpose is to tell a story and at the same time to exalt the Five Constituents of Worth, which according to Confucian ethics mark the perfect man. They are: Love, Righteousness, Ceremony, Knowledge, and Faith.[18] It shows also what Korea thought of her neighbors at the time when Napoleon Bonaparte was telling Europe what he thought of his. The composition [zzz zzz] is partly in prose and partly in verse. As there is no possibility of equalling the elegance of the original, I leave the form to take care of itself and try to interpret faithfully the points noted therein.

"Setting Free the Wild Goose" by Hong Yangho

In the late autumn of a recent year[19] a peasant of the Tumen River caught two wild geese, cut their wings, and gave them to me. I kept them in the court-yard and had the steward look after them. One day he came to me and said, "These birds are better flavoured even than pheasant; I advise Your Excellency to order them prepared for the table."[20]

"Tut, man," said I,[21] "have you never noticed that when these birds fly they preserve the strictest order? – they thus understand the Laws of Ceremony[22] (禮); when they mate they never [zzz], there is no free-love[23] – I [zzz zzz] Righteousness (義); in their migrations they follow

---

17 Presumably the *Kukcho inmul chi* (國朝人物志), published in three volumes by An Chonghwa (安鍾和, 1860–1924) in 1909. In the *JWM* version, Gale writes that the author "is noted in the sacred book of writers as one of the famous *literati.*"

18 The preceding two sentences explaining the five virtues of Confucianism were omitted from the *JWM* version.

19 In the *OC* version, Gale writes, "In the late autumn of the *chungyu* (1777)." The *JWM* version reads: "In the late Autumn a peasant of Kyŏnghŭng (on the Tumen near Vladivostok) caught two wild geese." The town in question is Kyŏnghŭng (慶興) in North Hamgyŏng province.

20 Here the *OC* version is used, whereas the *Pen Pictures* version reads simply, "I advise Your Excellency to kill and eat."

21 The *OC* version adds: "These are not for slaughter, wonderful birds they are."

22 In *OC*, "they thus understand the Laws of Ceremony" is translated instead as "which the great masters call *ye.*"

23 In *OC*, "there is no free-love" is deleted.

the path of the sun – surely that is Knowledge (智); though they go and come you can always depend on them – that surely is Faithfulness (信);[24] they never make war on other creatures, or scratch with bill or claws – that is Love (仁).[25] Only a bird with feathers, and yet possessing the Five Virtues! Its ways and habits are recorded in the classics, its note in a song! The great *Yi King* [*Book of Changes*][26] talks of it; at weddings, too, it is carried along to give good luck to the ceremony, and so its virtues and superior attainments are manifest. To make soup of, or to fry it like a pheasant, quail, or chicken would be an offense.[27] Feed these birds every day on grain and give them water to drink, fix them a coop to keep out the cold; shut them up at night from foxes and weasels; let a month or so go by, till their wings lengthen out, then take them to the peak, and let them fly away with this message:[28]

> Keep away from the North – Keep away!
> (Keep away from the North! (the Mongol World))
> The deep pine woods where your quills will lie;[29]
> (In the sand woods deep your quills will lie),

---

24 This section reads as follows in *OC*: "in their migration they follow the warmth of the sun, *chi* (wisdom); though they go far you can always depend on them to arrive with the season, *sin* (trustworthiness)."

25 In equating the bird's traits with the five virtues, the *JWM* version is much more succinct: "strictest order, that is *ye* (ceremony) … that is *ŭi* (loyalty) … that is *chi* (wisdom) … that is *sin* (trustworthiness)." As for the final virtue, the *JWM* writes "that borders on *in* (love)."

26 In the *OC* version, Gale writes that "the Yi-Keui, or Book of Ceremony, talks of it," presumably a reference to the *Yegi* (禮記, usually referred to as the *Book of Rites*); the *JWM* version claims that "The *Book of Yi* talks of it."

27 From this point until the beginning of the poem, the voice differs in the *Pen Pictures* and *OC* versions: whereas in this version the narrator is commanding his steward to take care of the geese and eventually release them, in the *OC* version the author is describing what he himself actually did. The *JWM* version concurs with *Pen Pictures*. The original *hanmun* version seems to allow for either reading.

28 There are significant variations between Gale's translation of the following verses in *Pen Pictures* and *OC*. Therefore, the translations appearing in *OC* have been presented line for line under the *Pen Pictures* version. The *JWM* version is nearly identical to the *Pen Pictures* version, except that "keep away" is not repeated at the end of the line starting each of the poem's four subsections (north, south, east, west).

29 *JWM*: "The long sand woods where your quills will lie."

And the inky Amoor that goes greedily by,
(Where the inky Amoor goes sullenly by),
The cracking ice that will spoil your bill,
(Where cracking ice will split your bill),
And the sneaky old bear to claw and kill,
(And the rude old bear will claw and kill);
And the round-spot tiger that loves you dear,
(And the round-spot tiger will love you dear),
And the savage bow, and the whistling spear.
(And the savage bow and whistling spear).
Keep away from the North, keep away!
(Keep away from the North, keep away!)
Keep away from the South – Keep away!
(Keep away from the South! (the Loochoos))[30]
There's red-hot earth and a boiling sea,
(The red-hot earth and the boiling sea)
And snakes in the air that fly,
(Have snakes in the air that fly;)
That stand on their tails and hiss and strike,
(That stand on their tails and hiss and strike)
Till the geese that are bitten die.
(Till the geese that are bitten die).
There are fiery hills that scorch the sun,
(There are fiery darts from off the sun)
And flames that glare by day;
(And flames that glare by day),
If you go to the South your breath is done,
(If you go to the South your breath is done)
And your feathers are burned away.
(And your feathers are burned away).
Keep away from the East – keep away!
(Keep away from the East! (Japan))
[Zzz zzz] we look for the 'Sea of the Child,'[31]

---

30 This refers to the Ryukyu Islands (琉球諸島), an archipelago stretching from southwest Kyushu to Taiwan, today officially called the Southern Islands (南西諸島) by Japan. Gale's romanization is based on the Chinese pronunciation of these islands. The Ryukyus existed as an independent kingdom centred in Okinawa until annexation by Meiji Japan in 1879.

31 *JWM*: "There's the Sea of the Child."

(For there, in sooth, the waters are piled)
With its waters pitching, heaving wild,[32]
(With the swell of the ocean pitching wild);
And whales that swallow a ship down whole,
(Where whales can swallow a ship down whole)
And jumping beasts that squirm and roll;
(With jumping beasts that squirm and roll);
And the black-toothed man with tattoo band (Japanese),[33]
(Where the black-toothed man with tattoo band)
And a cunning heart and a clever hand,
(And a cunning heart and a clever hand),
With a deadly bullet, and eye to aim,
(With a deadly bullet and eye to aim),
And a thunder flash and a burst of flame,
(And a thunder flash and a burst of flame!)
Where you never would get away at all,
(Where you never would get away at all)
And your bones and nerves would be ground up small.
(But your bones and nerves would be ground up small).
Keep away from the East, keep away!
(---)

Keep away from the West – keep away!
(Keep away from the West! (China))
Where the yawning gulf of the Yalu flows,[34]
(There the yawning gulf of the Yalu flows)
By the land of sin and dirt,
(By the land of sin and dirt);
Where the words they talk with nobody knows,
(Where the words they talk with nobody knows)
And the coat they wear's a shirt;
(And the coat they don's a shirt);
Where a spear is hung in the girdle string,
(Where a spear is hung in the girdle-string),
With a deadly blade beside,
(And a deadly blade beside);
Where they hunt for the life of each living thing,

---

32 *JWM*: "heaving, pitching wild."
33 *JWM* omits "(Japanese)."
34 *JWM* omits "yawning."

(Where they hunt the life of each living thing)
To gorge on its flesh and hide;
(To gorge on its flesh and hide);
Where the smell of oil they dote upon,
(Where the smell of oil they dote upon),
And the tents are decked with quills.
(And the tents are decked with quills),
If you venture there you are dead and gone,
(If you venture there you are dead and gone)
And a ghost among the hills.
(As a ghost among the hills).

But here in this land of green mountains, where the day first shines; and the Silver Constellation stretches across; and the Horn Star hangs over; and the warp and woof of heaven glisten with light; and mountains interlace; and waters circle round; where heat and cold are just what they ought to be; and fertile lands stretch three hundred miles; and grain grows plentifully; and the Doctrine of the Sages is taught; and where grace abounds; where the young of animals, and eggs of birds are not molested; and where all things flourish, stay here, fly nowhere else. Come with your wives and families and all your relatives, sail in with the clouds and sing out to the moon; dine off the reeds, but watch out for the stray arrow and the fish-net; go southward in autumn and come back north in spring, and live out your life in peace."[35]
(1905)

放鷹辭
季秋之月。孔 [慶興一號孔州] 之野人。生得二鴈。剪其翮以獻。余歸其
　直 而畜于庭。饔人曰。是味旨於雉。請膳之。余曰。毋。是鳥也, 羣而
　有序, 其有禮乎, 侶而不亂, 其有義乎, 飛必隨陽, 是其智也, 至必如期, 是

35　In the *JWM* version, Gale signs his work Esson Third, his nom de plume when he wrote for the *North China Daily News*; this seems to have been a reprint from that periodical. Gale wrote intermittently for the *North China Daily News*, a Shanghai-based newspaper, as a correspondent from the end of October 1899 until August 1905, with a short hiatus in 1903 when he was absent from Korea. Richard Rutt writes of the newspaper that "it is practically impossible to trace with certainty all the articles Gale wrote for the Shanghai paper, because complete files of the *North China Daily News* no longer exist outside Peking. Some of the articles were unsigned, but most were signed 'Esson Third' in honor of his Scottish grandmother's maiden name." Rutt, *James Scarth Gale and His "History,"* 35.

其信也。嘴不啄生，爪不攫物。　近於仁矣．羽蟲之微，具此五德。　故其居
載於書，其聲詠於詩。月令紀其來賓，嘉見執以成禮，凡以尙其德而昭其靈
也。　如之何其羹之炙之，如雉鶉鷄鴨然。乃日餕以粟，盆水濟其渴，茅薦禦
其寒。　夜則密其藩扃其竇，以遠狸鼠。旣月翮始長可擧。於是升高而放之，
送之以辭曰。

爾之飛兮無北。白礫林兮氈毳落。

黑水吼怒兮層氷攢角。

朱鬐綠睛兮熊攫豹食。

大弓長鏃兮捷投遠弋。

爾北徂兮爲彼得。

爾之飛兮無南。

赭墳潟洳兮沸水淫淫。

蝮蛇騰空兮尾豎舌銛。

火山爍日兮揚芒皷炎。

爾南翔兮毛將燖。

爾之飛兮無東，渡幼海兮洪濤潏汩而溯洄。

巨鯨吞帆兮奔鰌躍噬。

烏齒鏤身兮心巧手銳。

毒丸伺物兮霆擊焱駭。

爾不避兮骨筋碎。

爾之飛兮無西　過鴨水兮赤縣蒙穢而幽昧。

左言短衣兮腰槊臂矢。

逐肉充饑兮腥臭是嗜。搖翟揷幢兮毛羽之不棄。

爾適彼兮爲羈鬼。

於樂青丘日初暘兮。箕張角垂經緯光兮。

山嶸水繚適燠涼兮。膏壤千里足稻粱兮。

有聖涵育澤溥長兮。不爍日兮揚芒不卵物殷昌兮。

爾莫他方之逝。返舊鄉兮。携妃兮喚族。嬉雲兮叫月。

唧蘆兮避矰。色舉兮遠罿。

春去兮秋來。終汝天兮愉佚。[36]

辭曰。奮長翮兮挾浮雲。　超鬼門兮上磨天。

豜朔野兮跨鐵關。　度金城兮集華巓。

遊漢都之赫戲兮。　舞德輝以翩」。

朝刷翼於上林兮。　夕弄影於天津。

揚淸音之嘐唳兮。　近玉樓之蟬蜎。

爲報孤臣兮滯塞垣。　髮盡白兮心彌丹。

36　Gale's translation in *Pen Pictures* and *Old Corea* ends here.

A New Style of Courtship

"A New Style of Courtship" combines the conversion narrative with more of Gale's observations of love, marriage, and courtship, subjects that resurfaced intermittently in his writings. Gale seemed particularly struck by the rapid and perfunctory way in which Koreans approached marriage. At the time of his writing, arranged marriages still constituted the vast majority of marriages, to the extent that the very concept of romantic love and courtship became a celebrated and controversial cause of the so-called new woman (*sin yosŏng*). "New women," who championed women's education, freedom of mobility, and ease of divorce, among other causes, argued that in a system where "girls were being bought and sold like commodities" and love and marriage rarely coincided, women should be free to divorce their husbands for the sake of their own happiness, and to enter into relationships based on free choice and affection.[1]

The courtship described in this chapter is indeed that of a "new style," combining an arranged aspect with an added measure of agency, topped off with a religious twist, as the newly converted couple exchange Bible verses as part of their courtship. Although not quite a "modern" form of courtship where the couple is able to meet and converse directly, their clandestine *p'iltam* (筆談 brush talk), presumably on the subject of marriage and accomplished without the knowledge of their parents, still imbues their courtship with a sense of novelty and hybridity. In the end it seems convention and tradition hold sway, and Kyehwang-i is obliged to bow to the wishes of "Treasure Daughter's" father, waiting a full six months for a wedding that cryptic Bible passages told him would be imminent.

---

1 Yoo, "The 'New Woman' and the Politics of Love," 306–7.

A New Style of Courtship
Pen Pictures, 38–9; *Old Corea*, 111–12;
Korea Mission Field 2, no. 6 (1906): 119–20

A little quiet man with brown face and still browner beard lived under the ancient shadows of the Yellow Dragon Mountain.[2] His name was Kyehwang-i[3] and might be translated Cinnamon Brown. He had no worldly ambition except to see his farm of rice and beans do well, and to keep from entanglements with all doubtful and suspicious men.

A missionary had crossed his path, and him he viewed for a time from a distance, and, later on, a little closer, till he came into touch with and learned to know and trust the peculiar long scraggy being who hailed from the barbarian haunts of the West.[4]

Cinnamon became a Christian, learned to pray, and, in his own mind, to sing. Cinnamon's songs were all of a kind, the overbubblings of a grateful soul, and were wonderful for the ears to hear. He had a wife and a little baby girl, and few men on the round planet, be they magnates or millionaires have ever, in their domestic felicity, touched higher water[5] than Cinnamon Brown, who dwelt under the lee-side of the Yellow Dragon Mountain.[6] Cinnamon would kill the fatted calf, and make no end of grateful effort[7] when the missionary came his way. He was thankful and his world was peopled with expressions of good-will and peace to all mankind.

Mr. Cinnamon Brown left his home to spend a week or two in the world of the missionary, where there was a gathering of many men for prayer and Bible study. This was a great event in the life of Cinnamon.[8] A continental trip, a service in St Paul's, the Hallelujah Chorus, none of these could possibly compare with so great a dream as this outing for the little man.[9]

---

2 This seems to refer to Hwangnyongsan (黃龍山), a mountain with an elevation of 134 metres that lies northwest of Seoul, just north of the city of Koyang.

3 桂黃이.

4 *OC*: "the barbarian quarters of the distant West."

5 *OC*: "a higher water mark."

6 The phrase "who dwelt under the leeside of the Yellow Dragon Mountain" is deleted from the *OC* version.

7 *OC*: "grateful preparation."

8 *OC*: "This was a great occasion."

9 *OC*: "with this outstanding event in the life of the little man."

But life is uncertain at best, and even when our cup brims over, sorrow falls. Word came that the wife and baby of Mr. Cinnamon Brown were down with smallpox.

He left and a day or two later came the message, "Be it known to all, that wife and child have 'returned home.'"[10]

His reddish beard and pitted face were seen no more at the worship.[11] He was at home in his cheerless cabin amid the sorrowful silences that gathered at the foot of the Yellow Dragon Mountain. How was it that this ruthless robber *mama*[12] (`small-pox`), to whom he used to pray in his darkened days, could come with so high a hand and rob him of all?[13] He would pray and keep on praying until some answer came. After the conflict was finished, he gave as the result of his lonely experience, "God is good, all ends well."[14]

Usually Koreans marry in a week or two[15] after burying a wife when they are as well off as Cinnamon, but a year passed round and the uncomplaining[16] little man was still the sole occupant of his [zzz].[17]

He was urged[18] to take unto himself a wife and to take her quickly, but the answer was, "God will give when He chooses."[19]

On an unexpected day Cinnamon Brown called at the home of the missionary with cheerful countenance and passed a smiling salutation. Said he, "I have some important news for the honorable teacher, which I have not even whispered to anyone. It is this: I am to be married."

"Indeed!" said the missionary, "and to whom?"

"To the daughter of Mr. Oh, whose given name is Treasure, and very beautiful and good she is said to be. I've not seen her yet," said Cinnamon, "but I've carried on a correspondence with her and I want to ask the missionary if I have done it in accord with the laws of Christian enlightenment. She has answered me and we are going to be married," and here he unrolled a number of crumpled papers, the complete correspondence.

---

10 *OC*: "Be it known to all that wife and child are 'gone home to heaven.'"

11 *OC*: "at the sessions."

12 *Mama* is the colloquial Korean word for small pox (*ch'ŏnyŏndu* 天然痘).

13 *OC*: "and pillage his home?"

14 *OC*: "'God knows best; He is good.'"

15 *OC*: "in a week."

16 "Uncomplaining" is deleted from the *OC* version.

17 *OC*: "of his home."

18 *OC*: "He was urged by the neighbours."

19 This sentence has been deleted from the *OC* version.

"This is the first note that I sent her," said he. All that was on it was "Mark X:7; For this cause shall a man leave his father and mother and cleave unto his wife."[20] It had neither address nor signature.

"But how did Treasure know who it was from?" asked the missionary.

"Know? Why she saw from the man that brought it."

Treasure's answer was: "Mat XXII:3 and 7;[21] And he sent forth his servants to call them that were bidden to the wedding, and they would not come. But when the king heard thereof he was wroth, and sent forth his armies and destroyed those murderers and burned up their city."

"Was that not a wonderful answer for her to send?" asked Cinnamon.

"Really it is wonderful," replied the missionary, "I don't understand it at all."

"No?" said he, surprised at the lack of insight that it indicated.

"It simply means that if I have faith to believe, I'll be present at a wedding."

Again Cinnamon sent "I Peter III:7; Likewise ye husbands dwell with them according to knowledge, giving honor to the wife as unto the weaker vessel, and as being heirs together of the grace of life, that your prayers be not hindered."

Treasure at once answered, "John I:8; He was not that light but was sent to bear witness of that light."

Again Cinnamon remarked that her answer was very deep. "I don't understand it at all,"[22] said the missionary.

"The *moksa*[23] does not understand it"? he inquired with surprise, and then he undertook to elucidate it with that skill for the interpretation of a hidden mystery that pertains to the Farthest East.

"It means that our letters are bearing witness even though we have not yet decided."

Still another answer was "Mat IX:1: And he entered into a ship and passed over, and came into his own city."

"But truly," remarked the missionary, "this is past my comprehension too, what can it mean?"

---

20 These and subsequent Bible passages are from the King James Version of the Bible, which seems to be Gale's preferred version, as elsewhere in his writings he also cites "KJV."

21 The *OC* version mistakenly records this verse as "Matthew xxiii," but it is in fact Matthew 22.

22 *OC*: "I don't understand it again."

23 Preacher, pastor (牧師).

"The thought here," calmly proceeded Cinnamon, "is that we sail together to our own city, or heaven."

On a crumpled piece of paper the final answer that completed the correspondence was Mat VII:1; evidently written in Treasure's own hand: "Judge not that ye be not judged."

The missionary appealed to Cinnamon for an interpretation, hoping that he might make his prospects a little clearer.

"This also is very deep," was the answer, "and shows Treasure to be a wonderful woman. It means do not say anything about our plighting our troth as yet, or give anyone[24] a chance to judge."

Cinnamon's countenance beamed with trustfulness – so much so that the missionary had not the heart to say, "I'm afraid you have built a castle in the air."

He was evidently disappointed that the wise Westerner should be so slow to read the deeper meanings of these letters. He asked if he might tell others without breaking church rules. "Certainly," replied the missionary.

He then called on a worldly careless kind of man[25] named Yi[26] in the outer room, and told him, but Yi laughed and said, "Have you asked her father?"

"Why, no!"

"Well, you are mad," was Yi's reply, "She evidently has no idea at all as to what you are driving at."

Cinnamon, much cast down, went home to pray about it.

Six months of silence passed by and then one day, all unexpectedly there came in as on light fantastic toe, a familiar piece of crumpled paper, addressed to the missionary. It read in jubilant but irregular letters: "PLEASE COME AT ONCE TO THE YELLOW DRAGON MOUNTAIN AND MARRY TREASURE DAUGHTER OF OH TO THIS HUMBLE AND INSIGNIFICANT PERSONALITY.[27]

Signed CINNAMON BROWN"

---

24 *OC:* "them."

25 *OC:* "a worldly-minded kind of man."

26 This is evidently one of at least three of Gale's "pundits" with the surname Yi: Yi Ch'angjik, Yi Wŏnmo, or Yi Kyosŭng.

27 *OC:* "humble personality."

Korea's Receding Pantheon

"Korea's Receding Pantheon" appears with minor variations in both *Pen Pictures* and *Old Corea*, and was ultimately published in the December 1917 issue of *Korea Magazine*, suggesting the importance that Gale placed on the sentiments expressed therein.[1] In *Old Corea* the essay appears under the subheading "Religious and Allied Themes," alongside Christian conversion narratives and descriptions of Korean spirituality. "Korea's Receding Pantheon" represents a clear distillation of Gale's proselytization strategy as a missionary in Korea: to present Korean religious forms, and in particular Confucianism, as a sort of unfulfilled prophecy, somewhat akin to a Christian's view of the Old Testament without the fulfilment of the New Covenant. For Gale, Confucianism was inextricably intertwined with Literary Sinitic learning, and so one of the key thrusts of his evangelical work was to connect both spiritually and academically with the literati class.[2] To that end, "Korea's Receding Pantheon" and other of his writings are replete with parallels between

---

1 The content of the published version was virtually unchanged, save for slightly different numbering. Gale, "Korea's Receding Pantheon," *Korea Magazine* 12 (1917): 541–7.

2 For example, in *Korea Magazine*, Gale writes, "If we take the Century Dictionary's rendering, namely, 'the recognition of a super-human power to whom allegiance and service are justly due' as a correct definition of religion, then surely Korean literature is deeply impregnated with religious thought, from its earliest days down to 1894, when state literature ceased to be." See Gale, "Korean Literature," *Korea Magazine* 2, vol. 7 (1918): 293. This essay is not to be confused with the identically titled chapter appearing in *Pen Pictures*.

Judeo-Christian and East Asian history. Unlike many of his colleagues, Gale's knowledge of East Asian history through primary source material was substantial, giving his religio-historical allusions weight that he knew would not be lost on his literati interlocutors. Also in contradistinction to most of Gale's missionary colleagues, from this and other of his writings it is clear that he considered Confucianism to be a religion of sorts, albeit an imperfect and earlier iteration of Christianity. The final sentence of the essay encapsulates Gale's view of the "complementarity" of Christianity and Confucianism, as well as his sense of ambivalence at the inevitable passing of a religio-literary tradition he so valorized.

Korea's Receding Pantheon
Pen Pictures, 40–3; *Old Corea*, 44–8; *Korea Magazine* 1 (1917): 541–7

In the changes taking place in this country, there is a general exit noticeable on the part of former gods that ruled in the spiritual sphere.[3] Worship is disappearing from its ancient haunts, where it held sway through the slow-going and unchanging past.

Of these changes we notice first, the *Sajik*, or Worship of Heaven,[4] *Sa* being applicable to God, and *jik* to earth. God and Mother Earth they were, the spiritual originals of all parental existence, before whom the king used to bow, asking that rain be given and that good crops come forth to bless the land. The people had no part in this worship, only the king, whose ceremonial resembled that of the Emperor of China when he visited the Temple of Heaven. But now the *Sajik* gates are closed. The spirit of the crops goes unpropitiated. No complaint is made or word of regret spoken regarding him. The grass of the future will grow over his grave, and his name will be a far-off memory only.

3　In the *OC* version, "spiritual" is crossed out and replaced by "religious." It is unclear whether this suggests that Gale considered the enumerated belief system to be "religious" in the Western sense, on par with Christianity and other Abrahamic faiths, or simply that they shared certain religious characteristics and so could be included in the same discussion as Christianity. The *Korea Magazine* version also records "spiritual."

4　*Sajik* (社稷) refers to the worship of the gods of soil (*t'oji*) and crops (*koksik*) in order to ensure a prosperous, bountiful year without calamity.

Second, the *chongmyo*,[5] or Royal Ancestors, have likewise had written across their immovable countenances, "Finished." Near the middle of Seoul, just before the East Palace, is this abode of the spirits of the ruling family. In 1396 AD[6] a famous minister of the House of Plum[7] was given the responsibility of rearing this spirit temple. He made in it twenty-eight rooms, each room intended for one spirit.

T'aejo,[8] the king, asked, "Why twenty-eight?"

Chŏng Tojŏn[9] replied, "Twenty-eight will be sufficient," and so twenty-eight rooms were made in these Halls of Hades.

Chŏng was again asked to name the building and he called it Ch'angyŏp chŏn (蒼葉殿)[10] or Green Leaf Palace.

"That's a peculiar name," remarked the king.

"Peculiar it is, but will Your Majesty let it stand? Its meaning will be evident in days to come."

"Very well," said T'aejo, and Green Leaf Palace is the name to-day for this quiet house of departed spirits.

Now let us take these characters apart and see in how far they are prophetic.[11] "Green" (蒼) is made up of "twenty" (廾) and "eight" (八), which, thrown together, would mean "twenty-eight." The lower part of the character (君) is *kun* or "king." "Twenty-eight kings" is what "green" expresses when resolved into its component parts, and this is the number of kings that have actually ruled from T'aejo till the [zzz][12] emperor made his exit.

---

5 Chongmyo (宗廟) is a Confucian shrine at which kings and queens of the Chosŏn dynasty were honoured. Established in 1396, it is the oldest preserved royal Confucian shrine in the world.

6 *OC*: "I am told that in 1396 AD."

7 The sinograph for "plum tree" is (李), which is also the character for the Yi family name, the reigning monarchy of the Chosŏn dynasty.

8 King T'aejo (太祖, 1335–1408) was the founder and first monarch of the Chosŏn dynasty. In the *OC* version, the name T'aejo is left out.

9 Chŏng Tojŏn (鄭道傳, 1342–98) was the first prime minister of the Chosŏn dynasty and the principal architect of Chosŏn ideological, institutional, and legal frameworks.

10 The front gate of Chongmyo today is called Ch'angyŏmmun (蒼葉門), or Green Leaf Gate.

11 *OC*: "and see how far the prophetic element enters into them."

12 In the *OC* and *Korea Magazine* versions, "last emperor" appears; in *Pen Pictures*, "annexed" emperor has been crossed out, replaced by an illegible word in the margin that may possibly read "deposed."

We shall try "leaf" now and see what it is resolvable into.[13] (葉) is made up of "twenty" (卄), *se* or "generation" (世) and *mok*, or "tree" (木). This character, then, might be read, "Twenty generations of the House of Plum." Twenty-eight kings, but only twenty generations is, strange as it may seem, what it actually reckons up to be. The spirit of the prophets was in Chŏng Tojŏn.[14] The twenty-eight rooms are occupied; the twenty-eight kings of "green" have come and gone; the twenty generations of "leaf" are completed; the temple is closed, the story is ended, no jot or tittle[15] of the prophetic name having fallen to the ground.

Third, there are the Confucian Temples, one located in each county, and the large Sŏnggyun'gwan in Seoul.[16] At appointed seasons, the officials, aided by the literati, repaired to these temples and made their obeisance before the tablets of the Greater Sages and Lesser Sages. There were in all one hundred and thirty-seven of them, of whom one hundred and twenty-one were Chinese, and sixteen Korean.[17] Sacrifices

---

13 *OC*: "and see what it becomes."

14 Richard Rutt writes that the entire Presbyterian mission in Korea was deeply influenced by prophecy and millenarianism, the teaching that "the second coming of Christ [would] be followed by his reign on earth for a thousand years." Gale himself was involved with translating into Korean premillenarian texts such as W.E. Blackstone's *Jesus Is Coming* (1913) and the Scofield Bible, and elsewhere wrote extensively on Korea's being prophetically positioned for the reception of the Gospel. Gale was more generally drawn to matters of the occult, and the Korean literature that he chose to translate often reflects this interest. See Rutt, *James Scarth Gale and His "History,"* 63–4.

15 Invoking the Bible verse "For verily I say unto you, till heaven and earth pass, one jot or one tittle shall in no wise pass from the law, till all be fulfilled" (Matthew 5:17), Gale is again drawing a parallel between Abrahamic faiths and Confucianism.

16 Sŏnggyun'gwan (成均館) was the highest institute of learning in Chosŏn Korea. Its predecessor, the Kukchagam (國子監), was established in 992 by King Sŏngjong, then rechristened Sŏnggyun'gam (成均監) in 1298 before gaining its current title in 1304 at the behest of An Hyang, the father of Neo-Confucianism in Korea. The vast majority of students desiring to sit for the highest civil service examination (*kwagŏ munkwa sihŏm*) matriculated at this institution. Confucianism is the twelfth and last form of worship to appear in the *OC* and *Korea Magazine* versions, whereas here it is placed third. This may be an attempt in these later versions to transition more seamlessly from a form of worship that Gale views as most legitimate (Confucianism) to its "rightful" successor, Christianity.

17 There are actually eighteen Koreans honoured in the Confucian shrine (Munmyo 文廟), and collectively they are called *Tongbang sipp'al hyŏn* (the eighteen

of raw food material were offered, never cooked fare. To-day the temples are forsaken. Where the spirit sat enthroned, dust gathers, and the paper on the wall hangs in loose tag-ends and flaps in the wind.[18]

The fourth object of worship is the tablet of the family ancestor.[19] This has really been Korea's symbol of divine allegiance from time immemorial. To lose the tablet from the home; to fail to bow before it on the 1st and 15th days of the month; to forget the "greater" or "lesser" sacrifices, would mark one as cut off from the house of Israel.[20]

There are few or no temples in Korea to be seen by the passer, for the temples of the tablet are the home and quiet grave, and these truly exist. Sackcloth, and ashes, and tears, and loud wailings, have accompanied this diminutive symbol of the world of departed spirits, and its hold as a household god is the strongest of all.[21] But the ancestral tablet, too, is receding into the dim vista of forgottenness. Christianity has had a part in cutting into ancestral worship,[22] but apart from its influence, the spirit of the new age is one that pays little heed to the common everyday kind

---

sages of the Eastern Land [Korea]). The vast majority of these figures lived during the sixteenth and seventeenth centuries: Pak Sech'ae (朴世采, 1631–95), Song Chungil (宋浚吉, 1606–72), Song Siyŏl (宋時烈, 1607–89), Kim Chip (金集, 1574–1656), Cho Hŏn (趙憲, 1544–92), Kim Changsaeng (金長生, 1548–1631), Sŏng Hon (成渾, 1535–98), Yi I (李珥, 1537–84), Kim Inhu (金麟厚, 1510–60), Yi Hwang (李滉, 1502–71), Yi Ŏnjŏk (李彦迪, 1491–1553), Cho Kwangjo (趙光祖, 1482–1520), Chŏng Yŏch'ang (鄭汝昌, 1450–1504), Kim Koengp'il (金宏弼, 1454–1504), Chŏng Mongju (鄭夢周, 1338–92), An Hyang (安珦, a.k.a An Yu 安裕, 1243–1306), Ch'oe Ch'iwŏn (崔致遠, 857–908), and Sŏl Ch'ong (薛聰, 658?–?).

18 The preceding two sentences have been omitted from the *OC* version. However, the extremely significant following passage appears in the *OC* and *Korea Magazine* versions, clearly displaying Gale's sentiments toward Confucianism: "The Master, Confucius, has been one of the greatest prophets of the ages, and his teachings have had incalculable influence for good on the Far East. His worship, however, is very closely locked up with the scholarship of the literati, and as this is on the wane, one asks, 'Will his worship not also go?'" This perhaps more than any other of his statements encapsulates Gale's deep respect for the literary and intellectual nature of Korea's Confucian tradition, and the ambivalence of his Christian triumphalism.

19 This is often referred to in scholarly research as "spirit tablet" (*sinju* 神主).

20 This is an additional parallel between Western religions and Confucianism.

21 *OC*: "the most revered of all."

22 The preceding phrase on Christianity was removed from the *OC* and *Korea Magazine* versions.

Illustration 6. "One Section of the Pantheon," in *Pen Pictures*

of ancestor. The tendency, if any exists at all, is towards hero-worship.[23] Democracy is disappearing from the world of spirits, and only the god-like among men will remain to be remembered and prayed to.

The fifth form of worship to be noticed is that of Kwan kong.[24] The only great temples in and about Seoul, if we except the Sŏnggyun'gwan, are Kwan kong's. Kwan was a Chinaman of the Han dynasty, who died in 219 AD. A seller of bean-curd he was, who yet, through various temptations, proved his constant fidelity. The Korean calls him a master of *ŭi*[25] or "righteousness." He is regarded as a special guardian

---

23 Although this chapter is undated, most articles in *Pen Pictures* seem to have been completed during the first decade of the twentieth century and prior to annexation, a period that coincided with a succession of fictional biographies of "great men" and "heroes" of Korean history. Andre Schmid writes extensively on these nationalist histories as part of a broader movement to de-Sinify Korean culture by resurrecting indigenous cultural figures through writing. See Schmid, *Korea between Empires, 1895–1919*.

24 Guan Gong (關公 Lord Guan), also called Guan Yu (關羽), was a general during the late Eastern Han dynasty, one the most renowned historical figures in China and throughout East Asia and considered a paragon of righteousness and loyalty.

25 義.

divinity of this peninsula. In the Japanese invasion of 1592 AD he is said to have appeared at the South Gate of Seoul, where a temple to-day marks the spot, to have passed over the city and disappeared outside the East Gate, where another temple stands. He is to come again, they say. He is called *Sŏngjegun*,[26] the Holy Imperial Ruler, and is regarded as the special intercessor with the Jade Divinity.[27] His image and portrait represents him as very fierce and awful. He has blazing eyes, a thunder cloud for a face, and a threefold bristling beard, with whiskers that blow off wrath and fiery indignation. The worship paid him must be given in an atmosphere of fear and uncertain expectation.

The worshipper thinks that if he but repeat Kwan kong's formula, that deals with truth, faithfulness, etc., he will be free from all forms of danger by land and sea, and will finally reach the happy home of the Jade Divinity.

But no longer does the state share in the worship of the Kwan kong. The crowds that used to frequent the temple have fallen off. Wind-bells tinkle disconsolately over the grass-grown courtyard. Kwan is dead.

The sixth form of worship, universally spoken of and believed in by the Korean, is that of the Hills and Streams. The Hill, everywhere present, is the guardian of the human pigmies[28] that congregate under its wing. Seoul was safe in the shadow of the Three Horned Mountain,[29] Songdo,[30] likewise, under its protector. Each hill had its attendant spirit, called the *san sillyŏng*.[31] He is represented as riding comfortably on the back of a tiger, one of his special menials. He is great in power and

---

26　聖帝君.

27　Usually referred to as the Jade Emperor (*Okhwang* 玉皇), he is one of the representations of the first god in Chinese cosmology.

28　Referring to Koreans as "pigmies" is almost certainly due to the widely read "Korea, the Pigmy Empire," written by the American Orientalist William Elliot Griffis and published in the *New England Magazine* in 1902. Griffis, whose main area of specialty was Japan, was also the author of *Corea: The Hermit Nation* (1882), though he had yet to visit Korea at the time. Griffis was in close contact with Gale, Homer Hulbert, and other missionaries in Korea. See Griffis, "Korea, the Pigmy Empire."

29　The Three-Horned Mountain refers to what is today called Pukhansan, meaning "mountain north of the Han River." The three main peaks of this mountain are Paegundae, Insubong, and Man'gyŏngdae.

30　Songdo (松都) was the capital of the Koryŏ dynasty, today called Kaesŏng and located in North Hwanghae Province, North Korea, close to the border with South Korea.

31　山神靈.

can apportion special attainments in the way of strength, making men *charyŏkkun*[32] so that they can pull apart a bar of steel, can jump over the moon, or bite through armor-plate. The hunter prays to the mountain deity for success, in the chase and for a never-failing aim. The writer once met a man with a gun going into the hills[33] at the fall of night. I asked if he did not fear to enter thus into the realm of darkness. But he answered, "No, I am an attendant upon the Mountain Spirit (san sillyŏng), and have no cause for fear."

The seeker for ginseng, too, prays to this spirit that his eyes may be enlightened so as to see the precious weed.

"A hundred days of prayer" is one of the common sayings that have to do with the Taoist worship of the hills. Away alone where scarce the fall of a leaf can disturb the quiet, is this mystic worship carried on. The temple stands ever open. It requires no rickety old gate-keeper to dispute the right of entrance with anyone; it is forever and forever in good repair, a great temple, high-roofed with the lamp-light of the sky, and walled by the green eternal hills, accompanied by the silent flight of birds or the murmur of falling water. It would seem indeed a grand kind of worship, beckoning all hearts to come to its bosom and taste of the inner quiet of the soul. Will it go like the other deities of the Korean Pantheon? Undoubtedly.[34]

The seventh form of worship is Buddhism. For several centuries it [had] been in a decadent state and needed a great revival if it ever hoped to live. To-day has this revival come? From Japan Proper new Buddhist forces have entered, and are seeking to revive the fallen fortunes of the sect, but its task will be a difficult one.[35] Already adverse associations cluster about Buddhism that will make a revival of it all but impossible. For generations that state, while frowning with one eye on Buddhism,[36] nodded and winked at all sorts of requests with the other. Prayers were asked,

---

32 自力君.

33 *OC*: "Once I met a man going into the hills."

34 Gale's sensitive, even reverent description of Taoist worship, coupled with his benign certainty as to its eventual passing, seem like a particularly poignant example of the tension between his poetic, romantic inclinations and his Christian triumphalism.

35 In the *OC* version Gale writes "Buddhist faith" instead of "Buddhist sect." The *Korea Magazine* version reads: "For several centuries it has been in a decadent state and needed a great revival if it ever hoped to live."

36 In the *OC* version, "Buddhism" has been replaced with the word "Sakyamuni," another title of the Buddha derived from Sanskrit, meaning "hermit or sage of the Sākya tribe."

sutras were said and sung at her bidding, bell ringing, *kong* pounding and intoning have kept many a mountain dell in a state of discordant uproar at the bidding of the king and queen.[37] The common classes went to the Buddha to ask a son, or long life, or happiness. The silent god, never vindictive or threatening in face, as Kwan kong, gave a quiet hope for the future. To-day we find temples given up, we see gilded Buddhas stowed away. Buddhism, for the present, seems likely to still further decline.[38]

The eighth form is what was called in Hebrew parlance "the worship of the host of heaven." Attached to every Buddhist temple, and sometimes off in a quiet valley by itself, is the Ch'ilsŏnggak,[39] or Temple of the Dipper. The Seven Stars circling round and round the Pole, had to do in some way with the fortunes of the family, and so were worshipped. Many a little boy in Korea wears the name Ch'ilsŏng-i (Seven Stars), under whose favouring influence his birth came to pass. "You may thank your stars" illustrates the same faith on the part of our ancestors. Good fortune is said to attend the star in the ascendant here as it did with us. But the spirit of the age upon which we have entered will pay but little heed to the Seven Stars or any other deity unless quick returns are made in the way of profit.[40]

The ninth form of worship is associated with the roadway. The pilgrim must be accompanied with well-intentioned spirits. At each pass-way or elevation, there is usually an old tree with rags and tatters hanging to it, a pile of stones underneath and often a tumble-down shrine. The passer spits or casts an extra stone on the heap at the foot of the tree, or ties a rag to the branch, in the hope that the frowsty spirit that has to do with the place will give him a safe journey and good luck. These wayside shrines are nasty places[41] that look like pest-houses gaping at you as you go by, marring the beauty and the sweetness of the eternal hills.

---

37 *OC*: "Prayers were asked, sutras were said and sung at her bidding. The ringing of bells, the call of the *kong*, the intoning of prayers have awakened many a mountain valley at the bidding of the king and queen." The *kong* is a cymbal-like instrument used in Korean Buddhist ceremonies. Made of bronze or iron and shaped like a cloud, it is sounded in order to save creatures of the air.

38 *OC*: "Buddhism for the present seems likely to decline." "Still further decline" appears in *Korea Magazine*, as well.

39 七星閣.

40 In the *OC* version, "in the way of profit" has been deleted.

41 *OC*: "unsavoury places." In *Korea Magazine*, in response to a reader who queries "the significance of piling up stones before trees situated in narrow defiles or

The tenth form of worship is that of trees and rocks in general. The Koreans say, "When a thing grows old it becomes a spirit." Trees, especially the ginko, and rocks have an unchanging character, which suggests eternal life, unending posterity, and the like. Women will say their tearful prayers to the hoary tree, and the adamantine rock, in the hope that the spirits will hear. They will cut off the bark and make spirit tea of it, believing themselves to great and lasting benefit therefrom. The writer has a ginko tree that he has had to defend as with a shot-gun against the old and crazy wives[42] of the neighbourhood, who, beaver-like, if left alone would strip the bark all round the stem. One old dame lay down in front of the tree and had a "conniption" fit because she was interfered with in the holy exercise of peeling bark and saying prayers. Only by main force was she dragged off the premises, all the time protesting in language that would have made an ordinary spirit's hair stand on end.

As the tortoise, that never dies, presents a back from which Sages read all sorts of spiritual mystery, so the horny back of the tree, like the weather-worn surface of the rock is full of messages of spiritual intent.

The eleventh form of worship includes in its embrace household gods, and spirits of rats, snakes, and weasels. Some are bottled up and buried, some are seen alive in the flesh and prayed to, some are invisible. They are petitioned, sacrificed to, and called on imploringly for help and protection against this troubled world. This form of worship is on the wane in the more enlightened parts of the country and will disappear largely with this generation.

The twelfth and last is the worship of the dragon, be he snake or fish in form. He frequents pools and waters. Sailor lads in Korea, instead of singing out about the "good ship tight and free" pray to the sea-dragon and feed rice over the gunnel[43] into his seething, dusty gullet. The dragon will probably stay, for a time at any rate.

---

passes, and spitting on them," Gale links the piles of stones to the Korean custom of stone fights (see "Stone Fights," *Pen Pictures*, this vol.) and claims that Koreans stacked stones in case of foreign invasion, so that they could defend gods that they believed lived in trees. As for the custom of spitting on these stones, Gale makes the bizarre claim that this was to drive away centipedes. See Gale, "Questions and Answers," *Korea Magazine* 1 (May 1917): 237–8.

42 *OC*: "old wives."

43 The top edge of the side of a boat, more often spelled "gunwale."

Illustration 7. "The 'General of Hell' – a Spirit Guard" (地下大將軍), in *Pen Pictures*

These twelve forms of worship that have beckoned the Korean of the past to pay his vows, his prayers, his tithes, his tears, are receding into the vistas of the by-gone and forgotten. Soon we shall see them only in folk-lore records, and among customs defunct and dead. We watch them recede with something akin to sorrow, unless a better be on hand to take their place, and make good the defects that were inherent in them.

Stone Fights

Stone fights (石戰 *sŏkchŏn*) seem to be a cultural phenomenon of purely Korean provenance. The earliest records of such battles appear in the *History of the Sui* (隋書 K. Susŏ), the official history of the Sui Kingdom of ancient China (581–619) compiled in AD 636. This record describes a stone fight in neighbouring Koguryŏ (37 BC–AD 668), where the practice was thought to have originated: "At the beginning of each year the subjects would gather at the Taedong River and play games, and the king would ride his palanquin there to watch the festivities. After the games the king entered the river fully clothed and divided his subjects into two teams, after which time the teams would chase one another through the water, splashing, yelling, and throwing stones." Stone fights continued through the Koryŏ and Chosŏn dynasties, promoted by royal patronage of varying intensity to cultivate martial skills.[1] Originating as a palace sport, the battles eventually shed their martial origins and came to be adopted by the wider public throughout the

---

1 For example, King Sejong the Great (世宗大王, 1418–50) cultivated a volunteer stone fighter corps, attracting recruits by granting privileges such as government posts to volunteers, many of whom came from humble backgrounds. Yi Ihwa states that "when [King Sejong] learned of the frequent cross-border pillage by barbarians from the North, [he] ordered an immediate deployment of stone battle units to the northern borders." Despite his initial patronage of the sport, repeated and serious injuries each year in Seoul led to a ban on the practice by the Correctional Tribunal, which was nonetheless rescinded in 1469. From that time until 1910, stone fights more or less continued unabated. See Yi, *Korea's Pastimes and Customs*, 113–14.

peninsula, where the activity was called *ch'ŏksŏkhŭi* (擲石戲 throwing-stone game), although the most enthusiastic centres for stone fights were said to be P'yŏngyang, the ancient capital of Koguryŏ where the sport originated, Seoul, and Songdo.[2]

Records indicate that stone fights were staged each year around the beginning of the Lunar New Year, which coincides with early spring in the Gregorian calendar, a time when vast, barren fields provided optimal battlegrounds. Generally, neighbouring villages were pitted against each other, often fuelled by specific grievances among respective residents. The most dramatic stone fight where the greatest numbers participated occurred on the hills of Malli-dong outside the South Gate of Seoul, where residents from beyond the city gates battled against Seoulites from Ahyŏn-dong, present-day Mapo District.[3] Stone fights also functioned as predictors of fortune for the year, with a win for the team from outside the city gates auguring a high crop yield for the Kyŏnggi region, and a win for the Ahyŏn-dong team heralding a bumper crop nationwide.[4] Homer Hulbert offers a detailed account of a typical stone fight in *The Passing of Korea* (1906), which may serve to balance Gale's sparse and anecdotal account:

> Out they pour into the empty, fenceless fields, some armed with thick clubs and protected by heavy padded helmets, while others merely throw stones. The champions of either side prance up and down before their respective factions, twirling their clubs and breathing out threatening and slaughter. Stones begin to fly, most of them falling short of their mark, and the rest being deftly dodged. After the two warring factions have reinforced their courage by streams of most libelous invective, and have worked themselves up to the fighting pitch, they move toward each other warily, the stones fly more thickly, the champions prance more vaingloriously. Meanwhile the multitudes of white-clothed non-combatants, who cover the surrounding hills, shout encouragement to their respective favorites … Suddenly a deafening yell goes up from one side and a wild charge is made. The opposite side gives way, and it looks as if the day were won, but as soon as the first ardour of the pursuit is over the fugitives turn and make a counter-charge … and so it goes on by the hour, rush and

---

2 Hulbert, "The Stone Fight," *Korea Review* 5 (1905): 50.
3 Yi Ihwa, *Korea's Pastimes and Customs*, 115.
4 Ibid.

counter-rush, wild shoutings of delighted spectators, clouds of dust, broken pates, profanity unlimited and gruesome gaps where erstwhile were gleaming teeth.[5]

As Gale points out, "There is no special ceremony in connection with stone fighting, no bowing or repeating of verses, no special sacrifices offered, no prayers said." An inexplicable paroxysm of violence in the land of the literati scholar, stone fights were an ancient and curious Korean tradition that was anathema to Korean Buddhist or Confucian doctrine, but yet one that continued unabated for centuries. The practice was forcefully suppressed by the Japanese from 1910, but unlike many Korean traditions that met a similar fate, the stone fight was not to be mourned by wistful cultural nationalists.

Stone Fights
Pen Pictures, 44–5

At one of the frequented corners of the city while waiting for the trolley I fell into conversation with a policeman.

"Glad to see the people use the car freely," I said, "no longer any fear of the spark fiend or the electric current."

"Wait till this afternoon," said the policeman, "if you wish to see a proper crowd."

"What is on for this afternoon?" I asked.

"*Pyon-ssam*,"[6] said he, a stone fight.

Outside the West Gate they were making great preparation, stones were being collected from all quarters, and by noon crowds of spectators began to gather. Stone fights are a part of the New Year celebrations that have been handed down from the past, and any interference with

---

5 Hulbert, *The Passing of Korea*, 277. The following accounts by foreigners may also be found: Carles, *Life in Corea*, 173; Saunderson, *Notes On Corea and Its People*, 299–316. There is also gives an extensive account in Hulbert, "The Stone Fight," *Korea Review* 5 (1905): 49–53.

6 *P'yŏnssaum* (便싸움), *p'yŏn* meaning "side." Hulbert confirms the spike in passengers on such days: "The heaviest traffic on the electric tramway is when the crowds go out of the city gates to watch these stone fights. One day last year thirty-four thousand people were carried, a number twice as large as the average." See Hulbert, *The Passing of Korea*, 278.

them has been regarded as a violent laying of hands on the people's rights. It is the one case in which the Jews have said to Caesar, "Hands off." Caesar has kept his distance, regretful no doubt of the fact that he too could not be spectator.

There is no special ceremony in connection with stone fighting, no bowing or repeating of verses, no special sacrifices offered, no prayers said. They meet at a point mutually agreed upon, and those hired to kill each other enter the lists, one side representing the city and one the country. It is considered a good omen for the year to have a good, stiff stone fight. The old regent formerly encouraged the gladiators and gave them a bountiful reward.

On the day mentioned by the policeman they met and fought, rushing upon each other pell mell, retreating and advancing in the face of hail that flew like projectiles. Where a loose-jointed being like a Korean learned to throw as they do is a mystery, for when it comes to hurling rocks he revives the memory of Ajax and Hercules. We goose-livered foreigners seek the shelter of a tree or stand-off at a safe distance, but the Korean who usually runs on the merest suggestion of fear "faces the music" amid the shoutings of the crowd.

On this day two "strong men" bit the dust not to rise again and it was voted a great success. One unfortunate fell and before his friends could carry off the body, the enemy was upon him pummelling his lifeless clay with clubs and stones. If it came to settling questions between the powers by means of stone fights no doubt Korea would win. Why this current of surplus energy and activity cannot be switched into some useful line of life is also a mystery.

I imagine Caesar must have been reminded by some merciful Westerner that two men had been killed that day, and that we were now in the 20th century which regarded stone fights as out of date, for His Majesty sent troops to stop it, and so instead of having fifteen days of it we have had only seven. A friend who has been unwell told me yesterday that he did not dare to take medicine for the first eleven days of the new year as that would mean illness for him for all the months to follow. It may be that the stone fight being cut off before its time may affect the normal course of the year.

But if stone fights be barbarous, surely the gentle art of kite flying fitly represents peace. Within the city enclosure, these days, all eyes are heavenward while the little square kite dances and dodges and cuts capers to the delight of all the people. Two will manoeuvre a whole afternoon sometimes before a string is cut and the contest finished.

Korean kites have no tails and are never made in fantastic shapes, or with whiskery wings like those of China.

The kite is built for great deeds, not for "look-see," a little square homely specimen he is, but his feats are marvellous, and quite beyond my power to describe.

Yesterday morning as I passed "Great Peace Gate," guards, police, soldiers, civilians, gentry and coolies all alike were facing North Mountain, gazing excitedly at two kites that were having a tournament in the blue sky. Children, even the little girls, were transfixed with interest over the contest. Surely it is one of the prettiest national customs that exists to-day.

It requires skill to fly them too, for every motion intended must be telegraphed along the string to the kite as quick as thought can fly.

I once undertook to show a lad how we flew our kites, but before I could think to gather my wits the thing had taken a wild header straight for the earth. The Korean boy laughed and said all that was wrong with my kite flying was that I didn't know how.

(Feb. 26th, 1901 Seoul)

Standing for One's Rights

Like many social commentators of his day, Gale often compared his area of interest, Korea, with other countries of the world on a teleological continuum of civilization and enlightenment, with the Christian West as the unquestioned pinnacle of progress. The international stage was for Gale a competition among races, and while Gale argues that the Korean race had inherited many negative traits from generations of ancestors, a people were not irredeemable and could be improved and enlightened through right teaching and guidance. Gale's Social Darwinist views are evidenced by his response to an 8 October 1904 article in the *Outlook* by George Kennan, titled "The Land of the Morning Calm." In this article, Kennan, an American explorer and special correspondent, provides an extremely negative description of the Korean cities he visits. One representative example of Kennan's assessment, and the passage which Gale is presumably responding to, is as follows:

> To one who comes fresh from the perfect order and immaculate neatness of Japan, the choked drains, the rotting garbage, the stinking ponds, the general disorder, and the almost universal filthiness of Korea are not only surprising and disgusting, but absolutely shocking. Tourists who visit China speak of the smells in certain parts of Canton as the worst in the East; but Canton is clean and sweet in comparison with Chemulpo [Inch'ŏn], Seoul, Chi[n]nampo, or Pingyang [P'yŏngyang].[1]

---

1 George Kennan, "The Land of the Morning Calm," *Outlook* 78, 8 October 1904, 366.

Kennan followed up with a series of three articles appearing in the October and November editions of the *Outlook*, presenting his assessments of the Korean government and emperor, the Korean people, and Japan's task in Korea, respectively. Taken together, Kennan's accounts are arguably the most devastating assessment of the country ever penned, relentlessly negative in tone and overwhelmingly pessimistic as to the potential for Korean "revival."[2] Roughly coinciding with the Russo-Japanese War and the Ŭlsa Protectorate Treaty of November of 1905, many writings on Korea appeared in the American media, most of them supportive of Japan's efforts to "civilize the barbarian Koreans," reflecting the largely positive view in the United States toward Japanese influence in Korea.[3] There were of course dissenting views as well, represented most vociferously by the American missionary and pro-independence activist Homer Hulbert. Gale himself seemed to fall somewhere in the middle, appreciating more than most Western observers the rich historical and literary traditions of the country, while criticizing its outdated customs and dangerous superstitions and acknowledging the inevitability of Japanese-led reform.

Kennan's articles are laced with direct quotes from Gale, who must have known what the tone and content of these articles would be upon

---

2 George Kennan, "Korea: A Degenerate State," *Outlook* 81, 7 October 1905, 307–15; Kennan, "The Korean People: The Product of a Decayed Civilization," *Outlook*, 21 October 1905, 409–16; Kennan, "The Japanese in Korea," *Outlook*, 11 November 1905, 609–15. The *Outlook* was published in New York and ran from 1870 to 1935. Daniel Metraux reminds us that along with the *Nation* and the *Independent*, the *Outlook* was one of the most widely read and influential periodicals of its time, counting among its distinguished writers and editors Booker T. Washington and Theodore Roosevelt. Thus, Kennan's views would have been highly influential at a time when relatively little was known of the "Hermit Kingdom." See Metraux, "How Western Reporters Chronicled the Japanese Seizure of Korea."

3 Kennan alluded to American public opinion on the matter when he wrote, "The impression prevails in America that Korea has a real civilization, but that it has been arrested in process of development, and has come to a state of stagnation like that which we observe in China." This perception, of course, led to the logical conclusion that a country like Japan should intervene to stimulate enlightenment. Kennan, "Korea: A Degenerate State," *Outlook* 81, 7 October 1905, 307–8; See also Metraux, "How Western Reporters Chronicled the Japanese Seizure of Korea," for contemporary Western accounts of Japan's growing influence in Korea.

publication. Gale's opinions are in fact some of the very few positive assessments to appear in Kennan's writing. Despite Gale's "defence of home and fireside," it is telling that of all the vicious attacks launched by Kennan, what Gale takes issue with is not any of Kennan's arguments about the degradation of the Korean race and culture, or the sanitary level of Korea per se, but only its comparison with the worst of China. In light of his years of positive descriptions of his adopted homeland and his deep knowledge and respect of its culture, Gale's half-hearted "defence" strikes the reader as somewhat of a betrayal. Perhaps Gale, too, naively viewed Japanese encroachment as magnanimous and ultimately necessary, though this was a view that was increasingly challenged with the tightening of Japan's grip and eventually abandoned in the face of the violent response to the March First Movement.

Standing for One's Rights
Pen Pictures, 46–8;
"Standing by Her Rights," *Old Corea*, 118–19

Mr. George Kennan, the famous American correspondent, in a recent article in *The Outlook* gives Seoul a very black eye by saying that it is dirtier, filthier, and more unsavoury than any town in China, not excepting Chefoo[4] or Canton. Now Seoul is surely bad enough, but this is putting it just a little too strong. We have not seen Canton, but in a comparison with Chefoo we take issue and maintain that Seoul is a clean and well-swept summer garden compared with the native quarter of that seaport.[5] Lest some may question this, we shall prove it beyond all possibility of argument so that even Chefoo people will acknowledge it and say "Most true!"

Not long ago there came to the Far East the agent of a famous locomotive works, who spent some days in Seoul, testing the flavours, enjoying the lay of the landscape, and keeping his eye open as to the possibilities of railways, etc. The agent of a locomotive works we naturally picture as a large man, well put together, with steady eye, good

---

4 Chefoo is the previous name of today's Yantai (烟台), a prefecture-level city on the northeastern coast of Shandong Province.

5 In the *OC* version Gale adds here, "which is a terrible composite of conditions indescribable."

lungs and stomach of brass or other durable material, a man by no means easily knocked off his feet, or daunted by unsavoury sights or questionable odours.

This agent after surviving Seoul sailed for Chefoo. He lodged at the "Beach Hotel," and in the morning after breakfast went out with a friend to see the town. Here was the Consular Hill with the murmur of the sea – charming; there the clean streets of the Foreign Settlement – most praiseworthy; and now he would see the native town and acquaint himself a little with the abodes of the Celestials. They moved on southwest by west, step by step, till every trace of the Occident disappeared. This was what might be called China Proper. The general flavour of the atmosphere was new to him and most extraordinary – such odours as the agent had never before encountered. The surroundings too, were in keeping with the atmosphere. Against every post and corner leaned some wretched creature trying to hold on to the few remnants of its existence, and withal struggling for force enough to draw a last breath. Female Chinese with faces of warlocks were cooking red messes that might have been Esau's pottage but for the absence of the sweet fragrance of the open fields.[6]

In the wake of the agent and his friend shuffled along a multitude of beggars afflicted with diverse diseases. Horrible remnants reminding one of the text *"sic transit Gloria mundi"*[7] protruded from the public pools – emblems of China's good-luck. Around and over and underneath were the sickening accompaniments of the Celestial [zzz],[8] a whiff of which can sometimes be felt far out at sea when the wind blows hard.

"I say," said the agent to his friend, "this is a corker. I feel my rivets giving way." The continental locomotive works can stand a good deal but not this.

"Wait till I lean up against this post," said he.

He leaned. A sickly hue overspread his countenance, and at last, there, in the presence of four hundred million Chinese, to the fullest extent of his ability, he yielded up the ghost.

---

6 This refers to Esau's sale of his birthright to his brother Jacob for a "mess of pottage" (lentil stew) after coming in from the fields famished (Genesis 25:29–34).

7 A Latin expression meaning "thus passes the glory of the world," emphasizing the transitory nature of life and worldly things.

8 In the *OC* version "kingdom" appears; in *Pen Pictures* "kingdom" has been crossed out and replaced by illegible scrawling.

"Carry me out of this," said he when he had come to life again, "I thought that yonder Korean *sheol* [*sic*][9] was bad enough, but it's a paradise compared to this."

It is sad to have to relate this harrowing tale, but I am compelled to do so in defence of home and fireside. Let not Mr. Kennan touch on this subject again.

My condolences and sympathies are herewith extended to the friends in Chefoo, whose fortune of fate compels them to reside in such a place as China.

Korea wags on much the same. Port Arthur may be in the throes of death but Korea's heart is at peace.[10] Her government may be little better than a bundle of rags and yet also be at peace. She may be infested with a hundred societies clamouring for what they know not, and still the heart reclines in blissful peace. Korea is the most peaceful country on earth.

Illustration 8. "The Attractive City of Seoul," in *Pen Pictures*

---

9 For the older spelling of Seoul as "서울 Syŏul," often romanized in this period as "Syeoul."

10 *OC*: "Corea's heart is at peace! Her government may be little better than a bundle of rags and yet also be at peace."

Nothing can disturb, she is peace at any price. Nickels may go down and rice go up but what has that to do with peace? She may have no prospect of a dinner to-morrow, but still she possesses the gift of peace.

My neighbor across the way has had about seventeen dogs snarling, grinning, yelping round his cornstalk paling for the last forty-eight hours. All the discordant canine notes imaginable have been repeated a million times. I inquired this morning concerning the neighbor and the neighbor's wife, of what they were made – of wood, or mud, or dry bones – that they could tolerate forty-eight hours of such a pandemonium. My words were understood but not my thought. What had these dog-noises to do with the makeup of Mr. and Mrs. Kim? Kim is at peace, I am told. For eighteen hours out of twenty-four his head reposes sweetly on a wooden block, his mouth comfortably open, and his nose ticking off peaceful slumbers, while the confusion of dogs keeps up.

Mrs. Kim, too, is at peace. She has no useless harp-strings in her soul that get all on edge at every noise the Orient throws off. I am struck by the difference between Mrs. Kim, for example, and Thomas Carlyle.[11]

---

11 Thomas Carlyle (1795–1881) was a Scottish philosopher, satirical writer, and historian. According to Ross King, Gale "was an avid reader of Carlyle, and shared his post-Scottish Enlightenment and Romantic proclivities." Ross King, personal communication, 1 November 2018. The Gale Papers, Box 10, Folder 6, "Annual Report 1926–1927" contains a typescript titled "Report of Literary Work, etc. by J.S. Gale (Feb. 5th, 1927)," in which Gale writes of Carlyle, "People who criticize are not always unsympathetic. Carlyle you know was accounted a most unsympathetic character. He slew all the world with his unsparing pen till people said he had not a particle of love for anybody; but when he entered the little room in Wartburg Castle, where, 300 years before, brave Luther had hammered out his Bible, the old Sage of Chelsea stood for a moment tears filling his eyes and then bent reverently down and kissed the time-worn table. A great heart of true appreciation!

"As I have said before the Korean has had a past to be proud of, and an ancestral line that any of us might envy. Centuries of ease and isolation have weakened her will so that if today she is to survive she has a hard fight ahead of her. I often think of Scotland as a model worth Korea's while. What a place Scotland has had in the world's doings, and yet, in land, she is only one-third of Korea, while in population, less than a third. Three things she has however that have made her great: poverty to overcome; hard work to do; and a mind to improve by reading and study. Foolish pride she has none. Stone mason Carlyle, proud of his stonemasonship to the very last, was the envy of the Duke of Buccleuch."

After forty-eight hours of yelpings, snarlings, screamings, she is at perfect peace, and her soul reposes blissfully. Carlyle had had one night of it at the hands of a small dog over the way. Says he: "By five o'clock in the morning I would have given a guinea of gold for its hind legs firm in my right hand by the side of a good stone wall." What a diabolical frame of mind this is compared with Mrs. Kim, who, after forty-eight hours of seventeen dogs, is unmoved.

Korea's peace is extraordinary; all the dogs on earth cannot disturb it. She moves in an atmosphere of peace, walks in it, sleeps in it.[12] She has no anxieties, no worries, nothing to think about, no wolf at the door, no question as to the future. She has arrived at a state of nirvana among the nations, known as "Peace."

One national event of importance is the return of Yi Yongik from Japan.[13] Japanese papers used to poke fun at Yi and call him "His Excellency the Yellow Bull." Whether he comes back now intending to make a smash in Japan's China shop, or whether he is converted to the Sunrise Kingdom and intends to carry Japan's load, remains to be seen. Yi is a shrewd old fellow. He has the gentle accent of Hamgyŏng Province, and also the stomach of a far-north man, and will go his gait unwavering, while the limp and calico-livered gentry of the capital have flopped round a dozen times.

Yi comes by the railroad. What an event this new railway is! "All aboard for Fusan" is heard for the first time in this abode of the ancients.

I would give almost as much as Carlyle would for the small dog, to know what the wrinkled-faced, old countryman really thinks of the huge snaky monster crawling past his door on its way to the capital; crawling sometimes, sometimes again roaring by with fifty different thunders, in the night, too, when all the goblins are abroad.

I ask the young man what the old man thinks of it, and he says he has just one thought, namely *manghaetttan saenggak io*[14] (condemnation).[15]

---

12 *OC:* "sleeps in it, wakes in it."

13 Yi Yongik (李容翊, 1854–1907) was a government minister during the late Chosŏn period, known for being one of the leaders of the pro-Russian faction and vehemently opposing Japanese encroachment in Korean affairs. It was during this same year, in 1905, that Yi founded Posŏng Hakkyo, forerunner of today's Korea University (Koryŏ taehakkyo).

14 "망했단 생각이오" translates roughly as "I think we are ruined."

15 *OC:* "(damnation, or perhaps we had better say condemnation)."

"We were at peace once," says he, "till the crazy foreigner came bringing in his wake all these uncanny beasts,[16] and the last and worst of everything are these eternally racing demons that keep going up and down the land. No escape for me but to get off among the shades and for that I pray daily."
(Mar. 1905)

Illustration 9. "Within the Palace,"in *Pen Pictures*.

____

16 *OC*: "uncanny creations."

That Old Dragon

Dragons have a long and storied tradition in the Sinographic cosmopolis. The mythological progenitor of Chinese and human civilization, Fu Xi (伏羲), possessed a hybrid human and serpent/dragon body, and was credited with the invention of hunting, fishing, and cooking, and the development of sinographic writing some four thousand years ago.[1] Dragon symbolism and iconography were subsequently developed in Korean civilization, where the spiritual powers of dragons were emphasized. The dragon is often depicted with an orb called the *yŏŭi(bo)ju* (如意[寶]珠 Cintamani Stone), which is said to bestow upon the possessor the wisdom of the Buddha. Whereas in the Western tradition the dragon, because of its resemblance to the serpent and the attendant religious associations, has represented evil and destruction, the dragon in Eastern folklore became associated with auspiciousness. Sightings of the dragon were, as Gale notes, a sign that a momentous occurrence was on the horizon.

---

1 Fu Xi (伏犧) is also credited with inventing, among other things, the trigrams of the *Book of Changes* (易經 Ch. *Yijing*) after observing patterns in the heavens and on living creatures. According to Bruce Rusk, writing on the *Appended Verbalizations* (*Xici zhuan* 繫辭傳, also known as the "Great Commentary"), one of the Ten Wings of the *Change Classic* attributed to Confucius, "Fu Xi got the idea for knotted ropes and nets from the trigrams, and such ropes were used for record-keeping until society grew more complex and later sages replaced them with true writing. By the late Warring States period, the inventor of writing had been identified as Cang Jie 倉頡, court historian under the legendary Yellow Emperor." See Rusk, "Old Scripts, New Actors."

This chapter was written on 9 May 1904, only three months after the outbreak of the Russo-Japanese War, a prime example of just such an event that would invoke "Yong the Dragon." Although at first glance an insignificant account of mistaken identity, allegorically it concerns the war over Korea's future. Korean observers, aware of the cataclysmic times in which they live, claim sightings of a dragon and are unable to contemplate any alternative explanations for what they perceive, their visions being dictated by tradition and superstition. The calculating, rational Japanese, with technology in hand, dispel such superstitions and lead their reluctant Korean charges purposefully forward toward enlightenment.

That Old Dragon
Pen Pictures, 48

St. George did away with the dragon in Europe, but he still lives in the Far East, on Japanese coins, called *ryō*,[2] on the Chinese flag, called *long*;[3] and in the heart of the Korean, called *yong*.[4] He is head of all intellectual and spiritual being, he figures in the *Book of Changes*, the profoundest classic of the Far East, and rides about on the clouds. He is seen far out at sea where water-sprouts whirl and caper; he crawls down over the plain underneath the mountain spurs. At one place in Seoul near the East Gate, the ridge of the hill is paved with heavy blocks of stone, for it is Yong's back [zzz] to protect and the pavement is to keep passers from tickling his spine. He is dreadfully fearsome, and is pictured with huge goggle eyes, pointed claws, whisking tail, and armor-plated scales. In Korea he has long been feared and worshipped. He appears only at great epochs in the history of man, at a crisis such as the present time when the Far East has changed from the quiet of Confucius into a camp of the God of War. At such a time as this there are sure to be appearances of the Dragon. People have been on the look-out for him these days till at last they discovered him.

---

2 The *ryō* (両; K. *ryang*) was a unit of gold currency based on the Chinese *tael*, in use in Japan from the Kamakura Period (1185–1333) until its conversion to the modern yen system following the Meiji Restoration in 1868.

3 The flag of the Qing Empire (1644–1912) featured a blue dragon on a yellow background.

4 龍.

A house in the west part of Seoul, that had an old rusty creaking tree in the courtyard, had been sold to a Japanese. A Korean family was left in care of it till the Japanese should move in. One morning they looked out on the world and the tree as they had done a hundred times before, but this morning something was different, for there, looking out of an opening in the hollow trunk was a – who would think it? – yes, no mistake this time, there was the face, and there the eyes of Yong the Dragon. This too, was in accord with tradition, Yong frequenting pools, and mountain streams, and old trees.

Some friends were called in and all agreed that it was a dragon. They bowed in fear before it. Rice was brought and sacrifice offered, but the head had withdrawn itself and there was only the mysterious opening, and the memory of that uncanny face.

Word went flying everywhere. A dragon had been seen looking out of the tree in so and so's yard. Hundreds of people came to "look-see."

"Yes," said they, "these are momentous days, and such a visitation is not to be wondered at."

There were tables of food offered and a prayer said:

"Oh, Dragon King, we are here to pray: guard us from catastrophe this year, and watch over winds, and clouds, and rivers, and keep things steady."

They bowed with their faces to the ground, most devout and reverent, for Yong the Dragon was in the tree.

News of it reached the Japanese owner and he found his yard full of worshippers.

"Listen," said the caretaker, "there is a dragon in the tree; everybody has seen his head, and the people are now worshipping."

The Japanese left and came back with a countryman or two, who had a pair of field-glasses, iron spikes and a hammer. They looked and looked at the hole up so high, and then one of the Japanese began driving in spikes. He would climb and find out. The Koreans begged him not to risk it. "It is the dragon," said they, "you will die."

"Nonsense," said the Japanese, "Leave me alone."

Up he went, step by step, till at last with a boldness that paralysed the on-looking Koreans, his hand went in after the dragon. There was a scrimmage and a flutter and out flew an *olppaemi* – not a dragon but an owl. The wretched beast was in the tree and it was not a dragon at all. With disgust the rice tables were removed and the worshippers went home. The poor Koreans' mighty dragon had turned out an owl.

(Seoul May 9th 1904)

Happy Yi

In "Happy Yi," Gale recounts people and events from his time in the eastern port city of Wŏnsan, a period of his life (1892–7) in Korea that he always recalled fondly, despite the hardships of "frontier" life. Richard Rutt describes a rather isolated, pastoral existence in Wŏnsan, where Gale, his new wife Harriet (Hattie) Heron, widow of the late Dr John Heron (1856–90), and her two daughters contended with an extreme climate, diseases, and prowling tigers.[1] During this pivotal period in Wŏnsan, Gale contributed two of the most lasting legacies to Korean language and literature. First, he completed the Korean translation of *The Pilgrim's Progress* (*T'yŏllo ryŏktyŏng/Ch'ŏllo yŏkchŏng* 天路歷程, 1895), the first Korean translation of an English literary work, completed with the help of his "pundit" Yi Ch'angjik and his wife, Harriet.[2] Second, Gale worked constantly on his *Korean-English Dictionary* (*Han-Yŏng chajŏn*, 1897), which was the first comprehensive work of modern Korean-English lexicography in Korea. A massive and unprecedented work of over thirty-five thousand entries, it remained the standard bilingual dictionary for half a century. Gale also made inroads in proselytization, establishing a modest mission in Wŏnsan, but by far his most

---

1 Rutt, *James Scarth Gale and His "History,"* 22–31.

2 Harriet Heron had begun the translation of Part 1 of *Pilgrim's Progress* during her widowhood, and Gale completed the work with Yi's assistance. Rutt accords considerable credit to Hattie for not only the inspiration to translate the work but also ongoing editorial decisions, claiming that Gale, "when writing with her assistance … produced better work than he did after her death." See Rutt, *James Scarth Gale and His "History,"* 27.

significant contribution during this period was to Korea's literary and lexicographical legacy.[3]

At a Christmas party at the home of the Gales in 1892 attended by the small missionary community and Korean Christian converts, gifts of Bibles, towels, and soap were given to Korean patrons, although whether one patron did proceed to consume the soap as related in this account is uncertain. Gale's anecdote concerning the "sackcloth hat" (*paengnip* 白笠), or white mourner's hat, parallels an episode that is well known from his days as principal of the Intermediate Christian School (Yesugyo chunghakkyo), later renamed the John D. Wells Training School for Christian Workers (Kyŏngsin hakkyo 儆新學校).[4] Whereas Gale's account in "Happy Yi" seems to give the bereaved more agency in deciding to doff the mourner's hat, the account from Kyŏngsin hakkyo in 1904 positions Gale as a more active force in dispelling this custom, which he reportedly disdained.[5] At any rate, this latter episode occurred well after the penning of "Happy Yi" (1901), suggesting his ongoing efforts to dispel what he considered to be outdated superstitions.

Happy Yi[6]
Pen Pictures, 49–52;
"Happy Ye," *Korea Mission Field* 2,
no. 5 (1906): 97–100

Ever-Plenty is the name of a little village in the north land of Korea, tucked in behind the hills, unnoticed from the roadway, hidden from the greedy eye of the passing official – a group of thatched huts asleep,

---

3　The dictionary was published in Yokohama, Japan, during Gale's fifteen-month stay in the country (December 1895–March 1897) and funded by the Northern and Southern Presbyterian Missions to the tune of 1,200 yen. See ibid., 29. Gale did not return to Wŏnsan until 1898, to oversee the sale of his house to the Canadian mission, and this bittersweet return seems to be the episode related in "Happy Yi."

4　This school exists today as Kyŏngsin Middle and High School in Hyehwa-dong, Seoul. See ibid., 36. Korean historical sources usually credit Horace Grant Underwood (1859–1916) with founding the school, but Gale in his papers treats the school as his own.

5　Ibid., 38.

6　This essay was also published in 1901 as an independent pamphlet of twelve pages by the Methodist Publishing House with the title *From Korea: Happy Ye* [*sic*].

so quiet and still and lifeless seen from the top of the Long Snake Mountain. In the centre of the village there is a house facing south in which lived Yi Sunwha, a man famous for drinking and riot and gambling. His son once came and said: "Father, our home is damned."

"Our home is what?" asked the father, and he took his son by the topknot and tugged and beat him, till the village whispered:

"There's a big affair on at Yi Sunwha's."

Many days went by while an old woman of seventy looked out from her darkened soul into a world that a lost son haunted. But she was a Korean woman, and had learned to know that she herself was born lost, would live lost, and die lost. It was not for her to speak, or hope, or pray.

Into this village came the news that one Jesus of Nazareth, born somewhere, Son of God, was moving among men. People had gone crazy about Him, and had cut themselves off from the ancient customs of their country. Two or three from the village of Ever-Plenty had been caught by the "doctrine." There was a celebration at the foreigner's home up on the hill, something was going on about Jesus' birthday, and the "doctrine folk" were invited. A man with one eye from the town of Ever-Plenty was there, decorated with wonderful things. They were divided among those present. He, with one eye, got a Testament, a towel, and a cake of soap. The Testament he would learn to read, the towel he would tie around his head on the hot days in summer and keep his brain cool, but the cake of soap was a mystery. What was it, and what would he do with it? He smelt it, and the smell was good; he ate part of it, but the taste was not equal to the smell. However, thinking that it would improve in flavour, he kept on and finished it on his road home to Ever-Plenty. He told his village friends that foreign food would never suit the taste of a Korean, but that the doctrine was true, every whit, and the taste of it just their own. Thus the rumor spread and the year went by.

In a little mud room eight feet by eight, floored with coarse reed matting, a man slightly gray is on his face, praying for his life.

"Oh, Thou of Nazareth, Son of God, I'm a Korean, Yi Sunwha, child of many devils. I am told you are come to save the lost, which is me. My name is Yi Sunwha, worst among men."

When he told me the story, I marvelled that a Korean could pass through such a wonderful experience.

"I was at the limit of agony," said he, "Mountains-high sin rolled over me. I prayed, but there was no answer. I was forever condemned, too vile and wicked, till one night in the midst of tears, great is God's grace, my agonies went out and peace and joy came in. I have been singing ever since," said he, the spirit of it in his step, and the sunshine in his face.

He had come with his mother, seventy-two years of age, to pay a call.

"You know," said he, "Mother's with me; no more idolatry, praise the Lord!"

Yi used to ride about the country on a small donkey, selling pick and shovel heads at the market fairs. I once rode twenty miles behind him on the way to South Mountain. The picture I still see. Perched high on his saddle bags he guided the wee beastie that told by its long ears the workings of its soul. Its willing nimble feet picked their nimble way over the stony road deftly. I could not but think of that other little donkey, announced by the prophet five hundred years before [Jesus' birth], that carried Him up from Bethany to Jerusalem. How crowned with honor this homeliest beast of burden!

I said, "Yi, how do you get along at the fairs?"

"Oh," says he, "mortal man is queer. If I tell him I am gathering rags, and know a plan to make good clothes out of them, he'll say, 'Fine! Tell us how you do it'; but if I say, 'I am around telling how good men may be made out of poor rags of the street,' he says 'Away with you, we don't want you here,' and out of town he runs me; hallelujah."

I heard Yi preach at South Mountain. He sat on a mat while the crowd pushed into a door space and courtyard, front and rear.

Said he, "Men, I've something to tell you! My name is Yi Sunwha. I was a gambler, a drunkard, a libertine. I was lost altogether till I heard of God, and he forgave me, and cleansed me, and put peace inside my soul, so that the worst man in the town of Ever-Plenty is the happiest man in the world. You know how he did it? Why he sent his son Yesu[7] to earth 1900 years ago to do it. He lived 33 years and did what only God can do. He cured lepers, drove out devils, and raised men dead for days. Then he submitted to a death by torture, nailed through, hands and feet. Do you know why? To answer for my sins, and your sins, and yours and yours. On the third day he came forth from the grave, and he's alive and in heaven now, running the whole world, and he wants you to listen and repent and trust him. He's coming soon to call all the dead to life, and to judge everybody. Do you hear? Trust him and he'll put peace inside your soul. He has done it for me, and it is better than drink, better than money, better than all the world."

"What's he talking about?" Asked a bystander.

"Who knows?" answered one rough-headed fellow.

"He's been eating foreign medicine and is crazy," said another.

---

7 Yesu, Jesus Christ, often accompanied by the honorific suffix ~*nim* (*Yesunim*).

Yi and his friend Chŏn called to see me. They were interested in the great evangelist Moody.[8] I told them about him, and how he gathered

---

8 Dwight Lyman Moody (1837–99) was an American evangelist and publisher who founded Northfield Mount Hermon School, the Moody Bible Institute, and Moody Publishers. Gale Papers, Box 9, Folder 42 is a four-page essay titled "These Fifty Years," dated 30 April 1934 and thus penned in Bath, England, in Gale's retirement; it begins as follows:

"These fifty years began when four noted saints were on the earth: Dwight L. Moody, Hudson Taylor, Frances Ridley Havergal and Fanny Crosby, two and two. Who would not rise and be a missionary at such a call? [his handwritten edits are illegible]

My own touch with these was light and yet nonetheless full of inspirational power. On my eve of departure to the East, Hudson Taylor led me by the hand to his bedside and kneeling down, asked God's blessing on Korea and on the lad bound thither. Such a little man and such a short prayer and yet it marked a moment of life and vision for fifty years.

Mr. Moody was speaking in Vancouver the very night before my ship sailed. Quite unsuspecting and all unexpectedly I was led before him.

"Whither?" He asked.
"Korea! Student volunteer!"
"Capital." Said the voice that thrilled all Anglo Saxondom in those days.
"I'll pray for you." Dwight L. Moody!

In a short article titled "Church, Prison, and School," written in 1904 for the *Korea Mission Field* 11 (1916), 219–21, Gale recounts another anecdote about Moody connected to the conversion of Kim Chŏngsik (citing his "Personal Report of Dr. J.S. Gale, September, 1904"):

"But perhaps the most hopeful part of all has been in the interest taken by a group of men who have passed through deep trial in their political and spiritual experience. A group of some six attend our services regularly. They are not yet baptized but are undoubtedly Christian. They learned of God's love first when they were victims of man's hatred, prisoners in the *Kam-ok-so* (common prison) … One is Yi Wŏn'gŭng, who, under the old regime, was secretary to one of the six Boards … There is also Hong Chagi, a former official, and Mr. Kim Chŏngsik, who was at the head of the police in 1895–1896, a tall handsome Korean, who found relief from the miseries of prison life in one of Mr. Moody's sermons translated into Chinese, and then sent word to have someone go tell his wife the good news."

Shortly before Gale retired from the missionary field in 1927, he co-translated with his trusty "pundit" Yi Wŏnmo and published through the Christian Literature Society, Seoul, *Mudŭi hăengsyul* [*Mudi haengsul*], in some 4 + 237 pages. It has not yet been established which of the many biographies of

in the meeting, and Mr. Moody dressed him[9] down with a stick so that he was converted ever after. But there was no special response, no expression of having understood what I said. An Oriental's understanding is so hidden away in the innermost recesses of his physical being that the words must perforate all sorts of tissue before they reach his soul; his ears are miles away from the region of his comprehension, and words are heard only as words, not as thoughts. Evidently the story of Mr. Moody had not been understood.

Later, I started off for a trip into the country, and asked six friends to accompany me, first and foremost among them Yi Sunwha, but an answer was returned.

"Very sorry, mother ill; must stay by her."

A week later on the way home we heard that in Ever-Plenty a good Christian had died, the mother of Yi Sunwha, aged seventy-three.

"For all thy saints, who from their labours cease," was the refrain that my spirit seemed naturally to take up, till I reached the town and then this was the story: "The whole church is disgraced; it is too serious to speak of; we shall come specially and lay the matter before you. We thought Yi Sunwha a Christian, but little did we know."

Thirteen church members with faces of sackcloth and heads bowed in shame sat silent.

"What has he done? Out with it."

Then Kim began, "Since I imagine the time of Yo and Sun[10] (2300 BC) ..."

I said, "I don't want Yo and Sun; I've heard of them ten thousand times. I want to know what Yi Sunwha has done."

"But," continued Kim "I'll have to begin at the beginning for the teacher to understand."

"Then I must pass on," said I. "Son, can you tell what Yi Sunwha has done?"

Moody already in print by this time was the basis for Gale and Yi's translation. Ross King, personal communication, 1 November 2018.

9　It is unclear to whom Gale is referring by "him."

10　Emperor Yo (堯 Ch. Yao, r. 2356–2255 BC) and Emperor Sun (舜 Ch. Shun, r. 2233–2184 BC) are legendary leaders of ancient China, regarded as two of the great "Five Emperors" (*oje* 五帝) of ancient China. They were renowned for their sage virtue and revered as models of leadership for the unselfishness displayed in forgoing their own sons in selecting worthy successors. When the names were combined in Korean discourse they referred to an era or world view in which sagacity, wisdom, and Confucian morality reigned.

Son began: "Yes, there are Western nations and there are Eastern nations; there are people who wear black clothes and there are those who wear white clothes."

"Next, Kang, can you tell me what Yi Sunwha has done?"

"From the time that he was a boy," says Kang, "he always wanted his own way; he had a mind that did not care what the people said or pleased to do."

"Is that all you have to say, Kang? Then next!"

They looked at each other, as much as to say, "Well, we are gagged, aren't we?" My cook whispered to me, "Yi Sunwha refuses to put on sackcloth for his mother; that's what he's done."

"Is that all? Then, brethren, dry your tears and let's be happy."

"No, no," said they, "this will ruin us. The teacher must make him put on mourning or the church will go to pieces."

I called Yi Sunwha in and made him answer for himself. Said he,

"What have I to do with wearing an eternal hat that hides all the face of heaven, and going round uncombed like a warlock, mumbling 'I have sinned, I am condemned, I've killed my mother! It is all [zzz], every bit of it. My mother has gone home to the happy heaven. I have no cause for sorrow."

The church fathers slunk home, saying to themselves, "We hate him and his notions, but he's right."

The funeral day of Yi's mother came round, and I was down with an attack of grippe unable to attend. I called the leaders, gave them the passage of Scripture to read, and the hymns to sing, told them to be quiet and orderly and make it a day to be remembered.

Late at night a messenger came to see me, in hot haste. There had been a fight at the funeral. Would I call Yi's friend and inquire?

"Chŏn," said I "What's this you have been up to? I can't imagine your fighting."

"It's all right," says Chŏn, "when the teacher hears he'll understand."

"Tell me, then, and don't begin with Yo and Sun, but give me just what happened."

"Then," says Chŏn, "we read and sang, and that man Fish over the way, stood outside the fence and shouted to us all through the service. Said he, "There she goes, wings and all. Give her a lift. Shoo! Send her up to glory. If she falls, catch her on the fly.'

"I concluded he was a man to be dealt with, so after the funeral was over, I cut a stick and went into his house and gave him such a dressing down. I wasn't angry. I did it for his good, and told him he couldn't insult God in that way. He prayed me to let up, and said he'd never do so again. You remember Mr. Moody," concluded Chŏn.

I was absent for a spell from that district, and then went back to the dear old north land, where so many kindly faces waited. The teacher's impatience about Yo and Sun was forgotten, forgiven. A group – it seemed to me a little gentler, a little kindlier – came out to meet me, among them Yi Sunwha. The days flew by all too swiftly, and I was to leave, this time for good. Kim, who once hated Yi because he would not don sackcloth, said, "He is number one good man." Then when we reached the parting of the ways,

"Teacher, I'm so sorry," said Yi, "but we will all come to see you in the Capital and have a jubilee."

"Come," said I, "Stay with me, see the great city, and tell what God [has] done for you."

Yi never came. Outside of Ever-Plenty a foot-path skirts the hills; in and out it winds, until all huts are left, and you are alone among the mountains and the pine. So far off and still, some might pass it by and never see. How sacred a spot. In the thought of it tears come back to me, and memories of him who was redeemed from his lost life. There two little mounds rest side by side, one the grave of Yi Sunwha's mother, and one the grave of Yi Sunwha.

We, too, are both passing pilgrims. Certain it is that when our eyes have been brightened by the beauty of that Land of Promise and we shall look among the groups of those most exultant, we shall find a certain Korean, once a "child of many devils," but by the grace of God gloriously redeemed.

(Written in 1901)

My Lord the Elephant

In December 1895 the Gale family moved from their quiet home in Wŏnsan to the bustling port of Yokohama, Japan, where they remained until March 1897. One of the primary reasons for Gale's trip to Yokohama was to supervise the publishing of his *Han-Yŏng chajŏn* (韓英字典 *Korean-English Dictionary*), representing the first comprehensive work of modern lexicography in Korean and financed, according to Richard Rutt, by a sum of 1,200 yen provided by the Northern and Southern Presbyterians.[1] Yi Ch'angjik (李昌植, 1866–1936), who was one of Gale's full-time literary advisors and worked with him for decades, until Gale's retirement and departure from Korea in 1927, accompanied the Gales to Japan and is the "Yi" who appears in this story. "Chŏng," on the other hand, seems to be Chŏng Tongmyŏng, who served on the Board of Bible Translators from at least 1902 with Gale, William Reynolds, Horace Underwood, George Heber Jones, Mun Kyŏngho, and Kim Myŏngjun. Yi Ch'angjik seems to have replaced Chŏng on the board by 1906.[2] Gale provides a poignant and personalized account of a generation of Korean "gentlemen" who made the often-painful decision to cut their "topknot" (*sangt'u*) to be in accordance with the modern world. Pious Confucians believed the body to be a sacred inheritance bestowed by parents upon their progeny, and thus any sort of bodily damage or alteration, including the cutting of hair, was considered a form of desecration.

---

1 Rutt, *James Scarth Gale and His "History,"* 28–9.

2 I thank Ross King for pointing out the likely identity of "Chŏng." King, personal communication, 1 November 2018.

Although in Gale's account Chŏng and Yi undertake this transformation more or less willingly, when the so-called Hair Cutting Ordinance (斷髮令 Tanbal-lyŏng) was passed as part of the initial phase of Kabo Reforms in 1894, massive revolts engulfed the country, directed mainly at the Japanese, who were seen as overstepping their bounds. Japan's complicity in the assassination of Queen Min in December 1895 added fuel to anti-Japanese sentiment, and the initially mandatory ordinance became optional. In *The New Far East* (1904), the pro-Japanese British author Arthur Diosy wrote the following on the aftermath of the ordinance:

The progressive minority, favouring Japan, cut off their topknots, and became objects of scorn in the eyes of all the other Koreans. The Japanese gradually recognized their mistake in attaching too great importance to a matter of detail. It was, they soon found, the *inside* of Korean skulls that needed reforming far more urgently than the topknots; the obnoxious "Hair-cutting Ordinance" fell into abeyance and went the way of the dragon and the spirit cat. In 1897 the topknot had become entirely optional, and the more advanced thinkers, the young men educated in Japan, or in Korea under foreign guidance, wore their hair in the Western fashion, whilst the great bulk of the nation retained the national distinctive coiffure, or reverted to it in many cases where it had been abandoned under Japanese compulsion. So the topknot flourished once more, and with it the Korean hat.[3]

As Ross King has demonstrated, Gale maintained a cordial, almost familial relationship with his Korean literary informants over the years, not only depending on them heavily for "insider" explanations of Literary Sinitic but also spending a considerable amount of time with them socially, visiting the grave of the literatus Yi Kyubo, travelling to the Diamond Mountains, and of course experiencing the Ueno Zoo in Tokyo, related in the account below.[4] His well-documented and intimate relations with his "pundits" suggest not exploitation or dominance, as in the classical Orientalist trope, but rather a dynamic of cordiality and mutual admiration and respect, and invite the reader to focus on the interpersonal aspects of such a cultural contact zone.

---

3 Diosy, *The New Far East*, 92.

4 See King, "James Scarth Gale, Korean Literature in Hanmun, and Allo-Metropolitan Missionary Orientalism."

My Lord the Elephant
Pen Pictures, 53–4; *Old Corea*, 113–14;
Esson the Third, *North China Daily News* (1896)

My Korean friends Yi and Chŏng were much interested in the Elephant. They had never seen him, but they had heard of his sagacity, his honesty, his gentlemanliness.[5] These virtues, coupled with his enormous size, greatly impressed them, for they, like all Koreans, are hero-worshippers, and one of the requisites of their hero is that he be big. Littleness they despise. A diminutive Westerner they pity. Insult from such as he they reckon as unworthy of notice. But the Elephant, *k'okkiri* (Long-noser) – think of him! Twelve feet high, twelve feet long, tipping the scales at 8000 pounds, living, like the gods, hundreds of years, lord of beasts, mightiest of the mighty! Certainly he belonged to a class to be worshipped; the rumor of him alone was enough to inspire enlightened men with reverence. They did homage afar off, hoping some day that they might set eyes upon him.

Fortune had shuffled us across the sea; Yi, Chŏng, and I were in the picturesque harbour city of Yokohama, where everything was wonderful, undreamed of, indescribable. Up to this date these two Koreans had lived unconscious of the world they moved in;[6] they did not even realize that they themselves wore gauze hats, white suits, and quilted trousers; now for the first time this fact, too, dawned upon them. Chŏng had been accustomed to a measure of respect at home, being a gentleman, no less, and therefore entitled to deference when he walked abroad.[7] He had power, too, to put uncivil loafers under the paddle if need be. Behold him now in Yokohama, the butt of all the world, man, woman, and child pointing, poking, jeering.

"The wretches have no manners," said he, and his desire was to leave at once, but this being impossible, with many tears and with much trembling at the thought of his ancestors, he had his top-knot cut off and his person dressed out in Western clothes. I taught him how to arrange his tie and fix his cuffs, and a neater, more respectable man was not to be seen on the streets of Yokohama. Yi followed after. The same boys who

---

5 *OC* version: "gentleness."

6 *OC*: "of the world they breathed in."

7 This is the older meaning of "abroad," meaning here "around," "outside," or "in public," rather than in a foreign country (i.e., Japan).

had pointed sticks at the padded trousers yesterday, took off their hats to-day as he went by. Chŏng had died of sheer mortification but had come to life again. His spirit revived and he began to take an interest in the world. Did I not tell him once that there was an elephant in Tokyo? Sure enough, we shall pay a visit to the Zoo and see His Excellency.

With clean linen, and a fresh suit in the crisp morning air, what could have been more hopeful than our arrival in the capital? We took rickshaws[8] and raced across the city. The desperate speed of these *kuruma* men impressed Chŏng and Yi with the importance of our visit, and enlarged their capacity of expectation. Under the grateful shade of the everlasting pines we paid our fares and passed in. There were echoes of whistles, and calls, and pipings, fierce snarls, and snappings – we were in the zoo. Here was a tiger behind the bars, whose conscience gave him no peace; backwards and forwards he went, flinging his head and swinging his lank, restless body. There was a leopard with a face like a fiend, his ears lying flat, his teeth shining, and his eyes glaring like a demon's.

The Koreans enjoyed this opportunity to inspect their ancient marauding enemies.

"They are vulgar brutes," said Chŏng, "and have a very disagreeable odor." Then he asked, "Where is the elephant?"

Just then a "h-u-r-r-u-mp" warned us of his presence. We looked through the bars and there chained by the legs was "Long-noser," read of, dreamed of, thought of, seen now for the first time. He needed a bath, but never mind that. His eyes were not large enough to provide any view of his soul, but he kept up a see-saw motion with his body, much as the Oriental does when he is studying the Chinese written character. This no doubt indicated his scholarly and gentlemanly predispositions.[9] His trunk, meanwhile, found amusement in picking up pebbles and rapping them against the bars. At times he would vary his quiet line of thought by saying, "h-r-r-u-m-p," meaning, I suppose, "I see through it." The Koreans read into his unvarnished exterior their ideal elephant, his sagacity, his honesty, his truthfulness.[10]

We continued our round and saw the bear, who bowed, and bowed, and bowed. "*Kom kach'i miryŏn hao*," said Chŏng (stupid as a bear). There were snakes, and camels, and badgers, all in need of a bath and a

---

8 "Rickshaw" is a corruption of the Japanese neologism for the device *jinrikisha* (人力車), meaning literally "man-powered cart."

9 *OC*: "gentlemanly attainments."

10 *OC*: "his gentlemanliness."

sprinkling of rose-water. Before leaving we concluded to just once more pay a final, a sort of official, call on the elephant when an unbroken row of spectators were enjoying him along the front. We had difficulty in finding a place, till two Japanese stepped out from a corner and Yi and Chŏng moved in. The elephant was still playing see-saw and appeared deep in meditation. His trunk wandered round aimlessly, doing as it pleased, lifting itself up in the air, swinging round and playing all sorts of pranks, most interesting. At last his lordship gave a yawn, and a "h-r-r-u-m-p" and opened his eyes; suddenly his nose pointed out the two Koreans definitely, as much as to say, "How d'e do, gentlemen! Welcome to Japan." The Koreans were just on the point of showing their appreciation for this mark of honor[11] when suddenly he unloaded upon them a deluge of water, with a force something enormous. For the host in Korea[12] to forget his duty of hospitality, and turn insult upon his guests is the blackest crime possible. I am unable to describe the expression of speechless horror that the faces of these two Koreans wore, as they appealed to me.

"By what law under heaven," says Chŏng, "is a man to be expectorated upon in this fashion?"

When a Korean is outraged he fixes a steady glare upon his antagonist, and holds him with it one, two, or three minutes, not saying a word. Yi was trying this upon the elephant, making muttering attempts at oaths in Japanese. Meanwhile his lordship had returned to his meditative state, his eyes half shut, and his body going see-saw.

"If the disgusting brute had only used clean water," said Chŏng, looking in a nauseated way at his coat sleeve.

We found a stream of water not far off, and did our best to wash away all remembrance of my lord the elephant. His name is no longer mentioned in our society.[13]

---

11 OC: "The Coreans were just on the point of appreciating this mark of
    distinction."
12 OC: "For the host in the East."
13 OC: "in our midst."

The Displeasure of the Rain God

"The Displeasure of the Rain God" captures the mood of uncertainty on the Korean peninsula at the outset of the twentieth century. The opening account itself may be read as an allegory for Korea's future, the various responses as to the possibility of rain reflecting the diversity of opinions as to Korea's political prospects. A rather rambling account, "Displeasure" touches on issues of famine, superstition, dragon iconography, and cannibalism, but employs the unifying theme of uncertainty and, in a more religious context, Eastern and Western modes of faith. In characteristic tenor, "Displeasure" is obliquely critical of Korean "superstitions" but not dismissively so, nor in a manner ignorant of the sincere beliefs that undergird them. In his typical style, blending anecdotes with a popular historian's approach to scholarship that often concealed the actual depth of research involved, Gale's accounts of Korean beliefs here and elsewhere are well informed and reasonably sympathetic, despite his largely unspoken assurance of Western reason and logic. It is significant that the "Rain God" to whom Gale refers is none other than *Hananim*, his preferred term for the Christian God as predetermined (he would claim) in indigenous Korean tradition, and so his sympathetic depiction of Korean behaviour in their sincere hopes for rain is itself an acknowledgment of the partial validity of such "prayer," though lacking the ultimate knowledge of God's true nature.

The Displeasure of the Rain God
Pen Pictures, 55–6

On one of the days in early August, when all hopes of rain were at the breaking point, I started out for a trip over the hills. The wind was from the east, the sky red and lowering, and all signs said rain, rain; tree toads and birds took up the chorus. I decided to ask passers along the way what their opinion was regarding the weather. An old man with a load of wood on his back came toward me, step by step.

"Say, father, is it going to rain?" I inquired.

"Well, yes, friend, it seems to me it will rain today; what's your name and where are you going?"

Half a mile further on, I asked a young fellow leading a cow:

"Are we in for rain?"

His answer was: "Who knows what God (*Hananim*) intends?[1] Don't ask me!"

Later on I saw a respectable-looking pedestrian and inquired of him:

"Will it rain?"

"No sign of rain whatever."

Again I encountered a farmer and ventured:

"Will it rain?

"Rain? What are you talking about? What is rain?" and he moved away.

Thus Korea has passed the summer, all weather signals having failed. Great threatening clouds counted to nothing, and morning skies, red as painted thunder, would fade away and the hot fierce sun come out and blaze till the rice fields caked hard and the gasping, panting earth at last, with the seeds and hopes of harvest in its bosom, lay down to die. All means were resorted to to capture, cajole, or win the wilful heavens. The altar in the west part of the city, named *Sajik*, was called into requisition. It stands for abundant harvests. There are two stone elevations in it, twenty-four feet square, three feet high, and eight feet apart; one to the east and one to the west; this for the Heavens and that for the Earth. Here sacrifice of raw meat and half cooked grain was offered; sheep, cattle, and goats were slaughtered, and heaped up to please the Rain God and the Spirit of the Earth, but no answer. Some hold that *Hananim*, Chief of spirits, gives rain; others again say that the Dragon gives it. It would seem that ancient belief ascribes it to *Hananim*, but another belief borrowed from the *Book of Changes* and China says it is the Dragon. There are many so-called dragon-pools throughout the country, deep wells of water in which this monster is said to hide. He goes up on rare occasions and then rain falls abundantly. In many cases, this summer, refuse and blood were thrown into the pools to defile his lair, in the

---

1 For a discussion of the origins and meaning of the name *Hananim*, see Baker, "Hananim, Hanŭnim, Hanŭllim, and Hanŏllim"; "Korea's Preparation for the Bible," *Pen Pictures*, this vol.

hope that he would call down rain and go in for house-cleaning, but the Dragon seems dead and *Hananim* or God to have forgotten.

A poor old Korean who had not seen the like for sixty years remarked, "We have many sins to answer for and God does not give us rain."

For a people who live so universally from hand to mouth, the situation is grave, indeed, and the prospects most ominous.

The Korean is a fatalist and mourns not over what befalls him. His Eight Characters,[2] his Stars, his Lucky Days, have decided these matters eternities ago, and so there is no use of worrying.

"Chugimyŏn chukko, salmyŏn salji"[3] (If I live I live, if I die I die) is what he says.

Sixty-one years ago there was a great famine. Stories are still told of the suffering in the year *kyŏngja* (1840).[4] In their desperate need, people fed on the bodies of the dead. My friend Ko tells me that his father witnessed this frequently. Koreans have never been cannibals, even in their darkest days, and they view South Sea Islanders as savages unspeakable. There are only two cases, to my knowledge, in which they use human flesh; one as a medicine for leprosy or ague, the other as a toothsome morsel in triumph over a hated enemy, when they dig out his liver and chew it.

In this fatal year *kyŏngja*, there was a great catch of herrings, and the people gorged themselves on them and died. We are told, too, that the Governor of P'yŏngyang, Kim Namsŏn, had his face read by a fortune-teller.

"You shall become Prime Minister," said the wizard, "but not until you have killed a thousand men."

The Governor sat long in thought, "Oh, to be first in the land!" Men were dying about him daily of famine, but it failed to count in his favour. At last, with more than ordinary intelligence in the matter of cause and effect, he laid his plans. The following day huge kettles of

---

2	The "Eight Characters" refers to *p'alcha* (八字), the eight sinographs that correspond to the year, month, day, and time of a person's birth (two characters each) which in Sinitic cultures supposedly determine a person's fate. The word *p'alcha* can also be used more generally as a stand-in for the idea of fate or one's lot.

3	Standard Korean should actually read *chugŭmyŏn* (If I die …), not *chugimyŏn*, as Gale has written, which is likely meant to render a regional accent.

4	This is the year *kyŏngja* (庚子) according to the Chinese sexagenary cycle, where each year is assigned a combination of two charcters, one each from a group of ten "heavenly stems" (天干) and a set of twelve "earthly branches" (地支), and where sixty years represents a complete cycle.

rice and meat stew were run out from his *yamen* into the street, and a proclamation read:

"The Governor loves his people so that he shares his best with them and [zzz]. Eat, eat, eat!"

They ate, and there died a thousand men.

Last year was *kyŏngja* again, and according to the revolving cycle we should have had famine. Its coming a year later may betoken additional severity, so some think.

It is dangerous to one's reputation to forecast events in the Far East. The law of cause and effect works on a different [zzz] from that at home. Naturally we would say that a large part of Korea would starve next year; but who knows? It may turn out the happiest year in their history. Yesterday morning one of my writers came, and with a broad smile that was intended to move me and win all sorts of favors, said:

"I've been troubled with 'wind' in my knees, wrists and feet now for three years, and have suffered various and sundry agonies; I have eaten bottles of foreign medicine[5] and am tired of it. I want to go off for four days to cure this confounded complaint once and for all."

"Have you a cure for it?" I asked.

"Of course," says he, "That's why I ask off."

"Where did you learn of the cure?"

"From Kŭnbae."

Now this Kŭnbae was an ignoramus from some outlandish place up north, as his accent bespoke.

"But what does Kŭnbae know about it, pray?"

"Oh, he has cured lots of people."

"How does he go about it?"

"By mixing this, and this, and this, mercury and red lead, and rabbits' teeth and cat-feelers, etc., burning them, and you inhale the smoke."

I inquired as to the law governing it.

Said he, "People who inhale get well as to knees and feet, and that's all the law I want to know."

He had the best of it, and now he is at home engaged in the delightful exercise of inhaling this miscellany of smell. If he comes out all right I shall bow to him; if he is not cured I shall expect him to bow to me.

(Seoul Aug. 30th, 1901)

---

5 Here Gale is attempting to approximate Korean speech, as the same verb, *mŏkta* (to eat), is used with both food and medicine in Korean.

Korean New Year's

In "Korean New Year's," Gale relates the traditional practice of *sebae* (歲拜) or "bow of respect," a deep bow or *k'ŭn chŏl* that is performed by younger Koreans before their elders on Korean Lunar New Year's Day (Sŏllal). Following the bow, elders present younger members of the family with money, which is called *sebaetton*. The lunisolar calendar, originating in China some three thousand years ago, was used in Korea throughout its recorded history until 1 January 1896 (of the Western calendar), when the Chosŏn government officially adopted the Gregorian calendar as part of the Kabo Reforms package.[1] Despite the official proclamation, as Gale notes, the general public continued to live according to the rhythms of the ancient lunar calendar.

Today, Korea's major holidays, including Sŏllal and Ch'usŏk (秋夕 Harvest Festival), remain bound to the traditional calendar. Older generations tend to observe their lunar birthdays and ignore their solar, while younger Koreans tend to vary depending on personal preference. Although the solar calendar eventually gained sway, Korea's history of numbering years is more complicated. Following the promulgation of the new calendar in 1896, Korea continued to number years according to the traditional system of royal reigns, until annexation in 1910 forced compliance with the imperial Japanese system. Under the auspices of the staunchly nationalist Republic of Korea government from 1948, years were counted from the legendary reign of the Korean progenitor Tan'gun (2333 BC), up until 1 January

---

1 Meiji Japan adopted the Western calendar in 1873, while China followed suit only after the collapse of the Qing dynasty in 1911.

1962, when the year count was officially shifted to the Western system beginning with AD 1.[2]

"Korean New Year's" dates from February 1901, shortly after Gale began teaching at the Chŏngsin Girls' School located in Yŏnmotkol, Seoul; he would continue work as an educator until 1910. Gale's cynical views on traditional Korean education reflect the general consensus of foreign educators in Korea: excessively narrow, stifling, and a poor fit for the modern world. However, unlike most of his colleagues, Gale did not view Literary Sinitic as a useless remnant of the past, and in fact invested in its maintenance with the publication of his own four-volume textbook *Yumong ch'ŏnja* (牖蒙千字 Korean Readers). The first three volumes consisted of highly-sinicized *kukhanmun* orthography, while the final volume, written entirely in Literary Sinitic, was a collection of select passages from Korean writers. In the following account, Gale's ruminations on the brightness and potential of Korean youth, coupled with the absence or inadequacy of a Korean (or Western) alternative, once again suggest a sense of ambivalence as to the future of the country. While the system was in need of reform, the Sinitic literary world still offered something of enduring value. The question was how to reconcile Eastern form and Western function.

Korean New Year's
(Feb.1901)
Pen Pictures, 57–8; *Old Corea*, 115

What could be prettier than the child world of Korea at New Year's season? Along through the laboured months that precede children are quite unnoticed, being obedient, respectful almost without exception, and content with what they have in their narrow world.[3] This world[4] is sparing of everything but rice, but not of that, for the little lad eats until his very soul twangs with distension. Then he sleeps it off with the dignity of a grown up, and goes quietly about his affairs in the most orderly way possible. He very seldom shares in boisterous games or makes any unseemly uproar. Western children are savages in comparison.

---

2 Lankov, *The Dawn of Modern Korea*, 63–5.
3 *OC*: "little world."
4 *OC*: "Corea."

The child world of Korea has many attractions. For the little mite that he is, one wonders where he has ever learned all the mystic forms of ceremony that are necessary for his conduct in the presence of seniors. He is quick to hear and slow to speak, ready with his eyes and ears, and modest with his tongue. Those black eyes of his tilted at the outer corners, fairly drink you in with unyielding gaze, until he knows your visible peculiarities, and can discuss them with special friends in a way that you would like to hear.[5] What is there he cannot learn? Give him a chance and this little lad will make his way with honors.[6] But there is no one to have mercy on his little soul, or to fit him out with chart and guide, for the ocean that he is launched upon. Schools worthy of the name there are none for him; he grows up to be an incapable, and when he has lost all the natural graces and gifts that he was born with, he demands that he be appointed officer to rule the land.

To-day they throng the main streets,[7] these fairy children, dressed in scarlet, yellow, spring green, and sky-blue. What a pretty picture with their gold embroidered hair-bands, ermine tipped head-gear, silk coats layer upon layer, colour upon colour, flying and fluttering in the sunshine and the breeze, making the Land of Morning Freshness fresher and more picturesque than ever. It is Korean New Year's; the Government follows the Western calendar but not the people. The people hold to this their own special season and all the children are out making their calls and bowing.

Two little dots aged 5 and 7, whose respective papas I know, came to call on me. Such perfect circles of girls[8] were never seen before, jackets shimmering in Chinese yellow, and heads oiled and combed till they shone like blackest satin.[9] Their skirts of dazzling red stood out all round, full from the arm-pits where the little waists belong. On

---

5 *OC*: "you would be amazed to hear."

6 The remaining sentences in this paragraph are absent from the *OC* version. Perhaps Gale's recent experiences as a teacher had prompted his ruminations on the state of early education in Korea, whereas by the 1920s these sentiments had subsided somewhat. At any rate, their inclusion here seems somewhat tangential.

7 *OC*: "On New Year's Day they throng the streets."

8 *OC*: "Such perfect orioles of colour."

9 In the *OC* version, "blackest satin" has been crossed out and "balls of jet" pencilled in.

entering, the younger of the two who was my special friend, in a great hurry to do her little part, piped[10] out their greeting.

"Dear me, I'm delighted," said I, "this is a most unexpected honor to have two such nice young ladies call on me."

The little faces were properly powdered, and the outfit so perfectly in keeping, that I turned them round and round to see, and then pronounced them immaculate. A nickel was accepted for each[11] embroidered pocket, and something to eat was wrapped away in the little kerchief.

All was now ready for departure but still they did not go. A cloud suddenly passed over the face of the younger and I saw her nudge her companion, who made no response. Then she leaned over and whispered in her ear, "We must *kow-tow* or make a courtesy,[12] you know."

I overheard what was said and knowing what a world of courage it takes to have a little girl go through such a formal exercise, I said: "Oh, never mind, your call is perfect without the bowing. Tell your mama and papa that I said it was all right without," and like two birds set free away they went.

They forgot even to say "Peace," but of course little girls forget so easily. A few minutes later footsteps were heard approaching, little footsteps, and I naturally thought, "More ladies." The door opened cautiously, without any announcement, and only just wide enough to admit two faces, my lady callers no less. They had come back to say "Allengi kesio"[13] (Rest in peace). This over, their little consciences were free, and in gorgeous bliss they fluttered off home.

---

10 *OC*: "peeped."
11 *OC*: "A nickel was dropped into each."
12 "Make a courtesy" is British English for "make a curtsy."
13 A regional dialect version of *Annyŏnghi kyesio*, which should more aptly be translated as "Stay in peace."

The Korean Woman

Like many of his missionary colleagues, Gale was sometimes critical of the state of women in Korea, and could not resist the occasional perfunctory admonitions about the potential of Christianity and Western morals in general to improve the lives of the poor, downtrodden Korean woman. As Hyaeweol Choi has demonstrated, however, it is necessary to critically examine the "continuing assumption" that Protestant missionaries "contributed positively to the formation of *modern* womanhood."[1] Choi claims that "without specifying the complex nature of modernity," previous studies often cite two factors that demonstrate the positive effect of Christianity on modern womanhood: the Christian notion of equality for men and women under God, and the missionaries' contributions to institutional and socio-economic reform, mainly in the shape of mission schools.[2] Yet as Choi points out, "there is ample evidence that Western women … readily accepted a subordinate role as 'helpmates' in the foreign mission field," undercutting a discourse of Western equality, while the simple presence of schools cannot in itself indicate modernity, in that schooling "can also be a powerful mechanism for reinforcing traditional gender ideology and repressing the desire for freedom."[3]

In this light, Gale's conversion narrative "The Korean Woman," despite the slightly self-congratulatory tone, confers upon the main

---

1 Choi, "An American Concubine in Old Korea," 134.
2 Ibid., 134–5.
3 Ibid., 135.

characters agency in their own socio-economic transformation. Gale was more optimistic about the state of Korean women than most, and recognized the unchallenged authority wielded by women in the domestic realm that demonstrated their potential in the work force. The achievements of the women cited by Gale are not explicitly credited to missionary guidance but rather to the ambition of the women themselves. Moreover, mere attendance at modern schools is not portrayed as an end in itself; the actual achievements of these women as leaders in their community take centre stage, evidence not of a "reinforcement of traditional gender ideology" but of social empowerment. In this sense, "The Korean Woman" assigns the most potent agency not to Korean government reforms or to missionaries per se, but to the Korean woman herself, who possessed enormous potential if only the possibility of advancement were proffered. This was in tune with many of Gale's writings – the belief that the old order had begun to break down, yet the trappings of "modernity" had yet to fill the void, creating a vacuum that required filling.

The Korean Woman
Pen Pictures, 59–60

The subject is a wide one and we cannot deal with it here. Is she, for example going to be able to hold her own with her Oriental sisters of China and Japan Proper? Has she in her qualities that will overcome in the face of a thousand odds against her? Will she take a larger share than her husband or brothers at the long pull together in bringing her people to the forefront in the movings of the East?

In the first place she has never been free like the women of Japan, to go and come as she pleases. A prison life has been hers and her ancestors'. Freedom denoted social inferiority, and a tanned face was like the mark of sin. In her tight little quarters, over the *kang* floor,[4] she has borne and brought up her race; has worked her nimble fingers over distaff and needle; has prepared her rice and condiments for her lord and master, and has pulled through it, and to-day appears, perhaps, the better and more hopeful sex of the two.

---

4 The *kang* (炕) is a raised platform making up the inside of a traditional Korean home, under which is installed the *ondol* heating system.

Now that the world has opened up she comes forth to greet the public, but unfortunately her dress and general outfit are against her. The baggy trousers, the loosely bundled skirt, the unfastened socks, the short jacket, loose from the skirt and gaping front and rear, her head garnished with cap and sleeveless mantle, all make her an oddity as she steps out onto the stage of the world's doings. A smile or a question naturally follows in her wake. To adjust herself to this world, and find her place, is the task for the day.

The writer recalls a very poor widow woman of years ago. She had no husband and no son, and four daughters were the special mark of her humiliation, four meaningless units to be fed, and clothed, and sorrowed over.

Theirs was a little mud hut called Home, of one cheerless room six by six by twelve, plastered inside with mud, and with no white paper or other relief to hide the monotony of the wall.

As the oldest of the children was able to look after the others, the mother went out to do washing. Day by day she toiled. How she managed to find sufficient [nourishment] for these hungry chicks of hers, it would be hard to tell. Those boney hands wielded the ironing sticks with a continuity of motion that would have done credit to the wife of Goliath of Gath. To one who tries for the first time to do Korean ironing and to keep it up, it is like holding out five pounds at the horizontal and keeping it up for half a day. The arms simply die under the agony of it. She had graduated through all the stages of weariness and pain, till the radius joint bone of each wrist stood out like a bursa bunion.

She became a Christian, this woman, why not? Might just as well you know, nothing could be worse than her lot now and Christianity talked of comfort and peace, etc. She would try.

The writer still recalls her cheery smile through the tanned and scarred and crinkled features. There was always a wholesome set of activities accompanying her presence, that more and more made amends for the place of humility in the social world that her lot called for. The four daughters were unschooled; when did Korean girls ever go to school in those days? More unreasonable that would be than to have a modern suffragette a member of the Cabinet. They were bright, strong girls, however, and would, doubtless, pick up the washing and ironing sticks in due time, and give the poor old faithful mother a rest.

Twenty years later the writer visited the old washer woman. To a clean, neat, cozy Korean house he wended his way. She greeted him with the same kindly smile of twenty years before, with a thinner and more spareful expression, however, such as age takes on. She has retired now from hard labor and the pressing burdens of life. In return these daughters of hers fed and cared for her.

The oldest was the matron of the home, with her own children about, a strong honest-faced Korean woman, such as gives one hope for the whole peninsula. She had once befriended a little foreign child in dire distress in days gone by, and her grateful name was ever afterwards cherished and remarked upon.

The second, a woman, once seen, not to be forgotten, head of one of the best middle schools in the capital; a perfect host in herself! Is it good order that is hoped for out of chaos, this number two will bring it; is it wise counsel needed, that will prevail, she will do; is it a question of talking to 500 women of various degrees of arrested intelligence, and having them see and learn, and know, she is the one. The passers-by who meet and see her have but one word, and that of grateful surprise and delight. She would be marked, and honoured, and used in any land where intelligence and efficiency were the requisites.

The third daughter is in charge of a large medical practice. How she got across the wide ocean, learned English, reached Philadelphia, and graduated from the School of Medicine and Surgery, I do not know. But this she did, and here she, who was number three nobody in the train of a submerged home, has brought healing, and comfort, and joy, to many thousands.

The fourth, a jolly little girl with round face, who played at mud pies and built castles in the air, is head of a Training School for Nursing, accomplished, a good English scholar, trained in music, and one of the best factors in the hopes of the city.

These are samples of the possibility of the Korean woman.

Korea's Preparation for the Bible

Gale had a special interest in proving the monotheistic character of Confucianism as a way of establishing an effective shortcut to proselytization. His unpublished journals are replete with attempts to explain and justify the equivalent nature of the Confucian *ch'ŏn* (天 heaven) with the Christian God. Another method employed by Gale to establish a beachhead between Christianity and ancient Korean beliefs is the equating of the characters from the Korean creation myth – Hwanin (God as Creator), Hwanin's son Hwanung (God as Educator), and the grandson Tan'gun (God as Ruler) – with the Christian concept of the Holy Trinity. Although Donald Baker claims the Taejonggyo denomination continues this teaching, in this case the explicit Christian influence is denied.[1]

In "Korea's Preparation for the Bible," Gale delineates five characteristics of Korean culture and society that would in his mind facilitate the smooth reception of the Gospel. Among these, the final two points are most intriguing. Gale reiterates Korea's traditional devotion to "literature," one of his oft-repeated maxims, as a reason why the Bible will be well-received. Although this new form of literature represented by the Bible did not equate with the Confucian canon in Literary Sinitic, the sine qua non of acceptable literature in the Sinographic cosmopolis, in this instance it was not the form or content of the literature itself that could potentially captivate the Korean

---

1 Baker, *Korean Spirituality*, 118–19.

literatus, but the general tradition of "sacred" textual reception in Korea. Gale believed that thanks to Korea's long and celebrated history of revering "scriptures," studying them, and committing them to memory, this general predisposition to sacred writings would invite a similar response to the Bible. Thus Gale did not envision the Bible as replacing the Confucian canon, or even occupying the same stylistic or literary space as that body of texts, but rather constituting an expanded textual universe that would receive the same reverential esteem and sustained, thorough engagement enjoyed by other sacred writings.

In Gale's final point he extols the practical virtues of the Korean vernacular alphabet, an argument well in tune with his missionary colleagues and yet slightly out of character for Gale, given his esteem for *hanmun* literature. However, an acknowledgment of the merits of the vernacular alphabet and a deep admiration and engagement with *hanmun* literature were not necessarily conflicting ideologies. Like most reform-minded Korean intellectuals of the day, Gale sometimes extolled the positive attributes of *han'gŭl* while eschewing such a transcriptional practice in his own writing, adhering instead to mixed-script orthography (*kukhanmun*). Where Gale was somewhat of an outlier was in primarily engaging with *hanmun* literature, although even he did not advocate *hanmun* for expository works conveying new knowledge. His language ideologies, which praised the potential of *han'gŭl* to spread literacy while promoting mixed script as an expedient bridge between cosmopolitan and vernacular textual universes, thus aligned with the majority of Korean intellectuals of the period, though they appear slightly more conservative than those of his missionary colleagues. The endurance of mixed-script orthography among Korean reformers who paid lip service to a desire for fuller vernacularization was probably attributable to the difficulty of imagining a pure *kungmun* idiom when the very concept and form of such a novel inscriptional practice had only recently emerged, and to the continuing legitimacy commanded by sinographs among intellectuals whose education often straddled premodern and modern epistemologies. For Gale, however, this slightly ambivalent language ideology sprung from his conflicted identity, which simultaneously extolled the transformative potentiality of the vernacular, while decrying the rapid deterioration of the cosmopolitan tradition.

Korea's Preparation for the Bible
Pen Pictures, 61–2;
Korea Mission Field 8, no. 3 (1912): 86–8;
Korea Mission Field 10, no. 1 (1914): 4–6

It would seem as though Korea had fallen within the circle of prophetic vision when we consider the marked preparation she has shown for the coming of the Word of God.

I shall mention five points specially noticeable.

First: The Name for God, Hananim, meaning the One Great One, the Supreme and absolute Being, suggesting the mysterious appellation "I Am that I Am," *hana* meaning "one" and *nim*, "great."[2]

Our Saxon word God used in the plural and applied to heathen deities had to be adjusted greatly before it could serve the desired end. The Greek "*theos*" like the Japanese "*kami*" was applicable to many so-called deities, also "Sangje" (上帝)[3] of China, it being the highest of many spiritual personalities. But "Hananim" strikes at once a note to which other names labor to attain to and arrive at only after a long period of service.

Second: By the associations and characteristics that Korea attributes to the one God.

---

2 Donald Baker, however, suggests that there were no indigenous Korean terms for God until quite recently, and that there is no basis for an indigenous Korean tradition of monotheism. The term *Hananim* mentioned above was a word created by Protestant missionaries to refer to the "supreme, singular being," the Christian concept of God, whereas similar terms such as the modified Christian *Hanŭnim*, the Taejonggyo (the Religion of the Grand Progenitor's) *Hanŏllim*, and the Ch'ŏndogyo *Hanŭllim* were newly coined terms for a singular deity because the "supposedly 'traditional' term of *Hanŭnim* sounded too Christian to Non-Christian ears." See Baker, "Hananim, Hanŭnim, Hanŭllim, and Hanŏllim." According to Ross King, defining "God" in this way is disingenuous on the part of Gale: "The traditional spelling for 'one' was *honah* while the traditional spelling for 'sky' was *hanulh*. This was different vocalism, and Gale would have known this. Any earlier renditions of *hanu'-nim* would have had the 'sky' spelling (i.e., *hano-nim*, which is indeed attested from 1800, but not *hona-nim*, which I am willing to bet is not attested)." King, personal communication, 19 October 2018.

3 "Lord Above," the Sinitic term used first by Catholics to refer to the Christian God.

How greatly Jupiter of the West fails in acts, in moral virtues, and in dignity [zzz] suggests the God of the Hebrews, so far also falls short the Eastern Okwhang sangje.[4] But let me give you the translation of a few passages that have been handed down through a thousand years of time (coming from China it is true in the first instance but nonetheless Korean to-day) that deal with Hananim translating the name in each case by God.

"The man who does right God rewards, the man who does wrong God punishes."

"He who obeys God lives, he who disobeys Him dies."

"Where is God that he can hear so well? So vast is the universe, I wonder still when I come to think of it, it is not a question of height or of distance, God is in the heart."

"Secret words that men whisper to one another God hears as a clap of thunder and the dark designs plotted within the inner chamber, He sees as a flash of lightning."

"When a man's measure of wickedness is full, God takes him away."

"When through wrongdoing [a man] wins great renown, do not be disturbed about it, for if he be not killed by his fellow man God will see to him."

"When you sow cucumbers you reap cucumbers, when you sow beans you reap beans; the meshes of God's fishing net seem very wide indeed, yet none of us shall ever escape through them."

"Life and death are ordered of God; so also are riches and poverty."

"God never made a man without supplying his need."

"The hidden wickedness of the heart is what we need to fear, for God's eyes, like wheels turning, see everything."

"Flowers bloom and flowers fall,
Men have hopes and men have fears,
All the rich are not rich all,
Nor have the poor just only tears.
Men cannot pull you up to heaven,
Nor can men push you down to hell,
God rules, so hold your spirit even,
He is impartial, all is well."[5]

---

4 Okhwang sangje (玉皇上帝 Ch. Yu Huang Shangdi) is the Jade Emperor, one of the representations of the first god, appearing in Chinese Taoist philosophy.

5 The above quotations are drawn from *Myŏngsim pogam* (明心寶鑑 The Mirror of the Heart), a collection of sayings attributed to Confucius. This work was

Third: By the conditions under which Korea lives. Customs, habits, and ages common to those of Scripture are found to a remarkable degree in the land of the Hermit. Listen: Is the dragon seen in Scripture? So is he here. Were there perils in those days that pestered and bedogged the footsteps of men? So are there here. Did they labor to cast them out? So do they here. Did they say "Go in peace" there? So do they here. Did their new year fall toward spring time? So did it here. Is the fifteenth of the first moon a date never to be forgotten? So was it here. Did they sacrifice there? So do they here. Did they wear long robes girt about with a fancy girdle? So did they here. Did they put off their shoes when they touched holy ground? So do they here. Did they go forth to meet the bridegroom? So do they here. Did they take up their beds and walk? So do they here. Did the mourners go about the streets? So do they here.

When western worlds are illimitable distances removed from the kind of life found in the Scriptures, Korea sees herself one with the Bible in the common walks and ways of men, and so prepared to appreciate the times of Abraham, Isaac and Jacob, as well as those of Peter, James and John.

Fourth: By her exaltation of Literature.

Literature has been everything to Korea. The literati were the only men privileged to ride the dragon up into the highest heaven. The scholar could not only look at the king but could talk to him. The pen was mightier than the sword. Could you but read, or intone, or expound the classics, you might materially be dropping to tatters, but still the world would wait on you, listen regardfully, and show honor. Many an unkempt son of the literati has the writer looked on with to see him receive the respectful and profound salutation of the better laundried classes. Korea is not commercial, not military, not industrial, but is a devotee of letters. She exalts books and so the Book of all books finds its pathway prepared, and as by a kind of prophetic prescience a welcome accorded which is perhaps greater than that seen in any other part of the world.

Fifth: By virtue of its simple and efficient script.

The East elsewhere has offered but a poor reception to the agent of the Bible Society and the missionary when we regard the question of

---

well known among all educated Koreans and served as a shorthand guide to practical Confucian thought. Gale's lengthier translation of this work appears in *Old Corea*, this vol.

general ability to read on the part of the masses. The Nearer East and India with their Arabic and Sanskrit and other complicated forms of writing, have made no provision for the wayfaring man. China, worse than them all, sails complacently by on her literary ideals while the poor and the unlettered live on the bones of rumor, hearsay, and superstition.

Korea, by what prophetic instinct we know not, prepared, four hundred and sixty years ago, a simple form of writing, so that the old and the poor, the toil-worn, the sorcerer, the witch-wife, the less than no man, all might read. To-day among successful church workers are those who never had a day's schooling in their lives. King Sejong's simple alphabet has served as a medium for the transmission of the Scriptures, and the land of the Hermit has been put into touch with all the familiar stories clear down from Eden to the Sea of Galilee.[6]

Thus has Korea prepared a way for the glad reception of the Gospel, by her special name for God, by the attributes ascribed to Him, by the associations of every day life, by the place accorded to literature, and by her easy and comprehensive writing.

May this all mean something for more than Korea and for even as wide a world as the whole Far East.

---

6 This refers to the promulgation of *Hunmin chŏngŭm* (訓民正音, Correct Sounds for the Instruction of the People), which is traditionally dated to either late 1445 or early 1446 AD, the uncertainty due to the discrepancy between the solar and lunar calendars. Credit for the script's "invention" is usually given to King Sejong the Great (世宗大王, 1397–1450, r. 1418–50), although the exact extent of his involvement in the script's creation is still a matter of debate.

The Waning Eunuch

The use of male palace attendants (*naesi* 內侍) extended as far back as the Three Kingdoms period (57 BC–AD 668) and continued throughout the Koryŏ and Chosŏn dynasties. Unlike those in later Chosŏn, Koryŏ *naesi* came from the most elite of family backgrounds, had passed the civil service exam, and were not castrated and so should not be equated with the English "eunuch."[1] Castrated men were employed in government service, but they were termed *hwan'gwan* (宦官) or *hwanja* (宦者), came from humble origins, and held much lower ranks.[2] In 1356, King Kongmin of Koryŏ established the Naesibu (Bureau of Palace Attendants), which managed both castrated attendants and previous *naesi*, and it is from this period when the lines between the positions blurred, ultimately resulting in the extinguishing of the elite *naesi* pedigree and the convergence of castration and the palace attendant designation.[3] With the promulgation of the *Kyŏngguk taejŏn* (經國大典 Great Code of National Governance, 1485), the status of this group of officials became well defined, and their decidedly non-hereditary nature was established.[4] The Korean term *naesi*, "internal" or "palace attendant," denotes the nature of the officials' main duties during Chosŏn: tasting food and drink meant for the king (presumably to guard against

---

1 Pak Ŭnbong, *Han'guksa sangsik paro chapki*, chap. 4.

2 Ibid.

3 Ibid.

4 Hong Sunmin, "Chosŏn wangjo naesibu ŭi kusŏng suhyo ŭi pyŏnch'ŏn," 259.

adulteration), conveying royal correspondence, both of a written and spoken nature, guarding the palace gates, and carrying out various custodial duties.[5] Although Chosŏn *naesi* were not necessarily civil service examination passers, they were required to be familiar with certain basic Confucian texts such as the *Elementary Learning* (*Sohak* 小學) and *Samgang haengsilto* (三綱行實圖 Illustrated Exemplars of the Three Bonds), and to possess *hanmun* reading ability and Confucian comportment – skills that were periodically tested, as Gale reports.[6] The Naesibu presided over eunuchs occupying an array of official ranks in the Chosŏn bureaucratic hierarchy, ranging from Level Two (*chong 2 p'um*) to Level Nine (*chong 9 p'um*), with Level One being the highest.

There were several reasons for the employment of eunuchs in palace duties. First, such men would have contact with women within the palace walls, including ladies-in-waiting and royal concubines, and so castration would eliminate a possible source of temptation or even threat to the monarchy. Second, because of the considerable amount of power and influence amassed by certain eunuchs, castration put a check on intergenerational ambitions by denying this particular government official an heir. Finally, for more practical reasons, the lack of immediate offspring forestalled any entanglements with the sensitive nature of palace work.

Gale was observing the last gasp of this ancient custom of eunuch employment. Records show that the number of eunuchs in government service was set at 140 according to the Naesibu established by the *Kyŏngguk taejŏn*, but had swelled to 264 by the final days of the Chosŏn dynasty.[7] Written in 1905, the *Pen Pictures* version of "The Waning Eunuch," though pessimistic as to the future prospects of *naesi*, describes the influence and power wielded by them in the present tense; the *Old Corea* version, undated though probably rewritten sometime in the 1910s or early 1920s, renders the eunuch's disappearance a foregone conclusion. Gale was indeed witnessing monumental changes before his very eyes, and parallel, diachronic essays such as these index these transformations in stark fashion.

---

5 Ibid., 258.

6 Ibid.

7 Regulations of the Finances of the Six Ministries (Yukchŏn chorye 六典條例), in ibid., 262.

The Waning Eunuch
Pen Pictures, 63–4; *Old Corea*, 116–17

One of the leading influences that has borne upon Korea for weal or woe during its history has been the eunuch. Smooth-faced and sallow, high-keyed as to voice, and with the shadow of an old woman looking out over his cheek-bones, the tall, gaunt figure has been seen for ages scuttling in and out of the palace. Mankind may be divided into three classes – male, female, and neuter – and into the last class falls the eunuch. He is a monstrosity, of course, a contradiction of the eternal law, the product of a deformity, which shows itself in his face, and renders him unpleasant to look upon if not repulsive.

How do eunuchs come about that Korea should enjoy such numbers of them, and that they should live and flourish so abundantly?[8] It is a hard question to answer, and yet any Korean will answer it at once, and they will all answer it in the same way. Their answer is recorded in the *Histoire de l'Église de Corée*,[9] and occasions no surprise on their part, but always surprise and incredulity on the part of the foreigner. The answer as given there will explain how eight out of ten are said to be made; one out of ten is born a eunuch, and the last one becomes a eunuch through the ambitions of a family, who desire his entrée to the palace.

When grown up, eunuchs are taller than ordinary men. Nature having been switched off one course projects itself along another. Then, as to the voice, how shall I describe it? It is a girl's voice, lacking that subtle something of softness and charm that makes it a girl's voice. It is the ghost of a voice, like the clack of a cheap talking-machine, and yet withal an excellent voice to whisper with.

In disposition they approach more nearly to women, so Koreans say. There is a common expression which runs "Naesi ch'ŏrŏm kollanda":

---

8 "and that they should live and flourish so abundantly" is deleted from the *OC* version.

9 *Histoire de l'Église de Corée* (History of the Church in Korea, 1874) is a two-volume work written by Charles Dallet (1829–78), a French Catholic missionary to Korea. The history is preceded by a long introduction (which Gale seems to be referring to) representing the most complete ethnographic study of the country in a Western language up to that time. The introduction was based largely on letters written to Dallet by French missionaries in Korea.

"as hot-tempered as a eunuch!"[10] Their rage, when once aroused, is said to reach beyond all bounds. They are liberal and generous, are unforgiving if once wronged, are partial and one-sided in their views, all of which traits, according to the Korean, belong to women. I have some friends among the eunuchs and one I know particularly well – a jolly, free and easy, lively girl style of person, most refreshing to meet. He usually has some good story to tell or some droll experience that would hold the attention of anyone.[11]

The rank and position of the eunuch in society is very high indeed. They are divided into three classes, called *chisa* [知事], *changbŏn* [長番], and *naech'ong* [內寵]. The *chisa* class have titles applied to them that are used to princes and officers of the first rank. Even the *naech'ong* are addressed politely and shown all deference. This, of course, is accounted for from the fact of their being the Emperor's body servants. They sweep his rooms, make up his bed, draw the blinds, spread the quilt, put on his clothes, tie his top-knot, fix his headband and hat, bring in his table, light his pipe. They are all around and about him with their sallow, clammy existences, turning whatever of life there is for him into their emasculated world. They move in and out of the kitchens and among the serving maids. There is not a corner of the palace, be it the Emperor's or Queen's apartments, that is not free to them. They take turns in waiting on His Imperial Highness, and when off duty return to their private homes. In order to be reckoned as men and not as mere women, they each have a wife and usually an adopted son.[12]

Originally the eunuch was intended for the household servant of the Palace, and was not supposed to mix in the affairs of state, but as time passed he tasted the delights of power, and found that buying and selling and trading in office were more interesting and lucrative than simply hanging out bed quilts to air, or tasting the king's cabbage pickle or chilli peppers. The eunuch has grown to be a mighty man in state affairs. He never heard of Liverpool or New York, but he is a master of all the intricacies of Korean "squeeze," and the dark ways that underlie the present government's methods. He is horribly superstitious and

---

10 The more widely accepted contemporary expression seems to be "Naesi ch'ŏrŏm kulmyŏn kollanda," or "as angry as a eunuch scorned," which equates to the English expression "Hell hath no fury like a woman scorned."
11 *OC*: "He usually has some story to tell or some droll expression."
12 In the *OC* version, this entire paragraph is rendered in the past tense, suggesting the end of the eunuch era, just as Gale had predicted.

plays on the Emperor's soul by these means. Like a raff of hobgoblins they gather round His Imperial Majesty and make his original darkness more intensely dark than ever. The palaces swarm with them. They are sought out by all "pullers" for office.[13]

These are dark days for the eunuch. Scores of them have been dismissed from the imperial service, through the influence of the Japanese, we are told. In the agony of it they have wept, they and His Majesty.[14] Koreans all understand that eunuchs are victims of fate in the fact that they are eunuchs, without hope of posterity, which is another word for eternal life. Some hidden law of the gods has found its satisfaction in striking the balance against them. Koreans say that men who hook eels in the eye for a living find their posterity afflicted with what is called *sap'al nun* (four-eight eye), eyes that are not mates, the one on one side being a number four eye, the other being a number eight. Mencius says there is prosperity in store for those who heap up good, but wrath in store for those who heap up evil. The Korean argues that since the *naesi* (eunuch) has fallen on such days as these, when tears flow over his beardless cheeks, he must have heaped up sins and done much evil. Evil brings desolation and desolation proves evil. Doubtless this may be true. At any rate the eunuch belongs to the age of the night-gown coat and the long fingernail, an age that is now forever past.

In the old procession days when His Majesty went forth in state to visit the gods, there rode about his chair a cohort of eunuchs, with the cheek, the eye and the chin of the inscrutable East. But, says the Korean, "there is no more East, the East is gone"; nothing is left but a hopper full of mortals, everyone struggling to tread down his fellow and push him under into the very mills of the same gods once worshipped. The eunuch is a half woman, great in chicanery, but helpless to hold his own in an age when brute force and muscle hold sway. Low down in the hopper lies the eunuch, and one of these times at the turning of the wheel of fate he shall go his way and shall appear no more.

(1905)

---

13 The preceding paragraph in *OC* again conveys the narrative in past or past perfect tense, emphasizing the passing of the eunuch's influence.

14 *OC*: "These are dark days for the eunuch. The imperial service has ceased and he has been disqualified forever. In the agony of it he has wept and died of mortification."

A Freak of Language

Gale wrote extensively on issues related to language in Korea. Being a lifelong student of both vernacular Korean and Literary Sinitic, he penned many essays on the language that appeared in various missionary periodicals, and conducted extensive lexicographic studies accompanied by detailed and groundbreaking introductions to Korean grammar. In the following essay Gale, despite his in-depth knowledge of the Korean linguistic landscape, echoes the Orientalist trope of othering "the Character" – his synecdochic term for Literary Sinitic – as a visual symbol of an exotic, fascinating, and enigmatic Orient. The idea that Chinese characters represented a sort of ocular language unconnected to vocal sounds had deep roots in European theories of ideography. Despite the deciphering of Egyptian hieroglyphics by Jean-François Champollion (1790–1832) and the debunking of the Chinese ideographic theory by Pierre Étienne Du Ponceau (1760–1844), the myth that Egyptian and later Chinese "hieroglyphs" functioned as a "language of the eye" maintained a strong grip on the European scholarly and missionary imagination into the nineteenth century. Although European ideographic theory would have been well known to Gale, his expertise in Literary Sinitic would have also precluded his believing that sinographs were predominantly ideographic in nature, and so his description here seems to be an attempt to exoticize Literary Sinitic for an uninitiated Western audience. Gale's description below of Literary Sinitic clearly betrays his own fascination with the language, but his positionality as a missionary translator of the Bible also engenders a frustration at this primitive tool of "duplicity" and "guile," confounding a clear and exact translation for such a critical document. "A Freak of Language" perhaps encapsulates better than any other essay in this volume Gale's ambivalence toward Korea's inevitable yet sterilizing modernization.

A Freak of Language
Pen Pictures, 65

Korea, which sleeps and dreams of Yo (堯) and Sun (舜), two Chinese Emperors who lived before the Flood,[1] has no less than three languages in which to express her dreamings: an eye-language, an ear-language and a hand-language.[2]

The eye-language comes from China in the form of ideographs or pictures. Its soul lies not in the sound but in the shape, for the sound changes according to the place in which it exists, while the shape remains ever the same. In Japan, in Korea, in China, in Manchuria, in Annam,[3] this picture 馬 means "horse," this 人 "man," this one 日 "sun," etc.[4] They have all sorts of names and sounds attributed to them. For example, the name that goes with 日 will vary according to the locality where it is used, but the meaning and the picture will remain ever the same.

These are samples of the eye-language that reaches the brain by way of the optic nerve, and never by way of the ear drum. These pictures are strung along like beads in a vertical line, and the Oriental's eyes have followed down the columns for so many thousands of years that they have seemingly become tilted at the corners, trying so hard to bring their alignment into accord with the page before them.

---

1 Gale often provided parallel Western chronologies when discussing events in Asian history for the benefit of his Anglophone readers. In this case Gale claims that Yo and Sun predated the great biblical flood, but the flood's traditional dating to roughly 2300 BC suggests overlap with Yo's life.

2 For a detailed description of the origins of European ideography and its application to Egyptian hieroglyphics and Literary Sinitic, see O'Neill, *Ideography and Chinese Language Theory*.

3 Annam (安南 the Pacified South) was one of the names given to Vietnam prior to 1945.

4 Gale was of course writing before official Chinese character simplification policies were carried out by the People's Republic of China (1956, 1964) and Japan (1946), at a time when the form of sinographs was largely identical across the Sinographic cosmopolis, save for a limited number of characters created specially in Korea and Japan that existed nowhere else.

Korean literature is nearly all written in the eye-language.[5] It cannot be heard by any mortal ear. The eyes must see it, and the mind translate it, and the voice sing it out in colloquial before the ear can hear and understand.[6] For that reason Orientals are great readers by the eye. The book they look at may be upside down, or end for end, or backwards or standing on its head, or pasted inside out, any way at all, if only the shadow of the character presents itself to the eye of the reader he will catch the thought and read it.

This eye-language is a sign and wonder in the land of Sinim, a marvel and a mystery among the sons of men. It is the oldest form of writing on the earth. It is the most widely distributed, being placarded on door-posts all the way from Tokyo to Tibet and from Harbin to Mandalay. It is the most sacred, for its forms are worshipped by millions of the race, yet I

---

5   By "Korean literature," here Gale is clearly referring to the Literary Sinitic tradi-
    tion and most definitely not vernacular literature. This is an important distinction
    to make when reading Gale's writings, and the period during which he is writing
    is also important to note. At the time of *Old Corea* and *Pen Pictures*, Gale usually
    failed to specify "Classical" literature when writing about Korean literature,
    because "modern" vernacular Korean literature in the Western sense did not exist
    and modern Koreans had not "invented" or rediscovered their pre-twentieth-
    century works as classics. However, with the emergence of modern Korean litera-
    ture in the late 1910s, Gale was often obliged to make a distinction.

6   Here Gale seems to be referring to the traditional Korean manner of interfacing
    with Literary Sinitic texts, a method espoused for centuries throughout Korea's
    Confucian education apparatus, including its network of village Confucian
    schools (*sŏdang* 書堂), higher private Confucian academies (*sŏwŏn* 書院), and the
    Confucian College (Sŏnggyun'gwan 成均館). According to Song Kich'ae
    (宋基采), Professor of Classical Chinese at the Sŏnggyun'gwan University
    Graduate School of Classics Translation, who received a *sŏdang* education dur-
    ing the late 1950s and early 1960s, when teaching texts at Confucian schools,
    the instructor would first read the text and have the students repeat it, and each
    student would have to memorize the text before being allowed to proceed to the
    next work. Although minimal oral explications of the meaning were provided,
    the learning process was not based on contemporary linguistic analysis and
    explanation but rather was primarily dependent upon gradual uptake through
    constant vocal repetition/recitation and memorization. While it is impossible
    to know in detail the conduct of *sŏdang* education in the late nineteenth century,
    Song claims that the method by which he learned had been passed down to his
    instructor. Song Kich'ae, personal conversation, Sŏnggyun'gwan University,
    1 December 2016. For a detailed description of the traditional process of Literary
    Sinitic interface in premodern Korea from a Western perspective, see Rutt, "The
    Chinese Learning and the Pleasures of a Country Scholar."

suppose it is the most hidebound and indefinite of all written languages. It has been the lurking place of subterfuge, evasion, white-lie, guile and duplicity. Through it men hint at what they are after, while covering up the real thought and motive that lies underneath; by it you can write one thing and mean another. It possesses no definite article and no indefinite, so that when it comes to an exact translation satisfactory results are impossible.[7]

The Korean reads John VI and 53 (Except ye eat the flesh of the Son of man, and drink his blood, ye have no life in you):[8] If-you-not-eat-man-son-flesh-not-drink-man-son-blood-you-without-life-inside-are. "Zounds," says he, "these foreigners are a vile lot of cannibals. Wife, keep your eye on the children!" Such are the misunderstandings possible to the Oriental on account of this indefinite eye-language of his.

But its measure is wide as the sea and its possessions include a whole continent of the earth. As the Anglo-Saxon has spread his tentacles over all the Western lands, so this eye-language is in possession of all the Farther East.

On board a steamer built by the Anglo-Saxon, we were forging our way up the Yellow Sea. A motley crowd was on board, all sorts of faces and dresses. In one corner squatted three men, their heads close together: one a Japanese, one a Chinaman, and one a Korean. They were passing a roll of paper around with written messages for each other; not a word could they speak, nor a sound could they utter that was intelligible, but this wonderful eye-language was one and the same for each and all of them.[9]

(March 1901) (Unfinished)

---

7   A common discourse among Western scholar-missionaries in Korea concerned the "lack" of equivalents in Korean for Western conceptual terms and other terminology related to the modern world, supposedly a fundamental cultural flaw that needed to be corrected by creating words anew. Although Gale reproduces this language ideology here, on the spectrum of Western scholars of the Korean language, he was less inclined to insist on such a lack, and this discourse attenuates over the course of his career.

8   This excerpt is from John 6:53 (KJV).

9   Gale was in fact observing what is referred to as *p'iltam* (筆談 brush-talk). This was a common method of communication between various envoys to China in the premodern Sinographic cosmopolis. For a discussion of a *p'iltam* between the Korean envoy to Beijing, Yi Sugwang (李睟光, 1563–1628), and his Vietnamese counterpart, *Phùng Khắc Khoan* (馮克寬, 1528–1613), see Pore, "The Inquiring Literatus."

An Affair of State

The remaining chapters of *Pen Pictures*, beginning with "An Affair of State," mark the most political of Gale's writings, replete with palace intrigue, pointed criticisms of Kojong, and stark predictions as to Korea's future. Gale again alludes to the influence peddling of the palace eunuch, who presumably served as his source for palace rumour that he so confidently reports. Gale writes that eunuchs "lost their innings during 1895 and 1896, but the emperor has since declared in their favor and they and the Palace maids are once again to the fore," yet it is unclear what relevant events occurred in 1895 and 1896. Gale seems to be referring to the Kabo Reforms, a series of three government reforms, the last round of which occurred from October 1895 to February 1896, although these specific reforms do not seem to have directly affected the status of eunuchs compared with previous reforms. A sweeping set of reforms instituted at the behest of an ascendant Japan and executed by a pro-Japanese Korean cabinet, some scholars claim that one of the motives of the reforms was to limit royal autonomy, and the influential eunuch was viewed as an impediment to this goal. As part of the first round of reforms, in July 1894 the Naesibu (Bureau of Palace Attendants) was renamed the Naesisa (Ministry of Palace Attendants), but the duties of eunuchs remained unchanged. With the second round of reforms in December of that year, the Naesisa was abolished, and the remaining eunuchs were reorganized under the Sijongwŏn (Office of the Chamberlain) involved with menial service duties, in an effort, according to Chang Hŭihŭng, to limit their sway with the Korean monarch. The presence of eunuchs in the palace, however, continued until 1908, which year marked the abdication of Emperor Kojong in favour of his son Sunjong and the virtual takeover of real authority by Japan.[1]

Gale also refers to the selling of government offices, a practice in which eunuchs were apparently deeply involved. The selling of official titles and *yangban* (gentry) status began in the aftermath of the Imjin Wars (1592–8) in the midst of massive dislocations, in order to shore up revenue. This practice became even more pronounced in the late nineteenth century as the Chosŏn government found it increasingly difficult to secure revenue to carry out much-needed reforms, mainly because of the growing monopolization of non-taxable revenue by the *yangban* class. In many ways the sale of office was simply a quick fix that exasperated a systemic problem, creating a vicious cycle: their sale raised quick cash but enlarged the pool of non-taxable resources that increasingly undermined the regime's fiscal solvency.

Political Sketches

An Affair of State
Pen Pictures, 66

His Korean Majesty is out of the city to-day worshipping the spirits of his ancestors. At six in the morning the procession moved out of the palace and passed through the East Gate to the tombs of the kings. It costs $25,000 to perform the ceremony to the satisfaction of the emperor. But it is worth it for it leaves the palace free from evil ghosts, prevents assassination, and permits of grateful, comforting sleep. The eunuchs are out in full force, every one of them, "oiled and shiny;" Korea is richly blessed with this particular order of Oriental. They seem to develop as by a kind of spontaneous combustion, from no one knows where, whole brigades of them. They lost their innings during 1895 and 1896, but the emperor has since declared in their favor and they and the Palace maids are once again to the fore.

At present the revenue is largely raised from lotteries conducted by them, and the selling of office under their administration. As a result pawn-shops ornament every corner of the city, and the bartering of the public proceeds. There is no question raised as to a man's fitness for

---

1   See Chang Huihŭng, "Kapo kaehyŏk ihu Naesibu ŭi kwanje pyŏnhwa wa hwangwanje ŭi p'yeji."

office; if he can but raise the amount, in he goes. Artemis Ward[2] used to placard his show entrance as follows: "You can't expect to go in without paying, but you may pay without going in." So [it] is on the door of Korea's Office Exchange. It costs just now $20.00 to enlist as a soldier, $25.00 to get into the police force, $1,000 to be made a lieutenant, and $7,000 for the office of Minister of Justice.[3] Other offices vary in price in accord with the possibility of "squeeze" attached to them.[4] The party purchasing is left in uncertainty as to how long he will be permitted to hold the same. It not only requires the ready money with which to secure entrance, but a constant supply must keep circulating toward the Palace in order that one keep his seat.

The outlook for the Government is a rather mixed one. Le Gendre is dead, and Greathouse has only a few hours to live, and so ends the influence of the Foreigner.[5] The power of these two combined has not been sufficient to lead Korea along a safe and encouraging pathway. Now they are gone and their pupil seems ready to die with them, but the Emperor is happy: all is peace with him. He never dreams that 12,000,000 mortals are eying him narrowly, fools they may be, but so much the worse for his reckoning day to come.

The band plays at night and bottles of champagne pop hilariously. The ancestral spirits of the dynasty are propitiated, *fengshui* is favorable, his Eight Characters are beneficent, and his stars shine down just where they ought to shine. Amen and amen.

(Oct 20th 1899)

---

2 Artemus Ward (1834–1867) was the nom de plume of Charles Farrar Browne, an American humorist.

3 As with most of Gale's claims, his source remains anonymous, and there is no explanation given as to the extremely wide disparity between the prices of these offices. In "The Waning Eunuch" (*Pen Pictures*), Gale states that he has several friends among this group, so we may surmise that these comprise some of his sources.

4 This seems to refer to the potential that an office provides its holder to enrich his personal finances through corruption, to "squeeze" the population he is charged to represent or defend through misappropriation of funds.

5 Charles William Joseph Émile Le Gendre (1830–99) was a French-born American advisor to King Kojong from 1890 until 1 September 1899, dying just weeks before Gale wrote this essay. Clarence Ridgley Greathouse (1846–99) was an American legal advisor to the Kojong court, most renowned for leading the prosecution against those Koreans involved in the assassination of Queen Min on 8 October 1895. Greathouse died the day after Gale penned this essay.

Private Minting

Along with the selling of office discussed in the previous chapter, another prominent characteristic of the late Chosŏn was the issue of "fallen *yangban*," or impoverished gentry, a designation that seems applicable to Gale's Korean acquaintance in this chapter. By the late Chosŏn dynasty many so-called fallen *yangban* had gradually drifted into poverty after failing to reproduce past successes in the civil service examinations, yet prohibitions on *yangban* commercial activity and manual labour resulted in a static condition of enforced idleness. Following the abrogation of the civil service examination in 1894 and the disappearance of this final imprimatur of the literati, idle, cash-strapped "gentlemen" had even fewer options in the new economy. The idle man of letters, or lazy *yangban*, as critics might have called him, became an object of derision for reform-minded Koreans and Western missionaries alike. For Gale, such a tragic figure was the embodiment of the ambivalence of Korean modernity: a living vessel of precious knowledge, and an endangered species ill-equipped for survival.

Private Minting
Pen Pictures, 67

Yesterday I was having tiffin[1] quite alone, when a cough at the door announced the arrival of a caller. He was admitted with his greeting of "Peace," and "Peace" was extended to him. He proved to be an old

---

1 A British English word meaning a light meal or luncheon.

acquaintance of years gone by, but he had been to Shanghai, Hong Kong, and other questionable places in the meantime and had drifted out of my remembrance. His "Eight Characters" had failed him, he said, and now he was in dire distress. His wife had gone crazy and his brother on whom he had depended was dead. He wished that he was dead himself.

Said he, "The way luck is distributed in this forsaken land beats me. Here I am, destitute, trying to be an honest man, but I'll give it up. I've decided to give up being good from now on, and to go in on the other line."

"What do you propose to do?" was my inquiry.

"To do?" said he, "This: I've bought a machine from a Japanese for making nickels, so it's a private mint I mean to run. His Majesty does not like that kind of thing, and so I am looking for a corner on some foreign compound to run it."

Then he grew confidential, and drawing up his chair to me, said, "It's the only paying business that's left in this benighted country, and the high-class gentry are going in for it. Yi Chaesun, the 'Fat Prince,'[2] formerly Minister of the Household has seven of these machines running night and day, and Min Kyŏngsik[3] has eight of them. These gentlemen are related to His Majesty, and so the police do not dare to take note of what is going on in their compounds."

"One hundred pounds of white metal," said the caller, "can be bought for one hundred yen, and it mints up into four hundred dollars worth of nickels. This is better than lending money at 8% a month."

I had not understood before why railway men and shop-keepers found so many nickels to argue over. In the olden days Korea had cash strung on a string and no one could afford to [zzz][4] the minting of it privately. Now, however, by the introduction of the nickel, a delightful field to be exploited lies open to the idle gentry and my friend, in spite of my warning, and my urging him to try honesty, as it is the best policy, left, saying, "It's the only business that remains for a gentleman of my standing."

(1900)

---

2 Yi Chaesun (清安君 李載純, 1851–1904) was a nephew of the previous King Ch'ŏlchong (哲宗, 1831–64). I have been unable to verify whether Yi was indeed involved in the counterfeit business.

3 Min Kyŏngsik (閔京植, 1871–?).

4 Here Gale has crossed out "sin in" and scratched in something illegible.

A New Korean

In this account Gale relates a chance encounter with Kwŏn Yŏngjin (權瀅鎭, ?–1900), a pro-Japanese government minister who served in the late Chosŏn dynasty during the Kabo Reforms. In conjunction with the Sino-Japanese War (1894–5), Japan took advantage of its enhanced position and influence to push through, with the help of pro-Japanese Korean government ministers, a sweeping set of reforms. These reforms included ending Korea's centuries-long suzerainty with China; abolishing the class system, all forms of slavery, and the civil service examination; establishing a modern education system; and designating the vernacular script (*kungmun* 國文) as the official writing system of the Chosŏn government.[1] A number of these reforms were controversial, perhaps none causing more unrest than the Topknot Law (*Tanballyŏng* 斷髮令), which ordered all adult men to remove their topknot (*sangt'u*). This, combined with the unrest caused by the assassination of Queen Min at the hands of Japanese agents, led King Kojong to declare from his seclusion in the Russian legation that pro-Japanese government ministers, including Kim Hongjip, Yu Kilchun, Chŏng Pyŏngha, Ŏ Yunjung, and Chang Pak, were traitors to the kingdom and were to be executed. Kim and Chŏng were immediately arrested and executed, while the escaped Ŏ was captured the next day and killed. However,

---

1 Despite this final provision, the "Edict on Public Writing" (*kongmunsik* 公文式), few government documents were actually drafted in pure *kungmun*, and Sino-Korean mixed script (*kukhanmun*) rather quickly became the preferred writing style of the elite. For a thorough discussion, see King, "Nationalism and Language Reform in Korea."

Kwŏn Yŏngjin, whom Gale encounters, along with several other ministers, sought asylum under Japanese protection. This account captures the human side of the tumultuous atmosphere in Korea at the turn of the century, and Gale's depiction seems to suggest optimism for the potential of reform, if not through the tragic figure of Kwŏn himself, then through many more like-minded compatriots.

A New Korean
Pen Pictures, 68

In the port of Fusan[2] I changed steamers, taking one for Chemulp'o.[3] There were in the saloon two first-class Japanese passengers. We left at one o'clock, and at six met round a table, four of us in all, the skipper included, to share our rice with chopsticks. The Captain spoke a little Korean, and with him I conversed, but the other two passengers were silent. One was dressed as a foreigner, the other, in silken kimono and Japanese slippers, seemed a refined and modest gentleman, with an intelligent expression stamped on a face rather badly scarred by small-pox.

Next morning, as I sat in the saloon looking over some views that happened to be there, this gentleman in silk glided in and sat opposite to me.

"Evidently *tangsin* (you) has been [*sic*] many years in our country," said he. I looked up with a start, for the accent was too truly Korean to ever come from a Japanese.

"I thought you had come from the Rising Sun," said I, "but it is evidently Morning Calm instead, is it not?"

"I am a Korean," was the answer, "and we've met before, if I mistake not, in Prince EW's[4] rooms in Tokyo four years ago"; and then I recalled the face and name, Kwŏn Yŏngjin.

---

2 This refers to Pusan, a port city on the southeast coast of the Korean peninsula. The tendency among resident foreigners in Korea at this time to spell the city's name with an "F" seems due to the influence of the Japanese pronunciation (Fuzan).

3 Chemulp'o (濟物浦) was the previous name of the port city of Inch'ŏn.

4 Gale has crossed out "Eui wha" in the original typescript version and left instead only the initials "EW." Perhaps this was done to protect the identity

He had been in exile five years, had been branded as one of the wick-edest and most influential of all the rebels, had formerly been Police Commissioner of the Capital, and had gone to Japan in January 1896, just before the fall of the Kim Hongjip Ministry.[5]

In surprise, I asked, "Where are you going?"

"Back with a message to my country," was the answer.

"They'll take no message from you but your head," was my reply.

"That's what I mean to offer," was his response. "I am going back to give myself up. They regard me as guilty of death, and will undoubtedly behead me, but through my death there is a plan to save my country."

I left the subject and called up other things to find if the man was mad, but a more sane intelligent gentleman in other respects, you might travel far to see. He was posted on the subjects of the day, spoke of the cancer which had eaten at the vitals of the Transvaal, and of how one

---

of the prince who had, at least briefly, harboured a fugitive of the Chosŏn government. Prince Ŭihwa (1877–1955, a.k.a Yi Kang 李堈) was the fifth son of King Kojong, by his concubine Lady Chang, and because of the status of his mother was not eligible to become king. Prince Ŭihwa would have met Gale in Tokyo in 1896, when he was on appointment as special ambassador to Japan to celebrate the country's victory in the Sino-Japanese War. Gale seems to have been close to him. For example, in the Gale Papers, Box 12, Folder 7, titled "Notes by Ada L. Gale on meeting and marrying Rev. J. S. Gale," and dated May 1943, contains the following mention on p. 1: "My earliest recollections of my beloved husband date back to 1897 when at the request of a friend, my mother and I called on him and his wife and her two daughters – children of Dr. J.W. Heron. He had come to Yokohama from Seoul Corea to have his first *Corean-English Dictionary* printed … He had a most charming personality, he and his family came to live near us and we were soon intimate friends. He was in touch with one of the Corean Princes who was in Tokio – and we often met him. He was taught English by Dr. Gale. After a year in Yokohama they returned to Corea."

Prince Ŭihwa went on to serve as special envoy to Germany, the United Kingdom, France, Russia, Italy, and Austria before attending Roanoke College in the United States. This anecdote provides a glimpse into Gale's brief time in Japan during the 1890s, rubbing elbows with government ministers and other enlightenment thinkers at the house of royalty.

5 Kim Hongjip (金弘集, 1842–96) was a pro-Japanese politician during the late Chosŏn dynasty, installed as prime minister during the Kabo Reform period. Following the assassination of Queen Min by Japan, pro-Japanese officials such as Kim were also assassinated.

selfish Kruger had ruined a whole country.[6] He touched on points of history, here and there, calling attention to Westerners such as Nelson,[7] who had given their lives for their country. "All this goes on," said he, "while we, in the East, sit in selfish contentment and see our countries die. These years that I have been in Japan have been years of plenty; I have many friends, but while I live, Chosŏn dies. It was not so with Sakamoni;[8] he left his palace and became a poor man. Jesus of Galilee elected to die on the cross for the sins of the world. These were acts of the Gods, but we men too have little ways in which we can imitate. My people look upon the ruling class as altogether selfish. 'To die for one's country' they never heard of, and to see such a thing will cause even the dullest to think, and it is to wake my countrymen that I die."

"Surely you will not die! Let's meet again in peace. God will watch over you."

"If I live, we meet. When you pray, remember me," was the request.

The steamer anchored at Chemulp'o, and a telegram was sent to police headquarters: "I am here, Kwŏn Yŏngjin; you may arrest me, my life is in your hands." He was at once arrested and hurried up to the Capital, where he now lies in his noisome prison awaiting sentence. He said to me last of all, "Others are going to follow." We certainly have fallen upon odd days in the history of Korea.

(June 1900) Note: Kwŏn was murdered a few nights later in the prison.

---

6   Here Gale is referring to Stephanus Johannes Paulus "Paul" Kruger (1825–1904), president of the South African Republic (Transvaal) from 1883 to 1900. Importantly, Kruger was the leader of the country during the First (1880–1) and Second (1899–1902) Boer Wars against Britain, the second of which resulted in victory for Great Britain and the exiling of Kruger until his death in 1904. Kwŏn's referring to Kruger as "selfish" may reflect the pro-British sentiment that prevailed in Japan at the time, although it is ironic that Kruger and Kwŏn shared the same fate as exiles.

7   Gale is referring to Horatio Nelson (1758–1805), the most celebrated admiral in the British Royal Navy, who served in the American War of Independence, the wars of the French Revolution, and most famously in the Napoleonic Wars. He died in the Battle of Trafalgar, defending the British mainland from a combined French and Spanish fleet.

8   Śākyamuni was one of the titles of the Buddha, or enlightened one, referring to Śakya, where according to tradition he was born. Śākyamuni literally means "hermit of the Śākya tribe."

The Burning of the Temple

In the early morning hours of 14 October 1900, a fire broke out in the Sŏnwŏnjŏn (璿源殿 The Hall of the House of Yi), a shrine on the grounds of Seoul's Kyŏngun'gung (慶運宮), today called Tŏksugung (德壽宮), the royal residence. Constructed just two months prior to house the royal portraits (ŏjin 御眞) of the Yi dynasty rulers, the fire claimed the building itself along with all seven royal visages: that of King T'aejo, the founder of the dynasty, as well as Kings Sukchong, Yŏngjo, Chŏngjo, Chunjo, Munjo, and Hŏnjong. The *Hwangsŏng sinmun* (皇城新聞 The Capital Gazette) reported briefly on the incident the following day, claiming that the "accidental" fire was being carefully investigated and that the more than thirty palace guards in charge of the grounds were being detained for questioning.[1] The *Veritable Records of the Reign of Kojong* (*Kojong sillok*) portrays an indignant king determined to get to the bottom of this brazen affront to the Yi lineage's propitiousness and fortune.[2] I am unable to uncover any other sources that suggest the event was the result of arson, with contemporary Korean sources unanimously describing it as a fire of "unknown origin" (*wŏnin morŭl*), and thus the identity of Gale's source remains a mystery. However, he was rather privy to palace activities through his various contacts in the foreign community, and so his version of events should be given careful consideration.

This account is one of many pieces in this volume assailing the competence of the Korean monarch Kojong in leading his country into the modern era. Although the critique here is more oblique than that

---

1 *Hwangsŏng sinmun*, 14 October 1900, 2.

2 *Kojong sillok*, vol. 40, 14 October 1900, in *Chosŏn wangjo sillok*.

appearing in other chapters,[3] King Kojong is depicted standing in the midst of a tumult he scarcely understands. His entourage of "eunuchs, dancing-girls, sorcerers, fortune-tellers, geomancers, grave vendors, exorcists, astrologers and medicine-men" fleeing the blaze along with him compound his image as a premodern, hackneyed monarch out of touch with or unwilling to confront the current state of affairs, depending instead on the logic of a bygone era. The figure of the Japanese firefighter rebuffed in his offer of help, meanwhile, is symbolic of Gale's view of the Japan-Korea relationship at the turn of the century. Korea, faltering in its efforts at reform, refuses the assistance of an "enlightened" and "prepared" Japan, instead succumbing to its own corruption and maladministration.

The Burning of the Temple
Pen Pictures, 69–70

On Saturday night last the city of Seoul was illuminated by a huge blaze of fire from within the Palace enclosure. The building sacred to the memory of ancestors, and containing the pictures and tablets of the founders of the illustrious dynasty, took fire, no one knows how, in the early hours of the morning. His Majesty, *sans ceremonie*, was hustled out of his apartment into a red-hot Hades, just in time to see the tablets and benign faces of his ancestors disappear in a most horrible holocaust. Without waiting to tie on garters, or do up his hair, he fled from the enclosure through the rear gateway, along the lane between the British Legation and the Customs compound, turned to the left and made for the Library Building, a host of eunuchs, dancing-girls, sorcerers, fortune-tellers, geomancers, grave vendors, exorcists, astrologers and medicine-men fleeing hard after him. A most fearful disturbance took place in the Library Building. The shades of all the twenty-five dead kings of this dynasty had it out for once.

On the other hand the uproar in the palace enclosure calmed down. Nothing but the crackling of flames was to be heard. In a few minutes the Japanese were on hand with their fire-engine, and tapped gently at the garden gate – Peace Gate, I mean.

---

3 For examples of such a critique elsewhere in *Pen Pictures*, see "Unconscious Korea" and "All Good Things Are Three."

"What do you want?" asked the guard.

"We'll help you to put out the fire and save the pieces," said the Japanese.

"No thanks," said the voice from within, "We're getting along very nicely here," or something to that effect; and the fire was left to work its will. When morning came there was an investigation, and it turned out that the Imperial storehouses had been looted by the guards and soldiers left in charge. Even the sacred sleeping chamber of His Majesty had not been inviolate. Several hundred arrests have been made and a dire tussle is pending. While it goes on, goods from the palace will be passed round for sale cheap, and the stealer and the buyer will rejoice together.

The Emperor has sent out a notice: "The pictures of my ancestors have been burned. I shall refuse to hear any music for a month, schools may shut down and affairs of state may go on as they please; the question with me is my ancestors. New pictures must be made, many sacrifices offered, and great attention given."

It is a holiday for the geomancer. The matter of the Queen's grave has been already talked over, at a cost of 1,500,000 yen (these figures are given me by a trust-worthy authority) but her picture also was burned on Saturday night, so that the whole matter must be taken up *de novo*. There are rumors that the palace is now rendered unpropitious by the fire and that another must be juggled for.

Guards stand three deep about the corners and gates of the unholy place, threatening with their ever fixed bayonets to perforate the innocent passer. A time of storm and stress is upon the spiritual props of the Empire, while the material elements are having a North-Western Indian pow-wow, with no fear whatever of law and order stepping in.

In keeping with these conditions a week ago we had the first highway robbery of foreigners that has taken place since the opening of the ports.[4] A Mr. Sidebotham[5] was in charge of a party journeying from

---

4 This refers to both the literal opening of Korean ports to foreign trade in conjunction with the Kanghwa Treaty with Japan in 1876, and the "opening" of Korea more broadly. Though it is difficult to believe that this was the first reported incidence of theft involving a foreigner, based on other reports by resident foreigners at the time, such incidents were exceedingly rare.

5 Richard Henry Sidebotham (史保淡, 1874–1908) was a British missionary posted at the Daegu Branch of the U.S. Northern Presbyterian Church mission. He is credited with bringing the first piano to Korea, a piano that he brought for his

Pusan to Taegu. Suddenly they were attacked by Korean robbers who stationed Mr. Sidebotham on a rock, prodded him gently with their swords, and then demanded clothing, money, and baggage, promising to leave him intact if he responded quickly. There was nothing to do but to yield, and the party in a most destitute condition reached the end of its journey.

(Oct.19ᵗʰ, 1900)

---

wife through the port of Busan and on to Daegu via the Nakdong River on 26–8 March 1900. Gale claims that this robbery happened a week prior to the penning of this essay on 19 October 1900, so it seems that the robbery did not occur during the transporting of the piano. Gale may have been reporting what he had heard by word of mouth, as I am unable to locate any information on a robbery involving Sidebotham.

A Royal Funeral

Following the elevation of Chosŏn Korea to the status of Great Han Empire (Taehan cheguk 大韓帝國) and the simultaneous promotion of King Kojong to the level of emperor in 1897, Kyŏngun'gung (慶運宮) was rechristened Tŏksugung (德壽宮). The fire on the grounds of this palace in 1900 that wiped out the Sŏnwŏnjŏn and the royal portraits housed within obliged the emperor, with the aid of his geomancers, to select a propitious site to shore up the good fortune of the newly established empire. The "Commissioner" in the account below who thwarts the construction plans of the shrine in Cromwellian fashion seems to refer to Horace Newton Allen (1858–1932), an American doctor and first Protestant missionary in Korea who was quite close to King Kojong. Allen served in the United States legation in Korea as secretary in 1890 and later as minister and consul general in 1897, before being recalled over disagreements with the United States government over its non-intervention stance in the Russo-Japanese War (1904–5). The new Sŏnwŏnjŏn, also known as Yŏngsŏnmun Palace (永成門), would indeed not be located at this site and was eventually erected in the northwest corner of the palace compound.

This account continues the narrative of King Kojong as a superstitious and conservative monarch out of touch with the modern world, surrounded once again by fortune-tellers and geomancers. However, even in his ultimate dismissal of such superstitious beliefs, Gale's description of geomantic practice is informed, accurate, and somewhat sympathetic, displaying a tone that echoes through many of his writings and embodying a dissonance between his missionary and Koreaphile personas.

A Royal Funeral
Pen Pictures, 71

A long row of carts, like Israel's going down to Egypt,[1] passed out of the Palace yesterday, loaded with charred embers, logs, tiles, old iron, rags, and other debris. Behind the bullocks dragging them came as many pennies with bursting hampers on their backs, filled with ashes. It was the funeral procession of the late monarchs of this dynasty, whose ghosts and spirits were burned the other night. These remains are bound for a Buddhist monastery outside of the East Gate, where they are to be prayed over, and fed, and sacrificed to, and wept for, and paid millions of cash to, in the hope of straightening out the national calamity that has befallen Korea, by the burning of the tablets and pictures of the ancestors.

His Majesty refuses to go anywhere near the haunted region of the fire. He has backed up into a foreign building bordering on the Customs compound, and there he is casting lots, reading horoscopes, and listening to the findings of witches and geomancers. He was informed the other night by this congress of experts, that the former site of the Tablet Hall was rendered unpropitious, and that it could never be built again; but that they had skillfully caught up a current of influence,[2] and found that it ran directly across the customs compound, and that it offered a most lucky site at a few yards from the palace rear. The site happened to be the tennis court of the Commissioner, but never mind that; it was Korean soil and His Majesty was Emperor, and the tablets must have a resting place, regardless of a thousand Commissioners.

So they went at it bright and early on the following day, measuring off lines from the "pig" point to the "dog": keeping the "monkey" and "rat" in

---

1 This refers to Jacob (a.k.a Israel), along with his descendants and all of his possessions moving to Egypt in carts, as related in Genesis 46:1–7.

2 This "current of influence" refers to the belief in Korean geomancy (*p'ungsu* 風水) that a vital force (*saenggi* 生氣) flows under the surface of the earth. Humans can manipulate this force by choosing "propitious sites" for establishing homes, capitals, and ancestral graves, locations where such vital forces are said to congeal. Wind and water are believed to yield the most influence on the movement of this vital force, hence the sinographs that constitute the term *p'ungsu*. For an overview of Korean geomancy, see Kitagawa, ed., *The Religious Traditions of Asia*, 342–3; Yoon, *P'ungsu*.

their proper places.[3] Everything was coming out in perfect order, "weasel" and "snake" just where they ought to be, when suddenly the Commissioner returned for tiffin. He saw an assemblage gathered on his tennis court, and made bold to march over and inquire after the nature of their visit.

The reply was something like this: "His Majesty wantchee catch one piece ground makee joss-temple.[4] Every man say this can do number one luck." Cromwell's smash up of the Parliament in 1648 was light compared to the damage done to this concourse of diviners,[5] who had assembled to locate a joss-house on the Commissioner's lawn-tennis court, Seoul, 1900.

(Oct.23rd, 1900)

Illustration 10. "The Trappings of a Funeral," in *Pen Pictures*

---

3 In geomantic practice, specific animals of the Chinese sexagenary cycle (the Chinese zodiac) are associated with specific compass directions, and in turn one of the five basic elements (wood, fire, earth, metal, and water) in any given year. In order to ensure good fortune, these must be in harmony with each other.

4 "Joss-temple" or "Joss-house" is a generic term for a "Chinese"-style temple or place of deity worship, a term that was popular in nineteenth- and early twentieth-century western United States.

5 Oliver Cromwell (1599–1658) served as Lord Protector of the Commonwealth from 1653 to 1658 and was an important yet controversial political and military leader. Gale is referring to Cromwell's forceful dismissal of the so-called Rump Parliament in 1653 because of their refusal to dissolve, despite an agreement to do so – a speech replete with harsh denunciations, moral indictments, and religious allusions.

"Belong" Small Boxer

At the time of writing, the Boxer Rebellion (1899–1901), also known as the Militia United in Righteousness Movement (義和團運動), was rocking China's capital, contributing to rumours that the anti-foreign, anti-colonial, anti-missionary sentiments fuelling this revolt would spread to Korea. The rebellion had a considerable impact on fanning the flames of racist rhetoric on the so-called Yellow Peril of Asia threatening to engulf the West, discourse that Gale reiterates when discussing the threat of a perennially backward and dangerously unstable Korea. Homer Hulbert wrote in 1905 of the sense of unease brought about by the revolt: "As the summer came on, all interest in things Korean was held in suspension, while the great uprising in China swelled to such monstrous proportions, and the investment of Peking and the siege of the foreign legations there left the world no time to care for or think of other things. There were fears that the Boxer movement would be contagious and that it would spread to Korea. Indeed it was reported in the middle of July that the infection had reached Korea; but unfortunately this proved false."[1] Although an uprising in Korea did not come to fruition, a Boxer "plot" was indeed uncovered involving the discovery of threatening letters sent to foreign legations. Whereas the Boxer Rebellion had considerable popular support in China and even split the allegiances of the Chinese monarchy, there is no evidence to suggest that this "Small Boxer" plot in Korea was anything other than a political machination by a specific faction in the government.

Enter the infamous Kim Yŏngjun (金永準 ?–1901), a justice in the Chosŏn Court of Appeals (P'yŏngniwŏn chaep'anjang 平理院 裁判長).

---

1 Hulbert, *The Passing of Korea*, 171.

The turn-of-the century Chosŏn government was divided into three factions: Kim was a pro-Japanese minister in competition with the pro-American and pro-Russian groups. Whether he was behind the plot to attack foreign interests in Korea is unclear. Although Gale seems to suggest Kim's guilt, Hulbert claims that Kim became a scapegoat for the real culprit, a member of the Min clan who orchestrated the clandestine sale of Roze Island (Wŏlmido) to the Japanese.[2] Meanwhile, a contemporary scholar, Chang Hŭihŭng, suggests that Kim's downfall was due to a collision with the pro-American eunuch official Kang Sŏkho (姜錫鎬).[3] Whatever Kim's involvement in the plot, his downfall was as swift as his meteoric rise, and his sudden, savage demise is related in the following chapters of *Pen Pictures*.

"Belong" Small Boxer
Pen Pictures, 72–3

We have had a week of persistent rumor that has ended in the unearthing of a plot to play boxer here in Korea. There is now no question but that an order was sent secretly, a month or more ago, to every prefect, commanding him to begin the task of housecleaning on the 15th of the 10th Moon (December 6th). They were to destroy all natives who had in any way been associated with Westerners or Japanese, and following the example of China, were to clean out the foreign settlements. The order is said to have been signed by a Yi, name unknown, and Kim Yŏngjun. The moment that the representatives called the attention of the Foreign Office to it, they replied saying, "Yes, we have discovered the same plot and are working like tigers to … " The last part of the reply is indecipherable. Of course no one knows the bad man who originated it, or the worser [*sic*] man who let it out. His Majesty says: "Dear me, there's some blunder somewhere, I shall have to exile the rascal who designed it to Chemulp'o," and probably the man who let it out to the Everlasting Shades.

The Supreme Court is working at the task of finding the guilty parties. Meanwhile, Kim Yŏngjun writes to the *Hwangsŏng News*:[4] "Somebody

---

2 Ibid., 172.

3 Chang Huihŭng, "Tae Han chegukki naesi Kang Sŏkho ŭi hwaltong."

4 *Hwangsŏng sinmun* (皇城新聞), often referred to in English as the *Capitol Gazette*, was a daily newspaper that ran from 1898 until Korea's annexation by Japan in

with a bad mind is trying to involve this original me in difficulties, speaking lies that have no roots, and saying that all foreigners are to be expelled from the country. They have even forged my seal and sent this order to the prefects. When I heard of this my flesh trembled and I shuddered in my soul. Do not trust this lying generation; do not even listen to them. (Signed) Kim Yŏngjun."

Kim Yŏngjun has only one eye, but he sees further than any two-eyed man in the land. His father was killed in the émeute of 1882[5] for withholding rice from the soldiers. Kim has had experience and is born of a generation that understands the ways of the Far East. In the good old days no man with a physical blemish could appear before the king; a one-eyed man would surely have given His Majesty a fit; but Kim the man with the single yellow eye, the yellow heart, and the yellow hand, is cuddled and loved and honored and made the first in the kingdom.

When His Majesty is in need of money, which is always, Kim is called, and the dust that makes the hand doubly yellow is poured out at his master's feet. There seems no limit to the gold that he is able to command. The yellow heart "belong Boxer," no question about it, and the yellow eye is piloting the peninsula whither? We pray that we may not be left long to the tender mercies of such a trinity. The rumor now is that Kim was to be killed with the foreigners. A little dust in the eyes and wool in the brain might lead one to think so, and think him innocent. A Christmas gift of 10,000 Japanese troops to ornament the city would be most acceptable. Now that the plot is discovered, we suppose it will not come off, but the conditions will still exist, will in fact be aggravated, and what guarantee is there of safety? The fact that there are

---

1910. The paper was conservative in tone and used *kukhanmun* (mixed-script) orthography. Kim's plea read, "有一惡心者가 欲爲陷人하야 以無根謊說노 稱以排斥外人하人 本人에 圖章을 僞造하야 匿名書로 或傳致外邑云하니 聞甚駭怪한지라 此等悖類謊說은 切勿信聽홈 金永準告白." See "Kwanggo," *Hwangsŏng sinmun*, 23 November 1900.

5 The Imo Incident or Imo Mutiny (壬午軍亂 *Imo kullan*) was named after the year in the Chinese sexagenary cycle (*imo*) in which the uprising occured, 1882 in the Western calendar. Although a number of theses have been put forth to explain the rioting among Korean soldiers, all seemed linked in some way to the perceived poor treatment of Korea's regular military forces in comparison to the newly formed and Japanese-trained "special forces" (*pyŏlgigun*), the first modernized military force in Korea. A lack of adequate rations and salaries for regular army members was blamed on the cost of the special-forces unit.

a few plucky Japanese soldiers in town is a safeguard, indeed, but yet they are so few in number.

Without being pessimistic, we may say that Korea is at present hopeless. Some of us have had hopes, and aspirations, and dreams with regard to the country, but the last two years have blotted them out. It is on the down grade, and the only thing that is moving rapidly is the course of degeneration.

Soldiers are being recruited in great numbers to defend His Majesty against his own people. The currency, bad enough before, is more than ever to-day the expression of official corruption; the Palace is a never-ending joss-house, and the nation is absolutely without guide whatever.

The ancient Code of the Mings that was formerly the reference book of every official, has, in recent upheavals, been discarded and each mandarin is a law unto himself, and in most cases a representation of lawlessness to everyone else. No kinder, quieter, more inoffensive people, up to a certain point, exist than Koreans, but beyond that they are a variety of "yellow peril," and one of these days, unless Japan steps in, we shall see in the land of Morning Calm a culmination of the influences that are now at work, that will assuredly absorb some of the spare attention of the Far East.

(Nov. 24th, 1900 Seoul)

The Foreign "Squeezer"

Until recently, the dominant assessment in academia of reform efforts initiated under King Kojong has been overwhelmingly negative. Chosŏn
government policy during the late nineteenth and early twentieth centuries has been characterized as fitful, half-hearted, and lacking conviction and clear direction.[1] Gale's assessment of Kojong's performance
certainly concurs with this perception. However, in the past decade or
so many scholars have begun to re-evaluate Kojong-era Korea, taking
into consideration the limitations and exigencies of the period to paint
a more nuanced portrait of a modernizing Korea committed to reform
but confounded by complex circumstances.[2] Perhaps the most critical
limitation on Korean reform efforts was the inability of the Chosŏn
government to access the revenue necessary to institutute significant
changes. In characteristic fashion, Gale invokes the wastefulness of

---

1 For example, *Silp'aehan kaehyŏk ŭi yŏksa* (A History of Failed Reform) depicts
  reform attempts under Kojong as the most recent episode in a long history of
  failed reforms, assigning ultimate blame for the failure to Japanese imperialism.
  See Yŏksa munje yŏn'guso, *Silp'aehan kaehyŏk ŭi yŏksa*. Sŏng Yŏnggu claims that
  up until roughly 2005, stagnation theory (*ch'imch'eron*) reigned in research on
  the late Chosŏn economy. For an overview of trends in research on the late-
  Chosŏn era, see Sŏng, "2008nyŏn Chosŏn hugisa yŏn'gu kyŏnghyang kwa chŏnmang," 83.
2 For a multi-faceted examination of reforms during the Taehan Empire period,
  see Kim, Duncan, and Kim, *Reform and Modernity in the Taehan Empire*. Yi T'aejin
  paints Emperor Kojong as a determined modernizer and is the first major
  scholar to point out the positive aspects of factionalism. See Yi, *Kojong sidae ŭi
  chaejomyŏng*; Yi, *Taehan cheguk*.

traditional ceremony – in this case the devotion of two million dollars, or a fifth of the entire budget, to moving the late queen's grave – as a short-sighted and foolish use of resources. However, this was not the only source of government insolvency. As mentioned in a previous chapter, the selling of titles and ranks in the government was a quick method for Kojong's Korea to raise revenue, but this simply enlarged the rolls of the non-taxed population. Kojong's father, the Taewŏn'gun (興宣大院君, 1820–98; r. 1864–73), attempted to access untapped revenue by abolishing in 1871 the private academies (*sŏwŏn* 書員) that had for centuries functioned as tax havens, but as James Palais demonstrates, this had limited impact on generating government revenue and instead created an anti-reform backlash among the literati.[3] Thus, the main impediment to reform seems to have been, in the words of Kim Tong-no, not the vision of reform itself but the indifference to financial modernization as a means of securing funding for reform.[4] Gale notes a "vision of reform" among certain brave Korean figures, notably his acquaintance Kwŏn Yŏngjin, in "A New Korean," and the brother of the governor of Kyŏngsang Province, who appears in this account, but like most observers of his day he did not accord the wherewithal or the conviction for reform to Korea's monarch.

The Foreign "Squeezer!"
Pen Pictures, 74–5

A great wet blanket spreads itself over the land, it rains and snows by fits and starts. The streets are deep with mire and the soldier huddles himself up in his sentry box at the corner of the street, a picture of anything but *la courage militaire.* Squads waken at times to splash dismally through to relieve their comrades. To intensify the extraordinary conditions of wind and weather, His Majesty is building watch-towers at the corners of the palace wall. The result of the present-day trend of affairs is that we are to have a Eurasian city. Standing now at Chongno in the centre, you are confronted by a combination of East and West that is surprising to behold. Overhead is a network of yard-arms, porcelain nonconductors, electric wires, arc-lights; underneath, ties, spikes, steel

---

3 Palais, *Politics and Policy in Traditional Korea*, chap. 6.
4 Kim Tong-no, "Views on Modern Reform in the *Hwangsŏng sinmun*," 67.

rails, car speeding after car. What the old bell that has hung for five hundred years thinks of these times we have not yet heard.

The Chancellor of the Exchequer has made his financial statement for the coming year, and it runs as follows: Taxation is to be increased something over one third, so as to bring the revenue of six million dollars up to ten or thereabouts. Four million is appropriated for the army, each soldier getting his uniform, and food, and five dollars a month. Two million goes to moving the Queen's Tomb; one million is to be spent in connection with the new Office of Ceremony of which Min Yŏnghwan is president.[5] As this is a new venture, the object of which is not very clear as yet to the general public, the likelihood is that it will cost more than the appropriation. This leaves three million for all other expenses, the whole reckoning being based on a venture, namely the proposed increase of taxation. It will require surely the ghost of a Gladstone or some other powerful spirit to pull them through.

Not long ago the Governor of Kyŏngsang province, being informed that taxation was to be increased one third, promptly resigned. In his opinion the proposed increase was greater than was possible to collect.

A brother of the said governor appeared before His Majesty a few days ago and said, "I know it will cost me my life, but I shall speak; These men" pointing to Yi, and Kim of the Boxer plan, "are the destruction of this country, be warned." The speaker was hustled out of the Palace and will, I suppose, be promptly dealt with. Long may he live. A dozen men like him in rank and courage would save this benighted land. When such as he face danger and speak there is hope for Korea.

There are new doings in Korean finance. His Majesty is endeavouring to extend the Palace grounds, but foreigners are in possession of territory on every hand, so that each plot has to be haggled for and screwed out of the avaricious Westerner. With some degree of justice

---

5 Min Yŏnghwan (閔泳煥, 1861–1905) was a government minister during the late Chosŏn dynasty who held various posts, including official in the Board of Personnel (*Ijo*) and first ambassador to the United States, a post he was unable to take up because of the murder of his aunt, Queen Min. He also served as Special Ambassador to Russia and Korean Envoy to Great Britain. He was an active supporter of the Independence Club (Tongnip hyŏphoe), and upon Korea's signing of the Ŭlsa Protectorate Treaty with Japan, committed suicide in protest.

Illustration 11. "The Imperial Gateway" (Kyŏngbokkung 景福宮), in *Pen Pictures*

he can say that *yangin*[6] are the greatest "squeezers" alive. Not long ago he was clearing a way out to the street on the east side, where lived a Teuton of long experience in the East.

"How much do you want for your pile of debris?" inquired the man from the Palace.

"Ten sousand dollars" was the answer.

"My, His Majesty will give you two."

"Aus," said the Westerner, "Ich habe viel work to see to und no time to shpend."

Again the messenger came and said, "His Majesty does not mind your being here or your shack, but if you should put up a light-house on the top of your roof, you would be able to see into the palace and that would be very bad."

"Very bad, would it?" and the messenger left.

---

6 *Yangin* (洋人), "Westerners," as opposed to *Tongin* (東人), "Easterners," or in the parlance of the day, "Orientals."

Immediately the foreigner called a Chinese carpenter, saying, "John, how much you take put up one piece light-house top-side my godown cheap; anyding can do."

"I takee thirty-seven dollar fifty cents."

"Gut," and the light-house went up.

In hot haste came the messenger from the Palace with ten thousand dollars.

"Here, here, down with that light-house quick."

The street is now clear and the genial foreigner smokes placidly over a comfortable fire, smiling broadly at times. I cannot vouch for the broad smile and one or two other details of this story, but in the main it is correct.

(Jan. 8th 1901)

The Awful Kim

In "The Awful Kim," Gale claims that the titular character, Kim Yŏngjun, was finally brought down by the combined strength of the Min clan, who banded together in defence of a jailed member; a slighted Lady Ŏm,[1] who feared usurpation by palace Lady Kang – who had been introduced by Kim; and a betrayed Kojong, who had finally had enough of his machinations. As Gale points out, Kim's ultimate undoing was the so-called Roze Island Incident (Wŏlmido sakŏn), or at least his perceived involvement in it. In *The Passing of Korea*, Homer Hulbert suggests that "Kim Yŏngjun became a political pawn in a scheme by the Min clan in the matter of the selling of Roze Island," an island in the harbour of Chemulp'o (present-day Inch'ŏn). Hulbert goes on: "The matter made a great stir, for it was plain that someone had assumed the responsibility of selling the island to the Japanese. This was the signal for a sweeping investigation, which was so manipulated by powerful parties that the real perpetrators of the outrage were dismissed as guiltless, but a side issue which arose in regard to certain threatening letters that were sent to the foreign legations was made a peg upon which to hang the seizure, trial and execution of Kim Yŏngjun, as before mentioned. Min Yŏngju was the man who sold the island to the Japanese, and he finally had to put down thirty-five thousand yen and buy it back."[2] Thus, the "Boxer" plot mentioned two chapters earlier

---

1 Lady Ŏm was a former lady-in-waiting to Queen Min and the mother of Prince Ŭn, the younger half-brother of King Sunjong. Sunjong ascended the throne in 1907 when his father King Kojong was forced to abdicate.

2 Hulbert, *The Passing of Korea*, 172.

and the Roze Island Incident, according to Hulbert, combined to seal Kim's fate.

But what was the identity of the shadowy figure in this chapter who leaked Kim's name to King Kojong and Lady Ŏm? According to Chang Hŭihŭng, this was none other than the pro-American eunuch minister, Kang Sŏkho.[3] Kim's downfall began when a secret message that he attempted to pass to Kojong was intercepted by Kang. The message averred that the pro-American official Kang, in collusion with the American diplomat William F. Sands and over ten pro-American Korean officials, were conspiring to establish a republic and to remove Lady Ŏm.[4] Kim's manipulation was then reported to Kojong, driving a wedge between them, enhancing Kang's credibility before the king and further precipitating Kim's decline.[5]

The Awful Kim
Pen Pictures, 76–7

The past week has whirled us along into the unexpected. To-night one-eyed Kim languishes in prison.

"But yesterday the word of Caesar might
Have stood against the world: now lies he there,
And none so poor to do him reverence."[6]

The yellow eye, the yellow heart, the yellow hand, have passed for the present out of the official life of the peninsula, and in the low dark prison house, where so many have suffered at his nod, he himself, guarded by a cordon of soldiers, lies shackled.

For months past, notwithstanding the giddy prosperity that bore him along, Kim has felt that there were dangers threatening his position. Behold him to-night, run over as by a railway train, or, to put it literally,

---

3 Chang Huihŭng, "Tae Han chegukgi naesi Kang Sŏkho ŭi hwaltong."
4 *Kojong sidaesa* 5, February 14, 1900; quoted in Chang, "Kang Sŏkho ŭi hwaltong," 97.
5 Chang Huihŭng, "Kang Sŏkho ŭi hwaltong."
6 This is an excerpt from Shakespeare's *Julius Caesar*, Act 3, Scene 2; Mark Antony is remarking on the sudden and dramatic fall of Julius Caesar.

in collision with Lady Ŏm. Some time ago at the bidding of his fickle lord, Kim introduced a new lady to the palace, who was so attractive that she absorbed entirely the imperial will. His Majesty was delighted, we are told, and ordered a castle to be built for her and a chain of gold to be put round her neck. Besides, he gave her two hundred dollars.

All this time Lady Ŏm was wondering why her visits had been interrupted, and why her opinion was no longer sought in affairs of state. Dark suspicion took possession of her soul and she prayed the gods to smite someone.

Suddenly, like a bolt out of a clear sky, came the announcement that Roze Island opposite Chemulp'o had been sold to the Japanese. A prominent peak, commanding entrance to the Capital, passing thus mysteriously out of the hands of His Majesty into possession of a foreign power was enough to knock even thoughts of Lady Kang from his mind, and arrests were made in high places; Min, called also the "Executioner," the "Buddha," and the "Tiger" going first to prison, accompanied by his son. One-eyed Kim had informed and secured their arrest. Following this the whole family of Mins turned out to save their chief. They produced evidence showing that Kim himself had sold the island, and up to the hour of their chief's arrest had been prime mover in bringing about the transfer. The Mins are not as powerful as in olden days when they were little shoguns, but they still have some vigor left, and when they band together, it behooves even Kim Yŏngjun to see to his tackling that all is made fast about the ship and ready for a typhoon.

Lady Ŏm had heard that a lordly mansion was to be built for someone.

"For whom?" asked she. "For me and my son, (Yŏngwang (英王), the Flowery King)?"

"Oh, no, for lady Kang."

"Lady Kang? Who is she? Stars and garters, if I catch her ***"

The castle was not built. His Majesty has decided to buy more land and needs all his money; besides, the mint was burned night before last, and no more can be coined, except what comes from private parties. It is fortunate that we have these or we might run out of money altogether. But never mind the mint; detectives are out in hot haste to run down the villain who introduced Kang to his majesty.

Seeing an ugly situation closing around him, One-eyed Kim made a desperate throw in order to sweep Lady Ŏm off his track. He appeared a day or two ago before His Majesty with a letter purporting to be from Prince So-and-So in America, urging the dismissal of Lady Ŏm. Kim most eloquently denounced the letter, and called upon the ancestral spirits to smite Ŭihwa for such a preposterous proposal. When Lady Ŏm had been as the apple of the eye to His Majesty, to think of removing her was treason itself.

Two whisperers that night wound their way through different parts of the city, stealing under walls and along shadows. One was to His Majesty and the other was to see Lady Ŏm. In a lull in the goings and comings of the palace there wriggled round and underneath, and over the ledges, the creepy, crawly whisperer, until he was behind His Majesty and unnoticed by the callers, who stand with bowed heads. Trained to movement and speech that would out-silence a spirit, the whisperer breathed forth, "Be it known – sh – sh – sh that His Highness Prince So-and-So never wrote the letter – sh – sh – sh; one-eyed Kim did it himself, for I saw him, sh – sh."

The other whisperer made his way to Lady Ŏm and said, "Ma-ma" (also the word for small-pox, but in this case a title of respect, as the same sound happens to be with Anglo-Saxons), "Ma-ma, the man who introduced the wretch Kang to the Palace was one-eyed Kim, for I saw him."

An hour later there broke on Kim's head woes from three quarters, one from his Majesty, one from the Min Family, and one from Lady Ŏm. Kim had forged the letter marked by the Prince; Kim had taken a "squeeze" of seven thousand dollars on the sale of the island and then had turned traitor; Kim had pretended a friendship for Lady Ŏm, and yet had introduced another to usurp her place. How will it go with Kim, think ye?

As I mentioned above, the mint was burned the night before last, just as the announcement had been made that Korea was to have a gold and silver currency. Everything was in readiness for the coinage and for the fire. It must have cost a huge effort to ignite the place, but the work has been done most successfully, for the machinery is ruined, a million dollars gone, and only the brick shell of the building remains. We shall continue to use nickels. None of your gold and silver coins or newfangled notions for this country, the home-made kind or those strung on a string, are quite good enough.

Country people call coins without the hole in the middle *maengjŏn*,[7] "blind money." "Blind money," they say, "means ruin to the country." Probably they are right.

(Mar. 8th 1901)

---

7 盲錢.

Exit Kim

On 18 March 1901, Kim Yŏngjun was officially implicated in the Roze Island Incident and sentenced to hanging, although the method of death was much more prolonged and violent.[1] Hulbert confirms Gale's account of the downfall and violent death of Kim: "Against Kim Yŏngjun was ranged the whole nobility of the country, who waited with what patience they could until his power to extort money began to wane, and then fell upon him like wolves upon a belated traveler at night. But it was not until the opening of the new year, 1901, that he was deposed, tried and killed in a most horrible manner. After excruciating tortures, he was at last strangled to death."[2] A last-ditch effort to exonerate Kim and the other defendants in the hours before the execution based on a claim that Kim's testimony was false was to no avail, and the sentence was carried out.[3]

It is unclear why Gale spilled so much ink over the personage of Kim Yŏngjun, a relatively minor figure, at a period of such political unrest and social upheaval. The rise and fall of Kim may be read as a cautionary tale in the vein of Confucian literature, admonishing immoral behaviour and meting out justice. Given Gale's pessimistic outlook for Korea's prospects at the time, however, this narrative should more accurately be characterized as a contribution to the discourse on Korean

---

1 *Kojong sillok* 41, 18 March 1901, in *Chosŏn wangjo sillok.*

2 Hulbert, *The Passing of Korea,* 171.

3 *Kojong sillok* 41, 19 March 1901, in *Chosŏn wangjo sillok.*

cultural stagnation and decay. In other words, Kim's behaviour was not just his own but the symptom of a broader Korean illness that demanded violent expulsion, from within or without.

Exit Kim
Pen Pictures, 78

The day of judgment of Korea has surely come, for last night the same one-eyed Kim, who till so recently held the power that moved the king, was tortured, mutilated, and strangled, by the same fickle lord that hung on his smile but a day or two ago.

"Ugh, we are well rid of him," says His Imperial Highness.

In the same courtyard where less than a year gone by Kwŏn and An[4] were murdered by his order, lie his shattered fragments, proclaiming to the city the vanity of all human things. He was a lover of ancient custom and by ancient custom he departed.

I said to an acquaintance, "If he has done anything worthy of death, hang him in a neat gentlemanly way."

"No, no," was the reply, "he himself loved the bastinado,[5] and the paddle, and the torture chair," and so by his own methods he died.

I read in an ancient history that in the year *kyŏngsin* (AD 1) the king of Korea was offering sacrifice to Heaven, when the pig to be offered ran away. His Majesty sent two officers Takni and Sappi to catch it. They chased the animal into Ch'angok Lake, caught it, and hamstringed it so that it could not run away again. The king on seeing the victim brought before him in this condition flew into a rage and said, "How dare you mutilate a beast that is to be offered to God? Take these men out and bury them alive."

They were so buried, and a month or two later the king fell ill.

The witch who waited on him said,

"The spirits of Takni and Sappi are after you for your life."

---

4 The identities of An and Kwŏn are uncertain, as Gale does not introduce them in previous chapters.

5 This is a form of punishment that involves whipping the exposed soles of the feet.

The king, realizing his danger, confessed that he had committed a great sin in killing two men for the sake of one pig, and so he prayed to them for mercy.

No doubt the poor wretch Kim prayed also; he had killed An and Kwŏn – for the sake of what? – and now their spirits were after him.

Let's drop the curtain on Kim; his sins are too dark and too many to bear even mention, and let us hope that His Majesty will be wiser in future and select one Mordecai at least, to offset the many Hamans of his court.[6]

(Mar. 19th, 1901)

6　Haman and Mordecai are the main figures from the Book of Esther in the Old Testament, in a story set in ancient Persia. Haman was a vizier under King Xerxes I and, having learned that one of his subjects named Mordecai refuses to bow and show fealty to him, hatches a plot along with his wife to destroy Mordecai and all of the Jewish people. Haman attempts to convince the king to carry out an order to exterminate all the Jews in the realm, but Queen Esther, a Jew herself, intercedes to save her people. Haman is hanged on the very gallows that he has prepared for Mordecai. Haman is considered to be the archetype of evil and injurious council for a monarch, hence the comparison here with Kim.

The Opening of War

The Russo-Japanese War lasted just over a year (February 1904–May 1905) and resulted in a resounding victory for Japan. Despite its swift resolution, the conflict would have far-reaching implications for the conduct of modern warfare, East-West relations, and the balance of colonial powers. It was the first war to demonstrate the destructive, deadly potential of modern warfare, resulting in over two hundred thousand killed or wounded among the victorious Japanese.[1] Although the war did not enter the collective memory of Europe as it did in Asia and especially Japan, the Russo-Japanese War foreshadowed the destructive potential for modern warfare that would be released a decade later in Europe. Moreover, the Treaty of Portsmouth that concluded the war created a temporary but an uneasy peace, as it propelled Japan into a collision course with U.S. interests in the Pacific.[2] The war finally determined the balance of power in East Asia, forestalling further Russian influence in Korean affairs, sealing Korea's fate as an eventual colony of Japan, and launching Japan into the ranks of major colonial powers.

Perhaps the most significant consequence of the Russo-Japanese War, however, was the psychological impact of the war's result. It is difficult to overstate the degree of shock that Japan's victory in the war engendered. Japan's victory over China in the Sino-Japanese War (1894–5), though a dramatic subversion of the traditional Sinocentric hierarchy in East Asia, had not been completely surprising to most informed observers, and its repercussions were largely limited to East

---

1 Jacob, *The Russo-Japanese War*, 3.
2 Jacob, *The Russo-Japanese War*.

Asia. Japan's victory over Russia, however, was the first defeat of a European country by a non-European foe, fuelling fears of a growing "Yellow Peril" in Western discourse but also vindicating the reform efforts championed by Japan and its Western supporters, establishing the country as a model for Western-inspired technological, social, and political transformation. In the early years of Japan's administration of Korea, Gale would be among those voices calling for a judicious Japanese intervention in Korea due its demonstrated lack of progress in modernization. The opening years of the twentieth century had unfortunately proven for many observers the failure of Korean attempts at modernization and the necessity of Japanese intercession, welcome for some and lamentable for others.

The Opening of War
Pen Pictures, 79–80

One hardly knows who has been the greater fool, Korea or Russia. Korea has been duped and Russia has made herself the laughing stock of the whole Far East. During these months she has lived in a Fool's Paradise, and has thought it clever to manifest contempt for Japan and the Japanese. They were quite unworthy of the notice of her imperial dignity. The Emperor of Korea, being morally and intellectually a feeble man, took his lesson from the Russians and smiled to think of the vanity of these little people who dared to oppose the seven-foot, bearded sons of Anak.[3] During the days of keen negotiations when matters began to veer toward the breaking point, the Emperor remarked, "Dear me! I had a dream last night and there were fierce trampling of feet and sounds of war; shall we die? What shall we do?"

"Your Imperial Majesty may abide in peace," said Mr. Pavlov, "There are two Russian Men-of-War in Chemulp'o, and I can have 5000 troops here from Port Arthur[4] in twenty-four hours. The Japanese cannot get

---

3　Anak was a figure in the Old Testament who was the progenitor of the Anakim, a people known for their large stature.

4　Port Arthur was the Russian-controlled port at the southern end of the Liaodong Peninsula, currently part of China. The land on which Port Arthur was built was part of the original land that was to be ceded to Japan after its victory over the Qing Empire in the Sino-Japanese War, but reverted to Russia following the

at you, our ships guard the sea, you are safe. If you are anxious, call on me, but don't let the Japanese Minister bother you; tell him you are sick and have as little to do as possible with the English or Americans. They are all creatures of the same kind of stomach, very bad, veera bad." And the hopeless Korean Emperor and his princelings prattled on with their toys and playthings, while Yi Yongik, the henchman of Russia, ran between the Palace and the Czar's Legation.

The long, drawn-out days of conference continued. There were many occasions of startling rumor, when His Majesty would send suddenly for Mr. Pavlov.

"What is this I hear? Are we still alive?" etc.

"Of course," says Pavlov, "there are two Russian Men-of-War in Chemulp'o, and seven battle-ships at Port Arthur, with no Japanese vessels in sight."

So the Emperor gathered about him his favourites of Russia; Yi Yongik, Minister of Finance, Kil Yŏngsu, the butcher, head of the peddler gang, etc.[5]

On the 21st of January (1904) a telegram from Tokyo said that the Japanese Government had sent the final communication, but that she would [wait for] a reasonable time before taking action. Some of us measured off ten days, thinking that reasonable, but the Russian Minister scoffed at the idea of war.

"What! Japan dare to attack the might of Russia? Preposterous!"

The ten days went by, yes fifteen, and on Feb. 6th Minister Kurino said to Baron Rosen,[6] "It is finished."

Triple Intervention by Russia, Germany, and France to block a Japanese foothold on the mainland, one of the smouldering points of contention between Russia and Japan that eventually erupted in war.

5 Kil Yŏngsu (吉永洙, ?–?) was of the butcher class, one of the lowborn classes of traditional Korea, but his proficiency in astrology (*chŏmsŏngsul* 占星術) facilitated his entry into the palace, where he earned the favour of King Kojong. He was the head of the pedlar's guild (Sangmusa 商務社), which was adamantly opposed to Japanese encroachment on the Korean economy.

6 Kurino Shinichirō (栗野慎一郎, 1851–1937) was the envoy extraordinary and plenipotentiary in Russia who attempted negotiations to stave off war with Russia prior to the outbreak of war in 1904. Baron Roman Romanovich Rosen (1847–1921) was a Russian diplomat who served as minister in Tokyo at the outbreak of the Russo-Japanese War, which he had tried to prevent. He negotiated the terms of the peace treaty (Treaty of Portsmouth) on terms very favourable to Russia.

There was a lull on the 7th and 8th, but on the 9th into Chemulp'o Harbor came a Japanese fleet with transports. The Russian Men-of-War, on which leaned hard the Emperor, were still there. Their flags flew unconscious of the situation, suddenly grown ominous.

"Please come out of the harbor," said the Japanese Admiral, "we want to talk to you," and he signaled the Asama and the Chiyoda to deal with these two Russians. Bravely, but fool-hardily, the Czar's ships cleared for action and went out with cheers and flags flying.

"What thunder is that I hear?" asked the Emperor of Korea.

"They are firing a salute, Your Majesty."

"It is well! I was so scared."

But there was no end to the salutes, five, ten, twenty-five, thirty, thirty-five, fifty minutes of wild bursts of thunder, that fairly made the Palace walls to rattle. All the ministers looked upon the Emperor with dead faces. A messenger to the Russian Legation could get no answer. In the agony of these reverberations it is said that royalty died many painful deaths.

They were having tiffin at the Russian Legation it seems and the word still was, "There can be no war, impossible!"

At last the fury of it died away – all was quiet, till an hour later, a fierce explosion, two of them, ended the confusion of the day. The two ships of Russia on which had leaned the Emperor of Korea, were in the bottom of the sea; the proud Variak on her side, so that she loomed up like a lost soul when the tide went out.[7]

At just what point the Russian Minister realized that war had actually begun, we do not know, but he said to an American that day, "Think of it, just fancy the audacity of these Japs."

It was of no use now to see the Emperor of Korea, the game was up. He, the most astute of all diplomatic tricksters, had been compelled to bow to the arguments of six and eight-inch guns. The Japanese fleet was undamaged: already she had risen a hundred points in the estimation of the Koreans, while Russia was reduced to a worthless rag.

The Japanese took on shore the wounded, treated them kindly, gave them the best of nursing and medical care. "Why don't they kill them?"

---

7 The *Variak* (a.k.a *Varyag*) was a Russian ship sunk by Japanese forces at the Battle of Chemulp'o on 9 February 1904. Refusing the Japanese ultimatum to sail out of the harbour or be attacked, the crew was rescued by British, French, and Italian cruisers.

asked the Korean countryman. "They are only medicating these rascals to have to fight them again, but it is a kind act. Truly Japan is great."

Later there came a message from the despised Japanese Legation to the Minister for Russia, "I shall have a train waiting for you at 8 o'clock to-morrow morning. Please move out with your nationals. I shall send you a Japanese guard for safety." So M. Pavlov, notwithstanding all the might of Russia, and his seventy three Cossacks, surrounded by Japanese infantry and cavalry, were escorted out of Korea, and so the Russian regime with all its good-for-nothingness and might came to an end.

(Seoul Feb. 1904)

Prospective

This poem was penned by Gale in February 1904, shortly after the surprise attack on Port Arthur by Japan on 8 February. Gale describes "an awful fight on the giddy height," referring to the Japanese naval attack on Russian shore batteries high on the hillsides surrounding Port Arthur, an attack that lasted until late 1904 and resulted in high Japanese casualties. The Russo-Japanese War was widely depicted in Western media, especially in the form of cartoons. One common trope, employed in Gale's poem, was the depiction of Japan as a well-trained, disciplined, modern soldier, short in stature, battling a much larger though bumbling Russian "bear." As the war increasingly turned in Japan's favour, the respective traits of each combatant tended to be more pronounced, with the Japanese soldier – alternately samurai warrior – appearing more menacing and brutal, and the Russian bear or hulking Cossack soldier depicted as increasingly incompetent, stunned, and hapless. One cartoon featured in the *Brooklyn Eagle* in the summer of 1904, by which time the war was going decisively in Japan's favour, portrays a well-equipped modern soldier routing an unprepared "animal," with the caption, "Isn't it time the S.P.C.A. interfered?" In the background are pictured caricatures of Qing China and Chosŏn Korea looking on in amusement, which seems to suggest that popular sentiment in each country leaned toward Japan, or at least was perceived as such in Western media. Defeated by Japan in the Sino-Japanese War just a decade earlier, China nonetheless sided with Japan in the conflict, though Japan declined military aid offered by Yuan Shikai. The Chosŏn official position was one of neutrality, though Kojong leaned toward Russia and depended – foolishly, in the eyes of Gale – on the military protection of its continental benefactor. The majority of Koreans, especially among the intellectual class, favoured Japan against the West, symbolized by an encroaching Russia. In the influential discourse of Pan-Asianism and Social Darwinism dominant at the turn of the century, Japan represented the vanguard of modern Asia and the best hope in a racial struggle against the West. This discourse remained especially appealing prior to the Protectorate Treaty, when Japan's intentions might still have been construed as benign.

Gale's poem contains much of the "Yellow Peril" racist discourse of the day in describing Japan – "a tilt-eyed flat in a horse-hair hat"; "a dynamite devil with a head that's level" – but the rhetoric is decidedly tongue-in-cheek. This seems to be the "lie" that Gale repeatedly refers to in the poem, the lie of Aryan racial superiority and Asian inferiority. In a humorous tone, Gale facetiously appropriates the dominant Social Darwinist discourse of the West and exposes its fatal flaw – gross misinterpretation of Japanese capabilities. The sentiments expressed herein and the result of the war itself confirmed what Gale had been warning for years: Japan's neighbours and the world underestimated the country at their own peril, and it was time to take Japan seriously as a modern nation state in the ranks of world powers.

Prospective
Pen Pictures, 81

(Written Feb. 1904 in Seoul Korea,
on hearing the opening guns of the Japan-Russia War)

Hurrah for the fight and the puffs of white,
In the port of the Hermit Seoul,
For the raring guns, and the rattling tons,
And the flash, and the crash, and the roll.
'Tis the judgment day with a debt to pay,
And more than enough to damn,
Of lies unwept, and faiths non-kept,
And pride, and show, and sham.
'Twas the dapper boy with his new ship toy,
All out for a bit of fun,

That brought him to, and rammed him through,
"Before the war's begun."[1]
So the ball is off at the Peterhoff,[2]
And along the Siberian road
It is "fight or die for the worn-out lie";
It is "reap where you've gone and sowed!"
Yes, the dapper lad's not half so bad,
At the trick, and the ruse, and the plan,
He's a Chinese spy, or a Chosen[3] guy,
With the soul of a fighting man.
He's a tilt-eyed flat in a horse-hair hat,
Or a pig-tail long and spare,
He's a dynamite devil with a head that's level,
To blow up the Russian bear.
And the trains will cease, while the boys increase,
Up the sides of the Yŏsun'gu (Port Arthur)[4]
Where an awful fight on the giddy height
Will square up the false and true.
And the Bear shall die for his brutal lie,
And the lads will bury the dead,
And the flag of the boys long after the noise,
Will float on the heights o'erhead.

1　The Japanese attack on Port Arthur commenced three hours before Japan's official declaration of war was received by Russia.

2　Peterhof was a country estate eighteen miles from the city of St Petersburg. Founded by Peter the Great in 1709, it was subsequently developed into an elaborate imperial summer residence, where many Russian monarchs, including Nicholas II (1868–1916), the tsar at the time of the Russo-Japanese War, spent much of their time.

3　This seems to be a deliberate play on the Japanese pronunciation of the word Chosŏn, or Korean.

4　Yŏsun'gu (旅順口 Lüshunkou) is located at the extreme southern tip of the Liaodong Peninsula and was one of the major battlefronts during the Russo-Japanese War. Japan first seized the port during the opening stages of the Sino-Japanese War (1894–5) and was awarded a portion of the Liaodong Peninsula containing the port as part of the Treaty of Shimonoseki, only to be forced to return control to China following the Triple Intervention of France, Germany, and Russia, a source of national humiliation for Japan. Russia then proceeded to increase its influence in the region before eventual confrontation with Japan.

All Good Things Are Three

"All Good Things Are Three" represents Gale's most damning portrayal of Kojong in all of his collected writings. The description was so disparaging that the American explorer and special correspondent George Kennan felt inclined to include a large excerpt in his article "Korea: A Degenerate State," appearing in an October 1905 edition of the *Outlook*.[1] This article, together with three others by Kennan on Korea appearing in this magazine in 1904 and 1905,[2] perhaps represents the most negative, unflinchingly pessimistic portrayal of Korea ever penned by a Western observer. Kennan prefaces Gale's lengthy description of Kojong in the following way: "An American gentleman of impartiality and sound judgment, who has lived many years in Korea and has had an opportunity to know him well, describes him as follows ..." Elsewhere in the series Kennan cites Gale by name, and the more or less "informed" sections of Kennan's writings owe a debt to Gale's expertise, but the question remains how two Western (North American) observers could begin from a set of shared criteria on Korea and yet arrive at such diametrically opposed conclusions. For all of his pessimism about the state of the Chosŏn government, Gale at least found the Korean character endearing and held out optimism for the eventual betterment of the Korean nation, albeit perhaps under Japanese tutelage. Gale, moreover, held a deep knowledge of and respect for Korean literary culture and found much

---

1 See George Kennan, "Korea: A Degenerate State," *Outlook* 81, 7 October 1905, 307–15.

2 For Kennan's other articles on Korea published in the *Outlook*, see "Standing for One's Rights," this vol., nn 1 and 2.

Illustration 12. "Son Ogong or O Pudong" (孫悟空 五不動), in *Pen Pictures*

Illustration 13. "The Lotus Pavilion" (Kyŏnghoeru 慶會樓), in *Pen Pictures*

worth protecting for posterity. Kennan, by contrast, was almost universally disparaging as to every conceivable aspect of Korea's culture, people, government, and future prospects. It is difficult to understand why Gale did not offer a firmer rebuttal to Kennan than that appearing in "Standing for One's Rights" (also included in this volume); perhaps the Russo-Japanese War and the subsequent eroding of Korean autonomy through the Protectorate Treaty (1905) that was unfolding at exactly this time began to engender in Gale a sense of helplessness and cynicism.

Illustration 14. "The Abode of Royalty" (Hyangwŏnjŏng 香遠亭), in *Pen Pictures*

All Good Things Are Three
Pen Pictures, 82–4

On the official gates of Korea along the tiles that cover the ridges of the corners, there are seated a number of earthenware figures commonly called Son Ogong.[3] Now, Son Ogong was once a monkey that turned

---

3 Son Ogong (孫悟空 Ch. Sun Wukong) is a mythological figure in Chinese writings dating back to the Song dynasty also known as the Monkey King. He

into a man, and journeyed as far as Tibet, performing all sorts of magic feats. He was entirely invulnerable and could not be done to death by either fire or water. A sword might pass through him without the slightest damage to his internal organism; and to drown him in the depths of the sea was merely to treat him to a pleasant and refreshing bath. Such was Son Ogong, and that is the name by which the odd little figures are called that ornament the ridge corners of the Palace gates. It is probably intended to indicate to the people that the government sitting behind is inviolable, invulnerable, impossible of being harmed, and that it will live on after all the gazers are dead.

There is still another explanation of the little figures on the gates, where they are called *o pudong* (the five that mutually balance),[4] each one being the enemy of his next neighbor, and no one of them being able to overcome all of the others. There are the elephant, the mouse, the man, the monkey, etc., grouped into a deadlock, each able to overcome its neighbor on the one hand, and yet in turn ready to be overcome by its neighbor on the other. This is said to insure the government against the danger of a Napoleon or a Caesar, and to leave the various offices balanced off so perfectly, that each prevents the other from moving or acting in an independent way whatever. Some think that the meaning of the little gods on the gates has come to pass in the three parties that now exist in the land.

There is the Emperor and his supporters, including nearly all of the official class; there is the people, which includes all of the uncombed millions and some of the others; there are the Japanese, present now everywhere. The Emperor has no confidence in the People, the People have no use for the Japanese, the Japanese have no faith in the Emperor. Reverse it and we are still correct, the Emperor mistrusts the Japanese, the Japanese have no confidence in the people, and the people despise the Emperor.

---

was the main character in the sixteenth-century Chinese novel *Journey to the West* (西遊記 Ch. *Xiyouji*), a monkey born from a stone who gained supernatural powers of invincibility through Taoist practices. He and other characters accompany the Buddhist monk Xuanzang to the "Western Regions" (Central Asia and India) to obtain Buddhist scriptures.

4   This may be translated literally as "the five immovables" (五不動). The more well-known version of this involves slightly different animals – the mouse, cat, dog, tiger, and elephant – which collectively are known as the five immovable beasts (K. *osu pudong* 五獸不動). The concept of "checks and balances" explained by Gale remains the same.

Some Koreans think that these are mutually equal, and so are happy in the thought of being at last in a fixed condition and destined to go nowhere. We shall see.

As one of these parties, the Emperor of Korea is a gentle little man who has sinned away his day of grace, and now sits unconscious of the crack of doom impending. He has a pleasant face and a gracious smile. Of late years his teeth have turned yellow, and he is getting puffy under the eyes, but still he is handsome as Koreans go. He has none of the marks of a savage, neither in his face lines nor in his voice, but seems admirably suited to a drawing-room of the time of Moab and Edom[5] could he have lived then. He is an abstemious man in his meat and drink and quiet in all his ways. He smokes little and chews nothing but an amber bead. He is a head shorter than the Crown Prince but wiser on the whole.[6] He likes dress and to play with the stars and garters of his Order of the Indian Empire, and the other decorations that have been brought to him from over the sea.[7] He has read nothing and has heard only flattery for forty years. The atmosphere that surrounds him is one of dense superstition, and consequently he is as timid as a fallow deer. He is extremely credulous, and makes up for his lack of book-learning by séances with spirit-rappers and consulters of the eternal shades. He

---

5 Moab and Edom were lands that once occupied the region due east of Israel, in present-day Jordan.

6 The version appearing in Kennan's "A Degenerate State" adds here the following footnote: "The Crown Prince has partially lost his mind as the result of spinal disease." Although the exact medical causes of the Crown Prince's infirmity have never been established, Christine Kim points out that many theories exist, including those averring psychological trauma from having witnessed his mother Queen Min's murder and an opium addiction initiated by his Japanese handlers. However, in a well-known episode in 1898 that came to be referred to as the Kim Hongnyuk Incident (*Kim Hongnyuk sakŏn*), the eponymously named Russian-Korean interpreter attempted to assassinate Emperor Kojong and the Crown Prince by spiking their morning coffee with poison. Kojong, finding the taste strange, did not drink, whereas Sunjong finished the coffee and proceeded to vomit and faint. The offender Kim was arrested, tried, and executed, but the attack reportedly left Sunjong "mentally and physically feeble," as well as impotent. See Christine Kim, "Politics and Pageantry in Protectorate Korea," 838.

7 In this *Pen Pictures* version the following sentence has been crossed out but appears in Kennan's "Korea: A Degenerate State:" "He is as unconscious as a child, stubborn as a Boer, ignorant as a Chinaman, and vain as a Hottentot."

loves his sorceresses, witches, wise-women, and ground doctors, and consults them constantly on affairs of state. Not a day passes but messages come to him from the spirits of the dead. He is kindly disposed and only lately sent a gift to help a poor old coolie, whose tumble-down hut and poverty-stricken condition he happened to notice when he was on his way from the burned Chŏngdong Palace.[8] He does not like his people because they scare him with their Independence Clubs[9] and Societies for the Propagation of Peace. He will have the head off his best friend if that friend gives him cause for alarm. He and his older brother are not on first-class speaking terms; in fact he would be very glad indeed to have his older brother move far away.[10] He is afraid of his nephew who is now in Japan.[11] His own son, now in America, keeps a safe distance, for he has failed on more than one occasion to obey his papa.[12] This

---

8 Tŏksugung (德壽宮).

9 The Independence Club (Tongnip hyŏphoe 獨立協會) was a private initiative
   begun by Sŏ Chaep'il (Philip Jaisohn) on 2 July 1896, which included many
   reform-minded Korean intellectuals and advocated Korean independence,
   democratic institutions, national self-strengthening, modern journalism, and
   language reform, among other causes. The club grew increasingly critical of
   the Crown, calling for the establishment of a constitutional monarchy and the
   curbing of royal authority, which brought it into conflict with King Kojong and
   other conservative elements in the Chosŏn government. It was disbanded in
   December 1898. For an exhaustive account of the organization and its activities,
   see Chandra, *Imperialism, Resistance, and Reform in late Nineteenth-Century Korea*.

10 Kennan, "Korea: A Degenerate State": "he would be very glad indeed to have
    his older brother depart this life."

11 This refers to Yi Chunyong (李埈鎔, 1870–1917), Prince Yŏngsŏn (永宣君), who
    was sent to prison in 1894 on charges of conspiracy against the king, after
    which he was exiled to Japan.

12 Large portions of the preceding two sentences in the *Pen Pictures* typescript
    have been crossed out here. The original reads: "He is afraid of his nephew
    Prince Chunyong who is now in Japan, and would like him to become a ce-
    lestial spirit or something non-earthly. His own son, Ŭihwa, now in America,
    keeps a safe distance, for he has failed on more than one occasion to obey his
    papa, and knows full well that if he returned unprotected he would feel the
    heavy weight of the law." The version quoted in Kennan's "Korea: A Degener-
    ate State" includes allusions to Kojong's possible execution of family members,
    albeit using slightly different wording. It is unclear why Kennan's 1905 version
    reintroduces these allusions that Gale had decided to excise, but it may have
    been an attempt to paint a more sinister picture of the Korean monarch in an
    article that was unflinchingly critical.

gentle little man who consults his horoscope through the medium of the soft-handed woman, can order the execution of a friend without a tear, and then go on playing with his trinkets.

He has never advanced[13] in the way of true reform, and yet he takes a deep interest in the drawing room touches of Western life. He knows the exact differences between the uniforms of the representatives that appear before him, and just how many gold strings there are in each country's epaulettes. He has studied clocks, watches, and barometers, not as articles for use, but as ornaments. He likes machine-guns, not to fire off but to make-believe with. He is indeed a spoiled child that regards his little country as something created for his special delectation, and all the people as flocks and herds intended for his slaughter. He is as incapable of grasping the meaning of the age he lives in as a ten-year old boy would be of taking Port Arthur.[14]

He dislikes his people because they scare him and keep him awake at nights. He gets all sorts of messages about them through the gods, and his command reads, "Don't meet or make a noise; don't talk about the government; don't shoot off guns; don't fight with each other or send petitions into the Palace. Just eat your rice and do your work and be good."

He dislikes the Japanese because they fill him with terror. Marquis Itō is a gentle old man and him he rather likes, but these spurred and sworded fellows, who call as they go by to death, are not mortals but a fearful brand of infernal being whom he shudders to think of. He cannot ever come into sympathy with the Japanese; as little could a chief of Kaffirs be companion to Henry M. Stanley.[15] It is an impossibility, and any attempt to find common ground between had better never be made.

The Emperor likes the Russians. Why? Because in the evil day once on a time, when he was scared beyond words to express, the Waebers took him in and a kinder and more beautiful hostess than Madame Waeber surely never lived in the Far East. Everyone who had the good fortune to know Mr. and Mrs. Waeber in the old days liked them. Why should not the Emperor like them, too? He drank lemon tea and ate the delights of perfect safety in the thick walled legation after a scare that

---

13 Gale has crossed out here "one step;" Kennan's version reintroduces it.

14 Kennan's Gale citation ends here.

15 Henry Morton Stanley (born John Rowlands, 1841–1904) was a Welsh explorer of central Africa, famous for his search for missionary and explorer David Livingstone. Kaffir is a derogatory term for African.

would have petrified the gods. He liked the Waebers, and to his narrow vision, the Waebers were Russia.[16]

The Emperor of Korea might best be described as a man of fear.[17] Why should he not be living as he does without any confidence in anybody, ignorant of everything, and threatened all the time by a thousand malignant spirits? He has no idea of self-government or self-defense, and is just beginning to hear confusing words like "liberty, equality, fraternity." Such, too, is the average Korean.

"I have read such a good book," said a friend who spoke English.

"What was it?" I asked.

"By a Frenchman; 'The So-ci-al Con-tract.'"

They are anxious, many of them, for a sweeping change and to be something that they have never yet been, while the Emperor is perfectly content with the world "as it was, is now, and ever shall be."

The Japanese are on hand and so these three are face to face at the corners of the triangle.

A few days ago the people held a stormy meeting in the centre of the city just as they used to do in the days of the Independence Club, but on this occasion there were some 200 Japanese soldiers on hand with bayonets fixed.

"Where under the sun shall we go?" says the speaker, "when the Japanese have taken our land? Shall we go up to heaven or down to hell, or walk out on the sea? I call on you to fight for your homes."

All of this time the Japanese soldiers stand fixed like statues.

"They are going to fire on us," shouts a voice, and there is a stampede and in a moment the square is cleared. The whole concourse has disappeared somewhere round the corners, into the side streets and into the canal; but the soldiers stand just as still when they have the whole square of the city to themselves, as when the white coats surge around them.

16　Karl Ivanovich Weber, a.k.a Carl von Waeber (1841–1910), a distinguished diplomat of the Russian Empire, was Russia's long-serving first Consul General to Korea from 1885 to 1897. During a one-year period, from 11 February 1896 to 20 February 1897, Kojong sought refuge at the Russian Legation, spurred by the assassination of his wife Queen Min by Japanese assassins. This period prompted a shift away from Japanese influence toward Russian influence in internal Korean affairs.

17　Gale has crossed out the following from the typescript: "Koreans are all more or less fearful."

In a little the crowds come back, and once more a speaker mounts the platform of earth that occupies the midway and harangues the people. There were insults hurled at the Japanese – they were thieves and robbers – but they made no reply. A day or two later, however, in response to these threatenings, the Japanese quietly planted guns on Nam San (South Mountain), and brought 6000 more troops into town. This is the grim sort of reply that Korea specially dislikes.

A day or two later came an order from His Majesty placarded on the posts of the Bell Kiosk: "Let there be no meetings, or shout-talk of any kind in the streets. You are commanded every man to stay at home and mind his own business."

The Emperor desires the land to remain as it always has been, a piece of plunder for him and his rapacious officials; the people want the land turned over to them, so that they can use it as they please; the Japanese do not intend to let either have their way, but are planning new and unheard of things for this benighted country.

(Aug. 1904)

Japan's Task in Korea

Gale's relationship with Japan, like his perspective on Korean modernization, was complex and evolving. His second wife, Ada Louisa Sale, whose father was a businessman in Japan, had grown up in the country, spoke decent colloquial Japanese, and was very fond of Japanese culture. Though a Koreaphile at heart, true to his Orientalist and Social Darwinist leanings, Gale initially welcomed many of the changes in Korea brought about by the more modernized Japan. For example, he applauded advancements in hygiene, modern transportation, finance, and an overall "spirit of capitalism" ushered in by Japanese administration. Taken together, however, his writings suggest that he was never truly convinced that Japan would win the hearts and minds of the Korean people, since they were almost diametrically opposed in character and disposition. Following the 1 March 1919 Independence Movement and violent Japanese suppression, even Gale's tacit approval of Japanese modernization efforts was challenged, and from this time on he seems to have discarded any remaining illusions of Japan's motives in Korea. By no means a champion of Korean independence like his colleague Homer Hulbert, Gale seems to have embodied the position of a majority of the missionary community: that of a politically detached, evangelically engaged, secondary participant in Korean modernization, a position undoubtedly facilitated by his allo-metropolitan positionality. Intriguingly, Gale's ultimate verdict on Japan's efforts in Korea once again boiled down to the literary: Japan was a country of the sword and Korea a country of the pen, a gulf that he doubted could ever be bridged, despite the perfunctory platitude expressed in the closing lines of the essay.

Illustration 15. "The Homes of the People," in *Pen Pictures*

Illustration 16. "Dead Man's Gate" (Kwanghŭimun 光熙門), in *Pen Pictures*

Illustration 17. "The Great South Gate" (Namdaemun 南大門), in *Pen Pictures*

Japan's Task in Korea
Pen Pictures, 85–8

Japan has before her the difficult and delicate task of placating Korea, and winning the hearts of this conservative people. It will cost nothing to take possession of Korea and of Korea's government, but it will tax all her skill to win Korea's heart and confidence.

There is in the peninsula to-day, as there has been for a thousand years, an ingrained dislike of Japan and the Japanese. As naturally as the Korean says "Kongjanim"[1] (the Master Confucius), he says of Japan "*Waenim*," or "*kŭkkajinnim*" (contemptible creature).[2]

---

1 This is a title for Confucius consisting of the sinographs 孔子 (Kongja; Ch. Kongzi) and the vernacular honorific suffix -*nim* (님).

2 In the word *Waenim* (倭님), the first syllable was used to refer generally to the Japanese in the premodern period. The first sinograph *wae* (倭) is also homophonous with the word meaning "midget" (*wae* 矮), a play on words that added to the epithetic force of the term, as Japanese were seen as small in stature compared to Koreans. The *han'gŭl* suffix -*nim* is clearly typed in the

It is in most cases an unreasonable, foolish dislike, but it is a part of his bone and fiber and breaks forth on all occasions.

Down through Korea's official records, Japan has been marked with no character to do her honor, or word written in her favor. She holds a lower place even than the Mongols or Manchus.

Turning to a history written about 1485 by order of King Sŏngjong,[3] I find the first mention of Japan runs thus: "In the year *sinmi* (50 BC)[4] the Japanese sailed over and plundered our coast, but when they heard of the virtue of our illustrious king, they withdrew ashamed."[5] Unfortunately, to-day Japan will have no occasion to withdraw on any such grounds.

Again, in the year 417 AD, the brother of the king of Silla, or Kyerim (鷄林),[6] as the state was also called, was held a hostage in Japan.[7] How

---

original typescript for both *Waenim* and *kŭkkajitnim* (그까짓님, "contemptible creature"), but in context it seems more likely that Gale intended to write the derogatory suffix *"nom,"* i.e., *"Waenom."*

3 King Sŏngjong (成宗, 1457–95; r. 1469–95) was ninth king of the Chosŏn dynasty.

4 *Sinmi* (辛未) is the year name according to the Chinese sexagenary cycle.

5 Gale seems to be referencing the *Tongguk t'onggam* (東國通鑑 Comprehensive Mirror of the Eastern State), chronicling the early history of Korea in four parts: "Oegi" (外紀 Unofficial Histories), "Samgukki" (三國紀 Record of the Three Kingdoms) "Sillagi" (新羅紀 Record of Silla), and "Koryŏgi" (高麗紀 Record of Koryŏ). Originally commissioned by King Sejo in 1458, it was completed during the reign of King Sŏngjong in 1485 by Sŏ Kŏjŏng (徐居正, 1420–88) and other scholars. It is the earliest extant record to list chronologically the rulers of Kojosŏn or Ancient Chosŏn (古朝鮮, ?–108 BC) following the mythical progenitor of the Korean race, Tan'gun.

6 Kyerim (鷄林), literally meaning "rooster forest," was another name for Silla. According to the *Samguk sagi*, Kim Alchi (金閼智), the progenitor of the Kyŏngju Kim clan that would rule Silla, was discovered in the forest inside a golden box accompanied by a rooster. The forest where he was discovered became known as Kyerim, which eventually became the sobriquet for Silla.

7 This refers to the nineteenth ruler of Silla, Nulchi Maripkan (訥祗麻立干; r. AD 417–58), whose brothers were exiled as hostages to Koguryŏ and Wa (Japan) by the previous ruler of Silla and Nulchi's father-in-law, Silsŏng. The loyal retainer Pak Chesang (朴堤上, 363–418), mentioned by Gale, was successful in rescuing one brother from Koguryŏ and was able to secure the release of the second brother from Wa, but nonetheless was captured in the process and died under torture, refusing to submit to the authority of the Wa emperor. Varying accounts of this episode may be found in *Record of the Three Kingdoms* (三國史記), *Memorabilia of the Three Kingdoms* (三國遺事), *Chronicles of Japan* (日本書紀), and *Comprehensive Mirror of the Eastern State* (東國通鑑). Gale seems to be referencing the

he came there I know not, but the fact would seem to indicate that Silla was subject at that time to the Eastern Empire.[8] Great was the mourning on this account. He himself spoke of his brother as the loss of his strong right arm: "Who will be the man to set him free?"

A minister by the name of Pak Chesang volunteered. Said he, "You might expect to win over states by fair words, but not Japan; to outwit her is the only way. My life is at the king's pleasure and such meager gifts as I have. One request only: Please imprison my wife and family when I am gone."

He took ship at Yulp'o[9] and his wife wept bitter tears at parting.

"This must not be," said he, "I have given my life for my country, and your part is to act as though I were a rebel and were making my escape."

The Japanese were in doubts at first as to this fugitive, but hearing that his wife had been imprisoned, and seeing him act his part so well, they believed, and ere long he became a full minister of the island empire. Little by little he laid his plans and one day, unexpectedly, he smuggled the king's brother away and sent him home westward through a thick fog where he eluded all attempts at capture. Pak himself was caught and the weight of the Emperor's wrath fell on him.

---

account that appears in the *Memorabilia of the Three Kingdoms*. All Koreans would have been familiar with Nulchi Maripkan through the *Illustrated Conduct of the Three Bonds* (*Samgang haengsilto* 三綱行實圖, 1434) and the *Illustrated Conduct of the Five Virtues* (*Oryun haengsilto* 五倫行實圖, 1797), widely disseminated texts produced by the Chosŏn government and featuring individuals who embodied Confucian ideals. Among those "honoured" in the pages were virtuous subjects; Nulchi Maripkan was Royal Retainer No. 30 in both works.

8 Gale seems to be referring to the controversial Japanese claim that the Wa (Japanese) under Empress Jingū (神功皇后, AD 169–269; r. 201–69) had established a "colony" in the southern region of the Korean peninsula called Mimana, sometimes associated with the Kaya Confederacy (AD 42–532). Physical evidence of Japan's ruling over a portion of the Korean peninsula is non-existent; the only written evidence of such a claim appears in the *Chronicles of Japan* (*Nihon shoki* 日本書紀), but the semi-legendary status of this document makes its claims dubious. In the period surrounding annexation, Japanese historians used this narrative to support irredentist claims and justify Japanese imperialism. Gale, writing in 1905, seems to have been swayed by these same imperialist discourses. Rather than a permanent settlement or "colony," in the problematic modern sense of the word, northeast Asia in the third and fourth centuries more likely witnessed mutual interaction and exchange between tribal federations on both sides of the Korean Strait at a time before consolidation into well-defined kingdoms had occurred.

9 栗浦.

He was asked, "How did you dare to act so and set this man free?"

Pak replied, "I am the servant of Kyerim and my king desired it."

"You are my servant," said the Japanese, "what do you mean by Kyerim?"

His Imperial Majesty then prepared five kinds of punishment, and with these in full view he said,

"If you will consent to be my servant, I will reward you."

Pak replied, "I may be a dog or a Kyerim pig, but a servant of Japan never. I would gladly accept whip or rod from Kyerim, but would scorn office from Japan."

The Emperor then made him walk bare-foot over sharpened rods.

"Now whose servant are you?"

"I am Kyerim's."

He made him dance on red-hot irons and the question was,

"Whose servant?"

"Kyerim's," was the last reply.

He was burned alive, and to-day a shrine stands in south Korea in his honour, and people who know scarcely anything else of Korean history talk of immortal Pak who died at the hands of the Japanese.

The great invasion of 1591[10] is still referred to as though it had happened but yesterday or the day before. In those days we read they burned down the hut and drove sharpened stakes through the helpless children; and mothers still, when youngsters cry, say *"Ch'ŏngjŏng-i* will

---

10 This refers to what in English is frequently termed the Hideyoshi Invasions, which occurred not in 1591, as Gale writes, but in April 1592. In Korea this invasion is known as the Imjin Waeran (壬辰倭亂) or "Wae (Japanese) disturbance in the *imjin* year," named after the year of the invasion in the sexagenary cycle. The invasion was waged by the Japanese warlord Hideyoshi Toyotomi (豊臣秀吉, 1537–98), who had recently unified Japan and was seeking to legitimize his rule militarily in the absence of imperial pedigree and also to reduce the threat of civil disorder posed by now-idle samurai. Hideyoshi's primary objective was to conquer China, but because of Ming's dispatch of supporting troops and fierce resistance, the invading army never reached China, and all the fighting took place on the Korean peninsula. Japan waged an initial invasion in 1592 and came to occupy much of Chosŏn, including the capital, before fighting resulted in a military stalemate. Following attempts at peace talks in 1596 between Japan and Ming China, there was an additional invasion in 1597. When Japan finally retreated in 1598, in its wake were left hundreds of thousands of casualties, the destruction of countless cultural and historical artefacts, the disruption of the social and even linguistic order on the peninsula, and a deep legacy of Japanese resentment which continues today.

catch you," *Ch'ŏngjŏng-i* being Katō Kiyomasa,[11] the general of the first division. Records regarding Japan are a tale of woe only and lead one well along into the region of present-day thought, where the natural heart of the Korean is all against the Japanese.

Today, a Chinese army might march through this country, plunder it from coast to coast and commit all kinds of outrage, but its evil deeds would be forgotten to-morrow. A hundred thousand Japanese might pass along the same way, silent as the dumb except for the tramp of their feet, paying for every bag of rice and every string of eggs, molesting no one, orderly, well-behaved, and yet be talked of as a plague of thieves, robbers and wretches.

What are the causes of this unnatural and extravagant dislike of the Japanese on the part of the Koreans? Let me say first – disposition. The Koreans say that the Japanese are deceitful and untrustworthy. No land could possibly make a greater showing for bribery and corruption than Korea herself. On no piece of ground have men deceived and been deceived more universally than in this peninsula. No government ever existed that was more infected with rottenness to the bones, cheating, lying, defrauding. But Korea has grown accustomed to, and unconscious of, her own way of doing such things and sees only the fault of others.

"But," they say, "the Japanese are such small people, little in thought and disposition, and are so exacting about particulars."

This is true; the Japanese are past masters of detail, as is proven by the present war. Nothing is forgotten, to the smallest items everything is planned for, and no doubt their success is largely due to this. Korea, on the other hand, is the most careless country imaginable. She never dreams of planning definitely or of carrying out anything exactly. "Any old way" is quite sufficient for her purpose. This is one characteristic that divides these people widely, and until Korea is willing to learn from Japan and come somewhat to her way of doing things she will never amount to anything.

Another matter that divides them is their difference in custom and ceremony. The Japanese are a punctilious people, not only in forms

---

11 Katō Kiyomasa (加藤清正, 1561–1611) was one of the three senior commanders during the Imjin Wars. Kiyomasa was responsible for capturing Seoul and Pusan and renowned for his skill at constructing military fortifications. Gale's *Ch'ŏngjŏng-i* is the Sino-Korean pronunciation of the sinographs in the general's given name (清正) plus the Korean diminutive *-i*.

of expression, but also in genuflexions [*sic*] and bowings. Korea has not a shadow of this except from the servile class. She stands erect and says "Peace" and there it ends. She will push by in the rudest way; she will puff smoke into your face and expectorate all round the horizon without regard to king or courtier. So different is she from Japan in forms of deportment. Why should a man bow twice to you if he does not intend to deceive you? Why should any human being draw in his breath unless he is going to tell a lie? Japan's way is not Korea's and therefore it is at once open to suspicion. Because of his lack of ceremony and seeming rudeness, the Korean often meets with a sharp open hand from the lower-class Japanese and, as he never dreams of the cause, he proclaims himself horribly outraged.

Still, Koreans are really a polite, considerate, and well-meaning people. They do not know how to express it in ceremonial form, but every-day life among them soon convinces that their hearts are right ceremonially.

Another great dividing barrier is dress. In Japan, as we all know, the freest, easiest custom imaginable prevails. A man is never hanged for appearing in public in simply a loin-cloth or for even going stark naked. In Korea, however, to act thus would be dreadful. Koreans never expose their bodies in any such way. A woman shows off her breasts in triumph, to proclaim the fact that she is the mother of a son, but to expose the body otherwise is the mark of a barbarian. I once journeyed with an Englishman who pitched his tent up on the hillside away from the village, where he would be unmolested. His habit was to strip on a snowy morning and to pour cold water over himself right there in view of the public. Anyone could see him on the hillside going through the delightful exercise. Of course all the village turned out to see. I lived in an inn and slept meanwhile. The village elders called on me and said, "You are a civilized guest and act as men ought to act, but the honourable gentleman up on the hill yonder, outrages the whole known world by standing naked and pouring cold water over himself. Think of our women and girls."

I remarked that I was mortified beyond words to express, but that the gentleman had an inside mind that required cold water all over his outside body every morning, and that if they would not look at him it would be well.

"What country is he from?" they asked.

"From Yŏngguk," I replied (England).

"Dear me, we thought England civilized."

"So it is," I said, "but this honourable gentleman has lived long in Japan and drunk much Japanese water, hence his present ways."

That explained it all; the Japanese were barbarians, and no man, not even an Englishman, could live there and not degenerate. So it is: Japan is responsible for everything.

The Chinese have smuggled along the coast and fished beche-de-mer[12] for years. I have sat on rocks and watched them, and yet only the Japanese are fish thieves and pirates.

Still another reason for this dislike is the fact that their ideals are different. Japan is a land of *jiujutsu* [*sic*] and the two-handed sword. Mere babies of the Sunrise Empire wear soldier cape, carry make-believe guns and shout *"banzai."* Their world is the battle-field and their ambition is to rout Kuropatkin.[13] The Korean has no such thought. The goal of his desire is scholarship where he can pose as Confucius or the Yellow Emperor, and lecture his fellow-citizens in the language of the ancients. One is the land of the sword and one is the land of the pen. With what contempt the Korean regards the Japanese cross-strokes, and down-strokes, and short-stops and dots of the written character. Not one of them will do, all is lacking strength, finish and form. The rascal may rout 400,000 Russians, but he is not civilized – behold how badly he writes that character.

Korea is saved from insular disgrace by being stuck fast to the main-land, while in this Japan fails also. The Japanese are referred to as "island savages," while Korea is "Little China."[14]

Among all the thousands of Chinese characters that express respect and honor, Japan is accorded not one of them, but is referred to by the ideograph "dwarf."[15] Away back before the invasion of 1591 the king of Korea dreamed that he saw coming in at the Palace gate a wench with a sheaf of rice on her head. He called the soothsayers in and made

---

12 The French *bêche-de-mer*, literally meaning "sea-spade," is a sea cucumber, eaten as a delicacy in many countries of East and Southeast Asia.

13 Aleksei Nikolaevich Kuropatkin (1848–1925) was the Russian Imperial Minister of War from 1898 until his relief from command following Russia's initial defeats under his command in the Russo-Japanese War (1904–5).

14 "Little China," *sohwa* (小華) or *sojunghwa* (小中華), refers to Korea's faithful maintenance of traditional Chinese cultural forms, especially those related to Confucianism. Such a designation would have been worn as a badge of honour by the Korean literati.

15 *Wae* (倭／矮).

inquiry: "a she-man with a rice sheaf on her head." The soothsayers pondered over it and at last brought forth the character: first the man 亻 then the rice 米 then the "she" 女 making, when bunched together, 倭, which is the character that stands for Japan, and thus the great Japanese invasion was first announced by way of prophecy.

In religion, too, they differ. Buddhism has been regarded by Korea for 500 years as the lowest form of cult. Not a Buddhist priest, be he ever so learned, but he has hurled at him day by day the lowest forms of address. He may be an old man and gentle as the spring zephyr, but gray hairs are forgotten in his case, and he is commanded with a "ya!"[16] by the commonest riff-rraff of the country. A land where Buddhism flourishes must of necessity be an inferior land. Korea, the land of the Master (Confucius), can never come to terms with the land of Sakyamoni.

In the matter of surnames, too, in which Korea is so particular, they differ. "Kim" and "Yi" and "Pak" and "Chŏng" and a few others hold sway. Usually but a single character is used for a surname, and that always in accord with what China has sanctioned, but in Japan no such proper custom prevails. A man may have one character for surname or two, or three, or four. Such surnames as were never dreamed of are being printed in all the newspapers. Even General Hasegawa[17] is ruled out by reason of his name. He is, to translate him literally, General "Long-valley-stream." No excellence of ability can quite atone before Korea for such a surname as this. Some men are even called "Inuyama" (犬山), "Dog-mountain." A name like this would make a Korean give up the ghost.

This is the way Korea reasons. To win a hundred fights against Russia means nothing in view of Japan's disposition, customs, dress, ideals, and religion.

To sum up the whole matter, Korea's view of Japan is based, not wholly, but to a large extent, on prejudice, ignorance and superstition. A dislike of Japan is a part of Korea's bone and fiber, and to eradicate it will tax Japan's skill to the utmost. She is wise, however, in her day and generation, and doubtless will win in this fight too.

(1905)

---

16 This refers to the familiar form of speech in the Korean honorific spectrum, a register of speech characterized by vocative endings in the form of ~아 (~a) or ~야 (~ya).

17 Hasegawa Yoshimichi (長谷川好道, 1850–1924) was a general in the Japanese Imperial Army and the second Governor General of Korea (1916–19).

Where Are We?

After a succession of resounding military defeats for Russia on land and at sea, the Russo-Japanese War finally culminated in the Battle of Tsushima (27–8 May 1905). On account of Japan's military blockade of Port Arthur, Russia was forced to mobilize its Baltic Fleet to the Far East to break the blockade. Under Admiral Zinovii Rozhestvenskii, the Second Pacific Squadron embarked on its long, trans-global journey in September 1905, a tragic mission fraught with low morale, mechanical failures, and minimal international cooperation. Great Britain, allied with Japan, had denied Russia access to the Suez Canal after it mistakenly fired on British fishing boats in the Dogger Bank Incident, forcing the fleet to sail around the African continent.[1] After learning of the Port Arthur capitulation to the Japanese in January 1905, the dejected fleet continued its long journey for another four months, only to meet humiliating defeat in the Tsushima Strait, where Russia lost twenty-two of its battleships and was eliminated as a major naval power for many years to come.[2] The Treaty of Portsmouth arbitrated by American President Theodore Roosevelt in September 1905 stipulated the evacuation of Russian forces from Manchuria, the return of its leases in Southern Manchuria, including Port Arthur, to China, and the release of Japan's uncontested interests in Korea.[3] On 17 November 1905, just

---

1 Jacob, *The Russo-Japanese War*, 32.

2 Ibid., 35.

3 Japan had originally demanded indemnities from Russia, as it had received from Qing China in 1895, but dropped these demands in return for cessation of Southern Sakhalin when Russia threatened to reopen hostilities. The denial

months after Gale wrote this chapter, the Japan-Korea Protectorate Treaty (Ŭlsa nŭngnyak 乙巳勒約) went into effect, officially relinquishing Korea's sovereignty in foreign affairs.

"Where Are We?" continues Gale's trope of infantilizing Korea as hopelessly naive in international affairs and a helpless victim of circumstance. The character who loses his hat in the account below is symbolic of the Korean Empire and its loss of benefactor and protector Russia. To seek the continued protection of a vanquished patron is futile, much like chasing after a lost hat in a deep ravine. Yet to appear before the world bereft of headwear, like "a common coolie," is likewise unimaginable, and so hapless Korea is left floundering in bewilderment and uncertainty, much like the unsuspecting passenger flung from a train barrelling relentlessly toward the modern world.

Where Are We?
Pen Pictures, 89

News has come of the battle of Tsushima, another unparalleled victory for Japan. For many days prayers have ascended from Korea to all the gods, that have in keeping the fates of sea and land, asking that they, just for this once, give the palm of Rozhdiestvensky and put Togo under the sea. But all the prayers have been as nothing, and we learn now that the Borodino, King of Battleships, is sunk, and that the Navarin, and the Monomach, and the Donskoi, and the Oleg, goddess of speed, are all deep under water, carrying with them thousands of men. We hear also that ships are captured, and with them the redoubtable Rozhdiestvensky. Hot tears are the only consolation at such a time as this. The Fates have gone mad and Japan looms up mightier and more ominous than ever on the horizon.[4]

---

of indemnities resulted in the Hibiya Riots of 1905. Jacob, *The Russo-Japanese War*, 35.

4 Zinovii Rozhdestvenskii (1848–1909) was commander of the Second Pacific Squadron in the Battle of Tsushima in May 1905, a battle that resulted in a resounding victory for Japan and the eventual resolution of the war with the Treaty of Portsmouth in September of that year. Tōgō Heihachirō (東鄉平八郎, 1848–1934) was Admiral of the Imperial Japanese Navy and victor of the Battle of Tsushima. The *Borodino, Navarin, Monomach* (*Vladimir Monomakh*), *Donskoi*

The other day an unsophisticated Korean was riding on the through-train from Pusan, the fast express, going at twenty miles an hour. For a time it amused and interested him to look about the painted wagon, beneath which the landscape seemed to be racing in all directions. He looked at this and examined that, and finally grew tired and yawned, and then poked his head out of the window to see how the world wagged. A gust of wind carried off his hat and the hat-string, and away it went sailing down the valley. "My hat!" he shouted, but the soulless wagon made no response. In an instant he was at the door and out on to the platform. Before you could think, headfirst he went down over the embankment into the yawning abyss after that hat. We saw no more of him but I imagined a poor crumpled mass low in the valley, a mixture of white clothes, black top-knot, and brown honest face, no voice to speak with any longer, fearfully crumpled up by this foolish plunge of his after a five-cent hat. Is he dead, poor chap, or is he like the other Korean, who sat on the open top of the construction train? The day was warm and he nodded in deep sleep. He was a man of the world, had seen much himself, and knew how to ride on railway trains. Deep were the nods and comfortable the sleep; but a curve struck them around which the train whip-lashed violently, and away went this son of the Orient over the edge, down the green bank, over and over, till he reached the bottom. In an instant he was on his feet, wide awake, with a flash in his eye, and a look on his face that said to the train, "What in thunder do you mean, anyhow?"

This is like Korea at the present moment, on board a fast express, racing who knows where? She has lost her face and her hat, and is in a fearful state of mind over it. How can she endure being seen before the world, hatless like a common coolie? Her honor is at stake and her name. There is nothing for it but a wild plunge over some embankment or other. Will it be the end of her, or will she survive it, and with a look of surprise say, "What do you mean?" Korea has prayed that Russia would come but it is finished for Russia. Korea has no desire to be a Westerner; she does not wish to learn, and has no use for the twentieth century or for Japan; what she wants is a few dancing girls, a handful of eunuchs, a witch or two, and to be left alone. But here is Japan sinking

---

(*Dimitrii Donskoi*) and *Oleg* were some of the many battleships and cruisers lost in the battle.

the whole Russian Armada, and bundling out eunuchs, witches and dancing-girls from the sacred precincts of the Palace.

If Korea only thought of what was best for her, she would smile at the loss of her hat, take her humbling gracefully, learn her lesson, and fall into line with Japan and the fast train she rides on; but she is having a hard time, she thinks.

(June 3rd, 1905 Seoul)

Illustration 18. "Fisherman's Luck: As the Fates Decree," in *Pen Pictures*

As Regards the Fates

One of the themes that continuously resurfaces in Gale's writing is that of fatalism. Gale seemed particularly impressed by what he regarded as the fatalistic character of the Korean soul. Yet he did not deny similar proclivities in the Judeo-Christian tradition. It is highly significant that Gale capitalizes both "God" and the word *Unsu* (運數) throughout this chapter, in a clear attempt to connect Korean and Christian fatalistic outlooks: the Christian deity and the Korean "higher power" were analogous, but the latter had simply been accorded far too much authority. It was necessary, in Gale's perspective, for Koreans to strike a balance between active engagement in the modern world and an appropriate amount of passive acceptance of one's fate, grounded of course in Christian faith.

Gale goes beyond mere Christian allusions, drawing on diverse sources ranging from Scottish poet Robert Burns, the contemporary Korean intellectual Yun Ch'iho, and the Greek myth of Prometheus. "As Regards the Fates" is a brief, reflective work that poignantly concludes *Pen Pictures* and an important chapter in Korea's history. Although writing in October 1905, just weeks before Korea's protectorate status would commence, Gale does not comment on this impending development.[1] Perhaps Gale had said everything he had

---

1 The signing of the Protectorate Treaty had already been ratified by Japan, but it is unclear whether Gale or others knew that Itō Hirobumi would soon arrive in Seoul to force such a treaty. However, news of the Portsmouth Treaty and Japan's now unimpeded reign in Korea meant that any careful observer like Gale must have anticipated such a move by Japan.

to say on the subject. The exasperation and helplessness expressed throughout *Pen Pictures* has now given way to resignation, and the future of Korea was, as Koreans themselves seemed to believe, in the hands of fate.

As Regards the Fates
Pen Pictures, 90

What people have not believed in Destiny and the Fates? The Greeks and Romans, the Teutons, the Celts, the Anglo-Saxons have all passed under their shadow. The theology, too, of many so-called Christian peoples is tinged deep with the same. For example, this from Burns:

> "Oh thou wha in the heavens dost dwell,
> Wha as it pleases best thysel'
> Sends ane to heaven, and ten to hell,
> A' for thy glory,
> And no for ony guid or ill,
> They've done afore thee!"[2]

This quotation illustrates perfectly the mind of the great God *Unsu* (Fate), as the Korean calls him. He is a vast wheel, ever turning, under whose ruthless revolution go down the hopes of men. He cannot be propitiated, he cannot be argued with, he cannot be bribed; he is implacable, irresistible, beyond the range of reason, ever sweeping on with all mortals entangled in his train. A few rise with him but most fall. The other day on a walk by the city wall, I saw a man sitting at the wayside smoking a long pipe. We fell into a conversation and touched on politics.

"The whole 'business,'" says he, "is *Unsu*. There is no use of complaining," and he proceeded to puff.

---

2 This is the opening verse of "Holy Willie's Prayer" (1785), written by the Scottish poet Robert Burns (1759–96). Burns, who has been designated the "national poet of Scotland," often wrote in the Scottish vernacular, an idiom that by his time had all but vanished thanks to continual Scottish assimilation into Great Britain. Several Scottish English words appear in this verse, which I gloss here: "wha" (who), "ane" (one), "ony" (any), and "guid" (good).

In one sense it is a comforting thought, as it relieves a man of all sense of responsibility, or sorrow over past failures. *Unsu* explains everything and all men so hear and so understand it.

A belief in the fateful law of *Unsu* occupies the innermost chamber of Korea's soul. If I fail in business it is *Unsu*; if I am dirty and miserable it is *Unsu*; if the state falls, no one is to blame, for who can withstand *Unsu*?

In a recent public lecture a well known Korean,[3] who is both a Westerner and Oriental, said to those before him, "Until you give up the word *Unsu* there is no hope. It is nonsense, there is no such thing. Every man is his own *Unsu*, and can make of life what he will."

Unsu is a great iron chain that has got itself forged to the soul of the Korean, and has rusted deep in, leaving him like Prometheus fast bound to Mt. Caucasus, where the eagles feed on his liver.

Seoul, Korea (Oct. 1905)

---

3 At this point in the text of the typescript, "Mr. T.H. Yun" is crossed out and
   "a well known Korean" is pencilled in. Judging by the sentiment expressed and
   the relative lack of individuals who fit the description of being both Korean
   and Western, this probably refers to the Korean reformer Yun Ch'iho (尹致昊,
   1864–1945), who spelled his name Yoon Tchi-ho in English.

PART TWO

Old Corea

Corean Literature and History

With its focus on Korea's literary heritage, "Corean Literature and History"[1] sets the tone for *Old Corea*, a collection of essays and translations completed by Gale in the late 1910s and early 1920s and dealing primarily with Korean traditional literature composed in Literary Sinitic. As its title suggests, this opening chapter is a summary of Korean history from the earliest times to the nineteenth century, through the lens of classical literature. Far from a comprehensive treatment, the chapter rather touches on what Gale considers to be the highlights of Korean literature, including works by Ch'oe Ch'iwŏn, Chŏng Mongju, Yi I, and Gale's favourite literatus, Yi Kyubo. Gale's historiography represents the orthodox Confucian view of history promulgated by such works as *Tongguk t'onggam* (東國通鑑 Comprehensive Mirror of the Eastern State, 1485) and the *Samguk sagi* (三國史記 History of the Three Kingdoms, 1145).

Gale cites four main influences on Korea's history and literature: Tan'gun,[2] Kija,[3] Buddhism, and Confucianism. As Han Young-woo has

---

1　Although the original table of contents lists the title as simply "Korean Literature," this alternate and more accurate title appears at the beginning of the chapter.

2　Tan'gun (檀君), or Sandalwood Prince, was the legendary founder of the first Korean kingdom of Kojosŏn (古朝鮮) and is considered traditionally to be the progenitor of the Korean race. The date 2333 BC cited by Gale is the date appearing in the *Samguk yusa* (三國遺事 Memorabilia of the Three Kingdoms, 1279), the earliest extant account of the Tan'gun myth, which states that Tan'gun established the state of Kojosŏn in the "fiftieth year of the reign of Emperor Yo." For an English translation of the Tan'gun myth by Peter H. Lee, see Lee and de Bary, ed, *Sources of Korean Tradition*, 1:4–6.

3　According to various Chinese sources, Kija (箕子 Ch. Jizi) was the relative of the last king of the Shang dynasty, and upon its overthrow was called upon to

demonstrated, the status of Tan'gun and Kija in Korean historiography fluctuated over the course of the Koryŏ and Chosŏn eras, depending on how "the historical and cultural consciousness of each era was reflected in the way available sources were interpreted." Han goes on: "Generally speaking, depending on the political and intellectual inclinations of the author and his period, Kija was projected as a symbol of either political independence or subservience to China, on the one hand, and as a symbol of either cultural distinctiveness or uniformity with China on the other."[4] The practice of Kija worship, which began sometime during the Three Kingdoms period and seems to have peaked in the late nineteenth century, became problematic after Korea's loss of sovereignty in 1905, when Japanese historians interpreted Kija Chosŏn as a Chinese colony, thus implying a colonial precedent in Korea's history.[5] It was from this time that Korean nationalist historians began to augment the role of Tan'gun in Korea's history and cultural heritage, emphasizing the purely Korean roots of this legendary figure. Thus throughout Korea's history, Tan'gun and Kija have functioned as metonyms for the Korean *Volk* (*minjok*) and Sinitic civilization, respectively, with the former accorded far more prestige in contemporary South Korea in both scholarly literature and the popular imagination. Written in the 1920s, shortly after the March First Movement, Gale's observations would have come amid a surge of nationalistic historiography championing the personage of Tan'gun and critical of Kija as an embodiment of toadyism and a discredited Sinitic world view. Gale seems to provide a balanced view of these figures, yet it is telling that the legendary Tan'gun, of which no concrete evidence remains, is equated with the Christian God, while the semi-legendary Kija, who is attested in various Chinese and Korean sources and whose tomb was allegedly discovered in the P'yŏngyang area, is treated as a more or less historical figure.[6]

From the late 1910s and early 1920s Gale focused increasingly on literary translation and analysis, activities that would occupy him for the

---

advise King Wu of Zhou. Kija, however, refused to swear allegiance to the new ruler, and in return for his fidelity to the principle of loyalty, Kija was enfeoffed by King Wu as ruler of Chosŏn (朝鮮). The *Samguk sagi*, the earliest extant Korean history, contends that the descendants of Kija reigned until their overthrow by Wiman Chosŏn (衛滿朝鮮, 194–108 BC).

4 Han, "Kija Worship in the Koryŏ and Early Yi Dynasties," 371.

5 Ibid., 350.

6 Ibid., 349.

remainder of his career and constitute his primary legacy. Many of the works in this chapter also appear in the missionary journal the *Open Court*, and several more would appear in Gale's *History of the Korean People* (1927). A number of other pieces appearing in this chapter and throughout *Old Corea* may also be found in *Korea Magazine*, a missionary periodical published from January 1917 to April 1919 and edited by Gale.[7] Clearly a labour of love, this magazine was also authored overwhelmingly by Gale himself, through which he sought to "contribute to a further light concerning this ancient and interesting people and also help to preserve in English something of what they have written."[8] In the Editorial Notes of the inaugural issue, Gale expounds on the significance of Korean literature and the role of this magazine in fostering knowledge of the country among Anglophone readers:

> The Magazine makes no pretension to possessing any superior knowledge, but it is sincerely interested in the East, and has an earnest desire to aid in its interpretation. We, Occidentals, must remember that the Far East represents the oldest civilization in the world, a civilization that has come down by a continuous line, not through centuries only, but through long millennia and surely nothing could be more interesting or profitable to those who desire to deal with the mind and spirit of a race, than to read into their souls and to see what their ideals are, what their hopes, their fears, their longings. This is the wish of the Magazine, to interpret sympathetically the great world in which we live, and of which we really know so little. It is not too much to say that while we modestly think we have something to teach Asia, we must also admit that Asia has much to teach us.[9]

This is the guiding principle that informed this chapter on Korean history and literature, and a principle that continually resurfaced in Gale's subsequent literary activities.

Despite Gale's admonishment to Westerners to "learn something from the Far East," the only element of Korean culture that seemed deserving of emulation to Gale derived from the hoary recesses of the premodern era.

---

7 For a thorough accounting of this largely overlooked periodical, see King, "Korean 'Classics' for Anglophone Readers."

8 Gale Papers, Box 6, Folder 33, "Annual Report 1917"; quoted in King, "Korean 'Classics' for Anglophone Readers," 3.

9 *Korea Magazine* 1 (January 1917): 2–3.

Gale's constitution of Korean literature as the realm of Literary Sinitic alone was a stark pronouncement of his literary allegiances and an oblique critique of emergent "modern" Korean literature in the vernacular. In Gale's historical account, after the passing of Kija, "long centuries [are] blank." He remarks, "What Corea was busying herself about when Confucius and Buddha lived, no one can say. Page after page goes by white and unrecorded." Genuine history for Gale, therefore, is inextricably linked with the written tradition, not the oral, and more precisely with the Sinitic tradition, not the vernacular. Gale abruptly concludes his historical-literary accounting with the early eighteenth-century writer Yun Chŭng,[10] excluding even more recent writers in Literary Sinitic, a conservative delimination no doubt instilled by his literati "pundits." Gale writes, "Since Yun's day many famous authors have lived, and literature has held unquestioned sway till the year 1894 when, by order of the new regime, the government examinations were discontinued. With this edict all incentive to the study of the Classics disappeared, and the old school system ceased to be." Crucially, Gale termed this "the tragic death of *native* literature" (my emphasis). Writing in the early 1920s, "twenty-seven years since this edict was promulgated," Gale still longed for the earlier days when the literatus and "native" literature reigned, and mostly ignored the renaissance in vernacular Korean literature that was occurring all around him. The English translations contained in *Old Corea* would represent Gale's curatorial intercession in Korean literary life, a last-ditch effort to preserve for posterity what was rapidly fading into the vistas of the past.

Corean Literature and History
Old Corea, 1–4;
Open Court 32 (1918): 79–103

The main thoughts that dominate Corean literature have come down from the misty ages of the past.[11] We are informed by credible historians that a mysterious being called Tan'gun, a *sinin*, god-man, or angel, descended from heaven and alighted on the top heights of the Ever-White

---

10 Yun Chŭng (尹拯, 1629–1714) was a mid-Chosŏn literatus and ideologue who founded the Soron (少論) faction, which broke away from the Westerners (西人) faction.

11 The *Open Court* version adds the sentence "How long ago who can say?"

Mountains where he taught the people their first lessons in religion, the date given being contemporary with Yo of China, 2333 BC.

Whoever he may have been or whatever he may have taught, remains largely a mystery,[12] but echoes of this strange being are heard all down through the ages.[13] Many writers have recorded the story of Tan'gun. Pages of the *Tongguk t'onggam*, the greatest history of the early kingdoms of Corea, written about 1450 AD, tell of his doings.[14] The earliest contribution to Corean thought seems to have come from him, reminding the world that God lives, and that righteousness should rule on the earth.[15]

---

12 *Open Court*: "must remain a mystery."

13 According to the *Samguk yusa*, Tan'gun "took charge of some three hundred and sixty areas of responsibility, including agriculture, allotted lifespans, illness, punishment, and good and evil, and brought culture to his people." "而主穀主命主病主刑主善惡. 凡主人間三百六十餘事. 在世理化." See Lee and de Bary, *Sources of Korean Tradition*, 1:6.

14 Gale often cited the *Tongguk t'onggam* (1485), which was perhaps the most widely read history of Korea during the Chosŏn period and was well known among Western residents as well. The *Tongguk t'onggam* was a chronicle of Korean history extending from the earliest times to the fall of the Koryŏ, compiled by Sŏ Kŏjŏng (徐居正, 1420–88) and commissioned by King Sejo in 1446. The earliest account of Tan'gun, however, appeared in the *Samguk yusa*, a book by the Buddhist monk Iryŏn (·然, 1206–89) based on the *Book of Wei* (*Wei Shu* 魏書, AD 554) and the no longer extant Korean source *Ancient Records* (*Kogi* 古記).

15 From the 1890s Western missionaries had begun to discuss the nature of the Tan'gun myth in relation to Christian theology. According to the myth, a celestial being Hwanin (桓因) had a son named Hwanung (桓雄) who desired to live in the human realm, and so descended upon Paektu, or White Head Mountain (白頭山), also known as Great White Mountain (T'aebaeksan 太白山) or Ever-White Mountain (Changbaeksan 長白山), as Gale writes. There, a tiger and bear prayed to Hwanung to become human, and the bear eventually transformed into a woman. Hwanung metamorphosed, lay with the woman and begot a son, Tan'gun. A number of missionaries, including Homer Hulbert, found in this myth clear parallels with the Holy Trinity of the Christian faith, equating Hwanin with God the Creator, Hwanung with the Holy Spirit, and Tan'gun with Jesus. At first suspicious of the shamanistic origins of the myth and doubtful as to the tale's historicity, by the time this essay was penned in the late 1910s, Gale seems to have reconciled to the then-majority Trinitarian view of the Tan'gun myth, hence the divine association posited here. For a discussion of the Tan'gun myth's reception among Western missionaries, see Oak, "North American Missionaries' Understanding of the Tan'gun and Kija Myths."

A temple erected in his honour in Py'ŏngyang, in 1429, still stands. A huge altar, also, on the top of Mari Mountain[16] not far from Chemulp'o, date unknown, tells of his greatness in the distant past. Poets and historians, Coreans and Chinese, have sung his praises.[17]

A second set of thoughts entered Corea more than a thousand years later, in 1122 BC. This is indeed the most noted period in the religious history of the Far East. Kings Mun and Mu of China came to the throne, "at the bidding of God," so reads the record.[18] Mun had a brother called Chu Kong who was a great prophet and preacher of righteousness.[19] This group usurped the throne and inaugurated an era of justice which China had not known before.[20] Kija, one of their associates, refused to swear allegiance, however, claiming that he would have to stand by the old king, good or bad. In this act he set the pace for all loyal ministers of East Asia who swear to serve only one master till death. Knowing Kija's desire, King Mun gave him Corea, or the East Kingdom, for his portion, and hither this great minister came.

---

16 摩尼山.

17 The Sungnyŏngjŏn (崇靈殿 Temple of Spirit Worship) was constructed in 1429 in P'yŏngyang during the reign of King Sejong as a shrine for the veneration of Tan'gun and King Tongmyŏng (東明聖王, 58–19 BC; r. 37–19), the founder of Koguryŏ (37 BC–AD 668). The shrine still stands today in North Korea, and is registered as National Cultural Artifact No. 6. The Kanghwa Island Ch'amsŏng Altar (江華島塹城壇), which also remains today, was the site where Tan'gun was said to have performed celestial ancestor worship.

18 King Mun (周文王 Ch. Zhou Wen Wang, 1152–1056 BC; r. 1099–1050), literally "The Cultured King," was king of Zhou during the late Shang dynasty and is credited with overthrowing the dynasty, though his second son, King Mu (周武王 Ch. Zhou Wu Wang; r. 1046–1043 BC), "The Martial King," actually overthrew the Shang dynasty in 1043 BC. "At the bidding of God" refers to the mandate of heaven (ch'ŏnmyŏng 天命), an ancient Chinese belief that conferred celestial legitimacy upon righteous rulers, and conversely sanctioned rebellion against a ruling family who had forfeited the mandate through misrule, evidenced by the deteriorating condition of the people or the occurrence of natural calamities. Korean dynasties would later establish their own legitimacy through recourse to this ultimate authority of the Chinese emperor.

19 Chu Kong (周公 Ch. Zhou Gong, ca 1085–ca 1022 BC), the Duke of Zhou, was the fourth son of King Wen and the younger brother of King Wu. He was critical in laying the political foundations of the Zhou dynasty (1045–256 BC), the longest in Chinese history, and was remembered by many subsequent sages, including Confucius, as a paragon of virtue. Durrant, "Zhou, Duke of Zhōu Gōng."

20 The phrase "which China had not known before" is deleted from the *Open Court* version.

Kija left an indelible impress upon the hearts of the Korean people and their future history.

In P'yŏngyang a temple was erected to his worship in 1325 AD. An earlier record by a stone of his life[21] was destroyed in the Japanese War of 1592. A new stone was erected in the last year of Shakespeare's life (1616), and on it I find the following sentences:

"Kija came, and his teaching was to us what the teaching of Pokhŭi ssi[22] was to ancient China. What was this but the plan and purpose of God?"[23]

"God's not permitting Kija to be killed (at the fall of the Ŭn Kingdom) was because he reserved him to preach religion to us, and to bring our people under the laws of civilization. Even though Kija had desired death at that time he could not have found it; and even though King Mun had determined not to send him he could not have helped it."[24]

Such an appreciation of the over-ruling sovereignty of God is something as indelibly impressed on the Corean mind as on that of the Scotch Presbyterian. It came in with the pre-Confucian teachings of the East, and has had a mighty influence on the poets and thinkers of the peninsula ever since.

Following this for long centuries there is a blank. What Corea was busying herself about when Confucius and Buddha lived, no one can say. Page after page goes by white and unrecorded.

We hear of the landing of bands of Chinamen about 220 BC. These men had made their escape from the arduous labors of the Great Wall, and had come to Korea to set up a kingdom on the east side of the peninsula, which they called Chin Han. Other kingdoms came later into being, called Ma Han and Pyŏn Han, three Hans in all, and so time dragged on uneventfully till the Christian era.[25]

Fifty eight years before, about the time when Caesar was attempting conquest of Britain, the Kingdom of Silla was established in the southeast

---

21 *Open Court*: "A stone recording his life and acts was set up just before it."

22 Ch. Fuxi 伏羲氏.

23 This is Gale's translation of the stone that stands in front of Sunginjŏn (崇仁殿 Hall for the Worship of Benevolence), which now faces the Sungnyŏngjŏn in P'yŏngyang. His translation is an abridgement of the following passage: "箕子之敎東方是猶羲軒堯舜之敎中土盖有不可得而已者此又非天意而誰歟."

24 "天之不死箕子爲傳道也爲化民也箕子雖欲死得乎武王雖欲不封于朝鮮得乎."

25 Chin Han (辰韓), Ma Han (馬韓), and Pyŏn Han (弁韓) are collectively known as the Three Hans (三韓), and sometimes referred to as the Proto-Three Kingdoms period. This period extends from roughly 300 BC to AD 300. The earliest extant account of these polities, and indeed the earliest eyewitness

corner of the Korean peninsula. A few years later, one called Koguryŏ was set up in the north, and another in the southwest called Paekche.[26]

Here we have three kingdoms occupying the peninsula when the greatest event in its history took place, namely the incoming of Buddhism. In 372 AD it entered the north kingdom.[27]

The wonderful story of the Buddha and his upward pilgrimage from a world of sorrow and sin to one of eternal bliss conquered all hearts. The Coreans took to it as a thirsty man to water, and while they did not cast aside the great thoughts passed on to them by Tan'gun and Kija, Buddha ruled supreme.

We are told that black men from India came preaching this religion. This was Corea's first introduction to alien races, a grateful and appreciated introduction. Their visits continued from 400 to 1400 as Chigong, one of the most noteworthy of the men beyond the Himalayas, died in 1363.[28]

---

account of the Korean peninsula, is contained in the *Sanguozhi* (三國志 *Record of the Three Kingdoms*, AD 297), a Chinese document recording the history of the three states that arose following the collapse of the Eastern Han dynasty (AD 25–220): Wei (魏), Wu (吳), and Shu (蜀). The portion of the *Sanguozhi* relevant to the Samhan of the Korean peninsula appears in the final section of the Wei Chronicle titled "Account of the Eastern Barbarians" (東夷傳 Ch. Dongyizhuan). The Samhan were not yet kingdoms, but may be more accurately described as federations of statelets (*so kukka*). For a range of articles on the Samhan period and an annotated translation of the Samhan account from the *Sanguozhi*, see Byington, *Early Korea*.

26 According to most historians, the traditional dates for the founding of Silla (57 BC), Koguryŏ (37 BC), and Paekche (18 BC) are much too early, and smaller polities such as the Three Han probably dominated the peninsula into the third century AD. Silla, supposedly founded first, appears latest in the historic record in the fourth century, its foundation date being calculated by counting back twelve sixty-year cycles from the fall of Paekche in AD 663.

27 Buddhism was adopted first as a state religion by Koguryŏ in AD 372, when the monk Sundo (順道) was sent by the former Jin (晉, 265–420) bearing Buddhist scriptures and statues. Paekche later adopted Buddhism in 384, but it was not until 527 that the more geographically remote Silla adopted the religion.

28 Paekche was first converted to Buddhism when Jin China sent the Indian monk Maranant'a (摩羅難陀) to the Paekche court. "Chigong" (指空 Ch. Zhi Kong, 1289–1364), or Dhyānabhadra, who at the age of nineteen left his native India and travelled through Yuan China and Koryŏ Korea, influenced Buddhist thought in those countries. He has been called "The Last Light of Indian Buddhism" in East Asia. For a detailed treatment of his Buddhist thought and its influence on Chinese and Korea Buddhism, see Dziwenka, "'The Last Light of Indian Buddhism.'"

The most interesting monument in existence today bearing witness is the cave-temple situated near the old capital of Silla, Kyŏngju. The writer once crossed the hills to pay it a visit. As he reached the highest point of the pass, he saw away to the east the Sea of Japan, with the mottled hummocks of smaller ridges lying between him and the shore. A short distance down the hill he came to this cave-temple. Entering by a narrow way he found himself in a large hall with a figure of the Buddha seated in the middle and many figures in bas-relief on the walls. One was Kwannon.[29] Others were stately and graceful women quite unlike any types seen today;[30] others again, seemed to represent the men of far-off India, who wear strange half-shylock faces, types of the visitors, doubtless, who came preaching the good news of the Buddha 1500 years ago.

Count Terauchi, the former Governor-General in 1915, had plaster casts made of them and placed in the museum of Seoul.[31]

Buddhism, besides being a religious cult, introduced Corea to the outside world and brought in its train arts and industries that made of this people a highly enlightened nation.

In the middle of the seventh century we find Corea disturbed by internal troubles. The three kingdoms were against each other with no likelihood of victory for any one of them. The great Tangs were on the throne of China, and Corea had already come to acknowledge it as the suzerain state.

A young prince of Silla, by name Kim Yusin,[32] disturbed by the unsettled condition of his native land, went to the hills to pray about it. We are told in the *History of the Three Kingdoms* (written about 1145 AD) that while he fasted and prayed to God and the Buddha, an angel came to him and told him what to do. He was to seek help

---

29 Kwannon is the Japanese pronunciation of the Buddhist Goddess of Mercy Kwanseŭm posal [boddhisatva] (觀世音菩薩 Sans. Aryavalokitêśvara), or "[The One Who] Perceives the Sounds of the World." Perhaps best known by the Chinese pronunciation Guanyin, she is among the most renowned of the bodhisattvas, one who wishes to attain buddhahood for the benefit of all sentient beings.

30 *Open Court*: "quite unlike any types seen in the peninsula or China."

31 *Open Court*: "The present Prime Minister and former Governor General of Chosen, had plaster casts made of them and placed in the museum of Seoul in 1915." Terauchi Masatake (寺内正毅, 1852–1918) was the third and last Resident General of Korea, and upon execution of the Annexation Treaty in 1910 became the first Governor General of Korea, where he served until 1916 before becoming the ninth Prime Minister of Japan.

32 Kim Yusin (金庾信, AD 595–673).

of the Tangs. Thither he went to the great capital Nagyang[33] where his mission was accepted and an army sent to take Silla's part.

The result was that in 668 AD all the country was made subject to Silla and placed under the suzerainty of the Middle Kingdom (China).

An old pagoda erected at that time, commemorating the event, stands near the town of Kongju. Its long inscription down the face is one of Corea's early literary efforts.[34]

From 700 to 900 AD there are no records existing that mark the progress of events and yet it was evidently a period of great literary activity. Many monumental remains tell of master Buddhists who lived through these two centuries. Some of the stones are eight feet high and four feet wide and have as many as two thousand characters inscribed on their face, constituting a careful and concise biography.

Here are extracts from one erected in 916 AD:[35]

"A life of the Teacher of two Kings of Silla, called by the State, Master Nang Kong ..."[36]
"His religious name was Haengjŏk,[37] Walking in Silence ..."[38]
"His mother's name was Sŏl. In a dream of the night she met a priest who said to her, 'From a past existence I have longed to be your son.'"[39]

Even after waking she was still moved by the wonder she had seen, which she told her husband. Immediately she put away all flesh food and cherished with the utmost reverence the object of her conception, and so on the thirtieth day of the twelfth moon of the 6th year of Taewha (832 AD) her child was born."[40]

---

33 Nagyang (洛陽 Ch. Luoyang) was an alternate name of the Tang capital, usually referred to as Changan (長安 Ch. Chang'an). The *Open Court* version has a typo: "Mak-yang."

34 *Open Court*: "is one of the early literary remains extant."

35 Gale is referencing the Stone Inscription of the Stupa of Great Master Nanggong Taesa Paegwŏl at T'aeja Temple (太子寺 朗空大師 白月栖雲塔碑). The *hanmun* passages that follow are drawn from Cho Tongwŏn, *Han'guk kŭmsŏngmun taegye*, kwŏn 6.

36 "新羅國故兩朝國師教誼朗空犬師自月相雲之塔碑銘并序."

37 Haengjŏk (行寂, AD 832–916).

38 "大師 法諱行寂."

39 "行母薛氏夢見僧謂曰宿因所追願為阿孃之子."

40 "覺後感其靈瑞備啟所天自屛膻腴勤爲胎教以大和六年十二月三十日誕生."

"His appearance and general behaviour differed from that of ordinary man; from the days of his childhood he played with delight at the service of the Buddha. He would gather together sand and make pagodas; and bring spices and make perfume. From his earliest years he loved to seek out his teacher and study before him, forgetting all about eating and sleeping. As years added their knowledge, he loved to choose great subjects and write essays thereon.[41] When once his faith was established in the 'golden words' of the Buddha, his thoughts left the dusty world and he said to his father, 'I would like to give myself up to religion and make some return to my parents for all the kindness they have shown me.' The father, recalling the fact that Nang Kong had been a priest in a former existence, realized that his dreams had come true. He offered no objection but gave a loving consent. So Nang Kong cut his hair, dyed his clothes, dressed in black and went forth to the hardships and labours of a religious life. He went here and there in search of the 'sea of knowledge' … finding among the 'scattered flowers' beautiful thoughts and pearls of faith."[42]

"His teacher said of him, 'Prince Śākyamuni was most earnest in his search for truth, and Anja[43] loved best of all to learn from the master (Confucius). I used to take these things as mere sayings but now have I found a man who combines both. Blue-eyed and red-headed priests of whatever excellence cannot compare with him.' (Men of India?)[44]

"In the ninth year of Taejung (855 AD) at the Kwanje Altar,[45] in the Pokch'ŏn Monastery, Nang Kong received his confirmation orders,

---

41 *Open Court*: "When he had attained to a thoughtful age he loved to choose great subjects and write essays thereon."

42 "大師生標奇骨有異凡流遊戲之時演為佛事每聚沙市造塔常摘菜」以為香愛自青襟尋師緯帳請業則都忘寢金言志遺塵俗謂父曰所願出家修道以報罔極之恩其父知有宿根合符前夢不阻其志愛而許之遂酒削染披絡苦求遊學欲尋學海歷]."

43 This refers to Yan Hui (顏回 ca 521–481 BC), the most revered of Confucius's disciples.

44 "選名山至於伽耶海印寺便謁宗師宗師精探經論統雜花之妙義該貝葉之眞文師謂學徒曰釋子多聞顏生好學昔聞其語今見其人豈與青眼赤髭同年而語."

45 Emperor Kwan (關帝), often referred to in Chinese as Guan Yu (關羽), was a powerful warlord during the Three Kingdoms period (AD 220–80), playing a prominent role in the fifteenth-century novel *Romance of the Three Kingdoms*, where he appeared under his given name, Guan Yu. Over the centuries he was elevated to the status of deity by both Taoists and Buddhists, and there are many altars today in China dedicated to his veneration.

and from that time with his pilgrim bag and staff, he went to live in the grass hut of the religionist. His love for the faith was very great, and he longed to enter into the hidden recesses, where he might attain the desires of the heart."[46]

"(Nang Kong visited the capital of China) and on the birthday of the Emperor was received in audience. His majesty's chief desire was to be a blessing to the State and to advance the deep things of religion.[47]

He asked of the Master, 'What is your purpose in coming thus across the Great Sea?'[48]

The Master replied, 'Your humble servant, blessed beyond measure, beholds now, with his own eyes, the capital of this great empire, and hears religion spoken favourably of within its precincts. Today I bathe in the boundless favour of this holy of holies. My desire is to follow in the footsteps of the Sages ... bring greater light to my people, and leave the mark of the Buddha on the hearts of my fellow countrymen.'[49]

The Emperor, delighted with what he said, loved him dearly and showered rich favors upon him ..."[50]

"In the seventh moon of the following year[51] (916 AD) Nang Kong realized that sickness had overtaken him. On the twelfth day he arose early in the morning and said to his disciples, 'Life has its appointed limits. I am about to die. Forget not the truth. Be diligent in its practice. I pray you, be diligent.'[52]

He sat as the Buddha, with his feet crossed on the couch, and so passed away. His age was eighty-five. For sixty-one years he had been a learner of truth.[53]

At his death clouds gathered dark upon the mountains and thunders rolled. The people beneath the hill looked up and saw halos of light,

---

46 "哉大中 九年於 福泉寺官壇受其具戒既而浮囊志切繫草情深像教之宗己勞力學
    玄機之旨盡以心求所以."

47 "降誕之辰勅徵入內懿宗皇帝遽弘至化虔仰玄風問."

48 "犬師曰遠涉滄溟有何求事?"

49 犬師對勅曰貧道幸獲觀風上國問道中華今日切沐鴻恩得窺盛事所求遍遊靈跡追
    尋赤水之珠還耀吾鄉更作青邱之印."

50 "天子厚加寵賚甚善其言猶如法秀之逢晋文曇鸞之對."

51 *Open Court*: "In the seventh moon of autumn."

52 "所至明年二月初大師覺其不念稱染微痾十二日詰旦告衆曰生也有涯吾將行矣守
    而勿失 汝等勉旃."

53 "趺坐繩床儼然就」滅報齡八十五僧臘六十一."

with the colours of the rainbow filling the upper air. In the midst of it a cloud seemed to ascend like a golden shaft.[54]

The Master's will had been submissive and so God had given him something better than a flowery pavilion to shelter him; and because he was a master of the Law, a spiritual coffin bore him into the heights. His disciples were left heart-broken as though they had lost their all ..."[55]

"For years Nang Kong had been a distinguished guest of the state, serving two kings and two courts ... He made the royal house to stand secure so that demon enemies came forth and bowed submission ... His departure from earth was like the fairy's ascent to the heights of heaven ... There was no limit to his wisdom, and his spiritual insight was perfect ..."[56]

"His disciples made request that a stone be erected to his memory and so His Majesty undertook the grateful task and prepared this memorial to do him honour. He gave him a special name, calling him Nang Kong, *Light of the Heavens,* and his pagoda Paegwŏl Sŏun (White Moon amid the Clouds)."[57]

A wise and gifted teacher he,
Born in Silla by the sea.
Bright as sun and moon are bright,
Great, as space and void are free ...[58]
"Written by his disciple, Member of the Hallim, Secretary of War, etc.
   Ch'oe In'gon (916 AD)."[59]

This is a sample of such were the men that ruled Corea in the earliest days of her literature.

While the priest Nang Kong lived, there lived also a man who is called the father of Corean literature, Ch'oe Ch'iwŏn (857–951 AD)[60]

---

54 *Open Court*: "In the midst of it they saw something that ascended like a golden shaft." "于時啼雲霧晦冥山巒震動有山下人望山頂者五色光氣衝於空中中有一物上天宛然金柱."

55 "口智順則天垂花蓋法成則空斂靈棺而已哉於是門人等傷割."

56 I am unable to locate the passage in the original text.

57 "新羅國故兩朝國師教詣朗空犬師自月相雲之塔碑銘并序."

58 "懿欺輝伯,生我海東, 明向日月, 量等虛空."

59 "門人翰林學士守兵部侍郎知瑞書院事賜紫金魚袋臣崔仁滾奉教撰."

60 Ch'oe Ch'iwŏn (崔致遠) was a government official of the late Silla period (AD 668–935), a member of the head rank six (*yuktup'um*) in Silla hereditary

whose collected works are the earliest productions we have. What did he write? On examination we find congratulations to the Emperor, to the King, to special friends; prayers to the Buddha; Taoist sacrificial memorials; much about nature, home life, etc.

Here are a few samples:

The Tides

Like a rushing storm of snow or driving sleet, on you come, a thousand rollers from the deep; thou tide! Over the track so deeply worn, again you come and go. As I see how you never fail to keep the appointed time, I am ashamed to think how wasteful my days have been, and how I spend the precious hours in idle dissipation.

Your impact on the shore is like reverberating thunder as if the cloud-topped hills were falling. When I behold your speed I think of Chong Kak[61] and his wish to ride the winds and when I see your all-prevailing might I think of the sleeping dragon that has awakened.[62]

The Swallow
History of the Korean People, *168*

You go with fading summer and come with returning spring, faithful and true are you; regular as the warm breezes or the chilly rains of autumn. We are old friends, you and I. She knows that I readily consent to her occupying a place in my spacious home, but you have more than once

---

bone-rank system (*kolp'um* 骨品). Ch'oe studied Confucianism for many years in Tang China (618–907), passed the imperial examination, and rose to high office. Upon his return to Korea he made ultimately unsuccessful attempts at reform, summarized in his Ten Urgent Articles of Reform (時務十餘條 , 894). As Gale correctly writes, Ch'oe's collected works are the first such extant collection in Korea's literary history.

61 Chong Kak (宗慤 Ch. Zong Que, ?–465) was a general during the Liu Song dynasty. His story is related in the "Tale of Chong Kak" (宗慤傳) in the *Book of Song* (宋書) and is the origin of the four-character set phrase *sŭngp'ung p'arang* (乘風破浪 Ride the wind and break waves), which means to endure many hardships to make one's wish come true.

62 "潮浪 驟雪翻霜千萬重。往來弦望蹋前蹤。見君終日能懷信。慙我趨時盡放慵。石壁戰聲飛霹靂。雲峯倒影撼芙蓉。因思宗慤長風語。壯氣橫生憶臥龍。" Ch'oe Ch'iwŏn, Si 詩, "Chorang" 潮浪, *Kyewŏn p'ilkyŏng chip*, 桂苑筆耕集.

soiled the painted rafters. Are you not ashamed? You have left hawks and uncanny birds far off in the islands of the sea, and have come to join your friends, the herons and ibis of the streams and sunny shallows. Your rank is equal to that of the gold-finch, I should think, but when it comes to bringing finger-rings in your bill as gifts to your master you fail me.[63]

The Sea-Gull

So free are you to ride the running white-caps of the sea, rising and falling with the rolling waters. When you lightly shake your feathery skirts and mount aloft you are indeed the fairy of the deep. Up you soar and down you sweep serenely free. No taint have you of man or of the dusty world. Your practiced flight must have been learned in the abodes of the genii. Enticements of the rice and millet fields have no power to woo you, but the spirit of the winds and moon are your delight. I think of Changja who dreamed of the fairy butterfly.[64] Surely I too dream as I behold you.[65]

Tea
Korea Magazine 1 (January 1917): 15

Today a gift of tea comes to me from the general of the forces by the hand of one of his trusted aides. Very many thanks! Tea was first grown in

---

63 "歸燕吟獻太尉 秋去春來能守信。暖風涼雨飽相諳 再依大廈雖知許。久汙雕梁却自慙。深避鷹鸇投海島。羨他鴛鷺戲江潭。只將名品齊黃雀。獨讓銜環意未甘。"
   As this version and that appearing in Gale's *History* differ considerably, I reproduce the latter here: "She goes with the fading summer, and comes with returning spring; Faithful and true is she, Regular as the gentle winds, Or chilly rains of autumn. We are old friends, she and I. You know, ungrateful bird, that I have always consented to your occupying a place in my spacious home, but more than once you soiled the painted rafters. Are you not ashamed? You leave hawks and uncanny birds far off in islands of the sea, and come to join your heron friends in streams and sunny shallows. Your rank is equal to that of the goldfinch, I should think, but when it comes, finch-like, to bringing home finger-rings in your bill, as gifts to your master, you fail me!" See Rutt, *James Scarth Gale and His "History,"* 168.

64 Changja (莊子 Ch. Zhuangzi, 369–286 BC).

65 "海鷗 慢隨花浪飄飄然。輕擺毛衣眞水仙。出沒自由塵外境。往來 缺二字 洞中天。稻粱滋味好不識。風月性靈深可憐。想得漆園蝴蝶夢。只應知。我對君眠。" Ch'oe Ch'iwŏn, Si 詩, "Chorang" 潮浪, *Kyewŏn p'ilkyŏng chip,* 桂苑筆耕集.

rarities in the garden of the Su Kingdom (589–618 AD).[66] The practice of picking the leaves began then, and its clear and grateful flavours from that time were known. Its specially fine qualities are manifest when its delicate leaves are steeped in a golden kettle. The fragrance of its breath[67] ascends from the white goblets into which it is poured. If it were not to the quiet abode of the genii that I am invited to make my respectful obeisance, or to those high angels whose wings have grown, how could such a gift of the gods come to a common *literatus* like me? I need not a sight of the plum forest to quench my thirst, nor any day-lilies to drive away my care. Very many thanks and much grateful appreciation.[68]

By Night
Ch'oe Ch'ung (986–1068 AD) [69]
History of the Korean People, *186;*
Open Court *32 (1918): 86*

The light I saw when I awoke,
Was from the lamp that yields no smoke (the moon).[70]

---

66 *Korea Magazine* (hereafter *KM*): "Tea was first grown in Ch'ok [蜀 Ch. Shu; defeated by Qin in 316 BC] and brought to great excellence of cultivation." The Sui dynasty (隋朝) unified the Northern and Southern dynasties under Emperor Wen of Sui after a period of civil war. Because of a series of disastrous military campaigns against Koguryŏ, including the infamous loss to the Koguryŏ General Ŭlchi Mundŏk (乙支文德) at the battle of Salsu where a Sui force of over three hundred thousand was reduced to only 2,800 men, the Sui soon collapsed, giving way to the Tang dynasty (唐朝 AD 618–907).

67 *KM*: "aroma."

68 Gale used the text in *Tongmunsŏn* 東文選, kwŏn 47 (狀), "Sa sin ch'a chang 謝新茶狀":
　　右某今日中軍使兪公楚奉傳處分。送前件茶芽者。伏以蜀岡養秀。隋苑騰芳。始興採擷之功。方就精華之味。所宜烹綠乳於金鼎。汎香膏於玉甌。若非靜揖禪翁。卽是閑邀羽客。豈期仙貺。猥及凡儒。不假梅林。自能愈渴。免求萱草。始得忘憂。下情無任感恩惶懼激切之至。 Gale Papers, Box 7, Folder 20, and Box 8, Folder 28 both have an almost identical version, except for the following: "Tea was first grown in Ch'ok and brought to great excellence of cultivation. It was one of the rarities of the Su Kingdom … The fragrance of its breath ascends from the white goblets."

69 Ch'oe Ch'ung (崔沖) was a literatus and Confucian scholar of the early Koryŏ period, credited with establishing several private study halls (*sŏjae* 書齋) for teaching the Confucian Classics.

70 "Was from the torch that had no smoke." Rutt, *James Scarth Gale and His "History."*

The hill whose shade comes through the wall,
Has paid an unembodied call.[71]
The music of the pine tree's wings
Comes from the harp that has no strings.
I saw and I heard, the sight, the song,
But cannot pass its joys along.[72]

Kim Pusik (1075–1151 AD) is the earliest historian of Corea. He it is who wrote the *Samguk sagi* or *History of the Three Kingdoms*, one of the most highly prized books today.[73]

Two selections from his pen are given herewith that furnish the reader with a glimpse of the far-off world of Corea in the days of William the Conqueror. Kim Pusik was not only a noted *literatus* but a great general. He was a man of immense height who overawed the world by his commanding stature.

The King's Prayer to the Buddha
(Written by Kim Pusik)

This is my prayer: May the ineffable blessing of the Buddha, and his love that is beyond tongue to tell, come upon forsaken souls in Hades, so that they may awaken from the misery of their lot. May their resentful voices be heard no more and may they enter the regions of eternal calm. If this burden be lifted from me I shall be blessed indeed, and this distressing sickness will give place to health. May the nation be blessed likewise and a great festival of the Buddha come to pass.[74]

---

71 Although the *Open Court* version records "unembodied," this word has been crossed out in *Old Corea* and an illegible word scribbled in the margin. Rutt, *James Scarth Gale and His "History"*: "unexpected call."

72 In the *OC* version the line "How shall I pass their joys along?" has been crossed out, replaced by illegible writing. Here I have followed the *Open Court* version. Rutt, *James Scarth Gale and His "History"*: "Would I could pass the joys along."

73 Kim Pusik (金富軾).

74   Gale's text is an excerpt from a longer prayer found in Gale Papers, Box 7, Folder 10. The entire text reads as follows:

The King's Prayer to the Buddha

By Kim Pusik

"The three worlds of the Buddha pertain to the heart, and the truth as regards religion, rests there likewise. Mortals are slow to awaken to this fact, and

The Dumb Cock
Open Court *32 (1918): 86–7*

The closing of the year speeds on. Long nights and shorter days that weary me. It is not from the lack of candle light that I do not read, but that I'm ill and my soul distressed. I toss about for sleep that fails to come. A hundred thoughts are tangled in my brain. The rooster bird sits silent on his perch. I wait. Sooner or later he will flap his wings and crow.

---

are wearied out treading the six ways of existence, with no means of escape there from but adding as the years unfold sorrow upon sorrow. The Buddha, however, with his perfect mirror stands ready to enlighten all alike pitying us poor unfortunates who have the treasure in the earthen vessel and know it not. He has made known to us the way of repentance and given us the law.

The desire that all may be good is expressed in the Whaŭn Bible. We see there that true sincerity can indeed move the Merciful Buddha. Its teaching is as endless as eternal life and its grace like the unnumbered sands of the sea. I (the king) a most imperfect being, have come to this high office, and have to bear the burden that my forefathers have passed on to me. I am opposed by the evils of accumulated years. Walking on the thin ice where the deep yawns black beneath me I am the constant child of fear. My spirit thought to revive beneath the soft dews of Buddha's grace and boundless blessing, but now alas I am suddenly fallen ill. I have called for physicians and fortune-tellers, yes, more than once and have prayed to the spirits but no relief has come, only a deeper sense of my misery.

In the year that His Majesty Sukjong came to the throne (1095 AD) he had many of the Yi's and others sent into exile so that even the world of the spirits was shaken, wrath filled the spheres and destruction threatened.

With the burden of their distressed souls upon me, and with a desire to bring them peace and to escape from the danger of the resentful dead, I find no other way open to me but only that of the Buddha. My ministers I here-with send to you your far-famed temple, that they may set up an altar in the hall of worship. May the clouds of incense, the diligent reading of the sacred books and the sincere heart move the Buddha till the blessing be obtained, and all the dead in torment be delivered from their woes and transferred to heaven. May the mirror of grace so enlighten the heart that the weary ones on the way to death may be delivered.

This is my prayer: May the indescribable blessing of the Buddha and his love that is beyond tongue to tell come upon these forsaken souls in Hades so that they may awaken from the misery of their lot. May their resentful voices be heard no more on earth but may enter the regions of eternal quiet. If this burden be lifted from me I shall be blessed indeed, and this distressing

I toss the quilts aside and sit me up, and through the window chink come rays of light. I fling the door wide out and look abroad, and there off to the west the night-stars shine. I call my boy, "Wake up. What ails that cock that does not crow? Dead is he or alive? Has someone wrung his neck, or has a weasel bandit done him ill? Why are his eyes tight shut and his head bent low, with not a sound forthcoming from his beak?"[75]

This is the cock-crow hour and yet he sleeps. I ask him, "Do you not break God's most primal law? The dog who fails to see the thief and bark;[76] the cat who fails to chase the rat, deserve punishment. Yes, death itself would not be too severe." Still, Sages have a word to say: "Love forbids that one should kill." I am moved to let you live. Be warned therefore and repent.[77]

Other writers follow, the best being Yi Kyubo (1168–1241 AD). He was not a Buddhist but a Confucianist, and yet all through his writings is to be found a note of respect for the sincere religion of the Buddha. He was an original character with a lively imagination, and a gift of expression quite exceptional.

---

sickness will give place to peace and joy. May the nation be blessed likewise and a great festival of the Buddha result."

In principle, Gale would have found this in either Kim Pusik's *Samguk sagi* or in the *Tongmunsŏn* (東文選), but I am unable to locate the original.

75 The version in *Open Court* reads: "Dead is he or alive? Has someone wrung his neck, or has a weasel bandit done him ill? Why are his eyes tight shut and his head bent low, with not a sound forthcoming from his beak?"

76 Here portions of the typescript are crossed out and replaced with illegible writing, and so I have followed the *Open Court* version.

77 The version in *Open Court* reads: "Be warned therefore and repent." From Kim Pusik, "A kye pu" 啞鷄賦, *Kim Pusik munchip* 金富軾文集 *Tongmunsŏn* 東文選: 歲崢嶸而向暯。苦晝短而夜長。豈無燈以讀書。病不能以自強。但展轉以不寐。

百慮縈于寸膓。想鷄塒之在邇。早晚鼓翼以一鳴。擁寢衣而幽坐。見牕隙之微明。遽出戶以迎望。參昴澹其西傾。呼童子而令起。乃問鷄之死生。既不羞於俎豆。恐見害於貍猩。何低頭而瞑目。竟緘口而無聲。國風思其君子。嘆風雨而不已。今可鳴而反嘿。豈不違其天理。與夫狗知盜而不吠。猫見鼠而不追。校不才之一揆。雖屠之而亦宜。惟聖人之教誠。以不殺而爲仁。倘有心而知感。可悔過而自新。

Tongmunsŏn (A Selection of Eastern Literature, 1478) was a compilation of select literature from the Three Kingdoms, Silla, Koryŏ, and early Chosŏn compiled by Sŏ Kŏjŏng (1420–88) under the royal patronage of King Sŏngjong (成宗, r. 1469–94). It is the largest and most comprehensive Korean literary anthology prior to the twentieth century.

Here are a few examples of what he wrote:

The Body
Open Court 32 (1918): 87–8

Thou creator of all visible things art hidden away in the shadows invisible. Who can say what Thou art like? Thou it is who hast given me my body, but who is it that puts sickness upon me? The Sage is a master to rule and make use of things, and never was intended to be a slave; but for me, I am the servant of the conditions that are about me. I cannot even move or stand as I would wish. I have been created by Thee and now have come to this place of wariness and helplessness. My body as composed of the Four Elements was not always here, where has it come from? Like a floating cloud it appears for a moment and then vanishes away. Whither it tends I know not. As I look into the mists and darkness of it, all I can say is, it is vanity. Why didst Thou bring me forth into being to make me old and compel me to die? Here I am ushered in among eternal laws and compelled to make the best of it. Nothing remains for me but to accept and to be jostled by them at their will. Alas, Thou creator, what concern can my little affairs have for Thee?[78]

My Dog[79]

When I behold your glossy shimmering back, I wonder if you are a descendant of the goddess Pano; while again your swift devouring speed would suggest that you are a child of the dragon. Your feet are like rounded bells and you have a black lacquered nose. All the joints in your body are alert and your tendons on the wing. I love you for your faithfulness to your master. Your office is to guard the gates. For this reason I regard your fierce ways as commendable, and your suspicious

---

78 From *Tongguk Yi Sangguk hujip* 東國李相國後集, kwŏn 1 "*Pyŏng chung chŏngyu kuwŏl* 病中 丁酉九月:"
   造物在冥冥 形狀復何似 必爾生自身 病我者誰是 聖人能物物 未始爲物使 我爲物所物 行止不由己 遭爾造化手 折困致如此 四大本非有 適從何處至 浮雲起復滅 了莫知所自 冥觀則皆空 孰爲生老死 我皆堆自然 因性循理耳 咄彼造物兒 何與於此矣.

79 This is one of the few literary selections in "Corean Literature and History" that does not also appear in *Open Court*.

questionings as quite the proper thing. I have reared you, cared for you, fed you, and though you are only a humble beast, you are really high bred and born of the influence of the Seven Stars (Great Bear).[80] For instinct and animal wisdom what creature can equal you? On the slightest call you are awake with lifted ears. Though your barkings are unregulated by any set of law, still no one is harmed; if your bitings were such and you laid hold promiscuously there would be consternation indeed.

Listen now till I give you good counsel. When you see a company of official servants come in at the gate with noise and confusion, let them go by, do not bark. When His Majesty, pondering over the Sacred Books, finds a difficulty and sends a eunuch post-haste to call his teacher, do not bark at him either. Even though it be night time let him go by. Whoever it is that brings a grateful offering of dainties, sauces, sweets, fragrant wines, soy, be courteous, say not a word. When a company of the literati, well-robed, and with books under the arm, come to inquire concerning the ancient sages, keep yourself under control and be mum.

I'll tell you just when to bark and when to bite. Listen now. The rascal who peeks in to see whether the palace is occupied or not, who worms his way over the wall and comes spying here and there; whose purpose is to carry off yellow gold, or whatever else he can lay his hands on then you give the alarm and grip him fast. Also the man who is fair and sleek on the outside, but full of dark design inwardly, who comes with purpose to injure or play the foul assassin, who goes with ladder against the wall to spy whereabouts, fasten your eye on him and pipe out the alarm.

Also when the old fakir or witch come poking their noses in wanting to show off sleights of hand, with no end of evils in their train to deceive and lead the mind astray, lay fast hold and grip them tight.

If unclean spirits, or goblins, take advantage and come glowering about in the night to ply their deceptive arts, bark aloud and drive them off.

If wild-cats, or rats, find their way in through waste-holes or along the gutter edges, grip them till there is no voice left in their bodies.

If there be meat in the cupboard do not play the thief yourself or touch it; if remains of a rice meal be in the kettle do not lick it over. Do

---

80 The Great Bear constellation, or *Ursa major*, is known as the Seven Stars (*ch'il-sŏng* 七星) in Korean, or the Seven-Starred Northern Dipper (*puktu ch'ilsŏng* 北斗七星). According to ancient Korean beliefs, this constellation is believed to influence human fortune and longevity. Gale also wrote on the significance of this constellation in Korean mythology in "Korea's Receding Pantheon," *Pen Pictures*, this vol.

not climb up into the hall or go digging the court-yard with your feet. Do not leave the gate unwatched or sleep too long at one time.

If you have puppy dogs to care for let them be fierce-jawed with yellow breasts like the tiger, and tails like the flying dragon. Thus may your breed long endure.

If you hear and obey what I say and let my words sink into your heart, in a thousand years when I have gone to dwell in the abodes of the genii, I shall obtain some of the elixir of life for you, feed you on it and take you with me to heaven. If any man says to you, "It is not so, never mind him," just mind what I say and all will be well.[81]

A Prayer to God Offered by the King and Ministers of Corea,
Asking Help against an Invasion of the Khitan Tartars[82]
By Yi Kyubo
Open Court 32 (1918): 88

We the King and officers of the State having burned incense, bathed and done the necessary acts for purification of soul and body, bow our

---

81 From *Tongguk Yi Sangguk chŏnjip* 東國李相國全集, kwŏn 20: *Chapchŏ-Unŏ* 雜著-韻語, "Myŏng Pano mun 命斑獒文:"

爾毛有文。槃瓠之孫乎。爾捷而慧。烏龍之裔乎。鈴蹄而漆喙。舒節而急筋。戀主之誠可愛。守門之任斯存。予是以嘉乃猛愛乃意。育之於家。以寵以飼。汝雖賤畜。斗精所寄。其靈且智。物孰類爾。主人有命。汝宜竦耳。吠嘗無節人不懼。齧不擇人禍之始。有岌岌戴進賢三梁。言言挾華輈兩廂。帶櫺具佩水蒼。驕哄塡坊。鏘鏘琅琅而至者則汝勿吠。有高文大冊不可稽滯。聖慮念臣儻可奉制。急遣內豎。徵主人詣天陛者至則雖夜汝勿吠。有飣殽盤 。皿腌鼎餾。樽醴壺醬。饋先生行束脩者至則汝勿吠。有衣縫腋挾緗帙。欲與主人橫訊直質。踦駮難詰者林林而至則汝勿吠。所可吠且齧者。亦聽於吾。頡實虛乘不虞。穴墻塴窺室廬。謀攫金規竊鈇者則汝速吠速齧勿徐。其或外脂柔內鉗忌。偵人是非。潛毒隱刺者。突梯嚅唲而至則汝吠可也。有老覡淫巫。瞪視橫眄。舞幻引怪。以詿以眩者。款扉而求見則汝齧之可也。有黠鬼妖魅緣隙以窺。伺黑以欺則汝吠而追之可也。有伏貍碩鼠鑽墻以處。廁匿睥睨則汝齧而殪之可也。橐有肉毋盜。鼎有湆毋舐。毋登堂。毋撥地。毋離門。毋嗜睡。生雛則惟獢惟獷。豹膚螭尾。以及于主人之孫子宜矣。嗚呼。汝若敬聽吾言。佩以周旋。千歲之後。主人登仙。飲汝以藥。牽而上天。孰曰不然。敬聽敬聽毋忽焉。"

82 The Khitan were a tribal, nomadic people who inhabited parts of modern Mongolia, northeast China, and the Russian Far East from the fourth century AD. They established the Liao in AD 907, which laid claims to much of the former Parhae (渤海, AD 698–926), and claimed to be the successors of the Koguryŏ Kingdom. The Khitan invaded early Koryŏ multiple times before

heads in pain and distress and make our prayer to God and the angels of heaven. We know there is no partiality shown in the matter of blessing and misfortune, that it depends on man himself. Because of our evil ways God has brought death and despair upon our state by an invasion of the Tartars. Without cause, they encroached upon our territory, devastated the outlying lands and murdered our people. More and more are they encircling us till now the very capital itself is threatened. Like tigers after flesh are they, so that those ravished and destroyed cover the roadways. In vain are all our thoughts of ways and means of defense. We know not what to do to meet the urgency of the situation. All we can do is to clasp our bowed knees, look up and cry.

These Tartars are our debtors really. They have received many favours from us, and heretofore we have never had cause to dislike them. Of a sudden has their fierce dread flood broken in upon us. This cannot be by accident but must be due wholly to our sins. The past is the past; our desire is to do right from now on. Grant that we may not sin. Thus it is that we ask our lives from Thee. If Thou, God, dost not wholly intend to destroy our nation, wilt Thou not in the end have mercy? This will be to us a lesson and so I write out this prayer as we make our promise to Thee. Be pleased, oh God, to look upon us.[83]

---

establishing a tributary relationship with the kingdom, which effectively severed direct contact between Koryŏ and the culturally dynamic Chinese Song dynasty (960–1279) for roughly a century. See Seth, *A Concise History of Korea*, 91–4. The Khitan Liao dynasty, however, had long since fallen to the Jurchen Jin dynasty in 1125, which in turn was conquered by the Mongol Yuan dynasty in 1234. Though Yi wrote "Khitan" (Kŏran) he was actually referring to the Mongols, who at the time of writing had begun their second attack on Koryŏ. For a discussion of the Korean tendency to conflate Manchurian tribal groups within the "civilized-barbarian" (*hwa-yi* 華夷) cosmology, see Breuker, *Establishing a Pluralist Society in Medieval Korea*, chap. 6.

83 *Tongguk Yi Sangguk chŏnjip* 東國李相國全集, kwŏn 25: *Chapchŏ* 雜著, "*Sinmi sibiwŏl iril kunsin maengomun* 辛卯十二月日君臣盟告文:"
右下土臣某等。熏沐齋戒。謹頓首再拜。哀顧于皇天上帝及一切靈官。夫禍福無門。惟人所召。今者以臣等不肖之故。天降喪亂于國家。彼達旦之頑種。無故犯境。殘敗我邊鄙。殺戮我人民。侵淫至于京畿。騰蹂四郊。如虎擇肉。民之被劫物故者。狼籍于道。君臣思所以捍禦之計。倉惶罔知所圖。但把膝環顧。長大息而已。且達旦嘗有恩於我耳。非有所憾者。而一旦更加殘虐如此。豈偶然者耶。向所謂臣等不肖所致然也。噫。既往不可追。庶幾從此已後。勿復行非法之事。以此請命于上天。天若不甚處劉我國。則其終忍而不矜耶。所可得行而爲戒者。備載于文底。盟于上天。惟帝其鑑之。

The Angel's Letter
Open Court *32 (1918): 89–91*

In a certain month and on such a day the official in charge of the Palace of God sent a shining angel[84] to earth with a letter to a man called Yi Kyubo of Corea. It read, "To His Excellency who dwells amid the noise and confusion of this mortal world, with all its discomforts. We bow and inquire on your honoured health. We think of you and long for you as words cannot express, for we too serve on the right hand of God and await His commands. You, our exalted teacher, were formerly a literary attendant of the Almighty, who took His commands and recorded them, so that when spring came, it was you who dispensed the soft and balmy airs, and brought forth the buds and leaves. In winter, too, you scattered frost and wind, and sternly put to death the glory of the summer. Sometimes you sent wild thunder, wind and rain, sleet and snow, clouds and mist. All the things that God commanded for the earth were written by your hand. Not a jot did you fail to fulfil of His service, so that God was pleased and thought of how He might reward you. He asked a way of us and we said in reply, 'Let him lay down for a little the office of Secretary of Heaven and go as a scholar among men, to wait in the presence of a mortal king and serve as his literary aide. Let him be seen in the palace halls of mankind, share the government of men, and make the world bright and happy by his presence. Let his name be sounded abroad and known throughout the world, and after that bid him come back to heaven to take his place among the angels. We think that in so doing Thou shalt fitly reward his many faithful services.'"

God was pleased at this and gave immediate commands that it be carried out. He showered upon you unheard of gifts and graces, and clothed you with the commanding presence of the Superior Man, so that you might have a hundred chariots in your train, and ten thousand horses to follow after. He sent you forth and had you born into the earth in that nation that first catches the light of the morning as it rises from the Pusang Mountains. Now several years have passed, and we have not heard of your special rank, or of your having won a name. Nothing sterling has been done by you and no great book written. Not a sound has reached the ears of God. We were anxious about this and so were about to send a messenger to find out, when, unexpectedly, there came one from earth to us of whom we made inquiry.

---

84 *Open Court*: "sent a golden messenger."

He replied, "The man called Kyubo is in greatest straits, most far removed from any sort of honour. He is given over to drink and madness; goes here and there about the hills and by the graves writing verses; but no seal of state hangs from his belt, nor wreath adorns his brow. He is like a dragon that has lost its pool, or a dog in the house of mourning; an ill-fated lonely *literatus*; and yet all, from the highest to the lowest, know his name. Whether it be that he is so extravagant that he has not been used, or because they have not chosen him I do not know."

Before he had finished this, however, we gave a great start and struck our hands in wonder, saying, "His earth companions are evidently haters of the good, and jealous of the wise. We must take note."

Thus it was we wrote a memorial embodying what had been told us and God regarded it as right. He has prepared a great lock and key for those offenders, and now meditates setting matters straight. Little by little your wings will unfold, and your footsteps will take their upward way toward the heights. Far will you enter into the halls of fame. To the Chamber of the Ministry, though not equal to heaven, you will proceed. How glorious your way will be. Now, indeed, you will drink joy,[85] and the splendour of its dusty way. We, friends of yours, who are in heaven, impatient wait your high return. The harp that ought to dispense sweet music has dust upon its strings, and sad, awaits your coming. Your halls are silent as they mourn your absence, longing once again to open wide their gates. God has made ready sweetmeats of red dew, and butter of the golden mists of morning, on which He feeds his angel hosts. Make haste to fulfil your office among men and come back to heaven. First, however, you must attain to greatness of name and merit, wealth and honour. What we urge upon you is, be diligent, be diligent. We bow with this and present our grateful honour.[86]

---

85 *Open Court*: "you will drink your fill of heart's best joy."

86 From *Tongguk Yi Sangguk chŏnjip* 東國李相國全集, kwŏn 26 "*Tae sŏnin ki yŏ sŏ 代仙人寄予書*" (also available in *Tongmunsŏn* 東文選 kwŏn 59):
月日。紫微宮使某甲丹元眞人某乙等。謹遣金童。奉書于東國李春卿座右。人閒喧雜。甚苦甚苦。伏惟道用何似。傾佇罔極。吾二人居帝之左右。出納天命者也。昔者吾子亦爲上帝之文臣。掌帝之制勅。凡春而布和氣。煦育草木。冬而振寒令。肅殺萬物。其或雷霆也風雨也霜雪也雲霧也。是皆帝之所以號令於天下者。制勅一出子手。無不稱旨。帝用德之。圖有以報爾之勞者。俯詢於臣等。臣等議曰。暫虛天上之文官。遣作人閒之學士。西掖北門。快草紅泥之誥。紫微黃閣。穩調金鼎之羹。澤潤生民。名振寰宇。然後勅還天上。更綴仙班。如是儻可以償其勞矣。帝卽肯允。於是輔子以沖和之氣。益爾以峻爽之資。凡載祿車百兩馬萬蹄。踵隨于後。遣生於東海扶桑隅日始出之邦矣。子去幾年。尙未聞調

  This is an unusual piece of imaginative work, evidently written as a protest against his own adverse fortunes from a political point of view.[87]
  Here is a translation of one of his poems:[88]

On the Death of a Little Daughter
"On the Death of His Little Daughter," Korea Magazine 1
(May 1917): 204;
Open Court 32 *(1919): 91*

My little girl with face like shining snow,	小女面如雪。
So bright and fresh[89] was never seen before.	聰慧難具說。
At two she talked both sweet and clear,[90]	二齡已能言。
Better than parrot's tongue was ever heard.	圓於鸚鵡舌。
At three, retiring, bashful, timid, she	三歲似恥人。
Kept modestly inside the outer gates.	遊不越門闌。
This year she had been four	今年方四齡。
And learned her first lessons with the pen.[91]	頗能學組綴。
What shall I do, alas, since she is gone?	胡爲遭奪歸。
A flash of light she came and fled away,	倏若駭電滅。
A little fledgling of the springtime, she;	春雛墮未成。
My little pigeon of this troubled nest.	始覺鳩巢拙。
I know of God and so can calmly wait,	學道我稍寬。
But what will help the mother's tears to dry?	婦哭何時輟。

一官除一名。著一奇跡。撰一大冊。以聞于帝耳者。吾等甚訝之。方欲使使詰其所然。適有自人間來者問之。則曰。所謂春卿者。困躓窮塗。阻霆一命。謫仙盃酒。頗事狂顛。元結溪山。空稱漫浪。腰未垂尺五之組。頭未峙三梁之冠。失水之龍耶。喪家之狗耶。特纍纍貿貿。一布褐之窮士耳。公卿搢紳。非不知名也。豈以其迂濶不切事。而不容揀採歟。言未終。吾等愕然彈指。尋讞爾國之嫉賢忌能者之罪。緘奏于上帝。帝已頷可。將大錮其人。而信爾之屈也。則子之翼將奮矣。子之步將高矣。玉堂有路。何深不入。鳳閣非天。何高不陟。紅塵下界。方酣一餉之榮。碧落故人。空望九還之就。瑤瑟兮生塵。將待子而弄。玉室兮無人。將待子而開。紫皇所賜丹露之漿金霞之液。獨吾等日猷飫耳。久矣不得與吾子共酌也。宜速償於素志。復超躡於玄都。噫。功名不可不遂。富貴不可久貪。吾等所以勗子者此耳。勉旃。頓首再拜。謹白。

87 The *Open Court* version adds the following sentences: "Yi Kyubo writes on a variety of subjects. He touches nature again and again."

88 *Open Court*: "Here is a translation of one of his poems on the family life."

89 *Open Court*: "So bright and wise"; *KM*: "So wise and bright."

90 *KM*: "free and clear."

91 *KM*: "her first wee lessons with the pen."

I look out on the distant fields,	吾觀野田中。
The ears shoot forth upon the stalks of grain,	有穀苗初苗。
Yet wind and hail sometimes await unseen.	風雹或不時。
And when they strike,[92] the world has fallen full low.	撲地皆摧沒。
'Tis God who gives us life;	造物既生之。
'Tis God who takes our life away.	造物又暴奪。
How can both death and life continue so?	枯榮本何常。
These changes seem like deathly phantoms drear.	變化還似譎。
We hang on turnings of the wheel of fate,	去來皆幻爾。
And give it up;[93] we are just what we are.[94]	已矣從此訣。

Seven hundred years ago flies were in existence and evidently just as lively as they are with us.

On Flies

I have ever hated the way in which the fly continually annoys and bothers people. The thing that I dislike most of all is to have him sit on the rims of my ears and settle squabbles with his neighbors. When I am ill and see him about me, I am afflicted with a double illness over and above my original complaint. In seeing the multitude of his breed swarming about, I cannot but make my complaint to God.[95]

Here is his own portrait:

To his Portrait and the Artist

'Tis God who gave this body that I wear,	天地生我身
The artist's hand sends me along through space.	傳之者君手
Old as I am I live again in you;	予老少與偕
I love to have you for companion dear.	甘與影爲偶
He took me as I was an old dry tree,	眞箇槁木形

---

92 *KM*: "When once they strike."

93 *Open Court*: "No answer comes"; *KM*: "Let's give it up since thus we are."

94 The original Literary Sinitic work is from *Tongguk Yi Sangguk chŏnjip* 東國李相國全集, kwŏn 5 "*To sonyŏ* 悼小女."

95 From *Tongguk Yi Sangguk chŏnjip* 東國李相國全集, kwŏn 1 古律詩 105首 "*U pyŏng chung chil sŭng* 又病中疾蠅:" 平生厭汝逐人偏 第一深憎鬪耳邊 病裏逢來 重值病 滋繁此物怨皇天.

And sitting down re-formed and pictured me.   君於隱几取
I find it is my likeness true to life,   望之雖肖眞
And yet my ills have all been spelled away.   未甚移吾醜
What power against my deep defects had he   吾醜子何嫌
That thus he paints me sound, without a flaw?   取人貌可後
Sometimes a handsome, stately, gifted lord   魁岸美丈夫
Has but a beast's heart underneath his chin;   心或如冠獸
Sometimes a cluttered most ill-favoured waif   叢陋可笑者
Is gifted high above his fellow-man.   才有出人右
I am so glad there's nothing on my head,   喜哉首不弁
For rank and office I sincerely loathe.   已厭名途驟
You have put thought and sense into my eye,   眉目頗洒然
And not the dust-begrimed look I wear.   不以今蒙垢
My hair and beard are lesser white as well;   鬚髮未全皓
I'm not so old as I had thought to be.   不以今之壽
By nature I am given o'er much to drink,   我性本嗜酒
And yet my hand is free, no glass is seen.   手曷無卮酒
I doubt you wish to point me to the law,   置我禮法間
That I a mad old drunkard may not be.   不許作狂叟
You write a verse as well, which verse I claim   況復投珠聯
Is equal to the matchless picture drawn.[96]   雙絕人知不

---

96 Gale Papers, Ledger 6, pp. 193–4, contains a very rough manuscript draft (see
below) of this poem titled "His Portrait" and labelled "이규보 Vol. II; 358,"
referring to the Chōsen Kosho Kankōkai reprint of 1913. The original poem
can be found in *Tongguk Yi Sangguk hujip* 東國李相國後集, kwŏn 5, koyulsi 89
su 古律詩 89首, under the title "Sa sajin 謝寫眞."

"His Portrait"
'Twas Heaven and Earth brought forth this mortal frame,
But tis your hand sends me along through space.
Though old I'm young again in you
Who paint this picture for companion dear.
You took me as I was an old dry tree,
And sitting down, hath drawn me ills and all.
Still my defects are not your fault;
Nor does it count, for who looks at the outer man?
A Master of angelic form may have a beast's heart
Underneath his chin, while one all wizened up
And pointed at with scorn, may wear the gifts that crown.
I have no cap of office on my head for which I'm glad.
I hate these marks of empty show.

With one more little verse that touches nature we bid farewell to Yi Kyubo.[97]

The Cherry
Open Court 32 (1918): 92

How wonderful God's work!	天工獨何妙.
So delicately mixed his sweet and sour!	調味適酸甘.
And yet your beautifully rounded shape,	徒爾圓如彈.
And rosy hue invite the robber bird.[98]	難防衆鳥含.

As time passes on other masters follow, and one Yi Chehyŏn is specially noted.[99] He lacks the versatility of Yi Kyubo but in power of expression even surpasses him.

My eyes too shine with lustre bright,
And all my face is clean of every flaw.
My hair is not so white nor are my years so full.
By nature I am fond of drink
And yet within my hand no glass is seen.
You picture me a sober master-sage
And not the mad old creature that I be.
Still you have missed me something that I claim
For who would know I wield the pen and write?

97 *Open Court*: "Here is one of his little quartettes that touches nature."

98 Gale's unpublished typescript book on Yi Kyubo carries a slightly different version of this poem on p. 54:

"The Apricot Cherry"

Vol. I; 252.
How wonderful God's work!
To mix thus marvellously the sweet and better; So delicately ????
And yet your beautifully rounded shape,
Invites all the robber birds to come and eat pounce upon you.

When Gale identifies a work of Yi Kyubo as "Vol. I" or "Vol. II," he is citing the Chōsen Kosho Kankōkai reprint of 1913, meaning that these "volume" numbers bear no relation to the fascicles of the *Tongguk Yi Sangguk chŏnjip* and *hujip*. The original of this poem can be found in *Tongguk Yi Sangguk chŏnjip*, kwŏn 16, under the title "Aengdo 櫻桃."

99 Yi Chehyŏn (李齊賢, 1288–1367) was a late Koryŏ government official and literatus.

He was sent in 1314 as a young envoy to China to the court of the Mongol Emperors. A memorial was presented about that time urging that Corea be made a province of China Proper. Yi Chehyŏn, startled at the proposal, wrote so powerful and persuasive a rejoinder that the Emperor cancelled the Memorial and let Corea stand.

He travelled much in China and so I give one of the selections that dropped from his pen.[100]

The Whangha River[101]
Open Court *32 (1918): 92–3*

Down comes the rolling Whangha from the west, with sources in the fabled peaks of Kollyun.*[102] The envoy of great Han built him a raft, and went to see its fountain-head. From the heart of the hills it gushes forth, a thousand measures downward to the sea. He found it was the Milky Way that pours its torrents eastward and comes sweeping on. By nine great circles it outspans the earth even to the farthest limits of the eye.

It is like a battle, fierce, between the Hans and Ch'os;[103] the crash of ten thousand horses in an onset on the plain. Slantwise never ceasing it comes rolling in big battalions. When it rises and overflows the field and meadows, people's hearts forsake them from pale fear. By the opening gates of the mountains its way is cloven eastward. The fierce strokes of its blade cut a thundering pathway to the sea.

When I was young I played upon the bosom of the deep and wished to ride the fabled Moni.[2] Now I would fain drink from the waters of this Western river. As fair they seem to me as the mystic lakes of dreamland that beckon to my thirsty soul. I would launch forth by boat from its sandy shallows. As I sit high and look upon it my spirit is overwhelmed

---

100　*Open Court*: "and so I give one of the selections that he wrote there."

101　The Whangha River (黃河江 Ch. Hwanghe jiang, Yellow River) flows westward across China, beginning in Qinghai Province and emptying into the Bohai Sea in Shandong Province. It is the third longest river in Asia and the sixth longest river system in the world.

102　The Kunlun Mountains (崑崙) are one of the largest mountain chains in Asia, forming the northern edge of the Tibetan Plateau.

103　This refers to the Han-Ch'o Wars (楚漢戰爭 Ch. Han-Chu zhangzheng, 206–202 BC) famously recounted in the *Records of the Grand Historian* (史記 Ch. Shiji, 94 BC).

with awe. The fishy breezes kiss my startled gaze. Great waves mount high in view like castled walls. The tall masts in the distance jostle the mountain tops. The sailor shouts his shrilly cry while sweat outlines his tightened chin. Though the day darkens, far he still must go before he lights upon the gentle village of the plain. I am not Maeng Myŏng ssi who set fire to his boats in order to settle accounts with the people of Chin nor am I the man who threw his jewels into the boiling deep.[104] Still, like them, my soul has longed to see this stately river. If the iron ox that stands upon its shore had wits to prompt his sleepy soul, he would laugh at such as me and say, "What brought you here through wind and weather and all the dangers of the way?[105]

* Mountains of Tibet where the Taoist paradise is situated.

[2] A great sea monster.

Before Yi Chehyŏn had passed away from the world there was born into Korea's circle of literati a most famous man to be called Yi Saek who dates from 1328 to 1396 AD.[106] He is regarded as the greatest of Korea's authors, and yet the writer must confess that the investigation of his works has not led to that conclusion. He is a most voluminous writer. His complete works, numbering some fifty volumes, cannot be bought for less than a hundred Japanese yen.[107] The charm of originality seems lacking.

He is however a master of the laws of Confucian composition. From that point of view his works are faultless.

One short example translated herewith gives only the thought, [but] the real power of his Chinese composition is not evident.

---

104 Gale's "Chin" here refers to the Chinese state of Qin 秦 (ninth century to 207 BC). Meng Mingshi (孟明視) was a Qin general who led two disastrous campaigns against the state of Jin 晉 but achieved victory in his third campaign after crossing the Yellow River with his army and setting fire to his own ships.

105 The original can be found in *Ikchae nan'go*, kwŏn 1, "Hwangha 黃河":
     黃河西流自崑崙。漢使乘槎昔窮源。崑崙山高幾千仞。天河倒瀉流渾渾。崩騰九曲轉坤軸。浩蕩萬里浮天垠。有如楚漢戰垓下。千兵萬馬驅平原。橫流往往不可止。泛溢田野愁黎元。擘開兩山俾東注。辛苦巨靈留掌痕。蹇予少年遊海上。豪氣欲跨莊生鯤。西江眞堪一口吸。雲夢不足胸中吞。今日沙頭欲解纜。兀坐不覺驚心魂。腥風打頭浪如屋。長帆遠與山相掀。篙師絶叫污流瀋。日暮未到南岸村。我不是焚舟孟明視。期爲秦民一雪無窮冤。又不是投璧晉公子。誓與舅氏不負平生言。鐵牛有知應解笑。胡爲涉險西南奔。

106 Yi Saek (李穡).

107 *Open Court*: "cannot be bought for less than thirty dollars."

Concerning Himself
By Yi Saek
Open Court *32 (1918): 93–4*

This form of mine is small and poorly built, so passers think me a hunch-back. My eyes are defective, and ears dull of hearing. When someone speaks I look around to see and act much like a frightened deer that haunts the busy mart.

Though someone might be found to be my friend, soon he would change his mind and cast me off. Though I would give my inner heart and soul to prove I am a grateful man, he would run the faster. So my friendships end. Although my face may shine and lips speak sweetest things to voice my heart, I still would be the northern cart that finds itself within the southern kingdom. Who is there then to fit my arrow-head or wing my shaft for me? Who lends the comfort or listens to my woe?

Away into unfathomed depths have gone the friends I once loved and trusted, like trees that hide within the evening mist. If I regard myself I am as lonely as a single lock of hair upon a bullock's back. Whose teeth will ever part to speak a grateful word on my behalf? Yet wherein have I sinned, or how departed from the rightful way? My wish and my desire stand firm toward the truth. Where have my deeds been sordid, low or mixed with cunning? I am a straight and honest man, why then this doubt and disregard? My one wish is to teach all men the way. Why is my learning held of no account? In study my desire is full attainment. Where are the flaws? What have I failed to do? I wish to hold the plummet-line of rectitude.

My failures, faults, and lack of round success are due to this one wish I have that right may rule. I may have failed, how far I cannot know, yet why expect success from him who's but a beast, whose name is counted over on the finger-tips, as though he were a bandit chief?

Faults lie with you, my critics. You must change. God who sees full well and knows will account me clear. With all its feet and inches I have kept the required law.[108] No matter who, if he confess his faults, his past is buried evermore. To say I'm right and good, what joy is that? To jeer and treat me with contempt, what matter? Let me but so conduct

---

108 *Open Court*: "The law required, with all its feet and inches I have kept."

myself that I be not an agent of the dark. To keep God's law this be my all in all.[109]

Chŏng Mongju who went as envoy to Japan in 1377 AD is also regarded as one of Korea's foremost literary men.[110] He is a model, too, of the faithful courtier, for like Kija, he refused in 1392 to swear allegiance to the new regime, and died a martyr. His blood marks are pointed out in all sincerity today on the stone bridge in Songdo where he fell. Perhaps the fact that he lived up to this golden rule of the Far East, "Serve Only One Master," makes his writings more valuable than they would otherwise be. He went several times to Nanking on messages from the state, and once was shipwrecked on the way. He is regarded by both Chinese and Japanese as a great master of the pen.[111]

---

109 The original can be found in *Mogŭn ko* 牧隱藁, kwŏn 1, Sa 辭, "Chasong sa 自訟辭":

汝之軀矮而陋兮。人視之若將仆也。視既短而聽又瑩兮。中人聲而左右顧也。驚麛駁鹿之入于市兮。孰肯從而相友。雖幸聚而乍成懼兮。倏背焉而旋詬。出肺腑肉以求可兮。藐異馳而莫之遇。柔爾顏兮甘爾言。瀉眞情之繼吐。猶北轅而適楚兮。夫誰鏃而誰羽。舒憂娛悲之何所兮。豁茫茫其天宇。惟情親之乖離兮。杳暮雲而春樹。觀吾身於霄壤兮。吹毛一於牛九。疇其置齒牙間兮。抑難知其所否。豈予德之回譎兮。予則懷其純一也。豈予行之奇邪兮。予則視其正直也。豈予言之訐詐兮。予則師其悃愊也。豈予學之鹵莽兮。予則至于其極也。豈予政之多疵兮。予則蹈夫繩墨也。惟吾之顚頓狼狽兮。莫知主善之克一也。夫惟一之罔知協兮。离獸之歸而何擇。宜仁人之不齒兮。罔之生也是敵。胡反觀之不蚤兮。上帝臨之而赫赫也。其循循而蹈禮兮。則不違於咫尺也。引罪辜以謝過兮。孰既往之追責。貸予褒兮何欣。附予毀兮何怵。雍容袍笏之班兮。不識不知而順帝之則也。

110 Chŏng Mongju (鄭夢周, 1338–92) was a late Koryŏ scholar-official, diplomat, and proponent of Neo-Confucianism who is credited along with Yi Saek with founding the Sŏnggyun'gwan (成均館 National Confucian Academy) in 1367.

111 The *Open Court* version includes here a piece titled "Japan and the Japanese (Written on the departure of Chŏng Mongju as special envoy, 1377 AD)," followed by a short paragraph explaining the Korean view of the Japanese, and Korea's current elevated state in the Japanese Empire. Given its relevance to Chŏng's writings, I include it here: "The Korean viewed the Japanese in those days much as the Englishman viewed the Frenchman. Beneath his highly contemptuous manner, however, there was also a high regard. So it has been. So it is today. Koreans enjoy a safety of life and property as never before, have a door of opportunity open to them that they never could have erected themselves, and they give promise of not only forming an honorable part of the great Empire of Japan but of contributing something original to this illustrious nation." *Open Court* 32 (1918): 95.

On Loyalty[112]

Yes, though I die, a hundred times, and die,
And my white bones become the dust they tread,
Though this my soul be here or there, uncounted,
My heart's the King's; my loyal blood is red.[113]

---

112 This piece is not included in *Open Court*.

113 This particular poem does not appear in *P'oǔn chip* 圃隱集 (Chǒng Mongju's
collected works), and is known in Korea exclusively as a vernacular *sijo* by
the title "Tansim ka" (丹心歌 Song of Loyalty). Chǒng Mongju is said to have
composed the *sijo* in response to a *sijo* titled "Hayǒ ka" (何如歌) and composed
by Yi Pangwǒn (i.e., T'aejong 太宗, first monarch of the Chosǒn dynasty).
The song is presumed to have been transmitted orally before being recorded
in many different vernacular and Literary Sinitic versions, starting with the
Haedong akpu (海東樂府, 1617). A typical vernacular version runs like this:

이몸이 죽고 죽어
일백번 고쳐 죽어
백골이 진토 되어
넋이라도 있고 없고
임 향한 일편담심이야
가실 줄이 있으랴

A Literary Sinitic version exists, but the *baihua* elements in it suggest it was
not likely to have been written by Chǒng Mongju himself:
此身死了死了
一百番更死了
白骨爲塵土
魂魄有也無
向主一片丹心
寧有改理與之
The Gale Papers, Box 7, Folder 29, titled "Korean Songs, Poems, Etc.," contains another version of this poem on p. 6:
"Loyalty to the King"
Though I die and die a hundred times and die
And all my bones turn whitened clay,
With soul and spirit gone I know not where,
My heart sworn loyalty to my lord the King
Shall never change, no never, never, never.
It is not clear what text Gale was referring to for his translation. For a dis-
cussion of problems in translating this *sijo* into English, see Skillend, "Have
I a Soul or Not?"

In Nanking
By Chŏng Mongju
Open Court 32 (1918): 95–6

I, Chŏng Mongju, in 1386, fourth moon, with my commission from the king was in China's South Palace in the Assembly Hall. On the twenty-third day the Emperor, while seated in the Gate of Divine Worship, sent a palace maid-in-waiting with a command saying that His Imperial Majesty desired me to come. I went and he talked with me face to face. What he said was most gracious. He ordered the yearly tribute paid by Corea, gold, silver, horses, cotton goods, etc. to be entirely remitted. Deeply moved by this I wrote the following poem:

A palace-maid at noon passed the command,	內人日午忽傳宣。
And bid me come before the Dragon Throne,	走上龍墀向御筵。
To hear his gracious words it seemed to me that God was near;	聖訓近聞天咫尺。
Unbounded favours from his hand reach out beyond the sea.	寬恩遠及海東邊。
I did not realize that in my joy my eyes were filmed with tears.	退來不覺流雙涕。
My only word is "May Your Majesty live on forever."	感激唯知祝萬年。
From this day forth we thrive, land of the Han, how blessed.	從此三韓蒙帝力。
We plough and dig our wells and sing our songs of peace.[114]	耕田鑿井「安眠。

In Japan
By Chŏng Mongju (1377 AD)
Open Court 32 (1918): 96

A thousand years have stood, these islands of the deep,	海島千年郡邑開。

---

114   The original is in *P'oŭn chip*, kwŏn 1, "Hwangdo sa su 皇都 四首," Part 2, but Gale has reversed the order of the poem and the introduction. The latter reads: 臣夢周於洪武丙寅四月。奉國表在京師會同館。是月二十三日。上御奉天門。內人傳宣促臣入內。親奉宣諭。敎誨切至。因將本國歲貢金銀馬布一切蠲免。不勝感荷聖恩之至。謹賦詩以自著云。

<table>
<tr><td>

By boat[115] I came and long I linger here;
Priests from the hills are asking for a song;
My host, too, sends me drink to cheer the day.
I am so glad we can be friends and kind to
    one another,
Because of race let's not be mean in mind
    or jealous.
Who then can say one is not happy on a
    foreign shore?
Daily we go by chair to see the plums in
blossom.[116]

</td><td>

乘桴到此久徘徊。
山僧每爲求詩至。
地主時能送酒來。

却喜人情猶可賴。

休將物色共相猜。

殊方孰謂無佳興。

日借肩輿訪早梅。

</td></tr>
</table>

In the next century, the fifteenth, a greater number of writers appear, historians as well, like Sŏ Kŏjŏng who wrote the *Mirror of the Eastern Kingdom*, the best history we have of the early days of his people.[117] All through it he shows himself a man of good judgement who draws a definite line between mere superstition and historical fact.

And yet it was a day of superstition, for one of his contemporaries, Sŏng Hyŏn,[118] writes endless stories like the following:

115　In the *Open Court* version, Gale writes here "raft," accompanied by the following explanation: "'Raft' is a reference to the supposed means of conveyance by which Chang Kŏn went all the way to Rome and the Milky Way." Chang Kŏn (張騫 Ch. Zhang Qian) was an early Han dynasty diplomat and imperial envoy who travelled extensively in Central Asia.

116　Gale's manuscript Ledger 16, p. 1 contains a much longer version titled "Chŏng Mongju Goes as Minister to Japan in 1377," of which this poem is the first paragraph (but not versified):

"A thousand years this state has lived and flourished in the sea. I came by ship and long have lingered. Priests from the hills request from me a poem the ruler sends me wine to cheer the day. Kindness is something not limited seen only at home. Let us not be greedy of gain or jealous of each other. Who can say that there is no joy in the other parts than just their own. I go by *Kango* daily to see the plum blossoms bloom."

These are the first lines in *P'oŭn chip*, kwŏn 1: "Hongmu chŏngsa. Pongsa ilbon chak 洪武丁巳。奉使日本作。"

117　The *Tongguk t'onggam* is the earliest extant Korean source listing the names of Kojosŏn rulers following Tan'gun.

118　Sŏng Hyŏn (成俔, 1439–1504) was a scholar-official of the early Chosŏn dynasty.

Odd Story of a Priestess
Open Court 32 (1918): 96–7

Once when Minister Hong was on a journey he was overtaken by rain and went into a side way house in which he found a young priestess about eighteen years of age. She was very pretty and possessed of great dignity. Hong asked her how it came that she was here in this lonely place by herself, when she replied, "We are three of us but my two companions have gone to town to obtain supplies."

By flattery and persuasive words he promised, on condition that she yield herself to him, to make her his secondary wife on such and such a day of the year. The priestess all too readily believed him and awaited the day, but he never came, and the appointed season passed without sound of his footfall.[119] The priestess fell ill and died.

Later, Hong was sent south as provincial governor of Kyŏngsang Province. While there he one day saw a lizard run across his room and pass over his bed quilt. He ordered his secretary to throw it out, and not only did he [do] so but he killed it as well. Next day a snake crawled stealthily into the room. The secretary had this killed also, but another snake came the day following.

The governor began to question the manner of this visitation and remembered the priestess. Still he trusted in his power and position to keep him safe from all such trivial evils, so he had them killed as they came and gave orders accordingly. As day followed day they grew larger in size and more evil in their manner, until at last great constrictors came pouring in upon him. He marshalled his soldiers with swords and spears to ward them off, but somehow they managed to break through. The soldiers slashed at them with their sabres; fires were built into which the snakes were flung and yet they increased in numbers and grew. In the hope of placating this enemy, the governor caught one of them and put it in a jar, letting it loose at night to crawl about as it pleased over his bed, returning it to its place when the day dawned. Wherever he went, about the town or on a journey, he had a man carry the snake along in the jar. Little by little his mind weakened under the strain of it, his form grew thin and shortly afterward he died.[120]

---

119 *Open Court*: "without sound of his footfall or shadow of any kind."

120 This story can be found in Sŏng Hyŏn's *Yongjae ch'onghwa* 慵齋叢話, kwŏn 4. The version recorded in the *Taedong Yasŭng* 大東野乘 (and which Gale almost certainly used) reads as follows:

This unsavoury thread of superstition runs through all the writings of East Asia and makes up a large part of the mental fabric of the race today. The law of reason that governs modern thought is making its influence felt more and more through newspapers and modern books, as this world is bound to disappear. The fairy part of it we would still see live; but the snakes and devils may well go.

As time passed on and the rumour became fixed that Koryŏ met its fate in 1392 AD through the evil influence of the Buddha, Confucianism became more and more the State religion and the literati were its Scribes and Pharisees who taught and explained the Sacred Books. While many of them were merely creatures of the letter, some were devoutly religious and apparently most attractive in character. One named Yi I, or Yulgok as he is called familiarly, lived from 1536 to 1584.[121] His name today is recorded in the Confucian Temple No. 52 on the east side of the Master, and is revered by his people above all others.

The Flowery Rock Pavilion
By Yi I
Open Court *32 (1918): 98*

Autumn has come to my home in the woods, how many things I try to write about. The endless line of river goes by on its way to heaven.

洪宰樞微時路逢雨。趨入小洞。洞中有舍。有一尼。年十七八。有姿色。儼然獨坐。公問何獨居。尼云三尼同居。二尼丐粮下村耳。公遂與敍歡。約曰。某年月迎汝歸家。尼信之每待某期。期過而竟無影響。遂成心疾而死。公後爲南方節度使在鎭。一日有小物如蜥蜴。行公褥上。公命吏擲外。吏遂殺之。翌日有小蛇入房。吏又殺之。又明日蛇復入房。始訝爲尼所祟。然恃其威武。欲殲絕之。卽命殺之。自後無日不至。至則隨日而漸大。竟爲巨蟒。公聚營中軍卒。咸執刀釰圍四面。蟒穿圍而入。軍卒爭斫之。又設柴火於四面。見蟒則爭投之。猶不絕。公於是夜則以櫃褌裹蟒置寢房。晝則貯藏於櫃。行巡邊徼。則令人負櫃前行。公精神漸耗。顏色憔悴。竟搆疾而卒。

121 Yi I (李珥), along with Yi Hwang (李滉, 1501–70), is widely regarded as one of the most prominent Neo-Confucian thinkers in the Chosŏn dynasty. Aside from his involvement in debates central to Confucian dogma in the sixteenth century, such as the primacy of *yi* (理 principle) or *ki* (氣 matter), and the so-called Four-Seven Debate involving the "Four Beginnings" of Mencius and the "Seven Feelings" of humanity, Yi was also deeply concerned with political, economic, and social issues, as seen in his "Memorial in Ten Thousand Words" (萬言封事, 1574) to King Sŏnjo (宣祖, 1552–1608; r. 1567–1608). See Lee and de Bary, *Sources of Korean Tradition*, 1:286–92.

The red leaves, tinted by the frost, look upward towards the sun. The hills kiss the round circles of the lonely moon. The streamlets catch the breezes that come a thousand *li*. Why are the geese going north I wonder? Their voices are lost in the evening clouds.[122]

God's Way
By Yi I
Open Court 32 (1918): 98–9

God's way is hard to know and hard to explain.[123] The sun and moon are fixed in the heavens. The days and nights go by, some longer, some shorter. Who made them so, I wonder. Sometimes these lights are seen together in the heavens; sometimes again they are eclipsed and narrowed down. What causes this? Five of the stars pass us on the celestial warp, while the rest swing by on the wings of the woof. Can we say definitely why these things are so? When do propitious stars appear, and when again such wild uncanny things as comets? Some say that the soul of creation has gone out and formed the stars. Is there any proof of this?

When the winds spring up where do they come from and whither do they go? Sometimes though it blows, the branches of the trees do not even sing. At other times trees are torn from their roots and houses are carried away. There is the gentle maiden wind and there is the fierce typhoon. On what law do these two depend?

Where do the clouds come from and how again do they dissipate into their five original colors? What law do they follow? Though like smoke they are not smoke. Piled up they stand and swiftly they sail by. What causes this?

The mists too, what impels them to rise? Sometimes they are red and sometimes blue. Does this signify aught?[124] At times heavy yellow

---

122 The table of contents to *Old Corea* lists this as "The Flowery Pavilion," but here the title is "The Flowery Rock Pavilion." Gale Papers, Box 7, Folder 29, "Korean Songs, Poems, Etc." contains another version, identical except for this line: "The streamlets catch the breezes that come to them a thousand *li*."

The original is in *Yulgok chŏnsŏ* 栗谷全書, kwŏn 1, titled "Hwasŏk chŏng p'alse chak 花石亭 八歲作 (Flowery Rock Pavilion Written at Age Eight)":

林亭秋已晚。騷客意無窮。遠水連天碧。霜楓向日紅。
山吐孤輪月。江含萬里風。塞鴻何處去。聲斷暮雲中。

123 *Open Court*: "Hard" is replaced with "difficult."
124 An archaic word meaning "anything at all."

mists shut out all points of the compass, and again a mothering fog will darken the very sun at noon.

Who has charge of the thunder and the sharp strokes of lightning, the blinding flashes that accompany them and their roarings that shake the earth? What does it mean? Sometimes they strike men dead. What law directs this I wonder?

The frosts kill the tender leaves, while the dew makes all fresh and green again. Can you guess the law by which these are governed?

Rain comes forth from the clouds as it falls, but again there are dark clouds that have no rain. What makes this difference? In the days of Sillong[125] rains came when people wished them and desisted when their hopes were fulfilled. In the Golden Age they fell just thirty-six times, definitely fixed. Was it because God was specially favourable to those people? When soldiers rise in defence of the right, rain comes; rain comes, too, when prisoners are set free. What do you suppose could cause this?

Flowers and blossoms have five petals, but the flakes of snow have six. Who could have decided this?

Hail is not white frost, nor is it snow. By what power has it become congealed? Some of its stones are big as horses' heads, and some again are only as large as chickens' eggs. Sometimes they deal out death to man and beast. At what time do these things happen? Did God give to each particular thing its own sphere of action when He made it?

There are times when the elements seem to battle with each other as when rain and snow compete. Is this due to something wrong in nature or in man's way?

How shall we do away with eclipses altogether, and have the stars keep their appointed course, so that thunder will not startle the world; that frosts may not come in summer; that snows may not afflict us, nor hailstones deal out death; that no wild typhoons may blow; that no floods prevail; that all nature may run sweetly and smooth, and heaven and earth work in gentle accord to the blessing of mankind? Where shall we find such a doctrine? You literati who are deeply learned, can any of you tell me this? Open your hearts now and let me know.[126]

---

125 Sillong (神農 Ch. Shennong), or the "Divine Farmer" is a mythological being believed to have taught ancient peoples methods of agriculture and herbal medicine.

126 The original is in *Yulgok chŏnsŏ* (栗谷全書), kwŏn X, titled "Ch'ŏndo ch'aek" (天道策), and is the first "question" part of a two-part question and answer essay. It reads as follows:

To prove that literary talent was not confined to the halls of the rich we find a number of authors who rose from the lowest social stratum to shine high in the firmament. One, a son of a slave, called Song Ikp'il, was born in 1534 and died in 1599.[127] His works were republished in 1762 and are regarded today as among Corea's best, almost sacred writings.

On Being Satisfied
By Song Ikp'il
Open Court *32 (1918): 100*

How is it that the good man always has enough, and the evil man always lacks? The reason is that when I count my lacks as best I have enough; but worry goes with poverty and worrying souls are always poor. If I take what comes as good and count it best, what lack have I? But to complain against Almighty God and then my fellow men means grieving o'er my lacks. If I ask only what I have I am never poor; but if I grasp at what I have not, how can I ever have enough? One glass of water, even that may satisfy, while thousands spent in richest fare may leave me poor in soul. From ancient days all gladness rests in being satisfied, while all the ills of life are found in selfishness and greed. The Emperor Chinsi's son

---

問。天道難知。亦難言也。日月麗乎天。一晝一夜。有遲有速者。孰使之然歟。其或日月竝出。有時薄蝕者。何歟。五星爲緯。衆星爲經者。亦可得言其詳歟。景星見於何時。彗孛之生。亦在何代歟。或云萬物之精。上爲列星。此說亦何據歟。風之起也。始於何處而入於何所歟。或吹不鳴條。或折木拔屋。爲少女爲颶母者。何歟。雲者。何自而起。散爲五色者。何應歟。其或似煙非煙。郁郁紛紛者。何歟。霧者。何氣所發。而其爲赤爲靑者。有何徵歟。或黃霧四塞。或大霧晝昏者。亦何歟。雷霆霹靂。孰主張是。而其光燁燁。其聲虩虩者。何歟。或震於人。或震於物者。亦何理歟。霜以殺草。露以潤物。其爲霜爲露之由。可得聞歟。南越地暖。六月降霜。爲變酷矣。當時之事。可得詳言之歟。雨者。從雲而下。或有密雲不雨者。何歟。神農之時。欲雨而雨。太平之世。三十六雨。天道亦有私厚歟。或師興而雨。或決獄而雨者。抑何歟。草木之花。五數居多。而雪花獨六者。何歟。臥雪立雪。迎賓訪友之事。亦可歷言之歟。雹者。非霜非雪。何氣之所鍾歟。或如馬頭。或如鷄卵。殺人鳥獸。亦在於何代歟。天地之於萬象。各有其氣而致之歟。抑一氣流行而散爲萬殊歟。如或反常。則天氣之乖歟。人事之失歟。何以則日月無薄蝕。星辰不失躔。雷不出震。霜不夏隕。雪不爲沴。雹不爲災。無烈風。無淫雨。各順其序。終至於位天地育萬物。其道何由。諸生博通經史。必有能言是者。其各悉心以對。

127 Song Ikp'il (宋翼弼) was a government minister and literatus of the mid-Chosŏn. Song was the son of a concubine (*sŏŏl* 庶孽), and his father's maternal grandmother was of slave status.

who lived within the Mang-hŭi Palace*[128] was heard to say, "Though I live out my life 'tis all too short," and thus his worries came. The ruler of the Tangs, we're told, cast lots to meet his love beyond the veil because his heart was cheerless here; and yet we, poorest of the poor, when we wish only what we have, how rich we are. How poor are kings and princes who reach out for more, while he who is poor may be the richest. Riches and poverty lie within the soul and never rest in outward things. I now am seventy and my house has nothing, so that men point at me and exclaim "How poor!" But when I see the shafts of light tip all the hilltops in the morning my soul is satisfied with richest treasure; and in the evening, when I behold the round disk of the moon that lights the world and shines across the water, how rich my eyes! In spring the plum trees bloom, in autumn the chrysanthemum. The flowers that go call to the flowers that come. How rich my joy! Within the Sacred Books what deep delight! As I foregather with the great who have gone, how rich! My virtues I admit are poor, but when I see my hair grow white, my years how rich! My joys attend unbroken all my days. I have them all. All these most satisfying things are mine. I can stand up and gaze above, and bend and look below. The joy is mine. How rich God's gifts! My soul is satisfied.[129]

---

128 Emperor Chinsi (秦始皇帝 Ch. Qinshi huangdi, 259–210 BC; r. 220–210) was the first emperor of unified China after the Warring States period. Gale's "Manghŭi Palace" is a mistake for Mang'i Palace (望夷宮 Ch. Wangyigung), where Zhao Gao (趙高, d. 207 BC) staged a coup against and assassinated Qin Ershi, the Qin emperor's youngest son.

129   The original is in *Kubong chip* 龜峯集 (Song Ikp'il's collected works), kwŏn 1, with the title "Chok pujok (足不足)":

君子如何長自足。小人如何長不足。不足之足每有餘。足而不足常不足。樂在有餘無不足。憂在不足何時足。安時處順更何憂。怨天尤人悲不足。求在我者無不足。求在外者何能足。一瓢之水樂有餘。萬錢之羞憂不足。古今至樂在知足。天下大患在不足。二世高枕望夷宮。擬盡吾年猶不足。唐宗路窮馬嵬坡。謂卜他生曾未足。匹夫一抱知足樂。王公富貴還不足。天子一坐不知足。匹夫之貧羨其足。不足與足皆在己。外物焉爲足不足。吾年七十臥窮谷。人謂不足吾則足。朝看萬峯生白雲。自去自來高致足。暮看滄海吐明月。浩浩金波眼界足。春有梅花秋有菊。代謝無窮幽興足。一床經書道味深。尙友萬古師友足。德比先賢雖不足。白髮滿頭年紀足。

Gale's Annual Report for 1916–17, a partial copy of which survives in the Gale Papers, Box 10, Folder 8, closes on pp. 4–6 with this essay. Gale prefaces it as follows: "At the end of this 33 years what is the standing of the foreigner missionary? Our value has of necessity fluctuated through the overwhelming changes of the last three decades. Sometimes we have been up and sometimes down. To-day no longer is there any halo of light surrounding the

* 220 BC, built the Great Wall

The time of Shakespeare was the most prolific day of Corea's long period of literature. Suddenly a great tragedy befell the land in the war of Hideyoshi in 1592. The mind of the new generation was filled with its horror as can easily be seen in the literature that followed.[130]

It would seem as though the spirit of destruction entered society in the fateful seventeenth century, for four political parties fought each other, not as Whigs and Tories, who talk a bit and then take afternoon tea together, but with knife and deadly potion. Song Siyŏl, the greatest literary light of his day (1607–1689 AD) had to drink hemlock when he was eighty-two and so depart this life.[131] These were the days of the Plague and the Great Fire of London. It would seem as though the spirit of trouble had spread even to East Asia.

Avarice
By Yi Sugwang (1563–1628 AD)[132]
Open Court 32 (1918): 102

Busy all my days with head and hand,	枉役身心不暫閑。
And now at last a mountain high I have of treasure;	積來金寶大於山。

---

missionary's brow, or any touch of the unearthly about him ... Let me close with a word of counsel for the modern missionary from the son of the Korean slave, Song Ik-p'il (1555) before the time of Shakespeare."

130 In the *Open Court* version the following paragraph appears, relevant for its discussion of Kim Manjung (1637–92), author of *Cloud Dream of the Nine* (*Kuunmong*), which is set in Tang China. Gale completed his translation of this fictional narrative in 1922, the first Korean work of literature to be translated into English: "Kim Manjung, the author of the *Cloud Dream of the Nine*, was born in 1617, the year after Shakespeare died. The echoes of the terrible war were not only echoed in his ears as a little boy, for his father and mother had seen it, but when he was nineteen years of age the Manchus came pouring in and extorted a humiliating treaty from Korea. By the side of the river, just outside Seoul, a tall stone with Chinese writing on one side, and Manchu script on the other, told how Korea was brought under the imperial heel. The stone stood till 1894 when some of the youthful patriots of that day knocked it over, and it still lies on its face."

131 Song Siyŏl (宋時烈) was a long-serving literatus of the mid-Chosŏn period and a leader of the so-called Westerner faction (*sŏin p'a*), which upheld the orthodoxy of Zhu Xi's commentaries on the Confucian Classics.

132 Yi Sugwang (李睟光) was a Neo-Confucian literatus of the mid-Chosŏn and a member of the so-called Southerner Faction (*Namin p'a*), named after the area of Seoul where its members were concentrated.

But when I come to die, the problem's how
    to carry it.   須知到死難將去。
My greedy name is all that's left behind me.[133]   唯有貪名滿世間。

Temptation
By Kim Ch'anghyŏp (1651–1708 AD)[134]
Open Court 32 (1918): 102

So many tempters lay siege to the soul,   衆慾交攻一箇心。
Who would not lose his way?   誰人不喪本來心。
For though the axe cuts deep the fateful tree,
The roots shoot forth anew.   斧斤山木猶萌蘖。
By early morning light awake, my friend,
    And try thy soul and see.[135]   試向平朝看此心。

Queen Inmok was one of the most famous literary women of this age.[136] She was a broken-hearted mother of royalty who spent her days of exile writing out with silver ink on black paper the sacred Mita Book of the Buddha. The relic is preserved as a special treasure in the Yujŏm Monastery[137] of the Diamond Mountains, where the writer had a chance to look it over in October, 1917.

Here is one of her poems:

The Worn-Out Labourer
By Queen Inmok (about 1608)
Open Court 32 (1918): 102

The weary ox, grown old with toil through
    years of labor,   老牛用力 已多年
With neck sore chafed and skin worn through
    in holes,   領破皮穿 只愛眠

---

133 The original is in *Chibong chip* 芝峯集 (Yi Sugwang's collected works), kwŏn
    20, with the title "Kyŏngse" 警世.
134 Kim Ch'anghyŏp (金昌協, 1651–1708).
135 The original is in *Nong'am chip* 農巖集 (Kim Ch'anghyŏp's collected works,
    kwŏn 5, in "U hwa sim cha" 又和心字, verse 2).
136 Queen Inmok (仁穆王后, 1584–1632) or Queen Dowager Sosŏng (昭聖大妃)
    was the Queen Consort of King Sŏnjo (宣祖, 1552–1608; r. 1567–1608), the
    fourteenth king of the Chosŏn dynasty.
137 Yujŏmsa (楡岾寺).

would fain find rest.[138]
Now ploughing's done, and harrow days
    are over

犁耙已休 春雨足

and spring rains fall,
Why does his master still lay on the goad
    and cause him pain?[139]

主人何苦 又加鞭

An Ode
By Yun Chŭng (1629–1715 AD)
Open Court 32 (1918): 102

Little there is that I can do in life,
I leave it all to God and go my way.
When brack and fern thick clothe the hills with green,
Why should I sweat to till and dig the soil?
And when wild hemp and creeping plants enclose the way,
What need I furthermore of fence or wall?
Although the breeze no contract written has,
Yet still it comes unfailingly to cheer;
And though the moon has sworn no oath of brotherhood,
It nightly shines its beams across my way.
If any come to jar my ears with earthly woe
Tell him no word of me or where I am.
Within my mystic walls I sit supreme,
And dream of ancients, honoured, reverenced, glorified.[140]

Since Yun's day[141] many famous authors have lived, and literature has held unquestioned sway till the year 1894 when, by order of the new regime, the government examinations were discontinued. With this edict all incentive to the study of the Classics disappeared, and the old school system ceased to be. It is twenty-seven years since this edict was promulgated, and a young man must have been at least

---

138 *Open Court*: "would fain go sleep."

139 Queen Inmok's heptasyllabic regulated verse, composed in 1613, can be found on Treasure No. 1627, a hanging scroll executed in her own hand, held currently by the Kyŏnggi-do Pangmulgwan in Yongin, Kyŏnggi Province.

140 I am unable to locate this poem in *Myŏngjae yugo* (明齋遺稿 The Collected Works of Yun Chŭng).

141 In *Open Court* Gale writes "Since Kim's day," but it is unclear to which author he is referring.

twenty-three at that time to have had even a reasonable grounding. The result is seen today in the fact that Corea has no good Classic scholars of less than fifty years of age.

The tragic death of native literature that followed the fateful edict is seen in the fact that a famous father of the old school may have a famous son, a graduate of Tokyo University, who cannot any more read what his father has written than an ordinary graduate at home can read Herodotus or Livy at sight; and the father, learned though he be, can no more understand what his son reads or studies, than a hermit from the hills of India can read a modern newspaper. So they sit, this father and this son, separated by a gulf of two thousand years, pitiful to see.[142]

Nevertheless the poems, the literary notes, the graceful letters, the inscriptions, the biographies, the memorials, the sacrificial prayers, the stories, the fairy tales of old Corea remain, a proof of the interesting civilization of this ancient people.

---

142 Gale expressed similar sentiments in "Father and Son," *Old Corea*, this vol.

Corea's Noted Women

The five selections constituting this chapter on Korea's notable women appeared in comparable form in *Korea Magazine*, with changes that I have noted. Gale seems to have envisioned an ongoing series of articles on famous women in Korea: in the first issue he announces he will "give in the *Magazine* twelve of the most distinguished [women], with the historical references and legends associated with them."[1] Gale, however, would fall short of his original goal of twelve: he included only three additional female personages, for a total of ten before the *Magazine* ceased publication in April 1919 because Gale was going on furlough – evidence of his central role in the magazine's publication.[2] The articles

---

1 Student of the Orient, "Korea's Noted Women," *Korea Magazine* 1 (January 1917): 26.

2 King, "Korean 'Classics' for Anglophone Readers." The additional women featured in the *Magazine* were Sŏ Wangmo (西王母 Ch. Xiwangmu), "The Western Queen Mother"; Sŏsi (西施 Ch. Xi Shi), whom the O Kingdom (吳 Ch. Wu) used to bring about the destruction of the Wŏl Kingdom (越 Ch. Yue) during the Spring and Autumn Period (771–476 BC); and T'ak Mun'gun (卓文君 Ch. Zhou Wenjun), who was renowned for her loyalty to her husband and mastery of the pen. See Student of the Orient, *Korea Magazine* 1, no. 7 (1917): 295–7; no. 9 (1917): 389–90; no. 10 (1917): 438–9. King provides brief summaries of all eight women in "Korean 'Classics' for Anglophone Readers," 5–6. Gale seems to have drawn much of his information on ancient Chinese personages, including Korea's noted women, from Mayers, *The Chinese Reader's Manual*. William Frederick Mayers was a British consular official, interpreter, and sinologist, and member of the Royal Asiatic Society, of which Gale was also a member.

appearing in the *Magazine* are signed "Student of the Orient," one of the many noms de plume he adopted when writing for the periodical. This appellation was in keeping with the broader mission of the *Magazine* as well. In the inaugural issue Gale writes, "The *Korea Magazine* believes that all missionaries should be thoroughly acquainted with the people among whom they labour, having a knowledge of their thought processes, the lives they live, their habits, customs, literature and religion, and that knowledge possessed by one should be passed on for the betterment of all."[3] Continuing this pedagogical theme, Gale adds, "It is imperative that students of the East put forth effort, not only to learn the language, but something of that much more difficult subject, the inner mind and soul of the people."[4] Thus, one of the primary objectives for Gale's literary and scholarly activities during this period was to spread knowledge of the "mind of the people," an endeavour that repeatedly drew his attention back to history and literature.

In the opening paragraphs of this section Gale offers an apt comparison between the bibliocentrism evident in the notable women of the West and Korea's own Sinocentrism in its selection of remarkable women, claiming that "no English, French, or American women" would appear on a list of those attaining to the highest honour, since it would be composed entirely of Jewish, biblical names. This may strike the contemporary reader as excessively Christian-oriented, and even in the context of the early twentieth century perhaps slightly so, but from such a Christian missionary perspective as Gale's, Korea's reverence for personages and events from another time and place would not have seemed misplaced. Gale's tendency to imbue the Confucian Sinitic world with theistic legitimacy further infused biblical parallels and allusions that forged philosophical and theological consanguinity.

Collectively, the selections in "Corea's Noted Women" attempt to illuminate the "soul" and character of the Korean people through the women they have chosen to elevate, revere, and emulate. The women selected for inclusion, besides all hailing from China, are also uniformly described as beautiful, suggesting the importance of this particular trait as a criterion for immortality, at least among the male-dominated literati who constructed such discourse. The utter sorrow expressed by Wang Sogun (王昭君) upon being taken as a bride by the "barbarian" Turk and her eventual suicide to prevent such a union, meanwhile,

---

3 "Editorial Notes," *Korea Magazine* 1 (January 1917): 1.
4 Ibid., 3.

represent a stark embodiment of *hwa-i* (華夷), or "Efflorescence-Barbarian" philosophy in Sinitic cosmology. Other common traits among the noted women include unswerving devotion to husbands, in the case of Ahwang and Yŏyŏng, and virtuous, wise mothering, as demonstrated by T'aeim, T'aesa, and Sin Saimdang, the latter whom Gale briefly introduces to draw a Korean parallel.[5] One characteristic conspicuously absent from Gale's noted women, save Sin, is literary achievement, a virtue that is uniformly invoked in "hagiographies" of male members of the Sinitic pantheon.[6] The figures represented by Gale therefore constitute a decidedly Confucian world view that emphasized the prescribed roles of women as wives and mothers while ignoring or viewing with ambivalence any scholarly attainments.

Corea's Noted Women
Old Corea, 19–25;
Student of the Orient, *Korea Magazine*
1 (January 1917): 26–7

In the Western world many women have attained to places of highest honour where their names will endure.[7] Yet, if we were to call to mind, say, twelve of the most distinguished, no English, French or American women would appear, not even Queen Elizabeth, nor Joan of Arc, nor Pocahontas. They would all[8] be Bible names, beginning with Eve and running down to a group of Marys.

---

5   T'aeim and T'aesa are revered not so much for their own achievements but for their effective roles in mothering the sage rulers King Mun, King Mu, and the Duke of Chu (周公 Ch. Zhou gong). Although Sin Saimdang is venerated today for her excellence in poetry and art, one of the primary reasons for her high esteem remains her wise management of the education of her son Yulgok Yi I (栗谷 李珥, 1537–84), today regarded as Korea's quintessential Confucian philosopher.

6   For example, Gale writes that "while [Yŏwa ssi's] brother was engaged in copying from the back of a tortoise the first Chinese characters, [she] mended the rent in the curtains and propped up the sky." In *Korea Magazine* (hereafter *KM*), Gale does include a biography of T'ak Mun'gun (卓文君 Queen of the Pen), who was, according to Gale, "adept at the Chinese character."

7   *KM*: "where their names will endure as long as the world stands."

8   *KM*: "They would doubtless."

Corea, too, has her list of famous women, and yet not one among them a Corean. Her heroines have come down to her through the Sacred Books of China;[9] some was of myth and folk-tale,[10] but they have all come to be definitely recorded and live as truly here in the homes of the people, as do the Hebrew[11] women in the Anglo-Saxon world.[12]

Yŏwa Ssi[13]

Yŏwa ssi was an angel who first made her appearance on the mountains[14] of prehistoric China. She was a soft and gentle maiden, sister of the famous Pokhŭi ssi,[15] the first of the Five Great Rulers (2852 BC). He is said to have evolved the Eight Diagrams[16] out of the circle of white and red that was seen on the old Corean flag. While busied thus[17] in setting in motion the philosophies of the East, his sister was exercised over a quarrel that was going on between two knights of the yellow kingdom, Konggong and Ch'ugyung.[18] It was a fierce battle.[19] It is said that Konggong butted the heavens and tore a great hole in the canopy thereof. Yŏwa ssi, while her brother was engaged in copying from the back of the tortoise the first Chinese characters, mended the rent in the curtains and propped up the sky.[20] The record simply says that she did it "By means of stones of the five colours."

---

9 *KM*: "Sacred Books of the East."

10 *KM*: "some of them by the medium of myth and folk-tale."

11 *KM*: "Jewish."

12 In *KM*, Gale adds the following: "The writer proposes to give in the *Magazine* twelve of the most distinguished, with the historical references and legends associated with them."

13 女媧氏.

14 *KM*: "in the Seung-pi Mountains."

15 *KM*: "She married and became the wife of Pok-heui-si (伏羲氏)."

16 *P'algwae* (八卦).

17 *KM*: "While her husband was taken up thus."

18 The *KM* version records "Kong-kong-si (空公氏) and Tai-jung-si (大定氏)," but it is actually Konggong (共工) and Ch'ugyung (祝融).

19 *KM*: "They were not her children, but her subjects, and a fierce battle they had."

20 *KM*: "How she did it is not quite clear."

Later she stopped a deluge that threatened the earth by means of dykes of ashes gathered from[21] burnt reed straw.

It was Yŏwa ssi who brought with her musical instruments that played in harmony and awakened the sweet sounds of earth. With a harp of fifty strings she made her worship to God. Sweet and tender was this, but too sad, so she changed it to twenty-five strings, and then set the notes of joy dancing in motion.

She was the first of all women to bind up sweetly her flowing locks. She rode in a chariot of thunder with six outspreading wings.[22] When she worshipped and cast the horoscope, a voice said, "You are the chosen one to be sun and moon, and to give light to the far-reaching provinces of China. Your mission is to comfort the world and bring peace to men."

We are told that she killed the black dragon and saved the East, and that she pitched her tabernacle and worshipped the Bright Spirit.

A later writer, named Cho Sŏlhang,[23] cast doubt on these myths, saying with some apparent heat, "To imagine that any woman ever went up three thousand miles into the sky, and with stones made whole the broken rifts in the immensities, is nonsense."

She was the first to make combs.[24]

When her mission was over she mysteriously disappeared from the earth but many hundreds of years after, when one of the kings of the Tangs was passing by night the region where she had lived, there appeared suddenly out of the shadows a woman bearing a basket of fish[25] who said she was Yŏwa ssi.

It seems she is counted the mother of all living. By some strange metempsychosis, too, she became part serpent. Was she Eve?[26] If you drop the *ssi* of her name which is merely honorific and simply say Yŏwa, its sound is not unlike that of the Hebrew H'a wa which is Eve.

---

21 *KM*: "gathered from."

22 *KM*: "aeroplane wings."

23 Cho Sŏlhang (趙雪航 Ch. Zhao Xuehang) was a Ming-era minister who popularized the phrase "to drive the tiger from the front door only to let a wolf in the back" (前虎後狼 Ch. *qianhu houlang*) to describe the dangerous politics of the Ming court.

24 *KM*: "and to set going this part of the woman's world."

25 *KM*: "a basket of live fish."

26 The preceding three sentences are deleted from the *KM* version.

Ahwang and Yŏyŏng
Old Corea, 20–1;
Student of the Orient,
Korea Magazine *1 (February 1917): 60–3*[27]

Among the mysteries of the Far East are the names of Yo and Sun.[28] All that is told of them in the *Book of History*[29] can be read through in a few minutes. Yet it constitutes a text for endless counsels to East Asia. The wisdom of Solomon, the gentle admonishments of King Arthur and the faultless rule of King Alfred the Great all pale before these two masters of ancient China. They date somewhere about 2300 BC and yet live today. The vigour of the sparkling eye and tinted cheek continues with them, so that modern officials and literati still take their measure from these mighty lords of antiquity.

Yo had many sons but they failed to come up to the imperial standard so he set them all aside. He cast his eye on Sun, the son of a commoner, and his requirements were to be as rigid and unbending as those of Samuel when he came seeking a king in the house of Jesse.[30]

Desiring to know more definitely what kind of mind and heart Sun had, before he made the final decision, King Yo gave him his two daughters, Ahwang[31] and Yŏyŏng,[32] as his wives. The State was the question with him; they were only two girls. The State is gone today, but these two live.

---

27 The *KM* version adds the following introduction: "These are not Korean women and yet they occupy the soul of this people as no women of their own race ever do. As I said in the last issue, their place here is much that of the Jewish women in the mind and soul of Europe."

28 For a description of these mythical emperors of ancient China, see "A Freak of Language" in *Pen Pictures*, this vol.

29 *Sŏgyŏng* (書經).

30 This refers to 1 Samuel 16, when God looked for a replacement for Saul, the first king of Israel, because of his disobedience. God ordered Samuel to go to the house of Jesse the Bethlehemite and passed over nine of his progeny as possible kings, saying, "Look not on his countenance, or on the height of his stature: for the Lord seeth not as man seeth; for man looketh on the outward appearance, but the Lord looketh on the heart" (1 Samuel 16:6, KJV). God eventually chose the youngest of the brothers, the shepherd, who would become King David. Incidentally, Yo also disregarded nine of his own sons in favour of Sun.

31 娥皇.

32 女英. Their names may be glossed as "Fairy Radiance" and "Maiden Bloom."

They consented and bowed their wills to that of their father, and became models for all the submissive daughters of the East. There was no question of their rights, or personality, or individual choice; they yielded willingly,[33] and they live today supreme in the celestial spheres. I ask my friend Kim what they did that was so wonderfully great.

His reply is that they were entirely given up to their husband as good wives should be. This self-sacrifice may be good for the wife but I question whether it is good for Kim. However, as truly as the moon has cast aside its soul and consents to ride across the sky, a dead and lifeless thing, so queens Ahwang and Yŏyŏng made their journey reflecting only the glory of their lord. They are known as princess-sages, sweet and dear. There is no word of their special beauty. It may be that[34] some compelling spirit attended their way, so that the world that came into contact with them was forever after chained a prisoner by their grace and loveliness.

King Sun, on a journey through his kingdom, fell ill and died at Ch'ango Mountains[35] in central China. These faithful women hastened to render him assistance but they arrived too late and found that he was already dead.

They wept for him on the banks of the Sosang River[36] and their tears spotted the stems and leaves of the bamboo. This tear-marked bamboo is almost like the cross before the fading eyes of the Christian, so deep is its hold upon women of East Asia.[37] The story runs that in the end they cast themselves into the river and were drowned.

I can get from Kim no other light than that they were wonderfully faithful, which fact I admit.[38] They had no vote; they had not even the shadow of a choice, and yet Asia, especially Corea, says, "Ahwang, Ahwang, Yŏyŏng, Yŏyŏng."

There is a famous story in Corea[39] of a girl called Ch'unhyang, "Spring-Fragrance," whose name in no small way reflects the glory of these daughters of King Yo.[40] She had been arrested by a cruel governor who required that she submit to his demands. She bowed her refusal

---

33 *KM*: "unquestioningly."

34 *KM*: "I imagine that."

35 Ch'angosan (蒼梧山 Ch. Cang wu shan).

36 Sosang kang (瀟湘江 Ch. Xiaoxiang jiang).

37 *KM*: "the women of Asia."

38 *KM*: "I surely admit."

39 *KM*: "in Chosen."

40 *The Story of Ch'unhyang* (Ch'unhyang chŏn 春香傳), penned by an anonymous author, is the best-known love story in premodern Korea. The present form was

and was beaten. This hardened her tender soul's resolve[41] and, setting
her lips, she made choice to die. She was beaten again and again till all
consciousness fled. "In the flash of a moment," says the story, "she had
gone thousands of miles[42] to the Sosang River. She dreamed not where
she was, but went on and on till she was met by angels dressed in beautiful white garments, who came up to her, bowed sweetly,[43] and said,
"Our Lady Superior invites you; please follow."

They trimmed their lights and led the way. Arriving at a raised
terrace with an inscription over it in large gilded letters, she read, "The
Hwangnŭng Temple of Faithful Women."[44] Her soul was filled with
dazzled wonder as she looked about her. Upon a raised dais she saw
two queenly ladies each holding in the hand a jewelled sceptre. They
invited her up beside them, but Ch'unhyang modestly declined, saying,
"I am but a humble dweller in the dusty world and dare not mount to
the place of honour to which you invite me."

Hearing this, the ladies replied, "Wonderful, beautiful! We always
said[45] that Chosŏn (Corea) was a land of courtesy and faithfulness.
The teachings of Kija remain with you still, so that even one born of a
dancing-girl is chaste and true of life. The other day when we entered
the glorious portals of heaven we heard your praises sung, filling the
celestial spheres with music. We longed to see your face and could not
further resist, so we have called you all this distance to the Sosang River.
We are greatly anxious, too, for having given one so precious[46] so much
trouble. Since the beginning of time, glory ever follows in the wake of the
bitter pains and crosses of life. The same pertains to women as to men."

Ch'unhyang bowed twice and said, "Though I am untaught, I have
read in the ancient books the story of your ladyships, and my wish was
ever to remember it waking and sleeping. I had even longed to die so
that I might look upon your faces. Today we meet and I behold you in

---

probably composed sometime in the eighteenth or early nineteenth centuries,
based on the *p'ansori* tale "Song of Ch'unhyang." *The Story of Ch'unhyang* recounts a love story between the son of a government official and the daughter
of a courtesan, or *kisaeng*, whom Gale refers to as "dancing girls."

41   *KM*: "This hardened her tender soul to flint."
42   *KM*: "thousands of *li*."
43   *KM*: "courteously."
44   Hwangnŭng chi myo (黃陵之廟).
45   *KM*: "We always said, from ancient times."
46   *KM*: "so good and dear."

this temple of the Yellow Shades. Now let me die, for I shall have no murmurings any more to offer."

Hearing this, the ladies said in reply, "You say you know us; come up here and sit beside us."

The waiting-women helped her up[47] and when they had seated her, one said, "You say you know us; let me tell you, the great Emperor Sun went on a tour though the southlands till he reached the Ch'ango Mountains where he died. We two, his consorts, having no longer hope in this life, went into the bamboo grove hard by and wept tears of blood. Today, still, you will see on each branch and leaf the marks of our sorrowing souls. Till the Ch'ango Mountains fall and the Sosang River dries up, the marks of our tears on the bamboo will never cease to show. For a thousand years we have had no place to tell our sorrow till at last we meet with you and our souls find solace."[48]

T'aeim and T'aesa
Old Corea, 21–3;
Student of the Orient,
Korea Magazine *1 (March 1917): 154–7*

T'aeim[49] was the wife of Wanggye[50] and mother of the famous King Mun, one of the master saints of China.[51] She was a woman of exalted virtue who has become a divine ideal for all the daughters of East Asia.[52]

We are told that when she was with child she avoided all sights unfit for the eyes to see. She guarded her ears as a knight guards his castle. No unkindly word crossed her lips. She ate no food prepared in a careless or unseemly way. She rested on her mat only after all things in the room had been arranged and put in order. When she stood, she stood in dignified and

---

47 *KM*: "saw her up."

48 *KM*: "companionship."

49 太任.

50 王季.

51 King Mun (文王 Ch. Wen Wang, 1152–1056 BC; r. 1099–1050 BC) is honoured as the founder of the Zhou (周) dynasty (1046–256 BC). His son and successor, King Mu (武王 Ch. Wu Wang, r. 1046–1043 BC) defeated the Shang (商) dynasty and became the first king of the Zhou dynasty. Kings Yao (K. Yo), Shun (K. Sun), Wu (禹), Tang (湯), Wen, Wu, the Duke of Zhou (周公), and Confucius together constitute the lineage of sages in ancient China.

52 The *KM* version adds, "Thus her motherhood."

graceful manner, evenly on her feet as one attentive to the call of others. Waking or sleeping, her life was ordered by the law of sweet decorum and thus she guarded her son to be. She dearly loved the stories of Yo and Sun.

Her son King Mun was born, and, "Under the guidance of Heaven,"[53] came to the throne of China. The Empire had fallen on evil days and the palace of the so-called Son of Heaven was the centre of vice. Mayers says, "Wild forms of debauchery were continually practised. The Emperor formed a lake of wine, and here he set men and women, naked, to chase each other before his eyes."[54]

But God's day of judgment came, Chu[55] was stricken and Mun Wang or King Mun was called to the throne under the guidance of his mother. We are told that he was like an angel among men. Sinners were moved to repentance at his presence. Prisoners were reformed and prison doors thrown open.

He found Kang T'aegong[56] fishing by the river bank and made him his minister though Kang was eighty years old. Here are some of Kang's quaint sayings: "If you serve your parents well, your children will serve you well; but if I fail in my duty, how can I expect my children to be faithful in theirs?"

"Diligence is a priceless jewel and gentleness in action a charm about the neck."

"If you would judge others well judge yourself first; words that hurt others hurt oneself first of all. If I spit blood[57] my own mouth is sure to be defiled."

"If you would have a loveable child spare not the rod; if you have a hateful child give it all it wants."

In the days of the wicked emperor Chu, King Mun suffered the hardships of prison life; and when he was behind bars he wrote his comments on the Eight Diagrams and the Sixty-Four Combinations of the *Book of Changes*, the greatest Classic in China.

He was like the Messiah for he made all the world to become gentle; made each man to give up to the other; inspired the young to carry the burdens of the old; made officials step aside and yield their place. T'aeim sat by and saw it all.

---

53   *KM*: "'Under the guidance of God.'"
54   Mayers, *The Chinese Reader's Manual*, 22.
55   Chu Sin (紂辛 Ch. Zhou Xin) was the name of the corrupt tyrant and last emperor of the Shang Dynasty of ancient China.
56   姜太公.
57   *KM*: "on others."

But who was T'aesa?[58] She was King Mun's wife. East Asia's *Book of Psalms* opens with a tribute to her which runs something like this:

"Two happy birds upon the river brink,
The modest mate (T'aesa) and her Superior Man (Mun Wang)."[59]

King Mun says,

I sought her far, the perfect, peerless one,
Awake, asleep, I dreamed, I longed to see.
This way I turned and that, but none
Appeared. No one appeared to me.[60]

At last T'aesa came and she was King Mun's dream. Asia lacks words to tell of her goodness. Some of the songs in the *Book of Poetry* are her composition. Here is one that pictures her weaving grass-cloth from the fibre of the creeper:

The creeper winds along the valley's length
With leaves and tendrils where the orioles dwell,
    How sweet their song!
The creeper winds along the valley's length,
And of its threads I twist, and wind, and weave,
    My dress to be.[61]

58　太姒. *KM*: "But where was T'aesa?"

59　This is Gale's translation of the opening poem of *Shijing* (詩經 The Classic of Poetry), which reads, "關關雎鳩, 在河之洲。窈窕淑女, 君子好逑." James Legge's translation reads, "Guan-guan go the ospreys, On the islet in the river. The modest, retiring, virtuous young lady; For our prince a good mate she." Legge, *Shijing*.

60　This is Gale's translation of the immediately following lines from the *Shijing*. The original reads, "參差荇菜, 左右流之。窈窕淑女, 寤寐求之. 求之不得, 寤寐思服。悠哉悠哉, 輾轉反側." Legge, *Shijing*, renders it as the following: "Here long, there short, is the duckweed, To the left, to the right, borne about by the current. The modest, retiring, virtuous, young lady: Waking and sleeping, he sought her. He sought her and found her not. And waking and sleeping he thought about her. Long he thought, oh! Long and anxiously; On his side, on his back, he turned, and back again."

61　This is the translation of the following excerpt from the *Shijing*, which reads, "葛之覃兮, 施於中谷, 維葉萋萋。黃鳥于飛, 集於灌木, 其鳴喈喈。葛之覃兮,

Out of the simplicities of the world of T'aeim and T'aesa have come the mightiest forces known for the betterment of ancient China, forces that have called men back to God. Not even the age of Yo and Sun, or that of Confucius can equal the time when T'aeim and T'aesa gently guided the thoughts of men. To these two women Asia owes more than even her unbounded admiration can pay.

T'aesa had ten sons and two of them were the sages King Mu and Chu Kong.[62] Mun, Mu, and Chu Kong with their matchless mothers make the greatest moral force that has touched East Asia.

The famous Yulgok of Corea, whose tablet stands number fifty-two on the east side of the Master (Confucius), is really Corea's greatest sage. He, like the Chinese masters, was taught by his mother, a highly gifted woman, skilled as a writer, a penman, an artist. Today her paintings adorn the East Gate Museum and her name stands high upon Corea's roll of honour. Her pen-name was Saimdang which might be rendered "My teacher is T'aeim."[63]

Wang Sogun
Old Corea 23–4;
Student of the Orient,
Korea Magazine 1 (May 1917): 218–19

There is another Chinese woman of famous name and note, called Wang Sogun,[64] whom Coreans sing and speak of as one of the most beautiful fairies that ever visited the earth.[65] They have learned of her

---

施於中谷，維葉莫莫。是刈是濩，為絺為綌，服之無斁." Legge, *Shijing*, provides the following translation: "How the dolichos spread itself out, Extending to the middle of the valley! Its leaves were luxuriant and dense. I cut it and I boiled it, And made both fine cloth and coarse, Which I will wear without getting tired of it."

62 The Duke of Chu (周公 Ch. Zhou Gong).

63 Sin Saimdang (申師任堂, 1504–51) was the pen name of Sin Insŏn, a noted poet, writer, and artist of the mid-Chosŏn period, whose likeness appears on the Republic of Korea ₩ 50,000 currency note. Her nom de plume may be translated as "Lady taught by T'aeim," where *sa* means "honour as one's teacher," *Im* (任) is the same character appearing in T'aeim, and *tang* is the title "Lady."

64 王昭君 (Ch. Wang Zhaojun).

65 *KM*: "whom Koreans not only know, but sing and talk of."

through the songs of the Tang Kingdom that are taught to the children at school.[66] Here is one of them rudely translated:[67]

The rule of Han was greatest of might,
And heroes filled the palace hall;
But I, alas, was bound and sold,
To the wild Turk[68] beyond the Wall.[69]

Wang Sogun was a palace lady-in-waiting who lived in the reign of the Emperor Wŏnje (48–32 BC)[70] of Han. In her day there appeared along the upper reaches of the Amur River the unspeakable Hyungno,[71] father of the modern Turk. His presence was so annoying that he frequently made it uncomfortable for the all-powerful Han Kingdom. Han asked this Turk to consider the question of friendship. In reply he said, "Yes, on condition that the fairest princess of the Palace be given to me."

The Emperor, unable to consent to such a humiliating proposal, gave orders that one of the less beautiful be given instead. He commanded his minister, Mo Yŏnsu,[72] to have portraits painted of them all, so that he might choose one with which to placate this outrageous barbarian.

Mo was a man who loved ill-gotten gain, and so he made this a means of extorting money from the well-to-do palace women. They begged him to make their faces beautiful and gave him rich reward to insure it. One only of their number refused, Wang Sogun, queen of all the beautiful women of her day. She ignored the corrupt minister and refused to contribute one penny to his avarice.[73]

---

66 This seems to refer to *Tang si sambaeksu* (唐詩三百首 Three Hundred Tang Poems), a collection of poetry from the Tang dynasty and taught as part of the *sŏdang* curriculum in Chosŏn Korea.

67 *KM*: "Here is the translation of one of them: " The *KM* version also adds the title of the composition, "Sogun's Complaint" (Sogun wŏn 昭君怨).

68 *KM*: "To please the Turk."

69 The poem is by Li Bai (李白, 701–62) "昭君怨:"

昭君拂玉鞍
上馬啼紅頰
今日漢宮人
明朝胡地妾

70 元帝 (Ch. Yuandi).

71 匈奴 (Ch. Xiungnu).

72 毛延壽 (Ch. Mao Yanshou, ?–33 BC).

73 *KM*: "contribute one *sou* to his avarice."

Mo, incensed at this, had her portrait painted with irregularities and defects that marred it. The Emperor, looking them over, picked out Sogun as the ugly woman and ordered that she be given to the barbarian.

By Imperial command, the hapless maiden came to make her final farewell to His Majesty while the Turkoman looked on. Her beautiful face and graceful form upset the Imperial court. The Emperor, beside himself with rage, had Mo beheaded, but even that failed to rectify matters as the law of Han was as unchangeable as that of the Medes.[74] Tearful Sogun had to mount her camel and start across the long weary waste of the Gobi Desert. Finally she reached the Black Dragon River,[75] the Amur, and here, when crossing the ferry, she plunged in and ended her sorrow. A high mound on the bank marks the place of her burial. The grass grows green upon it at all seasons of the year and has won for it the name, Verdant Tomb.

Sir John Davis, Governor of Hong Kong,[76] in 1844 translated the story of Sogun from a Chinese drama called *The Sorrows of Han*.[77]

She was not religious, or greatly talented, or almost divine, as were some of the other noted women of China, but for beauty of face and sorrow of heart she was first and these lie very close to the soul of Asia.

From the *Tangsi haphae*[78] we take the following, a song by Sang Kŏn:[79]

The Grave of Sogun

Would you had died within the palace hall,	漢宮豈不死
And not off here in loneliness and woe:	異域傷獨沒
The eyebrows of the butterfly have fallen away	萬里馱黃金
Your bones lie white and bare.	娥眉爲枯骨
I pass toward the north hard by your tomb,	廻車夜黜塞
And rest my horse a while to think of thee;	立馬皆不發
The artist's brush hath done the deed of shame,	共恨丹青人
I weep beneath the shining, silent moon.	墳上哭明月

---

74 The Medes were an ancient people that inhabited what is today Iran and Asia Minor from the ninth to seventh centuries BC before falling to the Achaemenid Empire.

75 Hŭngnyong kang (黑龍江).

76 John Francis Davis (1795–1890) was a British diplomat and sinologist who served as the second governor of Hong Kong (1844–8).

77 Han Kungch'u (漢宮秋).

78 唐詩合解 (Ch. *Tang shi hejie*).

79 常建 (Ch. Chang Jian, AD 708–65).

Princess Yang (Yang Kwibi)
Old Corea 24–5;
Korea Magazine *1 (August 1917): 345–7*[80]

Before the days of Saxons and Danes when China was in all its pristine glory,[81] there lived a famous woman named Yang Kwibi,[82] or Princess Yang, of a surpassing beauty that has dazzled all the dynasties of succeeding ages. Corea, forgetful of the fair faces that have adorned her own court, speaks still of Yang Kwibi as though she were wholly hers, and had lived but yesterday.

Yang Kwibi was the daughter of a certain Yang Hyŏndam[83] of western China.[84] So famous was her excellence that she was sought over long miles of distance and made a secondary wife of Prince Su,[85] eighteenth son of Emperor Hyŏnjong of the Tangs.[86] Three years later, on the death of the chief mistress, daughter-in-law though she was, she was mentioned as a possible successor. The Emperor, having caught a glimpse and become enamoured of her beyond all bounds, set the claims of his son aside and appropriated her at once as the leading princess in the land.

Then her sphere of action began. By a way[87] of her fairy wand she completely mesmerized his Imperial Highness and held him a prisoner for eleven years. China's sun, moon, and stars revolved around this fair maiden as if she was the centre of the celestial sphere.[88] What was there she could not do? Her brothers and sisters came trooping into the palace as ministers of state and ladies-in-waiting.

The arduous labours of kingship went by the board and China was left to go as she pleased while Princess Yang held high revel.[89]

---

80 The article in *Korea Magazine* is unsigned, but its inclusion in the *Old Corea* typescript makes its authorship unquestionable.
81 *KM*: "ancient glory."
82 Yang Kwibi (Ch. Yang Guifei 楊貴妃, AD 719–56).
83 楊玄淡 (Ch. Yang Xuandan).
84 *KM*: "far-off Western China."
85 Prince Su (壽王 Ch. Shou Wang, AD 715–75).
86 Emperor Hyŏnjong (Ch. Xuanzong 玄宗, AD 685–762).
87 *KM*: "By a wave."
88 *KM*: "who was indeed the centre of the celestial sphere."
89 *KM*: "held high revel in the ancient palace of the sages."

Once, as the happiest[90] of human affairs sometimes go, Princess Yang offended, and the Emperor, we are told, in a fit of temper ordered the eunuch, Ko Yŏksa,[91] to ship her away to her native country. Yang Kwibi, in tears, said to her jailer, "All I have of house and lands, everything I know of honour, were graciously given me by His Majesty the Emperor. My only possession is my hair," and she cut it off and sent it with a humble request for forgiveness. The Emperor, moved by this proof of her devotion, repented his anger[92] and had her restored.

Among the Emperor's companions was a Turk, called An Roksan,[93] a fat man and famous in his day.[94] Princess Yang, of the slender waist and pointed toe, called this mountain of flesh her little son, and got him to take his part in the imperial revels. An grew tired at last of unending days of idle sport. Some insult had been shown him and he decided to pay it back with interest. He rose in rebellion and in place of the endless delights of music and dancing, there arose a cry in the city of fear and the stampeding of frightened multitudes.

We are told that the Emperor had to fly for his life taking Princess Yang with him. They reached the Horse Pass amid the murmuring of the soldiers who at last rebelled, claiming that all these evils had been brought upon them by Yang Kwibi and demanding her execution. There was no help for it; she had to die and Hyŏnjong beheld his favourite come under the knife. To him she was all the world, and he joined her spirit shortly after.

We see, during the day of her ascendency, long lines of couriers riding furiously between Changan, her capital, and the distant borders of Annam.[95] What dust is this that rises as though all the motor-cars of the West were racing toward their goal, horses with foaming bite and

---

90 *KM*: "best."

91 高力士 (Ch. Gao Lishi, AD 690–762).

92 *KM*: "repented of his unkindness."

93 安祿山 (Ch. An Lushan, AD 703–57).

94 *KM*: "fatter than G.K. Chesterton and much more famous in his day." Gilbert Keith Chesterton (1874–1936) was a British writer, philosopher, and theologian of famously large proportions. An Lushan was a general in Tang China who rose to prominence defending Tang's northeastern frontiers. An was of Sogdian and Turkish decent, and is best known for instigating the Lushan Rebellion (AD 756) and the short-lived state of Yan (燕, 756–63).

95 Vietnam.

men at the last gasp? It is on His Majesty's service, hot haste; let all the world give way. What was the purpose of it with its lavish expenditure of human energy? Answer: To bring *lychee*, fresh and sweet-tinted, from the south so that Princess Yang might eat and be made happy.[96]

It is a far-gone age that of Yang Kwibi, for she died in 756 AD, but she lives in the Corean mind, beautiful and beyond compare, though not good.

---

96 *KM*: "eat and be refreshed."

Religious and Allied Themes

"Religious and Allied Themes" is another example of Gale's pros-elytization strategy in action: the forging of philosophical parallels between Christian theology and the Confucian world view. Gale's engagement with and selective adaptation of the Korean philosophi-cal tradition, namely, his appropriation of Confucian cosmology cou-pled with an initial dismissal of Buddhism, echoed earlier attempts by Matteo Ricci (1552–1610) and the Jesuit mission in China to present Catholicism as complementary to Confucianism rather than in conflict with it – until a papal ruling in the early eighteenth century forbidding certain Confucian rituals undercut such attempts.[1] Gale's lifestyle in Korea similarly harkened back to the approach of Jesuits in China: he immersed himself in Korean language, literature, and culture, attempt-ing to perceive the world as much as possible through the eyes of those under his spiritual care. Though his classical allusions and overall cul-tural empathy imbue his writing with a measure of intellectual author-ity and undoubtedly endeared him to the classically educated Korean, they were ultimately too little, too late. As Gale himself lamented, the Literary Sinitic tradition was by the 1920s evaporating rapidly as its philosophical underpinnings were challenged. Ultimately the path that Korean converts would take to Christianity involved not the deifica-tion of Confucian cosmology, as Gale attempted, but the broadening of indigenous spiritual philosophy beyond the "orthopraxis" demanded

---

1 Baker, *Korean Spirituality*, 66.

by Confucianism to encompass the concept of orthodoxy that accompanied Christianity.[2] In other words, though many Christian converts continued "Confucian" practices of performing rites to ancestors, supporting their parents, and respecting authority, rarely did they attempt to define the Christian deity according to concepts of *li* (理 principle), *ki* (氣 material force), or *ch'ŏn* (天 heaven).

Gale's literary selections in the following essay are drawn, like most material appearing in *Pen Pictures* and *Old Corea*, from his vast collection of personal ledgers, a hodgepodge of rough drafts of translations, essays, and personal observations, summaries of sermons he delivered, language study notes, and letters to family and friends. A rough draft of "The Korean's View of God," appearing in Ledger 10 of the Gale Papers (55–9) and dating from roughly 1915, reads as a stream-of-consciousness brainstorming session in which the author seems to be fleshing out his most effective evangelization strategy based on the historical material, in this case drawn from a selection "of over 100 examples … spacing a period of nearly 2000 years."[3] Various appearances of "God" in the Literary Sinitic corpus are organized according to the deity's disparate manifestations in the Judeo-Christian tradition – a loving God, a righteous God, a creative God – further evidence of Gale's attempt at parallel deistic development. The selections ultimately culled by Gale for inclusion display a fatalistic view of Christianity, more sympathetic with premodern modes of Christianity than with the more deterministic Protestantism, but nonetheless an approach that he believed to be compatible with Korea's inherent and all-pervasive tradition of fatalism.[4] The specific chronology of Western philosophers presented by Gale in this essay is especially telling. By claiming the lineage of Stoic philosophers immediately surrounding the time of Jesus as belonging to the spirit of Christian thought, Gale not only subsumes a substantial secular philosophical tradition under the Christian banner but also points to the imminent emergence of "true" Christian thought from the spiritually consanguinous Korean intellectual tradition.

---

2 Ibid., 61.

3 Gale Papers, Ledger 10, 57–8.

4 For a lengthy exposition of Gale's view of Koreans as inherently fatalistic in outlook, see "Eternal Life," in *Pen Pictures*, this vol.

The Corean's View of God
Old Corea, 26–8;
Korea Mission Field 11 (1916): 66–9

How far has the immanence of God been an appreciated fact in the lives of the Corean people? Is He the greatest force to be reckoned with? Does He have a near and vital relationship to the affairs of men?[5] Has He ways of communicating His thought? Is He a great and awful being only, or does He also have a kind heart and tender feelings of a father? These are questions that arise in the mind of anyone [with] special interest in the Farthest East.[6]

Corea has been said by more than one foreigner to be a land without religion, and the statement might at first seem to be correct. It is due to the fact that she has but few fixed dogmas to rule her world.[7] Dogma, however, does not always represent the highest and purest kind of faith. While without a definitely clear-cut religion, Corea has never been without a deep-rooted conviction that God lives and that He is near at hand.

The writer in this short contribution does not expect to answer fully the questions asked, but rather to give a few quotations and jottings that more or less bear upon them, and that are universal expressions of the soul.[8]

If we put aside the tradition of the god-man, Tan'gun,[9] not yet fully investigated, we find that Corea received her first revelation of God about the time of the Hebrew prophet Samuel. The announcement came from China, of a great Creator. He sits high above the heavens

---

5 *Korea Mission Field* (hereafter *KMF*): "with life's affairs."

6 *KMF*: "These are questions that arise in the mind of anyone interested in the Korean, especially the missionary who needs most of all, if he would know him sympathetically, to enter into the world of his spiritual experiences. It must have some bearing on the matter of bringing Christianity to his attention, and certainly on our knowledge of his real religion attitude." These sentiments seem to contextualize Korean thought and the Korean religious landscape more clearly for a missionary readership, the target readership of this magazine.

7 *KMF*: "spiritual world."

8 Gale has heavily edited the original typescript of this paragraph, crossing out many portions and adding illegible words in the margins. As the end result is unintelligible, the *KMF* version has been followed here.

9 According to Sung-Deuk Oak, Gale's thinking on the question of Tan'gun's divinity evolved over time. Although he had initially resisted equating Tan'gun with a monotheistic force, in contrast to his missionary colleagues Homer

untouched by earth's frailties, sin, change, or decay. He was the God of the Chu [周] Dynasty, with Whom the kings Mun [文王] and Mu [武王], their contemporary, Kija [箕子], and later Confucius were in touch, and Corea has preserved His memory and expanded His ideas during the centuries that have gone by.

As God was ever present to the true Hebrew and was spoken of and addressed by a wide variety of names, so it has been with the Corean. As the Hebrew wrote El, Elohim, Eloah, El-Shaddai, Jehovah, etc., expressive of the deity's different attributes but all the one God, so the Corean has used many names that point to the same Spirit, infinite, eternal and unchangeable, Who, though he dwells unseen to the mortal eye, controls all the doings of the earth. Some of these names are Hananim and Ch'ŏn (天), the One Great One, Sangje (上帝), the Supreme Ruler; Sinmyŏng (神明), the All-seeing One; Taejujae (大主宰), the Master; Ch'ŏn'gun (天君), the Divine King; Ch'ŏn'gong (天功), the Celestial Artificer; Okhwang (玉皇), the Prince of Perfection; Chohwaong (造化翁), the Creator; Sin (神), the Spirit, and many others.

He is evidently the God that Balaam[10] knew, the God of Cornelius,[11] of Epictetus,[12] of Marcus Aurelius.[13] They have talked of Him, feared

---

Hulbert and Horace Underwood, by this time (1916) Gale seems to have been considering such divine origins, though he withheld ultimate judgment. By 1917, with the publication of his "Tan-goon" in *Korea Magazine*, Gale affirmed his belief in the divine, monotheistic nature of Tan'gun. See Gale, "Tan'gun Chyosyŏn," *Kŭrisŭdo sinmun*, 12 Sept. 1901; "Tan'gun," *Korea Magazine* (September 1917); Oak, "North American Missionaries' Understanding of the Tan'gun and Kija Myths."

10 Balaam was a prophet whose story was told in the Old Testament Book of Numbers. He was famous for being both a bestower of blessings and layer of curses upon the Israelites during their forty years' wandering in the desert. Balaam spoke directly with God, and in the most well-known episode was only allowed to utter words that God would allow him to speak.

11 Cornelius was a Roman centurion, and one of the first Gentiles to be converted to Christianity. His conversion by the apostle Simon Peter is related in Acts of the Apostles.

12 Epictetus (AD 55–135) was a Greek Stoic philosopher whose teachings centred on the acceptance of external events as beyond one's control. Epictetus's influence on the Roman Emperor Marcus Aurelius (AD 121–80) is evident in the latter's *Meditations*, a series of personal writings including thoughts on Stoic philosophy.

13 *KMF*: "of Romans, Chapter One." This passage discusses the nature of God as revealed to the apostles.

Him, longed to please Him, trembled before Him, trusted in Him. In the multitude of Corean writers who have been buried so long from sight one finds abundant proof of this.

The immanence of a God Who rules the world, gives the blessing of the seasons, yet holds in His hand the thunderbolts of judgment, is much more evident in Corean literature than in many literary periods of the West.

From earliest times there have been in Korea men like Seneca who, though unillumined by Christianity, were true seekers after God.[14] As Tertullian,[15] Lactantius[16] and even St Augustine[17] himself quote Seneca's words with marked appreciation, so those who read Corean evidences of a like faith may well be inspired with a like regard.

The following quotations speak for themselves.[18] They are selected from over a hundred examples spanning a period of nearly two thousand years.[19] They are given in chronological order so that the reader may get a better appreciation of how this great name has been around through the ages:

---

14 Seneca (4 BC–AD 65) was a Roman Stoic philosopher and writer, best known for the manner in which he accepted his forced suicide for being implicated in the assassination of Emperor Nero. Though Seneca was not a Christian convert and none of his writings mention an ostensibly contemporaneous Christian presence in Rome, he is often considered a "Christian writer" based on correspondences of dubious origin between him and the Apostle Paul, "discovered" in the fourth century.

15 Tertullian (AD 155–240) was an early Christian author who produced an extensive corpus of Latin Christian literature. Seizing on the moral teachings of Seneca, Tertullian claimed the philosopher as part of the Christian tradition, writing that he had expressed sentiments of a "great moral teacher" that were "often our own."

16 Lactantius (AD 250–325) was a Christian apologist and advisor to the first Christian Roman emperor, Constantine I. His most significant work was *Institutiones Divinae* (ca 303–11), which sought to systematically explain the new Christian religion to educated individuals still practising traditional faiths.

17 Saint Augustine (Augustine of Hippo, AD 354–430) was bishop of Hippo Regius in North Africa, an early Christian philosopher and theologian, and one of the most important influences on the development of Western Christianity and thought.

18 *KMF*: "Herewith are a number of quotations that speak for themselves."

19 This more extensive cache of sources may indeed be located in Gale's personal ledgers. Ostensibly, the examples presented here provided the clearest evidence of monotheistic indigenous thought according to Gale.

22 AD

"In the year *imo* (22 AD) the King of Koguryŏ launched an army against the King of Puyŏ (a kingdom to the north) but in the campaign he was worsted and found himself surrounded by a great force of the enemy.[20] Food failed him and he was in dire straits, so he prayed to God who sent a mist that completely enveloped the whole world.[21] By means of this he made his escape."[22]

196 AD

"Teacher Paek-kyŏl,[23] his name was a Hundred Patches because of his tattered clothes, carried a harp with him wherever he went. Whether it were joy or sorrow, anxiety or gladness, the harp responded to all. At the New Year season when others were enjoying themselves Paek-kyŏl's home alone was in the direst straits of poverty. When his wife complained of this the teacher smiled,[24] pointed up toward heaven and said, 'Life and death are wrapped up in Destiny; riches and poverty are in the hands of God. What comes to us we cannot hinder; likewise what goes from us we cannot detain. Why should we be anxious?'"[25]

---

20 Puyŏ (夫餘, 3rd c. BC–AD 494) was a tribal confederacy centred on the upper
    Sungari River Basin in Central Manchuria, which according to Chinese sources
    shared linguistic and cultural similarities with its southern neighbour Koguryŏ.
    During the early Han Commanderies period (108 BC–AD 313), Puyŏ emerged as
    the most powerful force in the region. Seth, *A Concise History of Korea*, 20.
21 *KMF*: "that completely enveloped both armies."
22 Here Gale provides a short synopsis of the more detailed account appearing in
    Samguk sagi Koguryŏ pon'gi: "五年 春二月 王進軍於扶餘國南 其地多泥塗 王使
    擇平地爲營 解鞍休卒 無恐懼之態 扶餘王擧國出戰 欲掩其不備 策馬以前 陷不能
    進退 王於是揮怪由 怪由拔劍號吼擊之 萬軍披靡 不能支 直進執扶餘王斬頭 扶
    餘人旣失其王 氣力折 而猶不自屈 圍數重 王以糧盡士饑 憂懼不知所爲 乃乞靈
    於天 忽大霧 咫尺不辨人物七日 王令作草偶人 執兵立營內外爲疑兵 從間道潛軍
    夜出." Gale's translation in his ledger adheres more closely to the *Samguk sagi*
    version. Gale Papers, Ledger 8, pp. 54–6. The phrase Gale translates as "prayed
    to God" is "乞靈於天."
23 *Paekkyŏl sŏnsaeng* (百結先生).
24 *KMF*: "the teacher sighed."
25 *Samguk sagi* (三國史記, 1145), vol. 48. Paek Kyŏl (AD 414–?) lived during the
    early Silla period. The "harp" that Gale refers to is the *kŏmun'go*, a traditional
    stringed instrument in the zither family that originated in early Koguryŏ. "百

750 AD

"When King Sŏn of Silla died the state council made Chuwŏn his successor.[26] Now Chuwŏn's house was some seventy miles north of the capital.[27] At that time a great rain came on suddenly that cut off communication with the house of Chu. Then one of the counselors said, 'The high office of kingship is not for us to decide lightly. I wonder if this rain does not indicate that God is unwilling to approve our choice?' All felt as he did, so Chu's name was dropped and a brother of the late king made ruler instead."

857 AD

"In the 8th Moon of autumn the king fell ill and in giving his last message, said, 'I have nothing more to long for. To finish and make an end is my one great desire. Our days are fixed definitely by God and so my going is in accordance with His will.[28] You who remain have no need to mourn over much for me.'"[29]

結先生 … 家極貧, 衣百結若懸鶉, 時人號爲東里百結先生, 嘗慕榮啓期之爲人, 以琴自隨, 凡喜怒悲歡不平之事, 皆以琴宣之, 歲將暮, 鄰里春粟, 其妻聞杵聲曰, 人皆有粟春之, 我獨無焉, 何以卒歲, 先生仰天嘆曰, 夫死生有命, 富貴在天, 其來也不可拒, 其往也不可追, 汝何傷乎."

26 Here Gale is relating "The Dream of King Wŏnsŏng," appearing in both vol. 2 of *Samguk yusa* and in *Samguk sagi*, "Silla pon'gi," vol. 10. Only the latter version mentions the minister who invokes "God's will," Gale's translation of *ch'ŏn* (天), so it is clear that Gale's translation is of the *Samguk sagi*. King Wŏnsŏng (元聖王, ?–AD 798; r. 785–98), or Kim Kyŏngsin, succeeded King Sŏndŏk instead of Kim Chuwŏn (金周元) to become the thirty-eighth monarch of Silla. The *Samguk yusa* and *Samguk sagi* agree on the year 785, not 750 as Gale has recorded. "及宣德薨, 無子, 群臣議後, 欲立王之族子周元. 周元宅於京北二十里,　大雨, 關川水漲, 周元不得渡. 或曰, "即人君大位, 固非人謀. 今日暴雨, 天其或者不欲立周元乎. 今上大等敬信, 前王之弟, 德望素髙, 有人君之體. 於是, 衆議翕然, 立之継位. 旣而雨止, 國人皆呼萬歲."

27 *KMF*: "Now Chuwŏn's home was north of the capital (Kyŏngju) some 20 *li*."

28 *KMF*: "is according to His laws."

29 In his ledger Gale translates the dying words of King Munsŏng (文聖王, ?–AD 857; r. 839–57) in their entirety, but here translates only the following portion concerning the will of God: "夫復何恨! 生死始終, 物之大期; 壽夭脩短, 命之常分. 逝者可以達理, 存者不必過哀." *Samguk sagi*, "Silla pon'gi," vol. 11.

982 AD

Ch'oe Sŭngno[30] writes, "I pray that Your Majesty will do away with all useless sacrifices and prayers, and show instead a righteous life and a repentant spirit, with a soul offered up to God. If this be done trouble will naturally take its departure and blessings come down upon you."

1123 AD

Im Wan writes in the year *kyemyo* of King Injong of Koryŏ (1123 AD)[31], "God can be approached by sincerity of heart only, and not by any outward form. Sacrifice offers no fragrance to Him; He desires of us a righteous life."[32]

1352 AD

Pak Ŭijung wrote to King Kongmin,[33] "Have regard to your behaviour day and night, serve God with reverence and work unselfishly

---

30 Ch'oe Sŭngno (崔承老, AD 927–89) was a government minister of the early Koryŏ dynasty most noted for his presentation of Twenty-eight Proposals for Contemporary Government (時務二十八條) to King Sŏngjong when he ascended the throne. Here Gale has translated a portion of Ch'oe's twenty-first proposal on the restricting of ceremonies to malignant spirits (ŭmsa 淫祀) appearing in *Koryŏsa chŏryo* (高麗史節要) kwŏn 6, yŏlchŏn (列傳): "願聖上除別例祈祭, 常存恭己責躬之心, 以格上天, 則災害自去, 福祿自來."

31 *KMF*: "Im Wan writes to the King." Here and elsewhere in this piece Gale omits details of historical figures' identities, as his missionary readership would have had little frame of reference for Korean history. Im Wan (林完, AD 1088–1152) was a government minister of the Koryŏ period originally from Song China.

32 Gale is paraphrasing the following passage from *Koryŏsa*, vol. 98.11: 書曰, '皇天無親, 惟德是輔.' 又曰, '黍稷非馨, 明德惟馨.' 所謂德者, 豈他求哉? 在人君用心與夫行事而已. A lengthier portion of Im Wan's petition appears in Gale Papers, Ledger 8, p. 43. In the *KMF* version, Gale adds here a poem by Yi Kyubo titled "On the Death of His Little Daughter," which is included in "Corean Literature and History," *Old Corea*, this vol.

33 Pak Ŭijung (朴宜中, 1337–1403) was a government minister during the transition from Koryŏ to Chosŏn. Pak served under many kings during the late Koryŏ, including King Kongmin (恭愍王, 1330–74; r. 1351–74), who oversaw reform efforts in late Koryŏ following the disintegration of the Yuan Empire in

for the good of the people. By such means you will show a proper gratitude to the Most High for His appointment of you to this great office."[34]

1389 AD

Cho Chun,[35] who built the walls of Seoul, wrote to the last king of Koryŏ in Sŏngdo, saying, "My prayer is that Your Majesty will remember that God reads the heart as in a mirror. When you reward anyone think first if he is one whom God would reward, and when you punish think first if he is one whom God would punish."[36]

1547 AD[37]

Kwŏn Pal,[38] when seventy years of age, was arrested. People wondered how he would do but he accepted his fate with a happy countenance. A friend came, took him by the hand, broke down and cried, whereupon Kwŏn said, "Fie, man, I thought you were a hero. Why do you act thus? Life and death, blessing and sorrow are in the hands of God. It is for us to submit."[39]

---

the mid-fourteenth century, including the rolling back of Mongol influence on the Koryŏ court.

34　"夙夜孜孜, 小心翼翼, 常以敬天勤民爲務. 則可以答上天立君之意." *Koryŏsa* 112.25.

35　Cho Chun (趙浚, 1346–1405) was a statesman and literatus who served during the Koryŏ-Chosŏn transition. He was involved with directing the construction of the Seoul city wall (Hanyangdosŏng), which was completed during a roughly one-hundred-day period in 1396.

36　Gale is paraphrasing this longer passage found in *Koryŏsa*, vol. 118.31: "願殿下上畏皇天之鑑臨, 下畏億兆之瞻仰. 賞一人, 則恐不合於上帝福善之心, 罰一人, 則恐不合於上帝禍淫之鑒." Gale translates a longer portion of Cho Chun's petition in Gale Papers, Ledger 8, pp. 45–6.

37　This passage has been eliminated from the *KMF* version.

38　Kwŏn Pal is a misreading for Kwŏn Pŏl (權橃, 1478–1548) as recorded in the *Sillok*; Kwŏn was a mid-Chosŏn literatus from Andong.

39　"至碧蹄驛。李晦齋亦到。公戲曰。李貳相。權貳相一時之行。何赫赫也。咫尺不相見而行。李校理延慶見於路左。握手欷歔。公曰。死生禍福。天也。其於天何。至謫所。"

　　This passage may be found in Kwŏn Pŏl, *Ch'ungjae sŏnsaeng munchip* kwŏn 8 冲齋先生文集 8.

1600 AD

Kim Tŏksŏng[40] was seven times a magistrate but he saved no money and extracted none unjustly from the people. His friends reminded him laughingly about the destitution that lay ahead of him. "Don't be alarmed," said he, "God will have some way to help me out."[41]

1675 AD

Song Siyŏl wrote, "He who bears tales that separate one from another and cause strife is a bad man and will be rewarded accordingly. I have seen it again and again through long years of experience. God who sees as in a mirror will certainly punish."[42]

Song was a great master of Eastern philosophy but, like Socrates, he gave offence to the state and had to drink hemlock in 1689.[43]

---

40 Kim Tŏksŏng is a misreading by Gale for Kim Tŏkham (金德誠, 1562–1636), a mid-Chosŏn literatus and scholar-official famous for his integrity.

41 This is similar to an account found in *Yŏllyŏ sil kisul* (燃藜室記述) vol. 18, Sŏnjojo kosabonmal (宣祖朝 故事本末), Sonjojoŭi myŏngsin (宣祖朝 名臣).

42 Gale's manuscript draft can be found in Gale Papers, Ledger 10, p. 59, but no source is given. This seems to refer to Song's discussion of factionalism (*pungdangnon*), but I am unable to locate the original source.

43 Gale has removed this sentence on the fate of Song from the *KMF* version. Gale then concludes with the following lines, summing up the significance of his "findings" on religiosity in traditional Korea:

> These are but a few expressions that have been recorded. While these extracts might be regarded as somewhat meagre for one to attempt to draw a definition from, still the sum total of Korean sentiment regarding God might easily lead me to write, 'God is a Spirit infinite, eternal, and unchangeable, in His being, wisdom, power, holiness, justice, goodness and truth.' Surely this preparation of the heart and understanding has had no little to do with the Korean's ready acceptance of the fuller light of the Gospel. Let me close these illustrations by a quotation from a famous scholar, and a good and righteous man, Kang P'ilhyo who lived from 1764 to 1846 AD.

It seems that Kang P'ilhyo died not in 1846 but in 1848. See Academy of Korean Studies, *Encyclopedia of Korean Culture* (*H'anguk minjok munhwa tae paekhwa sajŏn*). Gale also included an essay by Kang in his elementary reader *Yumong sokp'yŏn* (牖蒙續編), the final volume of the four-volume *Yumong*

Concerning Prayer to God
By Kang P'ilhyo (1764–1846 AD)

Thou art a great and glorious God and yet Thou dost condescend to dwell in the heart of man. When first created, all men received equally the divine light, the thoughts of the heart,[44] and the emotions of the soul. These were the gifts of God. But man transgressed and went far away, and then he was as dead.[45] The difference between a saint and a sinner is that small departure that leads indefinitely away.

Alas, oh, man, why is it that thou hast destroyed and defiled thyself leaving the good way to enter steep and dangerous defiles? You have made passion your master and cast away truth.[46] You have turned out to be a ravenous bird and beast with only clothes to prove you a man. Once life departs from virtue it becomes a fiery conflict with destruction as its end. The sins of the mouth and ears, the wicked spirit of the eyes, the wandering thoughts become evils[47] that envelop the whole nature. The fact that man wholly lacks virtue is due to his sins and transgressions that cover all. Thus has he destroyed[48] the good gifts of God. As such I ought to be ashamed to face even the light that shines into my room. Only by humiliation can I hope once again to come to right relationship with god.[49]

When troubles arise and dangers thicken then thoughts of repentance fill the soul. How long this body of mine has been immersed in evil; let me be cleansed and never more transgress. Let me think of the Sages, how they burned sweet incense and worshipped the Most High. Let me recount the actions of the day and tell them over at night. If I do so faithfully I shall have no shame, and by so doing a reform will truly be wrought. Tell me, my children, that you will resolve to do this. A single fault cuts us off with a heart grieved and pained by its offence.

---

ch'ŏnja (牖蒙千字). Whereas the first three volumes feature readings in mixed script (*kukhanmun*), the final volume includes only literature in Literary Sinitic authored by Koreans. Yi Sanghyŏn has published extensive research on these readers.

44 *KMF*: "the principles of the mind."
45 *KMF*: "so that he was said to be dead."
46 *KMF*: "You have made the flesh your master and smothered out the truth."
47 *KMF*: "become diseases."
48 *KMF*: "Thus have I destroyed."
49 *KMF*: "to resume my broken converse with God."

I admit it is hard to give up old habits and yet with a brave and valiant spirit you can do it.[50]

With the heart fully in control take your place before God and put away all wandering thoughts. Religion is to be found here and here only. Virtue can be discovered nowhere but in the heart. Work hard during the day and at night guard your thoughts with reverence and fear, lest you run counter to God's will and cast away your opportunity. In the middle of the night rise up with reverence[51] and, emptied of all selfish desire, with hands joined and with dress decently arranged, burn your incense. If you do otherwise can you expect to be blessed?[52] My dear children, think well over these things. If you truly search with all the heart, God will assuredly answer your desires and will honour you in ways you know not. Do not lose heart or grow weary. As I write this I myself make new resolves. Great God Thou art the light.[53]

These are but a few of the expressions that have been recorded through the ages. As one reads them more fully one gathers from them a definition of God that is quite in accord with the Westminster Divines, "a spirit infinite, eternal and unchangeable in His beings, wisdom, power, holiness, justice, goodness, and truth."[54]

---

50 *KMF*: "and yet a brave and valiant with spirit we must rise above them."

51 *KMF*: "reverence and fear."

52 *KMF*: "If you do otherwise than I thus indicate can you expect to be blessed of God?"

53 A typed draft of this translation can also be found in the Gale Papers, Box 8, Folder 15, in Miscellaneous Writings No. 30, p. 96, where Gale cites his source as *Haeŭn chip* (海隱集), Kang P'ilhyo's collected writings. Gale here lists Kang's dates as 1764–1846, but the Academy of Korean Studies, *Encyclopedia of Korean Culture* gives them as 1764–1848. Kang's collected writings are in fact the *Haeŭn yugo* (海隱遺稿).

54 This paragraph does not appear in the *KMF* version. The Westminster Assembly of Divines was a council of church theologians and members of the British Parliament that met from 1643–53 in order to restructure the Church of England. Gale's statement on the nature of God is taken from the Westminster Shorter Catechism (1647) issued by this council. Specifically, it is the answer to the catechism's Question 4, "What is God?" Each characteristic of God is referenced with a particular Bible passage.

The Mirror of the Heart

The *Myŏngsim pogam* (明心寶鑑 Precious Mirror for Illuminating the Heart) is described by Richard Rutt as "an anthology of edifying remarks and tales" from a number of sources – a "textbook of Confucian ethics."[1] Along with the *Thousand Character Classic*, *Kyemong p'yŏn* (啓蒙篇 Children's Primer), and *Tongmong sŏnsŭp* (童蒙先習 First Reader), *Myŏngsim pogam* was among the first texts studied by students in village Confucian schools or *sŏdang* (書堂), the most widespread form of elementary education in premodern Korea. *Myŏngsim pogam* contained historical and Confucian works, edificatory material, and poetry drawn from the classics of Confucianism such as the *Classic of Poetry* (Sigyŏng 詩經), the *Book of Documents* (Sŏgyŏng 書經), the *Book of Changes* (Chuyŏk 周易), and *Mencius* (Maengja 孟子), all of Chinese authorship. In *Old Corea*, Gale places "The Mirror of the Heart" under the category "Religious and Allied Themes," contextualizing not only Confucius but the entire Confucian thought world within an overarching Judeo-Christian philosophical frame.

Gale's brief introductory note to his translations reveals certain misconceptions about *Myŏngsim pogam* at the time: "These are sayings handed down from the great Confucian Masters that Coreans have gathered together in a little book called *The Mirror of the Heart*." Although the material was primarily Confucian in character, the overall work is by no means strictly Confucian, and a limited amount of Taoist and Buddhist content is also included. The second part of Gale's

---

1 Rutt, "The Chinese Learning and the Pleasures of a Country Scholar," 37.

statement however, reveals, the central misconception about the work: it was compiled by Koreans for Koreans. Although *Myŏngsim pogam* was traditionally attributed to the late-Koryŏ Neo-Confucian scholar Ch'u Chŏk (秋適, 1246–1317), Kwŏn Sangu, following Yi Usŏng, has convincingly demonstrated that the late Ming figure Wulin (武林) Fan Liben (范立本) compiled the work in 1393.[2] The text gradually fell out of circulation in China while conversely enjoying wide distribution and considerable longevity in Chosŏn Korea. Considering the overwhelmingly Sinitic character of the textual landscape in Chosŏn Korea, especially that which constituted the *sŏdang* curriculum, what is striking about the pervasive influence of *Myŏngsim pogam* is therefore not its foreign authorship but rather its assumed *domestic* provenance.

Mingxin baojian has the distinction of being the first book ever translated from Chinese into a Western language, translated by the Dominican Friar Juan Cobo and published in Madrid in 1592 under the title *Beng Sim Po Cam of Espejo Rico del Claro Corazón, primer libro chino traducido en lengua castellana.*[3] The "Korean" version of this original represents a significant abridgement: while both Chinese and Korean editions contain twenty sections – with slight variation in title – according to Frits Vos, "the Chinese texts contain 771 or 774 paragraphs; the Korean selections, a minimum of 256 and a maximum of 265 paragraphs, i.e. ca. one-third of the original Chinese text."[4] Gale's translations presented below represent an even more substantial abridgement, as he treats only the first seven sections, and in cursory fashion.

The Mirror of the Heart
Old Corea, 30–3

Note: These are sayings handed down from the great Confucian Masters that Coreans have gathered together in a little book called *The Mirror of the Heart*.

---

2 Kwŏn Sangu writes that in the early 1970s, Yi Usŏng discovered the so-called Ch'ŏngju Edition (1454) of the *Myŏngsim pogam*, which claims that the original compiler was none other than Fan Liben. See Kwŏn, "*Myŏngsim pogam* ŭi todŏk kyoyukchŏk ŭiŭi," 190–1.

3 Vos, "A Chinese Book in Disguise," 336.

4 Ibid., 340.

Chapter I
To the Children
繼善篇

"The good are rewarded by God with blessing, and evil with punishment."

子曰 爲善者天報之以福爲不善者天報之以禍.

"Never regard a little evil as a matter of no account, or a little good as something not worthwhile."

漢昭烈 將終 勅後主曰 勿以善小而不爲勿以惡小而爲之.

"If even one day goes without its good act, a great host of evils will follow in its train."

莊子曰 一日不念善諸惡皆自起.

"Even though a man keeps up good deeds till the day of his death, he still finds a shortage, but the evils of a single afternoon abundantly overflow."

馬援曰 終身行善善猶不足一日行惡惡自猶餘.

"Though you heap up gold for your posterity, sooner or later they will fail to guard it, and even your books they will fail to read. Neither of these are equal to unadvertised worth as a heritage to posterity."

司馬溫公曰 積金以遺子孫未必子孫能盡守積書以遺子孫未必子孫能盡讀不如積陰德於冥冥之中以爲子孫之計也.

"Scatter your grace and favours widely and as assuredly you will meet your blessing-bearers later. Make no man your enemy, for who knows in what narrow street you may meet him when alone."

景行錄曰 恩義 廣施 人生何處不相逢 讎怨 莫結 路逢 狹處 難回避.

"I must do good to those who treat me well, but also to those who treat me ill. If I do no evil to any man, what man will ever do evil to me?"

莊子曰 於我善者我亦善之於我惡者我亦善之我既於人無惡人能於我無惡哉.

"Even though the day's good brings no blessing, it will drive trouble far away and though the day's evil brings no trouble, blessings will depart from before it. He who does good is like the grass in the springtime, for though one does not see it grow, it still increases daily. An evil man is like a whetstone, for though we cannot see its wearing down, it grows less daily."

東岳聖帝垂訓曰 一日行善福雖未至禍者遠矣一日行惡禍雖未至福者遠矣行善之人如春園之草不見其長日有所增行惡之人如磨刀之石不見其損日有所虧.

"Good seems as though it never could all be accomplished, but evil is as boiling water to the hands."

子曰 見善如不及見不善如探湯.

Chapter II
The Book of God's Commands
天命篇

"He who obeys God prospers; he who disobeys Him comes to destruction."

子曰 順天者 存 逆天者 亡.

"God hears in silence, not a sound doth fall;
Off in the azure, tell me, does He dwell?
　　Not there, not in the distant heights of heaven,
　　But in the heart, the heart, the heart of man."

康節邵先生曰 天聽 寂無音 蒼蒼何處尋 非高亦非遠 都只在人心.

"The secret words that men speak in silence, God hears like a crack of thunder; the thoughts indulged within the darkened chamber, He sees as a flash of lightning."

玄帝垂訓曰 人間私語天聽 若雷 暗室欺心 神目 如電.

"When man's evil comes to the full, God cuts him off."

益智書云惡鑵 若滿 天必誅之.

"Man may do evil that may not be known, but God will take account and deal with him."

莊子曰 若人 作不善 得顯名者 人雖不害 天必戮之.

"If one plants pumpkins one gathers pumpkins; if beans, beans; God's net is wide, but there are no broken meshes in it."

種瓜得瓜 種豆得豆 天網 恢恢 疏而不漏.

"If you sin against God there is no place of prayer left for you."

子曰 獲罪於天無所禱也.

Chapter III
God's Appointments
順命篇

"Life and death are in the hands of God; riches and poverty are with Him."

子曰 死生有命富貴在天.

"God has decreed all the affairs of earth; useless is it for mortals to worry over them."

萬事分已定浮生空自忙.
"There is no sleight-of-hand that will ward off trouble, and blessing
cannot be forced by any tricks of ours."
景行錄云 禍不可倖免 福不可再求.

"The foolish, deaf, the stupid, and the dumb,
Are seen as born to fame and fortune;
While wise, the deep-souled and the rare
Are often poor and mean.
The years and months and days and hours
 Swing random by.
We reckon up and see they're all of God."

列子曰 痴聾痼瘂 家豪富智慧聰明 却受貧 年月日時 該載定 算來由命不
由人.

Chapter IV
Filial Piety
孝行篇

"My father he begat,
My mother 'twas who bore;
For all my wants, for this and that,
They toiled and sorrowed sore.
It is my heart's most chief concern
For grace so wide to make return."

時曰 父兮生我母兮鞠我 哀哀父母 生我劬勞 欲報深恩 昊天罔極.
"The filial child waits on his parents with all due reverence. By his
kind attentions he makes them glad. When they are ill he stands guard
with deepest anxiety. When they die he is the man of sorrow who sacrifices to their spirits with exacting care."
子曰 孝子之事親也 居則致其敬 養則致其樂 病則致其憂 喪則致其哀
祭則致其嚴.
"When parents are alive go not far afield; let your every outing first
of all win their approval."
子曰 父母在 不遠遊 遊必有方.[5]

---

5 The following quotation on filial piety is omitted from Gale's translations: "父命
召 唯而不諾食在口則吐之. If your father calls you, answer immediately without
hesitation; if food is in your mouth, spit it out."

"If you serve your parents well, your children will also serve you well, but if you fail in your duty, how can you expect faithfulness on the part of others?"

太公曰 孝於親子亦孝之 身旣不孝 子何孝焉.

"True filial love begets its own again
While disobedience breeds a like full tale;
Look at the rain-drops from the eaves that fall
And see how one draws others in its trail."

孝順 還生孝順子 忤逆 還生忤逆子 不信 但看簷頭水 點點滴滴不差移.

Chapter V
Behaviour
正己篇

"When you see good acts in others, seek them in your own life, but when you behold evil, take note lest you do the same. Make this your rule and you will find profit."

性理書 云 見人之善而尋其之善 見人之惡而尋其之惡 如此 方是有益.

"Do not listen to words against another; do not behold the faults or defects of your neighbour. If you never speak of the faults of others you will indeed be a superior Man."

耳不聞人之非 目不視人之短 口不言人之過 庶幾君子.

"If gladness or anxiety be in the heart they will show in the speech; therefore be careful with exceeding care."

蔡伯皆曰 喜怒 在心 言出於口 不可不愼.

"You cannot carve on a piece of rotten wood or plaster on a crumbling wall."

宰予-晝寢 子曰 朽木 不可雕也 糞土之墙 不可汚也.

"Blessing comes from neatness and frugality, virtue from humility and a retiring mind. Religion shows itself in a peaceful, quiet spirit, and in a life filled with harmony and concord. Trouble springs from lust and unblessed ambition, calamity from covetousness. Faults come from regarding others lightly, sin from lack of love. Guard your eyes, therefore, that they do not see the faults of others, and guard your tongue so that you speak not of their shortcomings. Guard your heart against desire and anger, and guard your body against making companions of evil people. Never speak useless or idle words and never indulge in acts that are hurtful to anyone. Honour the king, be filial to parents, treat with reverence your seniors, serve those who are truly virtuous; distinguish between the wise and the foolish. Forgive the ignorant and unlearned. What comes to you naturally, receive. What has passed you by and gone on its way do not hanker after. Do not long for what you have not, and never worry over what is past. Even those said to be wise are full of darkness, and those full of calculation lose their peace of soul. If you injure others you will be injured. If you trust only in your ability, trouble will overtake you. Guard yourself from these things and keep your spirit pure. Families go to destruction for lack of good order, and for want of purity of motive, men lose their standing. Therefore set yourself to maintain these lest you sigh over their loss in vain."

紫虛元君誠諭心文曰 福生於淸儉 德生於卑退 道生於安靜 命生於和暢 憂生於多慾 禍生於多貪 過生於輕慢 罪生於不仁 戒眼莫看他非 戒口莫談他短 戒心莫自貪嗔 戒身莫隨惡伴 無益之言 莫妄說 不干己事 莫妄爲 尊君王孝父母 敬尊長奉有德 別賢愚恕無識 物順來而勿拒 物旣去而勿追 身未遇而勿望 事已過而勿思 聰明 多暗昧 算計 失便宜 損人終自失 依勢禍相隨 戒之在心 守之在氣 爲不節而亡家 因不廉而失位 勸君自警於平生 可歎可警而可思.

"From above God sees as in a mirror, and the Spirit of the Earth watches all our ways. In this world there is a kingly law that brings its retribution; spirits and devils follow you everywhere unseen. Go only by the straight and narrow way, for you cannot deceive your own heart. Be careful; be guarded."

上臨之以天鑑下察之以地祇 明有三法相繼 暗有鬼神相隨 惟正可守 心不可欺 戒之戒之.

Chapter VI
Contentment
安分篇

"If you are content, happy are you; but if you are full of ambition, anxiety will be your portion."

景行錄 云 知足可樂 務貪則憂.

"He who is content is happy, even in poverty and obscurity; but he who lacks contentment is miserable, even with riches and honour."

知足者 貧賤亦樂不知足者 富貴亦憂.[6]

"He who is content always has enough, and to the end of his days he will see no shame."

6　The following quotation has been omitted: "濫想徒傷身妄動反致禍. Useless thoughts only harm the body; rash behavior only causes calamity."

知足常足終身不辱 知止常止 終身無恥.

"He who counts his life enough,
Finds no shame along his way;
He who knows the gist of things
Walks in peace by night, by day.
Though he lives and moves and plans,
His world is God's world, not man's."

安分吟曰 安分身無辱 知機心自閑 雖居人世上 却是出人間.
"If you are not a sharer in its responsibility then do not plan or scheme in its affairs."
不在其位不謀其政.

Chapter VII
Guarding the Heart
存心篇

"Even when alone in your own room act as though many eyes were upon you."
    景行錄云 坐密室 如通衢 馭寸心 如六馬可免過.
    "The true-born man forgives another's fault, but never needs himself to be forgiven."
    景行錄云 大丈夫當容人無爲人所容.
    "Never think highly of yourself and lightly of others, or imagine that your greatness makes others small. Do not trust in your own strength to meet your enemy."
    太公曰 勿以貴己而賤人勿以自大而蔑小勿以恃勇而輕敵.
    "When you hear the faults of others, hear them as your parents' names – something you dare not utter. Let the ears hear but let the lips be silent."
    聞人之過失如聞父母之名耳可得聞口不可言也.[7]
    "When reprimanded by another, do not fly into a rage; neither be over pleased when others praise you."

---

7 This phrase should actually be under Chapter V (正己篇), number 4, not listed under Chapter VII as Gale has it.

聞人之謗未嘗怒　聞人之譽未嘗喜聞人之惡未嘗和聞人之善　則就而和
之又從而喜之其詩曰 樂見善人樂聞善事樂道善言 樂行善意 聞人之惡 如
負芒刺 聞人之善 如佩蘭蕙.

"When a man speaks of the faults of another, do not agree too readily,
but when he speaks in praise lend your full approval and show your
gladness."

聞人之惡未嘗和聞人之善則就而和之又從而喜之.

"Be glad to see the good,
And pleased with what is well;
Rejoice to speak the word that's right,
And haste the truth to tell.
Let tales of others' ill
Be thorns along your spine,
While faithful words that speak good-will
Be drops of fragrant wine."

樂見善人 樂聞善事 樂道善言 樂行善意 聞人之惡 如負芒刺 聞人之善
如佩蘭蕙.

"He who speaks my praise may be a thief and robber, but he who
paints my faults may be my teacher."

道吾善者 是吾賊 道吾惡者 是吾師.

"Diligence is a priceless jewel, and care in action is a charm about the
neck.

勤爲無價之寶 愼是護身之符.

"If you would live long, curb your desires; if you would save yourself from trouble, never seek fame."

景行錄曰 保生者 寡慾 保身者 避名.[8]

"The Superior Man has three evils that he guards against: when he
is young and full of animal spirits, sexual evils; when he has come to
strength and maturity, quarrels with his neighbours; and when he is old
and the streams of life run low, greed and avarice."

君子有三戒 少之時 血氣未定 戒之在色 及其長也 血氣方剛 戒之在鬪
及其老也 血氣旣衰 戒之在得.

"In great anger there is damage to health; in too much mental strain
there is danger to mind. When the mind is weakened the spirit easily
lends itself to lower passions. When vitality runs low, sickness enters;
therefore do not yield yourself to too much gladness or sorrow. In food

---

8　The original version concludes with the following phrase: "無慾易無名難,"
　　"Giving up greed may be easy, but abandoning fame and honour is difficult."

also be moderate and wise. Do not indulge in drink at night and do not fly into a rage in the morning."

孫眞人養生銘云 怒甚偏傷氣 思多太損神 神疲心易役 氣弱病相因 勿使悲歡極 當令飲食均 再三防夜醉 第一戒晨嗔.

"Eat your food with moderate mind,
And dreams and sleep shall sweetened be."

食淡精神爽 心淸夢寐安.

"If one have but a fixed purpose in life, even though he be uneducated he can indeed rise to the place of Superior Man."

定心應物 雖不讀書 可以爲有德君子.

"Avoid anger as you would fire, and lust as you would a flood of waters."

近思錄云懲忿如救火窒欲如防水.

"Flee thou from lust as from a deadly foe;

Avoid its winds as arrows winged with woe.

Drink not strong tea when you have fasted long,

Avoid all surfeit, eat with care, be strong."

夷堅志云 避色 如避讐 避風 如避箭 莫喫空心茶 少食中夜飯.

"Flee all useless words and wrangles and do not be too eager over unnecessary things."

無用之辯 不急之察 棄而勿治.

"Even though all men speak in favour of a thing, still look it carefully over; and though all speak against it, do the same before you decide."

衆 好之 必察焉 衆 惡之 必察焉.

"There is no gain in making fun of others but in diligence of life there is great gain."

凡戲 無益 惟勤 有功.

"In all things have a liberal spirit and you will be blessed in your ways."

萬事從寬 其福自厚.

The Worship of Confucius

In "The Worship of Confucius," Gale describes Sŏkchŏnje (釋奠祭 Grand Confucian Ceremony),[1] a ceremony originating in ancient China. Sŏkchŏnje pays tribute to Confucius and the other 112 sages (eighteen of Korean provenance) enshrined in the Munmyo (文廟 Temple of Confucius). The ceremony was first adopted in Korea during the Three Kingdoms period and performed at Koguryŏ's highest institute of learning, the T'aehak (太學), from AD 372, and subsequently performed at Koryŏ's Kukchagam (國子監). The ceremony described by Gale was performed at the Sŏnggyun'gwan (成均館), Chosŏn Korea's highest institute of education, but similar ceremonies were performed nationwide at *hyanggyo* (鄉校 provincial Confucian schools) in the spring and fall to commemorate the birth and death of Confucius, respectively. Aside from brief interruptions during the Imjin Wars and Manchu Invasions, the ceremony has been performed continually for almost two millennia, and as Gale alludes, whereas it was originally maintained in China, Korea is now the only country to continue performing it. Unlike many Korean cultural artefacts, the ceremony was not abolished under colonial rule but rather maintained, stripped of its royal patronage and redirected toward the purpose of constructing a Confucian bond within the Japanese Empire. The ceremony may be observed today, performed twice a year in February and September on what is now the Sŏnggyun'gwan University campus. While Sŏkchŏnje has retained the essential ancient elements that Gale and centuries of scholars before him would have observed, one dramatic break with the past is the significant involvement of women in the ceremony.

---

1 This may be translated as "the ceremony for making offerings (lit., alcohol 酉) [to Confucius]."

The Worship of Confucius
Old Corea, 34–5;
Spectator, *Korea Magazine* 1 (July 1917): 300–2

Confucius lived from 556 to 479 BC, a contemporary of Sakamoni of India, Daniel, the Jew, and of Themostocles, Pythagoras, and Phidias of Greece. So far off are his times, yet he was the last, not the first, of the Confucian sages and gave his name to a system that had been in existence for many centuries before his day.

Apart from the palaces, certainly the most interesting group of buildings in Seoul is the Confucian Temple that stands within the northeast angle of the city, in a silent retreat suitable to the highly revered name of the Master.

This site, chosen when the city was founded, was first built upon in 1398 but the temple was burned down in 1400.[2] Rebuilt in 1407 it stood till 1592 when it was burned again during the sack of the city. The present buildings date from 1601.[3]

In 1501 a famous scholar named Yun T'ak[4] planted the two ginko trees that stand in the main courtyard.[5] Twice a year, in spring and autumn, a service is performed to the memory of the Master under the beneficent shadow of these trees.[6]

On the right side of the court a stone was set up in 1407 telling the meaning of the temple and the worship. The inscription was written by Pyŏn Kyeryang,[7] one of Korea's famous scholars.[8] This stone came

---

2 *Korea Magazine (KM)*: "had its first temple erected on it in 1398, but it was burned down in 1400."

3 *KM*: "The present building erected in 1601, has thus stood for something over 300 years."

4 尹倬 (1472–1534).

5 *KM*: "One hundred years before the building of the present temple, in 1501, a scholar named Yun T'ak graduated, and we are told that he planted two ginko trees that stand in the main courtyard."

6 It is said that Confucius taught his disciples under a ginkgo tree. The *KM* version adds, "and this year, on February 24th, it was the writer's privilege to see it."

7 Pyŏn Kyeryang (卞季良, 1369–1430) was a government minister of the late Koryŏ-early Chosŏn period and an instructor at the Sŏnggyun'gwan (成均館) adjacent the Confucian Temple (Munmyo).

8 *KM*: "Near the trees, a few yards from the main gateway, on the right side of the court, a stone was set up in 1407 with an inscription on it by Pyŏn Kyeryang, one of the greatest of Korea's *literati*."

to grief in the terrible War of 1592 and a new one was set up in 1626 with the former inscription restored and a later note on the back by Yi Chŏnggwi.[9] Yi Chŏnggwi was born in the same year as Shakespeare but outlived him by nineteen years.

Pyŏn Kyeryang says, "When our king first set up his capital it was his desire to exalt the religion.[10] This thought to do honour to virtue and truth came to him from God. He beheld religion as the source of future happiness and the foundation on which his high office might continue for all time. It meant enlightenment for the hearts of men and long life to the state."

Yi Chŏnggwi writes, "Since the death of Confucius the whole world has with one accord done him honour, saying that there is no sage like him, and no master his equal. In the National Hall, as well as in the village shrine, the tablet of Confucius stands at the head, while his disciples are ranged on each side.[11] From the emperor down, all worshipped before this altar, acknowledging him as [zzz] Great Chief.[12] Such worship was never before given, even to U, Tang, Mun, or Mu.[13] We cannot but trust the word of the record that says, "Since man[14] became a nation, no one was ever born as great as Confucius."

These two statements give a fair idea of how Coreans regard the Sage.

In the hall at the north side of the compound stands the tablet of the Master.[15] He is never represented by an image, but only by a tablet. It is inscribed, "All perfect, most holy, King of Literature." Immediately at his side are the tablets of his four great disciples, Anja, Chŭngja, Chasa,

---

9 Yi Chŏnggwi (李廷龜, 1564–1635). In the *KM* version Gale writes "Yi Chung-koo," using an alternate reading of the final sinograph.

10 *KM*: "to exalt the place of worship and religion."

11 "National Hall" refers to the Taesŏngjŏn (大聖殿 Hall of Great Achievement) housed at the Confucian Temple where Confucius is honoured. Confucian "spirit tablets" (*sinju* 神主) would have been displayed at local village shrines as well, which were often built in conjunction with village Confucian schools (*sŏdang*) and private Confucian academies (*sŏwŏn*).

12 *KM*: "acknowledging him to be the Master."

13 *KM*: "Such worship as this was never received by even U, Tang, Mun or Mu." This refers to the traditional lineage of ancient Chinese emperors: Yo (堯), Sun (舜), U (禹), Tang (商), Mun (文), Mu (武), and Chu Kong (周公).

14 *KM*: "people."

15 *KM*: "In the Temple, at the north side of the Main Hall or Myŏngnyundang (明倫堂) stands the tablet of the Master."

and Mencius;[16] while extending out likes wings are sixteen others of his lesser disciples.

Many dishes of fruit, beans, meat, all uncooked, are placed in order before the tablets while the doors of the temple are thrown open for the service to begin.

This service is said to be of very ancient origin. In the whirlwinds of change that have overtaken China, she has lost much of her old forms that did honour to the Master, and Corea offers the best example there is today of this very ancient rite.

Two large frames hung with musical instruments stood in either corner of the temple platform to east and west. Some of the instruments were of stone, some of metal, some of wood, eight kinds in all, unlike anything ever seen before.[17] Two similar frames stood behind the assembled company on each side of the main entrance, hung likewise with instruments of music.

Just in front on the right of the courtyard, stood a laver at which the President of the College and his associates washed their hands. On the left side was stationed the musical band of Civil Rites, sixty-four men in all, who wore fez-shaped [zzz] coloured caps and red gauze gowns. Each held a wooden disc in one hand a mallet in the other. At set times they would swing round, one half of them to the right and one half to the left, to represent the *yang* and the *yin*, giving a clap with the hammer just as they completed the circle. Round they would go and clap would go the hammer, round once on wood.[18] Then the other bands would take up their part and metal would resound as well as clattering bamboo.

The Director of ceremonies stood on the terrace to call out the parts, while the President of the College and his assistants were seated in a line[19] that ran at right angles to the main hall.

The President, dressed in the fullest ceremonial robes,[20] approached slowly and with dignified step, washed his hands at the laver and dried

---

16 Anja (顏回 Ch. Yanzi, or Yan Hui, 521–481 BC), Chŭngja (曾子 Ch. Zengzi, 505–435 BC), Chasa (子思 Ch. Zisi, ?483–?402 BC), and Mencius (孟子 Ch. Mengzi, 372–289 BC).

17 *KM*: "all of them unlike anything of the kind seen before."

18 *KM*: "round once more and again the place would echo with the interesting impact of wood on wood."

19 *KM*: "were seated in the courtyard in a row."

20 *KM*: "ceremonial form."

them on a roll of linen that was kept constantly turning before him. He then ascended the dais and knelt before the tablet of Confucius. The band struck up the "Myŏngan" or Tune of Bright Peace[21] and the sixty-four dancers swung about and danced the *yulmu*.[22]

Offerings were made to the Master and to his disciples of incense sticks and rolls of cloth, while the music continued to play.

The President then retired and this closed the first part of the service.

In the second part he again ascended the dais, knelt before the tablet and poured out the first libation, while the music began and the dancers danced. He retired[23] three steps and knelt again, when the music ceased and the Reader offered a prayer. After this the President made further offerings before the tablets of the disciples and then retired.

The Chief assistant then approached, washed his hands, dried them, ascended and offered a second glass before the Master and then before his disciples, just as his chief had done, the music accompanying.

A third and final offering was also made by a second assistant.[24]

Once more the President went forward and knelt before the tablet. The Reader passed him the glass of spirit which he tasted. He also gave him some of the flesh, which he passed to his assistant who carried it away. The President then offered incense, after which all the special guests were invited to come forward and make their congratulatory offerings as well. Then again all present made obeisance.

To the west of the main hall was a place prepared for the burning of the cloth goods that had been offered. The President went forward and took charge of this part of the ceremony. A fire was lit and in great clouds of flame and smoke the rolls of cloth disappeared. This, too, was done to the accompaniment of music, and marked the close of this ancient and interesting ceremony.

---

21 The full name of this piece of music, which originated during the Koryŏ era, was "Myŏngan chi kok" (明安之曲).

22 Probably a mistake for *ilmu* (佾舞), a sort of line dance performed at Confucian rituals.

23 *KM*: "receded."

24 *KM*: "who then retired."

Corea's Filial Piety

In "Corea's Filial Piety," Gale describes the practice in Korea of self-mutilation to procure "medicine" for an ailing parent. The most common form of mutilation, as Gale writes, was to sever the index finger or "cut flesh from the lower limb" to mix into an "elixir of life," which apparently produced "marvelous results." Although the exact extent of such a practice is unclear, many such filial sons and daughters were commemorated in state-produced publications. Wang Sixiang claims, for example, that of the 706 "filial children" (*hyoja*) included in the *Tongguk sinsok Samgang haengsilto* (1617), two hundred of them had gained such recognition through self-mutilation.[1] The most renowned of these cases was that of Kim Sawŏl (金四月) who, owing to an accident of geography, became the object of veneration by generations of Ming envoys. After hearing of her filial act, King Sejong in 1422 ordered a memorial gate (*chŏngnyŏ* 旌閭) to be constructed in her honour in front of her home in the provincial town of Kwaksan (郭山).[2] Located along the route that Chosŏn envoys to the Ming travelled, Kwaksan subsequently gained the reputation as a place to express homage to the filial Sawŏl, and reverence for such behaviour became "a persistent subject of their envoy poetry."[3] However, such behaviour was potentially problematic; not only did this practice find no precedent in the Confucian canon, and in fact contradicted Confucian injunctions against harming the body, but such mutilation also had "resonances with Buddhist

---

1 Wang, "The Filial Daughter of Kwaksan," 177.

2 Ibid., 176.

3 Ibid.

notions, local religious traditions, and fringe medical lore."[4] The resolution, according to Wang, was a process of reinterpretation and rewriting that "converted a problematic category of behavior into symbols of a Confucian civilizing project by emphasizing the affective power of sincere filial devotion,"[5] a process that unfolded most visibly through government-initiated publication projects like the *Haengsilto* (行實圖) series. Reports of "filial self-mutilation" appeared in periodicals as late as the colonial period, but by this time government encouragement for such a practice had long since diminished, and such behaviour was met with derision by forward-looking cultural nationalists.

Gale relates in this chapter one of the most enduring accounts of filial children appearing in the *Haengsilto* series, "Nubaek Catches a Tiger" (Nubaek P'oho 婁伯捕虎). This story appeared in the original *Samgang haengsilto* (1434), the annotated version (1490), *Tongguk sinsok Samgang haengsilto* (1617), and *Oryun haengsilto* (五倫行實圖 The Illustrated Exemplars of the Five Relationships 1797), the version that Gale translates here.[6] There was considerable divergence between the fifteenth-century versions and the latter two versions,[7] variation that seems attributable to the shifting role of the vernacular in the Chosŏn textual landscape. Young Kyun Oh, following Yi Yŏnggyŏng, notes the "pivotal change" that occurred in the "textual correspondence between the Chinese and the vernacular": whereas the vernacular writing appearing in the 1490 version was positioned tangentially in the upper margin and represented more of a synopsis of the dominant Literary Sinitic text, in the 1617 (and later 1797) version the vernacular appears as a translation of the *hanmun*, "a meticulous and conscientious" editorial strategy resulting from the growing influence of the *ŏnhae* translational style that emerged in the intervening sixteenth century.[8] It is difficult to determine

---

4 Ibid., 175.

5 Ibid.

6 Gale more or less translates the entire story, but adds some clarifying remarks
   for the uninitiated reader. For example, he writes in the first line "in the
   Kingdom of Koryŏ, seven hundred years ago," presumably as clarification for
   a Western audience. Like the *Samgang haengsilto*, the *Oryun haengsilto* conveyed
   Confucian ethics through illustrations and narratives in both the vernacular
   and Literary Sinitic.

7 Though Gale vaguely indicates the version he consulted through his English
   title, a cursory examination confirms that *Oryun haengsilto* was indeed the version translated.

8 Yi Yŏnggyŏng argues that the *Vernacular Exegesis of the Elementary Learning* (Sohak ŏnhae 小學諺解, 1587) was particularly influential, being an elementary

which version Gale translated, though knowing his penchant for Sinitic literature, it is doubtful that he would have bothered himself with an "inferior" translation.

Corea's Filial Piety
Old Corea, 42–3;
Korea Magazine 1 (July 1917): 289–92

Are Coreans likely to lose that devotion to parents that characterized them in olden days? Will they hold to it in spite of change and perhaps express it in a different way?[9] It is one of the tenets of their faith, filial piety, the most binding of all cardinal relationships.

Their way of expressing filial piety in the past was peculiar, and cost a man something, as their history shows.[10] In one group of devoted children mentioned in the *Yŏji Sŭngnam*[11] in connection with Seoul, I find that out of eighteen, five of them took a sharp knife and cut flesh from the lower limb with which to feed a revered father or mother doomed to die, with the result that the parents lived and flourished. Five cut off one joint of the third finger and used the drops of blood as an elixir of life with marvelous results. Three made pictures of the deceased, hung them up, and bowed daily before them,[12] offering food and saying prayers. Two fasted and mourned through all the desolate years[13] of wearing sackcloth and ashes. Two built huts by the graveside, cut themselves off from the world of the living, and devoted themselves to the dead. One closed his lips to all passers and wept tears of blood, we are told.

---

    moral primer akin to the *Haengsilto* series. See Yi, "*Tongguk sinsok Samgang hae-ngsilto* ŏnhae ŭi sŏnggyŏk e taehayŏ"; Oh, *Engraving Virtue*, 249.

  9 *KM* adds, "This is a question."

10 *KM*: "as one can readily see who reads through their history."

11 *Tongguk yŏji sŭngnam* (東國輿地勝覽 Survey of the Geography of the Eastern Country, 1462) was an early Chosŏn text that described both the physical and cultural geography of Korea, including Confucian *sŏdang* and shrines, Buddhist temples, and virtuous local inhabitants of note.

12 *KM*: "bowed daily for three years before them."

13 *KM*: "desolate three years." The three-year mourning period was prescribed by *The Family Rituals of Master Zhu* (Chuja karye 朱子家禮 Ch. Zhuzi jiali), a collection of ritual prescriptions compiled in the twelfth century by the progenitor of

In the said encyclopaedia, the compilation of which was begun in 1478 AD, we find after a description of each county seat, mention made of the faithful children of the district, the "nameless" third fingers[14] that come under the knife are too many to record. It is always the third finger that suffers, as it is supposed to be a supernumerary digit, of little use compared with the thumb, the "mother" finger, or the first one, which is called the "rice" finger.[15]

Here is one of the many examples of ancient filial piety found in the stories of the Five Relationships,[16] one of the holy books recognized as a part of Corea's sacred literature: "There lived in Suwŏn, in the Kingdom of Koryŏ, eight hundred years ago a lad called Nubaek-i, whose father was a scribe in the official yamen. This father it seems went out hunting in the hills one day and was caught and devoured by a tiger. Nubaek-i was then but fifteen years of age. Though so young he decided to go forth like a knight-errant and pay off scores with the horrible beast but his mother forbade him. He said to her, 'I must go and square accounts with the enemy of my father's ghost,' so taking his axe on his shoulder found the foot tracks of the tiger and followed him to his den. There the huge monster with full stomach was curled up to sleep. Nubaek-i rushed in upon him, shouting, 'You killed my father and I shall eat your flesh for it.'

Neo-Confucianism, Zhu Xi (朱熹, 1130–1200). It was also stipulated that pious Confucians would spend these three years of mourning beside the grave of the deceased in a makeshift hut wearing only sackcloth. The Buddhist tradition had specified a more manageable hundred-day mourning period, which was the more commonly followed length of time, especially among the general population.

14 In Korean, the middle or third finger is called *mumyŏngji* (無名指), lit. "nameless finger."

15 An alternative term for *kŏmji son karak* (index finger) is *sikchi* (食指 food or "rice finger"), presumably on account of its primary role in manipulating eating utensils and perhaps for checking the temperature of food. The sinographic and vernacular terms for thumb meanwhile all seem to relate to "mother": the "ŏm" in *ŏmji sonkarak* is likely etymologically related to "ŏmi" (mother), while the sinograph in the terms *muji* (拇指) and *taemuji* (大拇指) each contain the character mother as the phonophoric element.

16 The Five Relationships (*oryun* 五倫) of Confucianism are as follows: between ruler and subject there is to be righteousness (義); between parent and child there is to be affection (親); between husband and wife there is to be differentiation (別); between elder and younger siblings there is to be precedence (序); and between friends there is to be trust (信).

The tiger with switching tail crouched low to spring, but a fearful blow from the axe cut his neck.[17] The carcass was ripped open and the bones and flesh of his father were gathered back into a receptacle and taken away for burial, while the carcass of the beast was placed under the running waters of the river. Nubaek-i entombed his father on the West side of Hongbŏp Mountain[18] and built a hut by the side of his grave. There he dreamed a dream one night that his father's ghost came and sang to him, saying:

> 'You have cleared away the thorns
> From my shrine like a faithful son.
> Such sobbing of devotion, such tears
> My eyes behold.[19]
> Daily you bear earth on your back,
> To round up this grave of mine.
> While I lived you were my faithful son
> And now that I am dead you watch beside me.
> Who dares say that filial devotion has ceased on earth?'

With this the spirit disappeared.[20] When the days of mourning were ended Nubaek-i unearthed the tiger's remains and ate of the flesh."

"翰林學士崔婁伯. 水原戶長尚翥之子. 年十五時. 父因獵爲虎所害. 婁伯欲捕虎. 母止之. 婁伯曰. 父讎可不報乎. 卽荷斧跡虎. 虎旣食飽臥. 婁伯直前叱虎曰. 汝食吾父. 吾當食汝. 虎乃掉尾俛伏. 遽斫而刳其腹. 取父骸肉. 安於器. 納虎肉於瓮. 埋川中. 葬父弘法山西盧墓. 一日假寐. 其父來詠詩云. 披榛到孝子廬. 情多感淚無窮. 負土日加塚上. 知音明月淸風. 生則養死則守. 誰謂孝無始終. 詠訖遂不見. 服闋. 取虎肉盡食之.

시崔父山中獵兔狐. 却將肌肉餒於兔. 當時不有兒郎孝. 誰得揮斤斫虎顱. 捕虎償寃最可憐. 山西盧墓又三年. 小詞來誦眞非夢. 端爲哀誠徹九泉."

But this leads us to a modern example of an unforgetful son of Chosen. Dressed in perfect accord with Western ideas was this young man to whom I call your attention. Caught in the whirl of a great city with a thousand delights to woo him from thoughts of his old father, living in a forgotten corner of the country, who would expect him to

---

17 *KM*: "cut through his body."

18 弘法山.

19 *KM*: "Such sobbings of true devotion, such faithful tears my eyes behold."

20 *KM*: "And so he disappeared."

remember?[21] To forget is easy where no common ground of sympathy remains, but this young man forgot not.

Once[22] the writer had a chance to view clearly[23] the routine of the son's fast-moving hours and it ran thus: He awoke, washed, dressed, spent some time in morning devotions, and then took from his desk a sheet of letter paper and marked it "261," writing below something like this: "Long distance has closed my lips from greetings of the night and salutations of the morning. I bow with deepest feelings[24] over this. In profound reverence I ask concerning You, my honourable Father: Your health, Your peace, Your prosperity.[25] In all my thoughts, You are ever-present, and so I, Your child, make my low obeisance, thus inquiring. Graciously condescend to read this my lowly letter."

"What does '261' mean?" I ask.

"It means that this is the two hundred and sixty-first day since I left my father, and consequently the two hundred and sixty-first letter that I have written him."

"Do you write daily?"

"Why, of course; God forbid that I should forget my father. As my devotions are remembered and my duty to God, so my duty to him who cared for me when I was a child and helpless, must be remembered too."

This modern young Corean has a wide influence over other young men and has a high standing in society.[26]

---

21 The *KM* version removes the sentence, "Who would expect him to remember?"

22 *KM*: "Once, recently."

23 *KM*: "view at close quarters."

24 *KM*: "longing."

25 *KM*: "His health. His peace. His prosperity." The use of the second person pronoun seems to serve as an even more elevated form of honorific, akin to "His Highness."

26 *KM*: "He is one modern young Korean who has a wide influence over other young men, and a high standing in his own place in society." Whereas the *OC* version seems to generalize about other young, modern Koreans who behave in such a filial manner, the *KM* version refers to a specific individual, though his identity is a mystery. In *KM*, Gale follows this essay on enduring filial piety with "Father and Son," a heart-wrenching account of the schism between the classically-educated father and the "modern boy" in the post-Kabo era. Clearly for Gale the Korean Father-Son relationship was a dynamic still in flux.

How She Moved God

"How She Moved God" employs Gale's familiar trope of Confucian-Christian theological equivalence. Also in characteristic fashion, Gale accords superior expression of religious sincerity to Koreans as compared to the average Christian, something that few of his missionary colleagues were wont to do. "While their knowledge of God was limited to the measure of its capacity," Gale explained, "such a life as Yi Ssi's puts to shame today Christians of all shades of belief." The Yi Ssi described in this account was wife of Sin Myŏnghwa *chinsa* and grandmother of Yulgok, one of Chosŏn Korea's most renowned thinkers. Gale's title "How She Moved God" is a translation of the title of Yulgok's early sixteenth-century "Yi Ssi kamch'ŏn ki" (李氏感天記). A concise version of this narrative was included in the *Tongguk sinsok Samgang haengsilto* (東國新續三綱行實圖 New Sequel to the *Samgang haengsilto* of the Eastern Kingdom, 1613). This was a continuation of a Chosŏn-government-initiated publication project that sought to edify the population in Confucian virtues by demonstrating the proper conduct of the Three Bonds of Confucianism, namely loyalty between ruler and subject, filial piety between parents and children, and fidelity between wife and husband. The *Samgang haengsilto* (三綱行實圖 Illustrated Exemplars of the Three Bonds) was first published in 1434 at the direction of King Sejong, and later supplemented with vernacular explications (*ŏnhae*) in the late fifteenth century. Thus, through a three-fold presentation of Literary Sinitic and vernacular narratives and illustrations, the Chosŏn government attempted to reach the widest audience to instil

Confucian virtue.[1] Gale considers this widespread circulation of discourse on Confucian sincerity, as well as the behaviour itself, as evidence of the "religious" atmosphere of traditional Korea, though one not as yet fulfilled by knowledge of the "true" God.

Below is the opening paragraph of the vernacular version appearing in *Tongguk sinsok Samgang haengsilto* (1613).

"강릉에 사는 이씨는 신명화의 부인으로 사람이 어질고 점잖았다. 지아비 신명화가 병에 걸려 죽을 지경이 되자 이씨는 선조의 무덤에 가서 남편의 병을 낫게 해달라고 지성으로 빌며 남편이 죽으면 함께 죽겠다는 맹세를 하고 손가락을 베어 피로써 간구하니 이 지성에 하늘이 감동하여 지아비의 병이 나았다. 그런후 이씨 부인의 딸 이 꿈에서 아비의 병이 나을수있는 약을 얻었다며 대추를 가져오자 이씨부인이 이를 달여 먹이니 과연 남편의 병이 쾌차되었다."

How She Moved God
Old Corea, 38–9

Note: This remarkable story is told by the famous scholar, Yulgok (1536–1584 AD) of his grandmother. There were deeply religious people in the land long before the missionary was known; religious not in form only but from the heart. While their knowledge of God was limited to the measure of its capacity, such a life as Yi Ssi's puts to shame today Christians of all shades of belief.

Yi Ssi, the wife of Sin Chinsa,[2] was the daughter of a graduate of the Confucian College, Yi Saengwŏn.[3] She had a very beautiful nature; she was sweet, retiring, reserved, diligent, and given to few words. She did

---

1 For a detailed examination of these Confucian moral primers, see Oh, *Engraving Virtue*.

2 *Chinsa* (進士) was the title given to one who had passed the eponymous lower-level civil service examination in Chosŏn Korea, which tested various forms of poetry and prose. The other examination, known as the Classics Examination (*saengwŏnsi* 生員試), tested knowledge of the Confucian canon. The most important benefit of passing either examination was the conferral of eligibility for the higher examination for government service.

3 By "Yi Saengwŏn," Gale is referring not to a name but to a member of the Yi clan with the title of *saengwŏn*, which refers to a Classics licentiate who had passed the lower or mid-level Classics Examination (*saengwŏnsi*), as opposed to the Literary Licentiate (*chinsa*) who had passed the literary examination (*chinsasi*).

everything with great care and was ever ready to lend a helping hand to others. Yi Ssi was educated in the "character" but never indulged in poetry or essay writing.

When Yi Ssi had grown up her father took her with him to Kangnŭng[4] where he lived in retirement. After her marriage she came to Seoul and lived with her husband's parents. Meantime her own mother fell ill and on hearing this Yi Ssi asked leave to return home. This was granted and Yi Ssi became her mother's guardian, seeing daily to her food and medicine. In her devotion Yi Ssi never left her mother for a moment.

Yi Ssi had three young daughters that she reared and taught with the greatest care, and she and her little family became the [zzz].

Sin Chinsa, the husband, came once for the purpose of having his wife go back with him to Seoul. In her perplexity, Yi Ssi wept, saying, "A woman has three duties to perform and must not fail in any one of them. I shall go as you bid me but still I cannot but remember that my father and mother are old and I am their only child. If I am absent, even for a single day, who will see to their wants? My mother has been ill for a long time, and I have been her physician. How can I leave her? Your humble wife's pain and 'tears of blood' are on this account. May I ask that once more you return to Seoul, and leave me here so that we each may care for our parents?"

Her husband was moved and gave consent.

In the year 1521 AD Yi Ssi's mother died. At the time of her death, Sin *Chinsa* was again on his way from Seoul to Kangnŭng and learned the news at Yŏju. He was greatly upset by it. His food lost its flavour and his strength began to fail, but he kept on his way till he reached the post-house at Un'gyo. There he became hopelessly ill. He grew deaf and was in a high fever. But he pushed on persistently till he came to Chinbuyŏk. Here his head-servant urged him to stay and await recovery.

Sin *Chinsa* said, however, "It is better that we push on. If we wait here I may become worse." As the day advanced he sank lower and at last he began to vomit blood. At this point a man of Kangnŭng arrived in haste, and seeing the urgent need sent a special message to Yi Ssi. Again they pushed on with the utmost haste till at last they reached the

4 Kangnŭng is located on the northeastern coast of present-day South Korea, in Kangwŏn Province.

Confucian school in Chosan. Yi Ssi arrived here with a male cousin and her daughters and met the procession. Sin *Chinsa* could only feebly nod his greetings.

At last they reached Yi Ssi's home and the patient's face was quite dark as though he were dying.

Yi Ssi who had so recently lost her mother was greatly oppressed in her heart. In her distress she burnt incense to God and to the Spirit of the Earth. She prayed most earnestly night and day. She bathed her body, dressed her nails, and taking a short knife that was hidden in her belt, she went up to the mountain peak at the back of the ancestral cemetery, where she prepared a sacrifice, burnt incense, bowed to God and cried out in her agony:

"Oh God, Thou givest blessing to the good and trouble to the wayward. The world is full of evil but my dear husband has been an honest, faithful man, in whose acts and words there is no guile. Even when orders went out that mourning need not be worn, he dressed in sackcloth for three years for his mother. He ate only the poorest fare till he was thin and worn, keeping close to his parents' grave and offering the libation with his own hands. Thou knowest how faithful he was, for Thou seest the good as well as the evil. Why is it that Thou hast visited him with so sore a trial as he now suffers?

We have each served our parents and have thus been separated for sixteen years. Only a few days ago I suffered the loss of my dear mother, and now my husband lies at the point of death. If he does I shall be left in utter desolation. The same laws that pertain to man pertain to God, for nothing is hidden from Thy sight, great or small. Great God, Highest of All, look down on me I pray Thee."

Yi Ssi then drew forth the short knife from her belt and cut off two joints of the big finger of her left hand. She beat her breast saying: "Evidently my faith and my devotion have proven a failure, so I have come to this place of distress. The body that comes to us through our parents we are told to cherish, but my husband is like God Himself. If he perish my body is useless. Please take my life instead of his. Great God, Highest of all gods, behold my severed finger as my pledge and accept this poor devotion of mine."

So she finished her prayer and on her way back passed the ancestral graves of Ch'oe. There she bowed and said, "When you were alive you were a just and faithful Minister. Now that you are dead I know that you are a beautiful spirit. Aid me, please, in my prayers to God."

Without a shadow of anxiety on her face Yi Ssi returned to where her husband was lying. She even feared that he might notice her expression of too great peace.

There had been a great drought with continued sunshine till the earth was baked and dry, but after her prayer thunder clouds gathered and rain fell in abundance.

Next morning the second daughter of Yi Ssi sitting by her fell asleep and dreamed that she saw an angel come down from heaven with medicine as large as a date fruit. On that day the *chinsa*, with eyes still closed, whispered, "I shall be better tomorrow."

Ch'oe Sumong, who sat at his side, gently touched him and said, "How do you know?"

He replied, "An angel came and told me."

The day following he was greatly improved and the people of the village were all filled with wonder. They said, "This is an answer to Yi Ssi's devoted prayer."

This happened in the reign of King Ch'ungjong (1526) and when His Majesty heard of it he gave a command that the story should be recorded in the nation's archives and that a shrine should be erected in Yi Ssi's honour.[5]

進士申公妻李氏。成均生員諱思溫之女也。生長于外祖參判崔公諱應賢之第。天資純淑。擧度沈靜。訥於言而敏於行。愼於事而果於善。粗識學文。常誦三綱行實。不以辭章爲學。旣長。父生員率歸臨瀛居焉。自適進士之後。進士之親在漢城。故歸侍舅姑。于時李氏母崔氏疾病。李氏遂告辭于始洪氏。東還侍病。親調寒煖。嘗藥以進。愁容慽顏。夜不就寢。竭力致孝。有女數人。訓之有方。以故夙著鄉譽。進士之來也。輒欲同歸漢城。李氏涕泣曰。女有三從之道。不可違命也。雖然。妾之父母。今已俱老。妾是獨女。一朝無妾。則父母奚託。況萱堂久病。不絕湯藥。何忍棄別乎。妾之長慟血泣。只爲此也。今欲一言以稟於君。君往京師。妾在鄉村。各侍老親。於意何如。進士亦感涕。遂從其言。正德辛巳。李氏母崔氏卒。是時。進士自京將向臨瀛。行到驪州。聞崔氏捐世。感愴之極。食不知味。氣漸不平。冷發腦後。行至橫城。腦後尤冷。至雲交驛遂疾病。耳不聞聲。熱氣方熾。至珍富驛。蒼頭內隱山請留。進士曰。留庫苦痛。不如速歸。行至橫溪驛。病勢尤重。吐血數匙。臨瀛人金舜孝適來見之。使通于北坪。 李氏所居 仍到丘山驛。臥不能起。强行入助山齋舍。李氏之外弟崔壽┌。與李氏及諸

---

5 Gale has handwritten the following sentence in the margin: "She dreamt that she saw an angel descend from heaven with medicine as huge as a date fruit and gave it to her father."

女迎于路畔。進士不能言。僅頷而已。扶入室。面黑嘔血。幾至不諱。
李氏初經哀毀。又遭奇厄。勞心竭誠。焚香祈禱。上下神祇。無所不
至。連七晝夜。目不交睫。乃沐浴剪爪。潛持小刀。登外曾祖崔公致雲
墓後山上設卓。燒香拜天。號泣曰。天乎天乎。福善禍淫。天之理也。
積善累惡。人之事也。惟我良人。志操無邪。行業無凶。短喪之際。身
丁父憂。疏食毀瘁。不離墓側。躬執奠饌。衰絰三年。天若有知。應察
善惡。今何降禍如是其酷耶。妾與良人。各奉其親。分在京鄉。十六春
秋。妾之一身。頃遭門殃。慈母旣喪。良人又病。若不可諱。則惸惸獨
立。四顧奚託。伏惟天人一理。顯微無閒。皇天皇天。鑑此下情。仍拔
小刀。斷左手中指二節。仰天撫膺曰。我之誠敬不至。以至此極耶。身
體髮膚。受之父母。不敢毀傷。雖然。吾之所天。良人也。所天若崩。
則如何獨生。願以妾身代夫之命。皇天皇天。鑑我微誠。禱天旣訖。又
下拜于崔公墓曰。生爲賢相。死必英靈。弼告上帝。以達我情。告畢。
還到臥內。略無難色。惟恐進士之知也。是時久旱。天氣甚朗。俄頃之
際。黑雲倏起。大雷下雨。明朝。次女侍坐。假寐成夢。則自天下藥。
大如棗實。神人取之。以服進士。其日。進士瞑目。忽微語曰。明日。
病愈。崔壽「從旁强問曰。何以知之。答曰。神人來報耳。及期果愈。
鄉里驚嘆。以爲誠感所致也。時中廟朝也。事聞旌閭。嗚呼。五倫之
中。三綱最重。而鼎立其位。而不可輕重者也。男子之於君親。婦人之
於父夫。其事雖異。而理則一也。雖然。天理人心之最重者。無過父母
而已。則是無輕重之閒。亦有輕重矣。世人之情。恒重於仕宦而輕定
省。多重於婚媾而輕骨肉者。吁可悲也。然而內親而外君。內父而外
夫。亦不可也。然則若何。在乎善處其閒而已。李氏。珥之外王母也。
其於父子之閒。夫婦之際。動以仁禮爲務。眞所謂善處婦道。而宜作閨
門懿範者也。伉儷之情。非不篤厚。而乃以侍親之故。異居十六餘載。
進士之病也。終運至誠。以感天意。儻非秀人之行。超古之節。烏能爲
乎。若使得列於士君子。而俾處君父之閒。則其所以具忠孝而正國家
者。從可知也。嗚呼。珥之錄此者。豈徒然哉。後之子孫。其可目覩而
已乎。男而處朝廷者。視此爲規。女而處庭闈者。體此爲法。則不患不
爲賢人哲婦矣。⁶

---

6 According to Gale Papers, Miscellaneous Writings No. 30, "Yi ssi kamch'ŏn" is
   taken from *Yŏji sŭngnam*, vol. 4, 269.

Father and Son

This essay appeared – with slight changes that I have noted – in a 1916 edition of *Men and Missions* published by the Laymen's Missionary Movement of the United States and Canada, and again in the July 1917 issue of *Korea Magazine*.[1] The intergenerational gulf that had opened up between traditionalist and modernizing Koreans was a topic that Gale broached in many of his writings. This was one of the fundamental issues that lay at the heart of modernization for Gale, concerning the rupturing of religious and literary traditions and the potential loss of an important lineage of knowledge in East Asia. The allegorical backdrop of the family, particularly the all-important father-son relationship, presented a poignant canvas on which Gale charted the dramatic and highly accelerated transformations taking place in Korea. During the process of modernization, few countries in the world had experienced such drastic changes during such a compressed time frame, and Gale's observations that "his father's world will have receded from him thousands of years" was no exaggeration. Gale was a prodigious lexicographer, and his sensitivity to issues of vocabulary and language use emerge intermittently, as when he notes in this essay that the younger generation used "such combinations of the character and such new expressions as his father never thought of in his wildest dreams." This was a period during which thousands of newly coined terms representing the vocabulary of a new era were emerging in East Asia, neologisms

---

1 Gale, "Father and Son in Korea," *Men and Missions* 8 (1916): 143–5, available at https://books.google.com/*books?id=GJNAAQAAMAAJ*; Gale, "Korea – *Father and Son*," Korea Magazine 1 *(July 1917): 292–5.*

created in Japan and based on sinographs that lent them an air of legitimacy coupled with a newfangled novelty that would have baffled the older generations.[2] This was part and parcel of the "vernacular Korean" that would come to replace Literary Sinitic in academic circles, a style of writing with which Gale developed a fraught relationship. Though he accepted neologism production and adoption as integral components of linguistic modernization, he was also troubled by their potential to engender *illiteracy* in Literary Sinitic over time. The ruptures of modernity that Gale observes in "Father and Son" encapsulate his ambivalence toward the modernization paradigm in Korea: inevitable "progress" coupled with an uncertain future.

Father and Son
Old Corea 40–1;
"Father and Son in Korea,"
Men and Missions 8 (1916) 143–5;
"Korea: Father and Son," *Korea Magazine*
1 (July 1917): 292–5

Edmund Gosse,[3] while librarian of the House of Lords in England, wrote a book called *Father and Son* in which he shows how widely two generations of the West may be separated in feeling,[4] but the race maladjustment of Corea is even more startling. "Chip off the old block," and such expressions have fallen out untrue, for in these two generations that sit, there we find side by side the times of Abraham yoked to the 20th Century AD.

---

2 Gale kept an inventory of neologisms that he encountered in contemporary Korean, most often in periodicals. See Gale, *Present-Day English-Korean*. For an excellent and comprehensive examination of neologism production and dictionary compilation in early modern Korea, see Hwang and Yi, *Kaenyŏm kwa yŏksa*.

3 Sir Edmund William Gosse (1849–1928) was an English poet, author and critic. His book *Father and Son* was an account of his childhood in which he tried to break away from his father's strict religious upbringing to pursue his literary interests, a motif that would have appealed to Gale's sensibilities. *Father and Son* has been described as the first psychological biography.

4 In the *KM* version, in place of "feeling" Gale writes "heart and sympathy."

A glance at mental conditions will show that this is not a theory but is literally true. The father with his face turned to the golden ages of the past, talks of Yo and Sun (2300 BC) who antedate Abraham. To him the heroes who ushered in the Chu Kingdom of China[5] are living realities. Kings Mun and Mu and the prophet Chu Kong (1122 BC)[6] – who can equal them? He repeats their sayings and tries to make their lofty ideals his own. He regards with reverent awe their knowledge of communion with God.

The modern son knows nothing about these persons,[7] nor does he wish to know. He regards mildewed ideas as the inheritance of a decadent race and puts them far from him. He thinks in terms of George Washington, Gladstone[8] and General Nogi,[9] and looks to the future with expectancy. He used to be afraid when in the presence of his father, whom he held in regard as the Greeks revered their mountain divinities. Today he consigns this father to a quiet corner where he may sit hermit-like and ruminate on the ages so long gone by.

5　The Chu Kingdom (周 Ch. Zhou, 1046–256 BC) occupied the eastern region of present-day China and followed the Sang (商 Ch. Shang) dynasty. It was the longest-lasting dynasty in Chinese history. Many of China's most famous philosophers such as Laozi, Confucius, and Mencius lived during this dynasty. In the *KM* version, Gale extends the biblical parallel here by writing, "To him the heroes who ushered in the Chu Kingdom of China, slightly behind Abraham, but far away BC arc living realities."

6　The Duke of Chu (周公 Ch. Zhou Gong, ?–?) was a statesman during the Chu dynasty, the son of King Mun and the younger brother of King Mu. The Duke of Chu is credited with writing the *Book of Changes* and the *Classic of Poetry* and is said to portend an important event when appearing in dreams. For a description of Kings Mun and Mu, see "T'acim and T'aisa" in *Old Corea*, this vol.

7　In the *KM* version the following phrase is added here: "who they were he could not begin to answer."

8　Although it is uncertain, given the time frame and the positioning between other world leaders, this seems to refer to William Ewart Gladstone (1809–98), who served as prime minister of Great Britain four times, more than any other person, in a career that lasted over sixty years.

9　Count Nogi Maresuke (乃木希典, 1849–1912) was a general in the Japanese Imperial Army who served as commander during the capture of Port Arthur in the Sino-Japanese War (1894–5), as well as commander of the forces that captured Port Arthur in the Russo-Japanese War (1904–5). In the version appearing in *Men and Missions*, "General Nogi" has been replaced with Bismarck, likely to appeal to a broader Western audience who may not have been familiar with the Japanese figure. General Nogi also appears in the *KM* version.

The scholar-father reads and sings the Classics. From the opening lines of the *Thousand Character* [*Classic*] to the profound pages of the *Book of Changes*, he has learned them by heart. Mencius, Confucius, the *Book of Poetry*, the *Book of History*[10] with the records of Chu, Han and Song.[11] There is little that he does not know in the way of old Chinese history. Night and day as a boy he went through the grind that today makes him master of this literature, difficult as the hieroglyph.[12] Once get him started he will unravel a complex page giving place and name for everything. As he speaks, Chinese heroes come trooping out of the mists. And how wonderful they are. The battles they fought live once again, and noble women too appear immortalized in his memory.

Meanwhile the son thumbs the daily newspaper, picking out with difficulty telegrams relating to Europe or the Washington Conferences,[13] helpless when he comes to a piece of composition with ten characters in a line. He is able to handle two or perhaps three.[14] Can he read what

---

10 *Book of History* (Sŏgyŏng 書經).

11 Han (漢, 206 BC–AD 220); Song (宋, AD 960–1279).

12 "The grind" is the term applied by Gale to the method by which "all learning, all knowledge, all skill" was acquired in the Sinographic cosmopolis in the premodern era. Gale argued that because this method was so deeply ingrained in the acquisition of knowledge in Korea, any attempt by Western educators and missionaries to coerce Western methods of education would "undoubtedly spell failure," and that the "grind" should instead be repurposed in service of conveying the Gospel. Gale noted that *han'gŭl* literature, specifically the Bible, did not inspire the same committed memorization instilled by the Literary Sinitic tradition, and so advocated the mixed-script Bible as an expedient tool for transitioning to more vernacular literature. See Spectator, "Grind," *Korea Magazine* 1 (October 1917): 460–2.

13 In place of "telegrams relating to Europe and the Washington Conferences," Gale writes in *KM* "telegrams relating to the war in Europe."

14 This refers to the number of sinographs in a line, but more crucially, the difference between Literary Sinitic and vernacular grammar. Whereas ten sinographs in a row undoubtedly designates Literary Sinitic grammar that would have required specialized training in order to parse, two or three characters refers to the deployment of sinographs in discrete units as words mediated by vernacular grammar written in *han'gŭl*, a method that came to be employed from the late nineteenth century. This type of Sino-Korean mixed script (*kukhanmun*) became the style of choice in expository and academic writing, signalling a break with the Literary Sinitic tradition and resulting in an intergenerational cleavage.

his father sings as a sweet song? By no means![15] He has no more idea of it than the young Britons made captive had of the meaning of S.P.Q.R. carved on the walls of Rome.[16]

A great volume of Corean literature has come down during a period of a thousand years beginning with Corea's Chaucer, Ch'oe Ch'iwŏn,[17] and ending with men like Viscount Kim Yunsik.[18] Of these books the son knows nothing, nor can he ever hope to read them.

In the old days an incentive was given to the study of Chinese by the honours of the *kwagŏ* or official examination.[19] The distinction and social standing that it gave meant a starry crown for all time. To win this place of honour, the children of the literati would study from dawn till dark, day in and out, and never know a weary hour. This has ceased. Now, as in Western countries, the bell rings at fixed hours and classes assemble. The students repeat their lessons in Corean and Japanese and recite arithmetic, geography and universal history. What time is

---

15 In the version published in *Men and Missions*, "By no means!" has been replaced simply by "Never!" "Never" also appears in *KM*.

16 S.P.Q.R. refers to the Latin initialism for *Senātus Populusque Rōmānus*, meaning
"the Roman senate and people."

17 Ch'oe Ch'iwŏn (崔致遠, AD 857–908 or later) was a Confucian scholar, government minister, and prolific literatus during the late Unified Silla era (668–935).
He travelled to Tang China, passed the highest civil service examination there,
and served in prefectural office for many years in China before returning to
Silla, where he made futile attempts to reform a declining Silla before turning
toward the life of a Buddhist hermit. In the table of contents to *Old Corea*, Gale
records the year of Ch'oe's death as 951, but it is likely that he died much earlier, in the first decade of the tenth century.

18 In *Men and Missions*, Gale adds the following: "and ending with men like
Viscount Kim Yunsik, who recently presented the writer with a set of his literary works." Viscount Kim Yunsik (金允植, 1835–1922) was a late-Chosŏn
scholar-official and head of the Confucian College. Three years after this essay
appeared, during the independence demonstrations of 1919, Viscount Kim was
sentenced to two years of penal servitude for sending a petition for independence to the Government General of Korea.

19 The civil service examination (*kwagŏ sihŏm* 科學試驗) was a mechanism by
which talented men were selected for government service based on erudition and knowledge of the Confucian corpus, mainly the *Four Books* and *Five
Classics*, and literary composition. For a discussion of the civil service examination and the system of educational institutions that supported it in premodern
Korea, see Pieper, "Korean as a Transitional Literacy," chap. 1.

there left to remember that Kwanu saved the Kingdom of Han,[20] or that Chegal Yang was a greater general than Napoleon?[21]

The writer foresees not many years hence a day when the literature of this land will be a closed and sealed book except to a few persons of exceptional and rare attainment. As the old man who now sits lonely in the shadow says his farewell and withdraws into the eternal quiet, he will carry away with him one of the most interesting varieties of literary achievement that the world has ever seen.[22]

The son, knowing nothing of these things, will doubtless be an up-to-date man, who reads the papers, and modern books, and writes a letter in the colloquial with as much skill and neatness as anyone could wish, but his father's world will have receded from him thousands of years. In religious matters too, father and son sit at the antipodes. The father, deeply imbued with the spirit of Confucius, has read and studied the Classics till the ordinary sacrifices of the East are as natural to him as the breath he draws. Rice and dainties to the gods are the order of his days. He does not smile or think it strange, but performs the services with entire seriousness of soul. The son has no appreciation of it and thinks such sacrifice errant nonsense. His religion is the religion of modern life, namely, no-religion.[23] He lives, eats, and sleeps in a world that has lost the knowledge of God. He has not found any other religion,[24] and that of his father has passed beyond recall. Confucianism that hangs on a knowledge of Chinese will depart as the Classics cease to be studied.

---

20 Kwanu (關羽 Ch. Guan Yu, ?–AD 220) was a great and celebrated general during the late Han dynasty. He is valorized in Taoist, Confucian, and Buddhist traditions.

21 Chegal Yang (諸葛亮 Ch. Zhuge Liang, AD 181–234) was a politician and renowned military strategist during the Three Kingdoms period (AD 184/220–80).

22 In *Men and Missions*, the following sentence has been added: "No reserved sweetheart was ever so hard to woo and win as she, this subtle mastery of Chinese composition which is his." This aligns with Gale's language ideology that tended to exoticize the sinograph as a mysterious and tempting presence, especially in this case for a Western male audience.

23 In the *KM* version, Gale expresses this slightly less cynical sentiment: "He has only that religion that appears in modern life, namely no religion."

24 In *KM* Gale writes, "He has not become introduced to any other religion," suggesting more emphasis on the intercession of the missionary.

In dress and ceremony, too, they differ. The father still wears the horsehair hat that marked him a gentleman in days gone by. The son wears a collar, cuffs, and tie.[25]

In public assemblies it used to be the father who occupied the chair, sitting as only lords sit. With loud reverberating voice he would read the coming generation a lecture that is accepted with down-cast maiden looks. He would use toward them such language as Nebuchadnezzar of Babylon used toward Zedekiah whom he roasted in the fire.[26] When all was over he would sail out with a train of attendants that would have done honour to King Darius.[27] Today the young man occupies the chair, and a very good chairman he makes. He talks in short polite sentences with such combinations of the character and such new expressions as his father never thought of in his wildest dreams.

Thus they live, these two of the same race, in thought widely sundered, the son regarding the father as a decided "back-number," and the father regarding the son as a representative of a modern wisdom that he can never hope even to glimpse afar off. On the wheel of fate the tables have turned. A quarter of a century ago this son could not sit in his father's presence. He might be seventy years old but to his father of eighty-five he was the merest child to be ordered and commanded at pleasure. He

---

25　The published version in *Men and Missions* adds the following on attire: "Buttons on the headband behind his ears, recall the day when he stepped forth into manhood, or rose to rank and office." This is followed by this poignant paragraph, which does not appear in *Old Corea*: "The son, as he comes to man's estate, gathers up his gear and sells it to the first callow globe-trotter as relics that belong to the antediluvian period. The father's precious documents that bear the signature of the king, and the royal seal, he pawns to the curio dealer, asking that nothing be said about it, accepting so much by way of return, and suggesting that they be put in a room somewhere next to Ramses II, of Egypt." Gale also wrote on sartorial transformations in Korea in *Korea Magazine*. See Gale, "Korean Clothes," *Korea Magazine* 3 (April 1919): 159–62.

26　Nebuchadnezzar of Babylon (Nebuchadnezzar II) "roasted" Zedekiah, whom he had installed as the King of Judah, for committing adultery with his neighbours and for speaking lies in the name of God. This episode is related in Jeremiah 29:21 (KJV). This is another attempt by the author to draw parallels between Christianity and Confucianism, a favourite proselytization strategy.

27　Darius I (ca 550–486 BC) was the third king of the Persian Achaemenid Empire, ruling at the height of the empire's extent and influence. Darius is mentioned in the biblical books of Zechariah, Haggai, and Ezra-Nehemiah.

went nowhere, said nothing without permission, married quietly whom his father gave him, and renounced self entirely on the altar of parental sacrifice. Today the father views the son with a wan and submissive expression, barely speaking above a whisper, sitting alone under his hermit thatch, and passively waiting till the sun goes down.

Was ever such a phenomenon seen before?

Social and Allied Subjects

In the chapters that make up the "Social and Allied Subjects" section of
Old Corea, Gale describes the lifeways and everyday habits of Koreans.
In contrast with the sections of the book focusing on the exclusivist literati realm of literature, or on narratives from the still-limited Christian
community, these accounts describe more democratic practices such as
smoking or drinking, or common denominators such as teeth or clothing. The result is a valuable ethnographic study of lasting significance
from a time when traditional Korean culture, while fading rapidly, was
still directly observable. Gale's thorough use of *hanmun* sources, though
frustratingly non-attributed in most cases, adds depth and texture to
his analysis, providing a scholarly and informed curatorial intercession
into "Old Corea." Also in contrast with other sections of the book, religious allusions are relatively subdued, rendering a more secular, sober
ethnographic study.

There is tension, however, between Gale's overarching attempt to
experience Korean culture from a native perspective and his seemingly
incessant need to draw comparisons with the West. Much like Franz
Boas (1858–1942) and Bronislaw Malinowski (1884–1942), contemporaneous pioneers in the burgeoning field of anthropology, Gale was
thoroughly committed to the concept of "participant observation" and
prolonged immersion in a foreign culture. However, Gale's deliberate and continual comparisons with Western culture, though far from
teleological, seem to forestall a sincere embracing of anthropological
"cultural relativism" and reflect his own self-perception as a cultural
ambassador to the Korean people.

Gale begins his cultural tour of Korea with a discussion of alcohol, or rather, a history of prohibition in the country. In a conservative tone befitting his Presbyterian moral sensibilities, Gale writes approvingly of Korea's "brave fight" against the "unmitigated evil" of alcohol consumption throughout its history, while wringing his hands in consternation as to the current state of degeneration. This is a subject that he did not often write about but deserves a lengthy discussion here, as alcohol consumption has become a major component of modern Korean culture and society.

Although hundreds of traditional alcoholic beverages were produced during the Chosŏn era, Korean alcohol may be divided roughly into two categories: fermented and distilled. Fermented beverages may be grouped under the catch-all term *makkŏlli*, which means "roughly filtered [drink]." Often referred to erroneously as rice "wine," it is an opaque, milky-white alcohol made from fermented rice, yeast, and water. First mentioned in the founding story of the Koguryŏ Kingdom some two millennia ago, it is the oldest of Korea's recorded alcohol beverages. Once Korea's most popular alcoholic drink, brewed and enjoyed primarily by the agrarian population, it gradually waned in popularity in favour of its distilled counterpart, the culturally representative and ubiquitous *soju*. The term *soju* is based on the sinographs for "burn" (燒) and "liquor" (酒) and is derived from a Persian distilling technique that made its way to Koryŏ via the Mongol Yuan Empire in the thirteenth century.[1] Though traditional *soju* was typically a whopping 80 proof, comparable to its Chinese counterpart *baijiu*, there has been a tendency from the 1920s and especially in the new millennium to adopt recipes that offer less potent, softer, and more drinkable varieties of this liquor.[2]

As Gale describes in his account, most instances of prohibition in Korea stemmed from the perceived effect of inebriation on one's comportment and maintenance of Confucian virtue, and more practically on the diversion of precious grain resources to alcohol production. The latter explanation had continuing relevance in the twentieth century and has had a profound effect on the nature of alcohol consumption in Korea and the content of the drink itself. In the case of *soju*, despite periodic moratoriums on production, domestic distilleries thrived until the Japanese Residency General in 1907 began to levy heavy taxes on

---

1 Harkness, "Softer Soju in South Korea," 1616; Ines Cho, "Moving beyond the Green Blur."

2 Harkness, "Softer Soju."

locally produced spirits in order to stimulate demand for Japanese beer, sake, and whisky.[3] The establishment of Jinro Ltd. in 1924,[4] the company responsible for the 50-proof *soju* in a distinctive green bottle and featuring the iconic toad mascot, ushered in the era of commercially produced *soju* for mass consumption, and the industry has never been the same. Echoing Chosŏn-era prohibitions, Park Chung-hee in 1965 enacted the Grain Maintenance Law (Yanggok kwalli pŏp) in response to the country's insufficient rice harvest, forcing producers to turn to alternative ingredients such as sweet potatoes and tapioca rather than traditional grains such as rice, barley, or wheat. By the time the ban was finally lifted in 1999, attempts to reintroduce traditional distillation methods with high-end *soju* offerings ended in commercial failure, as the public had become accustomed to cheap, efficient intoxication offered by alternative methods of distillation and increasing use of ethyl alcohol.[5]

For all of Gale's moral posturing on the ill effects of alcohol, Gale was not a teetotaler like many of his missionary colleagues and would occasionally imbibe in moderation. His reservations about the substance seemed more akin to the Confucian argument against alcohol, that is, the impediment it posed to moral betterment.

Excepting "Corean Artists," all of the chapters in this section also appeared in *Korea Magazine*, though with considerable edits that I have noted. Such ethnographies of traditional Korea were closely aligned with the mission of the *Magazine* expressed in the first issue, to thoroughly acquaint the missionary with "the people among whom they labor," to instill a "knowledge of their thought processes, the lives they live, their habits, customs, literature and religion."[6] In the second chapter, in response to the apparent incredulity among foreigners as to the unpopularity of tea in Korea, Gale discusses the rise and fall of tea on the Korean peninsula over many centuries, basing his remarks on solid scholarship. In "Tobacco," Gale, backed again by a thorough consideration of primary source materials, ruminates on the charmed existence the plant has enjoyed in Korea and around the globe.[7] He then provides

---

3 Ines Cho, "Moving beyond the Green Blur."

4 Gale's essay would have coincided almost exactly with the founding of Jinro, which currently accounts for over half of South Korea's domestic *soju* consumption.

5 Ines Cho, "Moving beyond the Green Blur."

6 "Editorial Notes," *Korea Magazine* 1 (January 1917): 1.

7 For an additional discussion of the origins of tobacco in Korea, including my own introduction, see "Tobacco in Korea," *Pen Pictures*, this vol.

a detailed firsthand account of the traditional process of manufacturing Korean paper (*hanji* 韓紙), one of premodern Korea's most prized cultural possessions, followed by a description of Korean traditional dress. Here Gale's ambivalence toward the passing of the old order is on full display: gone are the "long tinted robes made of the finest silk" and the world's only "really beautiful footgear," replaced by ordinary white robes, or worse, the "coarse tweeds and stodgy shoes" of the West.

In "Corean Artists," not included in *Korea Magazine*, Gale provides a less-than-stellar assessment of Korean art history, based mainly on native Korean sources of the eighteenth century. Curiously, Gale makes no mention of Koryŏ celadon (Koryŏ *ch'ŏngja* 高麗青瓷), pottery produced during the Koryŏ dynasty that features a distinctive blue-green hue and is today considered the pinnacle of Korean arts and crafts. Gale follows with an insightful comparison of Korean "chess" (*changgi* 將棋) and Western chess, contending that the latter was derived from the former. It seems, rather, that Chinese *xiangqi* originated from the Indian game of *chaturanga*, which was directly imported to Europe by way of the Muslim world and included the same pieces as its Chinese counterpart. Gale concludes this section with an amusing assessment of the state of teeth in Korea, expressing his envy at the country's dental endowments and seemingly endorsing Korea's cosmological argument – sweet (earth) eats into teeth (water), and Westerners eat a lot of sugar – for the soundness of Korean teeth and the tribulations of the foreigner.

Prohibition in Corea
Old Corea, 48–9;
Korea Magazine 2 (October 1918): 438–41[8]

"America gone dry!" Surely this is one of the most significant messages ever flashed around the globe. In these days of startling change,[9]

---

8 Although prohibition in the United States did not go into effect at the federal level until the passage of the Volstead Act, which was ratified in 1919 and went into effect on 17 January 1920, Gale seems to predict the coming of prohibition with this 1918 article in *Korea Magazine*. Prohibition would last until the rescission of the Volstead Act on 5 December 1933.

9 *Korea Magazine* (*KM*): "unheard of change."

nothing could mean more than what these three words imply. That the temptation that ever lures bright boys to degenerate into "bar-rats" and "whiskey-soakers" should be removed from a great continent is almost worth a war. The hideous results of the drink habit, seen and condemned in America, are scattered the world over. One need not enlarge on them: drunken fools made out of someone's hopes, with whom bleared eyes, red noses, and befuddled brains do not begin to express the half. Who would not strike it a blow as Lincoln did the auction-block and the brutal slave-trade?[10]

Had ancient Corea any convictions regarding strong drink and what were they?[11] She knows all the brands of alcoholic spirits,[12] soft and strong, and every variety of victim, from the man who takes on a full cargo to the quiet guzzler who is always ready to give a temperance lecture, forgetful of the fact that he himself is a standing proof of the truth of what he preaches.[13] Corea knows the science of making alcoholic beverages, fermented, distilled, cured, flavoured, bottled away. She has learned them all.

As long ago as the year 38 AD, we read that an edict prohibiting the manufacture of strong drink was promulgated in Corea on account of the scarcity of food. Similar prohibitions occurred again and again through Corea's history till in 1876 when famine once more caused the king to order, "No more drink."[14]

These acts evidently meant what they said, for as late as the reign of Sejo, 1465 AD, we read that the king, when on a visit to the hot-springs at Ollyang,[15] sent a secret messenger through-out the province of Ch'ungch'ŏng to see how the recent enactment against drink was being

---

10 *KM*. "slave driver."

11 *KM*: "This article, however, would inquire into Korea's past and see if she has ever had any convictions regarding strong drink, and just what they were."

12 *KM*: "all brands of whiskey."

13 *KM*: "standing proof that his temperance is whiskey-soaked."

14 The *Chosŏn sillok* (Veritable Records of the Chosŏn Dynasty) mentions the famine of 1876, as well as King Kojong's prohibition on alcohol (*kŭmju-ryŏng* 禁酒令). See *Kojong sillok* 14:545, 1877/1/6, and *Kojong sillok* 14:552, 1877/4/15, in *Chosŏn wangjo sillok*.

15 Ollyang Hot Springs (Onyang Onch'ŏn 溫陽溫泉) was a favourite spot among Chosŏn monarchs, known for its curative properties. This was famously the location where King Sejong convalesced in 1443 while treating an ocular malady and working on the Correct Sounds for the Instruction of the People (*Hunmin chŏngŭm* 訓民正音), the vernacular Korean alphabet.

carried out. The messenger on his rounds found the Governor, Kim Chinji, at the house of Prince Hong Yunsŏng drinking.[16] The king was incensed at this breach of trust and ordered Kim to be decapitated at once. The offender's head was sent round the province for people to see and take warning so that they might obey when their king commanded them not to drink.[17] Strong measures opposed to strong drink![18]

The opinion of Corea regarding drink is seen very clearly in her literature,[19] and while there are some like Burns who sing its praises, there has always been a great force in the state with sense[20] and unselfishness enough to see that it was an unmitigated evil.

In the year 1423 King Sejong, though twenty-six years of age, urged by the Prime Minister to take a little stimulant for his stomach's sake, answered, "When I forbid my people the use of intoxicants how can I think of using them myself?"[21]

In the same year, the King issued an edict against drinking[22] in which he says, "The evils resulting from drink are very great, not only in its wasteful use of grain and state supplies, but in its destruction of the heart and soul of man. Under its influence human personality becomes

---

16 The report by the secret messenger (*sahŏnbu* 司憲府) to the king may be found in *Sejo sillok* 36:687, 1465/5/25.

17 *KM*: "at once, and then had his dangling head sent all around the province for people to see, take warning from, and learn to obey when he told them not to drink."

18 King Sejo sentences the Ch'ungch'ŏng Provincial Governor, Kim Chinji (金震知, dates unknown) along with Inspector Kang Anjung (姜安重, ?–1465) to death by decapitation in the following passage: *Sejo sillok* 37: 701, 1465/9/2.

19 *KM*: "through her writings."

20 *KM*: "gifted with sense."

21 *KM* adds, "Good king, he!"

22 *KM*: "against the whole system." The text by Sejong that Gale refers to is titled "Kyeju p'yŏn" 戒酒篇, "A Warning against Drink," and was included by Gale and his "pundit" Yi Ch'angjik as Lesson Three in their co-edited Literary Sinitic chrestomathy, *Yumong sokp'yŏn* (牖蒙千字 The Thousand Character Series, *Korean Reader Number IV*) (1904), 6–7. Gale also translated and published in 1923 a work called *Chuch'o kyeŏn* (Temperance Book), the sinographs for which are presumably 酒草戒言, meaning "A Warning against Alcohol and Tobacco." This work of sixty-one pages, detailing the evils of drinking and smoking, appears to be a translation of Christine I. Tinling, *Temperance Tales for the Loyal Temperance Legion* (1913). Gale's translation is written entirely in *han'gŭl* and was published by the Chosŏn Yasogyo Sŏhoe (Christian Literature Society). See Sungsil Taehakkyo Han'guk Kidokkyo Pangmulgwan, comp., *Han'guk Kidokkyo Pangmulgwan sojang Kidokkyo charyo haeje*, 228. Gale's

a thing of disgust. Beneath its spell children disgrace those who brought them up.[23] Men become human wrecks stripped of their diviner nature with all decency thrown to the winds."

He cites examples of drunkards to prove his point, and in his survey goes back almost to the year one. "Paek Yu," says he, "used the small hours of the morning for the manufacture of strong drink and in the end had the house fired about his ears and died. Chin Chun of Western Han (206 BC),[24] who used to bar his gates and have his friends drink deep, went to the Hun Tartars as envoy and there in a drunk stupor was set upon and killed, so fulfilling the will of the Fates."

Chŏng Chung, a man of Later Han (25 AD),[25] used to drink so excessively that finally his intestines gave out and he died, says the record.

The great Sejong, who invented the alphabet and lifted his country up to a high plane of civilization was squarely set against this evil.[26] So was it many times in the history of Corea. Probably no other land[27] ever had so many edicts issued on prohibition as Corea and has faithfully carried them out.

We find in 1512 a royal order issued by King Chungjong,[28] who was then twenty-five years of age, in which he says, "My ancestors all sternly forbade use of drink, yet I realize that forbidding it will avail nothing unless the people's heart and soul approve.[29] My desire is to persuade you to this decision, for unless you are opposed to drink by conviction[30]

---

publication of this volume coincided more or less with the highly publicized visit to Korea of famous temperance activist Christine Tinling under the auspices of the World's Women's Christian Temperance Union. See Hortense Tinsely, "Miss Tinling's Visit to Korea," *Korea Mission Field* 18, no. 3 (March 1922): 99–101. Another anonymous report on "Miss Tinling's Work in Korea" can be found in *Korea Mission Field* 20, no. 1 (1924): 23–4.

23 *KM*: "brought them up in the hope of something better."

24 Chen Jun (陳俊, ?–AD 47) was a Chinese official instrumental in the founding of Eastern Han (東漢, 25–220, also called Later Han 後漢), as Gale writes in *KM*, not Western Han (西漢, 206 BC–AD 24, also called Early Han 前漢), as he writes here.

25 The Later Han was succeeded by the Three Kingdoms period (三國時代, AD 220–80).

26 *KM*: "He might have wired 'round the world in his day, 'Gone dry.'"

27 *KM*: "I wonder if any other land."

28 The Royal Order issued by King Chungjong (中宗, 1488–1544; r. 1506–44) may be found in *Chungjong sillok* 21:38, 1514/10/25.

29 *KM*: "heart and soul be set against it."

30 *KM*: "by your every conviction."

my edict will avail nothing. I beg of you to make yourselves an example to the world[31] and so lead the people to better things."

King Hyojong,[32] who was carried away captive in 1636 by the Manchus, and lived three years in Mukden, wrote the following, "Most of the misfortunes that befall the state as well as the individual are due to strong drink.[33] Those who hold office know this,[34] yet I hear that there are some who make this unspeakable evil their means of entertainment. For myself, from the time I became Crown Prince, I avoided[35] this deadly thing."

One of his ministers, Song Chun'gil, whose tablet stands No. 54 on the east side of the Master in the Confucian Temple, said, "When Your Majesty, who have absolute freedom to drink as you please, gives it up, how much more should we."[36]

It takes[37] character and courage to stand as Hyojong did, and Corea furnishes many examples of this kind of superior man.

King Sukchong,[38] who came to the throne in 1675, wrote poems about hard drinkers[39] holding them up to ridicule. He wrote of the drunkard, of how he grows confident, how he talks as though he were king,[40] how

---

31 *KM*: "to the people."

32 King Hyojong (孝宗, 1619–59; r. 1649–59) became king shortly after the fall of the Ming dynasty to the Manchus and the rise of the Qing dynasty in 1644. Hyojong is perhaps best known for his planned military campaign against the Qing, which was never brought to fruition.

33 *KM*: "come from drink."

34 *KM*: "know this without my telling it."

35 *KM*: "I avoided all touch."

36 Song Chun'gil (宋浚吉, 1606–72) was a Neo-Confucian scholar and government minister of the seventeenth century. This quote by Gale, however, seems to be attributed to one of the most well-known Neo-Confucian scholars of the mid-Chosŏn and good friend of Song Chun'gil, Song Siyŏl. In a discussion of the Heart Sutra (心經) between Song Chun'gil, Song Siyŏl, and King Hyojong, Song stated: "雖然, 此心易縱於毫忽之間, 伏願終始戒愼焉。" See *Hyojong sillok* 20:161, 1657/11/21. Hyojong also confirms here that he has not gone near alcohol since becoming Crown Prince and has subsequently "become unable to imbibe" (今則便爲不能飮之人矣).

37 *KM*: "After all, it takes."

38 King Sukchong (肅宗, 1661–1720; r. 1674–1720) was the nineteenth king of the Chosŏn dynasty and a skilful politician who balanced the competing factions within the Chosŏn court.

39 *KM*: "boozers."

40 *KM*: "He reminded the world of how they grow confidential, how they talk as though they were kings, and that wisdom would die with them."

he smiles one minute like a judge of the Supreme Court, and acts like a fool the next.

In 1632 a new enactment declared that any man found making drink should be punished with a hundred blows of the paddle and three years' imprisonment. Any official found drinking was given a berth in the *Ŭigŭmbu*[41] which corresponds somewhat to the American Sing Sing. A second offence brought a double dose of punishment.

This is sufficient to show that Corea has had a conscience concerning this great evil, and has fought against it bravely through many centuries.

If this were a former age, and rice and supplies were as dear as they are today, a law would have been passed prohibiting the manufacture and sale of drink.[42] But the modern age under far West influence[43] has no conviction on this matter. It is in favour of strong drink at all times, and unwittingly has degraded the standards of morals and good deportment in the Far East.[44]

Tea
Old Corea, 50–1;
Korea Magazine 2 (September 1918): 406–9[45]

The question is frequently asked why Corea should drink no tea when Japan and China are devoted to its culture and to the rites and

---

41 The *Ŭigŭmbu* (義禁府) or State Tribunal was at the pinnacle of Chosŏn's legal system and decided cases involving treason or other high crimes.

42 *KM*: "If this were one of the older ages and rice supplies as dear as they were to-day we should have a law passed prohibiting the manufacture and sale of drink at once."

43 *KM*: "which has come from the far West."

44 *KM*: "but is in favour of strong drink from six in the morning till twelve at night, and so has unwittingly set back the hands of the Far East's clock of morals and good deportment." The *KM* version adds the following conclusion: "Assuredly she has less conscience to-day concerning the matter than she ever had before. All honour to Uncle Sam who has the strength and courage to give the world a helping hand in its great and crying need, by this high order that echoes the edicts of old Korea."

45 A manuscript draft of this essay can be found in the Gale Papers, Ledger 14, pp. 7–9.

ceremonies that attend it. One's answer must be largely of the nature of, "I do not know."

Tea does not seem to appeal to the Corean. He prefers coffee, or almost any other drink. So true is this that one might imagine that[46] he never really made its acquaintance. But this is not so.[47] Call on Mr. Odachi, for example,[48] and ask him if he has any Corean teapots and he will show you some. Ask him the price of one and he will probably say "two hundred yen," or thereabouts, and he will get this price, too, from some keen-eyed passerby.

Graceful as a fairy are these dishes that come forth from the long forgotten chambers of the dead. Some are modeled after the bottle-gourd and have the spout standing almost perpendicular on one side, while the graceful handle balances it on the other. Some suggest a hen sitting on a nest. The head slightly raised serves as spout and the tail for handle. These pieces of pottery are usually[49] ornamented with beautiful flower designs.

In museums these tea pots are erroneously marked wine pots. Korea was a tea-drinking country in old times as their history shows.[50]

The delight of afternoon tea, as known in England,[51] was an everyday delight of the Corean people[52] long before England ever heard of tea. Queen Elizabeth with all her regal graces never sipped afternoon tea.[53] It arrived just in time to brace up the nerves of Oliver Cromwell for his rough tasks.[54]

We learn from the *Samguk sagi* (History of Korea)[55] and other sources that Corea first became acquainted with tea in the reign of

---

46 *KM*: "So markedly is this the case that one could easily conclude that."

47 *KM*: "But evidence proves otherwise."

48 *KM*: "who lives near Namsan."

49 *KM*: "frequently."

50 *KM*: "In museums they are marked wine-pots, but really they are tea-pots, for Korea was a tea drinking country when they were made, and all through their history."

51 *KM*: "as specially known to the Englishman."

52 *KM*: "were the delights of this people."

53 *KM*: "One feels quite a shock of surprise when he learns that Queen Elizabeth, with all her graces of soul, never served afternoon tea."

54 *KM*: "It came too late for her day, but just in time to brace up the nerves of Oliver Cromwell for the rough task he had on hand."

55 *KM*: "and other sources." Although there was a historical document no longer extant compiled in the early Koryŏ named *Samguk sa* (三國史), as Gale writes

Queen Sŏndŏk (632–647 AD). This wise woman built a high tower from which to watch the stars – the tower still stands – and she introduced tea as a refined substitute for the wildly intoxicating drinks the old poets used to enjoy.[56] Corea learned to drink tea for two hundred years, apparently, before she learned to grow it.[57]

The *Samguk sagi* also tells that the seeds of tea were first brought to Corea by T'aeryŏn,[58] the envoy to the Tangs in 828 AD. These were the days of China's greatest glory, when she beneficently overshadowed the smaller states,[59] who looked up to her and worshipped her. Tea was first planted in the Chiri Hills of Chŏlla Province.[60]

Sŏ Kŭng,[61] a Chinaman, envoy of the Songs, who came in 1124 AD, wrote a book called *Koryŏ togyŏng* (Korean Pictures).[62] He says, "The tea of Corea has a slightly bitter and astringent taste, almost disagreeable to a Chinaman. Our 'Dragon' and 'Phoenix' brands are the brands which the emperor uses as gifts and they are also sold by merchants in large quantities. Coreans specially like these. Of late, Corea has become a great tea-drinking country and makes many varieties of teapots."

---

in the original typescript, Gale is referring here to the *Samguk sagi* (三國史記), compiled by Kim Pusik in 1145, and usually glossed as *History of the Three Kingdoms*.

56 Queen Sŏndŏk (善德, r. 632–47) was the first of three reigning queens in the Silla dynasty and the second queen in recorded Asian history. During the second year of her reign, Ch'ŏmsŏngdae (瞻星臺 Star-Gazing Tower), the world's oldest extant astronomical observatory, was built in the Silla capital of Kyŏngju.

57 *KM*: "Korea thus learned to drink tea, but for two hundred years, apparently never learned to grow it herself."

58 *KM*: "大廉."

59 *KM*: "like Korea."

60 *KM*: "where it flourished and grew." The following account of tea's introduction to Korea appears in the *Samguk sagi*: "冬十二月, 遣使入唐朝貢. 文宗召對于麟德殿, 宴賜有. 差入唐迴使大廉, 持茶種子來, 王使植地理山. 茶自善德王時有之, 至於此盛焉." *Silla pon'gi* 10, Hŭngdŏk wang: 828/12.

61 *KM*: "徐兢."

62 *Sŏnhwa pongsa Koryŏ togyŏng* (宣和奉使高麗圖經 Illustrated Account of the Xuanhe Embassy to Koryŏ) was a forty-chapter work by the Chinese envoy to Koryŏ, Xu Jing, based on his personal observations in the country. For an excellent study and translation of this text, see Vermeersch, *A Chinese Traveler in Medieval Korea*.

"Teacups are decorated with golden flowers. There are black cups, too, and small pots of blue-coloured ware. On occasions of special ceremony the host provides tea and as the servants bring it into the room they walk very slowly and say, 'Please, have tea!' When guests are seated the tea things are angled on a central table[63] and covered with a red silk gauze until it is time to serve it. It is the custom to offer tea three times a day."

It is interesting to note[64] that when the envoy went to Peking in 1712 to pay tribute and receive the imperial gifts, no mention is made of tea. Tea had died for Corea long before this.[65] When did it die and what was the cause?[66]

In 1470 Kim Chongjik,[67] a famous scholar, went as magistrate to Hamyang, near the Chiri Hills. He was interested in tea and having read the *Samguk sagi* found that it had been grown in that neighbourhood. He made inquiry of the older men concerning it and finally found some tea growing on a plot of ground north of the Ŏmch'ŏn[68] Temple. He immediately bought the land and saw to the further cultivation of tea. Tea grew so abundantly that Kim Chongjik made it a part of his yearly contribution to the government.

This paragraph would indicate a decline in the cultivation of tea since the days of Sŏ Kŭng.

The old kingdom of the Buddha had passed away in 1392 and the silence that follows would seem to say that tea also began to pack its "grip" and depart likewise. Scotch whiskey (Corean soju),[69] which the Buddhists are not supposed to drink, and which Confucianists hail as a boon companion,[70] had elbowed itself into greater right-of-way.

---

63 *KM*: "they arrange the tea things on a central table."

64 *KM*: "By way of comparison it is interesting to note."

65 *KM*: "Tea had died to Korea long ere this and was no more."

66 *KM*: "what caused its death?"

67 Kim Chongjik (金宗直, 1431–92) was a scholar and government minister of the early Chosŏn period. The story of Kim's tea cultivation is related in his "Tawŏn" (茶園 Tea Field), http://news.joins.com/article/16433108.

68 嚴川.

69 Aside from their granular derivation, there is little shared in common between Scotch whisky and Korean *soju*, making Gale's conflation here puzzling. Korean *soju*, distilled according to traditional methods, is much more similar in taste and appearance to Chinese *baijiu* (白酒).

70 This statement is curiously in contradiction to Gale's preceding chapter, "Prohibition in Corea," where he claims that alcohol has always been considered an impediment to Confucian moral behaviour and comportment.

The latest mention of tea[71] is in 1658 when a special commissioner, Min Chŏngjung,[72] went to Kyŏngsang Province to adjudge some question of tax contributions. It seems that Kŏch'ang County[73] was obliged to pay so much in tea every year. It was found, however, that this county did not grow it, but purchased it elsewhere, giving as much as thirty rolls of cotton goods for one measure of tea. This had become a heavy financial burden on the people of the county.[74] The commissioner set the matter right[75] by enforcing Chinju[76] and other counties where tea was grown to pay in tea while their taxation contributions were transferred to Kŏch'ang.[77]

Tobacco came into Corea about 1616. For forty years tea and tobacco were in competition for the first place for after-dinner consolation.[78] Tea, it is said, awakens[79] the faculties, heightens the speed, and causes the soul to throw off sparks, while tobacco slows down the system, casts a spell over the eyes, and leads its disciple into the arms of sleep.[80] Tobacco has easily won the day in Corea.[81]

A well-known Corean[82] whom the writer asked about this, said that Koryŏ was much more closely related to China than was the succeeding dynasty of Chosŏn. China's style of dress, her method of life, her delights and luxuries, became Corea's, and so she made tea a part of her everyday life. This may be so. Tobacco, however, would seem to have had a casting vote as regards tea, so that with its entrance tea finally departed.

---

71 *KM*: "found regarding tea."

72 *KM*: "閔鼎重."

73 居昌郡.

74 *KM*: "on the people of this unfortunate Ku'chang [*sic*] County."

75 *KM*: "straightened it out."

76 *KM*: "晋州."

77 *KM*: "pay in tea while other burdens of taxation that they had to bear were transferred to Kŏch'ang." Although Special Commissioner Min Chŏngjung is mentioned many times in the *Veritable Records of Hyojong*, when this incident is supposed to have taken place, I am unable to find a record of this.

78 *KM*: "1616 and so already there had been a trial of skill 40 years and more as to who should win first place in the way of after-dinner consolation."

79 *KM*: "Tea is inclined to awaken."

80 *KM*: "into the arms of Morpheus."

81 *KM*: "Tobacco we acknowledge to have easily won the day." Gale discusses the history of tobacco in Korea at length in "Tobacco in Korea," *Pen Pictures*, this vol.

82 *KM*: "A well-informed Korean."

Tobacco in Corea
Old Corea, 52–5;
E.T., *Korea Magazine* 1 (June 1917): 248–54

The history of tobacco is one of the fairy tales of earth. Surely the touch of a magic wand must have speeded its[83] extensive travels, and quickened its power to overcome every opposition.

It landed in Corea by way of Japan somewhere about 1616, the year in which Shakespeare died.[84] Japan had got it, name and all, *tam-bak-ko*, from Western merchants who brought it from Europe.[85] Its grip upon the world has lasted 300 years without any apparent slackening of its youthful vigour.

In sixteen hundred and sixteen King James of England wrote his *Counterblaste* against tobacco. He hoped[86] by one regal sweep to rid the world of its presence, so he beheaded Sir Walter Raleigh, the first smoker, and wrote the following: "And for the vanity committed in this filthy custom, is it not the great vanity and uncleanness, that at table – a place of respect, of cleanliness, of modesty – men should not be ashamed to sit tossing of tobacco pipes and puffing of smoke, one at another, making the filthy smoke and the smell thereof to exhale athwart the dishes and infect the air, when, very often men who abhor it, are at their repast? Surely smoke becomes a kitchen far better than a dining-chamber; and yet it makes the kitchen oftentimes in the inward parts of men, soiling and infecting them with an unctuous kind of soot, as hath been found in some great tobacco takers that, after their deaths, were opened up."[87]

This was surely a stunning blow, yet tobacco went serenely on its way to conquer France and all the rest of Europe.

It passed to the East where, it seems, the Grand Vizier of Turkey was so incensed against it, that he ran the pipe through the nose of every

---

83 *KM*: "aided in its."

84 *KM* removes this comment on Shakespeare.

85 *KM*: "Japan had received it from Western merchants who brought it from Europe, name and all, *tam-bak-ko*."

86 *KM*: "expected."

87 "A Counterblaste to Tobacco" was penned by King James I of England in 1604, then reprinted in the *Workes of King James* in 1616, the year Sir Walter Raleigh was executed.

smoker he could find, while his fellow religionist, the Shah of Persia, cropped the ears and slit the nose of anyone venturing to blow tobacco rings in his territory.[88]

Undaunted by this opposition in high places, tobacco made its way to the Far East and finally reached Corea.

Much doubt was manifested[89] on its first arrival. The following comment by Yi Ik who was born in 1629 is of interest: "Tobacco became generally known in this country in the closing years of King Kwanghae (1615–1623 AD).[90] The common story is that it came from a place in the far south called Tam-ba, hence its name *tambae*. I asked Teacher T'aeho, 'Do you think tobacco is good for the health?'

He replied, 'It is good for those troubled with phlegm, or those who are inclined to have spells of nausea. Those who have indigestion and insomnia are benefitted by it. It allays bitter flavours in the throat and is also a protection against the cold of the winter season.'

'But is it not also hurtful?' I inquired.

He replied, 'There are dangers that go with it. It may be hurtful internally to a man's mentality, or externally to his eyes and ears. On its continued use the hair grows gray, the face becomes dark and thin, the teeth fall out, the flesh dries away, and old age rushes upon you. The dangers, I say, are very great. The smell of it, too, is dreadful, and no man using it need ever expect to come into touch with the immortal gods. It also consumes one's money to no end. In a world like this,

---

88 These anecdotes, along with the above excerpt from King James's "Counterblaste," can be found in Johnson, *The Great Events by Famous Historians, 1609–1660*. It is almost certain that Gale consulted this work when writing "Tobacco."

89 *KM*: "There was much doubt manifested as to its character."

90 Yi Ik (李瀷, 1681–1763) was a literatus and government minister of the late Chosŏn era. One of the so-called Silhak (實學 practical learning) scholars, Yi's interests covered a range of fields, including economics, politics, history, and education, and he proposed various reform measures, most notably more equitable distribution of land. Yi was also widely read in Western scholarship in *hanmun* translation, though he was dismissive of Western religious philosophy. King Kwanghae (光海君, 1575–1641; r. 1608–23) and King Yŏnsan (燕山君, 1476–1506; r. 1494–1506) were the only Chosŏn kings to have been deposed from office, hence the degraded title of *kun*. Recent historians have been more generous in their appraisals of Kwanghae's rule, portraying the monarch as a victim of factionalism and viewing positively his relatively neutral stance toward the Ming in an otherwise fiercely sinocentrically-oriented Chosŏn dynasty.

where men are rushed with work, to give up time every little while to the use of tobacco seems unthinkable. If a man were to take the time and strength so wasted and use it in study, he would undoubtedly become a sage; or if, instead of doting over tobacco, he gave the same attention to the affairs of his family, he would become a rich man.'"[91]

Cho Kŭksŏn (1598–1658 AD)[92] says of it, "There is an evil weed which bears the name of *tam-bak-kwai* [*sic*] that came to us about the year 1615. Those who use it cut the leaves fine and make a pipe of brass into which to place them. The pipe is round at the top and bent at the lower end. Into the bent end they fit a bamboo stem that has a hole drilled through it. Thus, by means of the stem, after they have set fire to the tobacco in the bowl, they draw the smoke through the mouth."

Chang Yu (1587–1638 AD),[93] who is supposed to have been the first to introduce tobacco to Corea, stood in the same light before his king as did Sir Walter Raleigh before King James. He was remonstrated with about it, but wrote in reply a verse of which this is the translation:[94]

---

91 "南草之盛行自光海末年始也世傳南海洋中有湛巴國此草所従来故俗稱湛巴云有
問扵太 湖先生曰今之南草益乎曰痰在喉咯不出則益氣逆而涎潮則益食不消而妨
臥則益上焦停飲而吐酸則益隆冬禦寒則益曰益而無害乎曰害尤甚內害精神外害耳
目髮得之而白面得而蒼齒得之而凋肉得之而削令人能老余謂害尤有甚焉者臭惡不
得齋戒而交神一也耗財二也世間固患多事人無上下老少終歲終日役役不得休三也
若移此心力為學則必至扵大賢為文則成章治産則致富矣易曰上六冥升利于不息之
貞." Yi Ik, "Manmulmun, namch'o 萬物門 南草," in *Sŏngho sasŏl* 星湖僿說, kwŏn 4.

92 Cho Kŭksŏn (趙克善, 1596–1658) was a literatus of the mid-Chosŏn dynasty.

93 張維. Gale Papers, Ledger 1, pp. 150–2, contains a manuscript translation
titled "Tobacco" by "Chang Yoo (Man-p'il), page 39," indicating that one
of Gale's sources was Chang Yu's *Kyegok Manp'il* (谿谷漫筆). Gale Papers,
Ledger 8, pp. 107–13 contains several additional manuscript translations from
multiple sources, including *Taedong Yasŭng* (大東野乘) VI 486, *Munhŏn pigo*
(文獻備考) XXIX; (CXLVII) 20, S.H.S.S. II 395 by Yi Ik, K.K.C. XII (XXX) 27 and
K.K.C. XIV(I) 39; Y.G.C. V(X) 30 "See page 90 Cho Kŭksŏn"; C.E.E. IV(XIII) 8;
T.T.C. (8) I (II) 17; T.M.K.J III (IX) 3; M.C.C. III (VI) 26; S.A.M.C. VII (XIII) 28;
and K.N.C. VII (XIV) 9. Gale Papers, Ledger 8, pp. 131–7 contain additional
manuscript material titled "Tobacco," including a draft version of "Last Song
of the Korean Pipe" (p. 137), for which see below. Some of this material may
be found in Rutt, *James Scarth Gale and His "History,"* 267–8.

94 KM: "a verse that runs about like this."

Thou loose-filled flower, with oily seed
And leaf that turns a brownish tan;
You were not born of Chinese breed,
But came to us from east Japan.
Across the sea in savage ships,
You made your way by lifted sail.
A master of the heart and lips,
Thou wonder-weed, thou fairy-tale![95]

His flippancy, however, nearly cost him his head.[96] His father-in-law, Kim Sangyong,[97] who, on the Chinese invasion of 1636, blew himself up on a bag of gun-powder,[98] informed against him, and it was touch-and-go for a time whether Chang's spirit would join Raleigh's or not. His fear of being seen smoking by his father-in-law accounts for the custom in Corea today of hurrying the pipe out of the mouth and hiding it away on the approach of a superior.[99]

One of Corea's chief ministers, writing in 1639, calmly says, "From officers of state to the lowest wood-carriers in the land, all use tobacco.

---

95 This appears to be a loose translation of the following poem by Kyegok Chang Yu, written around 1623 when he was in the southwest as a secret inspector (*amhaeng ŏsa* 暗行御史):

疎花穠葉擢纖莖
不入神農本草經
誰遣孤根來日域
却隨蠻舶過滄溟
五芝雖元無種
九節何奇漫自馨
功用會須煩火候
藥欄眞覺有神靈

Cited from An Taehoe, *Tambago munhwasa*. Richard Rutt cites the same poem, attributing it to *Kyegok chip* xxx 27; see Rutt, *James Scarth Gale and His "History,"* 57.

96 *KM*: "life."

97 金尙容 (1561–1637).

98 *KM*: "(the famous man who later blew himself up on a bag of gunpowder in Kanghwa)."

99 Additional information on Prince Chang Yu may be found in Gale's "Tobacco in Korea," *Pen Pictures*, this vol.

Its name does not appear in any of our works on *Materia Medica* and so we do not know its exact nature, its strength, or how it affects one. Its taste is bitter, with a slight suggestion of poison about it. You are not supposed to eat the leaves but only inhale the smoke. Anyone taking an overdose is made drunk by it and has to lie down; but those accustomed to it are not so affected.

In the treatment of 'red-nose' it is said to be very good. Still I have thought that since it has a heating and drying effect it must be bad for the lungs and consequently the nose.

My friend Cho, however, says it is not so, but that it is good and cures indigestion. I expect he is right."[100]

The same writer adds, "Though scarce a score of years has passed since the 'south weed' began its course it has grown out of all possible proportion to other things. In less than a hundred years it will vie with tea in its race for the world.

In ancient times people in southern climes used the betel nut. They said, 'This nut will make a drunken man sober, and a sober man drunk; it will satisfy the hungry, and give relief to those overcharged with eating.' Evidently this is the praise of one fascinated by its wiles. The world that uses tobacco today says the same, 'It makes the hungry satisfied; it helps digestion in the case of those overfed; it makes the cold warm, and cools the overheated.' Just the same as the betel nut, very funny indeed!

Those who oppose tobacco do so on the grounds that it comes originally from the barbarian and is not found in ancient herbs. This is quite an unreasonable argument and unworthy of a gentleman. The list of ancient herbs was made up in the time of Hwijong of the Songs (1101–1125 AD).[101] The names of those tasted and recorded by Sillong made up only one-tenth of the whole number. Since the times of the Tangs many new ones have come to us from the barbarian. There is *p'agoji* now, a most efficacious remedy.[102] It came originally from beyond the pale. If tobacco is to be condemned for coming from the barbarian, why not also *p'agoji*? I do not know whether this 'south

---

100 *KM*: "I suspect he is right in this matter."

101 Emperor Hwijong (徽宗 Ch. Huizong, 1082–1135; r. 1100–26) was the eighth emperor of the Song dynasty.

102 *P'agoji* (破故紙) refers to *Psoralea corylifolia*, a flowering plant native to India that came to be used to treat various maladies in Chinese medicine.

weed' is good for one or not, but, if it is we need not bother our heads about where it came from."

The following statement comes down to us from Yi Sik,[103] a contemporary of Shakespeare: "Tobacco comes to us from the land of the East Sea (Japan). The Japanese say that it is the soul of a certain virtuous woman. The story runs:[104] 'A certain man lay dying while his wife tried all possible means for his recovery but failed. He died, and in her distress she said, "I shall die with him and may my soul become a medicine for this troubled world." Her soul became a plant with leaves that came up like cabbage and had a slightly bitter-sweet flavour. It grew abundantly from the grave of her husband, very fresh and bright in colour. Eight or nine out of ten who tasted it were drunk. At last a noted physician made use of it as medicine by having the leaves mixed in wine and steamed. They were burnt and the smoke inhaled. Through an instrument of brass like the trunk of an elephant the smoke was conveyed to the mouth. On smoking it, all the phlegms and indigestions of the body took their departure, and the inner being became sweet and light.'"

Much anxiety was felt at times regarding the hold that tobacco was getting on the land of Corea and in 1732 a memorial was presented to His Majesty which is backed up by one of the ministers as follows:[105] "Some twenty years ago when on a visit to Chŏlla Province I noticed that in the cultivation of the 'weed,' farmers used only the waste corners of the fields; but, two years ago when I went again, I found that the best of the lands[106] were dedicated to it. In the counties of Changsu and Chinan the whole place seemed given up to the cultivation of tobacco. Also, places that I did not see, such as lands off the west coast, have fallen victim to tobacco culture.[107] Thus, agricultural land has been whiffed away in smoke.[108] There are no words to express my[109] indignation. If strict orders were given at seed time by every official, people

---

103 Yi Sik (李植, 1584–1647) was a literatus of the mid-Chosŏn era.

104 *KM*: "and they account for it thus."

105 *KM*: "in the following manner."

106 *KM*: "lands of the province."

107 *KM*: "have fallen victim to the same practice."

108 *KM*: "Thus, land useful for cultivation has been given up to this useless thing to be whiffed away in smoke."

109 *KM*: "one's."

would not dare to sow it. Will not Your Majesty issue such a command and have the abuse stopped?"

King Yŏngjo,[110] who was then thirty-eight years of age and had been eight years on the throne, replied, "Many have made similar propositions to me, but to issue an order for the wholesale extermination of tobacco would cause trouble; and yet, we cannot allow rice-land to be given up for its cultivation. We shall command the governors of the south to see that good lands are no longer used for raising tobacco."

Here is the warning appended by Nam Kongch'ŏl,[111] who died in 1840: "Chŏng Sŏng says that King Mu of China (1122 BC) had characters written on his clothes, his books, his boxes, and his staff, in order that they might serve as a warning to him. He had them written so that all could see. One can judge from this how careful the ancients were in the smallest matters, and how far-reaching was their thought. I write this as a preface to what I wish to say on tobacco.

> Let him who smokes, like those who fight,
> Watch lest his pipe should get control;
> For he who puffs and lights this light,
> Is kindling tophet[112] in his soul."[113]

The sum total of all comment in Corea is decidedly against tobacco.

King James of England was against it. The Shah of Persia and other masters of the East were likewise against it. Yet, with an air of light indifference tobacco encircled the earth and tightened its grip as the centuries have gone by. It is a sign and a wonder, a proof that somewhere, somehow, all mankind may be one. The East and West do not dress alike,

---

110 King Yŏngjo (英祖, 1694–1776; r. 1724–76) was the longest-reigning monarch of the Chosŏn dynasty and skilfully balanced the various factions in the Chosŏn court. The *KM* version records "King Yung-jong."

111 南公轍 (1760–1840).

112 *KM*: "May kindle Tophet." Tophet is a theological synonym for hell in the Christian tradition, named after the location of human immolation sacrifices according to ancient Phoenician religious practices.

113 This appears to be a loose rendering of the following lines from Nam Kongch'ŏ's *Kŭmnŭng chip* 金陵集, kwŏn 14, Yŏnjŏn myŏng 煙盞銘:

爾吸之。寧少毋多。慎厥終。焰焰不滅。炎炎若何。

do not eat, talk, or think alike. One prefers white, the other black; one inclines toward salt and pepper, and the other toward sugar and pickle; one sings down in his lungs and the other in the roof of his mouth. One drops off his shoes and puts on his hat, while the other takes off his hat and ties on his shoes. What is there that they do alike that can prove them to be of the same reasonable genus and order, and all sons of Adam? Shall we say that the answer lies in the familiar whiff of tobacco that scents every steamer's smoking room, the "prophet's chamber" of Princeton University, the atmosphere of all modern up-to-date cities, as well as the soul of the men, women, and boys who walk the hills of Old Corea?

"Supposed Song of the Old Corean Pipe"[114]

For length of stem and bowl attach (sometimes three feet long)
I was indeed a wonder;
I never thought to meet my match,
Much less of going under.
I held my own three hundred years (1616 to 1916 AD)
And grew as time expanded;
No man could puff and stroke my ears
Or light me single-handed. (bowl too far off to reach
  with match)
But who should come and show his face? (At first a great
  disgrace it was to be seen smoking a cigarette)
Most underhanded caper;
A three-inch cigarette disgrace
All wrapped around with paper.
I used to ride down people's necks (so carried, stuffed
  down the back of the neck).
Or whiff along in splendour
I was the friend of woman-sex (All Corean women smoked.)
Her solace and defender
Alas my job is up. Regrets (the long piper has almost
  ceased to be; cigarettes are everywhere).[115]
May ship themselves to Dover;
The fates are calling "cigarettes":
Let's die and have it over.

---

114 *KM*: "LAST SONG OF THE KOREAN PIPE."
115 Gale's explanatory notes for this poem do not appear in the *KM* version.

Corean Paper[116]
Old Corea, 57–9;
Korea Magazine 2 (November 1918): 487–91

Corea has excelled in the making of porcelain and cement but also in the making of paper. She developed paper manufacturing[117] at a very early stage in her history and became specially known thereby throughout East Asia. China, who always assumed the high and mighty part of suzerain toward her smaller eastern neighbour, had to acknowledge that Korea was more than her match in this art that has to do with the gentleman and scholar.

In old records there are many notes[118] referring specially to that variety of paper made from the inner bark of the mulberry (*Broussonetia kazinoki*).

The Munhŏn Encyclopaedia[119] says, "Dwarf mulberries grew in the south and in the islands of the sea. Paper made from the bark is very white and smooth."

Sŏng Hyŏn[120] (1439–1504 AD) says, "Paper-making in our country includes many varieties; some made of straw, some from willow wood, some from willow leaves, some from the fiber of Job's Tears, some from hemp stalks, and some from the mulberry. All these varieties are very fine. At the present time, most of it is made from straw, hemp stalks, and willow wood."

Kim An'guk[121] used to gather seaweed for making a choice and finished paper product. Paper from seaweed costs much less labour than other varieties. Kim An'guk advertised it abroad and wrote poems about it.[122]

---

116 A manuscript draft of this essay can be found in the Gale Papers, Ledger 14, pp. 190–5. Pages 195–8 contain additional draft translations of *hanmun* sources on Korean paper and the Korean mulberry.

117 *KM*: "This manufacture she developed."

118 *KM*: "Looking through the old records we come on many notes."

119 *KM*: "*Munhŏn pigo* (文獻備考)." Hong Ponghan, *Tongguk munhŏn pigo* (東國文獻備考 Encyclopedia of Documents and Institutions of the Eastern Kingdom, 1770).

120 *KM*: "成俔."

121 *KM*: "金安國 (1478–1543 AD)."

122 *KM*: "His desire was to make this kind of paper generally known and so he advertised."

The *National Biographical Record*[123] reads, "A man named Yun Hyŏn,[124] who graduated in 1537, while minister of finance, gathered together all the old straw mats, straw rugs, etc., that he could find and piled them up in his storehouses. People laughed at him and asked him what he intended to do with this collection of rubbish. Later he had it all sent to the paper manufactory and made into paper of a very fine quality."

We are told that in the far north where the mulberry does not grow, the people make a yellow variety of paper called *hwangmaji*[125] from oat straw. This paper has become of general use in official circles as well as among the common people.

King Sejong, who came to the throne in 1419, set up a Paper Office and made the department responsible for all paper required by the government, especially that used in imperial service. They made the paper from the various materials mentioned by Sŏng Hyŏn: straw, willow wood, willow leaves, seaweed and mulberry bark.

Chinese opinion of Corean paper is interesting. In the *Haedong soksa*[126] it says, "The paper of Corea is of a superior quality, very white, tough and smooth. Chinese[127] paper making has been but poorly developed and so we have to depend on other countries for our supply, on Corea especially." In the poems of the Tang Kingdom (618–905 AD) we find many references to Korean paper.

A thousand years before the first patent was taken out in England for paper manufacture (1665), it was manufactured of such high skill in Corea that it won the admiration of the great Tang kingdom.[128]

In the imperial archives[129] of China the finest models of penmanship, the noted writings of kings and princes, the masterpieces of Han, the

---

123 *KM:* "The Kook-cho In-mool-chi [*sic*] (國朝人物考)." *Kukcho inmulchi* (Korea's Record of Famous Men) was compiled in 1909 by An Chonghwa (安鐘和, 1860–1924).

124 *KM:* "尹鉉."

125 *KM:* "黃麻紙."

126 *KM:* "In the Hai-tong Sok-sa [*sic*] (海東續史) these are recorded, some few of which we mention." *Haedong soksa* (A Continuing History of Korea), also called *Haedong yŏksa sok* (海東歷史續) and *Haedong yŏksa chiri ko* (海東歷史地理考), is a cultural geography of Korea compiled by Han Chinsŏ (韓鎮書, 1777–?) in 1823, based on an unfinished manuscript, *Haedong yŏksa*, by his uncle Han Ch'iyun (韓致奫, 1765–1814).

127 *KM:* "Our Chinese."

128 *KM:* "it was known to Korea, and such high skill developed in its making that it won the admiration of the great kingdom of kingdoms the Tangs."

129 *KM:* "We are informed that in the imperial archives."

Three Kingdoms (220 AD), the Six States (439 AD), the Su Kingdom (600 AD) and the Tangs, were all preserved on Corean paper.[130]

The Chinese were so surprised at the excellent quality[131] of Corean paper that they made a microscopic examination to see what it was made of. They decided that it must be made from the silk cocoon,[132] and for many years this idea was current.[133] Corea was able to[134] befool the Chinaman for five hundred years about something that his hands could handle and his eyes could see. We are doubtless safe in saying that no other people in the world have ever done it before or since.

The great Kanghŭi[135] seems to have discovered the secret of its origin.[136] He says, "In the days gone by we were told that Corean paper was made of the silk of the cocoon, but now we find that we were mistaken and that it is made of the bark of the paper-mulberry. The skill with which it is manufactured surpasses everything. I tried a piece of it by fire and discovered that it was made of the bark of a tree, not of silk thread. Inquiring of the Corean envoy how they made it, he told me that it was made of the bark of the *tak* tree,[137] the white part of the bark alone being used. Tough, smooth and soft, it glistens as though made of the finest windings of the silk worm."

One who has seen the process of Corean paper manufacture says,[138] "The paper mulberry grows the best in the south where it escapes the severe frost. There you find it growing abundantly on the hills[139] and

---

130 The year "220 AD" refers to the first year of the Three Kingdoms period (220–80), whereas "439 AD" is the year that the Northern Wei dynasty reunified the northern part of China within what is more broadly known as the Six Dynasties Period (220–589). The year "600 AD" seems to be a rough place holder for the Sui Kingdom (581–618).

131 *KM*: "The Chinese in their astonishment over its excellent quality."

132 *KM*: "The wise among them decided that it was made as silk from the cocoon."

133 *KM*: "made from the thread of the silkworm."

134 *KM*: "It is rather interesting to think that Korea was able to."

135 *KM*: "emperor Kang-heui [*sic*]." Emperor Kangxi (康熙, 1654–1722; r. 1661–1722) was the fourth emperor of the Qing dynasty. The veracity and source of this story are unclear.

136 *KM*: "discovered the mistake."

137 Paper mulberry tree.

138 *KM*: "The writer has never seen it made, much he regrets it, but his friend Kim who watched the process as a little boy gives the following account."

139 *KM*: "planted on the hills."

waste lands. The annual growth of timber, six feet or so, is gathered when autumn comes and the stalks, as big as walking sticks, are bound in bundles like rice sheaves. A number of these may again be bound together and wrapped about with matting in preparation for being steamed.

The next step is to have a hole dug in the ground about one *k'an*, or eight feet square, and six feet deep. This is filled with large logs of wood, an opening being prepared below by which to feed a fire. On the top of this wood, stones are piled up, care being taken to see that none of them are of the splitting, exploding kind.

Then a fire is kindled; as the logs consume[140] and disappear, the stones settle down also. Old mats are thrown upon the fiery mass with earth hurriedly piled on top, covering the stones completely except the part in the centre reserved for the steaming.

The bundles, tied as tightly as possible together, are placed on end in the open centre, pressed firmly against the heated stones while earth is piled all round close about them.

A foot or so from the bundle of stalks holes are hastily dug round about in the new earth and water poured in, the holes being stopped up instantly. As it sizzles and roars down among the burning stones, the steam that generates is forced up through the mulberry sticks, fiery hot and in great quantity.

As the water pours in and the sound of boiling ceases,[141] the process is complete. The sticks are then hastily removed and the bark stripped off. The thorough steaming causes it to come away with perfect ease.

The next step is to strip the dark outer bark from the inner. This is done first by sprinkling and then by stripping off by hand. The white inner bark is then boiled in lye made from the ashes of buckwheat straw until it is perfectly macerated and falls easily apart.

It is then taken out, washed, and placed on a flat rock to drain off and dry. When thoroughly dried it is beaten with a switch till it works up soft like cotton wool.

It is then soaked in a vat[142] of water mixed with powdered soapstone. The soft finish and velvet edge of Corean paper is given by this process; otherwise its shining surface would be hard and uninteresting. The root of a plant called *takp'ul* (`hibiscus manihot` L.) is then taken and

---

140 *KM:* "settle down."
141 *KM:* "When the boiling sound in response to the pouring in of water ceases."
142 *KM:* "The next step is to subject it to a soaking in a vat."

beaten up slightly in a mortar. Hot water is poured upon it and it is well kneaded by trampling with the bare feet. The water from this root is very carefully strained off and a certain amount mixed in the vat where the pulp goes through its final process. It is stirred continuously so as to ensure its being evenly mixed. Without this admixture of hibiscus glue, the paper would not hold together.

Next the paper-maker brings his light filter-frame that is made according to the size of the sheets required. It has a narrow border of an inch or so, with a very fine bamboo screen for bottom. He dips this into the vat and takes up the required amount of watery mixture which he shuffles backwards and forwards till the water has slowly percolated through the sieve. He then turns it over onto a prepared stand where it strips off clean and lies flat. He places a straw at the corner to serve as a dividing medium between this and the next layer that follows. Thus the process goes on till he has built up a pile of pulp layers two feet high and more. This is taken to a place in the sun or a warm room where they are peeled off separately to dry.

Naturally each sheet curls up and dries unevenly, so several sheets are taken together and given final treatment by a hammer with an iron face. This hammer has two arms that extend back from the fulcrum, and being exceedingly heavy, requires the weight of three or four men on each arm to keep it pounding. The paper is not placed on a hollow mortar but on a flat rock so that it catches evenly the heavy strokes of the hammer face. The object is to beat it out perfectly flat and smooth."

This gives, in outline, according to an eye witness, the process by which Corea makes her world-renowned paper.

Corean Clothes
Old Corea, 59–60;
Korea Magazine 3 (April 1919): 159–62[143]

In the West, where most things are in a state of flux, and surprises confront one almost daily, men's dress changes comparatively little. True, we had wigs, long-tailed coats, and knickerbockers from the time of Cromwell

---

143   A manuscript version of this essay can be found in the Gale Papers, Ledger
       15, pp. 89–90.

to the period of George Washington, but during the last hundred years men's dress has remained pretty much the same. Frock coats, cutaways, dinner jackets, etc., come and go without any very noticeable surprise. In Corea, however, there have been most startling innovations in dress.[144]

When the writer came to Corea some thirty-three years ago,[145] men walked on the streets wearing long tinted robes made of the finest silk, with a girdle across the chest of blue, or green, or scarlet. Nebuchadnezzar himself was never so adorned. Wide sleeves hung down on each side, deeper and more capacious than aunt Miranda's pocket. Sometimes this robe was divided at the back, sometimes at the sides; sometimes it was a complete "roundabout" or *turumagi*. On a man's head a headband was tied, after long practice, tight enough to squeeze tears from the eyes. Above the head was a little cap of beautifully woven horsehair. Above this again sat a gauze hat, a sort of cage for the topknot that was dimly glimpsed through its meshes. Over a man's eyes was a huge pair of spectacles, much like those Americans affect today, though more startling[146] in appearance. At the back of his ears were gold or jade buttons; under his chin a string of amber bead; his right hand waved a fan; on his feet were the daintiest pair of shoes mortals ever wore, wedded to a pair of socks, white, as Malachi's fuller never dreamed,[147] the only really beautiful footgear in all the world.

As a Corean man walked along with measured tread, his long robe adding inches to his height, he was indeed one of the most startling surprises which the eye of the West ever rested on. With our coarse tweeds and our stodgy shoes, we must have fulfilled his idea of the barbarian mentioned in his literature of a thousand years.[148]

---

144 *KM*: "innovations in the way of dress during the last thirty years." Gale Papers, Box 8, Folder 15 is a fourteen-page manuscript in Gale's hand with the title "Notes on Korean Dress" in his wife's handwriting.

145 Gale first arrived in Korea in 1888. *KM*: "When the writer came to this country the first thing that bowled him over, metaphorically speaking, was the manner of dress."

146 *KM*: "stunning."

147 "To full" is to press or scour cloth in a mill in order to whiten, and a fuller was one who whitened clothing. Malachi 3:2 states, "But who may abide the day of coming, and who shall stand when he appeareth? For he is like a refiner's fire, and like fullers' soap."

148 *KM*: "we must surely have been to him like the barbarians he had read of for a thousand years but had never seen before."

Today the Corean gentleman wears a white robe fastened with common buttons under the arms and his sleeves are narrowed down to a commonplace size.[149] The top-knot, the headband, the cap, the gauze hat, are replaced by an ordinary "bowler" or a soft felt fur. His shoes are the mere ghost of what they used to be, or more often are an uninteresting pair of leather boots such as foreigners wear.[150]

The Corean dress fashions have an ancestry of a thousand years or more. A few notes on it [zzz] gathered from the *Yŏllyŏ kisul*, one of their great books, may be interesting.[151]

"In the year 648 AD King Munmu of Silla[152] paid a visit to the capital of the Tangs, China, and there decided to adopt their state dress as his own. The Emperor T'aejong,[153] in approval of this, gave him samples of the dresses used in the Empire."

"In the opening days of Koryŏ (950 AD), the fashions of dress which had fallen into confusion were specially considered, and the king commanded Ch'oe Yŏnhŏn[154] to collect all the ancient models and

---

149 *KM*: "Today the glory has departed from the Korean gentleman … narrowed down to the plainest commonplace."

150 The *KM* version adds here the following sentences, which are visible in the typescript version but have been scratched out: "This is the common costume, in which he goes with a pair of leather boots, crowned with a cheap felt hat, and covered with long white robe between. This is a fair illustration of the mixed, unpoetic world of dress in which we live today, a dress divested of all ornament and reduced to the Bolshevikian level of everybody looking alike and every man doing the same thing." Gale often railed against the destructive force of Bolshevism in his personal writings.

151 *Yŏllyŏ kisul* (燃藜記述 Narration from the Yŏllyŏ Study), also called *Yŏllyŏ sil kisul* (燃藜室記述), was a history of the Chosŏn dynasty from its founding to the reign of Sukchong (肅宗, 1661–1720; r. 1674–1720) by the historian Yi Kŭngik (李肯翊, 1736–1806). According to Michael Seth, "The first part deals with the various reigns and the second part with a number of special topics such as institutions, diplomatic relations, taxes, marriage customs, penal systems, and astronomy and natural phenomena." Unlike most historians, Yi strayed from strictly Confucian historiography and refrained from presenting moralistic judgments, including instead four hundred verbatim quotations that read in a more objective fashion. Seth, *A Concise History of Korea*, 200.

152 King Munmu (文武, 626–81; r. 661–81) was the thirtieth monarch of the Silla dynasty, according to the traditional lineage, and was the first king of Unified Silla.

153 太宗, 598–649; r. 626–49.

154 Gale's text writes "Choi Yun-heun" but this individual's identity remains a mystery.

improvise something new, using the best he could find from the Tangs as his chief pattern. This fashion continued till the time of the Mongols (1230 AD),[155] when Corea began to cut the hair of the head in front and plait a pig-tail behind. The dress of the Mongols was used for about a hundred years until the Mings came in, when we bowed to them and received what they gave us in the way of clothes."

A very curious discussion arose in 1275 about the proper colour for Corean dress. The Office of Historians maintained that as Corea hung on the eastern rim of Asia, its colour should be green, as its symbol was wood and its flavour sour.[156] White was the colour that pertained to the West, and might be worn by the Tibetans or the Mongols of the Gobi Desert, but not by the Coreans. It was argued by others that Corea took its rise in the Ever-White Mountains to the North,[157] the ruling compass-point, and that the colour of necessity then should be black. This idea carried the day and from that time on officials wore black coats and green hats, suggesting a tree, the symbol of Corea. Trees were then planted on the hills to make all the world as green as possible.

During the Japan War of 1592, dress fell again into great confusion. It would seem that whenever the state neglected to take dress into consideration the people reverted to white as the national colour. In 1592, in

---

155 The Mongols launched a series of invasions from 1231 to 1259, when Koryŏ became a tributary to the Mongol Yuan Empire, which lasted until the 1350s when Koryŏ began to force out the Yuan presence.

156 According to the Five Phases (*ohaeng* 五行), a Taoist philosophy formulated in Han China that attempts to explain the interactions and relationships between phenomena, there exist five elements that are associated with various tastes and colours, the cardinal directions, and the animals of the Chinese zodiac. Wood is rising, expanding, and growing, and hence associated with blue-green; it generates sour taste and is associated with the East. The other phases or elements are as follows: fire – south, red, bitter; earth – middle, yellow, sweet; metal – west, white, spicy; water – north, black, salty.

157 The "Ever-White Mountains" (Changbaek sanmaek 長白山脈) refers to the highest mountain range on the Korean peninsula and in northeast Asia, and the highest mountain in this range, straddling the present-day North Korean-Chinese border, is Paektusan (白頭山 White-Head Mountain), purported to be the mythical origin of the Korean race where Tan'gun descended from heaven in 2333 BC. The caldera that forms Heaven Lake (Ch'ŏnji 天池) at the pinnacle was formed roughly one millennium ago in one of the most violent eruptions in recorded history.

1660, and again in 1691, we find government orders issued forbidding the use of white.[158]

In 1767 the king made a proclamation which ran, "When we forbade the use of white someone said, 'Kija (1122 BC) wore white and therefore white is the national colour.' I am grieved to think that people have forgotten what Kija thought, and remember only what he wore." If any of the candidates for examination came dressed in white, the official classes, military and civil, banded together to boycott them and put them out.

Notwithstanding royal orders and Corea's point on the compass face or its love of gaudy colour, Corea still holds to Kija's dress – white. Even in these days of change and counter-change, white holds its own, and New Year's 1921 sees the streets of the capital lined as of yore with the sons and daughters of Kija.[159]

Corean Artists[160]
Old Corea, 61–2

Little remains of Corean Art except the record that So-and-So lived, and delighted his day and generation by the pictures he drew. Speaking generally, Corean Art has sunk very low. As for the sculptor's world,

---

158 A 1691 entry in the *Chosŏn wangjo sillok* (Veritable Records of the Chosŏn Dynasty) contains the following exchange between King Sukchong and his ministers: "'It is the tradition of our eastern land to revere white attire (*paegŭi* 白衣), but in previous times it was not common to wear mourning dress (*sobok* 素服) while green clothing was donned in daily life. However, we cannot simply abolish this based on old practices.' The King ordered a stern warning to be issued against wearing white." *Sukchong sillok* 23:1691/3/4. The Korean expression for conscription, *paegŭi chonggun* (白衣從軍), literally meaning "to join the military donning white clothing," appears frequently in the *Sillok*, concentrated particularly in 1592, the year of the Imjin Wars, when thousands of commoners were pressed into service to repel the invading Japanese. This expression suggests the ubiquity of white dress among the masses.

159 In the *KM* version Gale has written "and New Year's 1919 sees the streets of the capital lined as of yore." The *KM* version therefore was rewritten for inclusion in *Old Corea*, which unfortunately never came to fruition.

160 In the original typescript version the following passage appears at the top but has been crossed out, accompanied by the handwritten note, "rewrite"

one need but mention only the horses in the royal funeral procession. Whether they are intended for giraffes or for horses who can tell? Some of the portraits, however, that used to adorn the walls of the picture gallery of Prince Yi's Museum, now unfortunately gone, will remain a wonder of Corean Art. The two extremes are here.

The first great Corean artist was a man named Solgŏ.[161] His shadow falls somewhere across the eighth century. He worked with charcoal, and life was in his hand. "A man of Silla," he is called, "who was a god among artists." He made a picture on the temple wall of an old pine tree. The birds seeing it flew into the room and tried to alight on the branches.[162]

The last king of Koryŏ, Kongmin (1352–1374 AD) was a great artist, exact in detail and large in vision. In the long stretch of 700 years, two artists have left traces of their once having lived. One is Yi Nyŏng,[163] two of whose pictures in the possession of the writer were done in the year 1133 AD. One subject is an old man with a white beard on his way to the wine shop; the other is a group of ancient-day Coreans having an earnest talk.

The author of the *Yŏllyŏ kisul* says,[164] "The work of Yi Nyŏng was greatly renowned." Again in the *History of Koryŏ*[165] we read that a merchant of the Song Kingdom presented the king of Corea with a picture. When the king saw it he exclaimed, "What a remarkable proof of China's artistic skill!" Delighted, he called his artist, Yi Nyŏng, and

---

(ultimately, the piece remained unpublished): "In the lapse of years pictures are jostled out of existence and forever lost. Books are printed and though one copy disappears, others remain to take its place. Pottery, with its accompanying companions of the antique, has a running chance to hold its own against the 'whips and scorns' of time; but pictures done on frail material if they meet but the wear of the finger tips, or a single rude trust, are gone forever." The bound notebook of typescripts titled Miscellaneous Writings no. 30 in Box 8, Folder 15 contains another earlier version of this essay on pp. 26–8. Gale Papers, Ledger 1, pp. 99–114, 117, and 125 contain additional manuscript translations from *hanmun* sources on Korean artists, while Ledger 15, p. 86 carries an unrelated half-page note on "Korean Artists."

161 率居 (dates unknown).

162 This account of Solgŏ may be found in *Samguk sagi* (三國史記), vol. 48.

163 李寧 (dates unknown).

164 Vol. 14 of *Yŏllyŏsil kisul* (燃藜室記述 Narration from the Yŏllyŏ Study) contains information about artists.

165 高麗史.

had him look. Yi hesitated for a moment and then said, "But this is my brush, Your Majesty!" The king was doubtful till they tore off the back wrapping and there was the name, "Yi Nyŏng."

An Kyŏn[166] and Ch'oe Kyŏng[167] who lived in the fifteenth century were famous, this one in landscape, and the other in men and animals. The old record calls the two "spiritual beings in their skill." When Sŏng Hyŏn was royal secretary he saw in the King's possession a landscape picture by An that was a perfect wonder. An himself confessed that into it all his heart and soul had gone.

Another noted artist of Corea was the famous Buddhist priest, Naong. He was not only a painter but a sculptor. His "Three Buddhas"[168] carved on the face of a rock in the Diamond Mountains, and his majestic "Myogil sang"[169] though 500 years old, still delight the passerby.[170]

Many artists appear in the list that brings us down to 1650 AD when Kim Myŏngguk lived.[171] The record reads, "Kim did not follow the methods of others in his work but developed all kinds of unheard-of and extravagant eccentricities. The more he worked out his details the more beautiful they became. His themes and execution were well conceived, but his bent was for the odd and bizarre. He was a man inclined to worldly pleasure and loved drink. If anyone came requesting a picture, drink was the first thing called for. If Kim had no drink his skill

---

166 An Kyŏn (安堅, fl. mid-fifteenth century) was an official painter of the early
       Chosŏn court. His "Mongyu towŏn to" (Dream of Strolling in a Peach Gar-
       den), the only extant painting that can be definitively attributed to him, is
       considered today a masterpiece of Korean landscape painting.

167 崔涇 (dates unknown).

168 三佛巖.

169 妙吉祥.

170 Naong (懶翁, 1320–76) was a painter and sculptor of the late Koryŏ period.
       His iconic "Three Buddhas" ("Sambul am") and "Myogil sang" Buddhist
       carvings are currently designated as National Treasure Nos. 42 and 102 by
       the Democratic People's Republic of Korea. Gale would have had direct con-
       tact with these works of art, having visited the Diamond Mountains from
       21 September to 22 October 1917, a travelogue of which he published in *Trans-
       actions*. See Gale, "The Diamond Mountains," *Transactions of the Royal Asiatic
       Society – Korea Branch* 13 (1922): 1–67. Gale intertwines his narrative with
       those of Chosŏn literati who preceded him, creating a rich diachronic trave-
       logue replete with literary and aesthetic sensibility.

171 Kim Myŏngguk (金明國, 1600–62).

was not at its best; that alone freed his artistic soul." But the old record adds, "If he was over much drunk his highly conceived dragon fell to the level of a centipede."

Kim Myŏngguk once went to Japan as Envoy and all the world surged like a tidal wave to ask samples of his skill. A Japanese who had built the beautiful three-*k'an* pavilion,[172] lined with silk and adorned with every costly decoration, came to request Kim to paint him pictures on its walls. Myŏngguk consented, got desperately drunk, and took the pen in hand. The Japanese prepared a mixture of gilding and brought it to him in a dish. Myŏngguk took a deep drawn mouthful of the mixture and blew it over the dainty walls, again and again, till all the dish was finished. The Japanese, who was dismayed at this unheard of act, drew his sword and made a rush at him. Kim, however, laughed a great laugh, took up his brush and began to work. Little by little, mountains, streams, and people came forth. All nature seemed to wake at his touch and its result was the most wonderful example of artistic skill ever seen. The Japanese bowed down before him to express his unbounded admiration. The little pavilion descended to his children and was always regarded as one of the most wonderful sights of the kingdom.[173]

About this time there lived two other noted artists, one named Cho Chiun and one Hŏ Ching.[174] Cho, a member of the Noron, or as we might say, the liberal party, was in charge of a royal tomb when he was visited by Hŏ Mok, a Conservative[175] of high standing, and at that time a Minister of the Left. Hŏ asked Cho to paint a picture of his fan, and this Cho did to his great delight. But the other Norons, or Liberals, hearing this were highly indignant, and charged Cho with being a

---

172 *K'an* is a unit of measurement that refers to the distance between two columns, roughly 1.8 metres.

173 This account is related in "Ch'ŏngjuk hwasa" (聽竹畫史), artistic critiques penned by the late Chosŏn literatus Nam T'aeŭng (南泰膺, 1687–1740) which make up his larger collection of literary works *Ch'ŏngjuk mallok* (聽竹漫錄). Gale draws much of his information in this chapter from this work.

174 Cho Chiun (趙之耘, 1637–?); Hŏ Ching (許懲 (澄), 1614–?).

175 Hŏ Mok (許穆, 1595–1682) was a prominent government minister, educator, and literatus of the mid-Chosŏn dynasty, and one of the most prominent leaders of the Namin (南人 Southerner) faction, what Gale refers to as "Conservative."

traitor. It is said that Cho from that time on never did any painting or touched the brush again.

Hŏ Ching was a special painter of peach blossoms and orchids. When he first came from the capital, Cho Chiun put some paper in his sleeve pocket, went to pay a call and asked him for a picture. Not knowing who he was, Hŏ Ching said, "Why not call on Cho Chiun? He could paint you a picture, indeed."

Cho, however, insisted and Hŏ consented. So wonderful was the work, that Cho made deep obeisance and told him his name. They were delighted to meet and know each other.[176]

Hong Suju[177] was a Board Secretary, and a special painter of grapes and peach blossoms. Once, his young daughter borrowed a red skirt from a friend but unfortunately upset a dish of soy sauce upon it. She was in great distress till her father said, "Don't be troubled; I'll put it right." He took it and made the stain the base of a beautiful bunch of grapes. This he gave to the envoy's interpreter who was going to Peking, and told him to sell it. He did so and bought silk enough in its place for many skirts. The daughter, greatly delighted, paid for the damaged garment and had left over abundant material for others. She asked her father to paint again, but he laughed and said "Ho! Ho! Once is enough, my dear."[178]

In the year 1720, Yun Tusŏ,[179] at the special request of the King painted him a picture. It seems that Yun was a mourner at the time, and one of the ministers protested, saying, "In the *Book of Ceremony* it says, 'The Superior Man never interferes with the honour awarded to parents, and never allows them to be dishonoured through the wishes of another.' Why should His Majesty make such a request and why should Yun yield?"

On hearing this, Tusŏ was mortally ashamed and went to Haenam,[180] where he hid himself and shortly after died. He was one of the last great painters of Corea.[181]

176　This story may be found in Nam T'aeŭng, "Ch'ŏngjuk hwasa."

177　Hong Suju (洪受疇, 1642–1704).

178　This account is related in *Yŏllyŏ sil kisul*, vol. 14.

179　Yun Tusŏ (尹斗緒, 1668–1715).

180　海南.

181　This account appears in Nam T'aeŭng, "Ch'ŏngjuk hwasa."

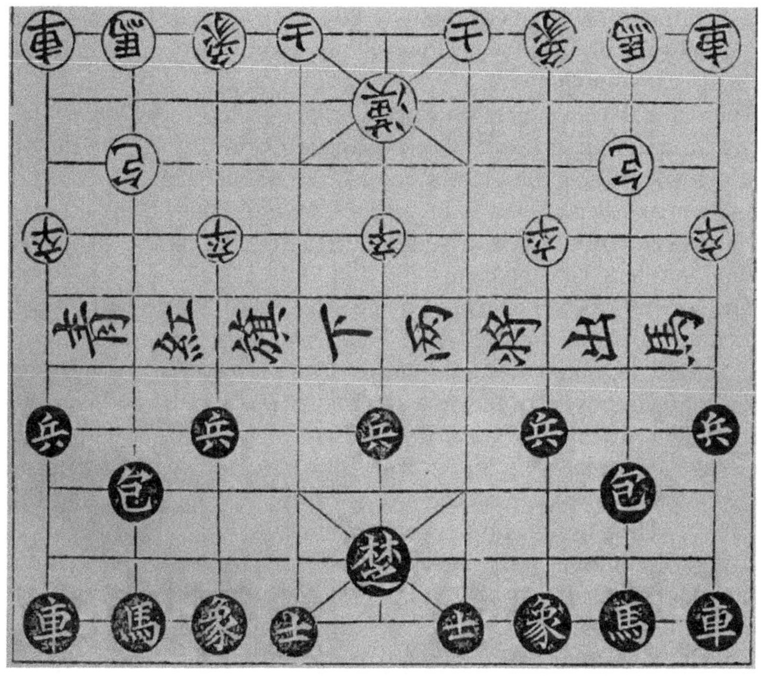

Illustration 19. "KOREAN CHESS-BOARD," *Korea Magazine* 2 (January 1918): 5

Corean Chess
Old Corea, 63–5;
"Chess – By Chang Yu (1587–1638)"
Korea Magazine 2 (January 1918): 5–9

Chang Yu (1587–1638 AD),[182] one of Corea's great writers, says, "Chess is a game that represents military operations on a marked board. The board is prepared by drawing nine lines from north to south, and ten

---

182 Chang Yu (張維) was a mid-Chosŏn government minister and literatus, and the father of Queen Dowager Hyosuk, wife of King Hyojong. This short mention of Chang Yu is absent from the *KM* version.

lines from east to west. On the two sides to the north to south[183] there are 'palaces' with nine rooms in each, marked by cross lines. In the centre of this sits the 'general.'

There are sixteen pieces on each side, one called *chang* known as the 'general' and marked *Han* (漢) on one side, and *Ch'o*(楚) on the other. At the back of the general are two *sa* (士), one on each side, his 'aides.' There are two *ch'a* (車) or 'war-chariots.' two *p'o* (包) or 'big guns,' two *ma* (馬) 'war horses,' two *sang* (象) or 'fighting elephants,' and five *chol* (卒) or 'soldiers' (兵) [*pyŏng*].

The *general* takes his place in the middle of the *palace*, while the *aides* stand behind on each side. The *elephants* stand to right and left one square removed from the aides. The *horses* take the next place, one square removed from the elephants. The *elephants* and *horses* may change places at will. The *chariots* stand at the extreme corners. The *big guns* take their places on the second cross, just in front of the *horses*. The *soldiers* take their places on the line in front of the *big guns*, standing at the two outside limits and at every other cross.

The *general* moves only one space at a time, forwards, backwards, to right or left, but always within the *palace* enclosure. The *aides* move as the *general* moves.

The *chariot* moves straight ahead, or at right angles, as many spaces as it pleases that are clear. The *big gun* moves with the *chariot*, but it must have some one piece to jump over in any line in what it moves. A *big gun* can never jump over a *big gun*. A *gun* also can never take a *gun*.

The *horses* move over two lines at once and always across the corner. The elephant moves across an angle of six squares (a quadrangle of three by two), any of the six that stand before it. If the cross line immediately in front of the *horse* is occupied he cannot move; nor can the *elephant*, if there is a piece immediately in front or in the middle of the second line.

The soldiers move one space forward or one space to the side, but never backwards.

If a piece gets in the way it is taken, and the person who first takes the *general* wins the game. When both sides fail it is a draw. The varieties and possibilities of the game rest with the player."[184]

---

183 Here Gale seems to mean "running from north to the south," or the borders running vertically.

184 "象戲者。局戲象兵勢也。其爲局也。東西九道。南北十道。南北之邊。畫九宮焉。斜通而湊于中。將之位也。子各十有六。將一將軍也。士二謀士也。車二戰車也。包二礮也。馬二騎也。象二戰象也。卒五徒也。將居九宮之中。士居其

Hong Yangho (1724–1802 AD)[185] writes,

"Chess and draughts represent low forms of diversion. The ancients said that they were the amusements of the pig-keepers, and ought to be cast into the river. But the Sage, Confucius, maintained that a game played was better than nothing;[186] how about that?

When God made man[187] he gave him his special work to do wherever he happened to be. Yet if a man merely eats well and dresses warmly without any other thought in mind, his soul will wander off into a thousand extravagances. Unless there is an effort put forward to fix the attention on something, up goes the imagination to heaven, or down again in the depths beneath, till what the eyes see and the ears hear become a snare and a temptation.[188] Therefore, thought must have something to rest upon, if one would master himself and not suffer the spirit to wander aimlessly about. Those who play chess and draughts, though these be rather low games, have constantly before them the matter of winning or losing, and so find in them that which occupies the attention. Thus it was that the Sage, referring to chess and draughts, taught us to keep the mind well occupied. But his words are by no means an encouragement to play games. The Superior Man finds a thousand other ways better than this to occupy his time. Can you not see it?"

Oriental chess, if we judge from tradition, is much older than ours. Granting this, we can easily see how our chess has come to be modeled on the Eastern board. It appeared since the Christian era,[189] sometime during the Middle Ages.

We have, first of all, changed the *general* into a *king*, a most natural proceeding in an age when the ruler combined kingship with leadership.

後之左右。象居士之左右。馬居象之左右。象與馬。雖互列焉可也。車居馬之左右。包居車之前二罫焉。卒列居包之前行而各間一道以竟局焉。將行一道。前却左右無拘。然不出九宮也。士行如將也。車行直。長短縱橫前却無拘也。包行如車焉。然必有乘也。惟包與包。不相乘也。亦不相食也。馬行二罫也。象行六罫。經三而緯二也。然馬有阻其前。象有阻其前及二罫者。皆不得行也。卒行一道。可左右而不可却也。敵當其行。欲食者食之。先得其將者勝。不能相勝者平。將與將相對。以將就之者請平也。此其大勢也。奇正之妙。存乎其人。"

Chang Yu, "Chapchŏ, Sanghŭiji," *Kyegok sŏnsaeng chip* 谿谷先生集, kwŏn 3.

185 Igye Hong Yango 耳溪 洪良浩. Gale was quite fond of Hong's writings.
186 *KM*: "better than doing nothing."
187 *KM*: "When God (Ch'ŏn) made man."
188 *KM*: "to the soul."
189 *KM*: "Eastern board, and made within the Christian era."

Instead of *aides* we have a *queen*, who is the *king*'s most powerful help-meet. Woman had already come into a measure of her own in Europe when chess was decided upon, though she has no place on the Chinese board.

Instead of a *cart*, or *chariot*, we have a *castle*, reminiscent of the age of chivalry.[190] It seems absurd for a *castle* to move toward the four points of the compass,[191] until we remember that the *castle* borrowed its powers from the oriental[192] *cart*, without troubling about this incongruity.[193]

Our *knight* is like the Eastern *horse* and moves in the same irregular manner. The prominent place won by knighthood in early days would easily account for its place on the board.

We in Europe had no idea of elephants and so, of course, the chess *elephant* had to go. What more natural thing to fill his place than the *bishop*? As the elephant had to do with the imperial splendor of the East,[194] so had the Bishop in the West.

A glance at the board will show that our *bishop*, like the Chinese *elephant*, crosses the squares diagonally,[195] six at a time, of the shortened or the elongated group.

Our gunpowder is supposed to date from the 14th Century, and as the beginning of our chess game is earlier than that, we would not know at that time what to do with the pieces representing Chinese artillery that used gunpowder, so we did away with them and blended them into the rank and file of the soldiers (pawns).

A Christian age, the Age of Chivalry, antedating gunpowder, evidently modeled our chess game after the Chinese or Corean, for they are virtually the same.[196] How our forefathers got it, or by what route it came to them, seems unknown.

The oriental game is more difficult than Western chess because of the board having the two pieces, the *gun* and the *elephant*. Good players[197] use

---

190 *KM*: "how like the age of chivalry."
191 *KM*: "It seems very absurd, however, for a *castle* to go moving about with all freedom toward the four points."
192 *KM*: "Chinese."
193 *KM*: "without troubling about the inconsistency of the thing."
194 *KM*: "splendor and imperial moving of the East."
195 *KM*: "our *bishop* gets his powers from the Chinese *elephant*, for he crosses the squares diagonally."
196 *KM*: "modeled our chess game after the Chinese."
197 *KM*: "Good Oriental players."

these pieces with great effect, but they are very hard for the Occidental to handle. The irregularity that attends them both causes the difficulty.[198] With the exception of our *knight*, all our pieces run on straight ways and avenues with much regularity, but it is not so with the *elephant* and *big gun*.

The pieces number thirty two on each board. As to shape, our love of regularity would at once make the oblong board a square, so we have sixty-four squares while the Corean board has seventy-two crosses or corners. Faithful to the spirit of doing things the other way, we move on the squares while the Oriental moves on the angles.[199]

The Corean scholar looks askance at chess, not because he is averse to a good game, but because chess suggests military operations, which he, a man of the pen, considers to be beneath his dignity, for he is a scholar and a gentleman.[200]

Teeth
Old Corea, 66–7;
Korea Magazine 1 (March 1918): 114–16

The question of teeth is one that interests the whole world. From the time that they come in with their fever and fits of temper, till they drop with a wrench into the dentist's gruesome receptacle, they are among the oddest riddles that confront human experience.

The day may come, let us hope so, when human beings will be able to dispense with teeth altogether and take their nourishment by some kind of concentrated tablet that will but touch the tongue and leave the recipient with a satisfied feeling of soup, and fish, and entree, and pudding and all the rest of an abundant meal. Under such gentle tutelage teeth may resolve themselves back into the original dark elements from which they sprung, and leave the earth free of one of the worst evils bequeathed it by old Adam.

---

198   *KM*: "that attends them is where the difficulty arises."

199   The *KM* version adds the following paragraph: "The Chinese board differs
        from the Korean in this, that it has what they call a river running down the
        middle of it where you see, on this board, the sentence, 'The generals ride
        forth under the red and blue flags.' This sentence, as a mark, is common
        to many boards." The board pictured at the opening of this chapter is the
        Chinese version, featuring this phrase in the middle.

200   *KM*: "regards as beneath his dignity, for he is a gentleman and a scholar."

They are a contradiction all the way through. Naturally their presence should spell health and cheer. A man with good white teeth, all sound, should be as strong as Ajax, and hale and hearty as Michelangelo's David. But this is by no means so. Some of the worst cases we have ever seen of dilapidation, dyspepsia, yellow blotches, and no end of bilious eructations have had back of them a perfect set of ivory teeth, the envy of the gods. Truly they are a great and insoluble mystery![201]

If I were an Oriental and should set about explaining the defects and ailments of the foreigner, I should start with teeth and conclude that there must be some devil or other who sows seeds of infection in every Western[202] baby's mouth, and then dances with glee over the pains and aches that follow, till he sees his prey drop finally into the dentist's box. What a world of expense, of misery, and of humiliation are teeth!

Three Corean friends happened to be sitting by me as I wrote and I asked:[203]

"Kim, how old are you, please, and how many teeth have you missing?"[204]

"I am fifty-one," said he, "and all my teeth are sound," opening his mouth to show.

The next man was Yi, fifty-one also. He has two unbroken rows of molars. They can crack walnuts and peach stones with an echo like the shot of a small revolver. Of late, however, I have noticed a twinge across his countenance that tells me he fears there is a "worm" working at the root of one of his teeth, planted at some unwary moment by the tooth-devil. Let us hope not.

The third friend is Yi also, forty-three years of age. He has not a defective tooth in his head; all are sound and well. "When a Corean's teeth go," said he, "he dies."[205]

---

201 In the original typescript version, the entire preceding section has one cross-though. Generally, when Gale wanted to delete a section he would cross it out several times, whereas a single cross-out through an entire essay accompanied by a date indicated that the piece had been published on that date in a certain periodical; this single cross-out of a section, however, is somewhat of a mystery. This paragraph did, however, find its way into *Korea Magazine*.

202 *KM*: "foreign."

203 *KM*: "Three Korean friends, who happened to be sitting by when these notes were made, were inquired of."

204 *KM*: "have you out?"

205 Gale employed many Korean informants to aid in his literary studies, several with the surnames Yi and Kim, and so it is difficult to know to whom he may

I ask them what they make of us foreigners and our teeth trouble[206] and they say: "foreigners eat sweets, and the flavour sweet is associated with the element earth, and earth devours water. Water has to do, not with liver, lungs or kidneys, but with teeth." So thus you have it: Sweet, that has to do with earth, eats into the teeth that are in the category of water, earth's sworn enemy.

Here we find ourselves in the region of the Five Elements with a large measure of proof in favour of what they say.

As I peer into the Oriental world I feel that teeth are a greater mystery than ever.

Once we saw exhumed[207] the bones of an ancient lord from a mound that had adorned a Corean hillside for a hundred years. The bones were all counted[208] and from the skull not a tooth was missing. The ancient record said that he had died at sixty years of age.

I had just come to the conclusion that Asia, especially Corea, was blessed with sound teeth above her kind when I found the following paragraph by Yi Kyubo written about 1200 AD.

"Man lives by eating, and he eats by means of his teeth. If his teeth ache he cannot eat. It looks as though God intended that I should die. If we have our aching teeth pulled out we get relief from the agony, but the toothless gum that shows puts us to shame.[209] The few I have left are all loose. They have no grip at all upon the jaw. These, too, begin to ache and my whole head suffers, for tooth-ache goes clear up to the crown. With it, one cannot drink cold water, nor can one drink hot. Even rice gruel has to wait till it cools before one attempts it, and this is eaten not with the teeth, but with the tongue. As for meat it is quite out

---

be referring. This essay seems to date to the early 1920s, when Gale had in his employ at the Christian Literature Society three men: Yi Wŏnmo (李源謨, 1875), Yi Ch'angjik (李昌稙, 1866–1938), and Yi Kyosŭng (李敎承, ?–1951). But he also worked closely with two Kims: Kim Wŏn'gŭn (金瑗根, 1870–1940), and Kim Tohŭi (金道熙, 1866?–1924). The three friends referred to here must be Yi Ch'angjik and Kim Tohŭi (both born in 1866 and thus aged fifty-one in 1917), and either Yi Wŏnmo or Yi Kyosŭng. It is frustratingly difficult to secure biographical data about any of Gale's "pundits." For a detailed discussion of Gale's expert informants, see King, "James Scarth Gale, Korean Literature in Hanmun, and Allo-Metropolitan Missionary Orientalism."

206 *KM*: "what they make of us in this respect."
207 *KM*: "We saw exhumed once on a time."
208 *KM*: "all counted, every one of them."
209 *KM*: "If you have them pulled out you get relief from the agony, but the toothless gum that shows, puts me to shame."

Old Corea

of the question and has to be left untouched in the dish. This is all a sign of age.[210] One really must get rid of the body altogether to be well."[211]

This extract proves[212] that there were toothache woes[213] in ancient days. But taken all in all, Corean teeth are as superior to ours[214] as the soldiers of the Western Front would be superior to a loose-flung Chinese mob.

Hard chewing and salt wash every day have kept Corean teeth strong and white as ivory. You could marshal an army of a hundred thousand men in Corea without a missing tooth. Would this be possible anywhere else in the world?

The coming generation, alas, with sugars, and ices, and *ami*'s and chocolates, and the thousand other accompaniments of the twentieth century, will soon develop aches and pains and a "worm" for every tooth in their head, till they know all the tooth-aching ills and woes of the West.[215]

---

210 *KM*: "proof of age."

211 The original can be found in *Tongguk Yi Sangguk hujip* (東國李相國後集) kwŏn 1, Koyulsi 古律詩 105 su 首, "U ch'it'ong 又齒痛 Another Tooth-ache:"

"人以食而生, 食必以其齒. 齒痛莫加飱, 天殆使我死. 剛折亦云經, 老豁更堪恥. 餘有幾箇存, 浮動根無寄. 今者又復痛, 延及頭亦爾. 水寒不可飲, 湯亦不可試. 糜粥候冷熱, 然後僅能舐. 矧可齕肉為, 有肉空在杦. 是實老所然, 無身始洒已."

212 *KM*: "It is not wholly as I thought, for this extract proves."

213 *KM*: "toothless woes."

214 *KM*: "Koreans are as superior to us in the matter of teeth."

215 *KM*: "till they know all the ills and woes that the West is heir to."

Ancient Remains

"Ancient Remains" contains two chapters on Korea's ancient tombs, both dating from the Koguryŏ period some 1,500 to 2,000 years ago. The third chapter continues this lineage of ancient funerary customs by detailing the funeral procession of Korea's Emperor Kojong, the last such procession carried out according to the ancien régime. The final chapter describing the forgotten narrative of the shipwrecked Dutch sailors in seventeenth-century Korea is neither ancient nor concerned with funerary customs, and so its inclusion in this section is difficult to explain. With the exception of this final piece, these chapters seek to introduce to the Western reader the art and culture associated with death and the afterlife in premodern Korea.

The section begins with "The Tombs of Uhyŏlli" (遇賢里), the old name for the location of the Koguryŏ tomb murals dating to around AD 500 described in the chapter. Located west of the Taedong River in the vicinity of P'yŏngyang, the third capital of Koguryŏ, these tombs are collectively known as Kangsŏ taemyo (江西大墓), and the murals contained therein represent perhaps Korea's greatest contribution to the world's artistic heritage. In "Ancient Burial Remains" Gale traces Korea's archaeological history even further into the distant past, describing royal tombs found at the Manchurian-based ancient Koguryŏ capitals of Cholbon (卒本) and Kungnae (國內), the latter the location of the capital until being moved to P'yŏngyang in AD 427. These ancient Korean capitals, especially the Manchuria-based capitals, represent for contemporary South Korean people a glorious and martial past, where their people presided over vast expanses of territory and vied for supremacy with great Chinese dynasties. As Gale aptly writes in "Ancient Burial Remains," "It is Chinese territory but all its memories are Korean, its proofs of greatness and its glory." The representation of ancient history also presents a geopolitically sensitive issue today, where the Democratic People's Republic of Korea (DPRK) claims its own historical legitimacy through recourse to the country's northern geographical orientation and martial posturing, while the "Korean" tombs of present-day China embody a contested historical heritage and a target of irredentist sentiment.[1]

In this section Gale touches on the topic of live burial (*sunjang* 殉葬) – not to be confused with the practice popularly known as Koryŏ burial (*Koryŏjang*), which refers to the unsubstantiated Koryŏ-era tradition of abandoning those over sixty in the mountains. Archaeological evidence has demonstrated that *sunjang* was observed in royal burials and by some nobility in Koguryŏ as well as in Silla, the Kaya Confederacy, and Paekche.[2] Those who suffered such a fate could be men or women of any age, of slave status or the sons and daughters of ministers, as claimed by Gale. The following passage from *Samguk sagi*, from which Gale seems to be drawing his information in this section, relates the practice of *sunjang* surrounding the death of the Koguryŏ King Tongch'ŏn (東川王, AD 209–48; r. 227–48):

> In the ninth month during the fall, the king departed this world and was interred at Siwŏn (柴原). His title was King Tongch'ŏn. The people of the land, pondering over his goodness and benevolence, were moved to sadness. Many of the subjects close to the king wished to offer their lives and die with him, but the new sovereign declared this to be counter to propriety (禮) and forbade it. Nevertheless, on the day of the funeral upon reaching the burial site, a large number of people offered their lives and died. Many of the people gathered brush and buried the bodies, thus the burial site came to be called Siwŏn (Brushwood Mound).[3]

Sunjang was discontinued earliest in Kuguryŏ in the fourth century, then in Kaya in the late fifth, and finally Silla in 502. In the latter, there seems to have been a progression from a period when any number of

---

1 Andre Schmid has written extensively on the subject of historiography and the contestation over historical legitimacy in the Koreas. See Schmid, "Rediscovering Manchuria," and Schmid, *Korea between Empires*.

2 No, "Han'guk kodae ŭi kyesesasang."

3 "秋九月, 王薨. 葬於柴原, 號曰東川王. 國人懷其恩德, 莫不哀傷. 近臣欲自殺, 以殉者衆, 嗣王以爲非禮, 禁之. 至葬日, 至墓自死者甚多. 國人伐柴, 以覆其屍, 遂名其地曰柴原." *Samguk sagi*, Koguryŏ pon'gi 17, 248/9.

victims could be buried to a period when the number was limited to five men and five women, before the practice was finally banned.[4] A passage from the *Samguk sagi* records the abolishment in sober terms: "In the third month of the third year [of the reign of King Chijŭng] a royal proclamation was issued outlawing the practice of *sunjang*. Previously when a king was buried, five females and five males were buried along with him, but the practice was from this time abolished."[5] Although there are many theories as to why *sunjang* was eventually abolished, Chu Yongnip suggests that the practice was perceived as a disruption to the development of agriculture by depriving society of labour, as well as an affront to the Buddhist tenet of protecting life, following the transmission of the religion to the peninsula.[6]

Another controversial legacy of Korea's ancient history that surfaces in this section is the Japanese contribution to establishing Korea's modern field of archaeology. Gale explicitly mentions in various places the contribution of Japanese archaeological methods in the location, excavation, and preservation of historical sites, which were often only vaguely referenced in traditional sources. Hyung-Il Pai reminds us that it was the Tōkyō Department of History, led by Shiratori Kurakichi (白鳥倉吉, 1865–1942) from the late nineteenth century, that combined knowledge of Sinitic historical literature with the imported Western disciplines of archaeology, art history, and physical anthropology to shift the focus away from reliance on dynastic Chinese textual sources to the collection, compilation, and study of Korean texts,[7] a development that revolutionized the approach to ancient history on the Korean peninsula. Concerning the sites described by Gale in "Ancient Burial Remains," Hyung-Il Pai writes that the first systematic archaeological studies of Koguryŏ burial sites were spearheaded by the sponsorship of the South Manchurian Railroad and conducted by scholars of Tōkyō Imperial University in the first decade of the twentieth century. Torii Ryūzō (鳥居龍蔵, 1870–1953) was the first to excavate a Koguryŏ fortress (fall of 1905), followed by Imanishi Ryū (今西龍, 1875–1932) and Kuroita Katsumi (黒板勝美, 1874–1946), who established the existence of not only Koguryŏ burials but those of Silla, Paekche, and Lelang.[8] While Korean nationalist

---

4 No, "Han'guk kodae ŭi kyesesasang," 11.

5 三年, 春三月, 下令, 禁殉葬. 前國王薨, 則殉以男女各五人, 至是禁焉. *Samguk sagi*, Silla pon'gi 4, 502/2.

6 Chu, "Han'guk kodae ŭi sunjang yŏn'gu."

7 Pai, *Constructing "Korean" Origins*, 23–4.

8 Ibid., 26; Pai, "The Politics of Korea's Past, 29–30.

historians and archaeologists during the later colonial and post-liberation periods would refute the findings of imperial Japanese scholars in their search for independent "Korean origins," Pai writes that this school nonetheless "appropriated mainstream nineteenth-century colonial historical and anthropological paradigms of racial invasions and territorial conquests to explain cultural change"; in other words, their attempts to propagate ideas of "Korean racial distinctiveness" and a "unique historical destiny" are embedded within "colonial-racist biases."[9]

The former Emperor Kojong, the target of so much of Gale's exasperation and frustration during the years preceding annexation, finally passed away on 21 January 1919, at the age of sixty-seven. His funeral procession, widely photographed and described by Gale in this section in great detail, was carried out according to the Royal Protocols of the Chosŏn dynasty (Ŭigwe). Gale's account is sober, devoid of emotion or investment, and instead dedicated to thoughtful and thorough description. Kojong's funeral procession took place on 3 March 1919, just two days after the Korean peninsula had been rocked by a massive independence movement. Following Kojong's death, talk began circulating that he had been poisoned by the Japanese and, inflamed by this rumour, crowds gathered in Seoul for the monarch's funeral, which morphed into full-blown demonstrations. Writing on the role of Japan in Korea in his personal diaries, Gale acknowledged Kojong's death as the impetus for the independence movement: "The death, in January of the present year, of the Ex-Emperor, Prince Yi, Sr., as he has been known since annexation, was one of the factors in starting the independence movement that is now stirring the whole land, for it was persistently rumored that the Japanese had either killed him because he would not, or that he had committed suicide to avoid being forced to sign a document that was used at the Peace Conference [at The Hague] which witnessed to the satisfaction of the Korean people under Japanese rule."[10] Ch'oe Yŏng-ho and Yi Taejin have claimed, based on the compelling eyewitness accounts of Yun Ch'iho and Princess Masako, daughter-in-law of Kojong, that Kojong was indeed the victim of poisoning at the hand of high Japanese officials,

---

9 Pai, *Constructing "Korean" Origins*, 56. For other articles on archaeology appearing in *Korea Magazine*, see "Ancient Burial in Korea," *Korea Magazine* 1 (October 1917): 436–8; "Antiquarian Studies," *Korea Magazine* 2 (January 1918): 2–5.

10 Gale, "Why Japan Has Failed in Korea," unpublished article, p. 5, reproduced in Yu Yŏngsik, *Ch'akhăn mokchya*, 646–51; 646. The same essay can be found in the Gale Papers, Box 24, Folder 22.

though the death was never officially investigated.[11] Though Gale mentions these rumours in his personal diary, in this account he seems more intrigued with the historical meaning of the event. Having ultimately failed in attempts at reform and leading a quiet palace existence since his deposition in 1907, in death Kojong seems to have wrought more momentous change than was possible during his life.

Gale's account of Dutchmen in Korea does not fit with the chapters on ancient Korean burial in this section, much like the shipwrecked sailors' own bizarre juxtaposition in seventeenth-century Korea. It seems that the Chosŏn government simply did not know what to do with these outsiders. As Gale writes, "Evidently in those days the Foreigner was outside the pale of recognition." In *The Dutch Come to Korea*, which remains the most comprehensive treatment of this largely forgotten and mostly inconsequential episode, Gari Ledyard writes, "On the Korean side it shows a civilization fully confident of its own values and much more vigorous than might be suspected after two generations of devastating wars with the Japanese and the Manchus."[12] The tale seems to support the narrative of a complacent Korea content within the cultural confines of the Sinitic sphere and blissfully ignorant of the "barbarian" West, a theme that repeatedly surfaces in Gale's writings. Gale no doubt felt a kinship, however, with these Occidentals who lived as exotic curios in their adopted land of Korea.

The Tombs of Uhyŏlli
Old Corea, 68–9;
Korea Magazine 2 (June 1918): 248–51

An interesting visitor came one day to Corea, Osvald Sirén,[13] Professor of the History of Art, Stockholm.[14] He arrived in P'yŏngyang where he stopped off a day in order to visit the famous tombs in Kangsŏ.[15]

---

11 Ch'oe and Yi, "The Mystery of Emperor Kojong's Sudden Death."

12 Ledyard, *The Dutch Come to Korea*, 11.

13 *Korea Magazine* (*KM*): "A very interesting caller came by the other day in the person of Osvald Sirén."

14 Osvald Sirén was a Finnish-born Swedish art historian who held a professorship in the History and Theory of Art at the University of Stockholm (1908–23) and was Keeper of Painting and Sculpture at the National Museum of Fine Arts (1928–45). Sirén wrote extensively on Chinese art.

15 江西.

These ancient palaces are well known in the world of art.[16] Their mural decorations, symbolic emblems, weirdly ancient yet almost modern-looking figures, are a world wonder.[17] Recently when the emblem of fire from these tombs was thrown on the screen in Boston, the audience greeted it with wondering applause. Evidently a world of strange beauty remains[18] in these old tombs of Koguryŏ.

What Professor Sirén desired specifically to see were the tombs of Uhyŏlli.[19] He gave the writer a hearty invitation to join him which he certainly would have done had duty permitted.

The three tombs of Uhyŏlli are placed close together.[20] The one to the south is called the Great Tomb. The diameter of the outer mound is about 170 feet while its height is about 30. Its masonry is of granite cut in large blocks and built in a most substantial way, the skill shown by the masons being of the highest order. In the inner chamber are two tables of stone evidently intended as stands for coffins.

The official record of this tomb says, "The walls and ceiling are of granite, decorated with coloured pictures strong in concept of beauty and grace[21] and exquisitely fine in execution." From the general appearance[22] of the decorations they belong to the times of the Divided Kingdom of China, 500 AD. Professor Sirén says that nothing equal to them of the same period exists in either China or Japan proper.

Four mural paintings that call for special attention[23] are drawn according to the symbolic law of Chinese philosophy. To the east is the Blue Dragon, blue being the colour that pertains to that compass point. This and all the figures are magnificently drawn with such power and wealth of imagination that the onlooker can only marvel about their origin.[24]

---

16 *KM*: "Already these ancient places have won the attention of the world of art."

17 *KM*: "are a wonder of the world just beginning to dawn."

18 *KM*: "Evidently a mine of artistic worth remains to be unearthed."

19 遇賢里.

20 These are the Three Tombs of Kangsŏ (江西三墓), consisting of three ovular burial mounds, small (*somyo*), medium (*chungmyo*), and large (*taemyo*) in size.

21 *KM*: "strong in concept, beautiful for grace."

22 *KM*: "It is considered from the general appearance."

23 *KM*: "that call the attention of the world."

24 *KM*: "point. Not only this one, but all the figures are magnificently drawn with a power and wealth of imagination that leaves a great wondering question as to whence they came."

The Blue Dragon, a dreadful monster with lifted paw and long spotted tongue curling upwards, rides on the clouds.[25] His long scaly back is curved with a grace of motion[26] while flames of fire like wildly driven torches blaze from his back.

The White Tiger, which is symbolic of the west,[27] is also a magnificent creation, its loose flung tail and strong rear foot expressive of the driving force that sends the beast hurtling through the air; the fierce claws, the wild flames of fire, the fanged jaws and hotly glaring eyes are splendid imagining. It is little wonder that artists came from the ends of the earth to see [zzz].[28]

On the south wall is the Red Bird, another surprising creation. It seems to have a double body with one leg to each, beautiful scimitar wings, and a sweep of uplifted tail. The figure has a highly crowned head, a tip of red above the eye, and a live coal in the beak. While the blue dragon has charge of wood in the east, and the White Tiger charge of metal in the west, the Red Bird has fire as its element in the south.

This bird, touched off by an unknown artist's finger one thousand five hundred years ago, holds the onlooker spellbound, so spectral-like yet so graceful[29] it seems. Touches of white ornament the body and the inner circle of the wings.

On the north wall is the strangest creature of all, an unimaginable turtle, lithe-limbed and long, with the snake, its mate, wound in folds around it. The name turtle, *kŏbuk*, though a native word, can be spelled out with Chinese characters, *kŏ* [居] meaning to reside, and *puk* [北], the north; the Turtle is the guardian creature of the north. The snake is its mate, and from these two in union, birth results at the new year, as the picture of the sun to the right indicates with life to all.[30] This would seem to mark the highest development of Chinese philosophy.[31]

Other interesting mural decorations are clouds, fairies, mountain peaks, racing horses, unicorns, the phoenix, angels with long sweeping

---

25 *KM*: "rides by us among the clouds."
26 *KM*: "grace of motion perfectly natural."
27 *KM*: "which has to do with the west."
28 *KM*: "No wonder Professor Sirén came miles on miles to see it."
29 *KM*: "graceful and real."
30 *KM*: "with life in general."
31 *KM*: "This surely marks the highest development of Chinese philosophy as pictured on the blackboard." This seems to be a transcript of a lecture delivered by Gale.

folds of light trailing behind them, the genii sitting among the rocks and hills of wonderland, odd conventional flowers, the honeysuckle, the lotus, and others.

These tombs are samples of the gilded palaces of the days of Koguryŏ when the living were interred along with the dead. Their wonder will only increase as time goes on.[32]

Ancient Burial Remains
Old Corea, 70–1;
"Ancient Korean Remains II," *Korea Magazine* 2 (September 1918): 400–4

The good people of Kanggye[33] would seem to live outside the pale of civilization, so far off are they, and so shut away from the immediate concerns of the nation. We were inclined to pity them until we came to look a little more closely into their world and its surroundings, and now we rather envy them.[34]

The town itself lies within the compass of three streams: the Tongno River[35] to the southwest, the North Creek[36] to the north-west, and the South Creek[37] to the south. There are five roads that branch out from it: one to the north that goes toward Chasŏng[38] past the old fire-signal station, one going east to Changjin,[39] one west to Manp'ojin,[40] and two to the south.

It is along the west road that the writer would like to accompany the reader. As it is the summer season,[41] let us dispense with the highway,

---

32 *KM*: "dead, objects of wonder they will continue to be as more time goes on."

33 Kanggye (江界) is the provincial capital of Chagang Province (慈江道), located in the extreme north-central region of what is today the Democratic People's Republic of Korea, in proximity to the Amnok or Yalu River and the Chinese border

34 *KM* adds here: "The writer has never seen Kanggye and yet he presumes to write something more or less related to it."

35 Tongno kang (禿魯江). Today this river is called the Changja River (將子江).

36 Pukch'ŏn kang (北川江).

37 Namch'ŏn kang (南川江).

38 *KM*: "慈城."

39 *KM*: "長津."

40 *KM*: "麻浦津."

41 *KM*: "and warm for walking."

take a boat instead, and glide gently down the Tongno for some thirty miles, picking up our road again at the end of the stage.

How long may you have to haggle with the boatmen before they sing out to heave away, how many dangers we may have to meet along the winding course of the river, I cannot say, but hardly anything could be more inviting than a run along the river's silver face as we pass the various peaks[42] and points of interest on either side. There is the Great Bear Mountain to the west, 3400 feet high, and a ferry some six miles below Kanggye with the highsounding name of "Righteousness and Virtue."[43]

We go southwest for a time and then we suddenly wheel north, circling the lowlands where the county offices huddle together, past Chungji Peak[44] that rides high up to the south, 4000 feet and more.

Keeping well north from this for about twenty miles more we come to the mouth of the Kŏnp'o, or Dry Creek. Here we disembark, load our pack on a coolie, and set out to walk nearly twelve miles to Manp'ojin on the Yalu. Half the distance is by the bank of a stream over a comparatively level road till we come to the pass of the Three Heroes[45] that rises some sixteen hundred feet and from there we swing down to Manp'ojin, one of the noted guard-stations of old Corea.

Following down the Yalu a mile or so, we cross the ferry and find ourselves on the site of the old capital of Koguryŏ,[46] one of the most interesting landmarks of this ancient people. It is Chinese territory, but all its memories are Corean, its proofs of greatness and its glory. Here are the remains of the ancient walls of T'onggu[47] that was the palace site of the kingdom from 37 BC till 427 AD, or nearly 500 years.[48]

---

42 *KM*: "watched by the various peaks."

43 *KM*: "Kindness, Righteousness and Virtue."

44 *KM*: "中支峯."

45 *KM*: "三傑嶺."

46 *KM*: "高句麗."

47 *KM*: "通溝."

48 There were in fact two Manchuria-based capitals of ancient Koguryŏ during this period. According to the *Samguk sagi*, the first was called Cholbon (卒本) and served as the capital until AD 3, when King Yurimyŏng (瑠璃明王, r. 19 BC–AD 18) moved the capital east to the Yalu River to Kungnae (國內), where it remained until the son of King Kwanggaet'o (廣開土王); King Changsu (長壽王, 394–491; r. 412?–491) moved the capital to P'yŏngyang in 427. Gale's T'onggu (通溝) is a variant name for this second capital of Kungnae.

Kim Pusik,[49] who wrote the *History of the Three Kingdoms*[50] in 1145 AD, was unable to locate it further than to say that it was beyond the Yalu. Other writers were equally indefinite. It awaited the expert knowledge of the modern Japanese archaeologist to definitely locate its limits.[51]

As we walk along the shore approaching the site of the walled city, we pass on our right a magnificent tomb built evidently by hands similar to those that shaped the pyramids. This vast pile is one hundred feet square and forty feet high, made of huge granite blocks, one layer above another in seven terraces capped with a kind of concrete that defies all modern attempts to imitate it.[52] It's called the "General's Tomb" but in reality it is a king's tomb.[53] Down through the valley there are grouped many tombs of kings, twenty in all. On the bricks[54] that served in the building we find inscribed, "May the great king be peaceful as the hills and live eternal as the mountain tops." "May his memory for all ages never, never end." No general would ever think of being buried here. This is a valley of kings and kings alone.[55]

From the tomb to the site of the old city is about five miles,[56] the road leading south-west parallel to the course of the river.

About a quarter of the distance along the way there is to be seen one of the most interesting monuments that remain of ancient Corea.[57] It is some twenty feet high and six feet across the face and was erected in 414 AD.[58]

---

49 *KM*: "金富軾."

50 *KM*: "Kim Pusik (金富軾) who wrote the *Samguk Sa*." Gale means *Samguk sagi*.

51 *KM*: "It required the expert knowledge of the modern archaeologist to definitely locate its borders." Gale writes elsewhere in *KM* on the positive contributions of Japanese archaeology, so the omission here of Japan does not suggest animus.

52 *KM*: "a kind of concrete that laughs to scorn all modern attempts to imitate it."

53 *KM*: "They call it in the Album the 'General's Tomb,' because the people of the place so know it."

54 *KM*: "This we know without a question for on the bricks."

55 *KM*: "Where 'Banzai' echoes today still from the fallen bricks and tiles, we may conclude that it is the valley of kings and kings only." *Banzai* (萬歲), or *manse* in Korea, is a phrase meaning "ten thousand years" and said to royalty, meaning "May Your Majesty live ten thousand years."

56 *KM*: "is about 15 *li*, or 5 miles."

57 *KM*: "along the way brings you to."

58 *KM*: "It is spoken of in 'Antiquarian Study' in the January number of the *Magazine*, 'some twenty feet high, and six feet across the face, it was erected in 414 AD and is the most ancient Korean monumental stone known today.' What it talks of cannot but be of interest to students of Korea. The story it tells you

Half-way to the city, we come to a group of eleven tombs only one of which we shall notice. It is the *Samsil*[59] or Tomb of the Three Chambers, built separate from each other but united by subterranean passages. The work has been done in the same substantial way as the tombs of Uhyŏlli[60] and the mural paintings and, like those, has outlasted all time.

This tomb is one of the halls of the buried-alive, a grim chamber of death.[61] Think of it! Five couples with bright cheeks and high hopes were pushed alive into this cavern to keep the dead king company. The door was sealed fast with a flat rock and marked with a signet-ring and ten thousand tons of granite between them and the blue sky. Imagine the sensations of these young left to die in the dark.[62] It was custom in these days for high officials to give their daughters as proof of their devotion to the dead king. Drop a tear of pity, ye who pass, for these gentle victims of fifteen hundred years ago.[63]

The writer recalls as if it were but yesterday his first reading of the Fourth Voyage of Sinbad the Sailor, and remembers how his hair stood on end as he accompanied that redoubtable prevaricator through the charnel house that had locked him in. Sinbad seemingly had made up his story out of whole cloth, but here is the real thing before our very eyes, among which we walk and wonder.

Two miles[64] further brings us to the town and three more[65] leads up to the hill fortress before which are five other tombs, one marked Older Brother and one Younger. Other tombs lie three miles[66] to the southwest on the flat lands of the Yalu.

---

will find outlined in the article mentioned above." The article Gale refers to is "Antiquarian Studies," *Korea Magazine* 2 (January 1918): 2–5. The monument Gale describes is the King Kwanggaet'o Stele (Kwanggaet'o wangnŭng pi 廣開土王陵碑), the earliest dated inscription in Korean, which details the military exploits of King Kwanggaet'o.

59 *KM*: "三室."
60 *KM*: "(June Magazine)."
61 *KM*: "a grim chamber of the dead as told of in *Korea Magazine*, October, 1917." See "Ancient Burial in Korea," *Korea Magazine* 1 (October 1917): 436–8.
62 *KM*: "Imagine the sensations of these gay young birds clipped of hope and wing forever, dying in the dark, shut away from the world for fifteen hundred years."
63 *KM*: "these gentle victims who had but to do and die."
64 *KM*: "five *li*."
65 *KM*: "and ten *li* behind it."
66 *KM*: "ten *li* further."

Illustration 20. "Emperor Kojong's State Funeral Procession and Citizen Onlookers," March 3, 1919.

This is one of the most interesting places in all Corea and yet not Corea. When the reader has the good fortune to visit the place he must look for a brick or tile marked,[67] *Ch'ŏnch'u manse yŏnggo*, "May your life endless be," and *Pogo kŏn'gon sangp'il*, "Keep sound and well a mate for Heaven and Earth."[68]

---

67 *KM*: "When the writer has the good fortune to visit the place he will look for a brick, or tile souvenir, marked." It seems as if the *Korea Magazine* version was written first and then revised into the *OC* version after Gale had visited the tombs.

68 *KM*: "*May Your Life Endless Be* (千秋萬歲永固). *Keep sound and well, a mate for Heaven And Earth* (保固乾坤相畢)." These inscriptions may be found on the so-called Tomb of a Thousand Autumns (Ch'ŏnch'u ch'ong 千秋塚), which draws its name from the former inscription.

When Kings Die
Old Corea, 72–5; Gale Papers, Box 9.31 "WHEN KINGS DIE"; *Korea Magazine* 3 (March 1919): 98–104

Note: The late Prince Yi, Senior, who died on Jan. 21st, 1919, and was buried on the 4th of March, was king of Corea from 1864 till 1907 AD,[69] and was likely the last ever that will be carried out according to ancient rites. The burial ceremony followed the State Book of Funeral Forms.[70]

All ceremonies respecting royalty have long since been decided on, even to the smallest details. Especially is this true of what pertains to the king's death, the greatest event that can happen in the land.[71] When it is seen that mortal illness is upon the king, he is taken to a specially designated place in the Palace and watched by his faithful eunuchs. As he breathes his last they test by cotton wool before the nose the exact moment when life ceases, then, turning the body with the head towards the east,[72] they remain for a time in silence.

Following the king's death, the first act is the summoning of the soul. A eunuch, with the king's inner coat in his hand, hastily ascends the roof of the palace and shouts, "*sangwi pok, sangwi pok, sangwi pok*" (Soul of the Highest, return, return, return!).[73] At this call, the spirit, that has been shot off into space by death, hurries back

---

69 The introduction appearing in the *Korea Magazine* differs markedly from this point: "According to present announcements it looks as though he would be interred after the manner of the ancient kings. If this be so, the funeral rites will follow somewhat this outline taken from the state Book of funeral ceremonies (國朝喪禮補編). Editor." Although the *KM* version hews more closely to the version in Box 9.31 of the Gale Papers, all three versions exhibit slight variations, noted below.

70 This refers to the *State Manual of Rites* (Ŭigwe 儀軌) of the Chosŏn dynasty, official records of the Superintendency (Togam 都監), which prescribed the proper conducting of rites by the state. Along with funerary rites (*hyungnye* 凶禮), these included ancestral worship rites (*killye* 吉禮), nuptial rites (*karye* 家禮), reception of foreign envoys (*pillye* 賓禮), and military rites (*kullye* 軍禮).

71 Gale Papers, Box 9.31: "than which there is nothing greater in all the happenings of the state."

72 Ibid.: "and then turning his head toward the east."

73 上位復.

into the garment, and remains the constant companion of the body till it is finally placed into the tomb.[74]

The remains are then set in order[75] – hands, feet and face. A small horn tablet is placed in the mouth to keep the teeth from setting too closely, for in the performance of the rites it is necessary that the jaws be kept slightly open.

A table of food is brought in and the attendants bow. Though the king is dead, his spirit lives, and food is faithfully prepared for it.[76]

The Crown Prince, now king, and other relatives, with hair down, outer garments off, and the left shoulder bared, begin the national wail of "*Aigo! Aigo!*" Ministers are called and the State is informed.

The whole land would seem to have fallen under an interdict. For seven months while the body awaits burial, all sacrifices except those to the *Sajik* (Mother-Earth God) are done away with. No markets are held for five days and no music is heard for three years. For seven months weddings are forbidden. Ordinary officials may not marry for a year; the highest, not for three years.

Three Officers of State are specially appointed: one to see to the mortuary, one to the funeral, and one to the tomb.

In the death hall the body is at once closed round with screens and covered with an awning. Eunuchs, with the aid of the king's relatives, perform a ceremonial washing with rice water mixed with incense. They comb the royal hair and put on specially prepared royal robes. Hair that comes off is placed in a pocket along with the parings of the nails to be buried with the body.

Food is again brought and officials take part in showing honour.[77]

Weeping places are assigned to the Crown Prince and others, the points of the compass always being kept carefully in mind.

The pouring of rice and pearls into the mouth of the dead is a solemn rite performed by the Crown Prince, the Prime Minister and others standing by.[78]

---

74 Gale Papers, Box 9.31: "and from this on is the constant accompaniment of the body till the final placing in the tomb."

75 Ibid.: "This done the body is then set in order."

76 Ibid.: "and food is as faithfully presented as to the living." The *KM* version follows this phrasing.

77 Ibid.: "When this is finished food is again brought and officials take various parts in doing honour." The *KM* version follows this phrasing.

78 Ibid.; *KM*: "and others, the horn tablet of course having been removed. The writer is unable to say as to the exact meaning of this ceremony."

During the preparatory days, if the weather is warm, ice is placed under the catafalque.[79]

Three days after death a minister is sent to make the announcement to the *Sajik*[80] and to the ancestral spirits in the Royal Mausoleum.

Then follows the wrapping of the body, a complicated ceremony, done in two parts: one on the fourth day and one on the fifth. When finished, the body is at once removed to the mortuary, a little brick-lined hut.[81]

The lacquered coffin is sealed up and the door of the hut on the east side is closed and papered so as to stop every chink. Outside to the south stands a chair with a folded silk tablet on it to which the soul retreats[82] after returning to the inner garment at the call from the roof. On the east of the mortuary is the *myŏngjŏng*,[83] a banner with the king's name written on it, stating that it is he who is lying in the coffin.[84] This accompanies the body to the tomb and is finally buried with it.

Beside this coffin-banner there is a red silk tent which is erected as a sleeping apartment for the soul, with quilts, pillows, etc. On the south side of the sleeping tent stands a table with the last will and testament of the king and his appointment of a successor.

During this time seven months pass by and food is offered daily, night and morning, to the spirit,[85] and the bed-chamber is kept in order.[86] The offerings are accompanied by prayers, sacrifices and wailings.

Three days before the great funeral procession, word is again sent to the *Sajik* and the ancestral spirits, saying that the funeral will take place. An audience is then held, before the spirit of the dead.[87] Incense is burned, candles are lit, libations and food are offered.[88] Prayers are read and followed by an order that the chamber of the dead is to be opened.

---

79 Gale Papers, Box 9.31: "catafalque but is never used before the 2nd moon."
    A catafalque is the wooden framework supporting the coffin of a distinguished figure during a funeral or while lying in state.

80 Ibid.; *KM*: "*Sajik*, the God Mother Earth."

81 Gale Papers, Box 9.31; *KM*: "a little hut built of bricks inside the main hall."

82 Gale Papers, Box 9.31: "to which the soul has retreated."

83 銘旌.

84 Gale Papers, Box 9.31: "with the name of the king written on it as the one lying in the coffin."

85 *KM*: "with the daily round of food offered night and morning to the spirit."

86 Gale Papers, Box 9.31: "the bed chamber is kept constantly ready."

87 Ibid.; *KM*: "Immediately an audience is held, not an audience before the new king, but an audience before the spirit of the dead."

88 Gale Papers, Box 9.31; *KM*: "libations offered, and food placed before the soul."

All the officers wail, pass before the seat of the soul and then retire to their appointed places. The prayer-roll is then burned and the soul's seat removed to the outside of the hall. The mortuary is then unsealed and the coffin is taken out and placed on the bier.[89]

The Chief Constable of the city rides ahead as a warning to evil spirits. Other officers following are the Mayor of Seoul, the Chief Justice, the Minister of Finance, and a division of soldiers. Then follow sixteen archers, armed and accoutered, and carrying red clubs. They march ahead as guardians of the burial implements.[90]

On each side red arrow flags announce to men and angels that this is the procession of His Majesty the King.

Here also are seen the four gods of the compass points. The Red Bird and Blue Dragon are on the left; the White Tiger and Black Warrior are on the right. These represent royalty and are protectors against evil spirits and baleful influences.[91] Riding high in the midst is the god of the Middle Region, a yellow dragon pictured on a flag. Thus was China the Middle Kingdom when yellow ruled.[92]

Then come cymbal and drum-bearers wearing red coats and leather caps and beating time as they march. Six pikes pass, three on each side having the character *chŏng* (丁) written on their tablet-board, *chŏng* being a great lord of the spirit world. Dragon-horses and flying creatures are pictured on flags.

A huge banner carried in the middle of the procession has written on it "Peace on Earth." One asks what this has to do with the king's death.[93] The answer is, "Though the king is dead his spirit lives and all is well."

Six trumpeters pass, three on each side. Two have long trumpets, two have smaller ones, two have still shorter ones and all are being blown.

Two huge bamboo horses, ready and saddled, come next, just as they do in the royal procession of a live king.[94] Six men, carrying bunches

---

89 Gale Papers, Box 9.31, and *KM* add here the sentence, "When all has been made ready the procession goes forth."

90 Gale Papers, Box 9.31: "They encircle as spirit guards the burial implements that follow."

91 Ibid.: "guardians against evil spirits and influences."

92 Ibid.: "rules."

93 Gale Papers, Box 9.31; *KM*: "One asks why this should be seeing the king is dead."

94 Gale Papers, Box 9.31; *KM*: "Two horses saddled and made ready come next just as in the royal procession when the king lived."

of leopard bones tied high on the end of a pike-pole, march, three on either side; other bearers have bear's bones.

Again saddled horses pass by, then flags and banners, and again horses. Ten bearers swing by, five on each side with long poles sloping over the shoulder.

As the procession advances, golden stirrups are seen and flags marked, "Long Live the King."[95] Then go sword bearers, gilded palanquins, purple coats, and cloth caps. Still the procession goes on and on with gods of the compass points, silver dishes for dipping water, silver bowls, horses with saddles, green umbrellas riding on either side.

Then comes a "spirit" chair[96] carried by thirty men wearing purple coats. The custom of the "spirit" chair comes down from the Emperor Chinsi,[97] who built the Great Wall of China. He used a false chair when he went out in order to mislead those who wished to do him harm. The practice has been followed by later kingdoms in China and Corea, and the custom is followed, be it a dead or a living king.[98]

Next come groups carrying halberts,[99] phoenix-fans, and dragon fans; then are followed by bands of music and a small chair carrying the last words and wishes of the king, and an officer with the royal seals.[100]

Next are officials dressed in black, bearing crystal staves and gilded halberts; then red lantern bearers; then the chair in which rides the spirit of the king borne by thirty men. Again amid green umbrellas, is a censer-chair[101] borne by fifteen men, then a wheeled chair for the soul borne by sixty men, then half a hundred banners with poems written on them, implements for burial, etc., chair after chair.

Next there is the high bier[102] that is used to convey the coffin from the large bier to the tomb, borne by a hundred and forty men, five hundred torch-bearers accompanying, two hundred and fifty on each side. Following these pass five hundred candle-bearers, many bell ringers,

---

95 Gale Papers, Box 9.31; *KM*: "On comes the procession with golden stirrups, flags marked 'Long live the King' though he be already dead."

96 Gale Papers, Box 9.31; *KM*: "an imitation spirit-chair."

97 Emperor Chinsi (秦始皇 Ch. Qin Shi Huang, 259–210 BC; r. 247–220 BC).

98 Gale Papers, Box 9.31; *KM*: "and as it s custom for the living king so the dead is likewise served."

99 Gale Papers, Box 9.31; *KM*: "Following come groups carrying battle axes."

100 Gale Papers, Box 9.31: "royal seals, and a chair with other seals attached."

101 Ibid.: "Again red lanterns, white lanterns, green unbrellas; then a censer-chair."

102 *KM*: "Then comes a light bier."

symbol flag bearers, metal lantern carriers, and finally the great coffin carried by two hundred men, with hundreds of torch-bearers wearing gags in their mouths to insure silence.

A general rides just in front as guardian of the dead, with two attendants, one on each side. Two directors dressed in mourning follow, twenty palace maids, numbers of eunuchs, grave guards with white sticks in hand, saddled-horses, bearers of the great seal, a false chair carried by thirty men, officers and soldiers armed and dressed in mail, forty stewards of the palace. Officers follow, some bearing the king's coat of mail, others his helmet, others his bow and arrows, others his clothes, then the princes' ministers, royal secretaries, and an endless throng of people.

Such is the general order of the procession.

On the day of the interment, sacrifice is offered at the sacrificial shrines[103] and at fifty other places as well as at the hills and streams along the way. With much form and ceremony, the tablet made of mulberry wood, with its case and stand, is carried to the tomb, but as yet no characters are written upon it.

On reaching the tomb which is built on the face of a hill, with two chambers, one inner and one outer, and an entrance in front, the eunuchs take off the outer cloth covering and carry the coffin into the first chamber. There the Prime Minister brushes it clean of all dust and defilement, and covers it with three palls, green, blue and red, while the name-banner or *myŏngjŏng* is placed on top.

At a call from the Minister of the Left the coffin is then taken into the inner chamber and put in its final resting place with head to the north. All wail, the Crown Prince and others included, bowing four times.

The condolences, written on silk or paper, are placed in a box and put in one part of the tomb while, to the south of it, is placed another box of presents, silk and jade ornaments. Symbol-banners are set up round about the chamber.

Eunuchs then bring the clothing formerly worn by the dead and place it on the coffin. Wailings and genuflections[104] follow.

Thus ends the service, and the new king or Crown Prince takes his departure.

------

103 Gale Papers, Box 9.31; *KM*: "On the day of the funeral sacrifice is offered at the ancestral shrines."
104 Gale Papers, Box 9.31; *KM*: "bowings."

The gates of the inner chamber are closed; a ceremonial dropping of clay about the outer circle takes place, and the final rounding off of the tomb.

The biographical tablets, made of porcelain, into which are burned the recorded life of the king, are buried just under the north side of the sacrificial table that stands before the mound. Not only does this large stone table stand in front, but a stone lantern as well, guardian pillars, sometimes called "Squirrel-stones," to protect the dead from any obnoxious spirits of the woods. Two civil officials and two military, cut in stone, stand one on each side. Four tigers and four sheep, also done in stone,[105] seated alternately with faces outward, encircle the large mound guarding the dead as well.[106] These animals represent the two classes that wait on the king: the sheep, the civil officials, the tigers, the military.

When the entrance is closed, the officials gather in the palace hall erected not far from the tomb to complete the last rite connected with the royal burial. The master of ceremonies places three stands in order,[107] one to the north of the tablet,[108] and two others at the side, one for the ink-stone and one for the pens. Everything needed is made ready: ink, towels of fine linen, incense water. The officers appointed to the service take their places, staff in hand, each bowing forward heavily as though to steady his trembling frame. The appointed official reads the prayer, bathes his hands,[109] steps before the "soul-seat," kneels, takes the box with the tablet in it and places it on the first stand. He removes the cover so that the tablet of mulberry wood may be seen. This he washes with incense water, dries with the linen towel, and places on its back so that it may be written upon. The Director then leads the Crown Prince (now king) in before the tablet, while the writer writes the names, titles, and honourable designations of his late majesty[110] down the face of the tablet. It is then lacquered over and placed on its stand. The silken tablet that occupied the "soul-seat" is buried, having fulfilled its duty, and the wooden tablet is placed in the royal palace in the capital for three years after which time it is removed to the mausoleum. Thus ends this outline of the burial of a king.

---

105 Gale Papers, Box 9.31 and *KM* omit "also done in stone."

106 Gale Papers, Box 9.31: "guarding the dead against evil."

107 Ibid.: "three stands in the hall."

108 Gale Papers, Box 9.31; *KM*: "one to the north of the Soul Seat for the tablet."

109 Gale Papers, Box 9.31: "The new king being present, the prayer reader bathes his hands."

110 Ibid.: "names, titles of his late majesty."

Hollanders in Corea
Old Corea, 76–8;
Korea Magazine 1 (March 1917): 101–6

There were Dutchmen in Corea from 1627 to 1666 (how much longer
we do not know) but this is not once mentioned in the writings of
that period. This is an interesting comment on the nature of the old-
time Corean.

The only record about these Hollanders that the writer has found is
in a book called *T'ongmun'gwan chi* that deals with Corea's relations
with China and Japan.[111] The Japanese Lord of Tsushima sent an inquiry about the Hollanders and his question is briefly noted in the
book. The paragraph notes erroneously that a Dutch ship was wrecked
off Chindo[112] whereas it was off Quelpart.[113] The Encyclopedia, *Munhŏn pigo*,[114] copies this statement from the *T'ongmun*, mistakes and all.
No one took the trouble to verify the facts or correct the statement.
Evidently in those days the Foreigner was outside the pale of recognition. Japan, on the other hand, accorded him a kindly welcome that
stands markedly in contrast.

In the year 1627 a Dutch ship, off its course, drifted to the coast of
Corea, as the ship's water supply had run short and three young men
were sent ashore to get some, but, instead of getting water, they found
themselves taken prisoner. Two died fighting for their captors against
the Manchu, and one, a man with a red beard called John Wettevree,
remained permanently at the Corean court.[115] At the time when Milton,

---

111 *T'ongmun'gwan chi* (通文館志 Records of the Office of Interpreters, 1720) was
     a record of the activities of the Interpreters' Bureau (Sayŏgwŏn 司譯院) com-
     piled by the interpreter Kim Chinam (金指南, 1654–?) and later supplemented
     in 1778, 1881, and 1888. There are in fact several Korean sources that mention
     this episode, sources that were, according to Gari Ledyard, "buried in large
     collections of annals, memoirs and literary collections" that have become
     available only in the post-war era. See Ledyard, *The Dutch Come to Korea*, 13.

112 珍島.

113 This is the English name for what is today more commonly known in English
     as Jeju Island (Chejudo).

114 文獻備考.

115 This information is based on "Account of a Shipwreck of a Dutch Vessel on
     the Coast of the Isle of Quelpart," the first eyewitness account of Korea in a
     Western language. Relating his first meeting with Wettevree, Hendrick Hamel

Cromwell and Jeremy Taylor were about their several affairs in England, Wettevree was dressed in Corean white garments and learning to eat *kimch'i* pickle with a pair of chopsticks.

On August 15th, 1653, another famous Dutch wreck took place. Out of sixty-four men, thirty-six managed to get ashore. A more miserable plight cannot be imagined. Pounded by wind and waves, exhaustion almost to the point of death, and huddled under a piece of driftwood-tarpaulin, the Hollanders made their first acquaintance with the people of Corea. They were made to bow in the dust to the magistrate and to humble themselves before a concourse of several thousand people.

The remnants of the unlucky ship were hauled ashore, which, however, meant nothing to them any longer. Their one thought was to escape at once from this inhospitable place. Vain thought! Long years were to pass over the heads of most of them before a day of hope dawned. To most of them it never came.

The men were brought before the governor of the island several times but neither questions nor answers were understood by either side. On October 29th, however, they were summoned to a new inquiry. Here they found a Corean sitting beside the governor wearing a great red beard. This was John Wettevree who had been a captive for 26 years. He could with difficulty speak his own language but little by little his understanding cleared.[116]

The first governor of the island where the ship was wrecked was a kind-hearted man, but a change of administration brought a bad successor. The prisoners were not fed and scantily clad. One night they made an attempt to steal away but the ubiquitous Corean dog gave notice and it fell through.

In May 1654 they were ordered to Seoul. Across the uncertain stretch of sea they made their way to Haenam, where Paul John Coole, a young

---

reports that two of Wettevree's companions, "Theodoric Gerards" and "John Pieters" "had been kill'd 17 or 18 Years since in the Wars, when the Tartars invaded Corea." This dates their death to the Manchu invasions of 1636. See Hendrik Hamel, "Account of a Shipwreck of a Dutch Vessel on the Coast of the Isle of Quelpart, Description of the Kingdom of Korea," *Transactions of the Royal Asiatic Society – Korea Branch* 9 (1918): 91–148.

116 Hamel wrote on their exchange, "It was very surprising, and even wonderful, that a Man of 58 Years of Age, as he then was, should so forget his Mother-tongue, that we had much to do at first to understand him; but it must be observ'd that he recover'd it again in a month." Ibid.

gunner of the sea, died and was buried.[117] The list of towns they stopped at on their way to Seoul is given by Hamel, the scribe of the party.

King Hyojong[118] was then thirty-five years of age, and it was the fifth year of his reign. He ordered the whole party of Hollanders be brought before him, informed them that it was not the custom of Corea to let strangers depart, and that they must resign themselves to end their days in his kingdom. He commanded them to show him something in the way of special skill, and the poor lads did the best they could in singing, dancing, leap-frog and the like. They were then enrolled in the king's bodyguard and for a time enjoyed a measure of comfort. Crowds of men, women and children came to see them, but the general of the forces found this a nuisance and put a stop to sightseers.

In August 1654 the Manchu Tartar came to collect his tribute and the Dutchmen were all hurried off to Namhan fortress to remain hidden until he departed.

The Hollanders, who were probably ill-clad, speak of the cold of the following winter as "vehement." The Han River was frozen over and they were imprisoned in a miserable hovel.

The Manchu came again in March 1655 and Henry Jans and Henry Bos, two of the castaways, rashly made petition to him to carry them back to China. The Manchu was inclined, at first, to listen but Corea got word of it. Money was paid over to square the matter, and the two culprits were brought to Seoul where they were put in prison and never heard of again.

An attempt was made by the leaders of the State to have the whole party destroyed, but the King, his brother, and the general of the forces, opposed this action. Once, when the King's brother, Prince Inp'yǒng,[119] was passing their place of confinement, a number of the prisoners bowed in the dust before him and prayed that he would have mercy. He was moved with compassion and Hamel says it was through him and His Majesty that they were not all destroyed.

---

117 Hamel writes, "The next morning having taken a very slender repast we came
     to the town of Jeham, where Paul John Cools of Piermerende, our Gunner
     dy'd, having never enjoy'd his health since our Shipwreck." Ibid. Haenam
     (海南) is a city in South Chŏlla Province on the extreme southwestern tip of
     Korea, adjacent to Chindo, though the location of Hamel's "Jeham" is unclear.
118 King Hyojong (孝宗, 1619–59; r. 1649–59).
119 麟坪大君.

Corea remained in constant fear lest these exiles should come into touch with the Manchu, make their escape to Peking, and so bring trouble on the State. It was finally decided to rid the capital of this anxiety by sending them all to Chŏlla Province. Thirty-three in number they were, "the miserable remains of our shipwreck," says Hamel. Thus they came to Kangjin[120] on the south coast. In 1657 we find them begging from door to door. Ignorant governors of the district treated them like animals but the common people were inclined to be charitable and kind.

In 1660 when they had already been prisoners and exiles for seven years, a dreadful famine overtook the land, the effects of which were felt till 1663. Eleven of their number seem to have died in this famine for only twenty-two are ever spoken of again.

They were found to be a burden on the county-seat at Kangjin, and were sent twelve to Suyŏng, five to Sunch'ŏn and five to Namhae.[121] The one thought that still possessed them was to get away and escape to Japan – risk any danger of life on the sea in order to make their exit from this place of torment.

The admiral of the province who resided at Suyŏng on their first arrival was a kind-hearted man, but he soon left and his successor seemed to be an incarnate spirit of evil.

Hamel tells of two comets that appeared in 1664 and the people in their anxiety asked the Hollanders what they thought of them. "Portents of evil," was their answer, "plague, war and famine." This was the Corean's interpretation also, so they found some common ground of fear at least in this. The year 1665 saw the Black Plague in London. Evidently the comet-signals were not in vain as far as the Western Hemisphere was concerned.

The next year was the year of the Great Fire in London. The misery of the little group of prisoners had reached its climax. A new governor used them with all the severity of his predecessor. He obliged them the live-long day to trample thick mud mortar with their bare feet, while the daily allowance of food was scarcely enough to keep them alive.

At last the chance of escape came and "with provisions, pots of water and a frying-pan" in their little boat, eight of them stole out of the harbour on the morning of the 5th of September.

---

120 康津.

121 Although the locations of Sunch'ŏn and Namhae, which Hamel renders "Siunschein" and "Naminan," may be confirmed, the final location where twelve of the prisoners went, "Suyŏng" (Gale: Sooyung; Hamel: Saysiano), is unclear.

On the same day, Sept. 5th 1666, Samuel Pepys is writing in London, "About two in the morning my wife calls me up and tells me of the new cryes of fire, it being come to Barking Church, which is the bottom of our lane. I up, and finding it so, resolved presently to take her away and did, and took my gold which was about 2350 pounds. Lord! What a sight it was by moonlight to see the whole city almost on fire."[122]

The Hollanders cleared the port, sailed all night, and next morning found themselves near the islands of Japan. They drifted about till the 8th when they were taken in hand by two sworded men. The Hollanders thought these must be dangerous warriors. The Coreans had told them that the Japanese killed everybody and they were afraid as none of them had ever been to Japan before. But their fears were groundless, for the warriors of Gotō[123] were kind in heart. They comforted them, gave them food and shelter, and by signs assured them they would take them to Nagasaki.

On Sept. 14th they arrived at their journey's end and found seven ships of Holland riding at anchor. After an exile of thirteen years and twenty-eight days they were once more among their countrymen.

After receiving much kindness from the Japanese they set sail on October 25th and arrived in Holland on July 20, 1668.

The fourteen who remained in Corea were never heard of again. There were five at Sunch'ŏn, five at Namhae, and four at Suyŏng.

It is strange that no Corean ever mentions the presence of the foreigner throughout the forty years (1627–1666). Men like Song Siyŏl, Yu Kŏ[124] and others who wrote on every conceivable subject, must often have seen Wettevree. The exclusive spirit of Corea that would have

---

122 *The Diary of Samuel Pepys*, Wednesday, September 5, 1666. Samuel Pepys (1633–1703) was an administrator of the British Royal Navy and a member of parliament in the seventeenth century. His private diary, covering a period from 1660 to 1669, was first published in the nineteenth century and is an important primary source on the English Restoration period.

123 Gotō (五島) is actually a five-island archipelago off the western coast of Kyūshū in the East China Sea.

124 Yu Kŏ (柳椐, 1613–91) was a government minister and literatus of the seventeenth century.

nothing to do with the outside barbarian, that foolish pride that looked down on every other race of men, was so common, and all pervading, that kind-hearted officials and even the king himself could not withstand it. No writer would sell his pen by recording the appearance, the doings, or the history, of these unspeakable outlanders.

Had the Mings been on the throne of China instead of the Manchus, it is possible that a conference would have been held and the wrecked crew sent to Peking to make their way home; but the Manchu was an imitation imperial whom the Corean wanted nothing to do with, and so the unfortunates were caught between the great unknown world and the Manchu Empire, neither of which Corea desired, for a moment, to be on speaking terms with.

Superstitions

This section continues Gale's foray into the supernatural and the occult, an exploration that seems to have intensified during his last decade in Korea. Gale's interest in such themes may be surmised from the Korean works he selected for translation later in his career and from various articles appearing in *Korea Magazine*.[1] The original typescript of this section is of a more substantial length, but two chapters, "Pak's Experiences" and "Concerning the Occult," are included in *Pen Pictures* and so have not been reproduced here. Considered in their original format, however, the chapters constituting "Superstitions" together represent an informed, sympathetic, and at times credulous accounting from a "Christian" writer genuinely captivated by his seductively supernatural subject matter.

Despite the somewhat dismissive title of the section, the subjects are treated not as baseless remnants of the premodern era but as strong beliefs and convictions, backed by an extensive cultural and in some cases literary tradition. Gale's discussion of the animal symbols of the Chinese zodiac is whimsical and somewhat perfunctory, a fitting addition to *Korea Magazine* and its mission of mediating East Asian culture for readers of various levels of familiarity. However, at no point in this essay on "animal superstitions" are such beliefs dismissed as groundless astrology, despite the complete lack of consanguinity with the Christian tradition. In "The Spirit Medium," Gale's Christian moral judgments

---

1 See, for example, "That Evil Spirit," *Korea Magazine* 1 (September 1917): 390–1, where he writes about the spirit medium.

begin to surface in his discussion of shamans. Although drawing his observations largely from mid-eighteenth-century descriptions by the scholar Yi Ik, Gale offers no counter to Yi's critiques and in fact takes liberties in translating Yi's more neutral *songmin* (氓俗 common people) as "stupid, unlettered country folk" who employ mediums to pray on their behalf, suggesting the gullibility of commoners in being deceived by such superstition. Curiously, however, even in this seeming antithesis of Christian faith – possession by spirits of the deceased – Gale draws a parallel to Christian beliefs and in the process subsumes Korean animism within his broader Confucio-Christian deistic discourse. Gale not only acknowledges the reality of spirit possession but claims this as the counterpart to "Christian" possession: "At the present time there are a great many such people throughout the country, but the spirit that possesses them is of the evil order, not the good." Thus for Gale the question of spirit possession in the Korean animistic tradition was not one of veracity but morality, where the spirit medium would have to be led away from the "evil," demonic force and toward the "good" of Christian faith, presumably the Holy Spirit. While the tone of "The Spirit Medium" is slightly judgmental, in characteristic fashion the main thrust originates from a preponderance of textual sources and thoughtful, bordering on anthropological, observation.

"One of the Immortals" is Gale's translation of a short story by the mid-Chosŏn literatus Hong Manjong (洪萬宗, 1643–1725), who wrote prolifically on literary critique, especially poetry, and Taoist philosophy. Although another version of this story appeared in the early nineteenth-century *Kimun ch'onghwa* (記聞叢話),[2] a collection of unofficial narratives (*yadam* 野談) from which Gale drew many translations that appear in this volume's "Short Stories" section, a comparison of these versions confirms that Gale's translation is of Hong's work. The book that contains this story, Hong's *Suno chi* (旬五志, 1678), combines themes of history with Taoist supernatural beliefs, a combination that would have appealed to Gale. This particular narrative reflects the feelings of despair, discord, and disillusionment that reigned in seventeenth-century Korea following devastating invasions by Japan from the south and the Manchus from the north less than two generations later. For Hong and many like him, the transcendental existence

---

2 The *yadam* genre and *Kimun ch'onghwa* in particular will be discussed below in the introduction to "Short Stories."

of the Taoist hermit removed from the secular world may have offered a comforting alternative to the Confucian capital, its confidence in the perfectability of man shaken by successive war and suffering.

Guardians of the Year
Old Corea, 79;
E.T., *Korea Magazine* 1 (January 1917): 25–6

The New Year season in the Far East is enlivened today by picture postcards and other illustrations announcing the tutelary animal of the year. Nineteen hundred and twenty one was the year of the Cock, and 1933 will be the next Cock year; 1922 is the year of the dog and his barkings may be heard all over the planet.[3] The twelve animal guardians of the great circles of the sun[4] are the Rat, the Ox, the Tiger, the Rabbit, the Dragon, the Snake, the Horse, the Sheep, the Monkey, the Cock,[5] the Dog and the Pig.

It may interest those[6] who have not yet discovered under which animal they were born to find out how far they resemble their presiding animal.[7] Nineteen hundred was the year of the Rat,[8] so is every year which adds or subtracts twelve. Taking the order indicated above and going backwards on the list to your birth year you can find out what animal claims you.[9] The last year of the Pig was 1911, that of the Dog 1910, that of the Cock 1909, and so on.

It would be interesting to guess your year from your knowledge of your inner self. For example, you might mark your leading

---

3 *KM*: "of the year. Nineteen and sixteen, that has just passed, was the year of the Dragon, and 1928 will be the next dragon year to come. This, upon which we have now entered, is the year of the Snake, an uncanny creature to have over us in control."

4 *KM*: "There are twelve animals in all that are set as guardians of these great circles of the sun."

5 *KM*: "Rooster."

6 *KM*: "the readers of the *Magazine*."

7 *KM*: "born under, to seek out and find just in how far each resembles the creature that presides over him."

8 *KM*: "1912 was also a Rat year."

9 *KM*: "Taking the order indicated above, you can find by going back on the list, a year for each animal, just when your own comes."

characteristics thus: I, So-and-So, dislike hard work, 90%,[10] love eating and sleeping, 10%.[11] Under these circumstances you would doubtless belong to the Pig, who is indifferent to hard work, and is one of the greatest eaters and sleepers in the world.[12]

Another person finds that he is inclined to grimace and make people laugh; he hardly knows why.[13] Doubtless it is due to the monkey that presided over his birth; 1884 would be his year, or perhaps 1896.[14]

Another is given to boasting of[15] what he has done and wants to be looked at. He cannot help it, for he is just twenty-five years old and the Cock is his guardian.[16] Some men are born to go steadily on with their daily work having no opinions about anything else. They eat their hay or bran-mash just as it is given them, and step through life at a pace of two and a half miles an hour. Such folks are thirty-three years old, or forty-five,[17] and have to do with the Ox. Others again who love cheese and Welsh rare-bit and are inclined to nibble in holes and corners in a way displeasing to their neighbours belong to the Rat 1876, or 1888.

The whole list might be run through thus; or we may judge of their year by a person's looks.[18] Some people wear the expression of a horse; you never see them without thinking of that noble animal. They belong to 1882 and are of the Horse year. Others have a timid glance and a peculiar flat note to the voice that suggests the Sheep, 1883. So the whole list may be expounded.

It is supposed that the idea of this guardian group came from the Tartars, and was introduced by Mongols who pitched their tents in the far distant region of the Altai Mountains. They were barbarians but

---

10 *KM*: "love of hard work, 10?"

11 *KM*: "love eating and sleeping, 50%, like crowing over other people, 25%, and so on."

12 *KM*: "making it evident that your year is that of the Pig, the greatest eater and sleeper in the world, or some other equally comfortable animal."

13 *KM* deletes "He hardly knows why," but adds, "He is evidently not born under the year of the cow, for the cow does not do this."

14 *KM*: "Undoubtedly his year is 1884, the year of the Monkey."

15 *KM*: "blowing about."

16 *KM*: "He cannot help it, for the rooster is his guardian, and he is just 32 years old."

17 *KM*: "Such fold are 28 years old or 40."

18 *KM*: "The whole list might be run through thus; or again we may judge of it by the looks of the person."

were conquerors and rulers of the Far East.[19] Genghis Khan probably brought animals with him into China, and China sent them to the farthest corners of the East. Fortune-tellers of the world never dreamed of anything so picturesque as this cycle of twelve animals that forecasts the future.[20]

One of the Immortals
By Hong Manjong (about 1675 AD)[21]
Old Corea, 84–5

Chŏng Kyŏngse was a native of Sangju, South Corea.[22] Once on return from examinations in Seoul he was passing Tanyang when he lost his way in the dusk of evening and suddenly found himself among the mountains. He had gone a distance of some three or four miles when the road, little by little, narrowed down and tall trees cast shadows across the way. He did not know where he was, or where to turn, when all unexpectedly he spied a little thatched hut that nestled among the bushes. Going up to the outer gate he rapped but no voice answered. He pushed in and peeked through the shutters and there he saw an old man, with a light, reading a book. There was something about his look that surprised and startled Chŏng, and so he pushed aside the sliding window and went in.

The old man closed the book and asked, "Who is this that calls on me in the shadows of the night?"

Chŏng told him where he was journeying and how he had lost his way, and added that he was very hungry.

---

19 *KM*: "Altai Mountains, always barbarians, and yet conquerors and rulers of the world."

20 *KM*: "Fortune-tellers at home never dreamed of anything so picturesque as these twelve animals of the cycle, in their forecasts of the future."

21 The book from which this selection was taken, *Sunoji* (旬五志), was published in 1678. Another version of this work with slight variations and an abridged conclusion appears in *Kimun ch'onghwa* as entry no. 609. Kim Tonguk provides a modern Korean translation and extensive annotations, which I refer to below, in Kim, *Kugyŏk Kimun ch'onghwa*.

22 Chŏng Kyŏngse (鄭經世, 1563–1633) was a Chosŏn-era government minister and literatus during the reign of King Injo.

The old man said, "We have no cooked food here in the hills," but he took from his hanging pocket a piece of cake and gave it.

It was round in shape, smooth and sweet as pine-nuts, but what it was made of, Chŏng did not know.

Before he had eaten half of it he felt satisfied and greatly refreshed. He wondered over this and asked, "As I behold the appearance and manner of your Excellency I take note that you are not one of us common mortals. How is it that I have not heard of you before, and that you have not taken occasion to announce your name to the world? Why stay here and let the fragrance of your presence be lost in the hills?"

The old man smiled and said, "You are evidently thinking of a name and fame, great deeds done, literary attainment."

Chŏng said, "Yes, that is my thought."

The old man laughed, "Ha, ha!" and said, "When the world talks of greatness and goodness its highest examples are Confucius and Mencius; and when it speaks of merit and deeds done, there is none who can equal Kwan Chung[23] or An P'yŏngjung,[24] but today they are dead and their bodies have mouldered into dust. A name is all that is left. Would you say that they are still alive? If we talk of writers we have had more of them since the days of Sama Ch'ŏn and Pan'go[25] than can be numbered. The crickets chirp when the dews of autumn begin to fall, and the birds come out in the glorious sunshine of the spring. They enjoy their life, have their little contests and live their day; but when the dew hardens into frost and the flowers pass on their way these voices cease and leave behind them only a touch of sadness. So it is with the writer, he ceases and is gone. My ideas of life differ from those of yours."

Chŏng then asked, "What is Your Excellency's idea?" The old man answered, "The grass first dies, then it rots, so with the trees; in fact it

---

23 Kwan Chung (管仲 Ch. Guan Zhong, 720–645 BC) was a government minister and legal reformer of the Spring and Autumn period (春秋時代, 771–476 BC). Guan carried out political and economic reforms as chancellor under Duke Huan of Qi (齊).

24 An P'yŏngjung (晏平仲 Ch. Yan Pingzhong, ?–500 BC), also known as An Yŏng (晏嬰 Ch. Yan Ying) or simply Anja (晏子 Ch. Yanzi), was an accomplished philosopher, statesman, and prime minister of the state of Qi during the Spring and Autumn period.

25 Pan'go (班固 Ch. Ban Gu, AD 32–92) was a historian of the late Han period best known for compiling the *Han shu* (漢書), or the *History of the Former Han*, the second of China's dynastic histories.

is so with everything, decay appears and death reigns. If there was no death there would be no decay."

Chŏng once again inquired, "Is there any place in the world where death does not reign?"

The old man said, "There certainly is; but the common saying runs, as you will remember, 'If you never go out at night you will never know whether people travel in the dark or not,' so if you never meet one of the immortals you will never know that there are those that never die. Let me tell you that if you breathe according to the law that governs their world for a thousand days you will attain to endless life. Though your body be buried a thousand years it will never decay, but the features will remain eternally the same. Also when the appointed time comes you will break the fetters of the tomb and awake victorious. This is called 'T'aeŭm yŏnhyŏng' (Rising from the dead).[26] The world has lost touch with this law and so I remain alone through the countless ages. This is what I mean by living forever. Why do you seek for that which is eternal among things that are transient?"

Chŏng arose and made a deep bow and said, "I would like to learn from your Excellency."

The old man looked at him for some time and then said, "You are not the material out of which Immortals are made. Do not try it."

He also said, "You will succeed in your examination this year but three times I see you locked behind prison bars. Still the end will turn out favourable. In seven years there will be a great war when ten thousand souls will perish. Thirty three years later an invasion of bandits from the west will take place. Seoul will be taken and the state gods will fall. You will see these things with your own eyes."

He twisted his face and said, "When these things come to pass you will know the world and its ways."

Chŏng asked repeatedly that he would tell him more, but the old man said, "By and by you will know, please do not inquire further."

Chŏng asked his name but the reply was, "I lost my parents in early life and so do not know my name."

---

26 The phrase that Gale translates as "rising from the dead" is *t'aeŭm yŏnhyŏng* (太陰鍊形), a phrase taken from the *Sinsŏn chŏn* (神仙傳 Ch. *Shenxian Zhuan*, Biographies of the Deities and Immortals), a work of Taoist literature dating to the fourth century AD. The passage reads "仙家有太陰鍊形之法" (There exists among Taoist immortals the law of disciplining the body).

It was now late at night and Chŏng being very tired put his head on the wooden pillow and went fast asleep. In the morning all trace was lost of the old man.

Chŏng, mystified, inquired of the host concerning him. The reply was, "Your humble servant knows very little about him. He is a scholar and his name is Yu. He goes hither and thither about the various temples and sometime passes here. He is exceedingly fond of nature. When he comes he sometimes stays several days and then again stays only one. I have never seen what he eats, but when he ascends the hills he seems to fly, not walk."

Chŏng hearing this was greatly bewildered.

In this year he passed his examination it being the 14th of Mallyŏk (1586).[27] Later the Japanese War came when Corea was invaded (1592). Again in the year *kapja* (1624) Yi Kwal's soldiers invaded Seoul,[28] and in *pyŏnja* (1636) the Manchoos came. Also in the spring of *kapsin* (1644) the Empire of the Mings came to an end.

Chŏng, on account of the doings of Yi Chin'gil,[29] was arrested and examined by the judges. Later, on account of Kim Chikchae[30] he was imprisoned in a distant part of Kangwŏn. He also found himself mixed up in the affairs of Kim Mongho[31] and was locked up for a year. This all took place as foretold by the genius.

---

27 Emperor Wanli (萬曆帝, 1563–1620, r. 1572–1620), whom Gale calls "Mallyŏk," was thirteenth emperor of the Ming dynasty.

28 Yi Kwal (李适, 1587–1624) was a military official of the mid-Chosŏn era who led a revolt to install Hŭngan'gun Yi Che (興安君 李瑅) on the throne. The revolt, which lasted just one week before it was suppressed, came to be known as the Yi Kwal Uprising (Yi Kwal chi ran 李适之亂).

29 Yi Chin'gil, the nephew of the government minister Chŏng Yŏrip (鄭汝立, 1546–89), who committed suicide amidst charges of plotting treason, was also implicated in this scandal and was beaten to death on suspicion of illicit correspondence with Chŏng Yŏrip.

30 In the Kim Chikchae Affair of 1612, the Greater Northern Faction (Taebukp'a), in order to eliminate the Lesser Northern Faction (Sobukp'a) from power, implicated Kim Chikchae (1554–1612) on fabricated charges. Under torture, Kim in turn falsely accused Great Northern Faction members in order to remove them from power.

31 Kim Mongho (金夢虎, 1557–1637) was a Chosŏn dynasty government minister and literatus. In 1615, because of the false accusation of Sim Kyŏng (沈憬), he along with Chŏng were interrogated but released due to insufficient evidence.

Chŏng wrote a verse which ran,

My life has hung three times in mortal pain,
And worldly things my soul has yielded up.
From the red dust of many a weary way
I long to hide me where Immortals dwell.

One of the scholars of Yŏngch'ŏn, Kwŏn Hu, was a disciple of Chŏng and a contemporary of my father. They were bosom friends. On his way by once, he told me this story, saying, "The world laughs at the idea of there being Immortals and says it is impossible, but I have heard from the lips of my master that those who betake themselves to the hills and follow this law, live long and have no desire for worldly notice, just like the old man of Tanyang. People no wiser than the beetles, who fly about in summer and question as to the possibility of ice in winter, by saying that there are no genii, prove themselves the laughing stock of those who are real masters. Chŏng told me to say nothing about this so I kept to myself for years and only now tell you."

鄭愚伏經世 [尙州人] 嘗赴擧洛中 路過丹陽 夜失道 投山谷間 約行十餘里 路逕漸微 松檜參天 不知所之 忽見茅屋數間 隱暎於林即 進叩叩其扉 寂然無人 遂從牕隙窺見有一老人 明燭看書 神采清癯 愚伏推牕而入老人掩卷問曰何來何客深夜到此愚伏具道其由且告之饑老人曰 山中無食因於 一團餅與之 甘滑如栢子 不知爲何物也愚伏吃未半 頓覺豊飽 心異之仍問曰 觀主人形貌 有異凡人 曷不顯名當世 呂圖不朽 而徒守此寂寞之境與草木同腐 何爲老人曰 子所謂不朽非立德立功立言者歟 愚伏曰然老人笑曰 世之稱道德者 莫高於孔孟 語功烈者莫盛於管晏 然求之於今日其人與骨皆已朽矣 獨其名存耳 可謂不朽乎 況文章小技 遷固 呂來 作者無數 而如蛩吟秋露 鳥弄春陽 爭嬌鬪妖 炫燿暫旹 而及其芳華謝盡 霜露交集 則聲沉響絶 寂然無聞 不亦可哀乎哉 吾所謂不朽異乎子矣 愚伏曰敢問何謂 老人曰 草死而後腐 木死而後朽 凡物之朽 皆由於死如其不死安可朽也 愚伏曰 世固有不死之理 歟曰 固有之矣諺曰子不夜行安知道上有夜行人 今子不遇不死者 則亦安知 山澤之間有不死者存乎 誠若按法運火千日功畢 能延年益筭 白日昇天 其或塵形未脫 托死呂解 則葬之雖千百年 全骨不朽 顏面如生 限滿之後 亦能破塚飛昇 所謂太陰鍊形 此法皆脫屣世界 歷萬劫而獨存 吾所謂不朽者此也 豈若子之求不朽於旣朽耶 愚伏拜曰 果若所敎願學焉隱者 熟視艮又 曰 子骨格未成 不可做得 且曰 科第則今年利矣 但不免三入王獄然終必無憂 此後七年 國有大亂 萬姓魚肉後三十三年 又有大賊 從西方起 都城不守 宗社幾覆 子皆身親見之矣因頓戲曰自 此以後天下事可知矣 愚伏再三請窮其說 老人曰 當自知之 不必强問 又問其姓名 老人曰 幼失怙恃 不知姓名耳 至夜深 愚伏困劇就寢

曉而視之 不知去向愚伏 怔問其家人 對曰此 卽號柳生員者也 浮遊諸寺
時或來過 愛此山水淨僻 或留數日或而未嘗見其所食之物 登陟岡巒 行步
如飛 愚伏聞之惘然若有失 是年果登第卽 萬曆十四年丙戌也 後壬辰倭亂
果大 至甲子适兵侵我 又甲申三月大明亡 愚伏當「李震吉事拿鞠 後又擘
連金直哉 自嶺外被囚 後又與於金夢虎之黨自江陵逮繫經年放歸 一如其
言 愚伏有詩一絶曰

  賦命每憐三不幸
  行身何啻七冝休
  東華久作紅塵客
  欲向丹丘訪道流

榮川文官權垕卽愚伏門人也 與先人同年相善 嘗過余談話偶及此事曰 神
仙之事雖稱誕謾不足信而以吾所聞扵□□者□□□□山澤以術自養延其
壽而不聞扵者 有若此丹陽老人則世之執夏虫之見而疑冬日之水者不爲大
方家之所笑乎 先生屬吾勿泄 故吾未嘗浪傳扵人云.

The Spirit Medium
Old Corea, 86–8

Note: The writer is little qualified to speak upon this subject, being
so superficially acquainted with it, but what he has read of Western
Spiritualism, and the findings of such investigators as Sir Oliver Lodge
and the late Mr. Stead,[32] it would seem as though the spirit-medium

---

32 Sir Oliver Joseph Lodge (1851–1940) was a British physicist and inventor who
    conducted groundbreaking research into electricity and magnetism and served
    as principal of the University of Birmingham from 1900 to 1920. Lodge was also
    a Christian Spiritualist who later in life became engrossed in the paranormal,
    including "thought-transference" (telepathy) and mediumship. In *Raymond
    or Life after Death* (1916) he documented his interactions with spirit mediums,
    who he was convinced had contacted his youngest son, Raymond Lodge, in
    the spirit world, a son who had died in the First World War. Lodge became
    convinced that the spirit world existed within the ether that enveloped the uni-
    verse. Although more than a mere object of "interest or curiosity" for Lodge,
    the driving force behind the belief in "mediumship" for Lodge and many of his
    generation seems to have been the desire to contact loved ones taken by the de-
    struction of the First World War, which stands in contrast to the function of the
    spirit medium in Korea. Brown, *Religion and Society in Twentieth-Century Britain*,
    103–4. Mr Stead refers to William Thomas Stead, a British newspaper editor

of the West was used simply as an object of interest or curiosity, to be exploited and investigated without any special benefit being in view from it. It is not so in Asia. The Medium here is used with a serious and definite purpose, to cure sickness, to cast out devils, to propitiate invisible spirits and win their favour. As viewed by East and West the subject resolves itself into two different questions, associated with entirely different thoughts, though accompanied by the same phenomena.

Mr. Yi Ik (1681–1763 AD) in his book the *Sŏngho sasŏl* says, "in the *Kugŏ*[33] we read that if a man's mind be set in its purpose with undivided aim, a spirit will come down upon him, and men and women so possessed we call mediums. At the present time there are a great many such people throughout the country, but the spirit that possesses them is of the evil order, not the good. The stupid, unlettered country folk employ these to say prayers for them, which they accompany with music. They call it the Spirit's work. There seems no way to put a stop to the practice, for the state encourages it. The reason for this is that the medium pays taxes and the state profits thereby. But we may ask, 'Where do these creatures get their money from?' They get it from the ignorant people for the prayers and services that they render.

"In the *Book of the Zhou Kingdom* (周禮) we find that there was an official of China called Master of Mediums. We would judge from this that there must have been a national cult at the time that did reverence to spirits."

"In our state affairs we never use the medium, which is right of course; and yet we do not decide to do away with him. Why should the government take taxes from such a source, levied, they say, as a regular due, and also, we are told, as a fine for the medium's evil ways. This will never put a stop to the practice but rather encourage it. From the Palace itself, to the most distant parts of the country, there are those in charge of spirit mediums who profit by their work. This means the degradation of the people.

"The Medium says, 'A spirit descends upon me and takes possession, but it must be asked for, prayed for, otherwise it will never force itself upon anyone.'

---

mentioned by Gale in "Concerning the Occult," *Pen Pictures*, who also became concerned with matters of telepathy and mediumship.

33 *Kugŏ* (國語 Ch. Guoyu, Discourses of the States) is an ancient Chinese text containing 240 speeches attributed to well-known figures from eight different states during the Spring and Autumn Period (771–476 BC), compiled some time during the fourth century BC.

In olden days there were both men and women so possessed; now, however, they seem to be mostly women. As women go freely into the inner quarters they are more suitable for mediums than men."

"In my village one woman I used to know would shout, 'The spirit has come down on me,' and then she would tremble and shake and say all manner of things. She had learned her part from an old hand who had acted as her teacher. I called her husband and remonstrated with him; also, I called the teacher and told her to cease her evil ways. At once the spirit departed from her and she was like other people. I judge from this that the matter could be easily stopped."[34]

Among Coreans the blind sorcerer has played a large part in the life of the people. He is called to diagnose a case of sickness or demon-possession, and if he gives judgment that is caused by a malignant spirit he is asked to exorcise it. Usually several other exorcists come with him, and after dressing up a stick with highly coloured paper and calling it *Sogŏ paengma taejanggun*,[35] the Great General of the White Cart, the White Horse, or some such name, proceed to carry out their operations.

With grain, money, cloth-goods, and tables laden with food, they begin repeating prayers from their books, usually from the Chinese Taoist Book, *Okch'u kyŏng*.[36] They keep up a succession of rapidly reeled off sing-song prayers till they are assured that the master-spirit has descended into the manikin, and then the leading medium takes it by the feet and sets it up before him. After a time it begins to dance. Up and down go its hands at the bidding of the spirit, active now as an electric current, and ready for any work it may have to do. The sorcerer begins

---

34 "國語民之精爽不携貳者則明神降之在男曰覡在女曰巫今世女巫遍扵國中其所降之鬼邪魔之類氓俗作樂祈祝謂之神事法不能禁非不能禁有以勸之也凡巫女皆有賦官利其物巫財所出何從從祈祝也如是而禁之難矣周禮立巫官意者古時崇信鬼道有災必禱故爾今國家祀典不用巫其儀極正宜斥絶之不暇又何收賦之為乎既收賦矣又罰其事鬼厚贖而利扵官非禁也意在錢布之入也扵是近自京輦遠至州邑皆有主巫出入隨意民風靡然矣巫者皆云有神来降此即人召之非鬼所强也古者有覡有巫今只有女巫盖出入外內親近媒利男不如女故男巫遂絶余村中有饗鬼者會中氓妻一人忽云神降通身戰掉作誑怔語遂徃從老巫師之余召其夫曉之又禁其師者鬼乃去終為平民以是知法足以禁之也." Yi Ik, *Sŏngho sasŏl* 星湖僿說 kwŏn 7, "Insamun Mu 人事門巫."

35 素車白馬大將軍.

36 *Okch'u kyŏng* (玉樞經 The Scripture of the Jade Pivot) is a Taoist scripture written around AD 1200 that contains various incantations that are to be invoked during spiritual medium ceremonies, or *kut*.

by asking, "What devil is it that possesses this sick man? Is it some resentful ancestor? Is it a spirit of the clan or the spirit of some other family? What spirit is it?"

The manikin waves backwards and forwards by way of saying "No," but up and down to say "Yes."

On receipt of the answer action is taken accordingly, whether a service of propitiation, or a chase and capture. If it be a malignant spirit, it is questioned something like this: "Why have you come here? Did you die here or elsewhere? Is it due to the cutting down of some sacred tree that you have come?[37] What is the cause? Has someone offended you? Let us know."

The manikin then leads the sorcerer here and there through the house, or outside, in quest of the spirit. A tablet is made with a string attached bearing the name and date of the supposed departed. Into this the spirit is said to take refuge when closely driven. After the spirit has entered it, the tablet is pushed into a bottle, rice and money accompanying; the cork is then clapped on and the whole buried safely in the ground.

Such is one of the common services of the male medium, the sorcerer.

The woman medium seldom undertakes to capture spirits or bottle them up. She comes with a great clamour of gongs and what-not to repeat prayers. The spirit that possesses her being is a master-spirit [that] drives out all others. She has power also to call forth from the unseen those who have died and left the earth long years ago. When these spirits come forth they talk through her lips with words that they alone know, to the surprise and often consternation of those who have asked that they be called.

The Medium has been considered a great danger to the state, and frequently efforts have been made to rid the world of her. Here is an extract from a famous book, the *Kimun ch'onghwa*.[38] "Nam Iung (1575–1648 AD), who was appointed teacher to the Crown Prince in 1607 and later made Prime Minister, was a man of undaunted spirit.

---

37 Gale writes about the significance of trees in the Korean animistic tradition in "Pak's Experiences," *Pen Pictures*, this vol.

38 This is Gale's translation of this work appearing under the following heading in *Kimun ch'onghwa* (記聞叢話), "Nam Iung" (1575–1648), 1:36. This is story no. 164 in the Yonsei University copy, translated in Kim Tonguk, *Saebyŏk kangka e haeoragi unŭn sori*; and *yadam* no. 20 in Gale, King, and Park, *Score One for the Dancing Girl*. This also appears in the Gale Papers, Diary 16, pp. 163, 164; translated 2 June 1921.

While he was Chief Justice a certain Medium was arrested and brought before him. When the death sentence was about to be passed on her she exercised her power in such a way as to cause the chair on which Nam sat to be shaken violently, so that he could not keep his place. The attendants were startled and turned pale. He, however, unshaken, was determined more than ever to carry out his decision and so he pushed the chair aside and sat on the mat. But the mat was also shaken beneath him, so that he had to throw it aside and seat himself against the wall. Here he found his footing firm and sat thus while he witnessed her being beaten to death."[39]

The power of the Medium is seen in the following story taken from the *Munhŏn pigo* [National Encyclopedia]: "There appeared in the fifth Moon of the year *muin* (1758) in the western provinces of Hwang-hae and P'yŏngan a medium who said she was a living Buddha and to whom all the people gave ear. She ordered the spirit shrines in these two provinces to be done away with and no worship offered to any but herself. The people followed her orders with abject submission and did exactly as she commanded. Other mediums threw away their swords and bell-rattles and gave themselves up to the orders of this special one.

Hearing of it, the King said, 'The spirit-shrine is something that the people believe in and honour with all their hearts; the medium too, is something that even I have no power to expel from the country, but this witch-woman with one word commands the whole world to her feet to do her will. I can only judge from this that she is no common medium but a woman of great power.' He sent a secret Commissioner, Yi Kyŏn-gok, with orders to arrest and have her beheaded and then exhibit her

---

39 "南春城以雄性剛果其爲都憲也有巫挾妖術惑衆者拿致憲府將刑之巫能施其術撓公所坐交椅使不得安身左右莫不驚惶失色公毅然不動却交椅而坐席巫又撓之公乃掇席及地衣倚軒壁而坐巫不能撓遂杖殺之." The version of the translation appearing in Gale's diary differs widely, and so I reproduce it here: "Nam Iung was a man of most determined disposition. When he was Chief Justice a certain *mudang* carried on much deception among the people. He had her arrested and was about to punish her when she brought her miraculous power into play and caused the chair where he was seated to be beaten. The people standing about were greatly alarmed and turned pale. Disturbed by this, Nam was more determined than ever to carry out his will so he pushed the chair away and sat on the mat. The mat also was shaken, and then he changed his place to a seat on the floor where he leaned against the wall. There he was solid and ordered her killed."

head throughout the towns and villages. Thus did he deliver the world from its deluding snare."

One can see from these scattered quotations that the Medium is a recognized member of Far-Eastern society; that she had played her part in its doings for many a day; that she is regarded with fear and suspicion; and that she never plies her craft for mere amusement, but orders it in the most serious way possible, as that on which hangs the fate of body and soul. She is not considered a make-believe by any means, though the nature of her profession makes it possible for frauds and counterfeits to attempt to duplicate her.

Short Stories

"Short Stories" consists of six of Gale's translations of short prose works in *hanmun* drawn from two different collections. The first four selections appear in *Kimun ch'onghwa* (紀聞叢話), an anonymous collection of unofficial *yadam* (野談) stories dating from the early nineteenth century. Si Nae Park writes of the *yadam* literary genre that "in their content *yadam* deal more often than not with historical events and persons from the Chosŏn dynasty, and are imbued with an air of historical veracity. However, the plot, characterization, and details of *yadam* tend to dwell more in likelihood, probability, and tropes than in verifiable facts."[1] Another characteristic of the *yadam* genre according to Park, a trait that illuminates Gale's approach to such texts in his translation activities, is the *yadam* as a form of "fluid textuality," a phenomenon that stemmed from both "intertextuality and manuscript culture."[2] Park points out that *yadam* transmission depended solely on handmade manuscript transmission and never on "xylographic or typographical reproducibility." Today, *yadam* collections such as *Kimun ch'onghwa* exist in various manuscript editions, and so such texts "should be understood as a sum of reader-produced compilations."[3] In his translational approach to such texts, Gale continued this tradition of participatory textual transmission but imbued his translations with an added dimension of translingual and intercultural connectivity. As I have demonstrated elsewhere in this work, Gale often domesticated his translations for an Anglophone

---

1 Park, "Translating to Inherit," xxviii.
2 Ibid.
3 Ibid., xxix.

audience, mentioning parallel events happening in Europe to contextualize events in Asia, and providing dates according to the Gregorian calendar when the original versions usually provided only reign dates. More significantly, however, Gale made certain editorial decisions – creative embellishments, strategic excisions – that harmonized with his own well-defined theory of translation prioritizing "sense" over "literalism," while demonstrating a reconfigured Anglophonic perspective on the tradition of participatory *yadam* transmission.

The four selections from *Kimun ch'onghwa* together project a condensed portrait of "Old Corea" for Gale, a synthesis of the morals and beliefs valued by members of the literati. In "The Spoiled Boy," the plot is driven by the spectre of an unlearned, unaccomplished son of a government official, perhaps the worst fear of any self-respecting literatus. The titular character in "Yi Changgon," meanwhile, is the victim of government purges and seeks protection among the lowest classes, only to return to glory when his name is restored, a common trope in such stories. Yi's harsh treatment by his father-in-law for being a "lazy lout," "a waste-basket into which to throw good food" further reflects a conscious awareness of the literati class within the broader Chosŏn social structure. Though somewhat misogynistic from a contemporary perspective, "Worthy Prince and Lucky Girls" presents the dilemma of a government official with no male heirs and five unmarriageable, "worthless" daughters. Gale returns to this theme of primogeniture predominance so often that the reader is led to believe that this was an all-pervasive sentiment within not only the official class but lower classes as well. Gale's motivations for including the remaining selection from *Kimun ch'onghwa*, "A Question of Conscience," may be interpreted as part of a broader evangelical strategy of drawing parallels between the Confucian and Christian moral universes.

The final two selections in this chapter, "Powers of Imitation" and "The Tartar Hunter," are taken from *Yongjae ch'onghwa* (慵齋叢話 Collected Talk from Idleness Studio),[4] a "bulky collection," according to one account, "of stories, biographical sketches, poems, and essays on

---

4 "Idleness Studio" (慵齋) was the pen name of Sŏng Hyŏn (成俔, 1439–1504), a government official and literatus of the early Chosŏn period. Ledger 11 from Gale's *Nachlass*, somehow separated from the rest of his papers and now in the Library of Congress, includes several additional manuscript translations from *Yongjae ch'onghwa*, demonstrating Gale's fondness for this particular author.

music, geography customs and other things … famous for its grace and wit."[5] These short works depart from the "representative samples of Confucian culture" embodied in the previous works and instead offer an idiosyncratic conclusion to the section.

The Spoiled Boy
Old Corea, 89–91;
"The Obstreperous Boy," *Korea Magazine* 2
(June 1918): 255–67[6]

This is an interesting story showing the workings of an unruly Corean boy's mind and also how to handle him. It proves as well how a kindly bearing can sweep away the long enmity of years.

(Translated from the *Kimun ch'ongwha*)

The magistrate of Hapch'ŏn had a son born to him when he was about sixty years of age. In his foolish love for the child he spoiled him completely and failed altogether in his teaching, so that at thirteen years of age the lad knew nothing and was quite unable to read.

There was a famous priest living then in Haein Monastery[7] with whom the magistrate had been on friendly terms for a long time. The priest called one day and, seeing the boy, said, "Your son is growing up and you have never sent him to school. What do you mean by it?"

The magistrate replied, "I have tried to teach him myself, but he is obstinate and will listen to nothing that I say. I cannot bear to beat him, so there you have it: a very distressful case."

The priest replied, "If a gentleman's son is not educated, he is of all men most useless. To merely lavish love on him and plan nothing for his improvement will surely never do. He is handsome and bright and

---

5 Pratt and Rutt, *Korea: A Historical and Cultural Dictionary*, 529.

6 The *Korea Magazine* (*KM*) version of this story appears under the title "The Obstreperous Boy" in Gale, King, and Park, *Score One for the Dancing Girl*, 187–98, and will be compared with the present version.

7 Haein Monastery (海印寺), located in Hapch'ŏn County in South Kyŏngsang Province, is the head temple of the Chogye order of Korean Sŏn Buddhism and houses the *Tripitaka Koreana*, the comprehensive Buddhist canon carved on 81,350 wooden blocks.

it seems a pity that he should be so neglected. Will you give me permission to take him in hand and teach him?"

"I would be delighted," said the magistrate, "but it seems overmuch to ask of anyone. To educate him and bring him to a place where he would be an honour to his forefathers and a master of the character, would be of all things most gratifying."

The priest then said, "If this is satisfactory there is one other matter that must first be settled. For better or worse I must have power to command him rigorously, and for this I would ask a written contract properly signed and sealed. Also, after sending him to the monastery, there must be no coming or going of servants, and you must give up your authority over him, here and now.[8] I shall see to his food and clothing myself, and if you have any occasion to send messages, let them be sent by priests who come and go, and addressed to me personally. Will Your Excellency consent to this?"

The magistrate replied, "I shall consent to anything you suggest."

Thus an agreement was made out, signed and sealed, and that day the boy was sent to the hills and all communication cut off.

He began by doing just what he liked, all license dispensed with. He answered his preceptor back, called him names, struck him in the face; in fact, there was nothing that he did not venture.

The priest pretended not to see, paid no attention, said nothing, and left him to do just as he pleased.

After four or five days of this, the master arose early one morning, put on his official hat and robes, took his seat in the place of command and had thirty or forty of his priests gather before him with their books. The strictest order was maintained with the most exacting ceremonial form. He then sent a young priest with orders to bring the magistrate's son.[9]

On being arrested the boy screamed and cried and took on in the most defiant manner, saying, "You dogs of priests, how dare you put your dirty hands on a gentleman? I'll go back and tell my father, and he will assuredly have you slaughtered, every one of you." Again he shouted, "Thieves and robbers, a thousand deaths to you! Though I die I'll not do your bidding."

The master then shouted out to have him pinioned and brought by force.

---

8 *KM*: "and you must give up your love here and now if I am to undertake the task."

9 *KM*: "the magistrate's son before him."

A crowd was on him at once, and, fastened like a criminal, he was brought to the master's presence.

The priest then unfolded the written contract that had been given him, spread it out and said, "Your father wrote this and signed and sealed it, and from now on your fate is in my hands – life or death. Here you are, the son of a gentleman, and yet you do not know a single letter. Evil deeds only and ungovernable[10] ways are your accomplishments. What use has the world for such a creature as you?[11] Without a definite reform you will be the ruin of your family and a disgrace forever. I shall have to punish you, and that severely."

He then heated an iron barb red-hot, had it turned against the boy, and speared his leg with it. The lad fell in a fit and for a time lay unconscious. A little later he revived and the priest again ordered him to be speared, when all of a sudden the boy dropped on his knees, prayed for his life and confessed that he had done very badly: "I shall hereafter do whatever Your Excellency commands. Please do not spear me."

While the master had him view in terror the threatened iron, he gave him a short but very impressive lecture.

He then had him unbound and told him to sit down beside him and begin his work on the *Thousand Character Classic*.[12] He gave him his appointed task each day so that he had no time to idle, and from this start, little by little, his knowledge grew and his general character developed. On hearing one thing he learned ten, and through ten he learned a hundred.

In four or five months he had mastered the *Thousand Character Classic*. Day and night he was constantly at it. So diligent and faithful a boy did he become that in less than a year he had made marked progress. In three years of this training at the temple he became a young man of liberal culture.

However, as he studied he had but one thought in mind: "I was insulted by these priests because I was ignorant. I shall study now with all my might, and when I pass my examination, I shall kill this master tyrant and wipe out the disgrace that I have suffered at his hands." With this purpose in mind he worked harder than ever.

---

10 *KM*: "ungoverned."

11 *KM*: "What use for the like of you to live?"

12 The *Thousand Character Classic* (Ch'ŏnjamun 千字文) is a sixth-century Literary Sinitic poem comprised of one thousand distinct sinographs. Considered a primer for the study of Literary Sinitic, it was the first text introduced to young students in the curriculum of premodern Korean schools.

The priest had him taught how to write Chinese composition, so that he soon acquired a practiced hand. One day he called him and said, "Your attainments now are sufficient for you to enter the examination lists as a candidate. Come with me tomorrow."[13]

The next day he took him to his father and said, "The young man's progress is such that if he keeps on, he will be able to pass the examination and hold office with honour.[14] I herewith resign my responsibility and give him back to you." Highly delighted, the father then planned for his wedding,[15] and they as a family returned to the capital.

For several years he was a candidate at examination contests, till finally he graduated with honours, and some years later became governor of Kyŏngsang Province. He thought with keen zest, "I shall now square up my account with that priest of Haein Monastery and wipe out the disgrace he did me."

He reached his official place and from there prepared to make a tour of the province, but before starting gave orders to his officer of justice, "Make ready special paddles and find me three or four skilled beaters. There is a priest in these hills whom I intend to have arrested and beaten to death."

He started then on his tour and finally reached Hongnyudong (紅流洞),[16] where the old priest of Haein Sa (Temple) came out with his disciples and stood by the side of the way.

The Governor, on seeing him, alighted from his chair, took him by the hand and spoke kindly.

The priest, now an old man, smiled and said, "I still live to see Your Excellency seated in the place of honour and surrounded by all the dignity and power of office. How glad my heart is."

He then led him to the temple and said, "The room I use now is the one in which you used to live and study, and tonight you will sleep there. I wonder if you would mind my occupying the same room with you?"

---

13 *KM*: "Come with me tomorrow and see."

14 *KM*: "hold office without shame."

15 *KM*: "The father then planned for his wedding."

16 Hongnyudong is a ravine near Haeinsa in Hapch'ŏn County, South Kyŏngsang Province. Gale, King, and Park, *Score One for the Dancing Girl*, 198.

The Governor said, "No, not in the least; I should be delighted."

When the night had grown late and all was quiet, the priest said, "When you were here and studied, you would like to have killed me, wouldn't you?"

The Governor said, "Yes, I would."

The priest continued, "Till after you passed your examination you had the same thought in mind, did you not?"

"Quite right," said the Governor.

"Also, the other day just before you started on your tour, you gave orders to prepare paddles and find skilful hands to beat me?"

"Yes, I did," said the Governor.

"Then why did Your Excellency not have me killed at once instead of dismounting from your chair and treating me so kindly?"

The Governor replied, "I did have that thought in mind all along till I met you. Seeing your kindly face, however, all my resentment melted away like snow in spring time and only delight and gladness remained."

The priest replied, "I followed you all along your course and noted your progress and attainment every foot of the way."[17]

陝川守某年六十只有一子 而溺愛而敎訓失 方年至十三歲 而目不識字 海印寺有一大師僧 自前親熟往來衙中矣 一日 來見而言曰 阿只年旣成童 而尙不入學 將何以爲之 倅曰 雖欲敎文字 而慢不從命 不忍楚撻以至於此 深以爲憫 大師曰 士夫子弟少而失學 則將爲世棄人 全事慈愛而不事課工可乎 其人物凡百可以有爲 而如是抛棄甚可惜也 小僧將訓學矣 官家其可許之乎 倅曰 誠好矣 固所願不敢請也 大師若敎訓而解蒙 則豈非萬幸耶 大師曰 若然則有一事之可質者 以生死惟意爲之 只可嚴立課程之意 作文記踏印而給小僧 且一送山門之後 限等乃 官隷之屬 一不相通 割斷恩愛 然後可矣 至於衣食之供 小僧自可辦之 如有所送者 僧徒往來便 直送于小僧 許爲宜官家其將行之乎 倅曰 惟命是從矣 仍如其言 書文記給之 自伊日 送兒于山門而絶不相通 其兒上山之後 左右跳踉 慢侮老僧 辱之頰之 無所不爲 大師視若不見 任其所爲 過四五日後平明 大師

---

17 Although Gale ends his translation here, Park notes that the original story goes on to relate an additional episode regarding the monk and the boy. While Gale's abrupt ending renders the story as one of "a prodigal son turning over a new leaf," the original story focuses on the "uncannily accurate prognostications" of the monk. The particularly violent nature of the original version sets it apart from Gale's tidy abridgement. See ibid., 190–1, 195–7.

整其弁袍 對案跪坐 弟子三四十人橫經侍坐 禮儀整肅[1]大師仍命一闍梨
僧拏致厥童 厥童號哭詬辱曰 汝以僧徒 何敢侮兩班至此也 吾可歸告大
人 將打殺汝矣 仍罵曰 千可殺萬可殺 賊禿云云 限死不來 大師大聲叱之
責諸僧 使之縛來 諸僧齊來 縛致之前 大師出示手記曰 汝之大人 書此給
我 從今以往 汝之生死在於吾手 汝以兩班家子弟 目不識字 全事悖惡之
行生而何爲 此習不 祛[祛] 將亡汝之門戶矣 第受吾罰 仍以錐末 灸火待
赤而刺于股 厥童昏塞 半晌而甦 大師又欲刺之 乃哀乞曰 自此以後 惟大
師之命是從 更勿刺之 大師執錐而責之誘之 食頃後始放 使之近前 以千
字文先授 而排日課程 不許少休 此童年既長成 智慮亦長 聞一知十 聞十
知百 四五朔之間 千字通 史[鑑]皆通曉 而晝夜不 輟[輟] 孜孜不懈 一年
之餘 文理大就 留山寺三年 工夫已成 每於讀書之詩 獨語于心曰 吾以工
夫受辱於山僧者 皆不學之致也 吾將勤工得科後 必欲打殺此僧 以雪此
今日之恨云 而一念不懈 尤用功力 大師又使習科工 一日 大師使近前而
言曰 汝之工夫 優可作科儒 明日可與我下山 翌日 乃率來衙中而言曰 今
則文辭將就 登科後文任亦不讓於他 小僧從此辭歸 仍留置而去 其童子
始議親成婚 上京後 出入科場 數年之後 決[登]科 數十年之間 得爲嶺伯
始乃大喜心語曰 吾今而後 可殺海印寺僧 以雪向日之憤云矣 及按到而
出巡也 申飭刑吏作別杖 而擇執杖之善者三四人以從 將到山門而欲撲殺
此僧之計也 行到紅流洞 此老僧率諸僧 祇迎于路左 巡使見之 仍下轎執
手而致款 老僧欣然而笑曰 老僧幸而不死 及見巡使威儀 幸莫大焉 仍與
之入寺 老僧請曰 小僧之居房 卽使道向年工夫之處也 今野移下處 與小
僧聯枕無妨矣 巡使許之 與之同寢 更深後僧曰 使道兒時受學時 有必殺
小僧之心乎 曰 然矣 僧曰 自登科至建節而皆有此心乎 曰 然矣 僧曰 發
巡時 矢于心而欲打殺小僧 至有別刑杖擇執杖之擧乎 曰 然矣 僧曰 若然
則使道何不打殺而下轎致款乎 巡使曰 向來之恨心乎不忘 及對君顏 此
心氷消雲散油然有欣悅之心故也 僧曰小僧亦已揣 知[之]矣 使道位可至
大官 而某年月日按節箕城也 當是時 小僧當送上佐矣 使道必須加禮 而
如見小僧樣 與之同寢可也 愼勿忘置 必須如是 巡使許諾 老僧乃出示一
紙曰 此是小僧爲使道推數平生而編年者也 享年幾許 位至幾品 昭然可
知 而俄所言箕營事 愼勿忘却 巡使唯唯 翌日 多給米布錢木之屬而去 其
後過幾年 果爲箕伯一日 閽者告曰 慶尙道陜川郡海印寺僧欲入謁矣 巡
使怳惚覺悟 卽使入來 使之升堂 把袖促 膝[膝] 問其師之安否 夕餐與
之聯床 至夜又與之同寢 至更深後 房堗過溫 巡使乃易寢席而臥矣 昏夢
之中忽有腥穢之臭 以手撫僧之背 則臥處有水漬手 仍呼知印 擧火而見
之 則刃刺於僧腹 五臟突出 血流遍地 巡使大驚 急使運置於外 翌日朝窮
查 則巡使所嬖之妓 卽官奴之所眄 而彼此大惑也 以是含憾爲刺巡使而
入來 意謂下堗之臥者卽巡使也 而刺之矣 仍拿致嚴覈則一一直招 遂置
之法 治僧之喪 送于本寺 盖大師預知有此厄 而故使上佐代受故也 其後
功名壽限 皆符大師之推數矣.

Yi Changgon
(Translated from the Kimun ch'onghwa)
Old Corea, 92–4;
"Yi Changgon 李長坤 (The Troubles of 1498 AD),"
Korea Magazine 3 (September 1918): 396–400[18]

In the year 1498[19] a great disturbance broke out in the capital of Corea, and among others who made their escape was a Mr. Yi who held the rank of *kyori*,[20] Keeper of the Records. He fled for his life to a distant county in Chŏlla Province. Overcome by thirst as he hurried along, and seeing a girl dipping water from a stream, he asked a drink. She dipped her gourd, but before passing it stripped some willow leaves from a branch that overhung her head and threw them into the water.

He thought this peculiar and asked, "When I am so thirsty and in so great a hurry, why do you scatter leaves over the water?"[21]

"Seeing you so overheated sir,[22] I was afraid you might take harm from drinking too fast, and so scattered the leaves," was her answer.

The man, impressed by this, inquired where she lived, and she replied, "I am the daughter of a basket-maker and live in yonder little cabin."

Yi followed her to her home and said to the master, "I desire a great favour, namely, to become your son-in-law[23] and live with you; please take me."

Being a very humble man, and guessing that the stranger was a gentleman, the basket-maker readily gave his consent.[24] There Yi lodged.

For a son of Seoul's ancient nobility, however, to become a basket-maker was out of the question. Day succeeded day with nothing done as Yi slept out the long hours. The father and mother-in-law, both

---

18 This *OC* version will be compared with the *Korea Magazine* (*KM*) version appearing in Gale, King, and Park, *Score One for the Dancing Girl*, 405–15.

19 *KM*: "In the reign of King Yŏnsan."

20 校理.

21 *KM*: "over the water that I have to drink?"

22 *KM*: "Seeing Your Excellency so overheated."

23 *KM*: "I desire to become your son-in-law."

24 *KM*: "Consent was given and there he lodged."

of them indignant at this, scolded him soundly. "We took you in order
that you might help us in our basket-making, but instead of a help you
are a total loss;[25] you simply eat your meals and sleep. You are only a
waste-basket[26] into which to throw good food."

From this day on they gave him only half the ordinary fare, though
night and morning, his young wife, sorry for him, brought him the
scrapings of the kettle, unknown to her parents.

Her kindness was rewarded, for his love for her deepened day by day.[27]

Thus three years passed till in 1506 a new king ascended the throne.[28]
Those who had been sentenced to death were pardoned, honourably
treated and appointed to office. Yi's name too, was on the restored list,
but he, like others, was lost to view and no one knew where he was.
Advertisement was made to all corners of the kingdom and the rumor
of it spread everywhere.

One fair day Yi was startled to hear the news, and as it happened to
be the first day of the month, the time for the basket-maker to pay his
tribute[29] to the magistrate, he said to his father-in-law, "On this occasion I'll take the baskets and see them safely to their destination."

The father-in-law replied in a high key, "You – you lazy lout[30] – you
don't know east from west; how could you take these baskets to the
magistrate? I never go myself without having a terrible tussle[31] with
the unreasonable creature, who constantly refuses this one and that
and orders them back, telling me to bring better. How do you think he
would treat you? No, no, no, you can't take the baskets."

But the daughter said, "Please try him father, it will do no harm."

Persuaded by his gentle daughter at last, the basket-maker sent Yi
with the load on his back to the official *yamen*, where he boldly walked
straight into the compound and shouted in a loud voice, "The basket-
maker has come with his baskets, ahoy!"

---

25 *KM*: "But instead of proving a help you are an abominable loss."

26 *KM*: "Nothing but a scrap bag you are."

27 *KM*: "Her kindness was rewarded, for their love for each other deepened by
    the day."

28 *KM*: "Thus three years passed till Chungjong ascended the throne (1506) and
    all the world was changed." King Chungjong (中宗, 1488–1544; r. 1506–44)
    assumed the throne when his half-brother Yŏnsan'gun was deposed in a coup.

29 *KM*: "offering."

30 *KM*: "lazy dog."

31 *KM*: "a terrible time of dispute."

The magistrate, who happened to be an old soldier friend of Yi's, was startled by this bold announcement. He looked for a moment, and suddenly realizing who the stranger was, hurried down the step-way, took him by the hand and led him up to the place of special honour.

"Friend of friends, wherever have you been, and how do you come to me in such a guise as this? The Government is out in search of you everywhere and a notice from the chief office[32] is here on your behalf. Go to Seoul at once, make no delay."

He had food and drink prepared and fitted him out with a new suit of clothes.

Yi said, "I was under sentence of death and so stole into a basket-maker's home and hid away, and thus have I survived these years. Never again did I expect to see such a day as this."

The magistrate sent word to the Governor saying that Yi *kyori* was alive and safe in Posŏng County. So he made ready post-horses to send him swiftly and safely to Seoul.

"But I cannot forget," said Yi, "the kindness shown me these past three years by my wife whom I greatly love. I must go now and say my word of greeting to her and to my master. Please come for me tomorrow morning."

The magistrate finally gave consent to the plan.

Yi again changed his dress to the old basket-maker's garb and went forth to his home. He greeted his father-in-law thus: "This time he took the baskets and all without a word."

The old man replied, "He did, did he? Well, well! They say that even a thousand-year-old hawk can be taught the work of a falcon. This must be true, for even my son-in-law has done his work for once as a man. Wonderful! Wonderful. Give him an extra spoonful of rice,"[33] he shouted to his wife.

The next morning Yi got up and swept the court; seeing it, his old father-in-law shouted out, "Yesterday my son-in-law made a success of the baskets, and today he sweeps the court clean as a whistle. I shouldn't wonder to see the sun rise in the west tomorrow. Ha! Ha!"

Yi then took out a mat and spread it on the ground and when the old man asked, "Look here, what are you about? Do you put a good mat like that out on the dirty ground?"

Yi replied, "The magistrate is coming today and so I am making ready."

---

32 *KM*: "Governor's office."
33 *KM*: "Give him an extra spoonful or two of rice."

The basket-maker laughed an ironical laugh and said, "What wild talk is this? The magistrate come to such a place as this?[34] Addle-headed dolt![35] Seeing what a fool is about now, I begin to mistrust his journey yesterday. I should not wonder if he threw those baskets away and came home to make an empty boast of it."

Before he had finished speaking, however, the magistrate's servant came bounding in all out of breath with a beautifully coloured mat that he spread out in the court, saying, "His Excellency is on the way!"

Hearing this, the man and his wife were greatly alarmed and ran to hide. A moment later they heard the official criers shouting to clear the way, when suddenly the magistrate arrived, alighted from his horse and went into the room. He greeted Yi *kyori* most politely and asked him how he had spent the night. A moment later he inquired, "Where is our sister? I pray, have her come in."

Yi called, "Come and make your bow to the magistrate."

With a plain wooden pin through her hair and in simplest linen dress she appeared and made her bow. Though evidently poor in circumstances, her face and form marked her as a young woman of good intelligence.

The magistrate treated her with marked deference and said, "Dr. Yi in the days of his desperate need, found you to be his friend and your service has proven more to him than any other person's could possibly have been. You will certainly be rewarded."[36]

The woman drew her dress modestly around her and replied, "I am a woman of the lowest class,[37] and though it fell on my lot to care for this, my master, I had no idea who he was, and so I fear that my treatment of him has been very defective and has lacked no end of honour.[38] Faults and failures rise up before me and render me speechless[39] at the kind words you have spoken. Your coming today to our poor home means honour beyond every dream, I fear, it being so great, it may bespeak[40] misfortune."

Hearing this, the magistrate sent a servant to call the basket-maker and his wife, had them treated to refreshments, and spoke kindly to them.

---

34 *KM*: "to such a place as we have?"

35 *KM*: "Addle-headed idiot!"

36 *KM*: "Are you not to be honoured?"

37 *KM*: "I am a woman, the lowest of the low."

38 *KM*: "and no end of lack to do him honour."

39 *KM*: "unworthy."

40 *KM*: "presage."

A little later other magistrates began to come in. The Governor sent his secretary to present his word of greeting. The court of the basket-maker's house was crowded with horses and servants of state.

Yi *kyori* said to his friend, "This little wife of mine belongs to the lowest class undoubtedly,[41] but she and I are one and we cannot be separated. For these years she has served and aided me with the most loyal heart[42] and now that I have come to a place of honour I cannot forget her.[43] Please provide a palanquin that she may go as well."[44]

The magistrate at once acceded to this request, had a "chair" made ready and saw her start with him.

When Yi went to the palace for audience,[45] His Majesty King Chungjong admitted him at once.[46] He inquired all about where he had been, and what had befallen him, and Yi told him the story.

On hearing it the King nodded and said, "She must never be treated as a woman of low station; I make her your wife to take the place of your kindred who have been killed, with all the honour that goes with it."

Long years they lived together, Yi and his faithful wife. There was no honour of state that did not come their way.[47] Many sons and daughters were born to them. This Yi Changgon was an honourable officer of the first rank, a great and noted minister.[48]

李長坤

---

41 *KM*: "Yi *kyori* said to his friend concerning his wife, 'She belongs to the lowest class, undoubtedly.'"

42 *KM*: "with all her strength."

43 *KM*: "I cannot forget her faithfulness."

44 *KM*: "Please provide a chair so that I can take her along."

45 *KM*: "When Yi went to the palace to bow his thanks before King Chungjong (1506)."

46 *KM*: "His Majesty gave command that he be admitted at once."

47 *KM*: "his way."

48 *KM*: "This Yi *kyori* was Yi *p'ansŏ*, Changgon (李長坤), a great and noted minister." The *KM* version follows the original *hanmun* more closely: "此是李判書長坤之事云耳." Si Nae Park writes that Yi Changgon (1474–?) was "a scholar-official under King Chungjong" who was "exiled to Kŏje Island in 1504 during the Literary Purges of the Kapcha Year, but fled to Hamhŭng [South Hamgyŏng Province] and lived among the low-born who were hereditary butchers and wicker craftsmen (*paekchŏng* 白丁). After the 'Rectification of King Chungjong,' he was reemployed at the court. His father was Yi Sŭngŏn 李承彦 [dates unknown]." Gale, King, and Park, *Score One for the Dancing Girl*, 415.

燕山朝士禍大起　有一李姓人　以校理亡命　行到寶城地渴甚　見一童女
汲於川邊　趨而求飮　其女以瓢盛水　而摘川邊柳葉　浮之中而給之　心竊怪
之　問曰　過客渴甚　急欲求飮　何乃以柳葉　浮水而給之也　其女對曰　吾視客
子甚渴　若或急飮冷水　則必也生病故　故以柳葉浮之　使之緩緩飮之之故也
其人大驚異之　問是誰家女　則對曰　越邊柳器家女云　其人隨其後而往柳器
匠家　求爲其婿而托身焉　自以京華之貴家［客］安知柳器織造乎　日無所事
以午睡爲常　柳匠之夫妻怒罵曰　吾之迎婚［婿］期欲助柳器之役矣　今焉新
婚　只喫朝夕飯　晝夜昏睡　卽一飯囊也云　而自伊日　朝夕之飯　減半而饋之
其妻憐而悶之　每以鍋底黃飯加數而饋之　夫婦之恩情甚篤　如是度了數年
之後　中廟改玉　朝著一新　昏朝沈廢之流　一幷赦而付職　李生還付官職　行
會八路　使之尋訪　傳說藉藉　李生聞於風便　而時適朔日　主家將納柳器於
官府矣　李生乃謂其婦翁曰　今番則官家朔納柳器　吾當輸納矣　其婦翁責曰
如君渴睡漢　不知東西　何可納器於官門乎　吾雖親自納之　每每見退　如君
者　其何以無事納之乎　不肯許之　其妻曰　試可乃已　盍使往諸柳匠始乃許
之　李乃背負而到官門　直入庭中　近前高聲曰　某處柳匠　納器次來待矣　本
官乃是李之平日切親之武弁也　察其貌　聽其言　乃大驚起而下堂　執手而延
之上座曰　公乎公乎　晦跡於何處　而乃以此樣來此乎　朝廷之搜訪已久　營
關遍行　斯速上京可也　仍命進酒饌　又出衣冠改服　李曰　負罪之人　偸生於
柳器匠家　至于今延命而度　豈意天日之復見也　本官仍以李校理之在邑　成
報于巡營催發馹騎使之上京　李曰　三年主客之誼　不可不顧　且有糟糠之情
吾當告別主翁　今將出去　君須於明朝　來訪吾之所住處　本官曰　諾　李乃換
着來時衣　出門而向柳匠家言曰　今番柳器　無事上納矣　主翁曰　異哉　古語
云　鴟老千年能搏一雉云　信非虛矣　吾婿亦有隨人爲之事乎　奇哉奇哉　今
夕當加給數匙飯矣　翌日平明　李早起灑掃門庭　主翁曰　吾婿昨日善納柳器
今則又能掃庭　今日日可出於西矣　李乃鋪藁席于庭　主翁曰　鋪席何爲　李
曰　本府官司　今朝當行次故如是耳　主翁冷笑曰　君何作夢中語也　官司主
何可行次於吾家乎　此千不近萬不近之荒說也　到今思之　昨日柳器之善納
云者　必是委棄路上而歸　作誇張之虛語也　言未已　本官工吏持彩席而喘喘
而來　鋪之庭中而言曰　官司主行次　今方來到矣　柳匠夫妻　蒼黃失色　抱頭
而匿于籬間　少焉　前導聲及門　本官騎馬而來　下馬入房　與敍別來寒暄仍
問曰　嫂氏何在　使之出來　李乃使其妻來拜　其女以荊┌布裙來拜於前　衣裳
雖弊　容儀閑雅　有非常賤女子　本官致敬曰　李學士身在窮途　幸賴嫂氏之
力　得至于今日　雖意氣男子　無以過此　何不欽歎乎　其女斂┌而對曰　顧以
至賤之村婦　得侍君子之巾櫛全昧如是之貴人　其於接對周旋之節　無禮極
矣　獲罪大矣　何敢當尊客之致謝　官司今日降臨於常賤陋湫之地　榮耀極矣
窃爲賤妾之家　恐有損於福力也　本官聽罷　命下隸　招入柳匠夫妻　饋酒賜
顔矣　已而隣邑守宰　絡續來見　巡使又送幕客而傳喝　柳匠之門外　人馬熱
鬧觀光者如堵　李謂本官曰　彼雖常賤　吾旣與之敵體　必作配矣　多年服勞
誠意備至　吾今不可以貴而易　願借一轎偕行　本官卽地得一轎　治行具以送
李於入闕謝恩之時　中廟命入侍　而俯問流離之顚末　李乃奏其事甚悉　上再

三嗟歎曰 此女子不可以賤妾待之 特升爲後夫人可也 李與此女偕老 而榮
貴無比 多有子女 此是李判書長坤之事云耳.

A Question of Conscience
Old Corea, 95–6
Gale Papers, Vol. III, 60; Diary XIV, 10–11;
Typescript in *Miscellaneous Writings* 30, 161–2

The question is sometimes raised as to how far conscience rules in East
Asia. To be found out in a wrong, we know, is a dreadful misfortune; or
to be exhibited to the public with loss of "face" is often more feared than
death itself; but the inner heart, which no eye sees, how far is its condemnation to be reckoned with? Can it readily influence the understanding
and the soul?

Two hundred years ago there lived in Corea a well-known man by the
name of Hwang In'gŏn.[49] He graduated from the Confucian college in
the year that George I came to the throne of England, 1714 and rose to
be an officer of the first rank. While preparing for the rigid examination
of that day he spent much of his time in a Buddhist monastery. The
quiet of the surroundings, pine trees, and rippling streams were condu-
cive to study, and the priesthood were always more than ready to run
his errands and do him service.

Among those he met was a young man of more than ordinary ability,
a sincere disciple of the Buddha who took great delight in waiting on
him and attending his every wish. Hwang made him part and parcel
of his service, and kept him as his special help till he rose to a place of
great influence, when suddenly the priest disappeared.

Some years later he was appointed Governor of Kyŏngsang Province,
and one day, while making his round of the different districts, he
suddenly caught a glimpse past his chair-flap of someone standing by
the side of the way who reminded him of his former friend. He sent a
servant to inquire and lo, it was the man.

---

49 Hwang In'gŏm (黃仁儉, 1711–65) was a late-Chosŏn government minister during the reign of King Yŏngjo (英祖, 1694–1776; r. 1724–76), the longest-reigning
Chosŏn monarch.

Overjoyed, Hwang took him back into his employ, had a horse provided for him and had him accompany him wherever he went. On return to his official quarters in Taegu he had a room set apart for him
next to the library and saw to his needs with the greatest care.

One day he called the priest and said, "There is an old saying that
runs, 'Every spoon of rice merits its return of favour.' How many spoons
have I received from you? I have silks and stores in great abundance,
and yet if I gave you half of all I possess I would still fail to express my
heart. Unfortunately, you are a priest who dresses in coarse cloth and
eats poor vegetarian fare. What is silk or gold to such as you? If you
could only cut yourself off from the Buddhist connection I would see
that you had a beautiful home with lands and abundant goods to spare.
How does this strike you?"

The priest replied, "I thank you very much for your kind thought,
but I have made a vow with my soul and can never go back on it."

Hwang, thinking this strange, inquired, "What vow, I pray, and for
what reason?" But the priest only laughed and made no reply.

Hwang was determined, however, to know and asked again and again.

The priest's answer was, "What reason for Your Excellency to know?"

Hwang then followed this with other questions but the priest gave
no answer. Then Hwang ordered his attendants and other listeners out
and went on to say, "You have some secret hidden from me, and you
know we keep nothing back from each other; let me know."

The priest, unable to refuse further, replied, "Before I knew you I was
an irreligious young man who had no thought of the Buddha, or the
Law, and sought my own will only. One day as I passed along the road
I saw a very pretty girl quite by herself digging greens among the grave
mounds. No one being near I went up to her and made evil proposals,
but she drew back, resented what I said, and seemed determined to resist me at all costs. Unable to persuade her, I used force, tied her hands
and feet, and having done her every dishonour, I unfastened her and
hurried away to the inn where I slept the night.

In the morning I overheard people talking together and learned that
a young woman of known integrity had committed suicide. A word
was added, 'Some rascal must have wrought her ruin to cause her to
take her life.'

I was terribly frightened on hearing this. Pity also, for the poor girl
took possession of my soul. Wishing to know whether the awful rumor
was based on fact or not, I made my way to the neighbourhood to find
that it was really so. I went in to view her body and there on her hands

and feet were the marks of where I had bound her. The people said, 'Someone must evidently have violated her when she was thus made fast. We shall let the magistrate know and have the scoundrel sought out and punished.'

On hearing this, my hair stood on end and in the altar of my soul I said, 'Why did I ever do such a thing? My guilty passion has brought this innocent girl to a dreadful death. There is surely no pardon for such a sinner as I in heaven above or earth beneath. God will assuredly smite me.' I thought of it, and thought of it till I was almost mad, and wondered if there was any atonement for such a sin as mine. I finally decided that only the hardships of the world could make amends, and that they must be my portion hereafter, with not an atom of joy entering my life. In this decision I became a priest of the Buddha and donned the coarse black coat as a mark of the oath I had sworn. It is, therefore, impossible for me to accept of your kindness and break with my soul's decision. Never again can I go back to earth. This happened long ago and only because you insisted on knowing do I tell it today."

Hwang had seen before in the list of crimes in his province that there was one not yet requited from long years ago. The time agreed, the day, the month, the year – just as he had been told.

On seeing this, the Governor said, "Though you and I are the best of friends, and love each other dearly, the law must take its course," and so he handed him over to the judges. The priest was condemned to die, and after his death the Governor gave him a great and honorable funeral.

黃判書仁儉 少時讀書山寺 有一僧盡誠使役 糧資如缺 則渠每間間自當 有無相資 終始不怠 黃頗感其誠而愛其人 及顯達 其僧絶迹 黃每念之 而 不得見 心常恨嘆 其爲嶺伯 出巡之路 有一僧避坐路傍 黃自轎中 瞥眼見 之 似是厭僧 乃命隸招使近前 則果是此僧 不勝欣幸 仍命一騎 載而隨後 夜每同寢 撫愛如子侄 及還營 置之册室 供饋甚豊潔 一日 招而謂曰 古 人有一飯之德必報 吾於汝 奚但一飯而已哉 吾則錢帛裕足 雖割半而與之 無所不可 而汝以山僧 衣葛食草 錢帛雖多 將安用哉 汝若長髮而退俗 則 非但家産之饒足 吾當爲汝圖拔身之計矣 汝意如何 僧曰 使道爲小僧之意 非不感謝 而小僧有區區迷執 欲以此終 無意於出世也 黃怪而問之 則僧 笑而不答 黃再三强問 終始牢諱 黃又詰之 則僧終不言 黃辟左右 促膝而 問曰 汝之所執 必有所以 而吾於汝之間 有何諱秘之事 從實言之可也 僧 始乃勉强而言曰 小僧不知使道之前卽俗人也 某年偶經山谷中 有一新塚 前有一素服女子採蔬 而貌頗妍美 四顧無人故 逼而欲犯 則抵死不從故 乃以衣帶 縛其四肢而强奸之 仍解其縛 而行數十里 宿於店幕 翌朝聞傳 說 則以爲某處守墓之節婦 昨夜自決 不知何許過人 必也强淫而致死云云

故 心甚驚動而哀憐 猶慮傳聞之未詳 委往其近處而探之 則果是的報 而
其手足縛痕宛然 人皆曰 必也縛其手足而强淫 至於此境云云 卽報于地方
官 使之跟捕兇身云矣 一聞此說 毛髮悚然 悔之哀之 仍以自量 則吾不忍
一時之欲 致使節婦至於此 卽天地間難容之罪也 神明必降之以殃矣 左右
思量 欲得贖罪之方而不可得 又自念以爲吾旣負此大罪 當喫盡天下之風
霜 小無生世之樂然後 庶可贖罪 仍削髮爲僧 以不脫緇衣矢于心矣 今何
以使道之厚恩 變幻初意乎 以是之故 不欲還俗矣 事已久遠 下問又切故
不得已吐實矣 日前巡使適見道內殺獄文案 則有此獄事 而殆近數十年 兇
身尚未得捕者也 年月日無一差爽 乃嘆曰 吾與汝 雖親切之間 公法不可
廢也 仍命隷拿下抵之法厚給葬需云矣.

Worthy Prince and Lucky Girls
(Translated from the Kimun ch'onghwa)
Old Corea, 97–9;
"High-Born Prince and Worthy Girls,"
Korea Magazine 2 (November 1918): 502–7

Note: On account of his faithful service during the trying days of the
Hideyoshi invasion, Yi Kwangjŏng was made Prince Yŏnwŏn, or Duke
Yŏnwŏn, as would be said in England.[50] He went as envoy to the Mings
in 1602 AD and by his upright character and high attainments won
great respect of the Chinaman.

Yi Kwangjŏng, while magistrate of Yangju County, had a falcon, and
a keeper who used to hunt with him. One day this hunter went out in
search of game, but did not return till the next morning. He had hurt his
foot, it seems, and came limping home. Seeing this, the master asked
what had befallen him. He laughed as he replied, "Yesterday when I
let the falcon loose after a pheasant he missed it and let it go. After
searching right and left in vain, he finally alighted on a tree in front of
Deputy Magistrate Yi's house. With much difficulty I finally induced
him to come back to me and perch on my arm and then turned to make
my way home.

Just at that moment I heard voices from the magistrate's garden talking in a very lively manner, and I glanced through the paling to see what

---

50 Yi Kwangjŏng (李光庭, 1552–1627) was honoured as Prince Yŏnwŏn
(延原府院君).

it was about. There, would you believe me, I saw five great rollicking girls, hand in hand, swinging along the hillside.[51] I was filled with fear as I looked upon them, afraid lest they might pounce out upon me, and so I ran for my life, but in doing so fell and sprained my ankle."[52]

"It was late in the day and growing dark. On second thought, I wondered who they were and what they were about, and resolved to hide behind the fence in the long weeds and hear what they had to say. They were talking together and one said, 'We are quite alone here; let's play county magistrate.'

'Delighted!' answered the others.

The tallest among them, about thirty years of age I should think, took her seat on a rock with her sisters just before her. One she named Deputy Magistrate; one, Secretary of Justice; one, the Public Crier; and one, the Constable Runner.[53]

She, the Chief Magistrate, then issued the following order, 'Arrest the Deputy and bring her here.'

The Secretary of Justice called to the Crier and gave the order that the Deputy be arrested. The Crier shouted to the Runner to carry out this command at once. The Runner made off at full speed and in a trice had the Deputy arrested and brought.

She knelt humbly before the judge, who, in a loud voice, gave forth the charge thus, 'Marriage is one of the primal laws[54] of society and yet even your youngest daughter, we take note, is past the marriageable age. What shall we say as to her older sisters? How comes it that you have disregarded this law of nature in such a shameful way, and left your children uncared for?[55] Surely you deserve to die.'

---

51 *KM*: "There I beheld five strong, husky girls swinging along the hill-side, hand in hand." The *KM* version seems closer to the original *hanmun*, which describes the women as "healthy [husky] and man-like" (豪健如壯男樣).

52 *KM*: "fell and hurt my foot."

53 Gale, King, and Park describe these positions in the following way: "Deputy Magistrate" (*agwan*; 座首 or 亞官) is equivalent to *suhyang* (首鄉), the head of a local yamen (*hyangch'ŏng* 鄉廳); "Secretary of Justice" (*hyŏngbang* 刑房) is a petty clerk (*ajŏn* 衙前) in charge of penal administration at the local yamen; the "Public Crier" (*kŭpch'ang* 及唱) is "a crier servant boy at the local yamen," and the "Constable Runner" (*saryŏng* 使令) is "a page boy at the local yamen." Gale, King, and Park, *Score One for the Dancing Girl*, 488.

54 *KM*: "first laws."

55 *KM*: "left your children unmarried."

The Deputy bowed low, with her face to the ground, and said, 'How is it possible that your humble servant could be ignorant of this fault? I know it full well, but I am as poor as carking poverty can make me, and so have no means by which to arrange a marriage.'

The Chief replied, 'Marriage should be carried out according to one's means. All it needs is a pair of mats[56] and a bowl of water across which to plight one's troth. How dare you say, "No means?" Such talk is nonsense.'

The Deputy said, 'Your humble servant's problem is not that of one daughter only, nor even two. How could I ever expect to find husbands for all these?'

The Chief[57] stopped her at once saying, 'Let me not hear a word of it. If you had any zeal in the matter you would find them soon enough. I have heard that Deputy Song, of such-and-such a place, has a son, and Vice Deputy An of another place, also Deputy Chŏng and Vice Kim and Ch'oe. They all have sons. You could apply for any of these. They are all of your own social class – what reason, pray, for not taking the necessary steps to approach them?'[58]

The Deputy said, 'I'll do as Your Excellency commands, but I am so poor that they are not likely to respond to my invitation.'

The Chief went on, 'You ought to be soundly paddled for this sin of yours, but for the present I'll let you off. Get the matter seen to at once. If you don't, you'll be severely dealt with, rest assured.'

She called the Runner to have the Deputy led out and dismissed.

The five of them laughed over this and with many words and much hilarity dispersed. It was a most amusing performance. Leaving the place I found an inn where I passed the night and so returned."

Hearing this story, Prince Yŏnwŏn laughed likewise, and calling the present deputy, asked about Yi as to his antecedents, how he was circumstanced, his children, etc.

The deputy replied, "He is the senior deputy of this county, but he is as poor as poverty. He has no sons but five daughters. Because of his being poor, his five daughters have all passed the marriageable age without a chance to wed."

Prince Yŏnwŏn, on learning this, sent through his secretary a letter, signed by him, asking Deputy Yi as to his health, etc. Shortly after, Yi appeared at the official headquarters and Prince Yŏnwŏn remarked,

---

56 *KM*: "a pair of quilts."
57 *KM*: "The Magistrate."
58 *KM*: "for not taking the necessary steps?"

"You were a deputy of this county, I understand, and know all the points of law. I have wanted to consult with you for some time on important matters, but have had no opportunity."[59] He then inquired as to how many sons he had.

The Deputy replied, "My luck is surely the worst you ever heard of, for I have not a single son, but only five useless daughters."

"Have you not married them off?" inquired Prince Yŏnwŏn.

His reply was, "Not a single one of them."

The Prince again asked,[60] "How old are they?"

He replied, "The youngest of them is past the marriageable age."

He then went on to ask the same questions that the daughter who had played at magistrate had asked, and the old Deputy answered just as the deputy daughter had done.

Prince Yŏnwŏn then added, "In such-and-such a deputy's house there are sons, and in such-and-such another house …," just as the daughter had said at the mock trial.

The Deputy's reply was, "I am so poor that I am sure none of these would consent."

Prince Yŏnwŏn said, "I'll be your go-between and see that your daughters are properly married," and with this he dismissed him.

He then dispatched his secretary to the five officials referred to and had them summoned. "Have you any unmarried sons?" he inquired.

The reply was, "Yes, we have."

"Have you not decided on their marriage?"

"Not yet," was the answer.

Prince Yŏnwŏn then said, "I have heard that in such-and-such a home[61] there are five daughters; why should you not marry there?"

The five hesitated over this and gave no answer.

The Prince then assumed a severe attitude: "He is a county official; so are you. Your station in life is the exact counterpart of his. Your not wanting to marry is solely on account of his being poor. Shall the poor man's daughters then have no chance to marry at all? I am socially a step higher than you, and yet my good office in this matter seems hardly acceptable to you." He then took out five sheets of paper and gave one to each.

---

59 *KM*: "but have had no chance to meet you."
60 *KM*: "The Magistrate again asked."
61 *KM*: "such-and-such a deputy's home."

"Write, each of you," said he, "the Four Points that constitute a marriage application." His words were stern and full of command.

The five, fearing trouble, knelt humbly before him and said, "We'll do as Your Excellency commands," and so they wrote each his application. The Prince took them in the order of the sons' ages, and appointed them to the daughters accordingly.

He then called for drink and refreshments and entertained them bountifully, giving to each as he left a large roll of grass-cloth. "Have an outer robe made of this," said he. Then he added, "I'll see to all the expense involved in these weddings so you need have no anxiety on that score."[62]

He sent supplies of cloth, cotton goods, silk, money, and grain in abundance to Deputy Yi's house, and on the day of the wedding he himself went and took a most interested part. The screens used, the mats, and the awnings were all sent from his official headquarters. Five tables were placed side by side in the wide court where five bridegrooms and five brides bowed toward each other and plighted their troth.

Sightseers crowded about till they formed walls on the four sides[63] and all were most appreciative of the goodness of the Prince.

Later many children were born to these five homes who passed their examinations and attained to high rank and responsible office. How much this unexpected favour of Prince Yŏnwŏn had to do with happy homes and joyful faces!

延原府院君李光庭爲楊牧時　養一鷹　使獵夫每作山行　一日　獵夫出去
經宿而還　傷足而行蹇公怪而問之　笑而對曰　昨日放鷹獵雉雉逸而鷹逃
四面搜訪　則鷹坐某處李座首門外大樹上故　艱辛呼鷹而臂之將欲復路之
際　忽聞籬內　有喧撓之聲故　自籬間窺見　則有五介處女　豪健如壯男樣　相
率而來　氣勢甚猛故　意其或被打　急急避身　足滑而傷　時日勢幾昏心甚訝
之　隱身於籬下叢「之中而聞之　則其五處女相謂曰　今日適從容　又當作太
守戲乎　僉曰　諾　其中大處女　年可三十　高坐石上　其下諸處女　各稱座首刑
房吸[及]唱使令名色　侍立於前　而已太守處女出令曰　座首拿入　刑房處女
呼吸[及]唱處女而傳分付　吸[及]唱處女呼使令處女而傳分付　使令承令
而捉下座首處女　拿而跪于庭下　太守處女　高聲數其罪曰　婚姻人之大倫也
汝之末女　年已過時　則其上之兄　從此可知矣　汝何爲而使汝之五女　空然
幷將廢倫乎　汝罪當死　座首處女　俯伏而奏曰　民豈不知倫紀之重乎　然而
民之家計赤立　婚具實無可判[辦]之望矣　太守曰　婚姻稱家之有無　只具單

62　*KM*: "on that account." The *KM* version adds here the following sentence: "He had the day chosen at once and in due time the marriages were celebrated."

63　*KM*: "The sightseers were packed like walls on the four sides."

衾 勺水成禮有何不可之理乎 汝言太迂﹁矣 座首曰 民之女 非一二人 郎
材亦無可求之處矣 太守口叱曰 汝若誠心廣求 豈有不得之理乎 以鄉中所
聞言之 某村之宋座首吳別監某村之鄭座首金別監崔鄉所家 皆有郎材 如
是則可定汝五女之匹矣 此人輩與汝地醜德齊有何不可之理 座首曰 謹當
依下敎通婚 而彼必以民之家貧不肯矣 太守曰 汝罪當答 而今姑十分參酌
斯速定婚而成禮可也 否者後當嚴處矣 仍命拿出 五介處女 仍相與大笑一
閧而散 其狀絶倒仍而作行 寄宿於旅舍 今始還來矣 延原聞而大笑 召鄉
所 問李座首來歷 與家勢子女之數 則以爲此邑曾經首鄉之人 而家勢赤立
無子 而有五女家貧之故 五女已過時 而尙未成婚矣 延原卽使禮吏告目請
李座首以來 未幾來謁 公曰 君是曾經鄉所而解事云 吾欲與之議事而未果
矣 仍問子女之數 則對曰 民命途奇窮 未育一子 只有無用之五女矣 問俱
已婚嫁否 對曰 一未成婚矣 又曰 年各幾何 對曰 第末女 已過時矣 公乃
以俄所聞太守處女之分付 一一問之 則其答果如座首處女之答 公乃歷數
某座首某別監某鄉所之家 而依太守處女之言而言曰 何不通婚也 對曰 渠
必以民之家貧不願矣 公曰 此事吾當居間矣 使之出去 又使禮吏 請五鄉
所而問曰 君家俱各有郎材云 然否 對曰 果有之 問已成娶否 對曰 姑無定
婚處矣 公曰 吾聞某村某座首之家有五女云 何不通而結親乎 五人﹁踧不
卽應 公正色曰 彼鄉族此鄉族 門戶相適 君輩之不欲 只較貧富而然也 若
然則貧家之女 其將編髮而老死乎 吾之年位 比君輩 何如不少之地 旣發
說 則君輩焉敢不從乎 乃出五幅簡 使置于五人之前曰 各書其子四柱可也
聲色俱厲 五人惶恐俯伏曰 謹奉敎矣 仍各書四柱以納 公以其年紀之多少
定其處女之次第 仍饋酒肴 又各賜苧布一疋曰 以此爲道袍之資 又分付曰
李家五女之婚具 自官備給 本家勿慮也 卽使之擇日 期在數日之間 仍送
布帛錢穀 使備婚需 伊日 公出往李家 屏﹁布陳之屬 自官借設 列五卓於庭
中 五女五郎 一時行禮 觀者如堵 無不欽嘆延原之積善 其後承繁衍而顯
達者 皆由積善之餘慶云爾.

Powers of Imitation
By Sŏng Hyŏn (1479–1504 AD)
Old Corea, 100

I had a neighbour once called Ham Pukkan, who hailed somewhere
from the east provinces. He knew how to blow a whistle wonderfully well, tell all kinds of odd stories, and act the part of a clown
generally. He could mimic anyone he saw and speak and act exactly
as they did. He would pucker up his mouth and pipe out sounds like
a flute, clarinet, or piccolo, loud and strong so that it could be heard
a mile off.

He could also imitate the harp and make sounds that twanged to any tune you wished. He used to be invited to the palace at times and was always rewarded most liberally.

I knew another man called Tae Moji who could imitate geese, ducks, chickens, or pheasants perfectly. One note from him and all the roosters of the place would take up the chorus.

We had a servant, too, named Pul Man-i who could imitate the barking of a dog. I once took him along to Kangwŏn [Province] with me, and when we reached a town at night he would set up a barking that put all the dogs of the neighbourhood into a state of wild excitement.

吾隣有咸北間者。自東界出來。稍知吹笛。善談諧倡優之戲。每見人容止。輒效所爲。則眞「莫辨。又能魘口作笳角之聲。聲甚宏壯。倡徹數里。至如琵琶琴瑟之聲。鏗鏘發口咸中節奏。每入內庭。多受賞賜。又有大毛知者。善爲鵝鴨鷄雉之聲。聲若出口。隣雞鼓翅而來。又耆之有奴曰佛萬者。善爲狗吠。嘗遊嶺東到一村。夜半發聲。隣犬皆集。[64]

The Tartar Hunter
Old Corea, 100–1;
"The Hunter," *Korea Magazine* 2
(October 1918): 455–7

Kim Soksi was a Yŏjin Tartar who came to Corea with his father when he was a young man. He was a strong athletic fellow and knew something of literature and letters as well. His home was among the hills of the Chojong[65] ward and the chase was his means of livelihood. He once told me a story of how he took deer. Said he, "In summer when the grass is long, the deer come out early in the morning to feed. When they have had their fill they retire to the hills and lie down. In hunting them I take beaters along with me and follow up their tracks[66] till I come to where they are.[67] We then surround them while two or three of the beaters go up to the top of the hill and perhaps sing, or call, or imitate the sounds of ploughing a field. The deer, hearing this, and counting them

---

64 Sŏng, *Yongjae ch'onghwa*, kwŏn 5.

65 朝宗.

66 *KM*: "and follow up these marks and tracks."

67 *KM*: "where they were."

familiar sounds, sit close and listen. Then is the time for me to string my bow and let fly my arrow. If not fatally wounded the deer unfailingly gets into the toils of the beaters when he tries to escape."[68]

"When the leaves and grass are gone in the autumn, my way is to find one of their runs, lie quiet nearby and shoot them as they pass."

"As for hunting bears, I may say that the bear is a fierce, powerful and fearless beast. If he meets a tiger he picks up a stone with one paw; with the other he takes the tiger by the throat and then gives him a smashing blow that crushes in his head. He also breaks off limbs of trees and fights with them. If he uses a limb and happens to let it fall, he does not know enough to pick it up again, but takes a fresh one instead. His turning to break off another gives the tiger a chance to pounce upon him."

"The bear knows how to climb trees. He sits down just as though he were a man, reaches out, turns the twigs toward him, and picks off the acorns and eats them. He frequently betakes himself to the edge of a stream and fishes for crabs, which he eats greedily. When winter comes he goes into his hole and sucks his paw. If he hears thunder in the 10th moon he refuses a hole for his winter quarters but covers himself with leaves instead."

"When grass and leaves are abundant, in summer, I frequently find him in a tree. On such occasions I take off my coat and go in as near as possible, but always behind his back.[69] While he is busy picking acorns I let fly my arrow so as to take him just behind the foreleg, and then I roll over and lie in the grass as though I were dead. Not a breath do I breathe."

"The bear shot, and with the arrow still in him, falls from the tree. He starts on a hunt for his enemy, scurrying about on all sides, but even though he finds me, he has no idea of harming me as I am dead. In his agony he cries like a human being, pitiful to hear, then goes down to the water's edge where he dies."

"As for tigers, I have shot many of them. Once, in the days of Sejo (1456–1468), His Majesty went on a trip to the hot-springs at Onyang, when a messenger came from one of the homes of the *literati* to say that a girl of sixteen years of age had been carried off the previous night from her inner room where she had been sitting, the door being open. A fierce

---

68 *KM*: "Though not fatally wounded he would only get into the toils of the
   beater if he tried to run away."
69 *KM*: "but always behind so that he cannot see."

tiger had suddenly pounced in upon her, and now the prayer was that His Gracious Majesty would do what he could to destroy the creature.

King Sejo ordered his officers to follow up the beast, and he sent me as well. I went first and inquired about the girl, and then started up the hill. About half way up we found her red coat, part of it torn away and hanging to the limb of a tree. A little further on we found the body near the edge of a stream, partly eaten. Later still, a sudden roar from the pine grove startled us. Looking up I saw a huge tiger with glaring eyes staring at me. I was wild to get at him so I dashed in with my horse and let fly an arrow. I then turned to get out of his way when suddenly I was stopped by the brushwood and my horse fell. He pounced on me and caught my arm in his teeth. There we had a fierce struggle till finally the others came up and dispatched him, so I escaped."

He pulled up his sleeve and let me see his arm, and there were the marks of the brute's teeth.

金束時女眞人也。少時隨其父出來。武藝絶倫。頗知經史。家在朝宗縣山谷間。日以畋獵爲事。嘗謂余言射鹿之事曰。當夏草茂之時。獐鹿凌晨出喫草。腹果入臥林藪。余率虞人數輩。尋蹤知所在。張網四面。又令一二人登山上。或歌或呼。爲畊田驅犢之狀。獸若聞之。則以爲尋常而不走出。屏氣而伏。余持滿而進。一箭而中之。不能中則退罹于網。百無一失。如草木黃落之後。潛立要蹊。俟其至而射之耳。言射熊之事曰。大抵熊勇敢多力。若見虎則以一手取大石。以一手搤虎項而壓之。又折樹枝而搏之。一搏之後。更折他樹枝。以故虎良久盡力去石。而復與之鬪。熊又能升大樹。蹲踞如人狀。以兩手攬枝柯。摘橡實而啖之。或遵澗搜小蟹。至冬則投巖穴。不食一物。只舐其掌而已。如十月有雷則不能投穴。惟以樹葉裹身而坐。余當夏草茂之時。見熊升樹。則盡脫衣服。而掛弓以入。隨熊背而坐。熊伸臂攀枝。遂持滿而射之。退臥草間。屏氣如死尸。熊被箭則狼狽而下。捫摸四旁。雖及吾身。而亦不知不能害。少頃不堪其苦。如人哀號之聲。伏澗而死矣。言射虎之事曰。平生射虎無算。昔世祖駐溫陽。有士族來告曰。年十六女子。昨夜在閨閣適窓開。惡獸攬之而去。仰冀聖德以伸冤抑。世祖命將往捕。亦令余隨之。至婦家問其狀。到山半腹。有紫衫。半裂掛林杪。又至數步。見尸在澗旁。半遭啖矣。俄聞松間有咆哮之聲。顧見之則大虎耽耽而視。余不勝憤。躍馬而進。一箭而中之。退爲松枝所掛馬躓而仆。虎來攬余臂而嚙之。與之相抗。虞人射而殪之。遂脫而免。去衣而視之。臂有所傷之痕矣。 [70]

---

70 Sŏng, *Yongjae ch'onghwa*, kwŏn 5.

Miscellaneous

Like the earlier section "Superstitions," the original typescript version of "Miscellaneous" is of a substantial length, but over half of the chapters (some with slightly different titles), including "A New Style of Courtship," "My Lord the Elephant," "New Years," "The Waning Eunuch," "Standing by Her Rights," *Broken Earthenware*, and "On and Off the Tram-Car" were included in *Pen Pictures* and so have been omitted here. The chapters are a truly eclectic mixture of themes befitting of the section title, with chapters ranging from music to transportation to insects.

The overarching theme that unifies the disparate chapters runs throughout both *Pen Pictures* and *Old Corea*: monumental change accompanying the eclipsing of the old order. In "The Dancing Girl," not to be confused with Gale's eponymously titled translation of a story from *Kimun ch'onghwa*, Gale skilfully traces the lineage of the *kisaeng* from the fall of Silla to the present day. Reserving his own moral judgments, Gale instead utilizes the Korean textual corpus as his own proxy denunciation, but suggests that ultimately it was not moral indignation or Confucian piety that triumphed but rather the modern world itself that sealed the fate of this ancient institution. In "Music," Gale explores the collision of Eastern and Western music, or rather, the vastly different affect engendered in Koreans' approach to each. In rather humorous fashion, Gale suggests not the demise of the East Asian tradition at the hands of an overwhelming Western force (his more common trope) but rather the emergence of a hybrid musical sensibility, an appropriation of Western musicality nevertheless devoid of "proper" function. "Corean Transportation" charts the technological progress of Korea, beginning with the ubiquitous pedestrian and ending with modern means of machine conveyance, hinting at the coming changes on the horizon. In "Flies," a seemingly random rant on that pesky insect, Gale similarly notes a dramatic shift in modern Korea. Reminding the reader of the ubiquity of the pest throughout history through detailed textual references, Gale notes that thanks to the "police and city authorities who have wrought his destruction," flies have "suddenly ceased to be." Unlike many aspects of "Old Corea," the disappearance of the fly would not engender the same feelings of regret or nostalgia. In a similar vein, Gale writes approvingly of the progress Korea has made in weathering the rainy season (*changmach'ŏl*). For those who have endured this humid, damp experience that marks midsummer in Korea, Gale's descriptions are evocative and oddly nostalgic.

In the final chapter, Gale narrates an ill-fated journey to the coastal resort area of Sorae. Though the article itself is unremarkable, the location it describes is nonetheless significant in the history of missions and Christianity in Korea. Sorae was the location of Korea's first Presbyterian church, founded by Sŏ Sangnyun (徐相崙, 1848–1926), one of the Koreans hired by the Scottish missionaries John Ross and John MacIntyre to translate the *hanmun* Bible into vernacular Korean. After completing this task in China, Sŏ returned to Korea and tried to open a church in Sinŭiju, but the state's still-adverse stance to Christianity forced Sŏ to the remote coastal farming village of Sorae, where he and a small group of followers founded a church in 1884.[1] Hearing of this church, the American Presbyterian missionary Horace Underwood, who arrived in Korea in 1885, acquired land in the area and built a house overlooking the beach shortly thereafter.[2] This was also how the first vernacular Bible, in possession of Sŏ and his congregation, was brought to Seoul by Underwood and came to be mass-produced.[3] From the 1880s until 1941, when the last of the missionaries were forced to leave Korea, Sorae Beach remained a popular vacation spot and resort area for foreign residents in Korea. In the chapter Gale relates one of his journeys from Seoul to this remote village, a narrative that ties in with the evolving nature of transportation related in a previous chapter.

---

1 Y.S. Kim, personal website, http://ysfine.com/kobak/soraech.html.

2 Ibid.

3 Ibid.

The Dancing Girl
Old Corea, 102–4; "The Kisaeng
(Dancing Girl),"
Korea Magazine 2 (May 1918): 198–202;
Gale Papers, "The Kisaeng," Box 7, Folder 11

One of the noticeable features of Corean life is the *kisaeng*[4] or dancing girl. You see her on the tram-car, dressed in all her fluff and feathers, coloured like a bird in pink, and green, and, I forget whether she has touches of red in her gear or not. However, she appears seemingly in all the colours of the rainbow, with ermine-tipped edges, a picture for the eye to see; not often pretty from a Western point of view, but striking. She rides about in the best rickshaws with up-to-date pneumatic tires, and holds her head up like a queen.

It might seem to a Foreign passer that a woman who would not only sell her gift of song and her grace of foot to dance, but her body as well, ought to hide her head, or be seen only lurking about hidden corners, or be dodging here and there in the twilight as do our castaways at home.

But not so the *kisaeng*. She is as blithe a bird as ever hopped, with not a shadow lying across her little old conscience, happy in the role she is called upon to play, and feeling that she is a very necessary and important part of what the East calls Society.

If we reckon up her ancestry according to the books and records on hand, she is a thousand years old, and probably, as far as society is concerned, comes down from some of the best classes of the day in which her fathers lived.

Mr. An Chŏngbok,[5] a strict old Confucianist, who spent some of his best strength in attacking Christianity, and who died in 1791, says that[6]

---

4 妓生.

5 An Chŏngbok (安鼎福, 1712–91) penned his treatise against Catholicism titled *Conversation on Catholicism* (Ch'ŏnhak mundap 天學問答) in 1785, in response to what he viewed as an alarming growth of Catholic influence among his Confucian peers. In this work, structured as an exchange with his Catholic-leaning son-in-law, An points out the immorality of Catholicism for placing personal salvation ahead of one's family and community. For a translation of this text, see Baker and Rausch, *Catholics and Anti-Catholicism in Chosŏn Korea*.

6 *Korea Magazine* (KM): "says in his book *Sŏngho sasŏl*." This is, however, a misattribution: *Sŏngho sasŏl* (星湖僿說) was written by Sŏngho (星湖) Yi Ik (李瀷, 1681–1763).

the official *kisaeng* comes down from the basket-making class. When Koryŏ conquered Silla in 918 AD one group of people absolutely refused submission and so lost their family records and their social standing. They betook themselves to the hills, where they wandered about as gypsies, hunting and making wicker baskets.

Later in their history a certain Yi Chiyŏng took one of their number, whose name was Red-Cloud-Fairy, as his concubine. Thus they became known to the outer world. After that date, if their women were pretty and won the favour of the official in charge of the district where their wanderings took them, they were dressed in silk, taught music and dancing, and called *kisaeng* or dancing girls.

The class to which she belongs, namely the basket-makers, was evidently like the "wild" Irish, "agin"[7] the government for all time, for we find them in 1217, or three hundred years after their defection, charged with aiding and abetting the Khitan Tartars in an attack upon Corea. The basket-makers petitioned the king against this suspicion and made considerable noise about it.[8]

Until recently, Corea classed basket-makers with executioners, acrobats, witches, and shoemakers, and marked them the lowest in the land.

Thus the dancing girl took her origin.

Mr. An goes on to say that the habit of cultivating the dancing girl increased and grew till she was found in every county in the state. She became the musician, not only on official occasions, but at private entertainments as well. He adds, "The impure language and foul acts that attended her way put one's eyes and ears to shame."

In 1430 AD there was a discussion in state circles as to how to do away with her, when Hŏ Cho,[9] a minister of great note, and a severe and correct man in his own life, remarked, "Such women must be had

---

7 Against.

8 The preceding three paragraphs constitute Gale's paraphrasing of the following account found in *Koryŏsa chŏryŏ*, kwŏn 129. "初李至榮爲朔州分道將軍, 楊水尺多居興化·雲中道, 至榮謂曰, '汝等本無賦役, 可屬吾妓紫雲仙.' 遂籍其名, 徵貢不已. 至榮死, 忠獻又以紫雲仙爲妾, 計口徵貢滋甚. 楊水尺等大怨, 及契丹兵至, 迎降鄉導故, 悉知山川要害, 道路遠近. 楊水尺, 太祖攻百濟時, 所難制者遺種也, 素無貫籍賦役, 好逐水草, 遷徙無常, 唯事畋獵, 編柳器販鬻爲業. 凡妓種, 本出於柳器匠家. 後楊水尺等帖匿名書云, '我等非故反逆也, 不堪妓家侵奪故, 投契丹賊爲鄉導. 若朝廷殺妓輩及順天寺主, 則可倒戈輔國矣.' 忠獻聞之, 乃歸其妓紫雲仙·上林紅于其鄉. 順天寺主, 亦恃勢自恣, 與妓爲亂者也, 聞之亡去."

9 Hŏ Cho (許租, 1369–1440).

for officials who go to far-distant out-stations and cannot take their wives with them, otherwise decent women will run great danger," and so the custom was maintained.[10]

We read that in the year 1519 an edict was promulgated doing away with the *kisaeng*, but the force of public opinion was too strong against it and failed to carry.[11]

Yu Hyŏngwŏn,[12] a noted scholar who died in 1673, says, "The *kisaeng* is an instrument to teach men evil ways."[13] The *Book of Ceremony*[14] reads, "Officials should never speak of women." A word even regarding them was not allowed, much less their near approach.

"In ancient times in the Court, in the Temple of Heaven, at the Ancestral Shrines – in fact, all places of the state – whether teaching, dressing, eating, feasting, or entertaining, men did everything in accord with the laws of God, but later these laws fell into disuse and society gave itself up to unlawful pleasure. Laws, regulations, and even punishments were not sufficient to keep back the flood of evil."[15]

"Men's passions rise at sight and hearing, therefore the ancients ordered the greatest care in what one saw and heard, so that the eyes should not behold a sight that tempted, nor the ears hear a sound that suggested wrong. Unchaste women were put far away. Now, however, officials rear and breed a race of low women that they can use in the entertainment of their guests. They dress and adorn them and have them await the stranger who comes. They serve to give him drink and sing him songs and so arouse his passion. Because of these the heart is taken captive and the victim drowns as in water, while state affairs go by the board and the customs and habits of the day degenerate.

---

10 Sŏng, *Yongjae ch'onghwa*, kwŏn 9.

11 The *Chosŏn wangjo sillok* (Veritable Records of the Chosŏn Dynasty) record extensive discussions in government circles during the years 1519 and 1520 regarding the issue of "female musicians" (*yŏak* 女樂).

12 Yu Hyŏngwŏn (柳馨遠, 1622–73).

13 In the *KM* version Gale adds the source of this quotation as *Pan'gye surok* (磻溪隨錄 1670), a twenty-six-kwŏn work resulting from two decades of extensive first-hand research and investigation by the author. It was completed in 1670 but not printed until 1769.

14 禮記.

15 古者。上自朝廷郊廟。以至官府閭巷。政敎號令。衣服飲食燕樂。莫非以天理。而爲之制度。故人皆習其事。安其俗。而不自知其日遷善遠罪也。Yu Hyŏngwŏn 柳馨遠, *Pan'gye surok* (磻溪隨錄) kwŏn 25, 1.10 "Yŏak uhŭi" 女樂優戲.

Resolutions toward better purposes in life are undermined and true service is gone forever."[16]

"A man who can associate with *kisaeng* and yet never yield himself to them is a rare individual. Few men can do so. If there were no singing girls it would be possible for many a man to live a life of virtue who otherwise falls. Anyone overcome by passion to the extent of taking forcible possession of another man's wife or daughter is a low criminal, and his case falls outside the realm of ordinary discussion."[17]

"Laws and ordinances are intended to conserve good form and keep right the heart, but for the sake of the lowest of the land to prepare these creatures of evil is only another way of encouraging vice. Is it right? As well prepare goods for a thief to steal, in order to meet the evil bent of his thievish nature, as to legalize the dancing-girl."[18]

"*Kisaeng*, too, are human beings. If those above them never teach them morals, but rather encourage them to sin, what hope is there for them? Are such laws and customs just? When Confucius saw dancing girls being used by the king of No he resigned office and left."[19]

All down through history we find Coreans out fighting this evil, honest men whose names would do credit to any state, but they were crushed under the rough feet of the ruling classes, one of whose greediest aims and ambitions was to possess the dancing girl.

16　人欲之起。皆由於視聽。所以古人。必尊其瞻視。而放淫聲。遠邪色也。今也畜淫娼。一聞使客之來。必令冶容姿。姱衣裳而待之。及其來也。則行酒以侑之。執樂以挑之。稱之曰房妓。而公然眠寢。彼爲使客者。亦曰官物取之無妨。而不以爲嫌。因以牽情溺欲。害政事。傷風敎。

17　夫有此而不爲所奪者。上也。不可人人而責之。無此而安焉無失者。人人皆能。至若 不勝其欲。而奪民妻女。陷於罪戾者。至下之人也。本無足論。

18　Gale is paraphrasing the following passage:
國家立制。而不務明禮法。正人心。而唯爲至下之人。預設其具。以濟其私欲者。此豈理也哉。苟如其說也。則好貨。亦人欲之所不能無者。恐人之陷於罪。而預爲非義之貨。無妨之制。以待之乎。

19　This is likewise a paraphrase of the closing section of "Yŏak uhŭi":
且彼亦人也。上之人。旣不能敎以人倫。而編籍爲妓。使不得有定夫。欲有定夫。則輒罪之。是何等規制乎。

The sentence on Confucius's well-known though likely spurious account of resigning office in the Dukedom of No (魯 Ch. Lu) is Gale's addition and does not appear in in the *Pan'gye surok*. In classic fashion, Gale's translations here are very much concerned with conveying the sense of the original in concise style, at times sacrificing entire pharases and clauses for the sake of brevity.
For a much more literal translation of this section from *Pan'gye surok*, see James Palais's translation, "Kisaeng and Actors."

She has survived all these years of a long millennium and still moves about the capital undaunted as though her case was above reproach.

Yi Kyubo writes of her seven hundred years ago:

"Have you not heard that the glance of her eye is a sharpened blade; that her eye-brows are a double-faced headsman's axe; that her red cheeks are a deadly potion; and that her soft flesh is a hidden demon that demands the soul? With her axe she strikes; with her blade she thrusts; with her hidden wiles she seeks my life and endeavours to bring me to sorrow and shame. Is she not a danger? Among all my deadly enemies can anything equal her? Therefore she is called a 'thief,' a 'robber.' A robber means death to me; how dare I make friends with him? So, I say, 'Put her far away!' To the eye she is a delightful invitation, while in reality she is a fearful evil.

There is no doubt that the beauty of the dancing-girl is something that can overturn the world. Her fascinations surpass in the fierceness of their intent even the tiger and the leopard. The love of such as she is the cause of all jealousy and strife. Once caught by her, a man's name is gone and his good reputation tarnished forever. Kings and princes, ministers and men of state who have overturned thrones and wrought ruin, have done it at her bidding. She has blinded their eyes and be-clouded their understanding. By her they have begotten disaster and woe, and dynasties have toppled to their ruin."[20]

Music
Old Corea, 105–6;
Korea Magazine 1 (April 1917): 160–4

One of the most inscrutable things pertaining to the Orient is its music. A most marked accompaniment of the Far East it is, and one of the things of which this great world thinks it has no little understanding, and yet it is as far removed from what Eastern people call music as are the raspings of the cicada from the soft warblings of a canary bird.[21]

---

20 In his Index to Korean Literature in the Gale Papers, Gale includes "isgc i 83.96.172.206.237. ii 288. 327. 364" for "Dancing Girls," referring to *Tongguk Yi Sangguk chip*, or *The Collected Works of Yi Sangguk*. These portions contain various mentions of *kisaeng*, but none seem to conform exactly to Gale's above excerpt.

21 *KM*: "and yet it is as far removed from what Wesern people call music, as the star Sirius and its system is distant from the sun."

The subdivision MUSIC in the *Munhŏn pigo*,[22] or National Encyclo-paedia, occupies some eighteen volumes out of two hundred and fifty, and has under its name such subdivisions as Weather, Weights and Measures, and the Alphabet. I ask my friend Kim[23] what possible relationship the weather can have to music, and he explains it thus: "There are twelve instruments that follow the twelve months of the year, and so keep swinging in step with the weather. Their notes agree with the changes that come and go. The spring's soft gentle touch finds its note; the summer's heat with its grasshopper[24] has its song to sing, as well as the stern tightening breath of autumn, and the savage grip of winter. All are represented in the fundamental laws of music."

"As for Weights and Measures, have you not heard," asks Kim, "how the grain of sand in the ancient Chinese lute lowered the tone one degree or inch? Now here is a grain of sand one inch of space – weight and measure."[25]

"The Alphabet, too, has its relationship, for it is built on the Five Notes of music, and the other half tones." The makers doubtless sang as they laboured over their task – *kung, sang, kak, ch'i, u*[26] – just as Mr. Kipling whistled or hummed *"O de tum tum tum"* and then launched out:

> "Oh it isn't good for the Christian's health
> To hustle the Aryan brown."[27]

One can see how the alphabet might thus be very closely related to the great question of music.

This, however, is by the way of introduction to say that their musical world is a closed book, clasped with many seals. We can never hope to open it without a special pass from the angel who guards the treasure

---

22 文獻備考.

23 This almost certainly refers to Gale's "pundit" Kim Tohŭi 金道熙, who died in 1925.

24 *KM*: "and cicada."

25 *KM*: "I had not heard of that, but I understood Kim's meaning at once, for here was a grain of sand and one inch of space weight and measure."

26 These are the names for the ascending tones in Eastern music, equivalent to "do-re-me-fa-sol-la."

27 The complete couplet reads thusly: "Oh it isn't good for the Christian's health, to hustle the Aryan brown, For the Christian riles, and the Aryan smiles and he weareth the Christian down; And the end of the fight is a tombstone white with the name of the late deceased, And the epitaph drear: "A fool lies here who tried to hustle the East." Kipling and Balestier, *The Naulahka*.

houses of the yellow East. So too, our music is a perfectly unintelligible quantity to them.

I said to Kim, "If you don't mind I'll sing you one of the songs written by the great Master Uam.[28] I know them and like them very much." So I launch out with a quaver in my throat and high-keyed voice, well sustained till it comes to the proper drop and choke at the end, just as nearly like what I had heard all classes of the people sing a thousand times and more. But Kim says, "Please don't, I beg you. Your Excellency knows many things but not how to sing in Corean."

Then I ask, "How about your singing foreign hymns, for example?"

"I sing at church," says he.

"You think you can sing?" I ask.

"Why, of course!"

"How comes it that you can sing a foreign tune of which you have heard almost nothing, while I can't sing a Corean song though I have heard man and woman and boy sing it through long years."

"I imagine we are a more musical race, perhaps, than you."

"Indeed!"

I said further, "I like your music; do you like ours?"

"No, not especially," said he.

"Why do you sing it then?"

"It's the proper form of worship everywhere; that's why I sing."

"Does it ever melt you to tears or make you leap for joy?"

"I don't catch your meaning," says Kim.

"Let me suppose there are a hundred hardened sinners gathered in a meeting, and I call on the Corean choir to sing 'Receiveth Sinful Men'; would they be moved by it to confess and change their ways, do you suppose?"

"Moved by it? Why no, that would not move them. It has nothing to do with moving, it is the form by which you carry on worship."

"Does the hymn 'Rejoice and be Glad' make you think of joy?"

I found, however, that it was no use to talk to Kim in this strain as he had not the faintest notion of what I was driving at. Mr. Sankey's "The Ninety and Nine"[29] that could captivate the hearts of thousands

---

28 Uam Song Siyŏl (尤庵 宋時烈, 1607–89).

29 "The Ninety and Nine" is a hymn, the music for which was composed by American gospel singer and composer Ira D. Sankey (1840–1908), also known as "The Sweet Singer of Methodism," and the lyrics for which were written by Scottish songwriter Elizabeth C. Clephane (1830–69). Sankey would have been

gathered in the great tabernacle in London has no influence whatever on the East, and yet they too have their music. I quote from a famous Corean novel, "The musician played another when the young lady remarked, 'This tune is very sweet and tender, the tune of Ch'ae Munhŭi who was caught in the war and carried off by the barbarians. Cho Cho gave a fabulous sum for her ransom and had her brought back home. When she bade good-bye to the far north she wrote this tune. It is said the barbarians hearing it dropped tears on the grass, while the Minister from Han was melted by its strains.'"[30]

They know all about being touched by music and made glad. They know what it means to dance for joy, and to shed tears, but they would no more think of associating these emotions with Western music, than we would associate the notes of Paderewski[31] with the rattle of an anchor chain.

The writer is convinced after careful study through long years that the thoughts and associations of the Corean regarding church music are of an entirely different order from anything we have ever dreamed of.

I recall a case: The leader strikes up before the harmonium has given the key, and they launch but five notes apart, but no one in the

---

close to Gale's heart because Sankey was a close associate of famous evangelist Dwight L. Moody (1837–99), who met and prayed with the young Gale the evening before Gale set sail for Korea from Vancouver.

30 Gale's typescript writes "Cha Moon-heui" but the lady in question is Cai Yan 蔡琰, courtesy name Wenji 文姬, so Gale should have written Ch'ae for the surname. The "famous Corean novel" in question is the *Romance of the Three Kingdoms* (Samgukchi yŏnŭi 三國志演義), one of the four great novels of classical Chinese literature, but a work so thoroughly enjoyed by Korean readers for so many centuries as to be considered virtually a "Korean" novel. For the history of the reception of this work in Korea, see Hyuk-chan Kwon, "From *Sanguozhi yanyi* to *Samgukchi*." Cai Yan, daughter of renowned Eastern Han scholar Cai Yong (蔡邕, AD 132–92), was taken prisoner by the Southern Xiongnu in 195 when they invaded Han territory, and then ransomed back in 207 by warlord Cao Cao (曹操, 155–220). She left behind her Xiongnu husband and two children. The song in question is likely the "Poems of Lament and Resentment" (Pibun si 悲憤詩) attributed to her. See Frankel, "Cai Yan and the Poems Attributed to Her."

31 Ignacy Jan Paderewski (1860–1941) was a Polish composer, pianist, statesman, and promoter of Polish independence.

congregation except the Foreigner realizes it. It continues through the whole of the first line, five notes clear out of tune, while jarring sensations go up and down the back of the unhappy Westerner. Not only so but the whole verse is sung under these unheard of conditions, and to end the matter the whole five verses are driven through to a fine finish, the organist playing, and playing well too, and the leader holding to his point in the scale as tenaciously as though his life depended on it, all the time five notes apart. The jangle and noise of it never reached the Corean's soul.

A band of music, four men or five, trained by a skilful Western master, though now no longer under his keen gray eye, strikes out with that confidence that the Orient shows when it writes a sign-board in English, into a discord and confusion indescribable, and yet the only ones who sense it are the Foreigners. To all other listeners it is the proper thing – a noise of course, but a noise that conforms to custom. That it be sweet to the ear, that it mean something to the soul, that it carry one away on its wings and show him regions of delight that can never be forgotten, is not for one minute associated with anything of the kind or any other variety of Western music.

We would not be a whit better in any attempt of ours to render their music. We might be quicker to notice the incongruity of the thing, but would be quite as helpless to enter into its hidden mystery.

I am inclined to think that there is no exception to this rule in the East. Many will doubt the correctness of this position, especially those interested in teaching Western music, but I commend to them a careful examination along the lines suggested.

At best even those who acquire a good knowledge of Western music are only phonographs, victrolas, or music-boxes, lacking the expression and tenderness that goes with the soul. To truly touch the heart of the East you must awaken those chords dealt with in the article in the *Encyclopedia* that has Weather, Weights and Measures, and the Alphabet for its subdivisions.[32]

---

32 *KM*: Gale signs this piece "E.T.," which stands for "Esson the Third," in honour of his Scottish grandmother's maiden name. Gale also used this pseudonym when writing anonymously for the *North China Daily News* from 1899 to 1905. Many unsigned literary translations appearing in *Korea Magazine* resurfaced in Gale's *History of the Korean People*, confirming their authorship. Rutt, *James Scarth Gale and His "History,"* 35, 54.

Corean Transportation
Old Corea, 107–8;
Spectator, *Korea Magazine* 1 (April 1917): 150–4

One of the interesting sights to a newcomer in Corea is to see the number of people who are walking. Roads and pathways are dotted here and there with white coats swinging off down the valley, skimming round the corner of the hill, crossing the long stretch of rice-flat, or making up the steep face of some rocky cliff. The Corean owns[33] a poise and a swinging step, free and independent, that indicates a soul well balanced on its heels[34] that fears not the word called distance. He has the means of self-transportation always ready: an extra pull to his garter straps,[35] and an inch tighter for his girdle string, and away he goes.

We have traveled[36] the road with him for many a day, and for the first fifteen miles are quite his equal, if not superior. For the next ten, matters even up, and the last five, those long hollow-cheeked miles, with no stomach and an ache in the back – these miles are all in his favour.

The Foreigner, though gifted with an extra ten-inch length of leg, reaches his limit earlier, is ten times more tired in the end; in fact, ready to roll over and yield up the ghost. His white-coated companion is not so; he is just as he was, and steps out with a reserve of ease and equilibrium most remarkable.[37] The soul of the Foreigner sings through the first ten miles, sweats over ten more, and finally staggers – I almost said swears – through the last ten, muttering to himself his views as to the senseless way in which Coreans measure distance.

He is a fine specimen of humanity[38] who can step off thirty miles and be sweet and light and jovial at the end of it. The writer has heard of a Corean after all the tug of mud and weary distance, tell a good story, and give a cheery laugh to crown the day. A nation of fine walkers the Coreans surely are.

---

33 *KM*: "carries."

34 *KM*: "a soul that stands square on its heels."

35 *KM*: "garter wraps."

36 *KM*: "We have tried."

37 *KM*: "steps out with the same poise and an equilibrium of spirit most remarkable."

38 *KM*: "manhood."

The pony continues to be one of the common means of transportation. He was a queer animal twenty-five years ago and he is still as queer as ever. No amount of street repair or road-making can change his soul. He can kick and bite as his father Abraham did, and be nearly as agile and unexpected as a ball of shrapnel. Once on his back and you are all right.[39] While you sit thus, all goes well, but just let a sudden lurch throw you sideways, or lift your heels across the line of his vision and then see what happens. The rebound from a fifteen inch mortar is not greater than the surprise that lands you on the back of your neck in the middle of the road. The writer can still see, as in a vision, a tall Westerner endeavouring to take the worth of such a fall out of a little game-cock of a pony. He had the *mabu*[40] hold him tooth and nail, while he circled venomously round and round with intent to let him feel the weight of four inches of Montgomery-Ward sole-leather. His number ten boot, in its efforts, shot at Sirius and all the other stars of the firmament without once landing a kick in the wary pony's side. Finally he gave it up, and found as a reward that he could not get near enough the animal for love or money to mount. He had to walk the last five miles under the inspiration of a broken neck without any of the honour of it, and a feeling accompanying him as though his kicking leg had been permanently dislocated from the socket. Walking is bad, but it is nothing to this.

Another beast of burden is the ox. Broad of back and with a neck like Job's behemoth, he can carry loads, something enormous; and yet he is the most docile animal in the world. He can cross the Han River, fifteen in a boat, and never say "boo." Could Ramsey Macdonald MP,[41] Ford of the automobile, and other pacifists behold him, how their hearts would rejoice at this creature after their own kind. Gad-flies and stinging beetles may sit on him all day and take their fill and not one of them be whisked into eternity. Tears may come to his eyes but *pro bono publico*[42]

---

39 The *KM* version adds the following sentences: "While you sit there you are safe. He seems to have lost consciousness of your whereabouts; his ears do not hear you and his eyes fail to see backwards."

40 *Mabu* (馬夫) is a horse attendant or horseman.

41 The Scottish-born James Ramsay McDonald (1866–1937) was Prime Minister of the United Kingdom from 1931 to 1935 and one of the founders of the Labour Party.

42 The public good.

is his motto, and he feels that the gad-fly has his right to all he can hold and eight hours a day.

With a load of brushwood that would crush the life out of most animals, he makes his way to the Capital, guided and beaten and stormed at by an imp of a boy not more than four feet high.

One sometimes wonders if the pacifist[43] were driven into a corner by a brigand with horns and hoofs, whether or not he would awake from his dream, with his eye flashing and the old spirit of the warrior upon him. Or if his ship, for example, were foundering at sea whether he would set to and pull and haul for dear life, or go down simply with a wan smile on his face.[44] Doubtless he would do the latter, remembering that the crawling things of the deep have a right to their innings as well as he, and that a square meal to them once in a while is the real spirit of *pro bono publico*.

Still, I may be mistaken for I had thought the Corean bull an unmovable pacifist till one day riding a wheel with a friend I found out the contrary. The friend had pulled ahead and then had gone down the hill like a flash,[45] barely missing the bull who was tied by the nose to a stake in the ground. The animal, awakened thus suddenly and alarmed beyond measure, broke the rope and turned for his life, only to behold another bicycle coming with a wild creature upon it. A change developed, lightning flashed from his eyes, and a blaze of fire from each nostril. Down went his head forward and he bounded like a raging buffalo of the plains. There was a sharp collision, bull and bicycle, flinging the rider hopelessly into the air.[46] A hazy memory remains of a bull crossing the horizon, with tail erect,[47] and the light defiant step of a warrior seeking battle. He is not always a pacifist. The spirit is in him but it is well under control.

The *rickshaw* has come as a new and feeble representative of modern ideas. To ride in a *rickshaw* is considered "high-collar," but really it is not what it is "cracked up" to be. After being on a pony and seeing the mighty movings of the bull, I have no spirit to deal with the *rickshaw* or the cart either.

---

43 *KM:* "Ford."
44 *KM:* "with the wan smile of the pacifist on his face."
45 *KM:* "like a flash of lightning."
46 *KM:* "in all directions."
47 *KM:* "with tail in the air."

Born somewhere in the regions of Pluto, and harnessed up and made ready by his uncanny aides, comes the motor-cycle. Could Tongbang Sak[48] or some other ancient Chinese have seen it, I can imagine him noting down something like this: "Racing demon, spirit of negative principle, voice impossible locate five notes of Chinese music. Smell defying thinking powers of human man. Number one bad devil!"[49]

Railways, automobiles, motor-cycles, bicycles, *rickshaws*, carts, bulls, and horses are all whipped into service and share![50] Hardly a dweller in the most distant hills but has seen all of these waddling about or skating over the horizon.

The coolie, however, remains, the man with the *chige*[51] who can lift 100, 200, 300, 400 – yes – and sometimes 500 pounds. Get your Corean coolie square under his burden and he will lift the world. He could not handle a Japanese wrestler, or spar with Becket[52] in the ring, but he could lift them both on his back and carry them to the top of North Mountain.[53] Among all shades and varieties of transportation what can equal the coolie? In spite of his lowly calling he is a gentleman at heart. I lift my hat to him as one good man of the Far East.

---

48 Tongbang Sak (東方朔 Ch. Dongfang Shuo, 154– 92 BC) was a scholar-official during the Han dynasty (206 BC–AD 220), considered a Taoist immortal imbued with supernatural powers. He was also known for his humorous antics at court and nicknamed Hwalgye (滑稽), or "Buffoon."

49 The *KM* version links the words in the following stream-of-consciousness description: "Racing-demon-filled-spirit-*ŭm*-negative-principle, voice-impossible-locate-five-Chinese-notes, smell-defy-thinking-powers-human-man. Hope-my-speedy-die-pass-off-green-earth, number-one-bad-devil." This is Gale's attempt to reproduce Literary Sinitic in English.

50 *KM*: "horses are all whipped into service and share a part in the transportation of goods and chattels in the Land of the Morning Calm. What a change!" That the original name given to Korea, (Ko) Chosŏn (朝鮮), did not literally mean "morning calm" but was rather based on a sinographic approximation of the Korean native pronunciation of the country would have been known to Gale.

51 *KM*: "*chi-keui.*" This is a Korean A-frame carried on the back.

52 Joseph Beckett was an English boxer active in the 1910s and early 1920s. In the *KM* version, Gale compares "the coolie" with Bob "Fitzsimmons" (1863–1917), who was active much earlier, in the 1890s. As the *OC* version was penned roughly a decade later in the mid-1920s, Gale seems to have opted for a more contemporaneous reference.

53 *KM*: "and carry them to the top of Pukhan." Pukhan Mountain (北漢山) is a mountain on the northern edge of Seoul. *KM* adds the following: "Most

Flies
Old Corea, 109–10;
Korea Magazine 1 (January 1917): 18–21

Corea is a land in which the Imperial Government at times rolls up its sleeve and goes out to fight the fly. Flies suddenly cease to be, and we behold them no more. A shot-gun, a knight's lance or a long sword is of no avail against the fly. In fact, his breed seems well nigh invulnerable until the authorities take him in hand and most skillfully compass his destruction.[54]

We remember the fly as one of the ancient possessors of the city. He drew up his forces by battalions, brigades and fighting corps, millions strong, encamping everywhere. Particularly does he enjoy the warm sunny side of life and seek it out with remarkable perseverance and skill. He made his rounds daily something in the following order: Starting from his sheltered ledge where the new sun had quickened him into life he would make his way to wine-shops and other exposed places, and have a light breakfast. From there, as the day advanced, and the rays of light peered down into the holes and noisome dens of the city, he gaily took his flight, calling at the most unnamable pools and awful places for a substantial meal. He would then come back, delighted with himself, an optimist hopeful about everything, and join Kim Sŏbang or some other man of leisure in his afternoon siesta. He would take a long running jump from the corner of the swinging door right into the unconscious Corean's face. Automatically, though sound asleep, Kim would drive at him with his hand, vainly however, for just as well try to put salt on a live bird's tail as to catch a fly when you are sound asleep. Quick as light he would drop down again and continue his travels just where he had left off. Round and round and round he would go into the corner of Kim's mouth and under his chin. Fearless? The like was never seen. Then he would join the family in the evening

---

foreigners spell the name of this equipment 'jiggy' but that is incorrect. It is *chi-kŭi* [지긔] and my Korean friend, who knows, tells me that *chi* [智] stands for wisdom and *keui* [器] for implement, *wise implement*." Needless to say, this is a folk etymology. The word derives from verb stem *chi-* "carry on the back" and the derivational suffix *–ke* which denotes tools.

54 *KM*: "The past year (1916) has been specially interesting as regards flies. The interesting part is that they have suddenly ceased to be, and we now see them no more."

meal, play foot-ball all over the fresh pan-cakes,[55] or go sightseeing across the face[56] of Kim's heaped up rice-dish.

The fly is rather a stay-at-home creature unless he can get suitable conveyance abroad. One favorite mode of transportation is to ride on a coolie's warm back and go comfortably across town, entering the home and wiping his feet on the baby's eye-lashes, or the corners of his ears; cantering all round its little mouth and over its neglected nose. What a lovely day the fly used to have, but it has come to a sharp end; his picnic is over, and we practically see him no more.

These are modern ideas regarding the fly. Some more ancient views as to his character and habits may be interesting.

Yi Kyubo (1168–1241 AD), Prime Minister of Corea in the Koryŏ Dynasty and a contemporary of Richard Coeur de Lion, says, "I have ever hated the ways in which the fly continually pesters and bothers people. The thing that I dislike most of all is to have him sit on the rims of my ears and settle squabbles with his neighbour. When I am ill and see him about me, I am afflicted with a double illness over and above my original complaint. In seeing the multitude of his breed swarming about, I cannot but make my complaints to God."

> "Your buzz and fuss drown e'en the crowing cock,
> And all your marks speck every whitened thing.
> I chase you off and yet you fail to go;
> I trust the King will make an end of you."[57]

This seems almost to have come true today, for His Imperial Majesty's Government is a very uncomfortable one for the fly to live under.

Again he says,

> "I'm worn to death in driving off these flies;
> I wrap my head but fail, alas, to sleep.
> No use to scold, or rate at them, or swear;
> They drop into my wine and die with glee."[58]

---

55 *KM*: "the fresh-cooked *taegak* cakes [*taegak ttŏk*]."
56 *KM*: "across the mountain face."
57 "平生猒汝逐人偏。第一深憎鬪耳邊。病裏逢來重值病。滋繁此物怨皇天。"
    Tongguk Yi Sangguk hujip 東國李相國後集 kwŏn 1, Koyul si 古律詩.
58 "驅去還來力亦疲。掩衾謀睡夢成遲。干人身分何須責。飛墮盃觴自不知。"
    Tongguk Yi Sangguk hujip 東國李相國後集 , kwŏn 1, Koyul si 古律詩.

Sŏng Hyŏn (1439–1504 AD) leaves among his literary notes the following: "There was a military official once, whose name was Yang, sent south as governor of Kongju.[59] In summer, it seems, the place was particularly plagued with flies, and Yang hated them with unspeakable hatred. So he set his secretaries, his writers, his runners, his maids, slaves, everyone, in fact, to work, ordering that each bring him a bowl of flies every morning. He made it a serious matter and urged them under penalty. The company fought each other over these flies. They feared to fail and yet they hated the task. Some went about hiring others to catch flies for them, while they gave the governor the name *p'ari moksa* (fly-governor). If one were to rule his district with the same zeal that this man exercised in catching flies, he would be doubtless a model governor."[60]

Kim Inhu (1501–1560 AD),[61] one of Corea's great pre-Shakespearian writers, says, "I beat my fan about and swing it round till I have cleared the room of their breed, and now my books are free to rest beside my bed, flies like to come and walk around my eyes and peer into the regions of my nose. Their buzzing fuss outside my window-shade I leave to them to do just as they please."[62]

Kim Sanghŏn (1570–1652 AD),[63] who was taken captive in the Manchu invasion of 1636 and kept for a year or two a prisoner at Mukden, has recorded his opinion of the fly. Here it is:

"Among the trees the dainty oriole calls,
High on a limb cicada sings his song.

---

59 Kongju (公州) is a city in South Ch'ungch'ŏng Province and was the capital of Paekche from AD 475 to 538, when it was moved to Puyŏ (扶餘).

60 "武官梁某。爲公州牧使。暑月多蠅。梁厭之。令州中吏胥。下至伶妓僕隷。每朝捕呈蠅一升。嚴設法而督之。上下爭務捕捉。皇皇不少休。至有抱布買蠅者。時人謂之蠅牧 使。治邑如捕蠅。則令豈有不行者乎。" *Taedong Yasŭng* 大東野乘 Yongjae ch'onghwa 慵齋叢話 kwŏn 7.

61 Kim Inhu (金麟厚, 1510–60) was a Neo-Confucian literatus and the only of Korea's eighteen sages (*tongguk sipp'al hyŏn*) enshrined in the Confucian Temple (Munmyo) to hail from the Honam, or Chŏlla region. Gale seems to have assigned an incorrect birthdate of 1501.

62 扇撲肱麾一室虛。從今免汚枕邊書。沿眠集鼻非前日。窓外營營任所如。 Hasŏ Sŏnsaeng chŏnchip 河西先生全集, Ch'ilŏn kosi 七言律詩, kwŏn 7.

63 金尙憲.

My friend Yangsu writes of the fly he sees,
The filthiest creature that creation knows."[64]

Chang Yu (1587–1638 AD), who first introduced tobacco into Corea,[65] says of the fly: "I got a chill once and was laid up for a day, when all the flies in the neighbourhood, seeing my plight, came in troops and sat about me. In revenge I wrote the following:

"Through freezing frost you still live on, you fly:
Whence comes your breed and all your loathsome way?[66]
Stay in your holes, I pray, and leave me in peace.[67]
Where filth abounds, you fight as for a crown;
But what you win I fail to understand.
You drink, and scrap, and drown, and die;
Within my wine-cup e'en your corpses float,
No mortal pity meets your hapless fate."[68]

Song Siyŏl (1607–1689 AD), for many years the greatest of Corea's literati, writes: "Men, after all, are more hateful than flies. My Chinese friend Yangsu says, 'Why hate flies, when there are other creatures far more hateful[69] all round about you?' If flies could have spoken in the days of Yangsu, they could have put a world of men to shame."[70]

How grateful these old masters of the pen would have been to write us today ringing verses on the departure of the fly. The kindly

---

64 "深樹休怜巧舌鶯。高枝厭聽亂蟬鳴。歐陽漫著蒼蠅賦。無限人間止棘營。"
    Ch'ŏngŭm Sŏnsaeng chip 清陰先生集 *Sŏlgyo pyŏl chip* 雪窖別集 ch'ilŏn chŏlgu
    七言絶句 kwŏn 13.

65 For an account of tobacco's introduction to Korea and additional background on Chang Yu, see "Tobacco in Korea," *Pen Pictures*, this vol; "Tobacco in Corea," *Old Corea*, this vol. Despite the identical titles, the content in these two pieces is almost completely different.

66 *KM*: "noisome ways."

67 *KM*: "and leave us peace."

68 "余病寒而嘔。見群蠅逐臭而至。就食嘔器。因以溺死。伏枕漫成。癡蠅凍不死。群飛何提提。曷不守孔隙。與物無咎疵。營營嘔吐間。所得良已微。終然就溺沒。飽腹爲流尸。止棘古所疾。爾死無足悲。堪爲小人戒。一笑因成詩。"
    Chang Yu, "Oŏn kosi" 五言古詩, *Kyegok sŏnsaeng chip* 谿谷先生集 kwŏn 25.

69 *KM*: "unlovable."

70 "世人情狀甚於蠅。六一篇中怪獨憎。若使當時蠅有語。不公之謗似丘陵。"
    Songja taejŏn 宋子大全 si ch'ilŏn chŏlgu 詩○七言絶句 kwŏn 2.

compliments they would have paid the police and city authorities who have wrought his destruction can be more easily imagined than expressed.

The Rainy Season
Old Corea, 122–3;
Korea Magazine 2 (August 1918): 351–2

As time goes on and changes come, the whims and notions that attend the rainy season in Corea seem to change as well. Surely in old days we can remember the kind of deluge that marked the months of July and August, when, through every chink in the tiles, came muddy water pouring over bed and board till even husband and wife differed in their views as to how to meet the dire disaster. His idea, for example, was to go to bed under an umbrella guy-roped at the corners and let the pesky thing rain its fill. Hers was to spend the night chasing the leaks with pots, pans and kettles. This illustrates a difference of view point that frequently develops during the rainy season.

Says she, "My bed-spread will be ruined by this muddy drip from the rafters."

"Who can stop it?" answers he.

Behold him trying to sleep while lights chase each other through all the rooms and corridors, and the airy flittering form of his wife appears and disappears.

All this goes on while the drops, in varying succession,[71] lull his sleepy slumbers: one big fat drop goes *plak*, *plak*, two every three seconds; another, light and more nimble, goes *dook*, *dook*, *dook*, faster than the second-hand can register.[72] Another is heard in the dim distance echoing *pat, pat, pat*. The wife listens and says, "I declare, there's another leak. Where do you suppose that is?" It falls regularly and in rhythmic measure, but where? Unable to locate it, she glides softly to her husband's side, with candle in hand, and says, "Walter," or "William," as the case may be, "there is a leak somewhere that I can't locate. Will you get up and see what we had better do about it?"

---

71 *KM*: "in varying tones."
72 *KM*: "run."

"Sakes alive," says he, "have some sleep and let the blithering thing go; who cares where it is? The whole house is leaking."

"But I prefer to see where I am," says the wife. "I could not think of sleeping in such a mess as this."

She finally succeeds in getting her husband to ascend the unused staircase to the attic to look for the mysterious dropping. He finds it in the dark by one great globule falling square on the back of his neck and going down.

"Thunder and lightning," says he, "when you build a house next time please put a roof on it."

He seemed to be talking to his wife, but the point he makes is not at all clear.

Thus the night passes and a clammy day succeeds. Every kind of musty, moldy smell creeps forth from the shaded corners and rides on the air. Boots turn a grayish white, silver goes black, and kid gloves take on a look as though infected with a spotted fever. The *penicillium glaucum*, an artistic fungus, adorns the very bread you eat, the books you read, the thoughts you think, and the world you live and move in.

Frogs burst forth from who knows where, as by the touch of a button, and roar like a cannon on the Western Front; this keeps up for forty-eight hours after the downpour.

Walter, worn to a bedraggled remnant[73] by the experience of the past night, was in no humor or mood to stand nonsense from these frogs. He was overheard, so I learn from his wife, to use language[74] such as no missionary should ever use. However, we reckon the circumstances in a measure extenuating.

This is but the barest outline of the old-fashioned rainy season when the clouds came down in tin cans and buckets, with ceilings falling, walls giving way, and cockroaches and centipedes racing for dear life to find some protected hole or corner, with husband and wife at it by united or divided effort to save the fortunes of the day.

This period has passed, the rains have grown wiser and more gentlemanly in their deportment, and come now with a measured moderation that is much appreciated. Roofs leak less than they did; ceilings are not so inclined to fall, while walls and embankments seem better able to hold their own, and husband and wife are left with better chances of sweet accord.

---

73 *KM*: "edge."
74 *KM*: "language in regard to them."

Illustration 21. "Foreign Residents Playing Volleyball on Sorae Beach,"
(date unknown)

A Trip to Sorae Beach
Old Corea, 126–8

Sorae Beach[75] lies off in the Yellow Sea on the western rim of the sky-line and offers to the beholder a very charming picture. A bluff juts out in the sea that looks down on a circle of sandy shore, where in the soft summer days happy bathers bask in the evening glow and drink in the eternal freshness of the scene.

But the trip to Sorae is a dark and fateful venture. In old days it was the River Styx that called for courage and a dauntless soul; today the trip to Sorae demands the same.

A party sets sail, or rather boards ship and swings at anchor off Chemulp'o. When the hour weaves its darkest web, warp and woof twilled of murky midnight, up comes the anchor and away goes this shadowy craft out among the rocks and eddies of the Yellow Sea. A mill-race of ten miles an hour underneath, Egyptian darkness overhead, and

---

75 蘇萊.

every imaginable uncertainty all round about, make up the midnight picture. The engines puff and cough for a full two hours, driving no one knows where, when suddenly there is a shock and stoppage. All sounds cease except the clatter of feet on deck and the swish of the sea; all motion except a drunken veer to the right that gradually increases its angle with the outgoing tide and the upcoming wind. Fast the ship sticks, glued to what or where? Over, more and more goes the deck till the holiday voyagers hang by rods, hawsers and table-covers. It looks as though the whole "shooting-match," to put it in sporting language, would go clear over and so lie buried under thirty feet of advancing water in the next few hours. Just when hope fails, the tide turns and the old craft, as by the veriest miracle, maintains its hold on life and rights itself.

Dim lights from the east cast a glimmer across the face of the deep, to show the sobered party where they were, within an inch of a billet in the deep blue sea.

"No more Yellow Sea for me," says one pale voyager. But wait – we are miles from port yet, and a thousand possibilities may crowd themselves between us and our desired haven.

The wind is up and is blowing great guns from two points or so off Shantung. The full swing of the sea is under way. Neptune and his horses are going to show the party what they can do in the matter of lifting six feet of shallow water into waves twenty-five feet high. On comes the roaring thunder.

Gaffs, spankers, and mainsails rip out before it like red-cross linen. All hands to the pump and every man to his duty, is the word. The ship that lay like a log hoping to die in the night is making up for lost time. Talk about speed! No destroyer ever turned nose into the bristling North Sea with livelier men or less chance of coming through than did this make-believe greyhound on its wild race for Haeju:[76] one minute riding nose sky-ward, the next down within six inches of the primeval rocks that grin along the bottom of the deep. People who had never before tasted the exceptional flavours of sea-sickness had it now in full measure, a complete bill-of-fare, entrees between, salads, cups of tea and coffee. At last, at last, who can measure the relief? No party of submarined castaways could say a truer thanks, or vow a deeper vow, than did these when they stepped ashore at Haeju. "That ends that business for me," was the general expression.

---

76 海州, in Hwanghae Province.

But we are on our way to Sorae. We sleep the night; blessed sleep, on *terra firma*, in a Japanese inn, built by the gods. We were dead, doubly dead yesterday, but now we live. Fifty miles to Sorae! It will be but the merest summer's outing. You may go as you please, but we will go by automobile. A night like that aboard ship entitles one to a little comfort.

Away go the less fortunate – some by motor-cycle, some by rickshaw, some on horseback – while we, multimillionaires, recline in the arms of Ford and bless the name of Henry. Such a lovely morning, green hills and high hopes! Five miles already accomplished and not fifteen minutes out, six, seven, ten – splendid machine! Suddenly, all unaccounted for, it stopped, but the chauffeur would fix it. Off with the cover and a short round of inspection showed everything in order, aortic valves, perfect, but go it would not.

It was market day and all the passers were interested in this novelty. Here was a foreign electric "self-goer"[77] giving up the ghost in the middle of the road. They would see what was the matter. Two hundred and seventy-five heads all looking over the chauffeur's shoulder determined to see into the opening where the screw-nail went that held the wire! A word of exhortation was given by the Missionary, "Will all you honourable dukes and marquises please proceed on your way without stopping to bother." But no sooner had one relay gone than another was on hand to strain, and look, and listen, offering meanwhile suggestions as to what to do.

"Please move on," says the Missionary, his spirit backed by a load of perspiration that threatened to blow up. Still more and more came. Did so many curious people ever go to market before? If they would only stand off at breathing distance, or range themselves in rows on the surrounding hills, one might endure it; but no, nothing but a microscopic look with one eye closed will satisfy them, and heads jostle heads in their determination to find out these secrets of knowledge.

"Get out of this, you idiots," shouts the Missionary in fiery indignation, dukes and marquises being dispensed with under the pressure of the day. Still they come never less than two hundred at any one time, women and babies.

The hours wear on from 10 a.m. till 4 p.m. Meanwhile the smiling landscape of the morning has taken on a jaundiced look that will, in the mind of these voyagers, infect the province of Hwanghae for all

---

77 The Sino-Korean term for automobile, *chadongch'a* (自動車), literally means "self-moving (automatic) vehicle."

time. Help is called for and the maddening thing is hauled up to an inn where the party dismounts.

Sunday follows, a day of short prayers and unrelaxing effort. Monday morning hails a friendly bull and has him haul the impossible thing back to Haeju. "Compliments to Henry Ford and tell him to go to thunder," seems to express the cable that this party might have sent, were the War not on. But a second look shows it was not a Ford after all. How often we blame people who have no possible concern in our muddles. It is clear, however, as a result of those days' experience, that automobiles have gone down on the stock-exchange and bulls have risen. For a creature gifted with the sinews of Ajax, the patience of Job, and the docility of a yearling lamb, give me a Corean bull. Few are his wants and unsurpassed his faithfulness.

Next day saw the party loaded on a four-wheeled lorry, with a primeval bull in the shafts – one of those splendid animals that have come down from the *megalosaurus* period. Off they go with high hopes and hat-wavings. For rate of speed the bull is a wonder. He can walk all day without any visible shifting of hill or valley. Shut your eyes for a few hours while he keeps steadily at it and when you open them the question is, has any change taken place in the landscape? So the day began, sure and slow.

At 10 a.m., barely two hours after getting started, the gallant bull-man who had the beast in hand began to unhitch.

"What for?" asked the Missionary.

"Must feed up," said he, "the animal has gone his stint and must have something to eat."

"Too soon, only ten o'clock, and where is your feed?" asked the astounded traveler.

"There on the hills," points the man. So, while the bull is tied up in the shade of the only tree, and left to chew yesterday's cud, the driver takes a sickle and goes to the hills, the best part of a mile off, to gather grass. In less than two hours he is back with a load sufficient to keep the animal for a week, so you would think, but no, he must go again. The rate at which a bull eats grass keeps step with the pace he goes. Imagine then the time required to masticate all this gathered heap.

While the party sits blistering in July's noonday sun, the bull comfortably enjoys his tiffin under the spreading chestnut tree, till the clock marks 2 p.m.

What can the party do, the driver a mile away after more grass, and the bull impervious to language of any kind, even profane?

So it keeps up. When afternoon tea time comes, English is the bull, and more grass is gathered than the missionary ever hopes to see again while he dwells on this green earth. Three a.m. finds them shivering through the sleepless hours of the night, the roosters having their innings and the bull chewing on.

After many days of this unheard-of exercise they arrive safe and sound at Sorae Beach. The Missionary pays the fare, washes his hands clean of the very memory of the thing, and quietly pronounces a curse on all means of transportation, including the third and last, the Bull.

Poems

Gale's collected works exhibit an ongoing predilection for poetry, from his pioneering translations of *sijo* published in the *Korean Repository* (1895–8) to his short collection of translations appearing here. Although a number were published in Gale's short-lived *Korea Magazine*, the remaining works appear here for the first time in English translation. Far from a sampling of works by canonical poets, Gale seems to have judiciously selected various poems based on his own affinity for the author's style and the potential of the subject matter to speak to a Western readership. In characteristic fashion, Gale introduces each poem with a brief contextualization for such a readership: drawing a distinction between Western and Eastern animal symbolism in "The Wild Goose," drawing parallels between Buddhist and Christian theology in "A Far-Eastern Francis of Assisi," and highlighting the Korean "love of nature" evident in Yi Talch'ung's poetry by invoking the opening lines of Chaucer's contemporaneous "Caterbury Tales." Other than their being composed in Literary Sinitic, there is likewise little unity in the categories of verse: included are so-called old style (*koch'e si*), verses in five- and seven-character lines that do not follow rules of tonal parallelism, as well as both regulated verse (*yulsi*) and quatrains (*ch'ŏlgu*) constituting the major divisions of "modern style" verse (*sinch'e si*), known colloquially as Tang poetry.[1]

Gale includes several selections from the late-Koryŏ official Yi Talch'ung (李達衷, 1309–85), who served concurrently as inspector general and minister of taxation and provincial military commander of the northeast region. Three of his works featured here, which Gale

---

1 O'Rourke, *The Book of Korean Poetry*.

titles "Clouds and Mountains," "The Good and Bad of It," and "The Joys of Nature," were included in *Selections of Refined Literature of Korea* (Tongmunsŏn 東文選), a selection of Korean literary works dating from the Three Kingdoms to the Chosŏn periods, compiled at the command of King Sŏngjong in 1478; the poem "The Falling Flowers" by the Buddhist monk Wŏn'gam Kuksa (圓鑑國師) Ch'ungji (冲止, 1226–92) was also included in this collection. Several selections by the late-Chosŏn literatus and Gale favourite Hong Yangho also appear here, including a reproduction of his "The Wild Goose," introduced in the "Korean Literature" chapter of *Pen Pictures*. In this chapter, Gale mobilizes several other Koryŏ and Chosŏn-era literati in a thematic analysis of wild goose symbolism, noting the animal's perceived embodiment of Confucian virtue in the East. The remaining selections are attributed to the early Chosŏn literatus Sŏng Hyŏn (成倪,1439–1504) from his *Miscellany of Yongjae* (Yongjae ch'onghwa 慵齋叢話), which James Lewis describes as a diverse collection of "stories from government offices, conversations with famous personages, comments on classics, painting, music, poetry, history, geography, customs, rituals, foreign relations and women … a literary achievement of its age."[2]

This work, like the *Tongmunsŏn* from which Gale draws other selections in this chapter, has been described as *kwan'gak* literature, the term referring to the government agencies or *kwan* in charge of civil administration in Chosŏn-era Korea. According to one literary history, *kwan'gak* literature indicates the product of writings used for official purposes, significant as the literary trends of Korea changed according to the direction of these writings "in areas such as diplomatic documents exchanged with China, royal proclamations, academic works, and cases related to current affairs." Those in charge of official writings in such offices were more than government officials, but rather leaders of the literary style of a particular age.[3] Gale's poetry selections thus demonstrate not only his own literary proclivities but the orthodox view of Chosŏn literary canonization, perhaps influenced by his classically trained assistants.

One selection that diverges from the orthodox canon both in terms of author identity and compositional medium is "Tribute to a Needle." The original, thought to have been written in Kin Sunjo's time (r. 1800–34) by a widow of a *sadaebu* (literati) lineage, usually carries the title "Cho ch'im mun" (弔針文), but can also be found with the title "Che ch'im mun" (祭針文), and was composed in vernacular Korean. As such, it is

---

2 Lewis, *Frontier Contact between Chosŏn Korea and Tokugawa Japan*.

3 Ko, Jung, and Jung, *The History of Korean Literature*

a rare example of Gale translating from Early Modern Korean rather than from Literary Sinitic. This work is usually classified as prose, or as a "classical essay" (*kojŏn sup'il*), so at first blush it is somewhat odd that Gale included it in a section on poetry. However, some extant versions are classified as *kyubang kasa* (閨房 歌辭), or "Songs/*Kasa* of the Inner Quarters," and this is likely the way Gale treated it a hundred years ago. In his selection of poetry, Gale thus seems to overwhelmingly favour late Koryŏ- and Chosŏn-era *hansi* by male authors, although this is slightly misleading. While his bias toward literature in Literary Sinitic has been well demonstrated throughout this volume, Gale dedicated an entire monograph, entitled *Footprints of the Wild Goose: A Trip to the Diamond Mountains and the East Coast by Miss Kim Kŭmwŏn*, to the writings of a late-Chosŏn female poet, and a separate volume featuring Gale's substantial work on poets from Silla and Koryŏ is also extant. In other words, it is not as if Gale discounted literature from ancient Korea or works by women, but rather that he had different plans for such works. The poetry presented here thus represents his most concise and authoritative distillation of Korean literature for the unitiated audience in the face of what he perceived to be its rapid extinction.

<h1 style="text-align:center">My Shadow
By Yi Talch'ung (1328–85 AD)[4]
Old Corea, 129;
Korea Magazine 2 (November 1918): 411</h1>

Note: Yi Talch'ung was one of the most noted writers of the Koryŏ period, which lasted from 916 to 1392 AD.

I do dislike the shadow that I wear[5] and try to shake him off, but when I run, he runs. Were I not here, he too, would cease to be; but as I [zzz] he dogs my every step. However much I'd like to cut adrift and let him go, I know no way to bring the wish about.

我惡我之影。我走影亦馳。無我則無影。有我影相隨。有我使無影。有術吾未知。

A friend said once, "If you so hate your shadow, sit beneath the shade." But I reply, "You fool, what is a shade if not the very shadow that I hate?"

---

4 The birth date for Yi Talch'ung is in fact 1309, not 1328 as Gale writes.

5 *Korea Magazine* (*KM*): "that I have."

人言若惡影。處陰庶可離。陰亦物之影。

Where form appears you'll find the shadow there. When I am gone my
form will disappear; where then will this same shadow be, I wonder?
I shout it out and ask my shadow, "Where?" But not a word of answer
does he give. He's like the foolish An who never opened his lips but
only listened deep in thought to all the Master said. In every act of life
he imitates and does the counterpart except of my words.

人言洒更癡。物我苟有矣。陰影復在兹。無我亦無物。陰影安所施。舉聲我
間影。影也無一辭。有如回也愚。默識而深思。凡我所動作。一一皆效爲。

I wonder if it's because I'm overgiven to talk my shadow does not
copy this as well? He gives no answer to my call. I expect it is for deepest danger lies in words.

The shadow has no need to copy me, but I full sore have need of his
ways to learn.

唯我頗多言。影也不取斯。影也豈不云。言洒身之危。顧非影效我。我洒
影爲師。 [6]

Clouds and Mountains
By Yi Talch'ung
Old Corea, 129

The mountain sits deep anchored, even firm;	山本乎止本乎静
The clouds, unrestful, swing to east and west.	雲可以西可以東
One, changeless, seems a part of mother earth;	本乎止静者有體而 　　附地
One, child of motion, rides upon the wind.	可以西東者無心而 　　隨風
Our motion and our rest hang at the will,	一動一静將觀物 　　所性

---

6 The original can be found in Yi's *Chejŏng chip* 霽亭集, kwŏn 1, with the title
　"Chŭng yŏng 贈影."

As green and white stand with the opened eye.　或靑或白已累吾
　　　　　　　　　　　　　　　　　　之瞳

I close my eyes and enter into space;　閑目嘿坐入大素
The very stillness fills my echoing soul.　胸襟寥寥如秋空
And yet I can see hills and cloudlets there.　森然還有雲山態
Who is the poet; who, the artist, pray?　誰爲詩人誰畫工
The artist's mind is deep and hard to know,　畫工之神未易測
The poet likewise, has his measure broad.　詩人所見何能窮
Sometimes I see the hills green in the white,　靑山靑靑白雲外
And then soft clouds I see, white on the green.　白雲白白靑山中
The white and green blend in one picture fair,　靑山白雲爲一致
We ask which are the hills and which the
　　clouds?[7]

　方信胸無九疑峯

The Good and Bad of It
By Yi Talch'ung
Old Corea, 130

A man, not much of a man, once called on an old man, a foolish man
and asked him this, "There is a company of folk near here who meet
daily to talk over mankind, and among them some say you are a man
and some say you are not a man. How comes it Pater[8] that to some you
are a man and to some you are not a man?"

　有非子造無是翁曰。日有群議人物者。人有人翁者。人有不人翁者。
翁何或人於人。或不人於人乎。

The ancient listened and then replied, "Though there are those who
say I am a man, I am not pleased at that; and though there are others
who say I am not a man I am not distressed at that. When a real man
says I am a man, or when a man who is not a man says I am not a man
I am interested. What kind of man is he who says I am a man; and what
sort of man is the man who says I am not a man? If a real man says I
am a man I am pleased; and when one who is not a man says I am not a

---

7　The original is titled "Sŏrhŏn Chŏng Sangt'aek Ch'ŏngsan paegun to 雪軒鄭
相宅靑山白雲圖" and can be found in the *Tongmunsŏn* 東文選, kwŏn 7, *Ch'irŏn
kosi* 七言古詩.

8　Gale has crossed out the word "Father" in the typescript version, replacing it
with "Pater."

man I like that too. If a real man says I am not a man, then I am anxious; and when a man who is not a man says I am a man, I am anxious too. My one anxiety is to know whether the man who says I am a man, is really a man; and whether the man who says I am not a man is really not a man. The saying is, 'A good man alone can truly estimate others.' Is the man who calls me a man, a good man, or is the man who says I am not a man, not a good man? This alone I wish to know."

翁聞而解之曰。人人吾吾不喜。人不人吾吾不懼。不如其人人吾而其不人
不人吾。

吾且未知。人吾之人何人也。不人吾之人何人也。人而人吾則可喜也。不
人而不人

吾則亦可喜也。人而不人吾則可懼也。不人而人吾則亦可懼也。喜與懼當
審其人吾

不人吾之人之人不人如何耳。故曰。惟仁人。為能愛人。能惡人。其人吾
之人仁人

乎。不人吾之人仁人乎。

The questioner laughed and went away. The old man then made a record of the interview as an admonition to himself.[9]

有非子笑而退。無是翁因作箴以自警。

The Falling Flowers
By Wŏn Kam (A Buddhist of the 13th Century)[10]
Old Corea, 130

My first fair view of Seoul was in the deeps of winter, in December's moon, and yet 'ere I could turn my head nigh fourscore days had passed and

---

9 The original, titled "Aeo cham pyŏngsŏ 愛惡箴 幷書," can be found in the
   Tongmunsŏn 東文選, kwŏn 49, Cham 箴. Gale's translation omits the final lines:
   箴曰。子都之姣。疇不為美。易牙所調。疇不為旨。好惡紛然。盍求諸己。
10 Wŏn'gam Kuksa (圓鑑國師) Ch'ungji (冲止, 1226–92).

spring was here. The years that come, the years that go, are like the stream's fast-rolling flood. Todays and yesterdays, a troop of horses that gallop by. A week ago the flowers were just about to bloom; today their anxious thought is how to fall. I cannot hold them back or stop their hurried pace. How can we bridle in the spring that comes or shout halt to autumn's winged way?

臘月念六初入郭。轉頭春已七十有三日。去年今年同逝川。昨日今日甚奔駟。昨日看花始
開。今日看花花欲落。花開花落不容惜。春至春歸誰把捉。

The world's vain people see the flowers but never think upon themselves how they too bloom and fade. Have you beheld the pretty face, so fair reflected from the morning's mirror, which in the evening slowly wends its way with bier and trappings to the moundy hill? We see the flowers that bloom and fall, and ask, "Is this the law that governs life?"[11]

世人但見花開落。不知身與花相若。君不見朝臨明鏡誇紅顏。暮向北邙催
翣。

須信花開花落時。分明說箇無常法。

The Joys of Nature
By Yi Talch'ung
Old Corea, 131

Note: The Corean has always been a great lover of nature, and one of his sure retreats in time of trouble was the woods with its sound of bird and bee, its murmuring of the pines, and the rhythmic note of the passing water.

Here is a translation of a poem written by a Corean about the same time that Chaucer was trimming off his lines:

When that Aprille with his showres swoot
The drought of Marche had perced to the root.[12]

---

11   The original, titled "Sŏk hwa ŭm 惜花吟," can be found in the *Tongmunsŏn* 東文選, kwŏn 6, ch'irŏn kosi 七言古詩

12   These are the opening lines of "General Prologue" from *The Canterbury Tales*, written between 1387 and 1400 by Geoffrey Chaucer (1343–1400).

How green these pine-clad hills! They circle round my home where all the solitudes combine. I see the world with sadness sweeping by. The chittering of the spring is heard, when lo, the rice is ripe and autumn's here. I am an exile from no choice of mind, 'tis simply no one comes to call on me.

雲松何蒼蒼。　家在山之阿。　於焉守幽獨。　覽物悲年華。
嚶嚶聽春鳥。　又復見秋禾。　豈我事高潔。　人自無相過。

The laughing flowers look from among the grass, and red smiles greet the green. Whence comes this yellow-coated bee? He hums his song of comfort and of cheer. The jaunty high-hole with his gilded dress rings his hammer notes throughout the wood. His work is no concern of mine and yet he makes my eyes to shine.

嫣然草中花。　灼灼紅暎綠。　黃蜂來何方。　歌詠慰幽獨。
翩翩有珍禽。　剝啄韻枯木。　事無關我心。　足以娛耳目。

Since I came here to dwell the world and all its strife have ceased to be. I cannot meet the friends whom I recall for woodmen are my only guests. But they are busy with the fields and have no time to spare. Let them keep at it lest they miss the day, and so alone I think my thoughts and live.

自我來山中。　事事漸踈略。　不見我所思。　芻蕘相唯┌。
田疇事方急。　亦未共酬酢。　去矣勿違時。　吾當成獨酌。

I sow my millet in the stony field, and wait and wait until the harvests come. The yellow bird thinks naught of mine or me, and I spend hours in driving off his brood. You did not till this field or sow the seed, what call have I to fill your pocket, pray? Though you fill out and fatten on my grain your end will be the hawk who'll pick your bones.

種粟磽磽田。　望望待其熟。　黃雀不我貸。　竟日費驅逐。
既非汝所爲。　公然實汝腹。　噫汝縱得肥。　恐爲鷹所肉。

Yon lonely cloud without a thought in mind floats softly through the wide expanse. He has no anxious care but wears as dress the purest, whitest silk. He cannot bark and yet his name is "Heaven's Blue Dog." To the west he goes then swings him toward the east; without a care he halts, he vanishes. Yon cloud and I are just alike, both free from care, and friends of deepest heart are we.[13]

孤雲本無心。汎汎遊宇宙。無心而白衣。無心而蒼狗。
無心而東西。無心而去住。雲我俱無心。相與爲益友。

A Spell against the Tiger
By Hong Yangho (1724–1802 AD)
Old Corea, 132–3;
Korea Magazine 2 (January 1918): 9–12

(This article illustrates a very interesting fact: namely, that Coreans, in the old days, thought they could charm away evils like epidemics or tiger raids by means of written incantations. This Mr. Hong, a very enlightened scholar, who was head of the literati of his day, and had been more than once to Peking as special envoy, evidently believed in the same, and so lent his power of the pen to drive away the tiger from the Tumen River region).

Near the seacoast of Kyŏnghŭng[14] a terrible man-eater had made his appearance, and had gone about for a month or more carrying off numbers of people and devouring them. Great fear fell upon the district.[15] A prohibition against firearms at the time increased the anxiety and cut off all means of taking the beast, so I wrote the following[16] and carved it upon a tree where it could be seen by the tiger. From that time forth the place was delivered from the ravages of the beast.[17]

詛虎辭 慶興海邊. 有惡虎縱橫 一月噬人。或至三四。爲邑大患。
而邊地有砲禁。無以捕。余乃作此辭。刻木立之。虎患自此頗息。

---

13 The original is titled "Chaphŭng ojang kisa am 雜興五章寄思菴" and can be found in the *Tongmunsŏn* 東文選, kwŏn 5, Oŏn kosi 五言古詩.

14 Kyŏnghŭng County (慶興郡) is in the extreme northeastern corner of North Hamgyŏng Province in present-day North Korea, sandwiched between the Russian Maritime Provinces, China, and the East Sea.

15 *KM*: "A great fear fell upon the district and anxiety indescribable."

16 *KM*: "the following incantation."

17 *KM*: "creature."

THE INCANTATION

"Glaring-eyed monster, king of the hills, with awful countenance and wildly twisting tail, horribly bedecked with black stripes and lightning flashes of the eye, before whom a thousand beasts stand in fear! Revolting! Who, fiercely, when he whistles calls the winds to rise, and makes his mane to stand on end. Dreadful! Born in the brazen spirit, Soho, under the constellation *In* (the Dragon)![18] Ugh! Sitting grimly on the rocks, or lying hidden in some shaded grove,[19] keeping far aloof from men! Abominable! When once he fixes his hold there is no escape and his teeth are stained with blood. Fearsome! His tracks and bristling mane are not seen among men. Ugh! How he loves the bones of the tender child and the flesh of the fat old man. Sickening! The widow weeps for the husband and the orphaned child for the parent. Alas! He travels not by day, but, demon-like, awaits the night to crawl forth from his loathsome lair. Shocking! With the awful face of a madman, the flashing eyes of an ogre, and a roar that shakes the heavens, he creeps forth, till the spirits he has devoured pipe and wail from fear.

God in heaven made all creatures of the earth, beast and man, and gave to each its nature and its appointed place. Winged creatures he destined for the trees, and scaly creatures for the sea, so that there should be no confusion.

In ancient times King Sun commanded Paek Ik to set fire to the hills and clear out such vermin;[20] also Hŭihwa had destructive beasts[21] expelled from his kingdom. A virtuous king is now born to the East (Korea),[22] whose light shines forth as the sun, making righteousness and harmony to rule the land. Wild hawks are changed to pigeons by virtue of the King. All the woes and anxieties of humanity depart. The

---

18 Soho (少昊, fl. third millennium BC) is one of the five legendary emperors of ancient China and is associated with dominion over the west, as is the tiger. The tiger *in* (寅) is the third of the earthly branches (地支) in the Chinese sexagenary cycle. Gale's "dragon" must be an error.

19 *KM*: "forest."

20 *KM*: "noxious beasts." Paek Ik (伯益 Ch. Bo Yi) was a legendary figure, one of the retainers of Sage Emperor Sun (舜帝 Ch. Shundi) credited with assisting in controlling the Great Flood during the third millennium BC.

21 *KM*: "vermin."

22 Hong Yangho lived under the reigns of King Yŏngjo (1694–1776; r. 1724–76) and King Chŏngjo (1752–1800; r. 1776–1800).

gates of the devil, and the distant sea of the barbarian, are transformed into places of sweet refinement. All dwellers on earth partake of his favour and become his faithful people. How is it then that you, you awful monster, have not been changed? King of the hills, the hills are your home and not the dwellings of men. Yonder is the Tumen River beyond which the Yŏjin[23] people live. God has placed unlimited bounds before you, and wild tracts of uninhabitable forest. Under the Ever-white Mountains there is no end of far-reaching space. There is the Amur River with its pearls and its slimy deep. Scores of wild hogs, bears, fat deer and stag! You may take your choice and still have heaps to spare. There are nine-tailed foxes and other delightful dainties. Go there, I command; live in peace and set up your home for your young. King of the hills, away with you! Delay not but be gone: The spirit of the King has arisen to destroy all who do not yield obedience. His spears are like a forest and his swords gleam in the sun. His fierce guns roar like thunder to blow you up, flesh and bones. He will set fire to your home and break up your den, till you have no place to hide your tracks. Deadfalls and traps are round about you, and soon escape will be impossible. Though you hold on to trees and weep like a climbing monkey it will not avail. Like a pig bound by thongs and on the way to slaughter – so will you be. What will all your far-famed valour do for you then? Or your wisdom? You may shake your tail and plead for your life but who will take your part or speak for you? Your head will come off to serve as a pillow, and your skin for a mat to sit upon. Your bones will be ground down for hat-string beads, and your whiskers will ornament the headgear of the soldier. Then all resentful ghosts will dance for joy and scold your disembodied spirit. Though your nature be fierce, still you love your young; and though you like to kill, still your own life is precious to you. I give you three days grace, yes, ten days to take yourself out of this. Take your family, one and all, and go at once. As birds start in flight, or fires flash up, away with you to the far north. Don't stop your ears but hear what I have to say. King of the hills, delay not! Though I[24] may not take your life, God is watching. I say again, away with you! Now that spring has come and the hills are green, and the soft clouds gather over the dark forest where no huntsman is, wild sheep and pigs abound and a hundred other dainty creatures await your coming. Let

---

23 I.e., Jurchen.
24 *KM*: "men."

the winds be your wings and the rainbow your banner – off with you! Good luck to you, king of the hills! Away! Away!"

耽耽素威。山之君猗。隆額卷尾。負玄文猗。雙瞳電爍。百獸奔猗。風嘯霧變。

長毛羣猗。少皥肝精。辰象寅猗。巖踞藪伏。遠人隣猗。胡畔厥次。遨海濱猗。

有遷無釋。血牙齦猗。蹄鬣之不足。及齊民猗。稛骸者肉。恣噎吞猗。寡哭孺呱。聲沸喧猗。晝不單行。夜羼門猗。狂視矍矍。號蒼旻猗。哀鳴唧唧。鬼叫冤猗。

皇天之播衆萬。物物人人猗。各廬其宅。區域分猗。林則羽而水則鱗。罔敢糅紛猗。昔有虞命伯益。山澤焚猗。粤姬公驅猛獸。素翟賓猗。聖人出乎震。如日月新猗。革頑剗「。流氳氤猗。鷙鳥之化鳩。感陽春猗。凡民患害。靡遠不詢猗。鬼門瑟海。視庭「猗。含氣麗土之族。悉王臣猗。矧爾物之靈。曷不戢以馴猗。山君兮歸去。人間不可以久蹲猗。前有土門之江。其外女眞猗。天開大荒。草木蓁蓁猗。白山千里。壓厚坤猗。黑水漫漫。珠出蠙猗。德林之石磴。如雲屯猗。封豕玄羆。富橐麑猗。擇肉爲粮。積廩困猗。妖狐九尾。盛姬嬪猗。爾宴爾室。育兒孫猗。山君兮歸去。行不可以逡巡猗。王靈於赫。誅不循猗。長戟如林。劍嶙峋猗。烈砲如雷。

糜骨筋猗。燔巢剔窟。無處寄身猗。機置四張。飛不得騫猗。攀木悲嘷。如窮猿猗。束身就死。若孤豚猗。爾勇何施。爾智何存猗。始搖尾而乞命。夫誰假汝之恩猗。斷顱爲枕。皮作茵猗。磨骨絡纓。鬚挿巾猗。俍鬼羣跳。嗔爾魂猗。爾性雖猛。

有鞠子之仁猗。爾雖嗜殺。愛其生則均猗。吾今與汝約。三日五日至于旬猗。挈族兮引黨。行矣詵詵猗。鳥舉焱疾。渡彼北津猗。毋爾褰耳。聽我誓言猗。山君兮莫淹留。人不可殺。天孔神猗。重爲告曰。春風兮祁祁。陰山靑兮草菲菲。黃雲溁兮四盖。長楸潤兮獵夫稀。鳥獸兮毛澤。牛羊滿野兮鹿豕肥。百靈繽其並。迅風爲翼兮霓爲旆。偓佺騰踔兮壽且樂。山之君兮胡不歸。[25]

---

25 The original, titled "Chŏ ho sa 詛虎辭," can be found in Hong's collected writings, the *Igye chip* 耳溪集, kwŏn 1, Sa 辭.

Tribute to a Needle
By Mrs. Yoo (date uncertain)
Old Corea, 134[26]

Sad to relate, this year, this month, this day, I, So and So, write out the story of my sorrow that tells about my needle.

Of all the useful things that touch the hand of woman, first and foremost is the needle. That people of the world should think so lightly of it breaks afresh my broken heart. Thou dearest one! Seven and twenty years have passed since first you came between my fingers. Should I not love thee well? Thou precious one! I'll wipe away my tears and with my resolution firmly set, write out your life, and tell how, heart to heart, we've lived and worked together. Thus will I bid adieu and say my last farewell.

Long years ago my uncle was selected envoy to the Imperial Court of China. On his return he brought home many packages of needles, which he distributed among relations near and far. He gave the servants each a few.

From among them I selected you and used you with a practiced hand, and kept and guarded you most safely. Though all unconscious as you were, yet how I loved and cherished you. Alas, but what a pity and what a tale to tell.

Blessings to me have been but few and far between. No prattling child has ever played about my knees, and yet my life refused to yield its hold and I lived on. Poor and unblessed I was, my only joy, my needle. With thee I overcame my sorrow, and made my way through life, till now today, I am compelled to speak my last farewell. Alas, the Creator seems to have grown jealous of my joy, and the gods have wished me ill. My dearest needle, how graceful your form and sweet your finished shape. Among all created things you were a spirit dearly loved. Among metals, the finest of the fine! So sharp, and smooth, and swift, outdoing all thy fellows, straight and true, a faithful courtier of the King. Keen was thy point like autumn bristles; clear thine eye to see. When embroidered the phoenix and the peacock on the silken fabric, your flashing speed and high-wrought skill were wonderful to see, as though the gods gave fire and life. How could man ever hope to equal you?

---

26 Another typescript version of this translation can be found in the Gale Papers, Box 6, Folder 33.

However precious a child may be there comes a time to part; the best of servants, too, will fail. When I think of all your faithful years you were better than the truest son, or staunchest follower. Your little case of silver, tinted with many colors, that hangs suspended at my girdle string, is the maiden's sweetest ornament. I used to finger you when I ate my meals, and hold you in my hand all night asleep. You were my nearest friend. In the long days of summer and longer nights of winter, underneath the glimmering light, I basted, hemstitched, bound, fastened, and embroidered, using a double thread and working round the piece like a phoenix tail, jumping with fast, long-running stitches, till head and tail raced, flashing after one another. How wonderful your ways! My hope was that we might live our lives together, but alas to tell, on the 10th Moon and the 10th day when twilight fell and I saw underneath a dimly lighted candle, joining the collar to my master's robe, all unthinkingly I blundered, when suddenly a snap was heard, at which my heart stood still from fear. My needle, alas, alas, broken in two! My eyes failed to see and my soul sank within me as though a blow had struck me on the head. I was dazed and stupefied. At last returning senses sought and found the broken bits and fitted them together, but all in vain. There was nothing I could do. Even the greatest physician cannot retain the departing life. My needle, alas, alas! I feel my bosom now with you no longer there. I was not careful and thus you died. Who but myself to blame? Your high-wrought sense and gifted skill how can I ever hope to see again? Your glancing form that shines before my eyes? My heart bleeds for you. Though but a lifeless thing still you had sense and reason. Would that we might meet again in some future life and never part. Alas, alas, my needle!

The Wild Goose
By Hong Yangho
Old Corea, 135–6

Probably the most popular bird in the West is the eagle. It figures prominently in the Bible; its likeness appeared on the standards of the Roman Empire; it was one of the symbols of the Crusaders; the double eagle marked the German claim to the succession of the Caesars; and finally, the bald eagle is the national bird of the great republic of America.

If we turn to East Asia and ask what is the most prominent bird here, I imagine the answer would be the wild goose. The stork that dances to the music of the pipes might run a close claim, or the fabled phoenix, but with all in all the honours would doubtless go to the goose. In the sacred books, those of Poetry and History, that correspond to our Bible, the wild goose appears, and in the simple songs of the people she is always the friend, always welcome.

One of the odd sights of the capital of Corea is to see a gaily rigged out wedding procession, a goose being carried along, wearing as serious a look as though all the fortunes of the day hung on her part in the ceremony. The goose here is a sedate, wise, far-seeing, blameless creature, honoured by all people, so that East Asia has no expression whatever corresponding to our English colloquial, "You silly goose!"

Here is a translation of a popular song referring to the wild goose as the representative messenger from afar, the letter-carrier, who comes with uncensored news from regions beyond the border. The long-deserted wife speaks:

> Silvery moon and frosty air!
> Eve and dawn are meeting.
> Widowed wild goose flying there
> Hear my words of greeting:
> On your journey should you see
> Him I love so broken-hearted,
> Kindly say this word for me,
> That it's death when we are parted.
> Flapping off the wild goose clambers,
> Says she will if she remembers.

Yi Kyubo, seven hundred years ago represented the wild goose as the postman who brings the exile news from home. He drops messages from his fast-moving aeroplane for the waiting prisoner. How many longing eyes of Asia have followed the wild goose as it fades into the distance.

詠鴈

The exile of a thousand *li*	故人千里訊音疏。
Who hears not from his native land,	
Awaits the frosty wild goose call	只待霜天雁到初。
In vain; the birds have lost their wing	鳥亦隨時情意薄。
And shouting "Heavy!" nothing bring.[27]	唯嫌翅重不將書。

---

27 The original, titled "Yŏng an 詠鴈," can be found in Yi Kyubo's collected writings, *Tongguk Yi Sangguk chip* 東國李相國集, kwŏn 11, Koyulsi 古律詩.

Im Ch'un in the year 1220 AD[28] wrote this about the wild goose: "The priest Hyeun had me go and see his famous picture of the wild geese. There were thirty-nine in all and eighteen of them differed quite markedly one from the other. Some were flying, some alighting, some eating, some taking flight, some looking up, some stooping over, every attitude of the wild goose was pictured, nothing forgotten and all most skillfully done.

The priest said, 'This is a memento that I keep in my home. The artist I do not know but his work I have long kept by me. Formerly I counted it a treasure above rubies, but as time passed I have changed in my feeling somewhat and do not specially regard it now. My reason is that the man of religion ought not to find satisfaction in material things. He should merely see and pass by. The Buddhist who reckons not of life or death has put away all earthly desire. What special interest then can a picture of this kind have for him? Too great a love for anything may cause the loss of one's better self."

"I am now contemplating a journey to the south and am going to leave the picture with my younger brother. If you will kindly write me a note about it I will take that along instead, and when I read your words I will see the picture once again before my eyes."

I laughed and said, "The artist when he painted this evidently had it all in mind before he touched the brush. Thus it was that life and power flowed from his hand. He painted it as no words could express, not even the artist's own lips. Even though I behold it how can I tell it? A few of the outer features are all I can give. Here is a pair of geese sitting together, their necks crossed most lovingly. Here again goes a procession with their backs just showing over the brow of the hill. Some stand with wings out-stretched ready to fly; some stoop forward with their bills upon the ground; some stand with head erect and step off briskly; some are like statues; some crowd and talk together; some circle round the little pond; some dispute with much heat. One stands on one leg the other having quite disappeared; one measures his wings; one looks as though he were asking a question; one is trimming his feathers; one is evidently asleep.'

------

28   Im Ch'un (林椿 ?–?) was a literatus of the mid-Koryŏ era. After his short life his collected poems were printed in *Sŏha sŏnsaeng chip* (西河先生集 The Collected Works of Teacher Sŏha). Sources place his death in the late twelfth century, so it is unclear from where Gale derives the year 1220.

Thus I wrote two copies and gave them, not as a specimen of my composition but as a memento to a friend."

道人惠雲。持一畫鴈圖。就予以觀。凡三十九鴈。而狀之不同者十有八焉。其翔集飲啄起伏伸縮之形。曲盡而無遺矣。是亦精強之至者也。道人之言曰。此吾家舊物也。工之名氏則不知也。以其奇且古。蓄之久矣。始則甚寶惜之。今乃釋然。盖君子不可以留意於物。但寓意而已。況爲浮屠者。旣輕死生去嗜欲。而反重畫。豈不謬錯而失其本心哉。今將歸江南。以畫付吾弟某者而去焉。子若書其形數以「。則異日讀之。雖不見畫。可以閉目而盡識也。余笑曰。爲是畫者。當其畫時。必先得成形於胷中。奮筆直遂而後。乃得至此。則心識其所以然。而口不能言之。余雖巧說。若工之所不能言者。安得而盡之。必欲存其形與數之粗者。則有兩對伏而交頸相叉者。纍纍然微見背脊於崖岸之交者。聳翅欲翔而未起者。昂其首而伏者。伸其吭而跂者。且步且啄者。兀立而不動者。群聚者。圜而向赴飲者。駢而爭翹者。拳其足　者。披其羽其又傍睨者。迴眄者。刷者戲者睡者。此其大略也。余因其言。爲甲乙帳而授之耳。非所以爲記也.[29]

T'oegye (1501–1570 AD), one of Corea's great masters of the pen and religious teachers, draws a lesson from the wild goose thus:

斜陽落雁

<table>
<tr><td>An autumn night, when drop the wild geese down;</td><td>秋日悠揚下天畔。</td></tr>
<tr><td>Out from the dark with clamouring call they come,</td><td>一陣點破遙空雁。</td></tr>
<tr><td>On echoing wing and low-descending sweep,</td><td>渺渺冥冥羽翮低。</td></tr>
<tr><td>Close rank on rank, they light.</td><td>庚庚秩秩天機慣。</td></tr>
<tr><td>Aware of traps, they leave the millet fields</td><td>稻粱多處有網羅。</td></tr>
<tr><td>And seek the reeds where frosty dews descend.</td><td>風霜落後饒葭「。</td></tr>
<tr><td>Behold how careful birds are of their way,</td><td>君看禽鳥愼翔集。</td></tr>
<tr><td>How much more man with fogs and mists embound.[30]</td><td>世事茫茫歲向晏。</td></tr>
</table>

---

29 The original, titled "Hwa an ki 畫雁記," can be found in the *Tongmunsŏn* 東文選, kwŏn 65, Ki 記.

30 The original, titled "Sayang nagan 斜陽落雁," is the second of ten in a medley titled "Kijŏng sip yŏng 歧亭 十詠," and can be found in *T'oegye sŏnsaeng munjip* 退溪先生文集, kwŏn 3.

Hong Yangho (1724–1802 AD) who once went as envoy to China wrote:[31]

"In the late autumn of the *chŏngyu*[32] year (1777), a peasant from the Tumen River caught two wild geese, cut their wings and brought them to me. I kept them in the court where the steward looked after them. One day he came to me and said 'These birds are better flavoured than pheasants, I advise Your Excellency to order them prepared for the table.'

'Tut! Man' said I, 'These are not for slaughter – wonderful birds they are. Have you never noticed that when they fly they observe the strictest order, which the great masters call *ye* (ceremony); when they mate there is no confusion, *ŭi* (righteousness); in their migration they follow the warmth of the sun, *chi* (wisdom); though they go far you can always depend on them to arrive with the season, *sin* (trustworthiness); they never make war on other creatures with bill, or scratch with claw. Thus they show *in* (love). Only a bird with feathers, yet possessing the Five Virtues. Its ways and habits are recorded in the Classics; its note is a song. The *Yegi*,[33] or *Book of Ceremony*, talks of it. At weddings too, it is carried along to give good luck, and so its virtues and superior attainments are manifest. It would never do to make soup of, or fry, like a pheasant.'

I fed them every day on grain and gave them water to drink; fixed them a coop to keep out the cold; shut them up at night from foxes and rats and let a month go by till their wings lengthened out. Then I took them to the peak nearby and let them fly away with this message:

> Keep away from the North! (the Mongol World)
> In the sand woods deep your quills will lie,
> Where the inky Amur goes sullenly by,
> Where cracking ice will split your bill,
> And the rude old bear will claw and kill;
> And the round-spot tiger will love you dear,
> And the savage bow and whistling spear.
> Keep away from the North, keep away!
> Keep away from the South! (the Loochoos)
> The red-hot earth and the boiling sea

---

31 See *Pen Pictures*, "Korean Literature," this vol., for a comparison with another version of this poem.

32 丁酉.

33 禮記 (Ch. Liji).

Have snakes in the air that fly;
That stand on their tails and hiss and strike
Till the geese that are bitten die.
There are fiery darts from off the sun
And flames that glare by day,
If you go to the South your breath is done
And your feathers are burned away.
Keep away from the East! (Japan)
For there, in sooth, the waters are piled
With the swell of the ocean pitching wild;
Where whales can swallow a ship down whole
With jumping beasts that squirm and roll;
Where the black-toothed man with tattoo band
And a cunning heart and a clever hand,
With a deadly bullet and eye to aim,
And a thunder flash and a burst of flame!
Where you never would get away at all
But your bones and nerves would be ground up small.
Keep away from the West! (China)
There the yawning gulf of the Yalu flows
By the land of sin and dirt;
Where the words they talk with nobody knows
And the coat they don's a shirt;
Where a spear is hung in the girdle-string,
And a deadly blade beside;
Where they hunt the life of each living thing
To gorge on its flesh and hide;
Where the smell of oil they dote upon,
And the tents are decked with quills,
If you venture there you are dead and gone
As a ghost among the hills.

But stay here, here in this land of green mountains, where the day
first shines, and the Silver Constellation stretches across, and the Horn
Star hangs over, and the warp and woof of heaven glistens with light,
and mountains interlace and waters circle round; where heat and cold
are just what they ought to be; and fertile lands stretch for three hundred miles, and grain grows plentifully, and the doctrine of the Sages is
taught, and where grace abounds; where the young of animals and eggs
of birds are not molested, and where all things flourish. Fly nowhere

else, but come with your wife and family, and call all your relatives, sail in on the clouds and sing out to the moon; dine off the reeds, but watch for traps and fish-nets; go south in autumn and come back in spring and live out your days in peace."[34]

放鴈辭
季秋之月。孔 [慶興一號孔州] 之野人。生得二鴈。剪其翮以獻。余歸其
　　直 而畜于庭。饔人曰。是味旨於雉。請膳之。余曰。毋。是鳥也, 羣而
　　有序, 其有禮乎, 侶而不亂, 其有義乎, 飛必隨陽, 是其智也, 至必如期, 是
　　其信也。嘴不啄生, 爪不攫物。 近於仁矣. 羽蟲之微, 具此五德。 故其居
　　載於書, 其聲詠於詩。月令紀其來賓, 嘉見執以成禮, 凡以尙其德而昭其靈
　　也。 如之何其羹之炙之, 如雉鶉鷄鴨然。乃日餧以粟, 盆水濟其渴, 茅薦禦
　　其寒。 夜則密其藩扃其實, 以遠狸鼠。旣月翮始長可擧。於是升高而放之,
　　送之以辭曰。
　爾之飛兮無北。白礫林兮氄毛落。
黑水吼怒兮層氷攢角。
朱鬣綠睛兮熊攫豹食。
大弓長鏃兮捷投遠弋。
爾北徂兮爲彼得。
爾之飛兮無南。
赭墳潟洳兮沸水淫淫。
蝮蛇騰空兮尾豎舌銛。
火山爍日兮揚芒皷炎。
爾南翔兮毛將燖。
爾之飛兮無東, 渡幼海兮洪濤漰汩而瀰湃。
巨鯨吞帆兮奔鰌躍噬。
烏齒鏤身兮心巧手銳。
毒丸伺物兮霆擊焱駭。
爾不避兮骨筋碎。
爾之飛兮無西 過鴨水兮赤縣蒙穢而幽昧。
左言短衣兮腰槊臂矢。
逐肉充饑兮腥臭是嗜。搖翟揷幢兮毛羽之不棄。
爾適彼兮爲羇鬼。
於樂靑丘日初暘兮。箕張角垂經緯光兮。
山嶷水繚適燠凉兮。膏壤千里足稻粱兮。
有聖涵育澤溥長兮。不麛不卵物殷昌兮。
爾莫他方之逝。返舊鄕兮。携妃兮喚族。嬉雲兮叫月。

34　The original, titled "Pang an sa 放鴈辭," can be found in Hong Yangho's collected writings, the *Igye chip* 耳溪集, kwŏn 1, Sa 辭.

啣蘆兮避矰。色舉兮遠罿。
春去兮秋來。終汝天兮愉佚。 35
辭曰。奮長翮兮挾浮雲。 超鬼門兮上磨天。
狃朔野兮跨鐵關。 度金城兮集華巓。
遊漢都之赫戲兮。 舞德輝以翩「。
朝刷翼於上林兮。 夕弄影於天津。
揚清音之嘐唳兮。 近玉樓之蟬蜎。
爲報孤臣兮滯塞垣。 髮盡白兮心彌丹。

A Far-Eastern Francis of Assisi[36]
By Sŏng Hyŏn (1439–1504 AD)
Old Corea, 138;
Korea Magazine 1 (January 1917): 11–12

There was once a Buddhist priest who was very kind and very honest. He saluted everyone, even a minister of state, by his given name.[37] Whatever was given him, great or small in value, he accepted with all simplicity, and whatever was asked of him he gave willingly, even all that he possessed. He wore only a ragged suit and a battered hat, and went about Seoul, a sight familiar to all the people. He never asked for anything. If anyone gave him food he ate it; if no one gave him any, he fasted. If given the finest fare he made no special treat of it, but accepted it as a matter of course. Poor fare he took with equal appreciation. Whatever he spoke of, he called Brother. In speaking of a stone he called it Brother Stone, or of a tree, Brother Tree. Thus he addressed everything.

A group of Confucian scholars once saw this priest hurrying along the road toward evening time, and they shouted out,[38] "Hullo, where are you off to?"

---

35 Gale's translation in *Pen Pictures* and *Old Corea* ends here.

36 The original version appearing in kwŏn 7 of Sŏng Hyŏn's *Yongjae ch'onghwa* (慵齋叢話) does not have a title, but one recent translation into modern Korean (*kugyŏk*) gives the title "Chabisŭng ŭi chinsolham kwa kihaeng" (The Honesty and Eccentricity of the Buddhist Monk Chabi). Gale's manuscript draft appears in the Gale Papers, Ledger 10, pp. 169–70, where he indicates that he took the text from the *Taedong yasŭng* (大東野乘; colonial era reprint), vol. 1, p. 172.

37 *KM*: "by his own name."

38 *KM*: "and they inquired."

"I'm looking for a pair of trousers," said he, "and I'm off to the house of Brother Bird." All laughed at this.

He had an ugly scar on his face and someone asked him how he came by it. He replied, "Once I was out on the hills looking for wood, when I saw a bear and a tiger fighting. I went to them and said, 'Why do you fight? Why not be friends?' Brother Tiger, on hearing this, looked ashamed and went away, but Brother Bear was resentful and turned and scratched my face. Some of the hill folk came and helped me at the time."

Once when I (Sŏng Hyŏn) was sitting in conference with other Ministers of State this priest came and called on us. We asked him, "Why don't you go to the hills and study instead of knocking about in all kinds of wind and weather, building bridges, placing stepping-stones, mending roads, and digging wells as you do?"

The priest replied, "When I was young my teacher told me to go to the hills and spend ten years in earnest study, assuring me that if I did so, I would understand the meaning of the Buddha. I went to the Diamond Mountains for five years, and to the Odae Hills[39] for another five, and worked very hard, but no profit came of it. My teacher then told me that if I would read the Lotus Sutra[40] one hundred times I would understand. This I did and yet found no profit. From that time on I understood that the Buddha was hard to fathom. Nothing else was left to me in the way of rendering helpful service to my fellow men[41] so I turned to building bridges, placing stepping-stones, making roads and digging wells."

有慈悲僧者。性直無曲節。雖公卿大相皆以名呼之。人有施與。則雖重物不讓而受。人有丐之者。盡數與之。只著破笠破衣而已。日日糊口於京中里閭。與之食則食。不與之則不食。腴饌不以爲美。糲飯亦不以爲歉。凡言物必稱主。言石則云石主。言木則云木主。其他物亦皆類此。儒生見僧向晩怱怱去。問曰向那裏去。僧曰往尼舍覓鳥主家。蓋言覓袴具也。人皆笑之。僧腮有傷痕。人問其故。僧言曾入山採薪。有虎與熊相鬪。僧就前謂之曰。何故相害。宜各和解。虎主聽戒而去。熊主不聽僧戒。來咬僧面。適被山人來救而得免矣。予嘗與諸宰樞會一處。

---

39 Odae Mountain (五臺山) is in Kangwŏn Province, South Korea at the juncture of the T'aebaek and Ch'aryŏng mountain ranges. The P'yŏngch'ang Odaesan Depository of Histories (五臺山史庫) was located here, one of four locations that housed the *Veritable Records of the Chosŏn Dynasty* (朝鮮王祖實錄).

40 The *Lotus Sutra* (Myobŏp yŏnhwa kyŏng 妙法蓮華經) is one of the most profound scriptures of Mahayana Buddhism and is considered to be one of the definitive teachings of the Buddha.

41 *KM*: "to my fellows."

僧亦來到。座中人問云。僧不曾入山修道。何苦每在人間修橋樑路井小
事。僧曰。少時師僧戒云。入山苦行十年。則可以悟道。僧入金剛山五
年。臺山五年。勤苦繕性。竟無其效。師僧又云。讀蓮華經百遍。則可
以悟道。僧依敎誦遍。亦無其效。自是始知佛氏虛妄難信也。然僧無他
輔國。但欲修橋梁道井以施功德於人。人皆樂其眞率也。[42]

The Snow
By Yi Chehyŏn (1287–1367 AD)
Old Corea, 139

The wild north wind rolls up the trembling earth and flings its shadows
over hill and river. In the bosom of the clouds is heaped up snow that
gives the traveler anxious thought. All heaven and earth are blotted out
in whirl-winds of confusion. The ground is robed in glistening white, a
new and fresh creation. At first I thought it was the Milky Way had broken loose and fallen to earth, or that the hill-tops driven by the storm
were down upon us. The angels of the sky, robed in their rainbow garb,
fluttered around like phoenix birds. The fairies of the deep flashed forth
their dragon scales. My horse's hoofs slip as he stands in fear. He moves
not though I let him feel the whip. My woolen robe takes on a hundred
pounds of weight, while I, inside its folds, think of Maeng Yangyang,[43]
of how he rode his donkey in the snow and thought out verses to relieve his hunger. How gracious is the master of the inn who dips a glass
of wine to cheer me. I take my seat beside the cat that sleeps upon the
warm and cozy floor. Have you not seen Chu Saeng's fine pictures of
the snow, how on one little sheet he piles its vast creation?[44] The willows by the river bank are weighted down where crow-birds used to
light. The little inn has closed its door and not a breath of smoke appears. A guest is starting off upon his cart into the wilderness. Official
duties make him pull his bridle rein so hard and twist his horse's nose.
How happy is his lot who draws around his ears his quilt, and floats

---

42 Original text from Sŏng Hyŏn, *Yongjae ch'onghwa* 慵齋叢話, kwŏn 7.

43 Maeng Hoyŏn (孟浩然 Ch. Meng Haoran, 689–740) was a poet during China's
    Tang dynasty. Hailing from Yangyang (襄陽 Ch. Xiangyang) in present-day
    Hubei Province, he was also called Maeng Yangyang (孟襄陽).

44 Chu Saeng (朱生) or "Mr. Chu" was a landscape painter during the Eastern Wu
    (AD 222–80) during the Three Kingdoms period (220–80).

off into common country dreams to let the world of heat and cold drive forward as it pleases. I too, have known the world that Chu Saeng pictures and so shall ne'er forget the meaning of his pen. If we someday should meet, Chu Saeng and I, I'd clasp his hand and talk with him about the landscapes of the snow.[45]

雪

朔風卷地暗河津。塞雲作雪愁行人。兩儀洪荒盪元氣。萬物陸離含古春。初疑倒瀉銀河空。轉恐壓折靑山峯。天女霓衣戲鸞鳳。海仙貝闕翻魚龍。馬蹄凌兢鞭不動。身上氈裘百斤重。令人却憶孟襄陽。驢背吟詩忍飢凍。逆旅主人眞可人。爲我一發浮蛆瓮。誰能興盡到門迴。席暖且與狸奴共。君不見吳中朱生畫稱絶。短幅曾掃燕山雪。河橋老柳不棲鴉。小店閉門煙火滅。客子驅車欲安適。應被名韁牽鼻裂。豈知瓦油衣下黑甜鄉。一天歲月無炎涼。畫中之境今自蹈。畫中之意不可忘。白頭更有相逢日。握手披圖感嘆長。

The Cackling Priest
By Yi Chesin (1536–1583 AD)[46]
Old Corea, 140;
Korea Magazine 1 (February 1917): 55–6

There was once a cackling priest,[47] a dwarf, who had a limp in one leg. He went here and there through Seoul, day after day, entering the homes of the poor as well as those of great officials. In fact, there was not a spot that he did not visit. He was an exceedingly odd creature,[48] for he could crow just like a great coarse rooster, clapping his sides, and puckering up his lips. Sometimes[49] he would make a noise like two roosters in a fierce fight, and again he would cackle like a hen. All

---

45 The original text, titled "Sŏl 雪," can be found in the *Tongmunsŏn* 東文選, kwŏn 7, ch'irŏn kosi 七言古詩.

46 Gale incorrectly attributes this to Yi Chesin. This selection appears in Sŏng Hyŏn, *Yongjae ch'onghwa* 慵齋叢話, kwŏn 6. Gale's manuscript draft appears in the Gale Papers, Ledger 10, pp. 168–9, where he has the author correctly as Sŏng Hyŏn. He indicates no source, but must have taken it from the colonial-era reprint of the *Taedong yasŭng* (大東野乘).

47 *KM*: "Buddhist priest."

48 *KM*: "He was the strangest creature."

49 *KM*: "Again."

imaginable sounds, such as these creatures make, he could imitate to
perfection. He would set a whole village crowing by his antics. Then he
would shake himself and sing:

For my own self, one room's enough.
My body finds these rags most dear.
When old King Hell shouts out for me,
I'll simply say, I'm here, I'm here!
King Kwanŭm, oh Kwanŭm, oh King,[50]
This word I say, this song I sing;
When my time comes to say farewell,
Lend me a hand against King Hell.[51]

With such songs he entertained his hearers, singing them to tunes the
farmers use.

Crowds of children used to follow him and he would say, "My following beats the world. No minister of state could ever equal me." He
used to get as much sometimes as a bag of rice in a single day.

有僧容體矮小。一足微躄。每居長安。日日周遍城中。朱門貴宅。無
不歷到。常拍手作鷄鼓翼狀。蹙口作聲。或雄鷄長嘷。或兩鷄相鬪。或
雌鷄遺卵。千聲萬態。無不吻合。或有村鷄應鳴者。又作歌搖身而唱
曰。此生此生。一間第屋心可樂。此生此生。懸鶉百結亦不惡。閻羅使
者若來迓。雖欲住世那可得。又曰。觀音帝釋。帝釋觀音。此身若淪
化。全墮地獄間。其歌多類此。曲節似農歌。兒曹隨行。千百爲羣。僧
常曰。吾丘率之多。雖三公不能及也。一日所得。多至擔石。以是衣食
之。時人號曰鷄僧。[52]

---

50 Here Gale seems to be referring to the Bodhisattva Guanyin, the Buddhist
    Goddess of Mercy, but it is unclear why this figure is called "King Kwanŭm."
51 *KM*: "Save me lest I drop down to hell."
52 The *hanmun* text here is taken from Sŏng Hyŏn, *Yongjae ch'onghwa* (慵齋叢話),
    kwŏn 6.

The Story of Unyŏng (*Unyŏng chŏn*)

Unyŏng chŏn (雲英傳), which Gale also titled "The Sorrows of Unyŏng (Cloud Bud)," is one of Korea's best-known works of classical fiction (*kojŏn sosŏl*) in *hanmun*. Although it depicts events from the mid-fifteenth century, *Unyŏng chŏn* is thought to have been written sometime in the early seventeenth century and, as with most works of fiction during this time, the author's identity has remained a mystery. The story was originally penned in Literary Sinitic and subsequently "translated" into the vernacular, eight versions of which are extant.[1] Alternate titles of the work include *Susŏnggung mongyurok* (壽城宮夢遊錄 Dream Record of Susŏng Palace), a title that describes the genre of the work (*mongyurok*) and the primary setting of Susŏng Palace, and *Yuyŏng-jŏn* (柳泳傳 The Tale of Yu Yŏng), referring to the scholar who is said to have received the story from the ghost of Unyŏng and Kim *Chinsa*.[2]

    Unyŏng chŏn is unique among *kojŏn sosŏl* of the Chosŏn era for several reasons. First, unlike virtually all other premodern romance novels,

---

1 Yang, *Kojŏnsosŏl munhŏnhak ŭi silche wa chŏnmang*, 144. These versions differ in varying degrees from the originals. Although there is slight variation in the two best-known *hanmun* versions – the Changsŏgak Library version at the Academy of Korean Studies and the Asami version at the University of California Berkeley, they are, according to Michael Pettid, "almost identical." See Pettid and Cha, "*Unyŏng-jŏn*," 28. Pak Kisŏk also confirms that these *hanmun* versions are virtually the same, the reason being that they were copied and read within a limited readership. See Pak, "*Unyŏng chŏn* chaep'yŏngka rŭl wihan yebijŏk koch'al," 94.

2 Pak Kisŏk claims that the oldest extant copy of *Yuyŏng chŏn* is held at the National Library (Kungnip tosogwan). Pak, "*Unyŏng chŏn* chaep'yŏngka," 94.

Unyŏng chŏn has a tragic conclusion.[3] Secondly, *Unyŏng chŏn* is unique in that it is the first Korean novel to feature a female narrator.[4] Moreover, nearly the entire novel unfolds within the confines of the palace, in particular the women's inner quarters, giving the reader an intimate and rare perspective into the lives of upper-class women in the Chosŏn dynasty.[5] That the voice of the narrator depicts the world from such a realistically feminine perspective led Michael Pettid to question the assumption by most scholars that the author was an upper-class man, based on the author's knowledge of *hanmun* and the breadth of classical allusions demonstrated in the text.[6] Pettid also claims that *Unyŏng chŏn* was unique for its time in its focus on human freedoms, namely, the "right to select a lover, the right to follow one's own choices in life, and the right of women to have rights equal to men."[7] Pettid goes on in no uncertain terms: "For an early-seventeenth-century work, *Unyŏng chŏn* is centuries ahead of its time in the quest for basic rights that are taken for granted at present. Such a historic call for autonomy is unrivaled in the fiction of this period in Chosŏn."[8] Although Gale describes *Unyŏng chŏn* as simply "a typical Korean story" in the chapter heading, judging by the tragic conclusion of the tale and the unique narrative structure and perspective, it seems *Unyŏng chŏn* was anything but typical for its era.

Unyŏng chŏn has garnered considerable attention in academic circles, especially since the 1990s.[9] Some of the major themes examined have been the identity of the author, influences from other genres, the effect and purpose of vernacularization in the *han'gŭl* versions, conflict between characters' desires and social realities, the nature and source of tragedy in the story, and the significance of the Susŏng Palace setting. The first study, conducted by Ōtani Morishige in 1966 and examining two *han'gŭl* and three *hanmun* versions of *Unyŏng chŏn*, hypothesizes that the tale was written by none other than Yu Yŏng, the narrator of the story who

---

3 Pettid and Cha, "*Unyŏng-jŏn*," 1–2.

4 Ibid., 2.

5 Ibid., 1–3.

6 Ibid., 28–32.

7 Ibid., 2.

8 Ibid.

9 Yang Sŭngmin claims that close to thirty studies of *Unyŏng chŏn* were published in the period 1990 to 2002 alone. See Yang, *Kojŏnsosŏl munhŏnhak ŭi silche wa chŏnmang*, 147–8.

receives the manuscript from the phantom main characters, Unyŏng and Kim *Chinsa*. Ōtani also proposes that *Unyŏng chŏn* demonstrates influence from Chinese *chuanqi* (傳奇, tales of the strange), a genre of fiction dating mainly from the Tang dynasty, although the evidence for this as well as the authorship of Yu Yŏng is inconclusive.[10] Subsequent studies by Kim Illyŏl have focused on the spectre of Prince Anp'yŏng from a psychological perspective. Kim writes that rather than a mere individual who foils the affections of Unyŏng and Kim *Chinsa*, Prince Anp'yŏng symbolizes the systematic moral reality of the Chosŏn era.[11] Yi Sanggu, however, portrays Prince Anp'yŏng in a more sympathetic light, as something of a tragic figure who falls victim to the political factionalism and social realities of his time. Noting the prince's progressive belief in women's potential for higher learning, Yi describes Susŏng Palace as a "parallel world" that seeks to transcend social and political realities by providing a clandestine space for idealized rule denied Prince Anp'yŏng by political exigencies.[12] This inability to realize this ideal form of rule, moreover, causes tension between the prince and the palace women and ultimately results in the demise of Unyŏng and Kim *Chinsa*.[13]

Other studies have delved into the relationship between the *hanmun* and *han'gŭl* versions of *Unyŏng chŏn* in terms of style, content, and readership. For example, Pak Kisŏk, in his comparison of original and translated versions of *Unyŏng chŏn*, argues that through the process of translation into *han'gŭl*, the readership and possible authorship of *Unyŏng chŏn* gradually shifted to a still limited group of upper-class women, as demonstrated by the augmented dialogic passages among palace women evident in vernacular versions.[14] Yang, however, suggests that

---

10 Ōtani Morishige, "*Un'eiten* shōkō," *Chōsen gakuhō* (Jan 1966): 340–70, quoted in Yang, *Kojŏnsosŏl munhŏnhak ŭi silche wa chŏnmang*, 137–9.

11 Kim Illyŏl, "*Unyŏng chŏn* ko (I)"; Kim, "*Unyŏng chŏn* ko (II)."

12 Yi Sanggu, "*Unyŏng chŏn* kaltŭng yangsang," 135–8. Pettid, however, argues that this marginally progressive thinking is nullified by the psychological torture that the prince inflicts upon Unyŏng. Pettid and Cha, "*Unyŏng-jŏn*," 42. Anp'yŏng was the third son of King Sejong and was the loser in a political struggle with his older brother Grand Prince Suyang (King Sejo, r. 1455–68), the second son of King Sejong. Pettid and Cha, "*Unyŏng-jŏn*," 39–40. Chŏng Ch'urhŏn makes a similar point to Yi's when he describes Anp'yŏng's Suyŏng Palace as a distorted expression of his own foiled political ambitions. See Chŏng, "*Unyŏng chŏn* ŭi aejŏng kaltŭng kwa kŭ pigŭkchŏk sŏngkyŏk."

13 Yi Sanggu, "*Unyŏng chŏn* ŭi kaltŭng yangsang."

14 Pak Kisŏk, "*Unyŏng chŏn* chaep'yŏngka," 94.

given the considerable number of *han'gŭl* versions extant today, the readership was not quite as limited as Pak contends, and that considering the already significant role of palace women and women's dialogue in the original versions, the changes evident in the vernacular versions should not be considered a major shift in form or content.[15] What should be kept in mind, however, is that "vernacular" and "cosmopolitan" readerships were never mutually exclusive in Chosŏn Korea, notwithstanding enduring discourses reproducing a naturalized link between women and the vernacular script. Although exact numbers are uncertain, literate Chosŏn men engaged with texts in both *hanmun* and *han'gŭl*, though these were compartmentalized according to disparate socio-cultural functions, while certain upper-class women, albeit in more limited numbers, were able to read literature in *hanmun*. Thus, it would be amiss to conflate readership, or authorship for that matter, on the basis of gender alone.

In the mid-1920s *Unyŏng chŏn* experienced a revival of sorts, spurred in part by the publication in 1923 of a Japanese-language version. Through a textual comparison, Hŏ Ch'an demonstrates that the first *han'gŭl* print version (*hwalp'anbon*) of the work, *Yŏnjŏng Unyŏng chŏn* (演訂 雲英傳 *Unyŏng chŏn*, expanded and revised, 1925), originally thought to have been based on a *hanmun* original, was actually a relay translation from the Japanese version by Hosoi Hajime, which in turn inspired the 1925 film *Unyŏng chŏn*.[16] Richard Rutt claims in his biography of Gale that he had translated it in 1917 with his assistant Kim Tohŭi, at the cusp of this renewed interest, but the Gale Papers indicate that Gale completed the translation in 1918.[17] Since Gale's translation, the only other major English translation to be published was that by Michael Pettid and Kil Cha, in 2009.[18] In characteristic fashion and

---

15 Yang, *Kojŏnsosŏl munhŏnhak ŭi silche wa chŏnmang*, 144–5.

16 Hŏ, "1920nyŏndae *Unyŏng chŏn* ŭi yŏrŏ yangsang."

17 Rutt, *James Scarth Gale and His "History,"* 54. Rutt gives no evidence for this claim of co-translation with Kim Tohŭi, and no such evidence seems to exist in the Gale Papers, but as for the date, the manuscript draft of Gale's translation in the Gale Papers, Ledger 13, pp. 100–38, contains two dates: p. 111 contains a penciled date of 15 May 1918, which seems to indicate the date he typed up the completed translation, while at the end of the manuscript translation Gale writes "From the [zzz] Sep. 15th 1917." Gale Papers, Box 9, Folder 21 contains another typescript of the translation in twenty-one pages that indicates "Translated from the original by James Scarth Gale May 21st 1918."

18 An English translation was published in 1970 by students at Ewha Woman's University. See English Student Association, Department of English Language

in harmony with his general translation philosophy, Gale's version is much less literal than that of Pettid and Cha and tends to domesticate potentially unfamiliar aspects of Korean culture and history for increased accessibility, a task that Pettid and Cha reserve largely for footnotes. For example, the following lines from Gale's translation set the scene for Yu Yŏng's meeting with the ghosts of Unyŏng and Kim *Chinsa*.

> One spur of the hills that reaches out farther than the others became the site of this far-famed enclosure [Susŏng Palace]. Though not specially high, one could see from its top the busy mart and all the congregated houses within the city walls. Like squares on a checker-board they lay open to its view; at night dotted with sparkling lights that flashed like stars of the sky.
>
> Off toward the east the Palace Halls rose up through the mists and clouds that rested on them. Morning and night, beauty adorned the Susŏng Gardens so that they became known as the most wonderful fairyland in the world.[19]

The following is Pettid and Cha's translation of the same passage:

> The Inwang Mountains meandered up and down, forming a high peak near the spot of Susŏng Palace. Although not high, if one went to the top and looked down, the shops scattered along the road and the houses in the capital looked like a *paduk* board and also – like stars in the heavens – one could clearly see the details. The shape was as ordered as a loom clearly separates thread. If one looked to the east, the palace was in the distance, and the double road to it seemed suspended in the air. The clouds and smoke were bluer in the morning and evening, intensifying its elegance all the more; it was truly peerless in beauty.[20]

仁旺一脈, 逶迤而下, 臨宮*起, 雖不高峻, 而登臨俯覽, 則通衢市廛, 滿城第宅, 碁布星羅, 歷歷可指, 宛若絲列分派. 東望則宮闕縹｢, 複道橫空, 雲烟積翠, 朝暮獻態, 眞所謂絕勝之地也.

Although both translations mention Susŏng Palace and Inwang Mountains in their preceding paragraphs, only Pettid and Cha repeat these place names above, producing an arguably more exact translation. Gale's omission of these names at second mention, however, was in line

---

and Literature, Ewha Woman's University, trans. and eds., *Woon Young's Romance and Other Stories*.

19   Gale, "The Sorrows of Unyŏng (Cloud Bud)," *Old Corea*, this vol.

20   Pettid and Cha, "*Unyŏng-jŏn*," 64–5.

with his belief that repetition was unnecessary – indeed undesirable –
when the meaning could be inferred from context. The most representative example of this translation philosophy is his dramatic reduction
of the occurrences of the word "God" in the passages of the Bible that
he translated compared with those translated by his missionary colleagues.[21] Furthermore, Gale provides minimal interlinear or annota-
tional explanation to the reader, instead domesticating the text for the
target readership, again in service of a more "readable" finished product. For example, Gale renders the Korean board game *paduk* as simply
"chess" without further explanation. Pettid and Cha's translation, on
the other hand, provides ample footnotes here and elsewhere for the
target readership for a main text displaying minimal domestication.[22]
Finally, Pettid and Cha's version reads as a far more faithful translation
of the original text than that of Gale's. Gale's translation in fact, omits
entire portions of the original as discrete elements, instead subsuming
them into more broadly and vaguely conceived descriptive sentences.
For example, in the passage above, Pettid and Cha translate 宛若絲列
分派 as "The shape was as ordered as a loom clearly separates thread,"
whereas Gale omits any mention of a loom, instead drawing on the
implication of a chessboard's grid to convey the sense of orderliness.
Gale also deletes the "double road" (*pokto* 複道) that leads to the palace,
a minor but important detail referring to the dual-purpose road with an
upper path for the king and a lower path for all other travellers.[23]

The most significant divergence between the Literary Sinitic version
and Gale's translation, however, is Gale's omission of a majority of the
poems, a significant literary trope in the original version that arguably
functioned as the primary crux of plot development. For example, early
in the story, when Prince Anp'yŏng returns semi-inebriated and slightly
disappointed after an outing with his scholar friends and decides to test
the poetic skill of his palace women protégés against those of his literati
peers found to be wanting in poetic ability, the *hanmun* original presents
poems from all ten of the palace women. Gale, however, includes only
the first poem by Little Jade (小玉) and the final poem by Unyŏng, adding the following phrase in between: "The nine, all in order, one after

---

21 Yu Yŏngsik, *Ch'akhăn mokchya*, 838.

22 *Paduk*, for example, is explained in a footnote as "a board game played on a
    board crossed with horizontal and vertical lines." Pettid and Cha, "*Unyŏng-
    jŏn*," 65.

23 Ibid., 64. One other major difference is that Gale translates Yu Yŏng's encounter
    in the first person, whereas Pettid and Cha's translation is in the third person.

another, wrote their part, till my turn came and I wrote this." An examination of Gale's manscript translation of this story confirms, moreover,
that he did not make an attempt to translate these poems but rather
executed a conscious editorial decision to excise most of the poetic passages. Given his demonstrated proficiency, even knack at translating
hansi into fluent and highly readable English poetic form, Gale's reason
for deleting these poems is unclear. The strong presence of *hansi* in the
original version – a high proportion even for the classical fiction genre –
may have seemed tangential to the plot. Perhaps Gale also predicted
that a Western audience would have trouble perceiving the central role
of poetry in the daily lives of the literati class or grasping the Chosŏn
literary truism that poetry reflected the inner workings of the mind.

Thus Gale's translation encapsulates many aspects of his translation
philosophy, including free translation or "sense translation" (*ŭiyŏk*),
and domestication in the service of introducing a completely foreign
body of literature to a virtually ignorant audience. Furthermore, Gale's
translation features his special style of quaint vocabulary and slightly
antiquated idioms, already outmoded in his day, giving his translation
a charming provincialism.

The Story of Unyŏng
(Concerning the days of Prince
Anp'yŏng 1418–53 AD)[24]
written about 1600 AD
(A translation by the author)
Old Corea, 141–64;
Gale Papers, Box 9, Folder 17, Ledger 13, 100–38[25]

Susŏng Palace,[26] the ancient home of Prince Anp'yŏng, stood on the
west side of Seoul under Inwang Mountain.[27] Here the hills and streams

---

24 Prince Anp'yŏng (安平大君, 1418–53) was a painter, calligrapher, and poet of
the early Chosŏn dynasty and the third son of King Sejong the Great.

25 An additional typescript appears in the Gale Papers, Box 9, Folder 21,
pp. 1–21 with the note "The story of Oon-yung [*sic*] written about 1600 A.D.,"
"Translated from the original by James Scarth Gale May 21st, 1918."

26 Susŏnggung (壽聖宮).

27 Inwangsan (仁旺山).

unite in rarest combination, like coiled up dragons, or seated tigers. The *Sajik*,[28] or National Gods, are at the South, while the Royal Palace stands guard on the east.

One spur of the hills that reaches out farther than the others became the site of this far-famed enclosure. Though not specially high, one could see from its top the busy mart and all the congregated houses within the city walls. Like squares on a checker-board they lay open to its view; at night dotted with sparkling lights that flashed like stars of the sky.

Off toward the east the Palace Halls rose up through the mists and clouds that rested on them. Morning and night, beauty adorned the Susŏng Gardens so that they became known as the most wonderful fairyland in the world.

Great lords who loved pleasure, archers, singers, pipers, and masters of the pen, used to take advantage of the spring season, when the flowers were out, and the willow catkins hung low; and in the autumn, when the leaves were coloured and the chrysanthemums were in bloom, to come day by day in crowds as to enjoy the fresh air and sing to the moon.

I, an obscure literary man living in Ch'ŏngpa Ward,[29] hearing again and again of the beauty of the place, had long wished to see it but was ashamed to come, being so poor in money and homely of face, a creature to be poked fun at by others. Many times I decided to make the attempt but failed till the spring of the twenty-eighth year of Mallyŏk (1600 AD)[30] when I bought a bottle of wine, slung it over my shoulder, and without servant or anyone to accompany, went to the old site of the palace. Those who saw me pointed the finger with smiles and gibes of fun.

Ashamed, I made my way to the rear park where I clambered up a high cliff and looked off. It was shortly after the Great War (1592),[31] and the palaces and all the best houses of the Capital were still in ruins: walls down, tiles broken, wells filled up, and terraces fallen away.

---

28 Sajik (社稷). Gale describes the *Sajik* in more detail in "Korea's Receding Pantheon," *Pen Pictures*, this vol., and "Corea's Receding Pantheon," *Old Corea* (not included in this vol.).

29 Ch'ŏngp'a Ward (青坡洞) is a neighbourhood in Seoul, north of the Han River in Yongsan District.

30 Emperor Mallyŏk (萬歷 Ch. Wanli, 1563–1620) was the fourteenth and longest-reigning emperor of the Ming dynasty (1368–1644).

31 In English-language sources this is usually referred to as the Hideyoshi Invasions, or in Korean as the Imjin Waeran (壬辰倭亂 The Japanese Disturbance of the *Imjin* Year).

Weeds and grass occupied the courtyard of the ancient hall, while only a few were left of the servants' quarters on the east side.

I walked out into the garden where the rocks hid me from view. Here grasses and brushwood reflected their shade in the waters of the lake, while the ground was strewn with fallen flowers. No trace of human footsteps was to be seen. A soft breeze kissed my cheek, carrying the scent of the flowers with it. Thus I sat on a rock and sang to myself So Tongp'a's[32] opening lines:

> By early morn I view the rosy spring
> Whose fallen petals carpet wide the court.

I then unfastened the bottle of wine and drank deep, after which I lay down to sleep off the effects, a stone under my head serving as pillow. Sometime later I awoke and looked about me to find that all the guests had departed and that the moon had just risen above the mountain. The mists rested on the willows and a soft breeze kissed the faces of the flowers, when suddenly I heard the gentle accents of a girl wafted to me. I wondered who it could be and looked about, when suddenly I saw a young man seated on the grass in the company of a maiden who seemed beautiful beyond compare. They looked at me with kindly, open faces. I bowed and said, "Young friends, how comes it that you choose night rather than the day in which to meet?"

The young man smiled and said, "The ancients used to say that a new friend was oft-times better than an old one. I take this as referring to Your Excellency."

So we sat down, the three of us together, and spoke our greetings.

In a soft voice, the maiden, called for a servant, when two girls came forth from among the trees. She said to them, "Tonight I have met my lord here and another distinguished guest. How happy I am! Make ready refreshments and bring a pen and ink-stone that we may write."

The servants bowed and retired. In a little they returned like the flight of two pretty birds carrying their fairy wine in a crystal vase, and the fruits of the genii arranged on a silver platter. They poured out the

---

32 So Tongp'a (蘇東坡 Ch. Su Dongpo, AD 1037–1101) refers to So Sik (蘇軾 Ch. Su Shi), an influential literatus, calligrapher, and government minister of Song-era China (960–1279).

wine in white jade glasses and we drank, after which the maiden sang us a song to wake our joy:

> I meet my lord within this rock-bound vale,
> My destined mate, my sole companion dear.
> He is my cloud whom in my dreams I see;
> How oft he comes, how oft he melts away.
> The past is buried long, 'tis dry and sere,
> While ages new think o'er our loves and weep.

She ended her song, broke down and sobbed bitterly so that pearly drops bedewed her face.

Wondering at this, I arose, made a deep bow and said, "I am no great scholar and yet I am a student of the pen and know something of its ways. The song you have sung has greatly moved me and rendered me deeply sad. My heart is much disturbed. Under so glorious a moon as we have tonight, with all the flowers about us, and a world of beauty to enjoy, what is the cause of these tears, I pray? We have passed the glass together and yet do not know each other's names, and our inner thoughts are all unspoken. Most strange this seems!"

I then told them my name and asked the young man his. He sighed and said, "The fact that I have not told you my name is due to shame on my part, but since you desire to know it I can easily tell you. Our story, however, would take too long to tell. We are forever sad, I fear, for joy had little part in our poor lives."

A moment later he added, "My family name is Kim. When I was ten years of age I had already become a master of the pen and won a name at school. At fourteen I took my second examination, when everyone called me *chinsa* (`master`).[33] I was full of young and vigorous thought and longed to know the world, but failed to restrain myself as I should have done. On account of this young woman whom you see I lost my standing and misused the gifts that God gave me. An offender I became before heaven and earth. Why should you know the name of the one who has been so great a sinner? This woman's name is Unyŏng and

---

33 *Chinsa* (進士), or literary licentiate, was the title for one who had passed the Literary Examination in Koryŏ and Chosŏn Korea, an examination that tested knowledge of belles lettres literary composition. The counterpart of this test was the Classics (*saengwŏn* 生員) Examination, which tested knowledge of the Confucian Classics.

her two servants are called Songok[34] and Yŏnju.[35] They were maids-in-waiting in ancient days in the palace of Prince Anp'yŏng."

I said, "You give me only a hint but do not tell me all. Will you not tell me your story? I should like so much to hear a tale of Prince Anp'yŏng's days."

Kim *Chinsa* then looked toward Unyŏng and said, "Long years have passed and our grief has grown old. Can you recall it?"

Unyŏng said, "My heart of sorrow is filled to breaking. How could I ever forget? I shall tell it and my master can sit by and correct me where I fail."

She began, "King Sejong (1419–1450 AD) had eight sons, but among them all Prince Anp'yŏng was most handsome and highly gifted, so the King greatly loved him and showered favours upon him without number. Because of this he had lands and retainers, goods and high honours, beyond all his brothers.

When thirteen years of age he went to live in this special palace named Susŏng. Here he made the Confucian religion his deepest study. At night he read and by day he wrote the character. Not a minute did he waste or spend in aimless loitering. The best scholars and literati of his time came to measure their gifts and talents with him and kept up their studies till cock-crow of the morning. The Prince had great skill in penmanship, so that his name became far-famed throughout the land. When King Munjong was a young man,[36] he, along with others, paid special honour to Anpy'ŏng, saying, 'If our brother had been born in China he would have attained to the place of Cho Maengbu or Wang Hŭiji.'[37]

On a certain day Prince Anp'yŏng said to his maids-in-waiting, 'God has given various gifts to man, and yet, only after diligent study and special attention do these become manifest.'

---

34 宋玉.

35 Although Gale records the name as "Nokchu," the name should be read "Yŏnju" (緣珠).

36 King Munjong (文宗, 1414–52; r. 1450–2) was the eldest son of King Sejong the Great and succeeded him in 1450, only to die two years later of disease.

37 Cho Maengbu (趙孟頫 Ch. Zhao Mengfu, AD 1254–1322), or Cho Songsŏl (趙松雪 Ch. Zhao Songxue), was a calligrapher and painter of Yuan China (1260–1368); Wang Hŭiji (王羲之 Ch. Wang Xizhi, AD 303–61), also known as Wang Ilso (王逸少 Ch. Wang Yishao), was a famous literatus of the Eastern Jin (317–420) best known for his calligraphy.

Beyond the north gate of the Palace, where nature is quiet and the noisy city far removed, he built him a house of several *kan*, in the hope that his study there would come to full attainment. He wrote for the nameboard over the door, *Pihae tang* (The Busy Home)[38] and also built an altar at the side inscribed with, 'To the Poets' (Maengsi tan).[39] It became the meeting place of great writers and noted men. Among these was Sŏng Sammun the renowned master of the character,[40] and Ch'oe Hŭnghyo, the special penman.[41] Yet even they were not equal to the Prince himself in literary skill.

One day after his glass of wine the Prince called his maids to him and said, 'God has not given his special gifts to men only but to women as well. Today we have many scholars and yet not one of any special note; not one that China would call a great master. You maids, also, ought to make an effort to attain to the best there is.' So he selected from his household ten of the youngest, brightest, and prettiest and set them to study the *Lesser Learning*,[42] and after they were able to read that, to go on to the *Doctrine of the Mean*, the *Great Learning*, the *Analects*, the *Book of Poetry* and *History* till they had completed the whole course.[43] They also took up chapters of the Chinese poets, Yi T'aebaek and Tu Chami,[44] and selections of the Tang Kingdom so that in five years they were well trained scholars. When the Prince was in

---

38 匡㥘堂.

39 盟詩壇.

40 Sŏng Sammun (成三問, 1418–56) was a literatus and government minister of the early Chosŏn. He served on the Hall of Worthies (Chiphyŏnjŏn 集賢殿) and was involved in the creation of the vernacular alphabet (*hunmin chŏngŭm*) under King Sejong the Great.

41 Ch'oe Hŭnghyo (崔興孝, 1370–1452) was a master calligrapher of the early Chosŏn dynasty. Ch'oe handled foreign diplomatic communications with Ming dynasty China.

42 The original version reads "先授諺解小學." ([He] first gave them an annotated version [*ŏnhae*] of the *Lesser Learning*). *Ŏnhae* versions were basically translations of the classics into vernacular Korean using a mixed-script orthography and used by students of Literary Sinitic.

43 These works together constitute the bulk of the Confucian canon used in Chosŏn-era education.

44 The original version records simply the family names 李杜, which refer to Yi Paek (李白 Ch. Li Bai, AD 701–62) and Tu Po (杜甫 Ch. Du Fu, AD 712–70), two renowned masters of Tang-era poetry. Here and elsewhere Gale records their pen names, Yi "T'aebaek" (太白) and "Chami" (子美), respectively.

residence he would have us constantly before him to write, and then would select the best we had done, giving rewards to some and reprimand to others. Thus he urged us on. Though we never attained to such a mastery as he himself, we could sing and write in such a way as assured our admission to the outer courts of the Tang Temple of Literature. The names of the ten girls were: Little Jade (Sook), the Lotus (Puyong), Jewel (Pigyŏng), Peacock (Pich'wi), Bright One (Ongnyŏ), Golden Lily (Kŭmyŏn), Silver Toad (Ŭnsŏm), Red Phoenix (Charan), Matchless Bloom (Poryŏn), and Cloud Bud (Unyŏng).[45] I was Cloud Bud.

The Prince loved us dearly and kept us close within the palace where we saw no one else; nor did we speak to anyone.

Day after day he had his scholar friends come to call with whom he drank and wrote, but none of them ever had to do with us, or we with them. He desired to keep secret the fact that we were studying at all, so he constantly gave orders, saying, 'If any of you go beyond the gates you shall suffer for it; or if you let your names be known to outsiders you shall surely die.'

Once the Prince on return from an outing called us and said, 'Today I met a number of friends and after we had a glass together we wrote verses on the subject, A Cloud of Light on the Palace Grove, on the Walls, on the Hills.' 'I wrote first,' said he, 'and then I asked the guests to write as well, but what they wrote was a failure. Now I want you each to write in order of your ages.'

Little Jade wrote:

A soft blue cloud, a bolt of woven silk,
Upon the breeze comes gently through the gate.
How frail, how thin, its light unfolding form,
It melts into the shadows of the night.

The nine, all in order, one after another, wrote their part, till my turn came and I wrote this:

A thin light mist is wafted from afar,
A silken roll that winds from off its loom.

45 Sook (小玉), Puyong (芙蓉), Pigyŏng (飛瓊), Pich'wi (翡翠), Ongnyŏ (玉女), Kŭmyŏn (金漣), Ŭnsŏm (銀蟾), Charan (紫鸞), Poryŏn (寶蓮), Unyŏng (雲英).

The weaver hears the sighing of the breeze,
And longs to lift her wings o'er Fairy Hill.[46]

Seeing this, the Prince was much astonished and said, 'These verses
might be mixed with the best of the Tang Dynasty and still pass muster.
Sŏng Sammun's disciples could not do better.' He read them over two
or three times without being able to decide as to which was best. After
a while he said, 'Lotus' verse reminds me of Kul Wŏn[47] – very pretty!
Peacock's is a match for the ancients. Little Jade's is like the fluttering of the butterfly, with a far-off picture in the closing line. These two
I regard as best. When I first saw them I could not decide; but now as
I look again, Red Phoenix' verse brings tears to my eyes; again it makes
me dance for joy. The others too are all very sweet and beautiful. Cloud
Bud evidently thinks of someone with longing; I wonder who it can be?
I ought to ask of you to find out and let her be punished, but her refined
touch is so evident that I'll let her off this time.'

I at once descended to the court, bowed low with my face to the
ground, and said, 'I assure Your Highness that my verse is written without any such thought in mind, but now that I have caused my master to
question me I deserve to die many deaths.'

The Prince, however, called me back to my seat and had me sit down,
saying, 'A poem comes from the heart, something we cannot hide. Let's
say nothing more about it.'

He had ten rolls of silk ordered and gave us each one.

The Prince had never shown me any special favour, and yet the people of the Palace all thought he was in love with me.

We girls then withdrew to our rooms where we lit the lamps and
placed an open volume of the Songs of Tang [唐律] on the ornamented
table. We talked over the best that palace-women had ever written,
poor hearts who wrote in loneliness. I, however, sat by myself against
the screen in sad dejection, saying nothing to anybody but silent like
an image of the Buddha. Little Jade said, 'Just now in your verse on the

---

46 In the original, each woman offers her poem in turn, with Unyŏng going
    second to last before Poryŏn, but Gale has omitted these poems from his
    translation.

47 Kul Wŏn (屈原 Ch. Qu Yuan, 340–278 BC) was a member of the Ch'o (楚) royal
    clan during the Warring States period of ancient China. Together with the
    Classic of Poetry (詩經), the Songs of Chu (楚辭) attributed to him is consid-
    ered to be one of the two greatest collections of Classical Chinese poetry.

Cloud you gave the Master cause to question. Are you anxious about it and does that make you silent? Or is it that the Prince has passed you word to be ready for the embroidered coverlet and so you are happy and do not speak? Which is it? Tell me please.'

I drew my dress about me and replied, 'You and I are not of the same mould; how can you expect to know my heart? I was just now thinking out a verse and could not find a suitable character to express exactly what I wished; that is why I was silent.'

Silver Toad replied, 'When our thoughts are absent, our minds follow them, and talk of those who sit by is like the wind that wanders past the ear. I would like to know just what your silence means; I will find out. I suggest that the grape-vine outside the window be your subject and that you write me a verse on that.'

On hearing this I dashed off the following:

The winding stalks are like the dragon's form,
The shade beneath its leaves most cool and dear;
The sun's strong rays strike through the open rift,
While far away the blue sky hangs aloft.
The clinging tendrils clasp the railing close,
Like gems the fruit hangs rich and rounded fair;
If I should say just what you merit most,
I'd call the clouds to bear you to the sky.

Little Jade read this over slowly then rose, bowed and said, 'Heaven and earth behold your skill with wonder. The style is not anything special except that it is like the old-time songs; but your rapid exposition is a rare gift indeed. I am delighted to have seen it and bow to you as the seventy disciples bowed to the Master Confucius.'

Red Phoenix said, 'Be careful what you say. Why do you use such extravagant language? Still the verses are very pretty and the expression beautiful, while the thought rises on wings like a bird.'

All the others chimed in, 'That's so!'

Though I had by these verses turned their attention from myself, I had not yet fully dispelled their doubts and questions.

The following day we heard the sound of approaching carriages when the gate-keeper rushed in to say, 'Guests are coming.'

The Master had his east room specially set in order and there he met them. They were all literati of note and men of special attainment. He had them seated, and after some little time showed them what we had written regarding the Cloud. They were astonished, one and all, saying, 'We never dreamed to see a return to the old days of Tang. Assuredly we are no match for such songs as these. How did Your Highness come by them?'

The Prince laughed and said, 'Why do you think they are so fine? My Boy picked them up somewhere. I really do not know who wrote them; some gifted hand or other must live in this village.'

The guests looked in wonder at this, when a moment later, Sŏng Sammun appeared and said, 'Skill in composition does not appertain to any special age. During the six hundred years since the days of Koryŏ there have been many great writers as well as many lacking clearness; the light, the thin, the shallow. I have seen plenty of the latter, but these poems are beautiful, lofty in thought and dignified in expression, with not a shade of the dust of earth about them. Written they evidently are by those who dwell within the deep enclosure of the Palace and have never mixed with the common run of men. These writers have read only the songs of the Masters, and spent their days with them, until they have attained in heart to a style of beauty unexampled. They say that when the winds blow in songs of sadness it shows that thoughts of others possess one. Again the lonely bamboo that guards its green through all the seasons of the year tells of the virtuous woman; but if this bamboo bends to the wind that blows, it shows a lack of virtue. If thoughts go out to Kul Wŏn of Ch'o, it means an expression of loyalty to the king. When the dew hangs on the leaves it indicates that the fairy's hand is near. Though there is some slight difference in these efforts yet they are about all the same. I believe Your Highness must enclose ten fairies within the palace who write so well. I would like much to see them.'

Though Prince Anp'yŏng agreed in heart, outwardly he pretended to dissent. 'Who said that Sŏng Sammun was a critic of the character? What fairy folk could I be expected to have within the palace? You have altogether too high an opinion of me.'

All this time we ten maidens were watching through the chink, and hearing what was said, scarce drew breath in our wondering appreciation.

On this night Charan spoke sweetly to me saying, 'A girl, not only on her own account would like to marry with a good man, but for her parents' sake as well. All so desire; tell me truly whom you are thinking of. I see you growing more silent day by day and am anxious for you. I ask this in all kindness – tell me please and hide nothing.'

I thanked her for her loving words and said, 'There are so many people in the palace that even the walls have ears to hear, so that I dared not speak, but your kind heart moves me and I cannot but answer. Last autumn when the yellow chrysanthemums first came out and the leaves turned their colour, the Prince took his place in the main hall. There he had us maids make the ink ready and unwrap a roll of silk on which he wrote ten poems. Just then the house-boy came in to say that a young scholar, Kim *Chinsa*, had called and wished to see His Highness.'

The Prince was very pleased and said, 'Show him in.'

He wore a grass-cloth coat and a leather belt, and bowed as he came up into the hall like a splendid bird opening his wings. Then he sat down just in front; a fairy he seemed to me, one of the genii. The Prince seemed greatly drawn to him calling him *chinsa*. He sat aside and offered him a special place, though Kim bowed low and declined it, saying, 'I am unworthy of this welcome by Your Highness, and your addressing me thus covers me with shame.'

The Prince comforted him, saying, 'I have long heard of you and your high attainments. Your coming thus at my invitation is an honour to all the house, better than the rarest gift could be.'

While Kim *Chinsa* was being thus addressed, we were all seated together where we could see him and he us. The Prince, in view of Kim's youth, thought nothing of it, and did not command us to leave.

Said he, 'We have with us now the loveliest time of the autumn season; come write me a verse on it that will bring honour to my home.'

The *chinsa* arose and said in reply, 'You have mistaken my gifts and talents altogether, for I know nothing of poetry.'

Then the Prince had Kŭmyŏn sing, and made Puyong play, while Lily blew the pipe and Jewel brought some wine. He ordered me to prepare the ink and bring it. I was then a young girl and when I saw this handsome lad my soul was dazed with wonder and my thoughts rushed in upon me. He also looked at me and smiled, and glanced in my direction again and again.

Then the Prince said to the *chinsa*, 'My welcome to you is from the inner heart; you must not refuse to write me one of your gems, else my home will lose its name.'

The *chinsa* then took up his pen and wrote:

The wild-goose flocks sail to the distant south,
The Palace knows that autumn days are near;
The chilly pools unfold no lotus buds,
And lowly bends the Golden Flower its head.
On broidered mats with tinted cheeks I sit,

While snow-flake tunes are wakened from the harp.
The fairies' wine in brimming cups they bear,
I drink and find no power to stem my thoughts.

The Prince read these through and through, hummed them once or twice appreciatively, and said, 'Such a skillful hand is rare, most rare; how comes it that we have never met before?'

The ten maids all looked at each other and expressed their admiration by saying, 'This visitor is unquestionably Wang Chajin (32–7 BC) [48] come back to earth by the crane on which he rides. In this common world, how can there be such as he?'

The Prince took up his glass and asked, 'Who is the greatest poet that ever lived?'

The *chinsa* replied, 'In my narrow experience, I think first of Yi T'aebaek (699–762 AD). [49] He was a fairy from Heaven, who had long waited on God and then come down to Hyŏp'o the Garden of the Naiads. [50] He drank of the wine of the genii and, overcome by it, broke off flowerlet buds and tossed them into the abodes of mortal men. No Cho-rin and Wang Par-i [51] were fairies of the deep, the thick woods, the floating seaweed, the water-birds that cry, the dragons of the deep. I hold them all in heart – they are my greatest masters. Maeng Hoyŏn (689–740 AD) is sweetest of singers and nearest to the harp. Yi Ŭisan [52] was a master of the arts of the fairy, till at last he fell a victim to the demon who keeps his eye on poetry. What he writes is not the work of mortal man but of the gods. Why need one speak of others who are not of special note?'

---

48 Wang Chajin (王子晋 Ch. Wang Zijin), alternately called Wang Chagyo (王子喬 Ch. Wang Ziqiao) was an immortal legendary dating from the Zhou dynasty (1046–256 BC), making Gale's dating problematic. He was regarded as the temple guardian god of Mt Ch'ŏnt'ae (天台山 Ch. Tiantaishan) and is described as playing a reed instrument and riding on a crane in *Chronicle of Visiting Mt Ch'ŏnt'ae and Mt Ot'ae* (参天台五台山記). See Nikaido, *Asian Folk Religion and Cultural Interaction*, 65–6.

49 Yi Paek (李白 Ch. Li Bai, AD 701–62).

50 Naiads were a kind of female spirit thought to inhabit bodies of freshwater in Greek mythology.

51 No Chorin (盧照鄰 Ch. Lu Zhaolin, AD 634?–89) and Wang Pal (王勃 Ch. Wang Bo, 649–76 AD).

52 Yi Ŭisan (李商隱 Ch. Li Shangyin, AD 812–58) was a well-known poet of the Tang dynasty.

The Prince said, 'As I talk over poetry with the literati, most of them consider Tu Chami (712–770 AD)[53] chief. Why is this I wonder?'

The *chinsa* replied, 'The ordinary literati enjoy poetry as they do roast fish, and Tu Chami's poems are roast fish indeed!'

The Prince said, 'He has written every variety of poem. Charm and delight are everywhere evident; why should he not be appreciated?'

The *chinsa* replied modestly, 'I should never suggest that he be regarded lightly. Tu Chami's poems are like the soldiers that the Emperor Han Muje sent out in fierce battle array against the northern barbarian, a million bears bounding forth to meet their prey.[54] They are the peaches that the Western Queen Mother passed on to Han Muje.[55] When we think of these things we reckon Tu Chami the highest of the high; but to compare him with Yi T'aebaek is like comparing earth with heaven, or a river with the sea. As compared with Wang and No he rides a cart far ahead, while these two whip up their horses in the fast receding rear.'

The Prince made answer, 'Hearing what you say, my spirit rejoices and I feel as though I rode upon the clouds up through the firmament. Still Tu Chami is indeed a great scholar. Though his songs are somewhat unsuited for singing; how can one mention Wang and No in the same breath? Let that go. But once more will you not write me another poem for the glory of my house?'

The *chinsa* then wrote on peach paper as follows:

The mists lift off the gilded lake,
And leave the lights serenely pure.
The deep blue heaven's celestial sea
Roofs o'er the wide extended night.
The gentle breeze with loving thought,
Beats lightly on the hanging screen;
The white-faced moon comes like a friend

---

53 Tu Po (杜甫 Ch. Du Fu, AD 712–70), pen name "Chami" (子美).

54 Han Muje (漢武帝, 157–87 BC, r. 141–87 BC), Emperor Wu of Han, was one of the longest reigning and most successful monarchs in Chinese history, greatly expanding the territory of Han China, including through campaigns against the Xiongnu (匈奴), a nomadic confederation inhabiting the northeast Asian steppes.

55 The Queen Mother of the West (西王母), a goddess of Chinese religion and mythology, offered a banquet to Emperor Wu that included special teachings and the "peaches of immortality" (蟠桃), but the emperor ultimately failed to follow these teachings. This account is related in *Stories of Emperor Wu* (漢武故事).

With measured step soft through the room.
The darkness swings from out the court,
The peach tree shadows circle by.
Bright from the wine-cup's rosy brim
I drink the 'autumn daisy's' cheer.
And though I fall beneath its spell,
Mark me not ill but mark me well.

More delighted than ever, the Prince took the *chinsa* by the hand and said, 'Your gifts are not those of mortal man but of the genii. Your power of composition and artistic expression mark you God's appointee to Korea for some great purpose. Now let me see you write something – your penmanship.'

The *chinsa* took up the pen, when a drop fell from it onto my hand and spread out like the wings of a bird. I looked at it as a good omen and did not wash it off. The palace-maids on each side laughed at what they saw but still counted it a propitious sign.

When the night had fallen and the water-clock had counted off its watches – one, two, three, the Prince stretched himself, yawned and said, 'I am drunk; go now and rest, but do not forget the line that runs, "Bring your harp and come with the morning."'

The day following the Prince read over again the two poems that the *chinsa* had written, sighed, and said, 'The *chinsa* is even a match for Sŏng Sammun, yes – in grace and beauty he is superior.'

From this time on I did not sleep, my food failed me, and my mind was all perturbed. My clothes grew so large that everyone could see and take note.

Charan replied, 'I forgot about that but now that I hear what you say I seem like one awaking from a dream.'

The Prince frequently invited the *chinsa*, but he did not let me come into his presence. I could only look through the chink and see him. One day I wrote a verse on white duck-paper:

A scholar lord with coat and leathern belt
So fair his form, it seemed like to the Gods.
I look from out the shadow of the screen,
And count us mated by the moonbeam's ray.
I wash my face with endless tears that flow,
And from the harp-strings break my sighings sore.
My deepest longings his fair face to see
To God ascend. He knows, but only He.

I wrapped the poem round my ring ten times and more in hope to send it but every eye forbade me.

That night the Prince ordered a great feast, invited many guests, and praised the *chinsa* before them all, showing the poems that he had written. Each looked in admiration as he passed them round, and joined in approval of their excellence. A horse was then sent with an invitation to the *chinsa* to come.

When he arrived and took his place he looked thin and worn – quite a different man from what I had seen before. The Prince spoke feelingly of this, saying, 'Your Excellency has no anxiety for the state of Ch'o and yet you have grown quite thin.'[56]

All the guests joined in the laugh.

The *chinsa* arose, excused himself, and said, 'Your servant, a poor literatus, has found the love and favour of Your Highness more than he can bear, and has been worn down thin by it. I have fallen ill so that I cannot eat and have to be helped about by others. Once more Your Highness has done yourself the dishonour of calling me. I have come, as you see, with staff in hand.'

The guests all gathered their coats about them and sat in deepest respect as they made their salutation. The *chinsa*, being the youngest, sat in the lowest place and so his side was against the wall that joined our inner room.

The night was already far advanced and all guests were drunk so I gently pressed a hole in the partition paper and looked through. He was evidently aware of me as he sat by. I pushed the package through the opening. He picked it up and when he reached home opened and read it. He could not overcome his sorrow or lay aside the verses that I had written. His thoughts went out a hundred fold more than ever toward me. It seemed as though life had become impossible without his palace-maid. He desired to write and send me a reply but there was no 'azure pigeon' by which to speed it.[57] All he could do was to think, and think, and sigh.

---

56 This seems to be an allusion to Qu Yuan (屈原, ca 340–278 BC), who was a poet from the southern Chu (楚) and considered to be one of the first prominent Chinese poets. Twenty-five of his poems are included in the poetry anthology Chu Ci (楚辭 Songs of Chu or Songs of the South). Upon receiving news that the King of Chu was taken and the capital taken, Qu is said to have committed suicide in protest of the corruption of the era.

57 An "azure pigeon" (*ch'ŏngjo* 青鳥) represents good news or a welcome messenger in Sinitic literary tradition. According to a legend associated with Emperor

There was a wise-woman living outside the East Gate whom he had heard of. Frequently she went on errands to the Prince's Palace, and was greatly respected and feared.

The *chinsa* set out to look her up, and found that she was quite a young person, not yet twenty. She was exceedingly beautiful and a widow. She had of her own accord become a woman of public life, and seeing the *chinsa*, treated him royally to drink and sweets.

The *chinsa* took the glass, but set it aside without drinking, saying, 'I am in great distress today over a certain matter that concerns me, and so will come again tomorrow to speak to you.'

He went again the second day and again said the same. He did not venture to disclose his thoughts. 'I'll come again tomorrow' was all he said.

The wise-woman seeing that he was not an ordinary visitor, was delighted and yet his coming and going without any meaning seemed strange. 'I expect it is because he is so young that he is afraid to speak his wishes. I'll help him to what he desires so we may share the pillow together.'

The day following she bathed, dressed her hair, put on her best apparel, spread out her finest embroidered coverlet and had one of her slave maids await his coming just outside the door.

The *chinsa* came, but seeing this special preparation, rouge and powder, and all her decorations, he was disturbed by it.

The wise-woman said, 'What night is this that I should meet so fair a lord.'

The *chinsa* did not respond, but drew a sigh and looked deeply distressed.

The wise-woman then went on, 'How is it that you, a young man, should come so frequently to my house, I being a widow?'

The *chinsa* said, 'If you are indeed a person of spiritual insight, how is it that you do not already know the object of my coming?'

The woman then turned aside and, bowing to a spirit that stood in the corner, struck a bell and passed her hand over the strings of a harp.

Wu of Han (漢武, 157–87 BC), the scholar-official and court jester Dongfang Shuo (東方朔), an enigmatic character considered in Chinese mythology to be a Taoist immortal and occasionally planetary incarnation, seeing an "azure bird" considered it to be a messenger from the Queen Mother of the West (西王母), a mythological figure of even more ancient provenance associated with eternal bliss and good fortune and worshipped by many cultures throughout the Sinographic cosmopolis.

Then her whole body began to tremble. After a little she arose and said, 'My lord you are indeed to be pitied, for you are desirous of that which can never come to pass. Your wish will not only fail, but ere three years go by you will be a dweller in the Yellow Shades.'

The *chinsa* wept and said, 'Though you do not tell me why, I can guess, for I am oppressed in heart and no medicine can give me relief. If only I could send by you a little message that I have written, then I might die in peace.'

The woman made reply, 'Your humble servant sometimes goes to the Palace on messages from the spirit she serves, but only when I am called can I go. Still, I shall make the attempt and see what can be done for your lordship.'

The *chinsa* then took from his bosom a letter which he gave her, saying, 'Be careful, please; any slip in the giving may be a matter of life and death.'

With this letter in her safe-keeping, the wise-woman went to the Palace where all the folks regarded her coming with question. She stated that she had come on a special errand. Later, as opportunity offered, she gave me a nod, and when alone passed me this letter.

I went to my room, opened it, and read:

'Since I first saw you my soul has gone out toward you in endless longing; and my love for you overwhelms my whole body. My heart is moved within me every time I look toward this western Palace. I have your letter that you passed me through the soft partition. So precious is it that I bear its words on my heart all the day. Before I opened it my soul was enveloped in clouds of impetuous fire; and before I had read half, my eyes were dropping tears. Though I desire to sleep, no sleep comes; my food refuses to go down. I have been ill and nothing brings relief. I shall pass on into the Yellow Shades where I hope to meet you. May death soon come, but before that, may God have mercy on me and the spirits lend me help, so that just once while I live I may find relief from my distress. Then though I become dust, and my bones crumble away, I shall, with a contended heart, make my sacrifice to Heaven and to all the spirits of the upper air. As I lean over this paper to write you, my throat feels closed and dry. What further can I say?'

He added to the letter a verse which ran:

The halls and towers fade in the gathering mist,
The shadow trees recede from out the view.
The flowers that fall sail out upon the stream,

While twittering swallows hasten their homeward flight.
My pillow lends no dream, no butterfly;
No wildgoose comes to bear my message dear.
Your lovely form I see: why speak you not?
The grass is green, the oriole calls, but tears and only tears!

I read this and felt as though I would swoon away. Words failed me and my tears were like drops of blood. I hid behind a screen lest someone should see.

From this time on not a moment did I forget him. I was like one in a dream, half conscious, so much so that others noticed it. The Master's doubts of me and the talk of the others were thus based on fact.

Charan was also one who felt her wrongs (not being married), and hearing what I had to say, replied in tears, 'A poem comes from the inner heart and never deceives in what it says.'

One day the Prince called Peacock Feather to him and said, 'You ten all being together in one place have not as good an opportunity for study as I would like. I am going to separate you into two groups of five each and place one in the West Hall.' And so Charan, Ŭnsŏm, Ongnyŏ, Pich'wi and I were that day removed.

Ongnyŏ said of our new home, 'The flowers here with the grass slopes and the surroundings of hill and stream are like the delights of the country. This is indeed "The House of Study (Toksŏdang)."'[58]

I replied, 'We are not scholars nor are we priestesses; we are only prisoners. This place is none other than Pan Ch'ŏmyŏ's (BC 18 a famous lady in waiting) Changsin Palace.'[59] On hearing this, all faces looked sad.

I desired greatly to write an answer and tell my whole heart to the *chinsa*, and so sent an earnest message to the wise-woman begging her

---

58 The "House of Study" (讀書堂) was a Chosŏn government office-cum-scholarly academy, where promising young scholar-officials were given leave from government service to polish their academic skills.

59 Consort Pan (班婕妤 Ch. Ban Jieyu, 48–6 BC) was a palace woman and poet of the Western Han (206 BC–AD 23) and a concubine of Emperor Cheng (漢成帝). After falling out of favour with the emperor, she became a lady-in-waiting to the Empress Dowager and was relegated to the Changsin Palace (長信宮 Ch. Zhangxingong), where she penned her extant work "Song of Resentment" (怨歌行 Ch. Yuan Gexing), in which she ruminates on palace life and feelings of abandonment.

to come again, but she did not consent for she was angry that the *chinsa* had refused her offers and favours.

On a certain evening Charan said to me quietly, 'We palace-maids each year on the 15th of the 8th Moon go to the T'angch'undae[60] to wash silk and have a picnic. This year, I hear, we are going to Sogyŏk instead.[61] On the way how would it do if you called on the wise-woman yourself?'

I thought this an excellent suggestion and waited impatiently for the day. Every hour dragged by like a winter season. Pich'wi became aware of my impatience, but pretended not to notice it and said, 'When you first came to the Palace your face was like the pear blossom; you needed no powder or rouge and everybody called you the lady from the Kingdom of O,[62] but now you have lost your bloom and beauty; what's the reason, pray?'

I replied, 'I am physically not strong, and the heat of the summer has overcome me, but I shall be all right when the autumn leaves fall and the cool breezes return.'

Pich'wi wrote a verse making fun of me and treating my complaint as a bit of sport. The verse was beautifully written and I greatly admired her skill, but I was ashamed to be made fun of. Thus the months went by and autumn was here. The cool air of the evening had just returned and the chrysanthemums had begun to bloom; the cricket, too, had taken up his customary song, and the white moon flooded all the world with light. I was delighted that the season had come but I made no display or expression of joy.

Silver Toad said to me, 'To-night you will have a chance to pass on your letter and your joy will be equal to that of heaven itself.'

The reason that Silver Toad said this was because I had already told her my secret. I felt that I could not hide it from those with whom I was so closely associated, but I added, 'Don't tell the others in the South Palace, please.'

---

60 蕩春臺.

61 昭格署洞.

62 Guoguo Furen (虢國夫人 K. Koekkuk puin, State Mistress of Guo, ?–AD 756) was the elder sister of Yang Guifei (楊貴妃, 719–56) and said to be her equal in beauty. According to the *Historical Dictionary of Medieval China*, "In 756 she followed [Emperor] Xuanzong [of Tang] in fleeing the advance of An Lushan's army. From Mawei … where Yang Guifei was killed, she escaped to Chencang … where she committed suicide." Xiong, *Historical Dictionary of Medieval China*, 225.

That night we saw the wild geese begin their flight south and the gem-like dew-drops of autumn fall about us. This was the season for our washing silk at the fresh clear stream. The day was finally settled, though the place rather than the day was the question. Those in the South Palace said, '[T]here is no dearer spot than the stream beneath the T'angch'undae.' Those of the West Palace said, 'Not so, the springs of Sogyŏk are better still. Why pass aside what is near to take what is far-off?'

But the South Palace group was fixed in their determination and so won.

That night Charan said to me, 'Sook is the leader of the South Palace, and what she says they all do. I'll get hold of her and change her mind.' So, with lantern in hand, she went to the South Palace where she was received by Kŭmyŏn, who in great delight, said, 'Though we are divided like the ancient kingdoms of Chin and Ch'o,[63] so very far apart, yet my dear Charan has come to visit us. Thanks, so much.'

Sook then said, 'No need to thank her; she has come to influence us to her way of thinking.'

With all dignity, Charan drew her skirt about her and said, 'When Mencius announced that the Superior Man could read the mind of another, he evidently referred to you.'

Sook said, 'You folks in the West Palace wish to go to Sogyŏk and because I am opposed to it you have come here to see me. There is no need to thank our honoured guest, Charan.'

Charan made answer, 'Among us five of the West Palace I am the only one who wishes to go outside of the city.'

Sook replied, 'Then why is it, pray, that you come here to urge keeping within the city?'

Charan said, 'I have heard that Sogyŏk is a place where sacrifice is offered to the stars, and that it is called Samch'ŏng.[64] Now, we ten are Samch'ŏng fairies. In a former life we made a mistake you know, in reading the Hwangjŏng Book of the Taoists,[65] and were sent exiles to

---

63 Chin (秦 Ch. Qin) and Ch'o (楚 Ch. Chu) were two of the major combatants among the seven ancient Chinese states that comprised the Warring States period (475–221 BC). These states were eventually annexed by Chin in 221 BC under China's first empire.

64 三清.

65 *Hwangjŏng kyŏng* (黃庭經 Yellow Court Classic) is a Taoist meditation text received in the third century AD from Lady Wei Huacun, the founder of the Shangqing (上清) or Supreme Clarity sect of Taoism.

earth, so here we are amid its dust and confusion. Houses, villages, farms, fishing-towns, all lie before us, and yet we are locked behind bars like birds in a cage. Though occasionally we hear the voice of the oriole, we sigh in vain to catch a glimpse of the willow blossom. The swallows mate as well as our little birds that rest on the same bough when they sleep. There are flowers, too, that fold each other in their tendrils, and trees that cling close by their branches. Even inanimate things and little birds follow the dual law of the universe and join in love together, while we ten, for some sin or other, have to live unmated and alone. We pass these lovely autumn nights with only a lamp for companion while our souls melt away with longing. Our youthful years are cast uselessly aside, till at last, doomed to die, we are gathered back into the dust. Our lot, so cheerless, one wonders why; for when once youth is past and age comes on there is no return. Think it over, please. Will you not go with us and bathe in the fresh clear stream and then call at the T'aeŭl Temple,[66] to make our bow and pray for blessings for the ages to come so that we may not have such a lot as this in our afterlife. This is what I'd like to do. We ten here are like children of the same parents, and have our same little tasks for the day. Why should you question a matter that needs no question? This division of opinion is due to my having failed to win the faith and confidence of my associates.'

Hearing this, Sook thanked her and said, 'I did not think matters out clearly like you, and the reason I did not consent to the choice of the city was my fear of meeting idle fellows that hang about ready to insult one. But now that you have explained it so fully I am won over. From today on, whether it be walking on the sea or riding on the clouds, I'll follow you. Through your influence I shall share in this trip and share in its blessing.'

Puyong said, 'Whatever be the matter in hand, the heart is first of all. When we are divided in opinion nothing ever turns out well. Besides, our Master, the Prince, does not know we slaves count honour. You have done badly in yielding so readily to Charan, seeing it is a question that has occupied us for days. Your decision is not wise or good. As for clean water and surroundings that give joy, I do not agree with keeping inside the walls, for before our hall the water is clear and the rocks charming. Let's go where we have gone each year. If you attempt a change I shall oppose it. By such an act there are many things that we will lose; I will not go.'

---

66 太乙祠.

Poryŏn said, 'Words should be an ornament to one's person. If we are careful in their use we find blessing, so the real gentleman always guards his lips as you would a bottle.

'In the days of Han, Pyŏnggil and Chang Sangyŏ[67] kept silent all day long and yet their plans were more than carried through. A game-keeper may give an answer to all the questions asked, but Chang Sŏk-chi reminded the king that a ready speaker was not always safe.[68] I do not accept Charan's speech as the sincere expression of her heart. Sook's words do not really indicate her meaning; they merely show that she has been outdone in debate. Puyong's words are only meant for show. None of these speeches convince me and I'll join no such expedition.'

Kŭmyŏn said, 'Your discussion leads nowhere; I'll have to cast lots for you and see.' So she opened the *Book of Changes*, found a diagram and explained it, saying, 'Tomorrow Unyŏng will meet her husband. Now, we know that Unyŏng – one glance at her face suffices – is not a person of this world. The Master has long had thoughts of Unyŏng. Her refusal to accept any such relationship even though she die, is due to the many favours that she has received from the Princess. The Prince is all powerful, but for fear that some harm might overtake Unyŏng, he has not ventured to push the matter. Now, if we take her from this quiet, secluded place into the bustle and whirl of the city, where there are idle young men who may see her face, they will assuredly lose their heads over her and go crazy. Even though not brought face to face with her, they will point her out and that will be an insult. The other day the Prince issued an order saying, "If the maids go out of the gate or let outsiders even know their names, they shall die for it." I shall have no part in any such expedition.'

Charan, seeing that the matter had turned out a failure, was very much disappointed. She bowed and announced her going. Just then

---

67   Pyŏng Kil (丙吉 Ch. Bing Ji, ?–55 BC) was a government minister during the
     Western Han dynasty; Chang Sangyŏ (張相如 Ch. Zhang Xiangru?–165 BC)
     was a general and the Marquis of Dongyang (東陽侯) during the Western Han
     dynasty.

68   Chang Sŏkchi (張釋之 Ch. Zhang Shizhi, 206 BC–AD 8) was a Commandant
     of the Court (廷尉 Ch. tingwei) during the Han dynasty. He advised Emperor
     Mun (文帝, 202–157 BC; r. 180–157 BC) on matters of punishment, of which one
     such instance is related in Sima Qian's *Records of the Grand Historian*
     (史記), in "Biography of Chang Sŏkchi" (張釋之馮唐列傳).

Pigyŏng, with tears in her eyes, took hold of Charan's silk girdle and held her so that she could not go. Then, bringing a 'parrot'' glass and pouring out some 'cloud-milk' wine, she had them all drink.

Kŭmyŏn said, 'Our meeting tonight has been one most restrained and orderly; I am disturbed at Pigyŏng's tears.'

Pigyŏng made reply, 'When we first went to the South Palace I was the nearest friend of all to Unyŏng, and we made a contract, she and I, to live and die together. Now, though we are divided, I can never ever forget her. The other day when we had our audience before the Prince I noticed that her waist had grown so thin, her face worn away and her voice so weak, that she could hardly be heard. When she bowed she almost fell, so that I had to assist and steady her. The dear one replied that she was unwell and expected any day to die. "You have no need to bother about my poor little life," said she, "and yet I regret that I shall not share in the poems and letters of the nine, which will grow more beautiful and wonderful daily, till they become a volume that will delight and edify other states than ours, famous the world over. I am sorry about this and cannot stop my tears."'

'Her words and tears were more than I could endure and I, too, cried. Now that I think over it I am sure that her sickness is due to troubles of the heart. Alas, Charan is a friend of Unyŏng and her plan today was to place her companion on the Altar of Heaven. If she fails, nothing remains for Unyŏng but to go down unsatisfied to the Yellow Shades. Her resentment, then, will be against the South Palace. One good act and a hundred good results follow; one untoward deed and a hundred evils come in its train. Our decision just now was all right. I shall go for one and so there will be three of us. How can the others refuse? If any troubles arise with the Master it will be Unyŏng's fault only; what concern is that to the rest of us?'

Sook said, 'I have nothing more to say, only this: that I will give up my life for Unyŏng if necessary.'

Charan said, 'Half will follow, half refuse; this is not a happy conclusion.' She got up to go away but sat down again and seemed to think the matter over, and yet no one ever spoke, no one wishing to change her mind. So Charan spoke again, 'In the world there are direct methods and indirect methods. If the indirect succeeds it turns out to be direct. How is it that you cannot think of others and set aside the decision you have made?' Then they consented and all decided to go.

Charan again said, 'I was not trying to overpersuade you, but simply to do a kind act.'

Pigyŏng said, 'In ancient days So Chin united the Six States,[69] and now Charan has made us five all join hands. She is a skilful tongued courtier, sure enough.'

Charan said, 'So Chin became minister of the Six States: now what are you five going to give me in the way of special honour?'

Kŭmyŏn made answer, 'The union brought about was a matter of great profit to these states and so they honoured him who accomplished it; but simply agreeing to what you asked us to do, what profit is there in that, pray?' Thus they talked and laughed together.

Charan finally said, 'You in the South Palace have done a kind act, and have raised Unyŏng to life again. How glad and grateful she will be.'

Twice she made a low bow and Sook arose and bowed likewise. Then she said, 'You have made a solemn promise with God above, who sees, and Mother Earth beneath, who feels, and with all the angels round who guard us. Let no change of mind overtake you later.' So she bowed once more and then departed. The five also responded and saw her out of the gates.

Charan returned and told me, while I supported myself against the wall. I then arose, bowed twice to her and said, 'I am indebted to my father and mother for the beginning of my life, but how much more to your dear self, who has raised me from the dead and given me hope. Before I die I shall find some way to reward your kindness.'

I could not sleep that night, so impatiently did I await the morning. After my early greetings had been paid I returned to my place.

Sook said, 'The weather is beautiful, the water clear and fresh, and today we shall pitch our happy tents in Sogyŏk Village.' The eight others expressed their joy likewise but with no further word to say.

I then came out of the West Palace and wrote on a piece of white silk all my heart and soul, put it in my bosom, and with Charan fell behind the others as we moved on in our procession. We said to the little horse-boy who accompanied us with his whip, 'They say that there is a wise-woman living outside the East Gate who is a prophetess. We want to go and ask her about my sickness.'

---

69   So Chin (蘇秦 Ch. Su Qin, 380–284 BC) was a political strategist during the Warring States period and the proponent of the so-called Vertical Alliance system, which sought to unite the six states of Qi, Chu, Yan, Han, Zhao, and Wei against the more powerful state of Qin. The Vertical Alliance soon disintegrated due to internal squabbles.

The boy at once assented and took us to her home. There I introduced myself and said, 'My coming today is to see Kim *Chinsa*. Please send a messenger at once and have him come. If you do so I shall never forget your kindness, no – not till I die.'

The wise-woman did as requested, sent a messenger and Kim *Chinsa* came hurrying forth in one headlong response.

We met and yet not a word could we say. We looked at each other and only tears came. I gave him the letter I had written and said, 'I shall return in the evening on my way back; please wait for me.' Then I mounted my horse and left.

The *chinsa* opened the letter and it read, 'The letter that came to me by the wise-woman was dearer than the tinkling of choicest gems, and sweeter than the sweet. I held it open in my two hands and read it over and over again. Gladness and sorrow contended in my bosom. I could not control my thoughts and longed to answer you at once, but there was no one by whom to trust it; and fearing that it might get noised abroad, I just bowed my head and thought only. I wanted to fly to you but had no wings. My heart was broken and my soul seemed to die away, till I waited only for my day of earth's release. Once only before dying I wanted to give you this letter and tell you all my heart. My one wish is that Your Excellency may know my love.

My country is the south and of all our children my parents loved me best. They let me play as I pleased without restraint, in the garden, by the stream, among the bamboos, or in the orange groves. Happy day followed happy day. The fishers by the stream, the woodmen, the reapers, the boys who blew their pipes – all wore familiar faces. Such was my world. There were besides the hills in which lived the fairies – more than I could number.

My parents, first of all, taught me the Three Principles and the Poems of the Tang Kingdom till I was thirteen. Then I was called by the Palace. Never shall I forget how good my parents were. When I arrived in the city I was homesick beyond words. I left my hair uncombed, my face unwashed, and my clothes unkempt in hope that those who saw me would think me hateful and let me go. Thus I bowed with my face to the ground and cried. The maids of the Palace said, "A lotus flower, indeed, who comes from the country."

The Princess loved me dearly and treated me like her very own child, not like an ordinary maid-in-waiting. All my companions, too, were most dear. Once I began my studies I advanced quickly in book knowledge and in music and so grew up. All the maids and palace people were most kind to me.

After being moved to the west side I gave my whole time to the study of the character and the harp, so that I became a practiced musician, as well as a critic of the pen whom nothing could fully satisfy. Truly I realized what Confucius said that there are but few great writers. Not being a boy, however, I had no hope of ever leaving a name on earth. Only a girl I was, shut deep within the palace, to fall at last like a dead dry leaf. Once this little life was over, with death my portion, who would ever know that I had been here? Regret filled my heart and resentment inflamed my soul. I worked at my embroidery for a time then threw it down, and then again I cast my weaver's shuttle away in disgust. Many a time I have torn my woven piece of silk across, and flung my green-stone hair-pin as far as I could throw it. I have drunk wine to try to drown my sorrow; cast off my shoes and gone barefoot or pulled the weeds and grass with my own hand that grew within the court. I was like a naughty child or one that had lost its reason. Who can stifle the longings of the soul?

Last year, one night in autumn, I first saw your Excellency, your handsome face and courtly manner. I said to myself, "Here is one who has come to me from the gods." As for looks, I was the plainest of the ten; but there was a destiny for me, nonetheless, appointed from a former life that held, so that one drop of ink on my hand from your pen grew into a burning desire that consumed my soul. I looked from behind the screen and felt that I was chosen to be your slave. In my delight, too, I realized that your love was something I could never forget. We have not known the joy of being husband and wife, and yet the lovers' birds that call from the blossoms of the spring made me sad with anxious thoughts of thee. The grass in the court, or the call of the wild geese that flew dimly across the distant rim of heaven, were to me pictures of infinite sorrow. Sometimes I sat alone behind my screen; sometimes I stood leaning on the railing of the balcony beating my impatient breast; sometimes I changed from one longing attitude to another as I prayed to the far-off blue heaven wondering all the time if your Excellency ever thought of me. If I had died before I saw you I felt that the earth would grow old and the heaven pass away.

Today we are out for the ceremony of washing silk so I cannot stay long. My tears are mingled with the tears with which I write, and my soul is woven into the silken meshes that bear this message. My earnest humble wish is that my lord may read it well. With my poor stanza I desire to reply to your dearest verse to me. I have no wish to show you how I can write, or to make you smile, but only to convey to you my heart's deepest love and longing. In this love that lives between us you will find the sadness of the autumn season.'

As we came Charan led the way outside the East Gate and Sook laughed over our venture, making such fun of me. My heart was ashamed and I blushed at the mention of it, but I stifled my throat and went on.

Here is the poem that I wrote:

A group appears before T'aeŭl,
The gates that guard God's temple wide;
A gentle form unbuilt to stand the winds,
Is swept within the grove till night appears.

Pigyŏng wrote a verse likewise, and all the others as well, making fun of me.

When we first reached the wise-woman's house I saw that she was full of resentment and sat with her face to the wall, not giving me even a smile of recognition.

The *chinsa* read through my letter. All day long his tears dropped upon it. His soul was overcome, and his spirit dazed so that he scarcely recognized my return. The gold ring on my left hand I drew off and dropped within his bosom, saying, 'Think me not plain, please, but regard me as gold. I am not bright or lovely, but yet I am not made of wood or stone. Till death I am yours and so I pass this gold ring as a pledge of my word.'

With evening, the time being short, I arose to depart, saying my good-bye amid the tears that fell. I whispered in his ear, 'I am in the West Palace; come in the night over the rear wall and let us fill up the destiny of the worlds that are ours.'

I drew my skirt about me and hastened away. I rode first into the palace and the eight followed after, it being already the second watch of the night.

Sook came along with Pigyŏng, who carried a light with which to lead the way. She said, 'The verse I wrote today I wrote without thought. It made light of you, my dear, and so I have come to ask your pardon and to require that you punish me as I deserve.'

Charan said in reply, 'The five verses all came from the South Palace. Since we have been separated into two companies we are now two peoples like the noted ones of the Tang Kingdom. We ought to make no jokes about each other, and yet I am sure our love is none the less sincere. We have long been held prisoners, doomed girls, with only the candle-light for company and nothing to do but to play upon the harp. While the flowers open their buds and smile, and the swallows touch each other's wings, we, unfortunate ones, behind lock and bar see spring go by with hearts and souls full of unanswered longings. The fairy Cho Un often went in her dreams to see the king of Ch'o[70] and, Wangmo, though one of the genii, often joined in the feasts at Yodae.[71] We, too, are prisoners like you; how can we expect you in the South Palace to live like Hanga alone and never steal the elixir of immortality?'[72]

Pigyŏng and Sook exclaimed together, 'One person's heart proves all the hearts of earth to be alike. How true your words are; we are moved to tears.'

Then they arose and took their departure.

I said to Charan, 'I have a tryst to keep this night with the *chinsa*. Though he may not come early, he will be here by morning light, I am sure, over the wall. When he comes how shall we welcome him?'

Charan said, 'Behind the embroidered curtains with the silken mats spread out, with wines of the Milky Way, and good things to eat placed mountains high. What is there we cannot do? If he should not come that is the question; but if he comes there need be no anxiety about a welcome.'

He did not come that night.

---

70 Cho Un (朝雲 Morning Clouds) was a mountain spirit of Musan (巫山) that visited the King of Ch'o (楚王) in dreams at the Palace of the Cloud Dream to partake in earthly pleasures. On her departure she said, "In the morning I shall become clouds, and in the evening I shall fall as rain (旦爲朝雲暮爲行雨), never leaving this palace." This secret tryst is related in "Kodangbu" (高唐賦) by Ch'o era literatus Song Ok (宋玉 fl. third century BC) and gave rise to the four-character set expressions *Musan chi mong* (巫山之夢 dream of Musan) and *Unu chi chŏng* (雲雨之情 pleasures of cloud and rain).

71 Yodae (瑤臺) is a splendid royal palace.

72 Hanga (姮娥) was a Taoist immortal said to inhabit the moon. According to legend, she was the wife of the archer god Ye (羿), and together they were chased out of the celestial realm and forced to become mortal. In order to restore their status they received the "elixir of immortality" from Sŏ Wangmo, or the Queen Mother of the West, an elixir derived from the tree of immortality that bore fruit only once every three thousand years. Instead of achieving eternal life with Ye by imbibing the elixir together, Hanga takes the elixir in her husband's absence and absconds to the lunar realm. Because of her betrayal, Hanga's beautiful form transforms to that of a toad.

The reason was that when the *chinsa* came to look the place over, the wall was so very very high, that without wings it was impossible to scale it. He returned home in anxious disappointment. His distress showed itself in his face so that his servant, T'ŭg-i, a bright fellow, full of resource, seeing it, came and knelt before him, saying, 'Your Excellency will not live long, I fear,' and he bowed low and cried.

The *chinsa* then told him all his trouble, whereupon T'ŭg-i said, 'Why did you not tell me before? I shall help you to see it through.'

He then made a ladder of rattan-string, most light and easy to handle, one that could be folded up or let out. When folded, it was like a screen, and when let out it was five or six *kil*[73] in length, so light that one could carry it in the hand. T'ŭg-i said, 'With this you can scale the wall; let it out and go down on the other side. On returning you can do the same.'

The *chinsa* had T'ŭg-i try it and it worked beautifully. He was delighted and that night made preparations to go. T'ŭg-i brought a pair of socks made of dog-skin that he asked him to put on. 'You must wear these –' said he, 'they make no noise.'

The master tried them and they were light as feathers, and not a sound escaped them. Thus he made his way over the walls, the outer and the inner, and hid himself in the bamboo grove. The splendor of the moon was like the day and all was quiet within the great enclosure. In a little he saw someone come out of the palace and walk back and forth as though repeating the character. The *chinsa* then announced himself and said, 'I'm here.' She laughed and said, 'Come, please come.'

He stepped forth and bowed again, saying, 'Being young, I was unable to resist the joy of this meeting, and though I die a thousand times I must ask that you help me. Please give me your kind assistance.'

Charan replied, 'We have waited for your coming as the world waits for the clouds and rain after a long drought. Now that you are here we live again. Do not doubt me.' So she led the way.

The *chinsa* went up the stone steps, and following the turnings of the balustrade drew back his shoulders and marched straight on. I opened the silken window and with a lighted candle awaited his coming. The brazier before me was of brass with gold inlaid. Over it I sprinkled a suggestion of *ulgŭm* incense,[74] and on the glass-topped table at my

---

73 One *kil* is roughly the height of an adult.

74 *Ulgŭm* incense is the fragrance of the tulip (鬱金香).

side, had the famous book *Kwanggi* open.[75] When I saw him I arose and bowed and he bowed to me. We entered the room and sat together then, side by side. I had Charan bring special dainties, food and wine, of which we took three sips each to mark our marriage vow.

The *chinsa*, pretending to be tipsy, said, 'What time of night is this?'

Charan then drew the curtains, shut the door and left. I blew out the light, and, lo, we were together. How happy we were.

In a little the morning began to dawn and the cocks to crow so the *chinsa* arose and took his departure. From this time on he came with the returning eve. Each night our love grew deeper, beyond words. It knew no bounds.

In the snow on the top of the wall, however, were seen the footprints of someone and this rumour got abroad. Soon every one of the group knew of this coming and going, and all viewed it with intense alarm.

One day the *chinsa* said to me, 'I greatly fear that this delight of ours will end in disaster,' and so all day long he thought and thought and trembled.

T'ŭg-i came to him and said, 'Since my favours have been so helpful, does Your Excellency not intend to reward me?'

The *chinsa* replied, 'I have it in mind, and shall see that you are rewarded well; there is no danger of my forgetting.'

T'ŭg-i went on, 'Now that I see your face you are again the victim of anxiety; what is the cause, please?'

The *chinsa* said, 'When I do not see her, the longing enters my very bones, and when I see her, I feel that I am a sinner beyond words to express. Should I not be anxious?'

T'ŭg-i replied, 'Then why do you not take her with you and make your escape?'

The *chinsa* thought it a good suggestion and that night told me. 'A servant of mine,' said he, 'named T'ŭg-i, a resourceful fellow, suggests that we make our escape together. What think you of it?'

I replied, 'My clothes and other things are a question. When I came here I had a large supply and since then the Prince has given me many other things. If I were able to take them all ten horses would scarce suffice.'

---

75 *T'aep'yŏng kwanggi* (太平廣記 Extensive Records of the T'aep'yŏng Era) was a collection of various stories, mostly of a supernatural nature, dating from the Han to the early Song Dynasties. Though it was completed in AD 978, it was not published until the Ming era because the *sosŏl* (小說) or "insignificant stories" it contained were not considered important objects of study for students.

The *chinsa* on his return told T'ŭg-i of this. Greatly delighted, T'ŭg-i said, 'I have a friend who has twenty strong men who make their living by robbery. No one dare molest them and yet they are my special friends and will do anything I say. I'll get this group together and take the things. They'll carry a mountain if you wish it. When these twenty stand guard even a thousand soldiers would not dare pursue. Have no fear regarding the matter!'

The *chinsa* came again and told me, I thinking it a most happy plan; so night by night we sent the things off till by the seventh all had gone.

Said T'ŭg-i, 'If you take all these valuables and pile them mountain high in your home, your excellent father will be full of doubts regarding them; and if you put them in my house the neighbours will wonder where I got them. Let us take them to the hills and hide them.'

'But,' replied the *chinsa*, 'if we lose them, you and I will both be accounted thieves. Be careful what you do.'

T'ŭg-i said, 'I have plans enough and friends enough to see it through, so that I have no fear of anything on earth. Besides, I'll take a knife and stand guard myself, night and day. Though I lose my eyes I'll keep these treasures safe; and though my feet be cut off, nothing shall be lost of them. Have no fear, I pray you.'

Now, T'ŭg-i's real plan was to get us off into the hills where he and his accomplices could murder the *chinsa* and possess themselves of me and the things I had. The *chinsa*, however, being an unsophisticated scholar, never dreamed of this.

The Prince had formerly built a house outside the North West Gate that he called the Pihae tang[76] and was anxious now to get a specially well written name with which to decorate the entrance. All his friends suggested names but they failed to suit him. He then called Kim *Chinsa* and entertained him to the best of fare. Then he asked him to write a name and a verse. Taking the pen, the *chinsa* gave it a special flourish and wrote. All the beauty of the hills and stream was in this name as well as in the verse he wrote. The winds and rain when they saw it would assuredly be startled, and the very spirits would voice their wonder.

The Prince was greatly delighted. 'Truly,' said he, 'Wang Par-i[77] has once again visited the earth.' Before he had finished reading it over he suddenly turned to the line,

---

76 匪懈堂.

77 The original version reads Wang Chaan (王子安); Chaan (Ch. Zian) was the courtesy name of famed Tang poet, Wang Pal (王勃 Ch. Wang Bo, AD 649/ 650–75/676), hence Gale's Wang Par-i.

'He climbed the wall to steal the harper's tune.' He stopped for a moment, silent, then thought, 'What does this mean?'

The *chinsa* arose, bowed and said, 'Your Highness, I am dazed by the wine and so have failed of the proper form. I will now withdraw.'

The Prince called a boy and had him see the *chinsa* out.

On the night following he visited me again. Said he, 'We must fly; yesterday my verses gave occasion to the Prince to doubt me. If we do not escape now, sudden destruction will overtake us.'

I replied, 'Yesterday in a dream I saw a man with an awful face who said to me, "I am Muk T'ŭk Sŏnu,[78] and by an agreement from a past existence I wait here by this long wall for you."

'When I awoke I was dreadfully frightened, and even now I can see him. A most unlucky dream! What does Your Excellency think it means?'

The *chinsa* said, 'Dreams are vain stuff; why bother about them?'

I replied, 'Not so, "Beneath this long wall" evidently means our palace, and his name Muk T'ŭk doubtless refers to T'ŭg-i. Have you any idea of the designs of this servant of yours?'

The *chinsa* replied, 'This servant of mine is really a very wicked, hardened fellow, but he has been wholly devoted to me and our meeting today is through his help. How could he be so faithful in one case and yet prove faithless in another?'

I replied, 'Since you think so, I will let it rest. How can I thank you sufficiently for all your kindness? But Charan is to me a very sister and so I must tell her of it.' I called Charan and we three sat together while I told what the master had proposed.

Charan gave a great start, struck the palms of her hands together and said, 'We have been friends for long and now you are calling down death upon yourself. You have had a month and more of joy, let that suffice. To make your escape over the wall is surely a most impossible thing. The Prince has long had a special love for you, and so it would be the worst step imaginable. Your going would bring down wrath on your parents' heads which would finally fall on us as well. The world is really a great net. You cannot fly to heaven, nor can you go down into Hades; where will you go? If you are caught you will not be the only ones to suffer. I do not know anything about your dream, but even though it were a lucky dream, I would never think of your going. Your part is to stifle your impatience, stay where you are and wait on God.

---

78 The original reads Modon Tanu (冒頓單于 Ch. Maodun/Modu Chanyu, but known in Korean as Muktol Sŏnu or Mukt'ŭk Sŏnu), who was the fourth known ruler of and founder of the empire of the Xiongnu (匈奴).

When you grow a little older and your face begins to fade, the Prince will forget his special love. Then will be your opportunity to pretend sickness and if you keep abed long enough he will let you off to your country home. You can then join your master, make your way in each other's company and grow old together. Your joy will be without measure and undisturbed. To forget this and plan what is contrary to all best judgment, may deceive men but cannot deceive God.'

The *chinsa*, at last, realizing that flight could never be successfully accomplished, took his departure in distress and tears.

A day or two later, the Prince was sitting in his special hall with the azaleas in bloom before him. He suddenly ordered the maids of the West Palace to wait on him and write verses on the flowers. This they did.

Greatly delighted, he said, 'Your skill in poetry grows apace; I am charmed with these. Unyŏng's poem seems specially directed to some particular person, as it was before in the one on the Cloud. Who is it Unyŏng that you think of so constantly? When Master Kim wrote his verse for the dedication of the Pihae tang, he too, seemed to suggest something. Is it love for Kim that lies back of this?'

I at once hastened down into the court, bowed my face to the ground and said through my tears, 'Once before when Your Highness expressed doubt concerning me, I asked to die. But not being yet twenty and regretting to die without seeing my parents once more, I have stolen a greater length of life than I should have and have lived till today. Now, again, Your Highness doubts me, so I shall die this time without a question. God, Mother Earth, and the Spirits are my witness as they hover about me. We five never leave each other for a moment, and yet the name that is questioned is mine only. Assuredly I shall die.' I tied my scarf to my neck and fastened it to the banister, when Charan said, 'Your Highness, a great and gifted Lord, is permitting an innocent girl to go forth to death; from now on we shall drop the pen and give up writing forever.'

The Prince pretended to be full of wrath, and yet in heart he had no idea of letting me die, so he had Charan rescue me. Then he called for five rolls of silk and gave us each one as reward for the verses we had written.

From this time on the *chinsa* did not visit the Palace but closed his gates and lay ill. His tears wet his pillow, while his life hung as by a thread.

T'ŭg-i came and said, 'If Your Excellency dies, why you die; but simply because your wishes are not carried out and you cannot see the girl you want, why should you throw away your precious life? I have a plan that will make all easy. Just go at midnight when everything is quiet, and with your handkerchief stop her mouth, then take her on your back, and over the wall with her. Who is there that dare hinder?'

The *chinsa* said, 'That seems to me a very dangerous plan.'

That night again the *chinsa* came to the Palace but he found me ill so that I could not rise. Charan saw him and passed the glass to him three times. I gave him a letter and said, 'I shall never see you again in this life; our contract ends tonight. If this be not our full destiny as appointed by God, perhaps we shall meet again at the Nine Springs of Hades.'

The *chinsa* took the letter but was speechless. He beat his breast in tears and came away. Charan, unable to look upon it, leaned against the pillar behind which she hid her face and cried.

On reaching home the *chinsa* spread out the letter and found it to read, 'This unblessed self of mine bows twice before my lord. Most unlucky girl! I have been overwhelmed with love for you, and while we have met and seen each other, yet our love like the sea could never find a limit, and our meetings seemed like the passing of a moment. The Creator, jealous of the joys of life, as all in this palace know, has raised doubts in the mind of my lord, so that death dangles before my eyes. Die I must. My own wish is that Your Excellency, after this farewell, give up all thoughts of me, turn to your studies, win at the examination, ride upon the clouds of fame and fortune, and leave a name for future generations, an honour to your home and parents. Please take my dresses and jewels and make an offering of them to the Buddha, as the prayer of a sincere heart, so that our lives may be united again in the world to come.'

Before the *chinsa* had read all the letter his strength failed him and he fainted away. His servants finally brought him round and then T'ŭg-i came in and said, 'What answer did the palace-maid make that has given you such a death-stroke as this?'

The *chinsa* made no direct reply but said, 'Keep those things carefully that you took away; I intend to sell them, make an offering to the Buddha, and so fulfill her wishes.'

T'ŭg-i went back to his home thinking, 'The palace-maid has not come out, so those things are God's gifts to me.' He sat with his face to the wall and laughed the laugh of the brigand, no man seeing him.

A few days later, T'ŭg-i, with his clothes torn and a bleeding nose that he had given himself, his hair disheveled and his feet bare, came rushing in. He bowed low and in tears said, 'I have been attacked by robbers,' and without a further word pretended to faint away.

The *chinsa*, anxious lest T'ŭg-i should die without telling him where the dresses and jewels were, had medicine ordered for him till at last he brought him to. For ten days following this he had him specially cared for. At last when he had sufficiently come to himself he said, 'While I was alone on guard in the hills a band of robbers came rushing upon me with intent to beat me to death; so I made my escape at the risk of life itself. These goods and chattels are what endangered me. Such luck as this is worse than death itself.' He beat the earth with his feet and hands and cried.

The *chinsa*, fearful lest his parents should get to know it, restrained him, and with gentle words sent him away.

Some time later the *chinsa* awakened to the part that T'ŭg-i was playing, and went with a dozen friends and servants to T'ŭg-i's house, but found only the gold rings and the looking-glass. These, however, were witness of what he was about.

The *chinsa* desired to give information and have him arrested, but fearing that the whole story might get out and be made public, he did not dare to do so. On the other hand, if he did not recover the things, he would have no possible means of making the prayers. He really desired to kill T'ŭg-i out and out but had not the resolution necessary. So he stifled his feelings and remained silent.

Aware of his own faults, T'ŭg-i went and made inquiry of a blind sorcerer who lived near the Palace. Said he, 'Some time ago, in the early morning, I saw someone scaling the west wall of the Palace. Thinking it to be a thief I shouted and gave chase, when the rascal dropped what he had and ran for his life. I took the plundered goods that he left and hid them away, waiting for the owner to turn up. Meanwhile, my master, a *chinsa*, hearing that I had fallen heir to certain valuable things, most unjustly laid claim himself. I told him that I had nothing but a gold ring and a mirror; but he, not accepting this statement, came with his servants and went by force through my place taking these things away. Not being satisfied, however, he now seeks my destruction. I imagine there is nothing for me but flight, what would you advise?'

The sorcerer said, 'Good, fly!'

The neighbours, hearing of this, asked of T'ŭg-i, 'Who is your master that he should treat one of his servants thus?'

T'ŭg-i replied, 'My master is a man of great learning who expects to graduate with honours. He is brim full of avarice and greed. Later, if he ever enters office you will know assuredly of what breed he is.'

The word of what had happened got abroad and even to the palace itself. Some of his retainers told the Prince. He was terribly angry and sent a party to search the West Palace and see what was missing. They found that all my clothes and ornaments had been taken away.

The Prince then arrested the five of us and had us placed in the court where he made ready the instruments of torture. He gave orders, 'Kill these five and put others in their place.' He commanded the beaters, 'Lay on without counting the blows till they are dead.'

The five then made reply, 'We would say one word before we die.'

The Prince replied, 'What would you say?'

Ŭnsŏm wrote out her statement, which ran, 'The love that man and woman have for one another is born of nature. In this respect high and low are all alike. Shut behind palace walls we have been fated to live alone, no other sound or shadow ever crossing our path. Seeing flowers brings tears only, and looking up at the moon melts the soul within one. It is like cutting off the oriole from his mate in the plum tree, or holding up a screen between the swallow and his little partner. No other fault is ours than the envy of those who are happier than we. Once outside the palace walls, the joys of the world would be at our feet. We have had the possibility of escape more than once and the desires to do so, but the fear of Your Highness has held us prisoners and our decision was to live and die here unknown. We have done no sin, committed no wrong, and yet we are condemned to death. We may die but we shall not close our eyes even in the Yellow Shades.'

Pich'wi wrote, 'Your Highness' kind care has been high as the hills and deep as the sea. We have ever been most grateful and appreciative, giving our best thoughts to poetry and the harp. The sin for which we are arrested pertains to the West Palace only, but we had rather die than live. Let it be over quickly is my only prayer.'

Ongnyŏ said,[79] 'We have shared in the joys of the West Palace, and now in its misfortunes we must share also. When fire arises in the Kon'gang Hills[80] it burns jade as well as common stone. This death today we all shall share alike.'

Charan wrote,[81] 'We maids of lowly birth have no fathers like Yo and Sun; nor have we mothers like Ahwang and Yŏyŏng,[82] and yet we are fated to be the unhappy ones who know nothing of the love of man for woman.

---

79   Here Gale switches the order of the speeches by Ongnyŏ and Charan.

80   This is in reference to the following phrase from the *Thousand Character Classic*: "Okch'ul Kon'gang" (玉出崑崗), "*Jade comes from Kon'gang Mountain.*"

81   The following line which begins Charan's speech has not been translated by Gale: "今日之事, 罪在不測, 中心所懷, 何忍諱之." "The guilt we feel over what has transpired today is immeasurable; how can we possibly hide what is in our hearts?"

82   Ahwang (娥皇) and Yŏyŏng (女英) were the daughters of Emperor Yo of ancient China, becoming the royal consorts of Yo's successor Emperor Sun.

Though Emperor, Mok Wang[83] thought constantly of the joys of the Lake of Gems; and Hangu, though the greatest of warriors, was overcome by tears from behind the screen.[84] Why should Your Highness expect to stifle that natural impulse in Unyŏng? Kim *Chinsa* is a great and gifted man. Your Highness introduced him into our inner circle. Yours is the fault, no other's! Unyŏng's bringing the inkstone and rubbing the ink was by your order – not her act, but yours, Sir. Unyŏng, the prisoner, seeing this attractive young man, lost her heart and fell deathly ill. All the medicine in the world cannot avail to give her help. Like the dew of the morning her life has faded away. Even Your Highness was not sufficient for so deep a trouble as hers. My foolish thought is, that if only Unyŏng could be given her freedom where she and Kim *Chinsa* might meet and find their love's true satisfaction, it would be the greatest kindness you could bestow.

On a recent occasion Unyŏng did wrong, but the fault is mine, not hers. The reason I freely state, so as to hide nothing from Your Highness, and yet do no injustice to my companions. Thus our death today will be our glory. Unyŏng is innocent and so to pardon her would be worth a hundred ordinary lives. I pray my Lord to take my life and let Unyŏng go free.'

I, Unyŏng, wrote, 'The kindness I have received from Your Highness is high as heaven and deep as the sea. I have not guarded my virtue and so indeed am a sinner. My verses have on more than one occasion given my Lord cause to doubt me. This fact constitutes my second sin. My companions being arrested and put under condemnation today constitutes my third sin. These three sins I am guilty of and so have no face to live. Though Your Highness should pardon me, I should still have to die with my own hand.'

The Prince finished his examination and read once again what Charan had written. His anger seemed to have subsided somewhat. On this, Sook, kneeling in tears, said, 'The other day when we went for our outing, it was I who opposed the choice within the walls. Charan

---

83 Mok Wang (穆王) was fifth emperor of the Zhou dynasty (1046?–256 BC).

84 Hangu (項羽 Ch. Xiang Yu , 232–202 BC) was a warlord who defeated the Qin in 207 BC and ruled for a brief time as Hegemon-King of Western Ch'o until being defeated by Yu Pang (劉邦 Ch. Liu Bang), the first emperor of the Han. Hangu's military exploits are most famously recorded in *Records of the Grand Historian*.

then came by night to the South Palace and urgently asked that I consent. Feeling sorry for her, I turned all other opinions aside and cast my vote in her favour, so Unyŏng's sin is really mine, not hers. I pray Your Highness to take my life and grant pardon to Unyŏng.'

On this the anger of the Prince subsided. He said no more but shut me up in a special room and let all the others go free. That night I hanged myself with my silken scarf."

While Unyŏng was telling this story, the *chinsa* sat at her side writing it down. They looked at each other in tears and Unyŏng said to him, "Now you tell what happened to you."

The *chinsa* said, "On the day that Unyŏng committed suicide all the Palace was plunged into tears. A beloved sister had been taken and the sound of wailings was heard outside the Palace walls. I too heard it and fainted away, remaining long as dead. Some of my servants gave the death call on behalf of my soul, '*pok, pok, pok*,' and joined in weeping while others went for medicine. As evening came on I returned to consciousness and thought, 'It is finished, she is dead. I must not forget my promise to make offerings to the Buddha on behalf of her soul!' So I sold the gold ring, the mirror and other things, and bought forty bags of rice intending to go to Ch'ŏngnyŏng Temple[85] and there make my prayer. But I could not find a suitable servant to do the part needed, so I called T'ŭg-i again and said, 'I'll forgive you all your past offences if you'll but give your whole heart to what I ask now.'

T'ŭg-i bowed low in tears and said, 'I am a darkened and ignorant beast, and yet I am not quite a piece of stone or wholly a block of wood. My sins are greater in number than the hairs of my head, but Your Excellency has forgiven them all. It is as though leaves had sprouted from a dead dry tree, or flesh returned to whitened bones. I shall give life itself on behalf of my lord ...'

I said to him, 'I desire to make a prayer to the spirits of the hills and to the Buddha, but I have no one that I can trust with the errand. Will you do it for me?'

T'ŭg-i said, 'I'll do all that you command me.' He then went to the temple and for three days lay heating his legs. He called the priests and said, 'Why use all these forty bags of rice in a sacrificial offering? Let's have wine prepared, plenty of it, and food, and call your friends to a feast.'

At that time a woman of the village happened to be passing and T'ŭg-i took forcible possession of her, and had her stay with him in

---

85 清寧寺.

one of the rooms. Thus he carried on for several days till he forgot all about the offerings to be made. The priests, outraged by his lawless behaviour, were furiously angry. As the service was about to begin they said to T'ŭg-i, 'The service of the Buddha requires that the one sent take part. When this agent is a wretched fellow like you, we feel disgraced. Go and bathe and bring yourself to a place where you can do your part decently.'

T'ŭg-i, ashamed to reply, went and gave himself a hasty dip, then knelt before the Buddha and prayed, 'Let the *chinsa* die this day, and may Unyŏng live once more and be my wife.' For three days he kept up this prayer. Then he returned and said to me, 'The dead maiden will assuredly live again, for on the night the offering was made your servant had a dream in which she appeared and said, "Since you have offered this prayer with a sincere heart I cannot sufficiently thank you." She bowed and wept. The priests also dreamed the same as I.'

I believed this and lifted up my voice in tears. It was now the early days of spring when examinations are held, but I had no desire to take any part. Going instead to the Ch'ŏngnyŏng Temple, I remained for several days when I learned definitely of T'ŭg-i's doings. Though angry beyond words, I had no means of requiting the wrong. So I bathed and went before the Buddha, where I bowed twice and again three times. Offering incense with hands joined, I prayed, 'When Unyŏng died, her gentle words, like a knife, pierced my soul, so heart-breaking they were. I desired to carry out her wishes faithfully and so sent T'ŭg-i with all the necessaries. Now I learn that his prayers were evil only and that Unyŏng's last wishes have been wholly unfulfilled. Such being the case I come myself to make my proper offering. World-exalted One, will you not call back Unyŏng to life and let her be my companion once more? Also will you not grant that in the ages to come we may be free from such sorrows as these? Require the death I pray thee of the evil-doer, T'ŭg-i; bind him in chains in hell, and boil and feed him to the dogs. If Thou, Highest, will but do this, I shall build for Unyŏng a pagoda twenty stories high, with three great temples besides, and thus make some return for thine unbounded favours.'

When I had finished this prayer I arose, bowed a hundred times and more and then retired.

Several days later T'ŭg-i fell into a tiger-trap and was killed, and from this day on I had no longer any thought of the things of the world, but bathed, fasted, dressed in my best and lay down in my quiet room to die. I ate nothing for four days and then with a long sigh of grief passed away."

When he had finished he threw away his pen and the two sat and wept as though their hearts would break.

I, Yu Yŏng, comforted them, saying, "You two have come to meet again in another life; let the past be the past. The evil servant is dead; let your anger rest and have your souls refreshed. Is it because you cannot pick up life once more and live that you feel so bad?"

The *chinsa* wept and said, "Seeing that we two died in sorrow, the keeper of the region of the dead suggested out of pity that we go back and try this mortal life a second time, but when I thought it over I was unwilling. The joys of Hades may not be great, but they are quite as good as the best of this troubled world. What must the joy of Heaven be in comparison? So we have no desire to come back to earth. Our meeting tonight and our sorrow thus expressed is because the ancient palace of our Prince has fallen to decay, with only the sparrows and other birds about, and no one to come or go. Now also that the war is over we see how beautiful homes have been turned to ashes, and white walls have crumbled down. But the flowers of spring time bloom again with their unforgotten fragrance and the green of the grass is as fresh as ever; yet the affairs of men have so changed. Thus it is that we who come to see it weep for sorrow."

I asked, "Are you indeed a dweller in heaven?"

The *chinsa* said, "We two were originally attendants who waited before the throne of God till one day He took his place in the T'aech'ŏng Palace, and commanded me to bring some fruits from the Jade Garden. Whither I went, gathered peaches of the fairies, gem fruits, golden lotus seeds and secretly passed some of them to Unyŏng. This act of mine became known and as a punishment I was sent into exile into this dust-covered earth to try the temptations and hardships of mortal life. Now God has forgiven our offences and taken us back to the Third Heaven, where we are before His Throne and await his commands. Sometimes we ride the winds and come back to this old earth where we once existed, and weep again over our great sorrow."

He took Unyŏng by the hand and said, "The sea may dry up and the rocks crumble away, but our love will never, ever fade. The earth may grow old and the heaven pass, but our sorrow will live on and on. I meet you again this night to tell you of the burden of my heart. If there had not been an appointed destiny for us from a past existence, how could such a meeting as this ever have come about? I pray you (speaking to me) accept of this account that I have written and let it be made known to the world, but do not let it be told by those of a light or frivolous tongue."

Heartened by the wine he had drunk, the *chinsa* turned to Unyŏng and sang:

> We meet, the swallow and the sparrow here,
> Within this ancient hold where flowers have fallen;
> The spring smiles sweet as springs did long ago,
> But men have changed and loving hearts are gone.
> The moonlight floods the court with softened ray,
> The dew sits fresh upon our fairy garb.

Then Unyŏng sang in response:

> The ancient willows meet a new-born spring,
> The splendor of the past lives in the mind;
> We come tonight to find old tracks anew
> And tears fall fast upon our fairy robes.

Yu Yŏng, under the influence of the wine he had drunk, fell fast asleep and in a little was awakened by the birds. He looked and it was all dark, the birds being seen indistinctly in the shadows. He looked for his friends but they were gone and only the little book that the *chinsa* had written remained. With a deep feeling of loneliness he rolled it up, put it into his sleeve pocket and came away. When he reached home he hid it in his wall-box and only occasionally looked at it. Its experience, however, had taught him the transient nature of human life. He dwelt on this more and more and often forgot all about eating and sleeping. Later he went off into the hills and no man ever knew his end.

Note: The author Yu Yŏng[86] was the son of Yu Mongjŏng who matriculated in 1567 and graduated as a finished Chinese scholar in 1574. In the year of the Great War (1592) he was sent as special envoy to the Court of the Mings where he wept and asked for help against the Japanese. He died in 1593 on his way home from Peking. His son, Yu Yŏng, writes this story.

---

86 柳泳.

1 壽聖宮, 卽安平大君舊宅也, 在長安城西仁旺山之下. 山川秀麗, 龍盤虎踞, 社稷在其南, 慶福在其東. 仁旺一脈, 逶迤而下, 臨宮*起, 雖不高峻, 而登臨俯覽, 則通衢市廛, 滿城第宅, 碁布星羅, 歷歷可指, 宛若絲列分派. 東望則宮闕縹緲, 複道橫空, 雲烟積翠, 朝暮獻態, 眞所謂絶勝之地也. 一時酒徒射伴, 歌兒笛童, 騷人墨客, 三春花柳之節, 九秋楓菊之時, 則無日不遊於其上, 吟風咏月, 嘯翫忘歸.

2 靑坡士人柳泳, 飽聞此園之勝槪, 思欲一遊焉, 而衣裳藍縷. 容色埋沒, 自知爲遊客之取笑, 況將進而趑趄者久矣. 萬歷辛丑春三月旣望, 沽得濁醪一壺, 而旣乏童僕, 又無朋知, 躬自佩酒, 獨入宮門, 則觀者相顧, 莫不指笑. 生慙而無聊, 乃入後園. 登高四望, 則新經兵燹之餘, 長安宮闕, 滿城華屋, 蕩然無有, 壞垣破瓦, 廢井堆砌. 草樹茂密, 唯東廊數間, 巋然獨存.

3 生步入西園, 泉石幽邃處, 則百草叢芊, 影落澄潭, 滿地落花, 人跡不到, 微風一起, 香氣馥郁. 生獨坐岩上, 乃咏東坡, '我上朝元春半老, 滿地落花無人掃'之句, 輒解所佩酒, 盡飮之, 醉臥岩邊, 以石支頭. 俄而酒醒, 擡頭視之, 則遊人盡散, 山月已吐, 烟籠柳眉, 風東花腮. 時聞一條軟語, 隨風而至. 生異之, 起而訪焉, 則有一少年, 與絶色靑蛾, 斑荊對坐, 見生至, 欣然起迎. 生與之揖, 因問曰: "秀才何許人? 未卜其晝, 只卜其夜." 少年微哂曰: "古人云: 傾蓋若舊, 正謂此也." 相與鼎足而坐話. 女低聲呼兒, 則有二丫鬟, 自林中出來. 女謂其兒曰: "今夕邂逅故人之處, 又逢不期之佳客, 今日之夜, 不可寂寞而虛度. 汝可備酒饌, 兼持筆硯而來." 二丫鬟承命而往, 少旋而返, 飄然若飛鳥之往來. 琉璃樽盃, 紫霞之酒, 珍果奇饌, 皆非人世所有. 酒三行, 女口新詞, 以勸其酒, 詞曰:

4 重重深處別故人, 天緣未盡見無因.

5 幾番傷春繁花時, 爲雲爲雨夢非眞.

6 消盡往事成塵後, 空使今人淚滿巾.

7 歌竟, 欷歔飮泣, 珠淚滿面. 生異之, 起而拜曰: "僕雖非錦繡之腸, 早事儒業, 稍知文墨之事. 今聞此詞, 格調淸越, 而意思悲凉, 甚可怪也. 今夜之會, 月色如晝, 淸風徐來, 猶足可賞, 而相對悲泣, 何哉? 一盃相屬, 情義已孚, 而姓名不言, 懷抱未展, 亦可疑也." 生先言己名而强之, 少年歎息而答曰: "不言姓名, 其意有在, 君欲强之, 則告之何難, 而所可道也, 言之長也." 愀然不樂者久之, 乃曰: "僕姓金, 年十歲, 能詩文, 有名學堂, 而年十四, 登進士第二科, 一時皆以金進士稱之. 僕以年少俠氣, 志意浩蕩, 不能自抑. 又以此女之故, 將父母之遺體, 竟作不孝之子, 天地間一罪人之名, 何用强知? 此女之名雲英, 彼兩女之名, 一名緣珠, 一名宋玉, 皆故安平大君之宮人

7 也."生曰:"言出而不盡, 則初不如不言之爲愈也. 安平盛時之事, 進士傷懷之由, 可得聞其詳乎?"進士顧雲英曰:"星霜屢移, 日月已久, 其時之事, 汝能記憶否?"雲英答曰:"心中畜怨, 何日忘之? 妾試言之, 郎君在傍, 補其闕漏."乃言曰:"莊憲大王子, 八大君中, 安平大君最爲英睿. 上甚愛之, 賞賜無數, 故田民財貨, 獨步諸宮. 年十三, 出居私宮, 宮名卽壽聖宮也. 以儒業自任, 夜則讀書, 晝則或賦詩, 或書隷, 未嘗一刻之放過, 一時文人才士, 咸萃其門, 較其長短, 或知鷄叫參橫講論不怠, 而大君尤工於筆法, 鳴於一國. 文廟在邸時, 每與集賢殿諸學士, 論安平筆法曰:"吾弟若生於中國, 雖不及於王逸少, 豈後於趙松雪乎!"稱賞不已.

8 一日, 大君於妾等曰:"天下百家之才, 必就安靜處, 做工而後可成. 都城門外, 山川寂寥, 閭落稍遠, 於此做業, 可以專精."卽搆精舍十數間于其上, 扁其堂曰:'匪懈堂', 又築一壇于其側, 名曰:'盟詩壇', 皆顧名思義之意也. 一時文章鉅筆, 咸集其壇, 文章則成三問爲首, 筆法則崔興孝爲首. 雖然, 皆不及於大君之才也.

9 一日, 大君乘醉, 呼諸侍女曰:"天之降才, 豈獨豊於男而嗇於女乎? 今世以文章自許者, 不爲不多, 而皆莫能相尙, 無出類拔萃者, 汝等亦勉之哉!"於是, 宮女中, 擇其年少美容者十人敎之. 先授諺解小學, 讀誦而後, 庸學論孟詩書通史, 盡敎之, 又抄李杜唐音數百首敎之, 五年之內, 果皆成才.

10 大君入則使妾等, 不離眼前, 作詩斥正, 第其高下, 明用賞罰, 以爲勸․ 其卓犖之氣像, 縱不及於大君, 而音律之淸雅, 句法之婉熟, 亦可以窺盛唐詩人之藩․也. 十人之名, 則小玉, 芙蓉, 飛瓊, 翡翠, 玉女, 金漣, 銀蟾, 紫鸞, 寶蓮, 雲英, 雲英卽妾也. 大君皆甚撫恤, 尙畜宮內, 使不得與人對語, 日與文士, 盃酒戰藝, 而未嘗以妾等, 一番相近者, 盖慮外人之或知也. 常下令曰:"侍女一出宮門, 則其罪當死, 外人知宮女知名, 其罪亦死."

11 一日, 大君自外而入, 呼妾等曰:"今日與文士某某飮酒, 有祥靑烟, 起自宮樹, 或籠城堞, 或飛山麓. 我先占五言一絶, 使坐客次之, 皆不稱意. 汝等以年次, 各製以進."小玉先呈曰:

12 緣烟細如織, 隨風伴入門.

13 依微深復淺, 不覺近黃昏.

14 芙蓉次呈曰:

15 飛空遙帶雨, 落地復爲雲.

16 近夕山光暗, 幽思尙楚君.

17 翡翠呈曰:

18 覆花蜂失勢, 籠竹鳥迷巢.

19 黃昏成小雨, 窓外聽蕭蕭.

20 飛瓊呈曰:

21 小杏難成眼, 孤篁獨保靑.

22 輕陰暫見重, 日暮又昏冥.

23 玉女呈曰:

24 蔽日輕紈細, 橫山翠帶長.

25 微風吹漸散, 猶濕小池塘.

26 金蓮呈曰:

27 山下寒烟積, 橫飛宮樹邊.

28 風吹自不定, 斜日滿蒼天.

29 銀蟾呈曰:

30 山谷繁陰起, 池臺緣影流.

31 飛歸無處覓, 荷葉露珠留.

32 紫鸞呈曰:

33 早向洞門暗, 橫連高樹低.

34 須臾忽飛去, 西岳與前溪.

35 妾亦呈曰:

36 望遠靑烟細, 佳人罷織紈.

37 臨風獨惆悵 飛去落巫山.

38 寶蓮呈曰:

39 短墻春陰裡, 長安水氣中.

40 能令人世上, 忽作翠珠宮.

41 大君看罷, 大驚曰: "雖比於晚唐之詩, 亦可伯仲, 而謹甫以下, 不可執鞭也." 再三吟咏, 莫知其高下, 良久曰: "芙蓉詩, 思戀楚君, 余甚嘉之, 翡翠詩, 比前騷雅, 玉女詩, 意思飄逸, 末句有隱隱然餘意, 以此兩詩, 當爲居魁." 又曰: "我初見詩, 憂劣莫辨, 一再翫繹, 則紫鸞之詩, 意思深遠, 令人不覺嗟嘆而蹈舞也. 餘詩亦皆淸雅, 而獨雲英之詩, 顯有惆悵思人之意. 未知其所思者何人, 事當訊問, 而其才可惜, 故姑置之."

42 妾卽下庭, 伏泣而對曰: "追辭之際, 偶然而發, 豈有他意乎! 今見疑於主君, 妾萬死無惜." 大君命之坐曰: "詩出於性情, 不可掩匿, 汝勿復言." 卽出綵帛十端, 分賜十人. 大君未嘗有私於妾, 而宮中之人, 皆知大君之意, 在於妾也.

43　十人皆退在洞房, 畫燭高燒, 七寶書案, 置唐律一卷, 論古人宮怨詩高下, 妾獨倚屏風, 悄然不語, 如泥塑之人. 小玉顧見妾曰: "日間賦烟之詩, 見疑於主君, 以此隱憂而不語乎? 抑主君向意, 當有錦衾之歡, 故暗喜而不語乎? 汝心所懷, 未可知也." 妾斂容而答曰: "汝非我, 安知我之心哉? 我方賦一詩, 搜奇未得, 故若思不語耳."
銀蟾曰: "意之所向, 心不在焉, 故旁人之言, 如風過耳. 汝之不言, 不難知也. 我將試之." 卽以窓外葡萄爲題, 使作七言四韻促之, 妾應口卽吟, 其詩曰:

44　蜿「藤草似龍行, 翠葉成陰忽有情.

45　署日嚴威能徹照, 晴天寒影反虛明.

46　抽絲攀檻如留意, 結果垂珠欲效誠.

47　若待他時應變化, 會乘雨雲上三淸.

48　小玉見詩, 起而拜曰: "眞天下之奇才也! 風格之不高, 雖似舊調, 而蒼卒製作如此, 此詩人之最難處也. 我之心悅誠服, 如七十子之服孔子也." 紫鸞曰: "言不可不愼也, 何其許如之太過耶? 但文字蜿曲, 且有飛騰之態, 則有之矣." 一座皆曰: "確論也." 妾雖以此詩解之, 而群疑猶未盡釋.

49　翌日, 門外有車馬騈「之聲, 閽者奔入而告曰: "衆賓至矣." 大君掃東閣延入, 皆文人才士也. 坐定, 大君以妾等所製賦烟詩示之, 滿坐大驚曰: "不意今日復見盛唐音調. 非我等所可比肩也. 如此至寶, 進賜從何得之?" 大君薇笑曰: "何爲其然耶? 童僕偶然得於街上而來, 未知何人之所作, 而想必出於閨閣才士之手也."

50　群疑未定, 俄而成三問至曰: "才不借於異代, 自前朝迄于今, 而已六百餘年, 以詩鳴於東國者, 不知其幾人, 或哯沉濁而不雅, 或輕淸而浮藻, 皆不合音律, 失其性情, 吾不欲觀諸, 今觀此詩, 風格淸眞, 思意超越, 小無塵世之態, 此必深宮之人, 不與俗人相接, 只讀古人之詩, 而晝夜吟誦, 自得於心者也. 詳味其意, 其曰'臨風獨惆悵'者, 有思人之意. 其曰'孤篁獨保靑'者, 有守貞節之意. 其曰'風吹自不定'者, 有難保之態. 其曰'幽思向楚君'者, 有向君之誠. 其曰'荷葉露珠留'者, '西岳與前溪'者, 非天上神仙, 則不得如此形容矣. 格調雖有高下, 而薰陶氣像, 則大約皆同. 進賜宮中, 必儲養此十仙人, 願毋隱一見." 大君內自心服, 而外不領可曰: "誰謂謹甫有詩鑑乎, 我宮中豈有此等人哉! 可謂惑之甚矣."

51　于時, 十人從窓隙暗聞, 莫不歎服. 是夜, 紫鸞以至誠問於妾曰: "女子生而願爲有嫁之心, 人皆有之. 汝之所思, 未知何許情人, 悶汝之形容, 日漸減舊, 以情惘問之, 妾須毋隱." 妾起而謝曰: "宮人甚多, 恐有囑喧, 不敢開口, 今承惘「, 何敢隱乎?" 上年秋, 黃菊初開, 紅

51 葉漸凋之時, 大君獨坐書堂, 使侍女磨墨張縑, 寫七言四韻十首.
小童自外而進曰:"有年少儒生, 自稱金進士見之."大君喜曰:
"金進士來矣."使之迎入, 則布衣革帶士, 趨進上階, 如鳥舒翼.
當席拜坐, 容儀神秀, 若仙中人也. 大君一見傾心, 卽趨席對坐,
進士避席而拜辭曰:"猥荷盛眷, 屢辱尊命, 今承警咳, 無任悚恢."
大君慰之曰:"久仰聲華, 坐屋冠蓋, 光動一室, 錫我百朋."

52 進士初入, 已與侍女相面, 而大君以進士年少儒生, 中心易之, 不令
以妾等避之. 大君謂進士曰:"秋景甚好, 願賜一詩, 以此堂生彩."
進士避席而辭曰:"虛名蔑實, 詩之格律, 小子安敢知乎?"大君以金
蓮唱歌, 芙蓉彈琴, 寶蓮吹簫, 飛瓊行盃, 以妾奉硯. 于時, 妾年十
七, 一見郎君, 魂迷意闌. 郎君亦顧妾, 而含笑頻頻送目. 大君謂進
士曰:"我之待君, 誠款至矣. 君何惜一吐瓊「, 使此堂無顏色乎?"進
士卽握筆, 書五言四韻一首曰:

53 旅鴈向南去, 宮中秋色深.

54 水寒荷折玉, 霜重菊垂金.

55 綺席紅顔女, 瑤絃白雪音.

56 流霞一斗酒, 先醉意難禁.

57 大君吟咏再三而驚之曰:"眞所謂天下之奇才也. 何相見之晚耶!"
侍女十人, 一時回顧, 莫不動容曰:"此必王子晋, 駕鶴而來于塵寰.
豈有如此人哉!"大君把盃而問曰:"古之詩人, 孰爲宗匠?"進士曰:
"以小子所見言之, 李白天上神仙, 長在玉皇香案前, 而來遊玄圃,
餐盡玉液, 不勝醉興, 折得萬樹琪花, 隨風雨散落人間之氣像也. 至
於盧王, 海上仙人, 日月出沒, 雲華變化, 滄波動搖, 鯨魚噴薄, 島嶼
蒼茫, 草樹「鬱, 浪花菱葉, 水鳥之歌, 蛟龍之淚, 悉藏於胸襟, 此詩
之造化也. 孟浩然音響最高, 此學師曠, 習音律之人也. 李義山學得
仙術, 早役詩魔, 一生編什, 無非鬼語也. 自餘紛紛, 何足盡陳."大
君曰:"日與文士論詩, 以草堂爲首者多, 此言何謂也?"進士曰:"
然. 以俗儒所尙言之, 猶膾炙之悅人口. 子美之詩, 眞膾與炙也."大
君曰:"百體俱備, 比興極精, 豈以草堂爲輕哉?"進士謝曰:"小子
何敢輕之. 論其長處, 則如漢武帝, 御未央之宮, 憤四夷之猾夏, 命
將薄伐, 百虎萬態之士, 連互數千里, 言其短處, 則如使相如賦長楊,
馬遷草封禪. 求神山, 則如使東方朔侍左右, 西王母獻天桃. 是以杜
甫之文章, 可謂百體之俱備矣. 至比於李白, 則不啻天壤之不侔, 江
海之不同也. 至比於王孟, 則子美驅車先適, 而王孟執鞭爭道矣.'大
君曰.'聞君之言, 胸中惝怳, 若御長風上太淸. 第杜詩, 天下之高文,
雖不足於樂府, 豈與王孟爭道哉? 雖然, 姑舍是, 願君又費一吟, 使
此堂增倍一般光彩."進士卽賦七言四韻一首, 其詩曰:

58　烟散金塘露氣凉, 碧天如水夜何長.

59　微風有意吹垂箔, 白月多情入小堂.

60　夜畔隱開松反影, 盃中波好菊留香.

61　院公雖小頗能飲, 莫怪瓷間醉後狂.

62　大君益奇之, 前席┌手曰:"進士非今世之才. 非余之所能論其高下也. 且非徒能文章筆法, 又極神妙, 天之生君於東方, 必非偶然也." 又使草書, 揮筆之際, 筆墨誤落於妾之手指, 如蠅翼. 妾以此爲榮, 不爲拭除, 左右宮人, 咸顧微笑, 比之登龍門.

63　時夜將半, 更漏相催, 大君欠身思睡曰:"我醉矣. 君亦退休, 勿忘'明朝有意抱琴來'之句." 翌日, 大君再三吟其兩詩而歎曰:"當與謹甫爭雄, 而其淸雅之態, 則過之矣." 妾自是, 寢不能寐, 食滅心煩, 不覺衣帶之緩, 汝未能織之乎?"紫鸞曰:"我忘之矣. 今聞汝言, 怳若酒醒."

64　其後, 大君頻接進士, 而以妾等不相見, 故妾每從門隙而窺之, 一日, 以薛濤牋寫五言四韻一首曰:

65　布衣革帶士, 玉貌如神仙.

66　每從簾間望, 何無月下緣.

67　洗顔淚作水, 彈琴恨鳴絃.

68　無限胸中怨, 擡頭欲訴天.

69　以詩及金鈿一隻同裹, 重封十襲, 欲寄進士, 而無便可達. 其夜月夕, 大君開酒大會, 賓客咸稱進士之才, 以二詩示之, 俱各傳觀, 稱贊不已, 皆願一見, 大君卽送人馬請之. 俄而, 進士至而就坐, 形容癯瘦, 風槪消沮, 殊非昔日之氣像. 大君慰之曰:"進士未憂楚之心, 而先有澤畔之憔悴乎?"滿坐大笑. 進士起而謝曰:"僕以寒賤儒生, 猥蒙進士之寵眷, 福過災生, 疾病纏身, 食飮專廢, 起居須人, 今承厚招, 扶曳來謁矣."坐客皆歛膝而敬.

70　進士以年少儒生, 坐於末席, 與內只隔一壁. 夜已將闌, 衆賓大醉. 妾穴壁作孔而窺之, 進士亦知其意, 向隅而坐. 妾以封書, 從穴投之, 進士拾得歸家, 拆而視之, 悲不自勝, 不忍釋手, 思念之情, 倍於曩時, 如不能自存. 卽欲答書以寄, 而靑鳥無憑, 獨自愁歎而已.

71　聞有一巫女, 居在東門外, 以靈異得名, 出入其宮中, 甚見寵信. 進士訪至其家, 則其巫年未三旬, 姿色殊美, 早寡, 以淫女自處, 見進士至, 盛備酒饌, 而待之甚厚. 進士把盃不飲曰:"今日有忙迫之事, 明日再來矣."翌日又往, 則亦如之. 進士不敢開口, 但曰:"明日又再來矣."

72 巫見進士容貌脫俗, 中心悅之, 而連日往來, 不出一言. 意謂年少之
人, 必以羞澁不言, 我先以意挑之, 挽留繼夜, 要以同枕. 明日, 沐
浴梳洗, 盡態凝粧, 多般盛飾, 布滿花氈瓊瑤席, 使小婢坐門外候
之. 進士又至, 見其容飾之華, 鋪陳之美, 中心怪之. 巫曰: "今夕何
夕? 見此至人." 進士意不在焉, 不答其語, 愀然不樂. 巫怒曰: "寡
女之家, 年少之男, 何往來之不憚煩!" 進士曰: "巫若神異, 則豈不
知我來之意乎?" 巫卽就靈座, 拜于神前, 搖鈴祝說, 遍身寒戰, 頃
之, 動身而言曰: "郎君誠可怜也. 以齟齬之策, 欲遂其難成之計, 非
但其意不成, 未及三年, 其爲泉下之人哉." 進士泣而謝曰: "巫雖不
言, 我亦知之. 然中心怨結, 百藥未解. 若因神巫, 幸傳尺素, 則死亦
榮矣." 巫曰: "卑賤巫女, 雖因神祀, 時或出入, 而非有招命, 則不敢
入. 然爲郎君, 試一往焉." 進士自懷中出一封書, 以贈曰: "愼毋枉
傳, 以作禍機."

73 巫持入宮門, 則宮中之人皆怪其來, 巫權辭以對, 乃得間目, 引妾于
後庭無人處, 以封書授之. 妾還房拆而視之, 其書云: "自一番目成
之後, 心飛魂越, 不能定情, 每向城西, 幾斷寸腸. 曾因壁間之傳書,
敬承不忘之玉音, 開未盡而咽塞, 讀未半而淚滴濕字. 自是之後, 寢
不能寐, 食不下咽, 病入膏肓, 百藥無效, 九原可見, 唯願溘然而從.
蒼天俯憐, 神鬼ㄱ佑, 倘使生前, 一洩此恨, 則當紛身磨骨, 以祭于天
地百神之靈矣. 臨楮哽咽, 夫復何言, 不備謹書." 書下復有七韻一
詩云:

74 樓閣重重掩夕霏, 樹陰雲影摠依微.

75 落花流水隨溝出, 乳燕含泥趁檻歸.

76 倚枕未成蝴蝶夢, 回眸空望鴈魚稀.

77 玉容在眼何無語, 草緣鶯啼淚濕衣,

78 妾覽罷, 聲斷氣塞, 口不能言, 淚盡繼血. 隱身於屏風之後, 唯畏人知.

79 自是厥後, 頃刻不忘, 如癡如狂, 見於辭色, 主君之疑, 人言之怪, 實
不虛矣. 紫鸞亦怨女, 及聞此言, 含淚而言曰: "詩出於性情, 不可欺
也." 一日, 大君呼翡翠曰: "汝等十人, 同在一室, 業不專一." 當分
五人置之西宮, 妾與紫鸞, 銀蟾, 玉女, 翡翠, 卽日移焉. 玉女曰: "幽
花細草, 流水芳林, 正似山家野庄, 眞所謂讀書堂也." 妾答曰: "旣
非舍人, 又非僧尼, 而鎖此深宮, 眞所謂長信宮也." 左右莫不嗟惋.
其後, 妾欲作一書, 以致意於進士, 以至誠事巫, 請之甚懇, 而終不
肯來, 蓋不無挾憾於進士之無意於渠也.

80 一夕, 紫鸞密言于妾曰: "宮中之人, 每歲仲秋, 浣紗於蕩春臺下之
水, 仍說盃酌而罷. 今年則設於昭格署洞, 而往來尋見其巫, 則此第
一良策." 妾然之, 若待仲秋, 度一日如三秋. 翡翠微聞其語, 佯若不

80　知, 而語妾曰:"汝初來時, 顏色如梨花, 不施鉛粉, 而有天然綽約之恣, 故宮中之人, 以┌國夫人稱之. 比來容色減舊, 漸不如初, 是何故耶?"妾答曰:"稟質虛弱, 每當炎節, 則例有署渴之病, 梧桐葉落, 繡幕生涼, 則自至稍蘇矣."翡翠賦一詩戲贈. 無非玩弄之態, 而意思絶妙, 妾奇其才而羞其弄.

81　荏苒數月, 節屬淸秋, 凄風夕起, 細菊吐黃, 草虫歛聲, 皓月流光. 妾知西宮之人, 已不可隱, 以實告之曰:"願勿使南宮之人知之."于時, 旅鴈南飛, 玉露成團, 淸溪浣紗. 正當其時, 欲與諸女, 牢定日期, 而論議甲乙, 未定浣濯之所. 南宮之人曰:"淸溪白石, 無踰於蕩春臺下."西宮之人曰:"昭格署洞泉石, 不下於門外, 何必舍邇而求諸遠乎."南宮之人, 固執不許, 未決而罷.

82　其夜, 紫鸞曰:"南宮五人中, 小玉主論, 我以奇計, 可回其意."以玉燈前導, 至南宮, 金蓮喜迎曰:"一分西宮, 如隔秦楚, 不意今夕玉體左臨, 深謝厚意."

83　小玉曰:"何謝之有? 此乃說客也."紫鸞歛┌正色曰:"他人有心, 予忖度之, 其子之說歟?"小玉曰:"西宮之人, 欲往昭格署洞, 而我獨堅執. 故汝中夜來訪, 其謂說客, 不亦宜乎."紫鸞曰:"西宮五人中, 吾獨欲往城內也."小玉曰:"獨思城內, 其何意哉?"

84　紫鸞曰:"吾聞昭格署洞, 乃祭天星之處, 而洞名三淸云. 吾徒十人, 必是三淸仙女, 誤讀黃庭經, 謫下人間. 旣在塵寰, 則山家野村, 農墅漁店, 何處不可? 而牢鎖深宮, 有若籠中之鳥, 聞黃┌而歎息, 對綠楊而歎欷. 至於乳燕雙飛, 栖鳥兩眠, 草有合歡, 木有連理, 無知草木, 至微禽鳥, 亦稟陰陽, 莫不交歡. 吾儕十人, 獨有何罪, 而寂寞深宮, 長鎖一身, 春花秋月, 伴燈消魂, 虛拋靑春之年, 空遺黃壤之恨, 賦命之薄, 何其至此之甚耶! 人生一老, 不可復少, 子更思之, 寧不悲哉! 今可沐浴於淸川, 以潔其身, 入于太乙祠, 扣頭百拜, 合手祈祝, 冀資冥佑, 欲免來世之此若也. 豈有他意哉? 凡我宮之人, 情若同氣, 而因此一事, 疑人於不當疑之地耶? 緣我無狀, 言不見信之致也!"

85　小玉起而謝曰:"我燭理未瑩, 不及於君遠矣. 初不許城內者, 城中素多無賴俠客之徒, 慮有意外强暴之辱, 故疑之, 今汝能使余, 不遠而復通. 自今以後, 雖白日昇天, 而吾可從之, 雖憑河入海, 而亦可從之, 所謂因人成事, 而及其成功則一也."芙蓉曰:"凡事心定, 上言未定, 兩人爭之, 終夜未決, 事不順矣. 一家之事, 主君不知, 而僕妾密議, 心不忠矣, 日間所爭之事, 宵未半而屈之人, 人不信矣. 且淸湫玉川, 無處不有, 而必往城祠, 似不宜矣. 匪懈堂前, 水淸石 白, 每歲浣洗於此, 而今欲所轍, 亦不宜矣. 一舉而有此五失, 妾不從命."寶連曰:"言者文身之具, 謹與不謹, 慶殃隨之. 是故, 君子 愼之, 守口如瓶. 漢時, 丙吉張相如, 終日不語, 而事無不成, 嗇夫喋

85 喋利口, 而張釋之, 秦詆之. 以妾觀之, 紫鸞之言, 隱而不發, 小玉之
言, 强而勉從, 芙蓉之言, 務在文飾, 皆不合吾意, 今此之行, 妾不與
焉." 金蓮曰: "今夜之論, 終不歸一, 我且穆卜." 卽展羲經而占之,
得卦解之曰: "明日, 雲英必遇丈夫矣. 雲英容貌擧止, 似非人世間
者也. 主君傾心已久, 而雲英以死拒之, 無他故矣, 不忍負夫人之恩
也. 主君之威令雖嚴, 而恐傷雲英之身, 故不敢近之. 今舍此寂寞之
處, 而欲往彼繁華之地, 遊俠少年見其色, 則必有喪魂欲狂者. 雖不
能相近, 而指點送目, 斯亦辱矣. 前日, 主君下令曰: "宮女出門, 外
人之名, 其罪皆死."今此之行, 妾不與焉."

86 紫鸞知事不偕, 憮然不樂, 方欲辭去. 飛瓊泣把羅帶, 强留之, 以鸚
鵡盃, 酌雲乳勸之, 左右皆飲. 金蓮曰: "今夕之會, 務在從容, 而飛
瓊之泣, 妾實悶之." 飛瓊曰: "初在南宮時, 與雲英交道甚密, 死生
榮辱, 若與同之, 今雖異居, 寧忍忘之. 前日, 主君前問安時, 見雲英
於堂前, 纖腰瘦盡, 容色憔悴. 聲音細縷, 若不出口. 起拜之際, 無力
仆地, 妾扶而起之, 以善言慰之. 雲娘答曰: "不幸有疾, 朝夕將死.
妾之微命, 死無足惜, 而九人之文章才華, 日就月長, 他日, 佳篇麗
什, 聳動一世, 而妾不及見矣, 是以悲不能禁."其言頗極悽切, 妾爲
之下淚, 到今思之, 其疾實在於所思也. 嗟呼! 紫鸞, 雲娘之友也. 欲
以垂死之人, 置之於天壇之上, 不亦難哉. 今日之計, 若不得成, 則
泉壤之下, 死不暝目, 怨歸南宮, 其有旣乎? 書曰: "作善降之百祥,
不善降之百殃"今此之論, 善乎?不善乎?" 小玉曰: "妾旣許諾, 三人
之志, 旣已順矣, 豈可半塗而廢乎. 設或事泄, 雲英獨被其罪, 他人
何與焉哉. 妾不爲再言, 當爲雲英死之." 紫鸞曰: "從之者半, 不從
者半, 事不諧矣."欲起而還坐, 更探其意, 或欲從之, 而以兩言爲恥.
紫鸞曰: "天下之事, 有正有權, 權而得中, 是亦正矣. 豈無變通之
權, 而膠守前言乎."左右一時從之. 紫鸞曰: "余非好辯, 爲人謀忠,
不得不爾." 飛瓊曰: "古者蘇秦, 使六國合從, 今紫鸞能使五入承順,
可謂辯士." 紫鸞曰: "蘇秦能佩六國相印, 今吾以何物贈之乎?" 金
蓮曰: "合從者, 六國之利也. 今此承順, 有何所利於五人乎?" 因相
對大笑. 紫鸞曰: "南宮之人皆善, 而能使雲英復繼垂絶之命, 豈不
拜謝?"乃起而再拜, 小玉亦起而拜. 紫鸞曰: "今日之事, 五人從之,
上有天, 下有地, 燈燭照之, 鬼神臨之, 明日, 豈有他意乎?"乃起拜
而去, 五人皆拜送于中門之外.

87 紫鸞歸於妾, 妾扶壁而起, 再拜而謝曰: "生我者父母也, 活我者娘
也. 入地之前, 誓報此恩."坐以待朝, 小玉與南宮四人, 入而問安,
退會於中堂. 小玉曰: "天朗水冷, 正當浣紗之時, 今日設帳於, 昭格
署洞, 可乎?" 八人皆無異辭.

88 妾退還西宮, 以白羅衫, 書滿腔哀怨而懷之, 與紫鸞故爲落後, 謂執馬者曰: "東門外巫女, 最爲靈驗云, 我將往其家, 問病而行." 僮僕如其言. 至其家, 巽辭哀乞曰: "今日之來, 本欲爲一見金進士耳. 可急通之, 則終身報恩." 巫如其言送人, 則進士顚到而至矣. 兩人相見, 不得出一言, 但流涕而已. 妾以封書給之曰: "乘夕當還, 郎君於此留待. 卽上馬而去.

89 進士坼封書而視之, 其辭曰:

90 曩者, 巫山神女, 傳致一札, 琅琅玉音, 滿紙丁寧. 敬奉三復, 悲歡交至, 意不自定. 卽欲答書, 而旣無信便. 且恐漏泄, 引領懸望, 欲飛無翼, 斷腸消魂. 只待死日, 而未死之前, 憑此尺素, 吐盡平生之懷, 伏願郎君留神焉. 妾鄕南方也, 父母愛妾, 偏於諸子中, 出遊嬉戲, 姸其所欲. 園林溪水之涯, 梅竹橘柚之蔭, 日以遊翫爲事. 苔磯釣漁之徒, 罷牧弄笛之兒, 朝暮入眼. 其他山野之態, 田家之興, 難以毛擧. 父母初敎以三綱行實, 七言唐音. 年十三, 主君招之, 故別父母, 遠兄弟, 來入宮門. 不禁思歸之情, 日以蓬頭垢面, 藍縷儀裳, 欲爲觀者之陋, 伏庭而泣, 宮人曰: "有一朵蓮花, 自生庭中." 夫人愛之, 無異己出. 主君亦不以尋常視之. 宮中之人, 莫不親愛如骨肉. 一自從事學問之後, 頗知義理, 能審音律, 故宮人莫不敬服. 及徙西宮之後, 琴書專一, 所造益深. 凡賓客所製之詩, 無一掛眼, 才難不其然乎! 恨不得爲男, 立身揚名, 而爲紅顔薄命之軀, 一閉深宮, 終成枯落而已, 豈不哀哉! 人生一死之後, 誰復知之. 是以恨結心曲, 怨塡胸海. 每停刺繡, 而付之燈火, 罷織錦, 而投杼下機, 裂破罷幃, 折其玉簪. 暫得酒興, 則脫爲散步, 剝落階花, 手折庭草, 如癡如狂, 情不自抑. 上年秋月之夜, 一見君子之容儀, 意謂天上神仙, 謫下塵寰. 妾之容色, 最出於九人之下, 而有何宿世之緣, 那知筆下之一點, 竟作胸中怨結之祟. 以簾間之望, 擬作奉箒之緣, 以夢中之見, 將續不忘之恩. 雖無一番衾裡之歡, 玉貌手容, 恍在眼中. 梨花杜鵑之啼, 梧桐夜雨之聲, 慘不忍聞, 庭前細草之生, 天際孤雲之飛, 慘不忍見. 或倚屛而坐, 或憑欄而立, 搥胸頓足, 獨訴蒼天而已. 不識郎君亦念妾否? 只恨此身未見郎君之前, 先自溘然, 則地老天荒, 此情不泯. 今日浣紗之行, 兩宮侍女皆已集, 故不得久留於此. 淚和墨汁, 魂結羅縷, 伏願郎君, 俯賜一覽. 又以拙句謹答前惠, 非此之僑弄, 聊以寓咏好意.

91 其文則傷秋之賦, 其詩則相思之詩也.

92 是夕來時, 紫鸞與妾又先出. 而向東門, 則小玉微笑, 賦一絶以贈之, 無非譏妾之意也. 妾中心羞赧, 而含忍受之, 其詩曰:

93 乙祠前一水回, 天壇雲盡九門開.

94 細腰不勝狂風急, 暫避林中日暮來.

95 紫鸞卽次其韻, 翡翠玉女, 相繼次之, 亦皆譏妾之意也.

96 妾騎馬, 而先來至巫家, 則巫顯有含慍之色, 向壁而坐, 不借顔色. 進士抱羅衫, 終日飮泣, 喪魂失性, 尙不知妾之來矣. 妾解左手所着雲南玉色金環, 納于進士之懷中曰：“郎君不以妾爲菲薄, 屈千金之軀, 來待陋舍, 妾雖不敏, 亦非木石, 敢不以死許之, 妾若食言, 有此金環”行色忽遽, 起以將別, 流涕如雨. 與進士附耳語曰：“妾在西宮, 郎君來, 暮夜, 由西墻而入, 則三生未盡之緣, 庶可續矣.” 言訖, 拂衣而去, 先入宮門, 則八入繼至.

97 其夜二更, 小玉與飛瓊, 明燭前導, 而來西宮曰：“日間之詩, 出於無情, 而言涉戲翫. 是以不避深夜, 負荊來謝耳.”紫鸞曰：“五人之詩, 皆出南宮. 一自分宮之後, 頗有形跡, 有似唐時牛李之黨, 何不爲其然也. 女子之情則一也. 久閉離宮, 長弔隻影, 所對者燈燭而已, 所爲者絃歌而已. 百花含葩而笑, 雙燕交翼而戲, 薄命妾等, 同銷深宮, 覽物懷春, 情思如何. 朝雲岱神, 而頻入楚王之夢, 王母仙女, 而幾參瑤臺之宴. 女子之意, 宜無異同, 而南宮之人, 何獨與姮娥苦守貞節, 不悔靈藥之偸乎!”

98 飛瓊與玉女, 皆不禁淚流曰：“一人之心, 卽天下人之心也. 今承盛敎, 悲憾之懷, 油然而出矣.”起拜而去. 妾謂紫鸞曰：“今夕, 妾與進士有金石之約. 今若不來, 明日必踰墻而來矣. 來則何以待之?”紫鸞曰：“繡幕重重, 綺席燦爛, 有酒如河, 有肉如坡, 有不來則已, 來則待之何難.”其夜果不來.

99 進士密窺其處, 則墻垣高峻, 自非身俱羽翼, 莫能至矣. 還家, 脉脉不語, 憂形於色. 其奴名特者, 素稱能而多術. 見進士之顔色, 進而跪曰：“進士主, 必不久於世矣.”伏庭而泣. 進士跪而執其手, 悉陳其懷抱, 特曰：“何不早言?吾當圖之.”卽造槎橋, 甚爲輕捷, 能捲能舒. 捲之則如貼屏風, 舒之則五六丈許, 而可運於掌上. 特敎之曰：“持此橋, 上宮墻而還, 捲舒於內, 下之來時, 亦如之.”

100 進士使特試於庭, 果如其言, 進士甚喜之. 其夕將往時, 特又自懷中出給豹皮襪, 曰：“非此難越.”進士用着而行之, 輕如飛鳥, 所踐無足聲. 進士用其計, 踰墻而入, 伏於竹林中, 月色如晝, 宮中寂廖. 少焉, 有人自內而出, 散步微吟. 進士披竹出頭曰：“何人來此?”其人笑而答曰：“郎出郎出.”進士趨而揖曰：“年少之人, 不勝風流之興, 冒犯萬死, 敢至于此, 願娘怜我.”紫鸞曰：“苦待進士之來, 若大旱之望雲霓也. 今幸得見, 妾等蘇矣. 郎君, 願勿疑焉”卽引而入, 進士由層階循曲欄, 竦肩而入.

101　妾開紗窓, 明玉燈而坐, 以獸形金爐, 燒鬱金香, 琉璃書案, 展太平
　　廣記一卷, 見進士至, 起而迎拜. 郎亦答拜, 以賓主之禮, 分東西坐,
　　使紫鸞設珍羞奇饌, 而酌紫霞酒飲之. 酒三行, 進士佯醉曰: "夜如
　　幾何?" 紫鸞會知其意, 垂帳閉門而出. 妾滅燈同枕, 喜可知矣. 夜既
　　向晨, 群鷄報曉, 進士起而去. 自是以後, 昏入曉出, 無夕不然. 喜深
　　意密, 自不知止. 墙內雪上, 頗有蹬痕. 宮人皆知其出入, 莫不危之.

102　一日, 進士忽慮好事之終成禍機, 中心大┌, 終日不樂. 特奴自外而
　　進曰: "吾功甚大, 迄不論賞可乎?" 進士曰: "銘懷不忘, 早晚當重
　　賞矣." 特曰: "今見顔色, 亦似有憂, 未知何故耶?" 進士曰: "不見
　　則病在心骨, 見之則罪在不測, 何之不憂?" 特曰: "然則何不竊負而
　　逃乎?" 進士然之, 其夜, 以特之謀告於妾曰: "特之爲奴, 素多智謀,
　　以此計指揮, 其意如何" 妾許之曰: "妾之父母, 家財最饒. 故妾來
　　時, 衣服寶貨, 多載而來. 且主君之所賜甚多, 此不可棄置而去. 今
　　欲運之, 則雖馬十匹, 不能盡輸矣."

103　進士歸於特, 特大喜曰: "何難之有?" 進士曰: "若然則計將安出?"
　　特曰: "吾友力士十七人, 以日强┌爲事, 人莫能當, 而與我甚結, 唯
　　命是從. 使此輩運之, 則泰山亦可移矣." 進士入語妾, 妾然之, 夜夜
　　收拾, 七日之夜, 盡輸于外. 特曰: "如此重寶, 積置于本宅, 則大上
　　典必疑之, 積置于奴家, 則人必疑之. 無已則堀坑山中, 深┌而堅守
　　之可矣." 進士曰: "若或見失, 則吾與汝難免盜賊之名矣, 汝可愼
　　守." 特曰: "吾計如此之深, 吾友如此之多, 天下無難事, 有何畏乎?
　　況持長劍, 晝夜不離, 則吾目可抉, 此寶不可奪. 吾足可斷, 則此寶
　　不取, 願勿疑焉." 蓋特意, 得此重寶而後, 妾與進士, 引入山谷, 屠
　　殺進士, 而妾與財寶, 自占之計, 而進士迂儒, 不可知也.

104　大君以前搆匪懈堂, 欲得佳製懸板, 而諸客之詩, 皆未滿意, 强邀進
　　士, 設宴懇之, 一揮而就, 文不加點, 而山水之景色, 堂搆之形容, 無
　　不盡焉, 可以驚風雨, 泣鬼神. 大君句句稱賞曰: "不意今日復見王
　　子安!" 吟咏不已. 但一句有隨墙暗竊風流曲之語, 停口疑之. 進士
　　起而拜曰: "醉不省人事, 願爲之辭退." 大君命童僕, 扶而送之.

105　翌日之夜, 進士入語妾曰: "可以去矣. 昨日之詩, 疑入大君之意, 今
　　夜不去, 恐有後禍." 妾對曰: "昨夕夢見一人, 狀貌獰惡, 自稱冒頓
　　單于曰: '旣有宿約, 故久待長城之下.' 覺而驚起, 甚怪夢兆之不祥,
　　郎君其亦思之乎?" 進士曰: "夢裡虛誕之事, 何可信也? 妾曰: "其
　　曰長城者, 宮墻也. 其曰冒頓者, 此特也. 郎君熟知此奴之心乎?" 進
　　士曰: "此奴素頑兇, 然於我則前日盡忠, 今日與娘結此好緣, 皆此
　　奴之計也. 豈獻忠於始, 而爲惡於後乎?" 妾曰: "郎君之言, 如是懇
　　眷, 何敢辭乎? 但紫鸞, 情若兄弟, 不可不告也." 卽呼紫鸞.

106 三人鼎足而坐, 妾以進士之計告之, 紫鸞大驚, 罵之曰:"相歡日久,
無乃自速禍敗耶! 一兩月相交, 亦可足矣, 踰墻逃走, 豈人之所忍
爲也?主君之傾意已久, 其不可去一也. 夫人之慈恤甚重, 其不可去
二也. 禍及兩親, 其不可去三也. 罪及西宮, 其不可去四也. 且天地
一網罟, 非陞天入地, 則逃之焉往. 倘或被捉, 則其禍豈止於子之身
乎?夢兆之不祥, 不順言之, 而若或吉祥, 則汝肯往之乎?莫如屈心
抑志, 守貞安坐, 以聰於天耳. 娘子若年貌衰謝, 則主君之恩眷漸弛
矣. 觀其事勢, 稱病久臥, 則必許還鄕矣. 當此之時, 與郞君携手同
歸, 與之偕老, 計莫大焉, 不此之思耶. 當此之計, 汝雖欺人, 敢欺天
乎?"進士知事不成, 嗟歡含淚而出.

107 一日, 大君坐西宮繡軒, 矮躅「盛開. 命侍女各賦五言絶句以進.
大君大加稱賞曰:"汝等之文, 日漸就將, 余甚嘉之, 而第雲英之
詩, 顯有思人之意. 前日賦烟之詩, 微見其意, 今又如此, 汝之欲
從者, 何人耶? 金生之檄文, 語涉疑異, 汝無乃金生有思乎."妾卽
下庭, 叩頭而泣曰:"主君之一番見疑, 卽欲自盡, 而年未二旬, 且
以更不見父母而死, 九泉之下, 死有餘憾. 故偸生至此, 又今見疑,
一死何惜?天地鬼神, 昭布森列, 侍女五人, 頃刻不離, 淫濊之名,
獨歸於妾, 生不如死, 妾今得所死矣."卽以羅巾, 自縊於欄干. 紫
鸞曰:"主君如是英明, 而使無罪侍女自就死地, 自此以後, 妾等
誓不把筆作句矣."大君雖盛怒, 而中心則實不欲其死, 故使紫鸞
救之而不得死. 大君出素縑五端, 分賜五人曰:"製作最佳, 是以
賞之."

108 自是進士不復出入, 杜門病臥, 淚濺衾枕, 命如一縷. 特來見曰:"
大丈夫死則死矣, 何忍相思怨結, 屑屑如兒女之傷懷, 自擲千金之
軀乎?今當以計, 取之不難也, 半夜入寂之時, 踰墻而入, 以綿塞其
口, 負而超出, 則孰敢追我."進士曰:"其計亦危矣. 不如以誠叩
之."其夜入來, 而妾病不能起, 使紫鸞迎入. 酒三行, 妾以封書寄
之曰:"自此以後, 部得更見, 三生之緣, 百年之約, 今夕盡矣. 如或
天緣未絶, 則當可相尋於九泉之下矣."進士抱書佇立, 脉脉相看,
叩胸流涕而出. 紫鸞慘不忍見, 倚柱隱身, 揮淚而立. 進士還家, 折
而視之, 其書曰:

109 "薄命妾雲英, 再拜白金郎足下. 妾以菲薄之資, 不幸以爲郞君之留
意, 相思幾日, 相望幾時. 幸成一夜之交歡, 未盡如海之深情. 人間
好事, 造物多猜. 宮人知之, 主君疑之, 禍迫朝夕, 死而後已. 伏願郞
君, 此別之夜, 毋以賤妾置於懷抱間, 以傷思慮, 勉加學業, 擢高第,
登雲路, 揚名於世, 以顯父母, 而妾之衣服寶貨, 盡賣供佛, 百般祈
祝, 至誠發願, 使三生未盡之緣分, 再續於後世, 至可至可矣."

110　進士不能盡看, 氣絶仆地, 家人急救乃甦. 特自外而入曰:“宮人答之何語, 如是其欲死! ”進士無他語, 只曰:“財寶汝愼守乎? 我將盡賣, 薦誠於佛, 以踐宿約矣.”特還家自思曰:“宮女不出來, 其財寶天與我也.”向壁竊笑, 而人莫知之矣.

111　一日, 特自裂其衣, 自打其鼻, 以其流血, 遍身糢糊, 被髮跣足奔入, 伏庭而泣曰:“五爲强賊所擊.”仍不復言, 若氣絶者然. 進士慮特死, 則不知埋寶之處, 親灌藥物, 多般救活, 供饋酒肉, 十餘日乃起曰:“孤單一身, 獨守山中, 衆賊突入, 勢將剝殺, 故捨命而走, 僅保縷命. 若非此寶, 我安有如此之危乎? 賦命之險如此, 何不速死!”卽以足頓地, 以拳叩胸而哭. 進士懼父母知之, 以溫言慰之而送之.

112　進士知特之所爲, 率奴十餘名, 不意圍其第搜之, 則只有金釧一雙, 雲南寶鏡一面. 以此爲臟物, 欲呈官推得, 而恐事泄. 不得此物, 則無以供佛之需. 心欲殺特, 而力不能制, 囁不語. 特自知其罪, 問於宮墻外盲人曰:“我向者晨過此宮墻之外, 有人自宮中踰西垣而出. 我知其爲賊, 高聲進逐, 其人棄所持物而走. 我持歸藏之, 以待本主之來推. 吾主索之廉隅, 聞吾得物, 躬來索出, 吾答以無他寶, 只得釧鏡二物云, 則主人躬入搜之, 果得二物. 亦其無厭, 方欲殺之, 故吾欲走去, 走之吉乎?”盲曰:“吉矣.”驥隣在旁, 多聞其語, 謂特曰:“汝主何許人?虐奴如是耶?”特曰:“吾主年少能文, 早晚應爲及第者, 而爲貪婪如此, 他日立朝, 用心可知.”

113　此言傳播, 入於宮中, 告于大君. 大君大怒, 使南宮人搜西宮, 則姜之衣服寶貨盡無矣. 大君招致西宮侍女五人于庭中, 嚴俱刑杖於眼前, 下令曰:“殺此五人, 以警他人.”又敎執杖者曰:“勿計杖數, 以死爲準.”五人曰:“願一言而死.”大君曰:“所言何事?悉陳其情.”

114　銀蟾招曰:“男女情欲, 稟於陰陽, 無貴無賤, 人皆有之. 一閉深宮, 形單隻影, 看花掩淚, 對月消魂, 則可知人間之樂, 而所不爲者, 豈力不能而心不忍哉?唯畏主君之威, 固守此心, 以爲枯死. 宮中之計, 今無所犯之罪, 而欲置之於死地, 妾等黃泉之下, 死不瞑目矣.”

115　翡翠招曰:“主君撫恤之恩, 山不高, 海不深. 妾等憾懼, 惟事文墨絃歌而已. 今不洗之惡名, 偏及西宮, 生不如死矣, 惟伏願速就死地矣.”

116　鶯鶯招曰:“今日之事, 罪在不測, 中心所懷, 何忍諱之. 妾等皆閭巷賤女, 父非大舜, 母非二妣, 則男女情欲, 何獨無乎?穆王天子, 而每思瑤臺之樂, 項羽英雄, 而不禁帳中之淚, 主君何使雲英獨無雲雨之情乎?金生乃當世之端士也. 引入內堂, 主君之事也. 命雲英奉硯, 主君之命也. 雲英久鎖深宮, 秋月春花, 每傷性情, 梧桐夜雨, 幾斷寸腸. 一見豪男, 喪心失性, 病入骨髓, 雖以長生之樂, 難以見效. 一夕如朝露之溘然, 則主君雖有惻隱之心, 顧何益哉?妾之愚意, 一使金生得見雲英, 以解兩人之怨結, 則主君之積善, 莫大乎此, 前日雲英之毀節, 罪在妾身, 不在雲英. 妾之一言, 上不欺主君, 下不負同儕, 今日之死, 死亦榮矣. 伏願主君, 以妾之身續雲英之命矣."

117　玉女招曰: "西宮之榮, 妾旣與焉, 西宮之厄, 妾獨免哉?火炎崑崗, 玉石俱焚, 今日之死, 得其所死矣."

118　妾之招曰: "主君之恩, 如山如海, 而不能苦守貞節, 其罪一也. 前日所製之時, 見疑於主君, 而終不直告, 其罪二也. 西宮無罪之人, 以妾之故, 同被其罪, 其罪三也. 負此三大罪, 生亦何顔?若或緩死, 妾當自決, 以待處分矣."大君覽畢, 又以紫鸞之招, 更展留眼, 怒色稍霽.

119　小玉跪而告泣曰: "前日浣紗之行, 勿爲於城內者, 妾之議也. 紫鸞夜至南宮, 請之甚懇, 妾怜其意, 排群議從之. 雲英之毀節, 罪在妾身, 不在雲英. 伏願主君, 以妾之身續雲英之命."大君之怒稍解, 囚妾于別堂, 而其餘皆放之;其夜妾以羅巾, 自縊而死.

120　進士把筆而記, 雲英引古而敍, 甚詳悉. 兩人相對, 悲不自抑. 雲英謂進士曰: "自此以下, 郎君言之."進士曰: "雲英自決之後, 一宮之人, 莫不號慟, 如喪考妣. 哭聲出於宮門之外, 我亦聞之, 氣絶久矣, 家人將招魂發喪, 一邊救活, 日暮時乃甦. 方定精神, 自念事已決矣. 無負供佛之約, 庶慰九泉之魂, 其金釧寶鏡及文房諸具盡賣之, 得四十石之米, 欲上淸寧寺設佛事, 而無可信使喚者, 呼特而言曰: "我盡有前日之罪, 今爲我盡忠乎?"特伏泣而對曰: "奴雖冥頑, 亦非木石, 一身所負之罪, 擢髮難數, 今而宥之, 是枯木生葉, 白骨生肉, 敢不爲進士致死乎! "我曰: "我爲雲英, 設醮供佛, 以冀發願, 而無信任之人, 汝未可往乎"特曰: "謹受敎矣"卽上寺, 三日叩臀而臥, 招僧謂之曰: "四十石之米何用?盡入於供佛乎?今可多備酒肉, 廣招俗客而饋之宜矣."

121　適有村女過之, 特强劫之, 留宿於僧堂, 已過數十日, 無意設齋. 寺僧皆憤之, 及其建醮日, 諸僧曰: "供佛之事, 施主爲重, 而施主不潔如此, 事極未安, 可沐浴於淸川, 潔身而行禮可矣."特不得已出, 暫以水沃濯, 而入跪於佛前祝曰: "進士今日速死, 雲英明日復生, 爲特之配."三晝夜發願之設, 唯此而已. 特歸語我曰: "雲英閣氏, 必得生道矣. 設齋之夜, 現於奴夢曰, 至誠供佛, 不勝感謝. 拜且泣之, 寺僧之夢, 亦皆然矣"我信之其說矣.

122 適當槐黃之節, 雖無赴擧之意, 托以做工, 上淸寧寺, 留數日, 細聞
     特之事, 不勝其憤, 而無特如何. 沐浴潔身, 而就佛前面拜, 叩頭薦
     香, 合掌而祝曰: "雲英死時之約, 慘不忍負, 使特奴虔誠設齋, 冀資
     冥佑, 今聞所祝之言, 極其悖惡, 雲英之遺願, 盡歸虛地, 故小子敢
     復祝願. 能使雲英復生, 使金生得免如此之冤痛, 伏望世尊, 殺特奴,
     着鐵架, 囚于地獄. 伏乞世尊, 苟如此發願, 則雲英爲尼, 燒十指, 作
     十二層金塔, 金生爲僧舍五戒, 創三巨刹, 以報其恩." 祝訖, 起而百
     拜, 叩頭而出, 後七日, 特壓於陷井而死. 自是我無意於世事, 沐浴
     潔身, 着新衣, 臥于安靜之房, 不食四日, 長吁一聲, 因遂不起.

123 寫畢擲筆, 兩人相對悲泣, 不能自抑. 柳泳慰之曰: "兩人重逢, 志願
     畢矣. 讐奴已除, 憤惋洩矣. 何其悲痛之不止耶? 以不得再出人間而
     恨乎?" 金生垂淚而謝曰: "吾兩人皆含怨而死. 冥司怜其無罪, 欲使
     再生人世, 而地下之樂, 不減人間, 況天上之樂乎! 是以不願出世矣.
     但今夕之悲傷, 大君一敗, 故宮無主人, 烏雀哀鳴, 人跡不倒, 已極
     悲矣. 況新經兵火之後, 華屋成灰, 粉墻摧毀, 而唯有階花芬弗, 庭
     草藪榮, 春光不改昔時之景敬, 而人事之變易如此, 重來憶舊, 寧不
     悲哉!" 柳泳曰: "然則子皆爲天上之人乎?" 金生曰: "吾兩人素是
     天上仙人, 長侍玉皇前, 一日, 帝御太淸宮, 命我摘玉園之果, 我多
     取蟠桃瓊玉, 私與雲英而見覺, 謫下塵寰, 使之備經人間之苦. 今則
     玉皇已宥前愆, 俾陞三淸, 更侍香案前, 而時乘颷輪, 復尋塵世之舊
     遊耳." 乃揮淚而執柳泳之手曰: "海枯石爛, 此情不泯, 地老天荒,
     此恨難消. 今夕與子相遇, 攄此悃忱, 非有宿世之緣, 何可得乎? 伏願
     尊君, 俯拾此藁, 傳之不朽, 而勿浪傳於浮薄之口, 以爲戱翫之資,
     幸甚!" 進士醉倚雲英之身, 吟一絶句曰:

124 花落宮中燕雀飛, 春光依舊主人非.

125 中宵月色凉如許, 碧露未沾翠羽衣.

126 雲英繼吟曰:

127 故宮柳花帶新春, 千載豪華入夢頻.

128 今夕來遊尋舊跡, 不禁哀淚自沾巾.

129 柳泳亦醉暫睡, 小焉, 山鳥一聲, 覺而視之, 雲烟滿地, 曉色蒼茫, 四
     顧無人, 只有金生所記冊子而已. 泳悵然無聊, 收神冊而歸, 藏之篋
     笥, 時或開覽, 則茫然自失, 寢食俱廢, 後遍遊名山, 不知所終云爾

130 <國立圖書館本>

Retrieved on July 2, 2018 from: http://www.davincimap.co.kr/davBase/
Source/davSource.jsp?Job=Body&SourID=SOUR001299&Lang=
한문&Page=1&View=Text.

Conclusion

On 23 June 1927, the following brief announcement appeared on the second page of the Korean language newspaper *Chosŏn ilbo*, accompanied by a nondescript photograph of its subject:

> Dr. Gale, Elder Stateman of Christianity in Chosŏn, Returns Home: Will complete *History of the Korean People* upon return; Dedicated his life to Chosŏn
>
> At 10 a.m. on June 12th, the distinguished Christian missionary Dr. Gale, who for more than forty years has worked tirelessly for the people of this country, boarded the express train for Pusan to depart Chosŏn for the last time. During his four decades in the country Dr. Gale worked to propagate Christianity while contributing immensely to education, including the establishment of Kyŏngsin School and Chŏngsin Girls' School. Dr. Gale is also renowned for his research into Korean history, and upon departing he vowed that he would never forget Chosŏn, but until his dying day would continue his work, in particular complete his English-language manuscript *History of the Korean People* [Yŏngmun Chosŏnsa] seeking to introduce Korean history to the English-speaking world.[1]

A short article in the same newspaper the previous week reported on Gale's going-away party in similarly glowing terms, highlighting the missionary's four decades of service. However, this account provides

---

1 "Chosŏn Kidokkyo ŭi wŏnhun Kiil Paksa kwuiguk" [Dr. Gale, Pioneering Christian Missionary in Korea, Returns Home], *Chosŏn ilbo*, 23 June 1927.

some insight into alternate aspects of his academic activities, giving a more holistic summary of his accomplishments and legacy: "Dr. Gale is renowned among the missionary community as a scholar of Classical Literature (*Hanmunhakcha*), has put enormous efforts into literature translation, and was the first to translate the Old and New Testaments into the Korean language. Dr. Gale has also compiled Korean-English dictionaries and has translated numerous Classical works of Korean literature (*chaerae ŭi munhak*) into English, including *The Tale of Ch'unhyang* (Ch'unhyang chŏn) and *The Cloud Dream of the Nine* (Kuunmong). Through such translations, Gale received widespread recognition from the Western world."[2]

Upon his death ten years later in Bath, England, Gale was likewise remembered as a man who wore many hats, his contributions to Korean Christianity, modern education, literary translation, and lexicography all dutifully acknowledged.[3]

And yet, if we are to acknowledge the Gale Papers at the University of Toronto as the embodiment of his life's work relating to Korea, the picture that emerges is one of a dedicated mediator of Korean culture and literature to the Western world. More specifically, the mountains of unpublished works overwhelmingly fall into the category of English translations of Korean classical literature in Literary Sinitic. Thus, while the missionary and educational activities highlighted above and by subsequent scholars and church historians had an indelible effect on Korea, judging by the sheer number of hours that such a voluminous *Nachlass* would have required, it seems that Gale by the end of his career had discovered his true calling as the mouthpiece of Classical Korean literature to the Anglophone world. *Pen Pictures* and *Old Corea* thus serve as illuminating indices of his journey from neophyte cultural arbiter to sober literatus of the old school.

Despite Gale's voluminous literary legacy, the vast majority of his translations have remained unpublished. Being credited with such pioneering feats as the first translation of Korean literature into English, the first English literature into Korean, and an entire private translation

---

2 "Pujin sasip sŏngsang Kiil Paksa songbyŏl" [Dr. Gale Leaves Korea after a
   40-Year Odyssey], *Chosŏn ilbo*, 12 June 1927.

3 "Choson munhwa ŭi ŭnin Kiil Paksa ch'udohoe kaech'oe" [Memorial Services
   to Be Held for Dr. Gale, Great Benefactor of Korean Culture], *Chosŏn ilbo*,
   17 February 1937.

of the Bible would be enough to secure any translator's legacy, but the fact that more than 90 per cent of his translations remained unknown to the public is remarkable in its own right, and prompts us to ask why this was the case. Although many of his translations did see the light of day in various missionary publications such as the *Korea Repository*, *Korea Review*, and *Transactions of the Royal Asiatic Society – Korea Branch*, these were small publications with a readership limited mostly to the expatriate or missionary community in Korea, or at the widest, East Asia. *Korea Magazine*, where the majority of Gale's translations were published, enjoyed the shortest run and the most limited readership of all such magazines, representing more a fastidious medium for curatorial intercession into Korean literature than a vehicle for wide circulation. North American–based publications such as *Men and Missions* and the *Open Court* had more geographical reach but still remained more or less limited to missionary circles.

Gale's translations and other writings may not have found much of a readership beyond missionary circles or those based in East Asia, but the fundamental reasons for the relative neglect of his writings by his contemporary readership concerned the subject of his writing and his particular approach to that subject. Despite its "century of troubles," China was a populous, powerful country in the minds of Western observers, a cultural force that often stood as a metonymic symbol for all of Eastern civilization for a readership with only the most superficial understanding of such distant lands. Japan, on the other hand, was the upstart island nation that had defeated great powers in recent wars, the only Asian country that had successfully adopted Western ways and aspired to equal membership on the global stage. In this scenario, the tiny nation of Chosŏn unfortunately struggled to achieve a distinct identity – or rather establish an effective platform to voice such an identity – despite the best efforts of a cultural mediator acutely attuned to such a plight. With the deepening of Japanese colonial rule on the peninsula and the resignation of foreign powers to this status quo, Korean literature and culture to the casual observer in the West must have appeared increasingly as the fading subculture of a people gradually assimilating to the Japanese Empire.

Moreover, Gale's particular cosmopolitan conceptualization of Korean literature compounded the "obscurity" already associated with the country of Chosŏn, which not only potentially hampered wider recognition among an Anglophone readership but forestalled wider acknowledgment of Gale's accomplishments among subsequent Korean scholars. Like his missionary colleagues, Gale appreciated from a utilitarian perspective the potential of the vernacular script to convey knowledge to a semi-literate population, and his educational activities attest to this dedication to literacy and progress. And yet, the world of true literature for Gale was perpetually that of "the character," even after the advent of a "golden era" in vernacular literature in the 1920s during the closing years of his career. Tellingly, his final years in Korea during which this vernacular renaissance was in full swing also coincided with his most ardent, uncompromising commitment to Classical Korean literature, representing a complete disavowal of the vernacular inclination and a reactionary pledge to cosmopolitan orthodoxy. Thus, while his commitment to a "free translation" of the Bible that adhered to Korean spoken vernacular eventually prompted his resignation from the Bible's Board of Official Translators, Gale's cosmopolitan literary affirmation paradoxically eschewed such a vernacular Weltanschauung. As vernacular literature continued to develop, Gale's language ideologies and overall literary project appeared increasingly anachronistic, effecting a rupture with Korean cultural nationalists who found such an approach regressive and feudalistic while alienating or perhaps confusing an Anglophone audience who questioned how literature in "Chinese" represented the culture of a suppressed nation seeking to preserve its "national" heritage under colonial rule.

In the post-colonial era, Gale's perceived anti-nationalist literary agenda coupled with his supposed pro-Japanese affiliation has forestalled a more sustained treatment of his legacy in Korean academia. In North American academia, meanwhile, scholar-missionary figures have tended to fall into a grey area between church history and greater academia; in this paradigm, only Gale's missionary and educational activities have been considered part of the former, while his scholarly activities have been largely ignored. Despite the century that separates many of these writings from today's readership, the world view and literary sentiments contained herein reveal a dedicated Koreanist nevertheless coloured by the vagaries of his age, offering a fascinating snapshot of Korea's dramatic, contested, and often wrenching modernization process.

Bibliography

Online Digital Text Corpora

Academy of Korean Studies. *H'anguk minjok munhwa tae paekhwa sajŏn* [Encyclopedia of Korean Culture]. Accessible at https://encykorea.aks.ac.kr/.

Chosŏn wangjo sillok [朝鮮王朝實錄 Veritable Records of the Chosŏn Dynasty]. Accessible at http://sillok.history.go.kr/main/main.do.

Kojong sidaesa [高宗時代史 History of the Kojong Era]. Accessible at http://db .history.go.kr/item/level.do;jsessionid=10F3DE1C5833771BC522409136629510 ?itemId=sk.

Koryŏsa chŏryŏ [高麗史節要 Essential Koryŏ History]. Accessible at http:// db.history.go.kr/KOREA/item/level.do?itemId=kj&types=r.

Samguk sagi [三國史記 History of the Three Kingdoms]. Accessible at http:// db.history.go.kr/item/level.do?itemId=sg.

Suishu [隋書 The History of Sui]. Accessible at http://chinesenotes.com /suishu.html.

Tongmunsŏn [東文選 A Selection of Eastern Literature]. Accessible at https:// www.krpia.co.kr/product/main?plctId=PLCT00008012.

Yŏllyŏ sil kisul [燃藜室記述 Narratives of Yŏllyŏ (Yi Kŭngik)]. Accessible at http:// db.itkc.or.kr/dir/item?itemId=BT#dir/node?grpId=&itemId=BT& gubun=book &depth=2&cate1=Z&cate2=&dataGubun=서지&dataId=ITKC_BT_1300A.

Zhuangzi [莊子]. Accessible at Chinese Text Project. https://ctext.org/zhuangzi.

Newspapers and Periodicals

Chosŏn ilbo
Hwangsŏng sinmun
Japan Weekly Mail

Korea Bookman
Korea Magazine
Korea Mission Field
Korean Repository
Korea Review
Kŭrisŭdo sinmun
Men and Missions
Missionary Review of the World
New York Times
North China Daily News
North China Herald
Open Court
Outlook
Public Opinion
Sin yŏsŏng
Transactions of the Royal Asiatic Society – Korea Branch

Other Sources

An Chonghwa. (1909). *Kukcho inmulchi: Pu saegin* [Korea's Record of Famous Men, Indexed]. Sŏul: Myŏngmundang, 1983.
An Taehoe. *Tambago munhwasa* [The Cultural History of Tobacco in Korea, 1609–1910]. Seoul: Munhak tongne, 2015.
Baker, Donald. "Hananim, Hanŭnim, Hanŭllim, and Hanŏllim: The Construction of Terminology for Korean Monotheism." *Review of Korean Studies* 5, no. 1 (2002): 105–31.
– *Korean Spirituality*. Honolulu: University of Hawaii Press, 2016.
Baker, Donald, and Franklin Rausch. *Catholics and Anti-Catholicism in Chosŏn Korea*. Honolulu: University of Hawaii Press, 2017.
Breuker, Remco. *Establishing a Pluralist Society in Medieval Korea, 918–1170: History, Ideology, and Identity in the Koryŏ Dynasty*. Leiden: Brill, 2010.
Brown, Callum. *Religion and Society in Twentieth-Century Britain*. London: Taylor and Francis, 2016.
Byington, Mark E., ed. *Early Korea: The Samhan Period in Korean History*. Cambridge, MA: Harvard University Press, 2009.
Carles, William Richard. *Life in Corea*. London: Macmillan, 1888.
Carlyle, Thomas, and Alan Shelston. *Thomas Carlyle: Selected Writings*. London: Penguin Classics, 2015.
Chandra, Vipan. *Imperialism, Resistance, and Reform in Late Nineteenth-Century Korea: Enlightenment and the Independence Club*. Berkeley: University of

California, Institute of East Asian Studies, and Center for Korean Studies, 1988.

Chang Huihŭng. "Kapo kaehyŏk ihu Naesibu ŭi kwanje pyŏnhwa wa hwangwanje ŭi p'yeji" [The Post-Kapo Reforms Transformation of the Eunuch Bureau and the Abolishment of the Eunuch Minister System]. *Tonghak yŏn'gu* 21 (2006): 17–42.

– "Tae Han chegukgi naesi Kang Sŏkho ŭi hwaltong" [The Taehan Empire–Era Eunuch Minister Kang Sŏkho]. *Sahak yŏn'gu* 89 (2008): 87–117.

Chang Yu. "Oŏn kosi 162" [五言古詩 162 Five Character Classical Poetry 162]. In *Kyegok sŏnsaeng chip* kwŏn 25 [谿谷先生集 The Complete Works of Master Kyegok, vol. 25]. http://db.itkc.or.kr/search/group?q=query†%E4%BD%99%E7%97%85%E5%AF%92%E8%80%8C%E5%98%94%E3%80%82%E8%A6%8B%E7%BE%A4%E8%A0%85%E9%80%90%E8%87%AD%E8%80%8C%E8%87%B3.

Cho, Ines. "Moving beyond the Green Blur: A History of Soju." *JoongAng Daily*, 21 October 2005.

Cho Tongwŏn, comp. *Han'guk kŭmsŏngmun taegye* [Compendium of Korean Bronze and Stone Inscriptions]. Iri: Wŏngwang taehakkyo ch'ulp'anguk, 1993.

Ch'oe Ch'iwŏn. "Chorang" [潮浪 The Tides]. Si [詩 Poetry]. In *Kyewŏn p'ilkyŏng chip* kwŏn 20 [桂苑筆耕集 The Collected Works of Ch'oe Ch'iwŏn, vol. 20]. http://db.mkstudy.com/mksdb/e/korean-anthology/book/reader/1/?sideTab=toc&contentTab=image&articleId=1007246.

– "Hae ku" [海鷗 The Seagull]. Si [詩 Poetry]. In *Kyewŏn p'ilkyŏng chip* kwŏn 20 [桂苑筆耕集 The Collected Works of Ch'oe Ch'iwŏn, vol. 20]. http://db.mkstudy.com/mksdb/e/korean-literary-collection/book/reader/8197/?sideTab=toc&contentTab=text&articleId=894871.

– "Kuiyŏnŭm hŏnt'aewi" [歸燕吟獻太尉 The Swallow]. Si [詩 Poetry]. In *Kyewŏn p'ilkyŏng chip* kwŏn 20 [桂苑筆耕集 The Collected Works of Ch'oe Ch'iwŏn, vol. 20]. http://db.mkstudy.com/mksdb/e/korean-anthology/book/reader/1/?sideTab=toc&contentTab=image&articleId=1007238.

Ch'oe Sŭngno. "Ch'oe Sŭngno ka Sŏngjong ege simu ch'aek 28 cho rŭl ollida" [Ch'oe Sŭngno Submits Twenty-Eight Proposals to King Sŏngjong]. *Koryŏsa chŏryo* kwŏn 6 [高麗史節要 6 Essentials of Koryŏ History, vol. 6], yŏlchŏn [列傳 biographies]. http://db.history.go.kr/KOREA/search/searchResult.do?sort=levelId&dir=ASC&limit=20&page=1&pre_page=1&codeIds=PERIOD-0-3&searchTermImages=%E9%A1%98%E8%81%96%E4%B8%8A%E9%99%A4%E5%88%A5%E4%BE%8B%E7%A5%88%E7%A5%AD&searchKeywordType=BI&searchKeywordMethod=EQ&searchKeyword=%E9%A1%98%E8%81%96%E4%B8%8A%E9%99%A4%E5

%88%A5%E4%BE%8B%E7%A5%88%E7%A5%AD&searchKeyword
Conjunction=AND.

Ch'oe, Yŏngho, Peter H. Lee, and Wm. Theodore de Bary, eds. *Sources of Korean Tradition*. Vol. 2, *From the Sixteenth to the Twentieth Centuries*. New York: Columbia University Press, 2000.

Ch'oe, Yŏng-ho, and Yi Tae-jin. "The Mystery of Emperor Kojong's Sudden Death in 1919: Were the Highest Japanese Officials Responsible?" *Korean Studies* 35 (2011): 122–51.

Choi, Hyaeweol. "An American Concubine in Old Korea: Missionary Discourse on Gender, Race, and Modernity." *Frontiers: A Journal of Women's Studies* 25, no. 3 (2004): 134–61.

Chŏng Ch'urhŏn. "*Unyŏng chŏn* ŭi aejŏng kaltŭng kwa kŭ pigŭkjŏk sŏnggyŏk" [The Conflict of Affection and Its Tragic Nature in the *Tale of Unyŏng*]. *Han'guk kososŏlsa ŭi sigak* (1996): 575–613.

Chu Yongnip. "Han'guk kodae ŭi sunjang yŏn'gu." In *Son Pogi paksa chŏngnyŏn kinyŏm Han'guk sahak nonch'ong*, edited by Son Pogi. Sŏul: Chisik sanŏpsa, 1988.

Diosy, Arthur. *The New Far East*. London: Cassell, 1904.

Dredge, C. Paul. "Smoking in Korea." *Korea Journal* 4 (1980): 25–36.

Durrant, Stephen. "Zhou, Duke of Zhōu Gōng." In *The Berkshire Dictionary of Chinese Biography*, edited by Kerry Brown. Great Barrington, MA: Berkshire Publishing Group, 2014.

Dziwenka, Ronald. "'The Last Light of Indian Buddhism': The Monk Zhi Kong in 14th Century China and Korea." PhD diss., University of Arizona, 2010. https://core.ac.uk/download/pdf/143737554.pdf.

Edkins, Joesph. *A Grammar of the Chinese Colloquial Language Commonly Called the Mandarin Dialect*. Shanghai: Presbyterian Mission Press, 1864.

English Student Association, Department of English Language and Literature, Ewha Woman's University, trans. and eds. *Woon Young's Romance and Other Stories*. Korean Folklore and Classics, vol. 2. 1970.

Frankel, Hans H. "Cai Yan and the Poems Attributed to Her." *Chinese Literature: Essays, Articles, Reviews* 5 (1983): 133–56.

Gale, Esson M. *Salt for the Dragon: A Personal History of China*. East Lansing: Michigan State College Press, 1953.

Gale, James Scarth. *Korea in Transition*. New York: Young People's Missionary Movement of the United States and Canada, 1909.

– *A Korean-English Dictionary*. Han-Yŏng chajŏn 韓英字典. Yokohama: Fukuin Printing Co. Ltd., 1897.

– *Korean Sketches*. New York: Fleming H. Revell, 1898.

– *Old Corea*. [ca 1923]. Unpublished typescript in the Gale Papers, Thomas Fisher Rare Book Library, University of Toronto.

– *Pen Pictures of Old Korea. Chosŏn p'ilgyŏng* 朝鮮筆景. 1912. Unpublished typescript in the Gale Papers, Thomas Fisher Rare Book Library, University of Toronto.

– *Present-Day English-Korean: Three Thousand Words*. Kyŏngsŏng: Chosŏn yaso kyogwahoe, 1924.

– trans. *T'yŏllo ryŏktyŏng* 天路歷程. Translation of *The Pilgrim's Progress*, by John Bunyan. Seoul: Trilingual Press, 1895.

Gale, James Scarth, and Yi Ch'angsik. *Yumong ch'ŏnja* [Korean Readers]. Hansŏng: Taehan sŏnggyo sŏhoe t'akin, 1905.

Gale, James Scarth, and Yi Wŏnmo, trans. *Yŏng-Mi sinirok* [Strange and Marvelous Tales from England and America]. Sŏul: Christian Literature Society, 1925.

Goethe, Johann Wolfgang von, and Thomas Carlyle. *Goethe's Wilhelm Meister's Travels*. Columbia, SC: Camden House, 1991.

Griffis, William Elliot. "Korea, the Pigmy Empire." *New England Magazine* 26 (1902): 455–70.

Han, Young-woo. "Kija Worship in the Koryŏ and Early Yi Dynasties: A Cultural Symbol in the Relationship between Korea and China." In *The Rise of Neo-Confucianism in Korea*, edited by Wm. Theodore de Bary and JaHyun Kim Haboush, 349–73. New York: Columbia University Press, 1985.

Harkness, Nicholas. "Softer Soju in South Korea." *Anthropological Theory* 13 (2013): 12–30.

"Health Risks – Daily Smokers – OECD Data." https://data.oecd.org/healthrisk /daily-smokers. htm.

Hŏ Ch'an. "1920nyŏndae *Unyŏng chŏn* ŭi yŏrŏ yangsang: Iryŏkpon *Unyŏng chŏn* kwa Han'gŭlpon *Yŏnjon Unyŏng chŏn*, yŏnghwa *Unyŏng chŏn: Ch'onghŭi ŭi yŏn* ŭi kwangye rŭl chungsim ŭro" [Exploring Various Aspects of "The Tale of Unyŏng" through Connections between the Japanese Version, the Expanded and Revised *Han'gŭl* Version, and the Film Version *Unyŏng ch'onghŭi ŭi yŏn*]. *Yŏlsang kojŏn yŏn'gu* 38 (2013): 535–65.

Hong Ponghan. *Tongguk munhŏn pigo* [Encyclopedia of Documents and Institutions of the Eastern Kingdom]. Sungjŏngwŏn, 1770.

Hong Sunmin. "Chosŏn wangjo naesibu ŭi kusŏng kwa suhyo ŭi pyŏnch'ŏn" [Changes in the Structure and Personnel of the Chosŏn-Era Bureau of Eunuchs]. *Yŏksa wa hyŏnsil* 52, no. 6 (2004): 219–63.

Hong Yangho. "Chŏ ho sa" [詛虎辭 A Spell against the Tiger]. *Igye chip* kwŏn 1 [耳谿集 1 The Collected Works of Hong Yangho, vol. 1]. 1843. http:// db.itkc.or.kr/search/group?q=query†%E8%80%BD%E8%80%BD%E7%B4 %A0%E5%A8%81%E3%80%82%E5%B1%B1%E4%B9%8B%E5%90%9B %E7%8C%97%E3%80%82%E9%9A%86%E9%A1%8D%E5%8D%B7%E5 %B0%BE%E3%80%82.

– "Pang an sa" [放鷹辭 Setting Free the Wild Goose]. In *Igye chip* kwŏn 1 [耳谿集 1 The Collected Works of Hong Yangho, vol. 1]. 1843. http://db.itkc.or.kr/search/group?q=query†%E7%94%9F%E5%BE%97%E4%BA%8C%E9%B4%88%E3%80%82%E5%89%AA%E5%85%B6%E7%BF%AE%E4%BB%A5%E7%8D%BB.

Hulbert, Homer. *The Passing of Korea.* New York: Doubleday, 1906.

Hwang Hodŏk, and Yi Sanghyŏn. *Kaenyŏm kwa yŏksa, kŭndae Han'guk ŭi ijungŏ sajŏn: Oegugindŭl ŭi sajŏn p'yŏnch'an saŏp ŭro pon Han'gugŏ ŭi kŭndae* [Concept and History, Modern Korean Bilingual Dictionaries: Viewing Korean Linguistic Modernity through the Foreigner Dictionary Compilation Project]. Sŏul: Pangmunsa, 2012.

Im Ch'un. "Hwa an ki" [畫雁記 Picture of Wild Geese]. In Ki [記 Records], *Tongmunsŏn* kwŏn 65 [東文選 65 A Selection of Eastern Literature, vol. 65]. http://db.itkc.or.kr/search/group?q=query†%E9%81%93%E4%BA%BA%E6%83%A0%E9%9B%B2%E3%80%82%E6%8C%81%E4%B8%80%E7%95%AB%E9%B4%88%E5%9C%96.

Im Sangsŏk. *20-segi Kuk-Hanmunch'e ŭi hyŏngsŏng kwajŏng* [The Formation Process of Sino-Korean Mixed Script Style]. P'aju: Chisik Sanŏp-sa, 2008.

– "*Hanmun* kwa kojŏn ŭi pulli, pŏnyŏk kwa kukhanmunch'e: Keil ŭi *Yumong ch'ŏncha* (牖蒙千字) yŏn'gu" [Translation and Sino-Korean Mixed Script, and the Division of Literary Sinitic and the Classics: Gale's *Yumong ch'ŏncha*]. *Kojŏn kwa haesŏk* 16 (2014): 29–50.

Jacob, Frank. *The Russo-Japanese War and Its Shaping of the Twentieth Century.* London: Routledge, 2018.

Johnson, Rossiter, ed. *The Great Events by Famous Historians, 1609–1660.* The National Alumni, 1919.

Keith, Elizabeth. *Old Korea: The Land of the Morning Calm.* London: Hutchison, 1946.

Kim, Christine. "Politics and Pageantry in Protectorate Korea (1905–1910): The Imperial Progresses of Sunjong." *Journal of Asian Studies* 68, no. 3 (2009): 835–59.

Kim Illyŏl. "*Unyŏng chŏn* ko (I): churo simnihakjŏk ipchang esŏ" [A Consideration of *The Tale of Unyŏng* I: Taking a Psychological Perspective]. *Ŏmun nonch'ong* 6 (1971).

– "*Unyŏng chŏn* ko (II): churo simnihakjŏk ipchang esŏ" [A Consideration of *The Tale of Unyŏng* II: Taking a Psychological Perspective]. *Ŏmun nonch'ong* 7 (1972): 47–61.

Kim Pusik. "A kye pu" [啞鷄賦 The Dumb Cock]. In *Kim Pusik munchip* [金富軾文集 The Collected Works of Kim Pusik], *Tongmunsŏn* [東文選 A Selection of

Eastern Literature]. 1478. http://www.krpia.co.kr/viewer?plctId
     =PLCT00008012&tabNodeId=NODE07375961#none.
Kim, Tong-no. "Views on Modern Reform in the *Hwangsŏng sinmun*." In
     Reform and Modernity in the Taehan Empire, edited by Kim Tong-no, John B.
     Duncan, and To-hyŏng Kim, 37–70. Seoul: Jimoondang, 2006.
Kim, Tong-no, John B. Duncan, and To-hyŏng Kim, eds. *Reform and Modernity
     in the Taehan Empire*. Seoul: Jimoondang, 2006.
Kim Tonguk. *Kugyŏk Kimun ch'onghwa* [A Modern Korean Translation of
     Kimun ch'onghwa]. Sŏul: Asea munhwasa, 1996–9.
– *Saebyŏk kangka e haeoragi unŭn sori: kugyŏk Kimun ch'onghwa* [A Heron Cries
     by the Early Morning Riverside: *Kimun ch'onghwa* in Modern Korean]. Sŏul:
     Asea munhwasa, 2008.
Kim Uktong. *Pŏnyŏk kwa Han'guk ŭi kŭndae* [Translation and Korean
     Modernity]. Sŏul: Somyŏng ch'ulp'an, 2010.
King, Ross. "Dialect, Orthography, and Regional Identity: P'yŏngan
     Christians, Korean Spelling Reform, and Orthographic Fundamentalism."
     In *The Northern Region of Korea: History, Identity, and Culture*, edited by Sun
     Joo Kim, 139–80. Seattle: University of Washington Press, 2010.
– "I Thank Korea for Her Books": *James Scarth Gale, Korean Literature in
     Hanmun, and Allo-Metropolitan Missionary Orientalism*. Toronto: University
     of Toronto Press, forthcoming.
– "James Scarth Gale and the Christian Literature Society: Salvific Translation
     and Korean Literary Modernity." In *Corea, una Aproximación Humanista a los
     Estudios Coreanos*, edited by Wonjung Min. Santiago: Pontificia Universidad
     Católica de Chile, 2014. E-book.
– "James Scarth Gale, Korean Literature in *Hanmun*, and Allo-Metropolitan
     Missionary Orientalism." Lecture delivered at the Royal Asiatic Society
     – Korea Branch, Seoul, South Korea, 11 November 2017.
www.raskb.com/blog/2017/11/04/lecture-video-james-scarth-gale-korean
     -literature-hanmun-and-allo-metropolitan.
– "Korean 'Classics' for Anglophone Readers, Then and Now: *The Korea
     Magazine* (1917–1919) and Premodern Korean Literature in English
     Translation Today." Lecture delivered at Sunggyungwan University, Seoul,
     South Korea, January 2018.
– ed. *Cosmopolitan and Vernacular in the World of Wen: Reading Sheldon Pollock
     from the Sinographic Cosmopolis*. Language, Writing and Literary Culture in
     the Sinographic Cosmopolis Series. Brill (forthcoming).
– "Nationalism and Language Reform in Korea: The Questione della
     Lingua in Precolonial Korea." In *Nationalism and the Construction of Korean*

Identity, edited by Timothy Tangherlini and Hyung-il Pai, 33–72. Berkeley: University of California Press, 1998.

– "Western Protestant Missionaries and the Origins of Korean Language Modernization." *Journal of International and Area Studies* 11, no. 3 (2004): 7–38.

Kipling, Rudyard, and Charles Balestier. *The Naulahka: A Story of West and East*. New York: Macmillan, 1892.

Kitagawa, Joseph, ed. *The Religious Traditions of Asia: Religion, History, and Culture*. London: Routledge Curzon, 1989.

Ko, Mi Sook, Jung Min, and Jung Byung Sul. *The History of Korean Literature: From Ancient Times to the Late Nineteenth Century*. Translated by Michael Pettid and Kil Cha. Literature Translation Institute of Korea, 2016.

Kong, Wong Man. *James Legge: A Pioneer at Crossroads of East and West*. North Point: Hong Kong Educational Publishing, 1996.

Kwon, Hyuk-chan. "From *Sanguozhi yanyi* to *Samgukchi*: Domestication and Appropriation of Three Kingdoms in Korea." PhD diss., University of British Columbia, 2010.

Kwon, Jin-Won, Heeran Cho, and Sung-il Cho. "A Closer Look at the Increase in Suicide Rates in South Korea from 1986–2005." *BMC Public Health* 9, no. 72 (2009): 1–9.

Kwŏn Pŏl. *Ch'ungjae sŏnsaeng munchip* kwŏn 8 [沖齋先生文集 8 The Collected Works of Master Kwŏn Pŏl, vol. 8]. http://db.itkc.or.kr/dir/item ?itemId=MO#/dir/node?dataId=ITKC_MO_0107A_0130_010_0030.

Kwŏn Sangu. "*Myŏngsim pogam* ŭi todŏk kyoyukjŏk ŭiŭi" [The Significance of Moralistic Education in *The Precious Mirror of the Heart*]. *Minjok munhwa nonch'ong* 66 (2017): 187–213.

Lankov, Andrei. *The Dawn of Modern Korea: The Transformation in Life and Cityscape*. Sŏul: Eunhaeng namu, 2010.

Ledyard, Gari. *The Dutch Come to Korea*. Seoul: Royal Asiatic Society Korea Branch, 1971.

Lee, Peter H., and Wm. Theodore de Bary, eds. *Sources of Korean Tradition*. Vol. 1, *From Early Times through the Sixteenth Century*. New York: Columbia University Press, 1997.

Legge, James, trans. *Shijing* [詩經 The Classic of Poetry]. Chinese Text Project. https://ctext.org/book-of-poetry.

Lewis, James B. *Frontier Contact between Chosŏn Korea and Tokugawa Japan*. London: Taylor and Francis, 2014.

Mayers, William Frederick. *The Chinese Reader's Manual: A Handbook of Biographical, Historical, Mythological, and General Literary Reference*. Shanghai: American Presbyterian Mission Press, 1874.

McCarthy, Kathleen. "Kisaeng and Poetry in the Koryŏ Period." *Korean Culture* (Summer 1994): 6–13.

Metraux, Daniel. "How Western Reporters Chronicled the Japanese Seizure of Korea in 1905." 2015. https://www.academia.edu/31710762/How_Western _Reporters_Chronicled_the_Japanese_Seizure_of_Korea_in_1905.docx.

Nikaido, Yoshihiro. *Asian Folk Religion and Cultural Interaction*. Taipei: National Taiwan University Press, 2015.

No Chungguk. "Han'guk kodae ŭi kyesesasang kwa kŭ silhyŏn yangsang: *Ilbon sŏgi* 'Suingi' sunjang kisa rŭl tanch'oro hayŏ" [Beliefs on the Afterlife in Ancient Korea and Aspects of Its Practice: Searching for Clues of Live Burial in the "Suinin Chronicle" of *Nihonshiki*]. *Paekche hakpo* 7 (2011): 5–22.

Oak, Sung-Deuk. "North American Missionaries' Understanding of the Tan'gun and Kija Myths of Korea, 1884–1934." *Acta Koreana* 4 (2002): 1–21.

Oh, Young Kyun. *Engraving Virtue: The Printing History of a Premodern Korean Moral Primer*. Leiden: Brill, 2013.

Olsen, Leif. "Gendered Filiality and Heroism in the Tale of the Golden Bell, a Chosŏn Fictional Narrative." MA thesis, University of British Columbia, 2004.

O'Neill, Timothy Michael. *Ideography and Chinese Language Theory: A History*. Berlin: Walter de Gruyter, 2016.

O'Rourke, Kevin. *The Book of Korean Poetry: Choson Dynasty*. Singapore: Stallion Press, 2014.

– *The Book of Korean* Sijo. Cambridge, MA: Harvard University Asia Center, 2002.

Ōtani Morishige. "*Uneiten* shōgō." 「雲英伝」小考 [A Brief Study of *The Tale of Unyŏng*]. *Chōsen gakuhō* (1966): 340–70.

Pai, Hyung-Il. *Constructing "Korean" Origins: A Critical Review of Archaeology, "Korean" Historiography, and Racial Myth Origins in Korean State Formation Theories*. Cambridge, MA: Harvard University Press, 2000.

– "The Politics of Korea's Past: The Legacy of Japanese Colonial Archaeology in the Korean Peninsula." *East Asian History* 7 (1994): 25–48.

Pak Chŏngse. "Keil (J. Gale) ŭi *Tyŏllo ryŏktyŏng* kwa Kim Chungŭn ŭi p'ungsok sapdo" [The Illustrations of Kim Chungŭn Appearing in James Scarth Gale's *Tyŏllo ryŏktyŏng*]. *Sinhak nontan* 60 (2010): 63–91.

Pak Kisŏk. "*Unyŏng chŏn* chaep'yŏngka rŭl wihan yebijŏk koch'al" [A Preliminary Investigation of *The Tale of Unyŏng*: Toward a Reevaluation]. *Kugŏ kyoyuk* 37 (1980): 81–94.

Pak Ŭnbong. *Han'guksa sangsik paro chapki* [Grasping Common Themes in Korean History]. Sŏul: Ch'aekkwa hamkke, 2007.

Palais, James. "Kisaeng and Actors." https://digital.lib.washington.edu /researchworks/bitstream/handle/1773/23976/1–10-Kisaengandactors .pdf?sequence=10&isAllowed=y.

– *Politics and Policy in Traditional Korea*. Cambridge, MA: Harvard University Press, 1975.

Park, Si Nae. "Translating to Inherit: An Introduction to James Scarth Gale's Translations from the *Kimun ch'ŏnghwa*." In *Score One for the Dancing Girl, and Other Stories from the "Kimun ch'onghwa": A Story Collection from Nineteenth-Century Korea*, translated by James Scarth Gale, edited by Ross King and Si Nae Park, annotations by Donguk Kim, xv–xxxvi. Toronto: University of Toronto Press, 2016.

Pettid, Michael, and Kil Cha Pettid, trans. *"Unyŏng-jŏn": A Love Affair at the Royal Palace of Chosŏn Korea*. Berkeley: Institute of Asian Studies, University of California, 2009.

Pieper, Daniel. "Korean as a Transitional Literacy: Language Education, Curricularization, and the Vernacular-Cosmopolitan Interface in Early Modern Korea, 1895–1925." PhD diss., University of British Columbia, 2017. http://hdl.handle.net/2429/61132.

Pore, William. "The Inquiring Literatus: Yi Sugwang's 'Brush Talks' with Phung Khac Khoan in Beijing in 1598." *Royal Asiatic Society – Korea Branch* 83 (2008): 1–26.

Pratt, Keith. *Old Seoul*. Hong Kong: Oxford University Press (China), 2002.

Pratt, Keith, and Richard Rutt. *Korea: A Historical and Cultural Dictionary*. London: Routledge, 2013.

Rockhill, William. "Notes on Some of the Laws, Customs, and Superstitions of Korea." *American Anthropologist* 4, no. 2 (1891): 177–88.

"Rubaek P'oho" [Rubaek Captures a Tiger]. In *Oryun haengsilto* [Illustrated Exemplars of the Five Relationships]. 1797. https://www.flickr.com/photos/seoulmuseum/8570149373.

Rusk, Bruce. "Old Scripts, New Actors: European Encounters with Chinese Writing, 1550–1700." *EASTM* 26 (2007): 68–116.

Rutt, Richard. "The Chinese Learning and the Pleasures of a Country Scholar: An Account of Traditional Chinese Studies in Rural Korea." *Transactions of the Royal Asiatic Society – Korea Branch* 37 (April 1960): 1–100.

– *James Scarth Gale and His "History of the Korean People": A New Edition of the History Together with a Biography and Annotated Bibliographies*. Sŏul: RASKB, Taewon Publishing, 1972.

Said, Edward. *Orientalism*. New York: Pantheon, 1978.

Saunderson, H.R. *Notes on Corea and Its People. The Journal of the Anthropological Institute of Great Britain and Ireland* 24 (1895): 299–316.

Schmid, Andre. *Korea between Empires*. New York: Columbia University Press, 2002.

– "Rediscovering Manchuria: Sin Ch'aeho and the Politics of Territorial History in Korea." *Journal of Asian Studies* 56 (1997): 26–46.

Seth, Michael. *A Concise History of Korea: From Antiquity to Present.* Lanham, MD: Rowman and Littlefield, 2016.

Shin Eun-kyung. "A Reception Aesthetic Study on *Sijo* in English Translation: The Case of James Scarth Gale." *Seoul Journal of Korean Studies* 26, no. 1 (2013): 175–213.

Sin Kyuhwan, and Sŏ Honggwan. "Chosŏn hugi hŭbyŏn ingu ŭi hwakdae kwajŏng kwa hŭpyŏn munhwa ŭi hyŏngsŏng" [The Increase in the Smoking Population in Late Chosŏn and the Formation of Smoking Culture]. *Ŭisahak* 11, no. 1 (2001): 23–59.

Singh, Anna. "The 'Scourge of South Korea': Stress and Suicide in Korean Society." *Berkeley Political Review*, 31 October 2017. https://bpr.berkeley .edu/2017/10/31/the-scourge-of-south-korea-stress-and-suicide-in -korean-society/.

Skillend, William. "Have I a Soul or Not?: Some of My Problems with *Sijo*." In *Cheilhoe Han'gukhak Kukche Haksul Hoeŭi Nonmunjip*, 437–54. Inch'ŏn: Inha taehakkyo Han'gukhak yŏn'guso, 1987.

Sŏ Sŏngch'ŏl. "K'uba Hanin inminsa" [A History of Korean Immigrants to Cuba]. *Revista Iberoamericana* 11 (2000): 137–59.

Sŏng Hyŏn. *Yongjae ch'onghwa* kwŏn 4 [慵齋叢話 4 The Writings of Sŏng Hyŏn (1525), vol. 4]. In *Taedong Yasŭng* [大東野乘 Unofficial Histories of the Great East]. 1911. http://db.itkc.or.kr/search/group?q=query†%E6%B4%AA%E5 %AE%B0%E6%A8%9E%E5%BE%AE%E6%99%82%E8%B7%AF%E9%80%A2 %E9%9B%A8.

– *Yongjae ch'onghwa* kwŏn 6 [慵齋叢話 6 The Writings of Sŏng Hyŏn (1525), vol. 6]. In *Taedong Yasŭng* [大東野乘 Unofficial Histories of the Great East]. 1911. http://db.itkc.or.kr/search/group?q=query†%E6%9C%89%E5 %83%A7%E5%AE%B9%E8%BB%86%E7%9F%AE%E5%B0%8F%E3 %80%82%E4%B8%80%E8%B6%B3%E5%BE%AE%E8%BA%84.

– *Yongjae ch'onghwa* kwŏn 7 [慵齋叢話 7 The Writings of Sŏng Hyŏn (1525), vol. 7]. In *Taedong Yasŭng* [大東野乘 Unofficial Histories of the Great East]. (1525) 1911. http://db.itkc.or.kr/dir/item?itemId=BT#dir/node?dataId =ITKC_BT_1306A_0070_000_0010&viewSync=OT.

Sŏng Yŏnggu. "2008nyŏn Chosŏn hugisa yŏn'gu kyŏnghyang kwa chŏnmang" [Trends in Research on Late-Chosŏn History in 2008 and Future Prospects]. Yŏksa hakbo 203 (2009): 77–107.

Southerton, Donald G. *Colorado's Henry Collbran and the Roots of Early Korean Entrepreneurialism.* 2012. https://books.google.ca/books?id

=USzilH9-RMgC&pg=PT3&lpg=PT3&dq=Southerton, Donald+G.+%E2%80
%9CColorado% E2%80%99s+Henry+Collbran&source=bl&ots
= uKsEpZCtJx&sig=ACfU3U2hol4RmIJwJYOe4vq_1G9Gu-cr7Q&hl
=en&sa=X&ved= 2ahUKEwirmMHr 55jgAhUzoFsKHZW3DksQ6AE
wAnoECA0QAQ#v=onepage&q= Southerton%2C%20Donald%20G.
%20%E2%80%9CColorado%E2%80%99s%20Henry%20Collbran&f=false.

Sungsil Taehakkyo Han'guk Kidokkyo pangmulgwan, comp. *Han'guk
Kidokkyo Pangmulgwan sojang Kidokkyo charyo haeje* [Interpretation of
Christian Materials Housed at the Korean Museum of Christianity]. Seoul:
Sungsil Taehakkyo Han'guk Kidokkyo Pangmulgwan, 2007.

Unyŏng chŏn [The Sorrows of Cloud Bud]. http://www.davincimap.co.kr
/davBase/Source/davSource.jsp?Job=Body&SourID=SOUR001299&Lang
=한문&Page=1&View=Text.

Vermeersch, Sem. *A Chinese Traveler in Medieval Korea: Xu Jing's Illustrated
Account of the Xuanhe Embassy to Koryŏ*. Korean Classics Library. Honolulu:
University of Hawai'i Press, 2016.

Vos, Frits. "A Chinese Book in Disguise: Some Problems Concerning the
Myŏngsim pogam." In *Twenty Papers on Korean Studies Offered to Professor
W.E. Skillend*, edited by Robert C. Provine et al., 229–50. Paris: Collège de
France, Centre d'études coréennes, 1989.

Wang, Sixiang. "The Filial Daughter of Kwaksan: Finger Severing, Confucian
Virtues, and Envoy Poetry in Early Chosŏn." *Seoul Journal of Korean Studies*
25, no. 2 (2012): 175–212.

Whymant, Neville. *Colloquial Chinese (Northern)*. London: K. Paul Trench,
Trubner and Co., 1922.

Wŏn Kam. "Sŏk hwa ŭm [惜花吟 The Falling Flowers]. Ch'irŏn kosi
[七言古詩 Seven-character Classical Poetry]. In *Tongmunsŏn* kwŏn 6 [東文選
A Selection of Eastern Literature, vol. 6]. 1478. http://db.itkc.or.kr/search
/group?q=query†%E4%B8%96%E4%BA%BA%E4%BD%86%E8%A6%8B%
E8%8A%B1%E9%96%8B%E8%90%BD%E3%80%82%E4%B8%8D%E7%9F%
A5%E8%BA%AB%E8%88%87%E8%8A%B1%E7%9B%B8%E8%8B%.

Wŏnbon kugŏ kungmunhak ch'ongnim 5 (1617). "Rubaek P'oho" [Rubaek
Captures a Tiger]. In *Tongguk sinsok Samgang haengsilto* [New Continued
Illustrated Exemplars of the Three Bonds in Korea]. Sŏul: Taejegak, 1995.

Wŏn Hanil. "Na ŭi iryŏksŏ: Kumip'o haesuyokjang." [My Experience at
Kumip'o Beach]. *Han'guk ilbo*, 10 December 1981. ysfine.com/kobak/
underw81.pdf.

Xiong, Victor Cunrui. *Historical Dictionary of Medieval China*. Lanham, MD:
Scarecrow Press, 2009.

Yang Sŭngmin. *Kojŏnsosŏl munhŏnhak ŭi silch'e wa chŏnmang* [Classical Fiction
  Philology in Practice and Future Prospects]. Sŏul: Asea munhwasa, 2008.
Yi Chehyŏn. "Sŏl" [雪 The Snow]. In Ch'irŏn kosi [七言古詩 Seven-Character
  Classical Poetry], *Tongmunsŏn* kwŏn 6 [東文選 6 A Selection of Eastern
  Literature, vol. 6]. http://db.itkc.or.kr/dir/item?itemId=BT#dir/node?
  dataId=ITKC_BT_1365A_0070_010_0080&solrQ=query†이제현맹양양
  $solr_sortField†그룹정렬_s자료ID_s$solr_sortOrder†$solr_secId†BT
  _AA$solr_toalCount†4$solr_curPos†0$solr_solrId†BD_ITKC_BT_1365A
  _0070_010_00 80&viewSync=OT.
Yi Chunhwan. *"Yumong ch'ŏncha* (牖蒙千字) kukhanmun ŭi yuhyŏngbyŏl
  t'ŭksŏng koch'al" [An Examination of Special Characteristics of Various
  Sino-Korean Mixed-Script Styles Appearing in *Yumong ch'ŏncha*]. *Pangyo
  ŏmun yŏn'gu* 44 (2016): 13–58.
Yi Hwang. "Sayang nagan" [斜陽落雁 Wild Geese Alight]. In *T'oegye sŏnsaeng
  munjip* kwŏn 3 [退溪先生文集 3 The Collected Works of Master Yi Hwang,
  vol. 3]. http://db.itkc.or.kr/search/group?q=query†%E4%B8%80
  %E9%99%A3%E9%BB%9E%E7%A0%B4%E9%81%99%E7%A9
  %BA%E9%9B%81.
Yi, Ihwa. *Korea's Pastimes and Customs: A Social History*. Paramus, NJ: Homa
  and Sekey Books, 2006.
Yi Ik. "Manmulmun, namch'o" [萬物門 南草 The Record of Myriad Things:
  The Southern Weed]. In *Sŏngho sasŏl* kwŏn 4 [星湖僿說 4 The Learned Talk
  of Master Namho, vol. 4]. http://seongho.iansan.net/resource/Editorial
  .jsp?menuId=13004009&id=803¤tPage=2.
Yi Kyubo. "U pyŏngjŭng pyŏngsŭng" [又病中疾蠅 Flies]. In Koyulsi [古律詩
  Classical RegulatedVerse], *Tongguk Yi Sangguk chip* kwŏn 1
  [東國李相國集 1 The Collected Works of Yi Kyubo, vol. 1]. http://db.itkc
  .or.kr/dir/item?itemId=MO#dir/node?dataId=ITKC_MO_0004A
  _0450_010_0750&viewSync=TR.
– "Yŏng an" [詠鴈 Setting Free the Wild Goose]. Koyulsi [古律詩
  Classical Regulated Verse]. *Tongguk Yi Sangguk chip* kwŏn 11 [東國李相國集
  11 The Collected Works of Yi Kyubo, vol. 11]. 1241. http://db.itkc.or.kr
  /search/group?q=query†%E6%95%85%E4%BA%BA%E5%8D%83%E9
  %87%8C%E8%A8%8A%E9%9F%B3%E8%B8%88%E3%80%82%E5%8F%AA
  %E5%BE%85%E9%9C%9C%E5%A4%A9%E9%B4%88%E5%88%B0%E5
  %88%9D.
Yi Sanggu. *"Unyŏng chŏn* kaltŭng yangsang kwa chakka ŭisik" [An
  Examination of Conflict in and an Awareness of the Author of *The Tale of
  Unyŏng*]. *Kososŏl yŏn'gu* 5 (1998): 133–76.

Yi Sanghyŏn. "Yumong ch'ŏncha sojae Yŏng-Mi munhak chakp'um kwa Keil (J. S. Gale) ŭi kukhanmunch'e pŏnyŏk silch'ŏn: Kaesingyo sŏngyosa ŭi kŭndae munch'e rŭl hyanghan kihoek kwa kŭ nojŏng 1" [English Literary Works in Gale's *Yumong ch'ŏncha* (牖蒙千字) and His Sino-Korean Mixed-Script Translational Style: A Protestant Missionary's Project and Journey toward Modern Korean Style]. *Sŏgang inmun nonch'ong* 42, no. 4 (2015): 99–154.

Yi Sanghyŏn, and Yun Sŏlhŭi. *Oegugin ŭi Han'guk siga tamnon yŏn'gu* [Discourse among Foreign Observers of Korean Poetry]. Sŏul: Yŏngnak, 2017.

Yi Sŏng, and Chŏng Howan, eds. *Yŏkchu tongguk sinsok samgang haengsilto* [New Continued Illustrated Exemplars of the Three Bonds in Korea: Translated and Annotated]. Sŏul: Sejong taewang minyŏm saŏphoe, 2015.

"Yi Ssi kamch'ŏn" [李氏感天 How She Moved God]. In *Yŏji sŭngnam* kwŏn 4 [輿地勝覽 4 Survey of the Geography of Korea, vol. 4]. 1485. volhttps://www.krpia.co.kr/viewer/open?plctId=PLCT00005160&nodeId=NODE05192183&medaId=MEDA05391323.

Yi T'aejin. *Kojong sidae ŭi chaejomyŏng* [A Re-exploration of Kojong-Era Korea]. Sŏul: T'aehaksa, 2000.

– "Kyujanggak Chungguk pon tosŏ wa Chipokche tosŏ" [Chinese Books in the Royal Archives (Kyujanggak) and Books in the Royal Library of King Kojong (Chipokche)]. *Minjok munhwa nonch'ong* 16 (1996): 169–88.

– *Taehan cheguk: Ich'ŏjin 100nyŏn chŏn ŭi hwangjeguk* [The Great Han Empire: The Lost Empire of a Century Ago]. Sŏul: Minsogwŏn, 2011.

Yi Talch'ung. "Aeo cham pyŏngsŏ" [愛惡箴 幷書 The Good and Bad of It]. In Cham [箴 Injunctions], *Tongmunsŏn* kwŏn 49 [東文選 49 A Selection of Eastern Literature, vol. 49]. 1478. http://db.itkc.or.kr/search/group?q=query†%E5%AD%90%E9%83%BD%E4%B9%8B%E5%A7%A3%E3%80%82%E7%96%87%E4%B8%8D%E7%88%B2%E7%BE%8E%E3%80%82

– "Chaphŭng ojang kisa am" [雜興五章寄思菴 The Joys of Nature]. In Oŏn kosi [五言古詩 Five-character Classical Poetry], *Tongmunsŏn* kwŏn 5 [東文選 5 A Collection of Eastern Literature, vol. 5]. db.itkc.or.kr/search/group?q=query†%E9%9B%B2%E6%9D%BE%E4%BD%95%E8%92%BC%E8%92%BC%E3%80%82%E5%AE%B6%E5%9C%A8%E5%B1%B1%E4%B9%8B%E9%98%BF.

– "Chŭng yŏng" [贈影 My Shadow]. *Chejŏng chip* kwŏn 1 [霽亭集 1 The Collected Works of Yi Talch'ung, vol. 1]. http://db.itkc.or.kr/search/group?q=query†%E5%94%AF%E6%88%91%E9%A0%97%E5%A4%9A%E8%A8

%80%E3%80%82%E5%BD%B1%E4%B9%9F%EF%A5%A7%E5%8F
%96%E6%96%AF%E3%80%82.

– "Sŏrhŏn Chŏng Sangt'aek Ch'ŏngsan paegun to" [雪軒鄭相宅青山白雲圖
The Green Mountains and White Clouds of Sŏrhŏn Chŏng Sangt'aek]. In
Ch'irŏn kosi [七言古詩 Seven-Character Classical Poetry], *Tongmunsŏn* kwŏn
7 [東文選 7 A Selection of Eastern Literature, vol. 7]. 1478. http://db.itkc
.or.kr/search/group?q=query†%E9%9B%AA%E8%BB%92%E9%84
%AD%E7%9B%B8%E5%AE%85%E9%9D%91%E5%B1%B1
%E7%99%BD%E9%9B%B2%E5%9C%96.

Yi Yŏnggyŏng. *"Tongguk sinsok Samgang haengsilto ŏnhae ŭi sŏnggyŏk e
taehayŏ"* [The Nature of Annotated and Translated Versions of the *New
Continued Illustrated Exemplars of the Three Bonds in Korea*]. *Chintan hakpo*
112 (2011): 103–25.

Yŏksa munje yŏn'guso, ed. *Silp'aehan kaehyŏk ŭi yŏksa* [A History of Failed
Reform]. Sŏul: Yŏksa pip'yŏngsa, 2008.

Yoo, Theodore Jun. "The 'New Woman' and the Politics of Love, Marriage and
Divorce in Colonial Korea." *Gender and History* 17, no. 2 (2005): 295–324.

Yoon, Hong-key. *P'ungsu: A Study of Geomancy in Korea*. Albany: State
University of New York, 2017.

Yu Hyŏngwŏn. "Yŏak uhŭi" [女樂優戲 The Superb Performance of Women
Musicians]. In *Pan'gye surok* [磻溪隨錄 Free Writing from Pan'gye], kwŏn 25,
1.10. http://www.davincimap.co.kr/davBase/Source/davSource.jsp?Job
=Body&SourID= SOUR001386&Lang=한문&Page=25&View=Text.

Yu Yŏngsik. *Ch'akhǎn mokchya: Keil ŭi salm kwa sŏn'gyo* [The Kind Pastor: The
Life and Mission of James S. Gale]. Sŏul: Chinhŭng, 2013.

Index

Ahwang 娥皇, 341, 344–7
alcohol, 69, 129–32, 187, 403–5,
    406–11, 414n70
Allen, Horace Newton, 94–5, 97, 238
Analects of Confucius, 145, 573
ancestors, 42–3n103, 83, 116–18,
    123n6, 134, 136, 138–9, 160, 162–3,
    174, 195, 226–7, 235–6, 239, 298n17,
    357, 392, 409, 459, 462n103, 482
An Chŏngbok 安鼎福, 91–2, 513,
    513n5
angels, 84, 89, 132n13, 308, 315–16,
    346, 451–2, 460, 559, 591
Anglophone readership, 18, 36n87,
    222n1, 295, 295nn7, 8, 485–6, 626–8
An Hyang 安珦, 161n16
animals: bears, 149, 196, 262, 264,
    297n15, 313, 313n80, 453, 461, 509,
    547, 554, 558, 580; dogs, 68, 179–
    80, 239, 268n4, 279, 283, 311, 312–
    14, 317, 465, 472, 508, 544, 596, 606;
    donkeys, 188, 559; dragons, 11–12,
    77, 123–4, 167, 182–4, 198–200,
    214, 306, 312, 314, 317, 327, 343,
    435, 450–1, 460, 461, 472, 472n3,
    546, 559, 569, 576, 579; elephants,
    139, 193, 195–7, 268, 268n4, 421,
    438, 440, 441, 511; flies, 319, 512,
    523, 526–30; geese, 35, 66–7, 144n2,
    147, 537, 538, 539, 550–7, 578, 585;
    monkeys, 239, 267, 267–8n3, 268,
    472, 473, 547; pigs, 135, 239, 255–6,
    279, 439, 472, 473, 547; rats, 167,
    313, 554; snakes, 149, 167, 196, 240,
    329–30, 451, 472, 555; tigers, 106,
    135, 139, 149, 164, 186, 196, 268n4,
    297n15, 314, 315, 384, 386–7, 451,
    460, 463, 472, 509–10, 517, 545–8,
    554, 558, 606; turtles, 75, 451
An Lushan 安祿山, 354, 586n62
annexation, 4, 15, 30, 37, 114, 136,
    149n30, 163n23, 202, 278n8,
    301n31, 448
Anp'yŏng, Prince 安平大君, 564,
    564n12, 567, 568, 568n24, 572, 577
archaeology, 5, 445–6, 447–8, 448n9,
    449–56
art, 406, 432–6, 449–52
Aston, William George, 40–1
astrology, 259n5, 470, 472–4
automobiles, 523, 525, 534n77, 534–5

Ban Jieyu 班婕妤, 585n59. *See also*
    Pan Ch'ŏmyŏ